CREATING SPACES OF ENGAGEMENT

Policy Justice and the Practical Craft
of Deliberative Democracy

There is a growing need for public buy-in if democratic processes are to run smoothly. But who exactly is "the public"? What does their engagement in policy-making processes look like? How can our understanding of "the public" be expanded to include – or be led by – diverse voices and experiences, particularly of those who have been historically marginalized? And what does this expansion mean not only for public policies and their development, but for how we teach policy? Drawing upon public engagement case studies, sites of inquiry, and vignettes, this volume raises and responds to these and other questions while advancing policy justice as a framework for public engagement and public policy.

Stretching the boundaries of deliberative democracy in theory and practice, *Creating Spaces of Engagement* offers critical reflections on how diverse publics are engaged in policy processes.

LEAH LEVAC is an associate professor in the Department of Political Science at the University of Guelph.

SARAH MARIE WIEBE is an assistant professor in the Department of Political Science at the University of Hawai'i, Mānoa

Creating Spaces of Engagement

Policy Justice and the Practical Craft of Deliberative Democracy

Edited by LEAH LEVAC and
SARAH MARIE WIEBE

UNIVERSITY OF TORONTO PRESS
Toronto Buffalo London

© University of Toronto Press 2020
Toronto Buffalo London
utorontopress.com
Printed in Canada

ISBN 978-1-4875-0431-1 (cloth)   ISBN 978-1-4875-1989-6 (EPUB)
ISBN 978-1-4875-2325-1 (paper)   ISBN 978-1-4875-1988-9 (PDF)

Library and Archives Canada Cataloguing in Publication

Title: Creating spaces of engagement: Policy justice and the practical
   craft of deliberative democracy / edited by Leah R.E. Levac and Sarah
   Marie Wiebe.
Names: Levac, Leah R.E., 1977– editor. | Wiebe, Sarah Marie, editor.
Description: Includes bibliographical references and index.
Identifiers: Canadiana (print) 20200254057 | Canadiana (ebook)
   20200254286 | ISBN 9781487523251 (paper) | ISBN 9781487504311
   (hardcover) | ISBN 9781487519896 (EPUB)
Subjects: LCSH: Social policy – Citizen participation – Case studies. | LCSH:
   Deliberative democracy – Case studies. | LCGFT: Case studies.
Classification: LCC HN18.3.C64 2020 | DDC 361.2/5–dc23

This book has been published with the help of a grant from the Federation
for the Humanities and Social Sciences, through the Awards to Scholarly
Publications Program, using funds provided by the Social Sciences and
Humanities Research Council of Canada.

University of Toronto Press acknowledges the financial assistance to its
publishing program of the Canada Council for the Arts and the Ontario Arts
Council, an agency of the Government of Ontario.

Canada Council   Conseil des Arts
for the Arts   du Canada

ONTARIO ARTS COUNCIL
CONSEIL DES ARTS DE L'ONTARIO
an Ontario government agency
un organisme du gouvernement de l'Ontario

Funded by the   Financé par le
Government   gouvernement
of Canada   du Canada

Canadä

MIX
Paper from
responsible sources
FSC
www.fsc.org   FSC® C016245

Contents

Acknowledgments   ix

Introduction: Why Create Spaces of Engagement? Connecting
Theory, Policy, and Practice   3
SARAH MARIE WIEBE and LEAH LEVAC

**Part One – Across Disciplines and beyond the Academy: Stretching
Deliberative Democratic Theory**

1 Revelatory Protest, Deliberative Exclusion, and the BC Missing
   Women Commission of Inquiry: Bridging the Micro/Macro
   Divide   25
   GENEVIEVE FUJI JOHNSON

2 The Alberta Energy Futures Lab: A Case Study in Sociocultural
   Transition through Public Engagement   47
   STEPHEN WILLIAMS

3 Seeing and Believing: Reconciling Shared Outcomes and Shared
   Participation   72
   ELLEN SZARLETA

4 Northern Women's Conceptualizations of Well-Being: Engaging in
   the "Right" Policy Conversations   94
   LEAH LEVAC AND JACQUELINE GILLIS

5 Unsettled Democracy: The Case of the Grandview-Woodland
   Citizens' Assembly   117
   RACHEL MAGNUSSON

6 Opening to the Possible: Girls and Women with Disabilities
   Engaging in Vietnam   139
   DEBORAH STIENSTRA AND XUAN THUY NGUYEN

**Part Two – Centring Voices from the Margins: Expanding
and Evaluating Engagement Practices**

7 Collective Grist: Hacking Telecommunications Policy in
   Canada   163
   TARA MAHONEY

8 Engaging the "Heart and Mind": Building Community Capacity
   for Culturally Grounded Approaches to Substance Use on Post-
   Secondary Campuses   187
   CATRIONA REMOCKER, TIM DYCK, AND DAN REIST

9 Art-ful Methods of Democratic Participation: Listening,
   Engagement, and Connection   208
   JOANNA ASHWORTH

10 Power, Privilege, and Policy Making: Reflections on "Changing
   Public Engagement from the Ground Up"   226
   ALANA CATTAPAN, ALEXANDRA DOBROWOLSKY, TAMMY FINDLAY,
   AND APRIL MANDRONA

11 Engaging with Women in Low Income: Implications for
   Government-Convened Public Engagement Initiatives and
   Deliberative Democracy   253
   LEAH LEVAC

Part Three – Effective and Affective Spaces of Deliberation

12 The HeART of Engagement: Experiences of a Community-Created
   Mobile Art Gallery in Brazil   277
   BRUNO DE OLIVEIRA JAYME

13 Temporary Migrant Workers' Engagement and (Dis)engagement
   with the Policy Process   294
   ETHEL TUNGOHAN

14 Storytelling as Engagement: Learning from Youth Voices in
   Attawapiskat   312
   SARAH MARIE WIEBE

15 Making Spaces for Truth: Deliberating Reconciliation in
    Post-Secondary Education   332
    DEREK TANNIS

16 Global Goals with Local Relevance? "Glocal" Approaches,
    Tensions, and Lessons on Measuring Aid Effectiveness   353
    ASTRID V. PÉREZ PIÑÁN

    Conclusion: Reflections on Deliberative Democracy, Public
    Participation, and the Future of Policy Making   375
    LEAH LEVAC AND SARAH MARIE WIEBE

Bibliography   387

Index   435

Acknowledgments

First, we want to acknowledge that we are settlers living and working on Indigenous lands. We try to respect and honour this reality by practising humility, learning more about the territories we inhabit, and building meaningful and reciprocal personal and research relationships. We recognize that land acknowledgments are simultaneously important and fraught, but offer these words as part of our genuine commitment to helping shape a better shared future. Because many of the chapters in this volume are the result of collaborations with Indigenous research partners, we welcome continued conversations about working across Indigenous and Western knowledges and hope that this book can contribute to the ongoing, unfinished work of reconciliation. Writing across disciplines, nations, and oceans is no simple feat. This collaboration blossomed when Sarah was a postdoctoral fellow based in Coast Salish territory at the University of Victoria. There, she was deeply immersed in conversations about the arts of engagement and building meaningful research relationships with Indigenous communities. She reached out to Leah – by then at the University of Guelph, which rests in the treaty territory of the Mississaugas of the Credit – to partner in this work, given their shared interests in community-engaged scholarship, Indigenous rights, and more equitable policy processes and outcomes.

Editing a collection about *Creating Spaces of Engagement* required heartfelt and spirited collaboration. It was simultaneously an intellectual, emotional, and relational journey. Our aim in bringing together scholars and practitioners under the broad banner of public engagement was to contribute to meaningful discussions about the power relations embedded within policy-focused deliberations and public engagement initiatives. As critical, community-engaged policy scholars, we are indebted to the many diverse thinkers from inside and outside the academy who have influenced our reflections on the meaning-making practices that take shape when state officials reach out to affected people and communities, or vice versa. We hope that this praxis-oriented approach to exploring deliberative democracy will move us forward theoretically and practically, including by offering some new tools for undertaking meaningful participatory policy making and research.

Many democratic theorists and policy scholars influenced the emergence of this book. In particular, Sarah would like to thank several fearless, inspirational women who have informed her thinking and craft in community engagement, including: Leslie Brown, Maeve Lydon, Tara Ney, and Crystal Tremblay. In 2014, during an Arts of Engagement workshop at the University of Victoria, these women were part of an important conversation that provided the impetus for further reflection about the practical craft of public deliberation and constructing justice-oriented spaces of engagement. Sarah would also like to express gratitude to other community-engaged scholars for carving out creative spaces of public engagement for so many, and for the many conversations about how to be in service *to* community, including: Carly and Jennifer Bagelman, Michael Burgess, Noelani Goodyear-Ka'ōpua, Budd Hall, Kimberlyn McGrail, and Martin Taylor. Leah is immensely grateful to her academic mentors and colleagues – particularly those who work diligently to create space for community-engaged scholarship and socially engaged research in political science – and to the smart and thoughtful students with whom she has had the pleasure of working. She is also extremely grateful to the many community teachers and collaborators who have shaped not only her work, but also her personal and intellectual priorities and commitments. Leah and Sarah also want to thank the contributors to this volume, whose intentional and justice-oriented practices and scholarship are equal parts inspiring and challenging. Their knowledges and experiences are woven – as much as we were able – through the ideas presented in this book. We are grateful for their collective willingness to come together and create a community of sense and sense of community through many rounds of discussions and revisions. We are also sincerely appreciative of the editorial guidance and support offered by the University of Toronto Press. Our special thanks to Daniel Quinlan for believing in this work at all stages of the process. Sidey Deska-Gauthier – a graduate student at the University of Guelph – provided exceptional editorial assistance with the book's index and as we prepared these chapters in the final stages, and freelance copy editor Barry Norris incisively polished the pages as they went to press. The manuscript's anonymous reviewers provided insightful, thorough, intellectually critical, rich, and detailed feedback that strengthened the message, content, and tone of this project. We are so grateful for their comments and contributions. Several of the chapters in this book are based on research funded by the Social Sciences and Humanities Research Council of Canada; it is a testament to SSHRC that the scope of engaged research within these pages is possible through its funding streams. Overall, we are measured and hopeful about the future of community engagement in theory and practice as we continue to reflect critically not only on political processes, but also on what just policy outcomes for diverse sectors of society will look like. Through collective action, collaboration, and a continuous commitment to sustainable futures and research oriented to *policy justice*, we are cautiously optimistic about the possibilities for cultivating more dynamic and invigorated spaces of public engagement.

CREATING SPACES OF ENGAGEMENT

Introduction: Why Create Spaces of Engagement? Connecting Theory, Policy, and Practice

SARAH MARIE WIEBE and LEAH LEVAC

Elected officials and public policy scholars alike note a growing need for public buy-in as a requirement for the smooth operation of democracy. But from whom and where should this support come? And how broad should it be? And what happens when the public is deeply divided on the question at hand? During the 2015 Canadian federal election campaign, the Liberal Party platform articulated a partial response on the matter in relation to environmental assessments: "While governments grant permits for resource development, only communities can grant permission."[1] Fast-forward to the spring of 2018. After claims of extensive public engagement administered by the National Energy Board (NEB) – including public hearings and the submission of thousands of oral and written testimonies across two provinces – the same party, by then in power with a majority government, elected not only to endorse the expansion of the controversial Kinder Morgan Trans Mountain Pipeline, but also to buy the pipeline to undermine staunch opposition from the governing coalition between the New Democratic and Green parties of British Columbia.[2] The project would ease significantly the flow of oil from Alberta's tar sands through British Columbia and out to global markets by way of the Salish Sea. Many of those most directly affected stand in firm opposition. Members of local, provincial, and federal governments, as well as numerous Indigenous nations, including the Tsleil-Waututh, and a vast number of environmental advocates, have put their bodies on the line to protest the development and protect the pristine coastline.

Demonstrating frustration with the failures of the official environmental assessment process, over 150 people have been arrested defending the coast, including many citizens and activists, as well as high-profile politicians such as Kennedy Stewart, former Burnaby South NDP Member of Parliament, prior to his position as mayor of

Vancouver; then leader of the Green Party of Canada, Elizabeth May; and Union of British Columbia Indian Chiefs Grand Chief Stewart Phillip. Prominent musicians, including Sarah Harmer and Grimes, as well as young Indigenous leaders from the Tsleil-Waututh Nation such as Cedar George-Parker and Ocean Hyland, added their voices to the movement. In Ocean's words: "We're at the stage now where we're thinking about those future generations and how we're going to carry on those teachings and carry through those ceremonies to protect the land we're here on today."[3] These artful demonstrations reveal an ensemble of people expressing a deep love for the coast and a commitment to protecting the lifeblood of the lands and waters threatened by further extraction. More than human lives are at stake in this dispute. The NEB's own final five-hundred-page report highlights that the "effects from Project-related marine vessels would contribute to the total cumulative effects on the Southern resident killer whales, and would further impede [their recovery]," and thus would likely "result in significant adverse effects on Aboriginal cultural uses associated with these marine mammals."[4] Despite this constellation of concerns, the NEB recommended approval of the project by the federal government. Since then, the project has been stalled – by order of the Federal Court of Appeal, which disagreed with the sufficiency of the consultation process employed – and subsequently reinstated. The final outcome of the Trans Mountain Pipeline remains uncertain at the time of writing.

This example reveals multiple layers of power, disparate perspectives, and diverse processes tethered to public engagement, a term we use throughout the book to refer broadly to the processes, dynamics, invitations, and/or tools and activities associated with a wide range of efforts to engage citizens in policy development. Although sometimes used interchangeably with "public consultation," we intentionally use the term public engagement as a way of signalling our rejection of typical government-led public consultations, which frequently suffer from – among other things – an absence of two-way communication, a lack of opportunity for citizens to inform the questions being raised, and the general sentiment that citizens' voices are being used to advance the government's predetermined position on a matter. It is worth noting that public engagement – as we intend with our use of the term – does not necessarily depend on initiation by a government. Rather, the initiative must simply have a policy purpose. The ongoing conflict surrounding the Trans Mountain Pipeline also suggests that, at minimum, deliberation – a particular engagement activity characterized by a dialogic process of sharing and listening to each other's positions to come to a mutually acceptable decision – is lacking. Finally, this example highlights how the legitimacy of public engagement – especially when its processes or ambitions are truncated – can be disputed. Ultimately, it is one of many examples that remind us how much we still have to learn about the ideas and practices of public engagement, not to mention the relationship between public engagement initiatives and the public good. As we have seen within the contested context of Canada's resource extractive industries, public officials express a commitment to measuring their "social licence" to operate as they "consult" with citizens to make crucial policy decisions,[5] yet what this means in practice is far from clear. The term social licence itself is amorphous and evolving, but generally refers to the idea that public officials must go beyond regulatory and consultative processes to engage the public in diverse ways, to listen, and to garner community support to move initiatives forward.

Securing social licence then, requires building relationships and establishing trust between governing bodies and affected parties, as opposed to simply undertaking transactional processes that "check the box" of public consultation. Moreover, the time and mechanisms required for necessary trust and relationship building must be part of the legislative and regulatory processes that guide public policy development and implementation. From multijurisdictional pipeline projects to municipally based urban design and development projects like the one Rachel Magnusson describes in this collection (Chapter 2), the ways in which public officials engage with members of the public (and vice versa) can and should take many forms. From thinking about the role of protest and resistance, to considering more carefully the formation of policy problems, to exploring theories of complex socio-technical, economic, and cultural transitions, there are plenty of opportunities for expanding and strengthening our understanding of, and practices guiding, citizens' and residents' participation in democracy.

This is the essence of *Creating Spaces of Engagement*. Our argument is relatively simple: more careful inter- and transdisciplinary theorization and practice of public engagement are necessary for including – or being led by – affected communities in all aspects of policy development, and thus in striving for more just societies. Further, because the practices and outcomes of public engagement are heavily context dependent, the processes themselves can be part of advancing more equitable outcomes when local communities inform their framing, development, and implementation. Although our practical emphasis favours the language of public engagement, the theoretical foundations and contributions of this work are oriented to deliberative democracy. We distinguish deliberative democracy from participatory democracy by borrowing from Floridia's suggestion that "participatory democracy is today generally a very broad reference term indicating a set of [ideas and] practises embedding the *active* involvement of citizens *within* institutional decision-making processes."[6] Within the broad realm of participatory democracy is deliberative democracy, which includes a more intentional focus on the exchange of ideas (that is, the act of deliberating), founded on assumptions and reasons that are mutually understandable and acceptable and subject to change through future deliberations.[7] Some of the book's contributors stretch beyond deliberative democracy to offer ideas about participatory democracy more generally, a move that reflects one of our intentions, which is to expand thinking about deliberative democracy by expanding ideas about the practices that fit within its purview. However, because our work is substantially informed by deliberative democracy scholarship, including a critical approach that draws attention to its overly decontextualized, rational, and masculine origins, we primarily use the language of deliberative democracy throughout the volume. Ultimately, by building on the rich groundwork laid by participatory researchers[8] and interpretive, critical, and intersectional policy scholars and practitioners,[9] and by considering the interplay between context and policy development and the importance of dialogical exchanges, we can advance the ways we understand policy making, and help inform better strategies for meaningful public engagement and expectations for policy outcomes.

While our argument is simple, the related work is anything but. It necessarily includes attending to the difficult and time-consuming work of trust and relationship building, and ultimately must be driven by a commitment to *policy justice*. For us, *policy justice* includes a commitment to advancing public policy with intentionally anti-oppressive and social justice–oriented aims; in other words, public policy that acknowledges and aims to address the effects of racism, sexism, colonialism, ableism, heteronormativity, transphobia, and classism in all policy fields, in an attempt to seek equity. We are deeply concerned with persistent failures and paradoxes in these regards – including at the intersections between peoples' identities and their experiences with the policies and related structures to which they are subjected. In short, *policy justice* includes a commitment to intersectional praxis. *Policy justice* also depends on the inclusion of diverse people, knowledge systems, and forms of evidence in policy creation. In this sense, *policy justice* includes approaching policy making with the same anti-oppressive commitments that guide our desired policy outcomes. Taking a *policy justice* approach emphasizes the lack of neutrality in spaces of engagement by highlighting how power is applied, refracted, and practised, and by whom. Ultimately, *policy justice* requires innovation and imagination in theory and practice, and, like our core argument, insists on transdisciplinary approaches to knowledge creation.

Transdisciplinary research responds to problems that are difficult to define, contested, and characterized by uncertainty. A transdisciplinary research approach retains the complexity of the problem, "take[s] into account the diversity ... of life-world ... and scientific perceptions of problems, ... link[s] abstract and case-specific knowledge, and ... [helps us] develop knowledge and practices that promote ... the common good."[10] The commitment to accounting for life-world and scientific perceptions of problems advances the related concept of knowledge democracy. Knowledge democracy includes "recognizing and valuing the multiplicity of epistemologies and knowledge systems;[11] recognizing knowledge as produced and represented ... well beyond text and statistics to include ceremony, drama, video, poetry, and so on; knowledge as produced in social movements, community organizations, businesses, local governments, and elsewhere beyond the academy; and knowledge generated through partnerships."[12] The ideas highlighted and woven together in this collection take a transdisciplinary approach to building on current theorizations about deliberative democracy and associated public engagement practices.

Drawing on a range of political theorists, Genevieve Fuji Johnson (chapter 1) describes deliberative democratic theory as "[consisting] of principles of participatory inclusion, procedural equality, access to information, and respectful exchanges of reasons geared towards a consensus, agreement, or expression of a shared interest, which in turn provides the ethical and democratic justification for a collective decision." Deliberative democracy also includes careful consideration of the ways in which decision makers engage the general public through dialogical policy-making processes in order to inform, influence, and improve democratic outcomes, and, ostensibly, gain social licence. Deliberative democracy advances the idea that the best policy decisions emerge after careful and thoughtful dialogical interactions that include affected parties.[13] As Archon Fung points out, one useful way to think about the practices of deliberative democracy is to consider the extent to which the public's engagement addresses key concerns of democracy, including legitimacy, effectiveness, and justice.[14] Procedurally, this entails providing those affected by the problems and question(s) at hand with ample opportunities to consider relevant facts, gain exposure to alternative perspectives, and express preferences about desired outcomes. It also means – as is made clear in this collection – upending what we imagine as the most appropriate (or only) forums and tools for hosting or facilitating policy conversations.

As noted above, within the deliberative democratic tradition, critical, interpretive, feminist, and intersectional policy scholars have also pointed to deep sources of exclusion that can be created by, and/or upheld in, deliberative democratic exercises. Past traumatic experiences and lack of access to public space,[15] decisions about whose voices matter,[16] participants' deliberative capacities,[17] and the possibility that differences will be suppressed,[18] are some examples of sources of exclusion of which we must be aware. As Philippe Koch finds, state structures and privileged actors can interrupt the "empowering potential of participatory arrangements."[19]

In both literature and practice, and in line with our discussion above, the application of deliberative (and participatory) democratic ideas is variously referred to as citizen engagement, public participation, and public engagement. The International Association for Public Participation (IAP²), with member states in both the global North and the global South, is an example of an organization that focuses on applying deliberative democracy. It describes its mandate as including the promotion and improvement of "the practice of public participation in relation to individuals, governments, institutions, and other entities that affect the public interest in nations throughout the world."[20] As global initiatives such as IAP² and the Participedia project[21] draw into focus, engagement processes take many shapes and forms, ranging from online consultations to open houses to legislative hearings. Frequently, these processes are established in response to sticky, tricky, multilayered policy problems, ranging from waste management to health systems improvement. While often dialogical and collaborative, these processes cannot be separated from their inherently power-infused contexts.[22] Although decision makers have the political authority to represent publics and to determine policy outcomes, they must be willing to listen to and learn from those publics, and balance competing beliefs, priorities, and conceptions of justice, in order to gain social licence.

As raised in the vignette that opens the Introduction, the Canadian government continues to push pipeline projects ahead. Concurrently, it claims to uphold its commitments not only to climate change mitigation and adaptation, but also to rebuilding relationships with Indigenous peoples.[23] These seemingly incommensurate positions help to highlight the fact that public engagement creates – and takes place within – striated spaces.[24] By this we mean that public engagement efforts contribute to, and are affected by, a context that is nuanced and textured, laden with meaning, and often conflictual. We can also think about public engagement initiatives as spaces that are defined, yet malleable, overlapping, and often temporary. Critically, these spaces are not neutral. As many chapters in this volume emphasize, state-directed forms of public engagement are often imbued with asymmetrical power relations between governing bodies and communities, even when they are less cynical than "public consultation." Public engagement efforts are fluid, yet hitched to rigid statist hierarchies of governance. As such, they consist of messy, multilayered relationships, contingent upon the will of those with decision-making power. We are interested in envisioning alternatives to the asymmetrical, colonial status quo, and in imagining more democratic, just, and inclusive relations that can be manifested through public engagement. One way to do so, as several contributors suggest, is through the creative, emancipatory, and transformative potential of the arts. Many authors highlight how reaching and listening to a diverse range of voices can be enhanced through creative, emotive, and felt avenues.[25] This requires going beyond formal structured spaces, where public concerns are "heard," to creating spaces for meaningful listening.

Across jurisdictions, public engagement is governed by a patchwork of policies and legal frameworks, ranging from the Crown's Duty to Consult Indigenous Peoples and Nations, to municipalities' open government and citizen engagement plans. Existing research demonstrates that policy-making processes and related engagement strategies are not linear or straightforward,[26] and that the theoretical foundations and empirical outcomes are uneven. As Gaventa and Barrett note, a "large gap still exists between normative positions promoting citizen engagement and the empirical evidence and understanding of what difference citizen engagement makes."[27] Further, questions of inclusiveness remain, in addition to scepticism resulting from the paradox or "illusion" of engagement,[28] which is easily advanced by the transactional process of "checking the box" of public consultation.

Overall, as the practical work of public engagement races ahead and governments are hard pressed to measure their social licence to pursue emergent policy proposals, relevant theory and empirical evidence lag or conflict. Ultimately, then, this book is about the progression of theories of deliberative democracy and practices of public engagement towards the more complete inclusion of – and leadership from – historically marginalized citizens, residents, and communities. To advance our argument, we respond to the central question: What does meaningful public engagement in policy-making processes look like? To advance our core argument, *Creating Spaces of Engagement* documents public engagement initiatives locally (across present-day Canada) and globally, and exposes the edges of these deliberations to consider – and in some cases evaluate – their inclusiveness. In our effort to advance *policy justice*, this book contributes to a broader dialogue about how public engagement can be better understood and improved to promote democracy, challenge colonialism, and advance ideas about deliberative democracy. Several chapters in this collection work within the parameters of the colonial Canadian state. We acknowledge the limitations of this approach,[29] while also seeing value in trying to create spaces within the state for radical alternatives. As such, throughout the book, we argue that it is critical to examine various access points and techniques of engagement to explore the ways in which the public can both participate in and shape the terms of participation, particularly in response to concerns about lack of meaningful engagement. Cautious of the risk of consultation acting as a form of tokenism, contributors to this collection discuss various strategies and techniques of engagement. Many emphasize artful, creative forms of engaging the public across a spectrum of socio-economic backgrounds and life experiences. Several authors consider multidimensional processes that involve numerous policy actors who are engaged at various stages and in various spaces of the policy process. They also seek to expose structural hierarchies, issues of political marginalization, and power relations that maintain inequities – an effort that requires a close look at who is included and excluded from policy-making processes, who benefits, why, and how.

These efforts link to the conceptual commitments of *Creating Spaces of Engagement*, including transdisciplinarity and intersectionality, discussed above, as well as interpretive policy, which includes focusing on practices of meaning making and how citizens feel, enact, and "sense" policy in their daily lives.[30] Although policy is often understood to refer to specific actions, decisions, or frameworks that governments implement to achieve outcomes, through an interpretive lens policy is not just an output. It is made up of institutional processes, language, and stories that communicate particular ideas about people and situations and the practices of people involved in policy development and implementation.[31] In other words, policy is not simply a text, document, or course of action; it reaches beyond a centralized governing body or head of state into the capillaries of society, touching communities, places, and peoples' lives. This book documents how policies take shape and what power dynamics and relations are at play when non-state actors become engaged, entangled within, or excluded from these processes. In this context, the overall aim of this anthology is to share knowledge about the vital connections (and gaps) between public expression, policy responses, and decision making.

Our intended audience in *Creating Spaces of Engagement* is threefold. It includes: (1) researchers who study and teach about public engagement, public administration, and policy development; (2) students enrolled in classes related to public engagement and public policy, and who are interested in contributing theoretical or empirical research in participatory and deliberative democracy; and (3) practitioners (public servants, community organizers and community organization employees, and others) who design and implement public engagement policies and initiatives. Through a wide range of examples of public engagement, this book raises critical questions of relevance to policy scholars and practitioners alike, including:

- How do definitions and framings of policy processes shape the ways in which diverse actors and identities are represented?
- How can inter- and transdisciplinary theorizing contribute to deliberative democracy?
- What does meaningful engagement look like in the policy making process?
- How are members of the public expressing concerns and trying to reach policy makers and how do policy makers respond?
- How can public engagement processes lead to policy justice?

Contributing Chapters

The chapters in this collection draw on a wide range of theories and models of participatory and deliberative democracy, and are thematically integrated through three main points that contribute to our core argument. These points emphasize the need for inter- and transdisciplinary theorizing about deliberative democracy (part 1); the need for more creative and innovative thinking and practising in relation to framing, developing, and implementing policy-making processes (part 2); and the need for better understanding the interplay between public engagement and the contexts and striated spaces inside which meaningful, engaged, policy making occurs (part 3). Part 1 draws from across and outside disciplines to expand theorizations about deliberative democracy. Part 2 focuses more specifically on evaluating public engagement, and on ways of ensuring that the voices of marginal publics are included. Authors critique and examine the edges, limits, and paradoxes of engagement to expose underlying power relations in the seemingly smooth operations of many participatory and deliberative processes. Part 3 emphasizes connections between the space and context of policy processes and respect for situated knowledges. Overall, these chapters suggest that, in order to convene meaningful spaces of engagement, practitioners and scholars alike must look beyond efficiency and effectiveness to also account for affectedness and complexity. Despite the diversity of the chapters, each speaks to the central question: What is meaningful public engagement in policy making, and what does it look like?

Part 1 – Across Disciplines and beyond the Academy: Stretching Deliberative Democratic Theory

The analyses in the chapters in part 1 expand the idea of deliberative democracy. Our core argument picks up on Johnson's (chapter 1) assertion that formal public engagement processes can easily "[replicate] the same kind of exclusion and marginalization" that creates complex policy problems in the first place. We argue that, to address this risk, inter- and transdisciplinary theorization is necessary. This argument is supported by a second, related argument: because public engagement processes and outcomes are heavily context dependent, beyond the normative democratic principle of affected interests,[32] policy-making processes hold the most promise for advancing equitable outcomes when local communities inform their framing, development, and implementation. By rethinking policy making from an interpretive perspective,[33] and by considering the interplay between context and policy development, we can advance the ways we understand policy making more generally, and help inform realistic strategies for meaningful public engagement and expectations for policy outcomes.

The six chapters in part 1 use examples of policy problems and exclusions to advance arguments about the need to stretch or shift theorizations about deliberative democracy in relation to the state and in terms of the experiences of citizens and residents. Four of the chapters ask readers to consider the need for new theorization, or for linking theories across disciplines. As in other sections of the book, authors in this section use a number of theoretical foundations; for instance, micro and macro deliberation theory to explore protests and demonstrations and the social construction of policy to examine shifting public narratives. Work in this part also considers the significance of neoclassical economics as the context in which relationships between the public sector and public welfare are formed, and contests the necessary relationship between public engagement and democratic states.

Through an analysis of the British Columbia Missing Women Commission of Inquiry, Johnson (chapter 1) argues that, in order to counter the persistent exclusion of historically oppressed peoples from political decision making, a better understanding of bridging micro and macro forms of deliberation[34] is needed, as is an anti-oppressive (power-sharing) approach to governance. Using the case of the Alberta Energy Futures Lab, Stephen Williams (chapter 2) argues that the multilevel perspective,[35] which tries to explain how broad sociotechnical transitions (towards climate stability, for example) take place, can guide public and multipartner engagement in complex policy problems. Ellen Szarleta (chapter 3) asks how applying the collective impact framework[36] in public engagement can advance policy outcomes. In so doing, these and other chapters in the collection contribute not only to how we theorize about deliberative democracy, but also to how we might evaluate its effects. In chapters 2 and 3, respectively, Williams and Szarleta introduce citizen engagement projects that invite links between deliberative democracy and theories from disciplines other than political science. Williams's presentation of the case of the Alberta Energy Futures Lab highlights the use of the multilevel perspective in sociotechnical transition theory to advance policy systems change. Szarleta explores how collective impact asks us to theorize non-central roles for governments in policy processes. In chapter 4, Leah Levac and Jacqueline Gillis turn within political science to the social construction of policy framework[37] to highlight how the persistent exclusion of some people – in this case, northern Indigenous and settler women – results in an insufficient understanding of the policy problem to be addressed, thus raising questions about how we should theorize policy problems in deliberative contexts.

The other two chapters in part 1 theorize participants' experiences in deliberative democratic exercises as a way of expanding the theory. They also invite readers to reflect carefully on the representation of knowledge and what constitutes a "community." Magnusson (chapter 5) asks us to consider how being unsettled in citizens' assemblies – an increasingly discussed form of mini-public[38] – contributes to participants' democratic experiences. Finally, Deborah Stienstra and Xuan Thuy Nguyen (chapter 6) align their work with other global citizen engagement scholars[39] to argue – drawing on a collaborative project with women and girls with disabilities in Vietnam – that having a democratic state is not necessarily a precondition for meaningful deliberative participation. This chapter shows how thinking about disability, access, and inclusion helps to push theorization (and practice) in deliberative democracy. Broadly then, part 1 asks us to think more carefully about the idea of deliberative democracy and to consider not only how policy changes come about in collaborative forums, but also how these forums and their participants are shaped and determined.

Part 2 – Centring Voices from the Margins: Expanding and Evaluating Engagement Practices

The second part of the book focuses on practices of public engagement, and invites readers to consider a broad range of engagement tools and efforts, in terms not only of how they enable new voices to be heard, but also of how they can be evaluated and/or linked to formal policy-making processes. These chapters, like those in part 1, raise important considerations for designing more inclusive opportunities for public engagement. They engage with a range of theories and concepts. Counterdemocracy is explored in the form of "policy hacking" and arts-based engagement efforts that shift the analytical lens to non-democratic states and vulnerable populations. Authors explore the theoretical underpinnings of a health promotion framework to highlight the relationship between individuals and the world around them. The role of art practices in supporting meaningful public engagement – discussed in part 1 – is extended to include the importance of responsive political listening. Also in this section, feminist scholarship informs a critique of well-intentioned bottom-up policy consultation and development, and gender-based and intersectional policy analysis frameworks inform evaluations of public engagement by drawing from women's perspectives, voices, and experiences.

More specifically, chapters 7, 8, and 9 document a range of unique methods used in public engagement efforts. Tara Mahoney (chapter 7) describes the work of OpenMedia to consider the use of "policy hacking" for informing telecommunications policies. Using a provincial initiative aimed at better examining substance use on post-secondary education campuses, Catriona Remocker, Tim Dyck, and Dan Reist (chapter 8) describe the use of "culture-focused" dialogues, and explore how policy processes can enable broader community connections. Joanna Ashworth (chapter 9) draws on years of experience convening public dialogues to explore a range of "art-ful" engagement methods that open new possibilities for participation. Chapters 10 and 11 focus on how citizen engagement efforts can be assessed for their inclusive potential. Reflecting on two pilot initiatives aimed at increasing women's voices in policy-making processes, Alana Cattapan, Alexandra Dobrowolsky, Tammy Findlay, and April Mandrona (chapter 10) examine the complexities of honouring diverse women's voices, especially when Canadian public policies have been – and continue to be – tools of colonization. These authors create space through the creative mechanisms of their collaborative arts-based research for women to tell their own stories. As we take up in the concluding chapter, they encourage us to envision and enact "radical policy futures." Levac (chapter 11) considers a government-convened public engagement initiative to suggest design features that are important for ensuring the equitable participation of women, particularly women living in low income. These chapters focus on the design and procedural features of citizen engagement initiatives that are important for *policy justice*.

Part 3 – Effective and Affective Spaces of Deliberation

Where policy deliberations take shape, and how these processes are structured, is essential to understanding the often hidden and invisible power dynamics of public engagement. Part 3, the final section of the book, offers five important examples of engagement that push us to think more broadly about situated spaces where historically marginalized citizens (and non-citizens) are asserting their voices to advance policy change. This section investigates policy-making processes as spaces of inclusion and exclusion, and includes further examination of arts-based engagement. Authors reflect not only on participation in such initiatives, but also on the experience of publicly exhibiting resulting artwork. They explore mixed media storytelling as a method of engagement and a tool for reframing narratives, and build upon the broad theme of inclusion by looking to theories of the engagement and disengagement of migrant non-citizens in public policies, including theories of political quiescence. Bruno de Oliveira Jayme (chapter 12) describes the experiences of informal recyclers in Brazil with the creation of a mobile art gallery that invited new policy conversations and advanced new policy spaces. Ethel Tungohan (chapter 13) describes the acts of everyday resistance by Filipino migrant workers and associated civil society organizations to highlight spaces outside of formal politics where policy changes are provoked. Focused on a storytelling project in Attawapiskat, Sarah Marie Wiebe (chapter 14) suggests that crises open spaces for new conceptions of citizenship, environmental health, community well-being, and policy needs and preferences. In chapter 15, exploring one university's efforts to advance reconciliation between Western and Indigenous institutions and ways of knowing, Derek Tannis calls for opening up spaces for truth. In the final contribution, Astrid V. Pérez Piñán (chapter 16) uses three examples of engagement initiatives in Nicaragua to articulate how previously inclusive spaces of engagement can be closed off by globally imposed "development" frameworks.

Cross-Cutting Themes

Across the book's three parts, the sixteen chapters also touch on a broad set of themes, including: engagement through innovations in arts and technology; engagement by and with diverse communities, including Indigenous peoples, migrants, and women; and engagement for anti-oppression, social justice, and community health and wellness. Although differently focused, the chapters share several commonalities. First, each provides an overview of a particular engagement initiative or project, so that the book reads as a set of examples or cases of public engagement. These examples highlight who convened the engagement or deliberation and why; who participated (or not) and how; and how these processes could have been improved. Second, and related, each chapter intentionally links relevant theory and practice. Some chapters offer explicit theoretical contributions, while others draw on relevant theory to inform public engagement practices. Other cross-cutting themes are shared by clusters of chapters. These include: local (Magnusson; Tungohan), global (Stienstra and Nguyen; de Oliveira Jayme; Pérez Piñán), and quasi-governmental (Remocker, Dyck, and Reist; Tannis) initiatives; the use of creative arts and technology (Stienstra and Nguyen; Mahoney; Ashworth; Cattapan, Dobrowolsky, Findlay, and Mandrona; de Oliveira Jayme; Wiebe); and engagement by and with women (Johnson; Levac and Gillis; Cattapan, Dobrowolsky, Findlay, and Mandrona; Levac; Pérez Piñán; Stienstra and Nguyen), and by and with Indigenous peoples and nations (Johnson; Levac and Gillis; Cattapan, Dobrowolsky, Findlay, and Mandrona; Wiebe; Tannis). The chapters also speak to the cross-cutting themes of anti-oppression (Johnson; Levac and Gillis; de Oliveira Jayme; Tungohan; Wiebe) and environmental in/justice (Johnson; Levac and Gillis; Wiebe). From the prism of interpretive and intersectional policy analysis, the authors emphasize public engagement that is committed to action and justice.

Because of our orientation towards *policy justice,* we are interested in theorizations of power and critiques of the oppression evident in political structures. Several contributing authors focus specifically on government-convened engagement initiatives (Magnusson; Remocker, Dyck, and Reist; Levac), while others focus on government actors as participants in deliberative processes (Johnson; Williams; Szarleta). These contributions are multijurisdictional and multidimensional. Issues of health and the environment, which are taken up in four chapters (Johnson; Williams; Levac and Gillis; Wiebe), challenge the notion of neat separations between jurisdictions, scales, and levels of government. *Creating Spaces of Engagement* brings the messy multilayered scope of policy making to life in order to illuminate new understandings and policy priorities.

A final thread throughout many of the chapters is the value of the arts in making these connections and listening directly to historically silenced communities. Art making is a relational research and policy making approach. Rather than extracting, it centres community knowledges, as discussed in depth in several chapters (Ashworth; de Oliveira Jayme; Cattapan, Dobrowolsky, Findlay, and Mandrona; Wiebe). As such, the authors in this collection seek to create spaces for people to tell their own stories – respecting, engaging with, and responding to what Donna Haraway famously referred to as "situated knowledges."[40] Across the chapters, we articulate the importance of this idea for *policy justice*, particularly by highlighting the need to reach beyond hearing to listening, a progression that necessitates the transformation of power relations within administrative decision making processes. This book is thus a call to enact policy making that is relational, consensual, collaborative, and premised on the co-creation of solutions to the pressing policy problems of our times.

In advancing our core arguments, we also seek to serve some very practical ends. We seek to add to policy makers' toolkits as they develop and refine their approaches to framing and implementing public engagement initiatives in meaningful ways that are responsive to a diversity of community voices, interests and experiences. We also aim to contribute to classroom discussions. To this end, each chapter concludes with a series of discussion questions and suggested additional resources. The purpose of these questions and resources is to prompt readers to reflect on how best to further connect theory with practice and, ultimately, how to move citizen engagement processes and outcomes towards *policy justice*. Finally, the chapters in this book contribute to a broader dialogue about the importance of difference and the value of creating spaces for youth, migrant, Indigenous, and women's voices in policy processes. To take *policy justice* seriously, as more than a theoretical concept, requires asking difficult questions about what crucial policy conversations we need to have – and what engagement tools we need to mobilize – so that communities that are often rendered invisible can tell their stories, on their own terms.

NOTES

1 Liberal Party of Canada, "Environmental Assessments," online at https://www.liberal.ca/realchange/environmental-assessments/, accessed 30 June 2018.
2 Ashifa Kassam, "Canada: Trudeau vows to push ahead with pipeline plans in spite of protests," *Guardian*, 16 April 2018, online at https://www

.theguardian.com/world/2018/apr/16/canada-trudeau-transcanada
-pipeline, accessed 30 June 2018.

3 Canadian Press, "More than 150 protestors arrested so far at Kinder
Morgan Terminals in Burnaby, B.C.," *Globe and Mail*, 25 March 2018, online
at https://www.theglobeandmail.com/canada/british-columbia/article
-more-than-150-protesters-arrested-so-far-at-kinder-morgan-terminals-in/,
accessed 20 June 2018.

4 National Energy Board, "Final Report," *Trans Mountain Expansion Project*,
OH-001-2014 (Ottawa: May 2016), xii.

5 Tyee staff, "What is social license?" *Tyee*, 1 March 2017, online at https://
thetyee.ca/Presents/2017/03/01/Social-Licence-Debate-Vancouver-Panel/,
accessed 27 June 2018.

6 Antonio Floridia, *From Participation to Deliberation: A Critical Genealogy of
Deliberative Democracy* (Colchester, UK: ECPR Press, 2017), 4–5, emphasis
in original.

7 Amy Guttman and Dennis Thompson, *Why Deliberative Democracy?*
(Princeton, NJ: Princeton University Press, 2009).

8 We use "participatory research" as an umbrella term to refer to a broad set
of research practices and ideas that share a commitment to respectful and
reciprocal research that recognizes research participants as collaborators
and co-creators in the research process.

9 Olena Hankivsky, ed., *An Intersectionality-Based Policy Analysis
Framework* (Vancouver: Institute for Intersectionality Research & Policy,
Simon Fraser University, 2012); Olena Hankivsky and Renee Cormier,
"Intersectionality and Public Policy: Some Lessons from Existing
Models," *Political Research Quarterly* 64, no. 1 (2011): 217–29; Donna Har-
away, "Situated Knowledges: The Science Question in Feminism and the
Privilege of Partial Perspective," *Feminist Studies* 14, no. 3 (1988): 575–99;
Michael Orsini and Miriam Smith, *Critical Policy Studies* (Vancouver:
UBC Press, 2007); Peregrine Schwartz-Shea and Dvora Yanow, *Interpretive
Research Design: Concepts and Processes* (New York: Routledge, 2012); Iris
Marion Young, *Justice and the Politics of Difference* (Princeton, NJ: Princeton
University Press, 2001).

10 Christian Pohl and Gertrude Hirsch-Hadorn, "Principles for Designing
Transdisciplinary Research," in *Handbook of Transdisciplinary Research*
(Munich: Oekom Verlag, 2007), 431.

11 On this point, see also Leah Levac, Lisa McMurtry, Deborah Stienstra,
Cindy Hanson, Gail Baikie, and Devi Mucina, "Learning across Indigenous
and Western Knowledge Systems and Intersectionality: Reconciling Social
Science Research Approaches," May 2018, available online at https://www
.criaw-icref.ca/images/userfiles/files/Learning%20Across%20Indigenous
%20and%20Western%20KnowledgesFINAL.pdf.

12 Felix Bivens, Johanna Haffenden, and Budd L. Hall, "Knowledge, Higher Education, and the Institutionalization of Community-University Research Partnerships," in *Strengthening Community University Research Partnerships: Global Perspectives*, ed. Budd Hall, Rajesh Tandon, and Crystal Tremblay (Victoria: University of Victoria, 2015), 5–30.

13 In representative democracies, the interests of affected parties are intended to be sufficiently represented by elected officials. The inadequacy of this understanding is, at least in part, what has given rise to governments' efforts to attain "social licence."

14 Archon Fung, "Varieties of Participation in Complex Governance," *Public Administration Review* 66, no. s1 (2006): 66–75.

15 Frances Ravensbergen and Madine VanderPlaat, "Barriers to Citizen Participation: The Missing Voice of People Living in Low Income," *Community Development Journal* 45, no. 4 (2009): 389–403.

16 David R.H. Moscrop and Mark E. Warren, "When is Deliberation Democratic?" *Journal of Public Deliberation* 12, no. 2 (2016): article 4.

17 Guttman and Thompson, *Why Deliberative Democracy?*

18 Iris Marion Young, "Polity and Group Difference: A Critique of the Ideal of Universal Citizenship," *Ethics* 99, no. 2 (1989): 250–74.

19 P. Koch, "Bringing Power Back in: Collective and Distributive Forms of Power in Public Participation," *Urban Studies* 50, no. 14 (2013): 2976–92.

20 "International Association for Public Participation," online at https://www.iap2.org/page/history.

21 See "Participedia," online at https://participedia.net/, accessed 22 June 2018.

22 Our understanding of power dynamics and public engagement is informed by critical theorists such as Michel Foucault and his work on governmentality, as well as Chantal Mouffe's critique of consensus in *The Democratic Paradox* (London: Verso, 2000). The application of governmentality to public policy has been taken up extensively by others; see, for instance, M. Brady, "Researching Governmentality Studies through Ethnography: The Case of Australian Welfare Reforms and Programs for Single Parents," *Critical Policy Studies* 5, no. 3 (2011): 264–82; L. McKee, "Post-Foucauldian Governmentality: What Does It Offer Critical Social Policy Analysis?" *Critical Social Policy* 29, no. 3 (2009): 465–86; K. Murray, "Governmentality and the Shifting Winds of Policy Studies," in *Critical Policy Studies*, ed. M. Orsini and M. Smith (Vancouver: UBC Press, 2007), 161–84; and Sarah Marie Wiebe, *Everyday Exposure: Indigenous Mobilization and Environmental Justice in Canada's Chemical Valley* (Vancouver: UBC Press, 2016).

23 The veracity of the latter two commitments has been called into serious question by scientists and Indigenous nations, governments, peoples, and traditional knowledge holders. Without dismissing myriad significant

concerns, we also recognize a need to engage with colonial state efforts in the context of trying to better understand the ideas and practices of deliberative democracy. In this context, see, for example, the Truth and Reconciliation Commission of Canada's reports, online at the National Centre for Truth and Reconciliation http://nctr.ca/reports.php, accessed 10 December 2019.

24 We draw upon Gilles Deleuze and Félix Guattari's distinction between "smooth" and "striated" space as discussed in *A Thousand Plateaus: Capitalism and Schizophrenia* (Minneapolis: University of Minnesota, 1987). See also Flora Lysen and Patricia Pisters, "Introduction: The Smooth and the Striated," *Deleuze Studies* 6, no. 1 (2012): 1–5.

25 For more on the affective, felt dimensions of justice and engagement, see Dian Million, *Therapeutic Nations: Healing in an Age of Indigenous Human Rights* (Tucson: University of Arizona Press, 2013); and Iris Marion Young, *Inclusion and Democracy* (Oxford: Oxford University Press, 2001).

26 Fung, "Varieties of Participation in Complex Governance."

27 John Gaventa and Gregory Barrett, "Mapping the Outcomes of Citizen Engagement," *World Development* 40, no. 1 (2012): 2399–410.

28 Genevieve Fuji Johnson, *Democratic Illusion: Deliberative Democracy in Canada* (Toronto: University of Toronto Press, 2015).

29 Primary among them is the risk of overassigning legitimacy to a state that continues to pursue colonization.

30 Wiebe, *Everyday Exposure.*

31 Ibid.

32 Robert E. Goodin, "Enfranchising All Affected Interests, and Its Alternatives." *Philosophy and Public Affairs* 35, no. 1 (2007): 40–68.

33 Schwartz-Shea and Yanow, *Interpretive Research Design*; Wiebe, *Everyday Exposure.*

34 Carolyn Hendriks, "Integrated Deliberation: Reconciling Civil Society's Dual Role in Deliberative Democracy," *Political Studies* 54, no. 3 (2006): 486–508.

35 Frank W. Geels, "Technological Transitions as Evolutionary Reconfiguration Processes: A Multi-Level Perspective and a Case-Study," *Research Policy* 31, no. 8 (2002): 1257–74, doi:10.1016/S0048-7333(02)00062-8.

36 John Kania and Mark Kramer, "Collective Impact," *Stanford Social Innovation Review* (Winter 2011): 36–41; idem, "Embracing Emergence: How Collective Impact Addresses Complexity," *Stanford Social Innovation Review* (2013): 1–7.

37 Anne Schneider and Helen Ingram, *Policy Design for Democracy* (Lawrence: University Press of Kansas, 1997); idem, "Social Construction of Target Populations: Implications for Politics and Policy," *American Political Science Review* 87, no. 2 (1993): 334–47; Anne Schneider, Helen Ingram, and Peter DeLeon, "Democratic Policy Design: Social Construction of Target

Populations," in *Theories of the Policy Process*, ed. Paul A. Sabatier and Christopher M. Weible (Boulder, CO: Westview Press, 2014), 105–48.
38 Archon Fung, "Recipes for Public Spheres: Eight Institutional Design Choices and Their Consequences," *Journal of Political Philosophy* 11, no. 3 (2003): 338–67.
39 Gaventa and Barrett, "Mapping the Outcomes of Citizen Engagement."
40 Haraway, "Situated Knowledges."

PART ONE

Across Disciplines and beyond the Academy: Stretching Deliberative Democratic Theory

1 Revelatory Protest, Deliberative Exclusion, and the BC Missing Women Commission of Inquiry: Bridging the Micro/Macro Divide

GENEVIEVE FUJI JOHNSON

Introduction

In the Canadian province of British Columbia, serial violence against targeted women has been strikingly evident. For decades, women – Indigenous women in particular – have gone missing from, and been found murdered in, northern British Columbia, Vancouver's Downtown Eastside (DTES), and regions around that city.[1] In response to these profound tragedies and to the prolonged inadequacy of responses by police departments, municipal governments, and the provincial government, family members of missing and murdered women,[2] grassroots women's organizations, Indigenous organizations, community and advocacy organizations, and Indigenous and other public leaders mobilized in an attempt to pressure for an official inquiry into this violence and for the implementation of strategies to put an end to it.[3] For more than twenty years, they engaged in peaceful demonstrations that would evolve into political protest. For the purposes of this chapter, peaceful demonstrations include public events intended to memorialize, honour, or bring attention to an issue of significance. I define protest as public acts of either a legal or illegal nature carried out against state, or state-sanctioned, conventions, decisions, policies, laws, processes, or institutions that are perceived to be in violation of fundamental principles of social, distributive, and environmental justice. I understand protest to be a public declaration of disapproval or dissent designed to garner widespread attention to forms of injustice and oppression.[4] These forms of organization and expression were eventually successful in bringing about an official inquiry in 2010. Were it not for their efforts, it is very likely that an official inquiry would not have occurred. But, from its outset, the BC Missing Women Commission of Inquiry was seriously flawed, and when this became clear, women-led protests served to reveal the ways in which the inquiry replicated the same kind of exclusion and marginalization that contributed to the forsaking of so many missing and murdered women. My analysis of these demonstrations and protests highlights the critical role played by women's organizations in pressuring for an official inquiry and in exposing its troubling flaws.

In this chapter, I examine the case of demonstration and protest by grassroots women's organizations and ally organizations concerning missing and murdered women from Vancouver's DTES with respect to their critically important contributions to a system of collective governance based on an integration of micro and macro spheres of deliberative democracy. Examining this deeply tragic case contributes to a normative theory of governance that is informed by principles of deliberative democracy, but that does not reinforce forms of oppression, including exclusion, marginalization, and violence.

Theories of deliberative democracy – perhaps the largest and most significant area of contemporary Western political theory[5] – have given rise not only to an ideal approach to collectively binding decision making, but also to an ideal for the organization of collective life in constitutional democracies.[6] Developed over the past twenty-five years, theories of deliberative democracy consist of principles of participatory inclusion, procedural equality, access to information, and respectful exchanges of reasons geared towards a consensus, agreement, or expression of a shared interest, which in turn provides the ethical and democratic justification for a collective decision.[7] Recently, John Dryzek, Jane Mansbridge, and John Parkinson, to name a few scholars working in this area, have shifted both theoretical conceptualizations and empirical examinations away from single sites and forums and towards broader social and political systems of collective engagement.[8] While an important turn in deliberative theory and practice, the deliberative systems approach is likely not sufficiently radical to challenge aspects of constitutional democracy that perpetuate and reinforce oppression.

But it has potential. The approach can broaden our analysis of governance structures to explicitly include insights from demonstration and protest, especially by those who have been socially, economically, and politically oppressed. The approach necessarily enlarges focus to include both deliberative and non-deliberative practices within and among a set of interconnected entities contributing to systems that yield decisions that are binding – formally or informally – on a public or publics. Included in deliberative systems are multiple nodes of organization such as state and international bodies, political parties, interest groups, religious entities, unions, schools, police departments, voluntary associations, and social movements. Such systems also encompass a diversity of modes of expression and communication, as well as a variety of sources of knowledge – Jane Mansbridge et al. specifically include sources "of subjugated and local knowledge."[9] But in order for a deliberative system to be effective in addressing forms of deep inequality and persistent marginalization, there needs to be better integration between what Carolyn Hendriks has identified as micro and macro forms of deliberation.[10] Formal mechanisms of deliberative democracy in the political/juridical-institutional (micro) sphere need to be better connected to the activities of the broader civil society (macro) sphere.

Focusing on the official inquiry into missing and murder women in British Columbia as a micro forum and the demonstrations and protests by local organizations as macro activities, I argue that this case not only exemplifies the tension between the micro and macro; it also elucidates ways of resolving this tension. Despite being based on robust ethical principles, micro forums can be exclusionary, and can serve as rituals of state power.[11] Often unwieldy and contestatory, macro activities have many important functions that can enhance deliberation. These include, for example, organizing and mobilizing historically marginalized people, revealing new forms of knowledge and prodding shifts in public opinion, and scrutinizing and holding accountable those in political power. Although these spheres might clash, this case shows us the importance of better integrating them.

Some – especially Indigenous peoples, governments, and organizations – might understand deliberative democracy as yet another expression of settler rule, and might seek to disengage from or not participate in it.[12] Although sympathetic to these views, I believe that among the range of existing democratic practices and procedures, those of deliberative democracy have the greatest potential for the empowerment and autonomy of all, particularly where micro and macro activities are better integrated. With this in mind, I argue not merely that contributions of marginalized, subjugated, and experiential knowledges expressed in peaceful demonstration and protest *can* contribute to the development of more deliberative social and political systems, but rather that they are *necessary* in this endeavour. I claim that it is crucial to listen to, and act on the insights of, historically oppressed peoples to ensure that theories and practices of collective governance address the complexity and tragedy characterizing many social problems conditioned by deep structural inequalities and sexist, racist, and colonialist ideologies.

I begin with a brief overview of criteria expressed by Iris Marion Young and by Mansbridge et al. for assessing the relationships among protest, deliberation, and deliberative systems. I then discuss Hendriks's conceptualization of micro and macro deliberative democracy. Through this conceptual lens, and based on an interpretive analysis of published reports, letters, and statements, I highlight the role of organizations based in Vancouver's DTES in both bringing about a formal inquiry into missing and murdered women from the neighbourhood and exposing its replication of forms of exclusion and marginalization that contributed to the vulnerability of these women. I close with a discussion of critical lessons for the development of an integrated system of deliberative governance.

Protest, Deliberation, and Deliberative Systems

Achieving systems of deliberative democratic governance would require decentralizing agenda-setting and decision-making power in multiple areas of public policy and public life. It would involve realizing a range of empowered deliberative democratic forums and activities in the formulation, implementation, enforcement, and evaluation of public policy. Exposing and addressing oppressive, hegemonic discourses – discourses that uphold or, in Iris Marion Young's word, "mask" the reproduction of inequality and injustice – would entail attitudinal changes on the part of citizens, including traditional policy makers and stakeholders, experts and opinion leaders, and laypersons.[13] Moreover, a massive redistribution of social and economic resources would be necessary to eradicate structural inequalities and achieve the material conditions for genuinely inclusive and equal collective deliberation. In light of these challenges, it is important to resist assumptions that current instantiations of micro forums of deliberative democracy – for example, deliberative polls, citizen forums, participatory budgeting, and public inquiries – and interconnections among them are successes that can be built upon to forge sustained deliberative systems. They might instead be serving to replicate and reinforce existing forms of oppression, which might then be entrenched by broader systems of governance, effectively resulting in forms of deliberative oppression.

Young puts forth a compelling understanding of the conceptual and practical relationship between demonstration and protest and deliberative democracy, which she views as not only valuable but also necessary in endeavours for political and constitutional change that will end forms of oppression. Believing in the potential of deliberative democracy to curb political domination, curtail the imposition of partisan interests, and promote greater social and environmental justice through laws and public policies, the deliberative democrat "advocates processes and action to implement deliberative procedures in actually existing democracy, with all its conflict, disagreement, and economic, social, and political inequality."[14] The activist is much more critical, believing that "the normal workings of the social, economic and political institutions in which he [sic] dwells enact or reproduce deep wrongs."[15] Those who host deliberative forums and those who participate in them are generally "powerful elites representing structurally dominant social segments."[16] These elites wield significant influence over the deliberative processes, including setting the agenda, establishing the options, and determining the outputs.

From Young we can identify a broad criterion by which to assess the merits of demonstration and protest for deliberative democracy: these activities ought to expose oppression and oppressive forces that might not be visible to the broader public. Such injustices might be hidden in apparently fair and transparent processes of governance, and obscured by dominant discourses in the media, educational system, and political life. Demonstration and protest ought to be revelatory in the secular sense of the word. More specific principles emerge from writings on the importance of a systems approach to understanding and evaluating deliberative democratic practices and procedures. Mansbridge et al. argue that these movements can enhance "the deliberative system if they can be reasonably understood as giving voice to a minority opinion long ignored in the public sphere, or as bringing more and better important information into the public arena."[17] In other words, these movements can and should serve in achieving deliberative democratic ends, including a fuller constituency of participants (democratic), a more complete picture of the truth (epistemic), and a greater degree of empowerment for those who have been and are oppressed (ethical). In addition, these benefits must not be outweighed by "the partisan and aggressive tenor of many of the public protests and disruptions," which can create "chilling effects" or "a toxic atmosphere for deliberation."[18]

Seyla Benhabib was an early proponent of an inclusive and integrated system of public deliberation.[19] In her work, she develops a conception of deliberative democracy in broad terms, bringing to the fore the connectivity among the parts. Her deliberative democracy, conceptualized as a decentred public sphere, privileges "a plurality of modes of association in which all affected can have the right to articulate their point of view."[20] These include political parties, citizens' initiatives, social movements, voluntary associations, and consciousness-raising groups that ideally give rise to a *"public sphere of mutually interlocking and overlapping networks and associations of deliberation, contestation, and argumentation."*[21] More recently, Hendriks has analysed deliberative forums and practices in terms of the micro and macro – the former referring to more formal activities among those who are "willing and capable of participating" in structured deliberation, often in collaboration with the state, and the latter referring to informal and unstructured nature of political activities "both outside and against the state."[22] Ideally, in micro forums, "participants are relatively impartial, willing to listen to each other and committed to reaching a mutual understanding in view of the collective good."[23] Macro activities are "highly unpredictable" and include "more strategic forms of action such as protest, boycott and radical activism."[24] As Hendriks writes, the "very fact that macro deliberation is based on less stringent communicative norms renders it a more inclusive version of deliberative democracy."[25] Macro activities are valuable because they serve in organizing and mobilizing a wide range of members of the public, they can reveal new forms of collective knowledge, and they can scrutinize state actors and hold them accountable. But we need to ensure that the macro is integrated with the micro.

"Power of Women in the Downtown Eastside"[26]

Demonstrations and protests organized by grassroots women's organizations in Vancouver's DTES and their ally organizations show us why these activities are important and how they can contribute to ensuring that micro activities do not merely reinforce forms of oppression.[27] They can be understood as both intensifying the tension between the micro and macro and showing ways of resolving this tension. In this section, I focus on how women-led organizations based in the DTES mobilized a loud and clear call for an examination of the systemic conditions contributing to the vulnerability of women, and collectively pressured for an official commission of inquiry into missing and murdered women from the neighbourhood.

Vancouver's Downtown Eastside is a dynamic context characterized by both extreme violence against women living and working in the area, as well as the enormous perseverance of these women, family members, friends, and allies. Vancouver's DTES is one of the most materially impoverished neighbourhoods in Canada.[28] Women based in this neighbourhood have been abused, disappeared, and murdered for decades.[29] Indeed, the neighbourhood was the stalking grounds of a serial killer who was eventually charged with twenty-six counts of murder and found guilty on six counts in 2007.[30]

A site of great tragedy, the DTES is also a nexus of strength, perseverance, and organization, all of which contributed to effective political mobilization for an official inquiry into these murders.[31] In the late 1970s, women-led and women-serving organizations – in particular, the Downtown Eastside Women's Centre (DEWC) – began providing support to women in the neighbourhood. They also launched endeavours to increase social and political awareness of the violence against women occurring in the area. Numerous grassroots organizations, including the February 14th Women's Memorial March Committee, CRAB – Water for Life Society, and the Power of Women for Women, became engaged in important activities to increase public awareness and prompt an adequate investigation of the missing and murdered women. More formal organizations also became very involved, including the First Nations Summit (FNS), which consists of a majority of First Nations and Tribal Councils in British Columbia. Soon after its establishment in 1990, the FNS started advocating for the issue of missing and murdered women "to be taken seriously by the provincial government, local police, and various public agencies."[32] Alongside family members and friends of missing and murdered women, it demanded police investigations, but was often not taken seriously. The investigations that did take place were riddled with serious faults. Jason Gratl, in his report as independent counsel to the official commission of inquiry that eventually took place, would write, "Stereotyping, overt expressions of bigotry and discriminatory attitudes against sex workers, drug users, and Aboriginal women undermined the investigations of missing women."[33] Wally Oppal, as commissioner of this inquiry, would characterize many of the police responses to these tragedies as "colossal" failures.[34]

Perhaps the most visible women's grassroots organization is the Women's Memorial March Committee, which for more than twenty-five years has organized an annual march on 14 February to honour and remember missing and murdered women. The march, now held in cities across Canada, brings together thousands to express grief and anger at failures "to protect women from the degradation of poverty and systemic exploitation, abuse and violence."[35] As members of the committee write, women continue to go missing or be murdered "with no action from any level of government to address these tragedies or gendered violence, poverty, racism, or colonialism."[36] Over the years, the Memorial March has contributed to increasing the visibility of issues related to missing and murdered women, including biases within the Vancouver Police Department (VPD) and the Royal Canadian Mounted Police (RCMP), the judicial system, and the broader society, all of which have impeded a more timely and thorough search for them, investigation of their disappearance, and recognition of the possibility – if not probability – that they fell prey to serial murder. The persistent activity by family members of missing and murdered women, their ally organizations, and the Women's Memorial March Committee fed directly into a nascent awareness among city officials and provincial politicians of the imperative to take seriously the disappearances of women from the DTES. In response to the pressure from local organizations and pleas from family members, the BC Missing Women Commission of Inquiry was finally launched in 2010, chaired by the former attorney general of the province, Wally Oppal.[37]

"The Height of Unfairness"[38]

The Commission was charged with the responsibility of fact finding with respect to police activities and investigations concerning disappeared women from the DTES between January 1997 and February 2002. It was also responsible for fact finding with respect to the decision of the Criminal Justice Branch of the BC Department of Justice in January 1998 to enter a stay of proceedings against the serial killer, who months earlier had been charged with attempted murder, assault with a weapon, forcible confinement, and aggravated assault. This inquiry had the potential to realize deliberative democratic principles of participatory inclusion and procedural equality and to reach a resolution in terms of recommendations generally acceptable to all participants. In part, this is because inquiries are generally concerned with understanding and addressing systemic failures, as opposed to attributing legal responsibility to particular individuals.[39] But this potential was not realized. Here, I draw from published letters and statements to show how the macro activities of local organizations exposed forms of oppression reproduced by the Commission's terms of reference and procedures.

Very early in the inquiry, it became clear that the process would be exclusionary. The Women's Memorial March Committee and DEWC, as well as other women's organizations, sex worker organizations, Indigenous organizations, and ally organizations, would effectively be excluded. These organizations were important stakeholders, they had first-hand knowledge of the contextual circumstances in which many women went missing, and they had an ethical claim to participate.

In the fall of 2010, a number of these organizations applied for either full or partial standing in the inquiry's proceedings. Forming coalitions among themselves, they included DEWC and the Women's Memorial March Committee, as well as the Aboriginal Women's Action Network, Amnesty International, Asian Women Coalition Ending Prostitution, the

BC Civil Liberties Association (BCCLA), the BC Coalition of Childcare Advocates, the BC Council of Women, the Canadian Association of Sexual Assault Centres, the Carrier Sekani Tribal Council, Exploited Voices now Educating, the Ending Violence Association of BC, the Frank Paul Society, Justice for Girls, the National Congress of Black Women, PACE, Pivot, the Poverty and Human Rights Centre, the Vancouver University Women's Club, the Vancouver Rape Relief and Women's Shelter, the Union of BC Indian Chiefs, the West Coast Women's Legal Education and Action Fund (LEAF), and the Women's Information and Safe House Drop-In Centre Society (WISH).[40] The Assembly of First Nations, CRAB, FNS, the Native Courtworker and Counselling Association of BC, and NWAC also applied, but as independent organizations and not in coalition with other organizations.[41] Recognizing their direct interest in the Commission's findings and the importance of their participation, Oppal granted all of these organizations and coalitions among them either full or partial standing.[42] This standing was critical for a complete and accurate understanding of events concerning the investigation of missing and murdered women, as these organizations and coalitions had direct knowledge of their day-to-day realities and experiences, as well as the systemic factors contributing to their marginalization and the violence against them. Cross-examination by these groups would have ensured that evidence presented was challenged and probed.

But effective cross-examination would require legal counsel, which was denied by the BC attorney general in May 2011.[43] The result, as stated in a letter from Kent Roach and eleven other legal experts, all of whom had previously participated in official inquiries, was to ensure that "no party will be equipped or inclined to cross-examine witnesses with a view to addressing or revealing systemic issues."[44] They went on, pointing out that the VPD, the RCMP, and the Criminal Justice Branch "will all be present with highly trained counsel, with the lone lawyer for some of the families ... to cross-examine them on their conduct."[45] These perspectives were widely voiced, especially by women-led and -serving organizations.[46]

In the summer of 2011, Oppal unsuccessfully appealed to the attorney general to reconsider his decision.[47] He subsequently decided to appoint two independent lawyers, funded by the Commission and assisted by two *pro bono* lawyers, to represent the multiple and diverse interests that had been expressed by organizations based in the DTES and those representing Indigenous women that were denied funding for legal counsel.[48] Two lawyers, however skilled, would not be adequate to represent the many interests of the DTES and Indigenous women. Moreover, unlike counsel for the police and federal and provincial governments, these lawyers would function independently of their "clients."[49] Specifically, they would not be legally accountable to, and would not take instructions from, the groups they would purport to represent.[50] As opposed to correcting the unfairness and discrimination in the decision not to fund their legal counsel, the appointment of "independent" counsel was widely taken as a "further unfairness" and another "form of discrimination."[51] Given the inherent limitations of representation by these *amicus* lawyers, a number of organizations rejected the proposal. Key women-led organizations thus shifted their strategy away from calling for an official inquiry that was genuinely inclusive, to protesting and thus revealing the oppressive flaws of the BC Missing Women's Commission of Inquiry. Thus, in addition to organizing and mobilizing, these actors also played a crucial role in scrutinizing the activities of the inquiry and in holding official actors accountable when they perpetuated forms of oppression, which we shall continue to see in the following section.

Exclusion and Marginalization Exposed

Recognizing the virtual impossibility of self-representation, almost all of the organizations and coalitions started officially withdrawing from the inquiry. Their decisions to do so were extremely difficult to make, and only after serious deliberation within and among these groups.[52] Again, for decades, many had called for an official inquiry; now they were de facto being shut out of it and effectively forced to not participate. But in taking this important step, they highlighted democratic, epistemic, and ethical imperatives that formal deliberation must realize in order to end, rather than perpetuate, oppression. Without the meaningful participation of these groups, the inquiry's deliberations would be exclusionary, the truth would not come out, the crimes and contexts in which they occurred would not be comprehended, and justice would not prevail. The denial of funding made their participation impossible; these groups had little choice but to engage in protest that would reveal perpetuated oppression.

In early October 2011, following a discussion and vote among their members, DEWC and the Women's Memorial March Committee officially withdrew from the inquiry process.[53] The voices of those who were denied participation are instructive. In the words of Carol Martin, victim services worker at DEWC, "This Inquiry has a responsibility to highlight those systemic injustices that allowed the unimaginable deaths and disappearances of so many women from the Downtown Eastside. We have been raising awareness on this issue for over twenty years and demanding an inquiry for decades, but this Sham Inquiry is flawed and unjust. We cannot endorse it."[54] In the words of Beatrice Starr, a resident of the DTES for thirty years, "We are sick of this. This Inquiry was supposed to be about a measure of justice for us and the hope that things would change down here, but it is just more of the same injustices."[55] As stated by Diane Wood, a member of the Women's Memorial March Committee, "We have essentially been shut out from this Sham Inquiry that is actually supposed to be about us and our experiences. It is vital to this Inquiry that the voices of women and the community be front and centre when determining its recommendations. Without a commitment to the participation of women from the Downtown Eastside, the Inquiry is not legitimate and has no credibility."[56] According to Lisa Yellow-Quill, also of the Women's Memorial March Committee, "We were witness to the system's gross negligence as well as racism and sexism in investigating these disappearances and murders. It is unconscionable that ... the BC Government [is] demonstrating those same dismissive and discriminatory attitudes today. We want and continue to be committed to a just Inquiry, not a Sham Inquiry."[57] And finally, as stated by Harsha Walia of DEWC:

It is disgusting that the Vancouver Police Department and the Government of Canada – who are the ones on trial here – will have an army of publicly-funded lawyers to defend themselves. Women in the DTES have their own voices and critical information to share, but this Sham Inquiry has shut those voices out and maintained the status quo of inequality. This is representative of the very legacy of discrimination, racism, sexism, and colonialism that this Inquiry is supposed to interrogate. We have no faith that anyone or any institution will be held responsible for the deaths and disappearances of women from the DTES.[58]

Members of DEWC and the Women's Memorial March Committee, along with hundreds of others, protested outside the Commission's office for the first month and periodically throughout the hearings and study forums. On 13 February 2012, a day before the annual march, they held their largest, most vocal protest against the Commission in the heart of the business district of Vancouver. Hundreds attended the protest, while thousands attended the march. Consistent with the criteria articulated by Mansbridge et al., these protests were remarkable for their "non-toxic" and dignified characteristics. Moreover, the protests achieved Young's criterion related to exposing oppression not visible to the broader public. As the inquiry progressed, family members of the missing and murdered women, grassroots women's organizations from the DTES, Indigenous organizations, and their ally organizations continued carefully to reveal, document, and voice serious concerns with the Commission. What they found, exposed, and collectively articulated included many barriers to participation caused by not ensuring "adequate protection for the identities of vulnerable witnesses who agreed to come forward to tell their stories"; impossible time-lines thwarting "an appropriately diligent examination of all relevant issues";[59] conflicts of interest, with the Commission's hiring "a former Vancouver Police Department Officer to conduct witness interviews and to 'help' write an 'independent' report on the Vancouver Police Department and RCMP investigations"; allegations of "sexism and marginalization of witnesses by former staff of [the] Commission";[60] and limited witnesses and evidence, as the Commission did not "look into allegations of corruption and connections with organized crime."[61]

The Commission released its report in December 2012 to the pro-found disappointment of those who had called for it and those whose interests it was intended to serve. As stated in a letter signed by virtu-ally all of the community and advocacy organizations that had been granted standing in the inquiry but denied funding for legal counsel, this "failed Inquiry, far from assisting Indigenous women and women from the Downtown Eastside has ironically reinforced their marginali-zation."[62] Statements by grassroots women's organizations, Indigenous organizations, and ally organizations clearly indicate that they saw the Commission's process as an absolute failure in terms of both establish-ing the truth concerning police investigations and some reconciliation between the families and friends of the missing and murdered women and the VPD and the RCMP. This case clearly reveals the tension between the macro and micro, but also the importance of resolving it.

Critical Lessons: Towards a Micro/Macro Integration

Were it not for persistent efforts to scrutinize official activities and hold official actors accountable, the multiple ways in which the inquiry replicated and reinforced patterns of marginalization would have remained obscured by a veneer of impartial official procedures. The efforts by the Women's Memorial March Committee, DEWC, and many other organizations make clear the importance of understanding the context in which forms of formal collective deliberation take place, and of developing normative principles and practical procedures appro-priate to this context. Although these were called for by family mem-bers, community and advocacy organizations, and Indigenous and public leaders, the Commission's processes were artificially imposed.

The terms of reference, procedures for the hearing and study forums, and participants with legal counsel were based on decisions taken in exclusion of these voices. The design of the process, its management, and its oversight were made by those disengaged from the context in which the Commission's work took place. The micro should have been integrated with the macro from the beginning to ensure that marginalized actors could participate in a meaningful way and that the inquiry would not merely perpetuate oppressive state power.

Abstractly, the Commission's procedures might have appeared neutral and fair. Oppal had granted these groups standing, and the BC government had provided funding for legal counsel to families of the victims. The province was recovering from a fiscal crisis, and funding lawyers for groups granted standing was not among its spending priorities, nor was it legally required. Nonetheless, this veneer evaporates when the Commission's proceedings are understood within a context characterized by, on the one hand, material poverty, historical marginalization, and political exclusion, and, on the other, by individuals and organizations holding important information and knowledge about the lives of vulnerable women in the neighbourhood and the systemic factors contributing to that vulnerability. In this context, the Commission served to perpetuate marginalization and exacerbate power inequalities. This case makes vivid the importance of being acutely attentive to context and its oppressive forces, as they might be masked in formal procedures and hegemonic discourses. Although, in his final report, Oppal refers to "overarching social and economic trends" that contribute to the marginalization of women,[63] the inquiry's practices and procedures made a sustained and thorough examination of these context factors virtually impossible.

Darcie Bennett, David Eby, Kasari Govender, and Katrina Pacey – at the time of writing all associated with organizations working on behalf of marginalized communities in the DTES – elaborate on important concrete practices and procedures that could be implemented towards realizing the meaningful participation and deliberation of marginalized communities in formal procedures.[64] As they write, "commissions of inquiry that intend to work with marginalized populations as witnesses, or inquiries that are called in response to the concerns of marginalized communities, must consult thoroughly at every stage with those communities and the organizations that work with those communities."[65] In addition, marginalized individuals and groups must have "meaningful opportunity, including funding and legal representation if necessary, to participate."[66] Rather than imposing new measures to facilitate the participation of marginalized individuals and groups, it would be more effective to employ "the infrastructure, expertise and staff of existing community organizations ... by providing those groups with additional resources."[67] Bennett, Eby, Govender, and Pacey also point to the importance of "an educational component" to assist hosts and organizers of, and participants in, deliberative procedures, to aid in "understanding culturally appropriate and effective ways" to collect evidence, express arguments, and communicate.[68] They also argue for the provision of "[p]sychosocial, legal and any other supports that are reasonably required to facilitate" the participation of marginalized individuals and groups.[69] Through these concrete steps, the macro and micro spheres could be much better integrated.

This case sheds light on the critical importance of developing inclusive and contextualized deliberative systems of governance, especially where the lives of vulnerable people are at stake. In particular, it reveals a need to develop relational and institutional interconnections among community members, civil society organizations, entities responsible for making public policy, and those responsible for interpreting, implementing, and enforcing it. DEWC and the Women's Memorial March Committee, and many of their ally organizations, operate internally on the basis of principles of inclusive and collective deliberation. In principle, all participants – staff, committee members, and women living and working in the community – are respected, and each is given the time and support to articulate her views on an issue. Collectively deliberating, strategizing, and letter writing, these organizations acquire important information and develop important knowledge by enabling subjugated voices to surface and be heard. Members of these organizations participate in this deliberation on a daily basis; deliberation is a constant process, yielding important knowledge about what is going on in their communities. A more timely and comprehensive response to concerns about the missing and murdered women of the DTES could have transpired had a system of collective deliberation, composed of meaningful and respectful interconnections between these grassroots organizations and state officials, been in place. But police routinely dismissed both the concerns articulated by DTES community members and the wealth of knowledge they hold.

Conclusion

This case reveals deep tensions between the macro sphere of deliberative politics and the micro sphere of formal deliberation. It also highlights the importance of integrating these spheres so that a system of governance can be realized that achieves democratic, epistemic, and ethical aims. The activities of family members of missing and murdered women, grassroots women's organizations, sex worker organizations, Indigenous organizations, and their ally organizations bring into focus the necessity of expressing subjugated knowledge in order to keep a critical check on formal sites of collective deliberation, such as commissions of inquiry. Had it not been for their organization, mobilization, and tireless efforts, there very likely would not have been an official inquiry into the profound tragedies that occurred to women living and working in Vancouver's DTES. Had it not been for their letter writing, press releases, marches, and protests, the patterns of exclusion and marginalization evidenced in the Commission's terms of reference, the BC government's decision not to fund groups granted standing, and aspects of its procedures would have not been scrutinized, interrogated, and made widely known. This case shows us that peaceful demonstration and revelatory political protest are not only important, but might be necessary for developing a system of deliberative governance that includes the historically marginalized and addresses the tragedy and complexity of violence against them.

The activities of individuals and organizations, including the Women's Memorial March Committee and DEWC, contributed to prompting the provincial commission of inquiry. In turn, their persistent protests during the inquiry's hearings exposed exclusionary biases within the process itself. These protests were expressions of compelling arguments concerning the importance of including those directly affected not only for ethical reasons, but also for reasons related to the quality and validity of findings and recommendations. They were important public statements concerning the need to include, on equal terms, those directly affected by the inadequacies of the police investigations, realizing the meaningful collaboration and engagement of these individuals and organizations working on their behalf, and recognizing the extreme structural inequalities, marginalization, and vulnerability that characterize the reality of the missing and murdered women and many others. As proponents of deliberative democracy think more broadly in terms of a system of governance, we must be attuned to the possibility that exercises in its name might reinforce deep inequalities and perpetuate forms of oppression.

Discussion Questions

1 The author argues that marginalized groups can strengthen their role in micro deliberations through macro activities. Is it possible or even desirable for groups to have a role in both worlds? Can those

who criticize systems of power simultaneously participate in micro deliberations and maintain their credibility as independent critics?

2 Considering the extent of the activities Bennett, Eby, Govender, and Pacey say are required to realize meaningful participation and deliberation, is it possible to have micro deliberations that live up to their standards? Specifically, would it have been possible for the BC Missing Women Commission of Inquiry to produce an inclusive process that met their standards?

3 What do you find most attractive about inclusive and contextualized deliberative systems of governance? Where are they most likely to be effective? What shortcomings do such processes have?

NOTES

Although I write about vulnerable women, many of whom are Indigenous and many of whom are sex workers, I am neither. I cannot profess to fully understand their realities, but I am committed through my scholarship and my volunteer work to advancing the interests of the communities to which these women belong. In terms of my methodology, I have tried to draw strictly from public statements by organizations directly involved in supporting and advocating these communities.

1 It is important to point out that Indigenous women and girls are enormously overrepresented among the missing and murdered in Canada. In Canada, between 1997 and 2000, the homicide rate for Indigenous women was nearly seven times the rate for non-Indigenous women; see Vivian O'Donnell and Susan Wallace, "First Nations, Métis and Inuit Women," *Women in Canada: A Gender-based Statistical Report* (Ottawa: Statistics Canada, 2011). Based on data from the 2006 census, Indigenous women were eight times more likely to be homicide victims than were non-Indigenous women; see Holly Johnson, *Measuring Violence against Women: Statistical Trends 2006* (Ottawa: Statistics Canada, 2006). According to the Native Women's Association of Canada (NWAC), there were 582 documented cases of missing and murdered Indigenous women and girls throughout Canada between 1980 and 2010; see NWAC, "Fact Sheet: Missing and Murdered Aboriginal Women and Girls in British Columbia" (Ottawa: NWAC, 2010). In January 2012, NWAC added fifty-six additional occurrences of missing or murdered Indigenous women and girls between 2010 and 2012. In March 2013, NWAC updated this list of "new" occurrences to eighty-six, to bring the total close to seven hundred; see NWAC and Canadian Feminist Alliance for International Action, *Murders and Disappearances of Aboriginal Women and Girls in*

Canada: Information Update for the United Nations Committee on the Elimination of Discrimination Against Women (Ottawa, 7 June 2013), 7. According to the Royal Canadian Mounted Police (RCMP), Aboriginal women in Canada represent 4.3 per cent of the overall population of women, yet they are 11.3 per cent of the number of missing women; see RCMP, *Missing and Murdered Aboriginal Women: A National Operational Overview* (Ottawa, 2014), 7–8. It is also important to remember that women and girls of other ethnic and cultural backgrounds have also been the victims of these terrible crimes. The National Inquiry into Missing and Murdered Indigenous Women and Girls was launched in the fall of 2016, and released its report in spring 2019. In its report, it stated that the murder of Indigenous women, girls, and 2SLGBTQQIA people in Canada amounted to a genocide; see National Inquiry into Missing and Murdered Indigenous Women and Girls, *Reclaiming Power and Place: The Final Report of the National Inquiry into Missing and Murdered Indigenous Women and Girls*, vol. 1a (n.p.: National Inquiry into Missing and Murdered Indigenous Women and Girls, 2019), online at https://www.mmiwg-ffada.ca/.

2   As Wally Oppal would write in his report for the BC Missing Women's Commission of Inquiry, the "term 'missing women' is a terrible misnomer." He would go on: "'Missing' is a gentle euphemism for the stark, cruel reality that most of the missing women were murdered. 'Missing' does not come close to capturing the horror and brutality of the murders that befell most of the women, nor the depth of the continuous grieving caused by either certain knowledge of some of the women's terrible fate or the ambiguity of the unknown fate of the others"; see Wallace Oppal, *Forsaken: The Report of the Missing Women Commission of Inquiry* (Vancouver: Missing Women Commission of Inquiry, 2012), 1:4. For these reasons, in this chapter, I use the term "missing and murdered women."

3   For the broader Canadian context concerning efforts to bring about a formal inquiry into missing and murdered Indigenous girls and women, see Amnesty International, *Stolen Sisters: A Human Rights Response to Discrimination and Violence against Indigenous Women in Canada* (October 2004).

4   For more detailed discussions of the relationships among demonstration, protest, and deliberative democracy, see Archon Fung, "Deliberation before the Revolution: Toward an Ethics of Deliberative Democracy in an Unjust World," *Political Theory* 33, no. 5 (2005): 397–419; Francis Dupuis-Déri, "Global Protesters versus Global Elites: Are Direct Action and Deliberative Politics Compatible?" *New Political Science* 29, no. 2 (2007): 167–89; and William Smith, "Democracy, Deliberation, and Disobedience," *Res Publica* 10, no. 4 (2004), 353–77. Authors such as Temryss MacLean Lane have highlighted the long-standing reality that the word "protesters" is often preceded by "violent" in news reports of social

movement activities. This is particularly damaging when the phrase is used to describe Indigenous peoples' actions – people who are already stigmatized as violent. Instead, "defenders" and "protectors" have begun to be claimed as descriptors of Indigenous social activists. While I use protest and protesters to describe both Indigenous and non-Indigenous activists, I remain open to learning from others with greater insight into this important discursive challenge. See Temryss MacLean Lane, "The Frontline of Refusal: Indigenous Women Warriors of Standing Rock," *International Journal of Qualitative Studies in Education* 31 (2018): 197–214.

5 Carole Pateman, "APSA Presidential Address: Participatory Democracy Revisited," *Perspectives on Politics* 10, no. 1 (2012): 7–19.

6 See, for example, Seyla Benhabib, "Toward a Deliberative Model of Democratic Legitimacy," in *Democracy and Difference: Contesting the Boundaries of the Political*, ed. Seyla Benhabib (Princeton, NJ: Princeton University Press, 1996), 67–94; Joshua Cohen, "Procedure and Substance in Deliberative Democracy," in Benhabib, *Democracy and Difference*, 95–119; John Dryzek, *Deliberative Democracy and Beyond: Liberals, Critics, Contestations* (New York: Oxford University Press, 2000); and Amy Gutmann and Dennis Thompson, *Democracy and Disagreement* (Cambridge, MA: Belknap Press of Harvard University Press, 1996).

7 See, for example, Simone Chambers, "Deliberative Democratic Theory," *Annual Review of Political Science* 6 (2003): 307–26; John Gastil and Peter Levine, eds., *The Deliberative Democracy Handbook: Strategies for Effective Civic Engagement in the 21st Century* (San Francisco: Jossey-Bass, 2005); Genevieve Fuji Johnson, *Democratic Illusion: Deliberative Democracy in Canadian Public Policy* (Toronto: University of Toronto Press, 2015); John Parkinson, *Deliberating in the Real World: Problems of Legitimacy in Deliberative Democracy* (Oxford: Oxford University Press, 2006); Graham Smith, *Democratic Innovations: Designing Institutions for Citizen Participation* (New York: Cambridge University Press, 2009); Dennis F. Thompson, "Deliberative Democratic Theory and Empirical Political Science," *Annual Review of Political Science* 11 (2008): 497–520.

8 See John Parkinson and Jane Mansbridge, eds., *Deliberative Systems: Deliberative Democracy at the Large Scale* (New York: Cambridge University Press, 2012). See also John Dryzek, "Democratization as Deliberative Capacity Building," *Comparative Political Studies* 42, no. 11 (2009): 1379–402; John Gastil, *Political Communication and Deliberation* (Thousand Oaks, CA: Sage, 2008); and Carolyn Hendriks, "Integrated Deliberation: Reconciling Civil Society's Dual Role in Deliberative Democracy," *Political Studies* 54, no. 3: 486–508.

9 Jane Mansbridge, James Bohman, Simone Chambers, Thomas Christiano, Archon Fung, John Parkinson, Dennis F. Thompson, and Mark E. Warren, "A Systematic Approach to Deliberative Democracy," in Parkinson and Mansbridge, *Deliberative Systems*, 10.

10 Hendriks, "Integrated Deliberation."

11 See Adam Ashforth, "Reckoning Schemes of Legitimation: On Commissions of Inquiry as Power/Knowledge Forms," *Journal of Historical Sociology* 3, no. 1 (1990): 1–22.

12 See, for example, Taiaiake Alfred, *Wasáse: Indigenous Pathways of Action and Freedom* (Toronto: University of Toronto Press, 2005); and Glen S. Coulthard, "Subjects of Empire: Indigenous Peoples and the 'Politics of Recognition' in Canada," *Contemporary Political Theory* 6 (2007): 437–60. See also Joyce Green, ed., *Making Space for Indigenous Feminism* (Black Point, NS: Fernwood, 2007); idem, "Taking Account of Aboriginal Feminism," in *Making Space for Indigenous Feminism*, 20–32; Rauna Kuokkanen, "Globalization as Racialized, Sexualized Violence: The Case of Indigenous Women," *International Feminist Journal of Politics* 10, no. 2 (2008): 216–33; and Sherene H. Razack, "Gendered Racial Violence and Spatialized Justice: The Murder of Pamela George," in *Race, Space and the Law: Unmapping a White Settler Society*, ed. Sherene H. Razack (Toronto: Between the Lines, 2002), 121–56.

13 Iris Marion Young, "Activist Challenges to Deliberative Democracy," *Political Theory* 29, no. 5 (2001): 670–90.

14 Ibid., 672.

15 Ibid., 673.

16 Ibid., 677.

17 Mansbridge et al., "Systematic Approach to Deliberative Democracy," 19.

18 Ibid.

19 Benhabib, "Toward a Deliberative Model of Democratic Legitimacy."

20 Ibid., 73–4.

21 Ibid., emphasis in original.

22 Hendriks, "Integrated Deliberation," 487.

23 Ibid., 492.

24 Ibid., 494.

25 Ibid., 493.

26 This subtitle is drawn from the 2011 documentary by Alejandro Zuluaga, Harsha Walia, and members of Power of Women for Women entitled *Survival, Strength, Sisterhood: Power of Women in the Downtown Eastside*, available online at http://vimeo.com/19877895.

27 See also Dara Culhane, "Their Spirits Live within Us: Aboriginal Women in Downtown Eastside Vancouver Emerging into Visibility," *American Indian Quarterly* 27, no. 3–4 (2003): 593–606.

28 City of Vancouver Community Services and City of Vancouver Planning and Development Services, *Local Area Profile 2013* (Vancouver: City of Vancouver, November 2013).

29 NWAC, *Fact Sheet*.

30 Doug Lepard, *Missing Women Investigation Review* (Vancouver: Vancouver Police Department, August 2010), 33.

31 See also Carol Muree Martin and Harsha Walia, *Red Women Rising* (Vancouver: Downtown Eastside Women's Centre, 2019).

32 First Nations Summit, "Missing Women Commission of Inquiry," 12 October 2011, 5.

33 Jason Gratl, *"Wouldn't Piss on Them if They Were on Fire": How Discrimination Against Sex Workers, Drug Users, and Aboriginal Women Enabled a Serial Killer*. Report of Independent Counsel to Commissioner of the BC Missing Women Commission of Inquiry (Vancouver, 25 June 2012), 32.

34 Oppal, *Forsaken*, 1:77; See also Lepard, *Missing Women Investigation Review*.

35 Women's Memorial March, Justice for Missing and Murdered Women in the Downtown Eastside, "Their Spirits Live Within Us," 10 February 2012.

36 Ibid.

37 British Columbia Missing Women Commission of Inquiry, "Media Release: Oppal to head inquiry into missing women Vancouver," 28 September 2010.

38 This statement is from Wally Oppal, "Letter to BC Attorney General," 30 June 2011. The letter was posted on the BC Missing Women Commission of Inquiry website from early July to 29 August 2011 and possibly longer; see Wallace Oppal, "Statement by Missing Women Commission of Inquiry Commissioner Wally Oppal" (Vancouver, 29 August 2011). The letter has been removed.

39 Darcie Bennett, David Eby, Kasari Govender, and Katrina Pacey, *Blueprint for an Inquiry: Learning from the Failures of the Missing Women Commission of Inquiry* (Vancouver: BC Civil Liberties Association, West Coast LEAF, and Pivot Legal Society, 2012), 13.

40 Wallace Oppal, "Missing Women Commission of Inquiry: Ruling on Participant Funding" (Vancouver, 2 May 2011).

41 Ibid.

42 Ibid.; see also Kent Roach, Paul J. J. Cavalluzzo, Mary Eberts, Marlys Edwardh, et al., "Letter to Honourable Shirley Bond, Attorney General, Government of British Columbia," 7 September 2011.

43 David Loukidelis, "Letter to Honourable Wally T. Oppal: Decision on Funding for Inquiry Participants," 22 July 2011.

44 Roach et al., "Letter to Honourable Shirley Bond."

45 Ibid.

46 See Shelagh Day, "Urgent Letter to Hon. Barry Penner, QC, Attorney General of British Columbia, Missing Women Commission of Inquiry," 26 May 2011.

47 Loukidelis, "Letter to Honourable Wally T. Oppal."

48 British Columbia Missing Women Commission of Inquiry, "Media release: Missing Women Commission appoints two independent lawyers; two others to participate *pro bono*," 10 August 2011.

49 Ibid.; Roach et al., "Letter to Honourable Shirley Bond."
50 Roach et al., "Letter to Honourable Shirley Bond."
51 Ibid.
52 See The Family of Diane Rock, the Family of Georgina Papin, the Family of Marnie Frey, the Family of Cynthia Dawn Feliks, et al., "Joint Letter to Premier Christy Clark Regarding Missing Women Commission of Inquiry," 28 September 2011.
53 Women's Memorial March Committee, "Downtown Eastside Women's Centre and Women's Memorial March Committee announce non participation in sham inquiry, say will rally on first day of hearings," 3 October 2011.
54 Ibid.
55 Ibid.
56 Ibid.
57 Ibid.
58 Ibid.
59 The Commission was given an initial extension to 30 June 2012 and a second to 30 November 2012.
60 The law firm of Roper Greyell investigated the allegations of sexism and found that the "evidence received during the investigation did not corroborate allegations of inappropriate sexual remarks, comments, or behaviour occurring at the Commission workplace"; see Roper Greyell, "Missing Women Commission of Inquiry Workplace Investigation," 29 May 2012, 2, online at https://missingwomen.library.uvic.ca/wp-content/uploads/2012/06/Independent-Investigation-Report.pdf.
61 Aboriginal Front Door, Amnesty International Canada, Atira Women's Resource Society, BC Civil Liberties Association, et al., "Groups Affirm Boycott of Discriminatory Missing Women Commission," 10 April 2012. See also Joyce Arthur, "Honouring the Truth for Vancouver's Missing and Murdered Women," *Rabble.ca*, 2 November 2012; David Ball, "Amnesty International and Native groups release scathing open letter about Pickton inquiry," *Vancouver Observer*, 10 April 2012; idem, "Missing women: Dave Pickton among 20 outstanding witness requests ignored since 2011," *Vancouver Observer*, 19 April 2012; and idem, "Missing Women Inquiry Ends in Outrage: 'We Need More Answers, What Really Happened? '" *Rabble.ca*, 8 June 2012; Bennett et al., *Blueprint for an Inquiry*; and Harsha Walia, "Why the BC Missing Women's Commission of Inquiry Fails," *Rabble.ca*, 11 October 2011.
62 Aboriginal Front Door, "Community & Advocacy Groups Respond to Missing Women Commission of Inquiry's Final Report Joint News Release" 17 December 2012.
63 Oppal, *Forsaken*, 1:78.
64 Bennett et al., *Blueprint for an Inquiry*, 13.

65 Ibid., 5.
66 Ibid., 6.
67 Ibid.
68 Ibid.
69 Ibid., 7.

KEY RESOURCES

Bennett, Darcie, David Eby, Kasari Govender, and Katrina Pacey. *Blueprint for an Inquiry: Learning from the Failures of the Missing Women Commission of Inquiry*. Vancouver: BC Civil Liberties Association, West Coast LEAF, and Pivot Legal Society, 2012.
Johnson, Genevieve Fuji. *Democratic Illusion: Deliberative Democracy in Canadian Public Policy*. Toronto: University of Toronto Press, 2015.
Parkinson, John, and Jane Mansbridge, eds. *Deliberative Systems: Deliberative Democracy at the Large Scale*. New York: Cambridge University Press, 2012.
Young, Iris Marion. "Activist Challenges to Deliberative Democracy." *Political Theory* 29, no. 5 (2001): 670–90.

2 The Alberta Energy Futures Lab: A Case Study in Sociocultural Transition through Public Engagement

STEPHEN WILLIAMS

Introduction

Energy, starting with coal in the 1900s and more recently oil and gas, has been at the heart of Alberta's economy for over a hundred years.[1] The energy industry is also at the heart of Alberta's identity, extending even to the names of the two National Hockey League teams in the province – the Edmonton Oilers and the Calgary Flames. In the past few years, however, the dominance of the energy sector has been challenged by economic forces such as the collapse in oil prices,[2] political change at the provincial and national levels, and global pressures such as the COP21 Paris Agreement and the rise of the United States as an energy supplier, rather than just Canada's customer for energy.[3] The question of how the industry, and the province at large, should respond to these challenges is a pressing one. The Alberta Energy Futures Lab (EFL) is an attempt to do just that.

The EFL is a public engagement process launched in 2015 and led by environmental non-governmental organization (NGO) The Natural Step Canada (TNSC), and designed to accelerate Alberta's transition to a sustainable energy future. The EFL is a social innovation lab process[4] intended to answer the question, "How can Alberta's leadership position in today's energy system serve as a platform for the transition to the energy system that the future requires of us?" The EFL consists of sixty energy system leaders (known as Fellows) who are participating in a collaborative five-year leadership development and idea generation program. The EFL adopted the multilevel perspective (MLP) from sociotechnical transition theory as a core design principle, in large part due to my contributing the theory to the design process. I address my role in this process in more detail in a later section. The key questions of this chapter are whether, and how, the MLP can be a useful framing for groups designing public engagement processes aimed at fostering systems change, and what value the MLP provides such groups. To answer these questions, I examine the case of the EFL by engaging with the sociotechnical transitions literature, in particular the MLP, along with participatory process and deliberative democracy theory.

I begin with an overview of the multilevel perspective, its implications, and recommendations for the design of participatory processes. After a brief discussion of the methodology for the study, I present a detailed background of the EFL, then discuss key moments when the MLP has influenced the EFL in its design, delivery, and evaluation. I conclude with a discussion of key findings, suggestions for further areas of research, and thoughts on the value of this model for the design of participatory engagement processes. Overall, I argue that the use of the MLP has led the EFL to focus more strongly on system transition dynamics than on purely technical and policy innovations. The EFL has the potential to shift public narratives about energy in the province, engage with regime players and shift perspectives in industry and government in a more sustainable direction, and encourage the development, scaling, and adoption of niche innovations. An emphasis on transition dynamics makes this potential more likely to be realized than a focus on a collection of innovations or new policy developments.

Literature Review

Public Engagement for Systems Change

A recent turn to participation in the public engagement and deliberation fields promises increased engagement and better policy outcomes. Processes such as participatory integrated assessments,[5] citizen assemblies,[6] deliberative polls,[7] and social innovation labs[8] have been the focus of much attention. The literature suggests these processes should be designed to be inclusive and fair, and should present participants with unbiased information.[9] Outcomes may be described in terms of the impact of the process on participants (for example, in terms of increased knowledge or level of civic participation), the products of the process (such as reports), or the use of those products by policy makers.[10]

The kinds of participatory processes described above tend to be issue focused (for example, on transit,[11] urban development, or environmental assessment) or designed to elicit citizen preferences (for example, participatory budgeting).[12] Processes such as participatory integrated assessments[13] attempt to broaden both the constituencies engaged and issues considered, but are usually not framed around systems *change* or *transition*. A systems approach, with social innovation labs as just one example of sustainability transition experiments,[14] is promising, but needs a theoretical framework through which to determine which systems to change, where and how best to intervene, and how best to design processes to make that happen.

The Multilevel Perspective of Sociotechnical Transitions

The literatures discussed above do not talk about how or through what "mechanism" systems transitions take place. Nor do they address in detail the interdependencies and interconnections between levels of analysis. That is, they do not describe or evaluate the theory of change underlying the processes they examine. Sociotechnical transition theory attempts to do exactly this by focusing not only on how innovations are adopted, but also on how they shift the very systems of which they are a part. Of particular interest here is the multilevel transition theory perspective articulated by Geels[15] and others.[16] The MLP is a theoretical framework through which to examine these large-scale societal changes. It is situated within the broader sociotechnical transitions literature, and is closely related to the idea of transition management, which attempts to define how transitions might be guided or steered,[17] strategic niche management, which focuses on how best to support niche innovations to scale,[18] and technological innovation systems, which concentrate on how technical innovations develop and interact with institutions and systems.[19]

The MLP frames sociotechnical systems as consisting of three hierarchical levels: niches, regimes, and landscapes. Niches are protected spaces where radical innovations are generated "by small networks of dedicated actors, often outsiders or fringe actors."[20] Regimes define the "rules of the game" for sociotechnical systems and are often sources of incremental innovation. Regimes are not monolithic, and when examining transition processes, it is important to consider inter-regime interactions and interdependencies – for example, "battery-electric vehicles link transport and electricity systems."[21] Change (or resistance to change) in one of these linked regimes might have amplifying or dampening effects on the other.

Landscapes consist of "heterogeneous factors such as oil prices, economic growth, wars, emigration, broad political coalitions, cultural and normative values, [and] environmental problems,"[22] and provide a macro context for changes to the system. These exogenous landscape-level changes have a dramatic effect on transitions,[23] as landscape factors can create conditions for change, have a stabilizing impact on regimes, or induce a dampening effect on the impact of emerging disruptive niche innovations.[24] The MLP posits that changes in sociotechnical systems arise mainly from the intersection of two processes: one in which collections of niche innovations align to put pressure on the policy regime, and a second wherein landscape-level changes (economic pressures) create windows of opportunity within the regime for niche innovations to take hold.

Implications of the MLP for Public Engagement Processes

A review of the transitions literature suggests four key concepts that contribute to the design and evaluation of processes intended to facilitate or accelerate sustainability transitions. First, the MLP provides a framework with which to evaluate the current state of a system, its actors and relationships, and to assess whether sociotechnical system transitions have occurred or might be happening. These insights can help process designers understand where they might focus, which actors to engage, and what "success" might look like. Second, analysing the current state of a system through a transitions lens can help process designers identify opportunities and challenges for system transition and design a portfolio of interventions accordingly. For example, depending on the context, a lab process might choose to focus on accelerating regime transition through policy innovation, scaling niche innovations, or leveraging landscape-level shifts to influence cultural discourses that, in turn, can make the regime more open to adopting niche innovations.[25] Regardless of the specific approach, a portfolio of systems interventions is recommended, as the complexity of systems transition makes it unlikely that a focus on one particular intervention will lead to change at a systems level.[26] Third, the MLP literature suggests a set of process characteristics that lead to successful sociotechnical transition. These include providing space for learning and experimentation, developing multilevel actor networks that facilitate integrated decision making,[27] and providing space for mutually reinforcing dynamics between niche innovations that align to put pressure on the regime.[28] Finally, the dynamics and interactions among niche, regime, and landscape are a key feature of the MLP literature in that niche innovation success is highly "context dependent."[29] The implication is that engagement processes need to pay attention to systems changes, particularly at the landscape level, that will affect the design and implementation of interventions. Designers must also ensure that the process itself is designed for adaptation and reflexivity in response to landscape shifts by building in robust context monitoring and learning and evaluation systems.[30] This collection of insights from the MLP literature provides a clear set of recommendations for participatory process designers. In the balance of this chapter, I use the case of the EFL to assess how these recommendations were put into practice, and their value in systems transition processes.

The Energy Futures Lab

The EFL was led by The Natural Step Canada in partnership with the Banff Centre, the Pembina Institute, the Alberta government, and the Suncor Energy Foundation (SEF). Funding came from a range of partners, including the SEF (representing the large majority of funding), the Alberta Real Estate Foundation, the McConnell Foundation, and the Alberta government.[31] The EFL convening question was designed to be inclusive of different perspectives on the energy system and of different stakeholders, notably oil and gas companies. The goal of the EFL was to achieve "breakthrough results" defined as "New Partnerships, New Standards, Game-changing Business Models, Shifts in Public Narrative, and Changes in Public Policy."[32] Early Design Team discussions questioned whether the role of the EFL was to shift the system (a transitions approach) or to disrupt the system with innovations. The Design Team decided that the "goal is to *disrupt* the system in a way that accelerates the transition to a sustainable and resilient energy system."[33] The EFL set out to achieve this goal through three streams of activity.

The first stream was a cohort of Fellows who met for two-to-three-day workshops three or four times per year. These workshops were organized around different themes, such as prototyping, backcasting, and initiative development. Through the workshops, EFL participants learned about sustainability and systems change through different lenses, including the MLP, TNSC's Framework for Sustainable Systems Development (FSSD),[34] innovation processes, systems thinking, strategic foresight, the role of narratives, and a number of facilitation and process methods, such as open space (used to generate and explore new ideas) and fishbowl conversations (used to facilitate emotionally charged conversations in a safe space). This learning was facilitated by lecture-style presentations, hands-on workshop activities, and interactive games. The second stream was an organizational engagement process that conducted workshops inside participant organizations, such as Suncor and the National Energy Board, to deliver customized versions of EFL content. The final stream was public engagement that connected the EFL to the public through media, events, and public workshops.

During the Lab itself, participants used backcasting methods[35] to develop a shared vision of a sustainable energy future. As opposed to forecasting, which starts from the current state, backcasting starts with a vision of the future, then asks what steps are required to get there. The second EFL Workshop in January 2016 focused on this activity. The vision that emerged from this process says that, in a sustainable energy future:

Albertans are thriving because we produce and use energy in a way that the future requires of us. This means that we are ...

1 Home to the world's most innovative, entrepreneurial and responsible energy citizens.
2 Net carbon-neutral for electricity, heat, mobility and industrial processes.
3 The world's leading source of energy technology, products, know-how, and future-fit hydrocarbons.
4 A leader in energy-based partnership towards reconciliation with Indigenous peoples in Canada.[36]

Visions about future systems innovations play a number of important functions in sustainability transitions projects, including mapping the space of possible options, serving as a metaphor for building actor networks, and creating a shared narrative for mobilizing capital and other resources.[37] Especially in the Alberta context, it is important to recognize the significance of such a diverse group of actors coming to agreement on a shared vision of the future of energy in the province. One of the EFL Fellows described the value of the MLP in this regard as helping to gain "a better sense of the interplay between players [and become] better aligned when we better understand the roles we play." Although the vision was agreed to by all Fellows, there are still underlying tensions. For example, one Fellow challenged the strategy of the EFL to use existing hydrocarbon assets as a resource to invest in future transitions, saying that the "EFL has it wrong. There is no place for hydrocarbons in a sustainable energy future."[38] Nonetheless, there was enough agreement among the wide range of stakeholders to move forward as a group. At the time of writing, the EFL is continuing its work in modified form ("EFL 2.0"); however, this research study focuses on the design and implementation of the initial project ("EFL 1.0") from 2014 to spring 2018.

My Role in the EFL

It is important to note my role in the Energy Futures Lab. The EFL was the focus of my PhD thesis research,[39] and I have been involved with the project since its inception. I contributed to the original project proposal to the Suncor Energy Foundation in 2014, participated in design meetings, facilitated portions of EFL workshops, and reported interim findings from my research to both the EFL Design Team and EFL Fellows. Most relevant to this chapter, I introduced the MLP framework to the EFL Design Team in early planning meetings in 2014 and 2015, and have continued to share my observations, findings, and recommendations with the Design Team and with Fellows. This engagement puts me in an interesting position as a researcher. My theoretical background in systems transition theory and evaluation of participatory processes has led me to contribute knowledge from the literature to Design Team discussions and advocate for the adoption of the recommendations from the MLP described above, as I believe that this approach to systems analysis is most fruitful for organizations aiming for systems transition. In other words, I am not a disinterested observer of the process, and am in some ways assessing my own activities. To mitigate this inherent bias, I focus on the actions taken as a result of the MLP. As described below, I use evidence from design documents, workshop presentations, and meeting minutes to validate reported impacts from interviews. For transparency, I have included in my discussion points where I made direct interjections into the design process. Finally, I have engaged in an ongoing review process with the EFL Design Team to validate my conclusions and interpretations.

Methodology

For this study, I began with a review of the transition theory literature with a particular focus on the multilevel perspective in order to generate a list of process design recommendations. I then conducted semi-structured interviews with three EFL Design Team members in March 2017 asking how they learned about the MLP, how it was used in the EFL design and implementation process, what impact the MLP had on the EFL, what value was gained, and how the MLP might be used in the future. These interviews were complemented by semi-structured interviews with EFL Fellows in December 2016 and January 2017 (n=18), April 2016 (n=24), and January 2018 (n=34). In addition, I observed weekly team meetings of the EFL Design Team from January 2016 through to January 2018, observed eight EFL Fellow workshops,[40] and reviewed EFL design and planning documents for mentions and the application of the MLP. In addition, I reviewed the deliberative democracy literature with a focus on public engagement processes and their evaluation. After my review of the literature, I developed a set of codes[41] to represent key themes/recommendations, such as assessing the system and developing a portfolio of interventions, process suggestions, and context monitoring.

I used a secondary set of topic codes to capture challenges in the use of the MLP, systems transition, positive and negative contributions of the MLP to the EFL, and the use of other frameworks such as backcasting that also could have had an effect on EFL design and implementation. I used a final set of codes to mark mentions/use of specific components of the MLP such as niche, regime, landscape, and MLP itself. I then coded EFL design documents, meeting minutes, presentations, and selected interviews with EFL Fellows using this coding set. The focus of the coding effort was not just to look for evidence of where the MLP was referenced or had been used, but also where the MLP had made a contribution to changes in EFL design and delivery.

Key Moments of the MLP Effect

The MLP had noticeable effects on EFL design at a series of key moments. Unless otherwise noted, the quotations below are from interviews with EFL Design Team members conducted in March 2017.

Designing the EFL (2014–2015)

I first introduced the MLP to the EFL Design Team at an early planning meeting in September 2014[42] by briefly introducing transition theory and possible applications to the EFL. I followed this with a more detailed presentation in November 2014[43] in which it was first proposed explicitly to use the MLP – dubbed the "Geels framework" by the EFL Design Team – in framing the EFL transition strategy. The proposal suggested that "the Lab will work at all three levels," including niche innovation through Fellow projects; regime-level participation by engaging with policy makers (mainly at the provincial level) and businesses to better understand where policy shifts might be possible and how the cohort's innovations and networks could influence policy; and at the landscape level by leveraging cohort networks, targeted constituency messaging, and broad media engagement to disseminate FSSD principles into the narrative of energy in Alberta and to use narrative shifts to create more open conditions for innovations to be adopted at the regime level.

A concern in public engagement processes is that the participation of industry players can lead to *regulatory capture*[44] when industry advances its own interests in a regulatory or review process. The Energy Futures Lab made a conscious choice to include regime incumbents such as Suncor, Shell, and the Alberta government without a clear path to mitigating the risks of industry capture of the process. The inclusion of Suncor as lead funder was certainly beneficial in attracting support from, and demonstrating legitimacy to, the oil and gas industry and the provincial government. However, this also affected the legitimacy (or at least the perception thereof) of the EFL by other system actors such as environmental NGOs. Although no EFL participants reported pressure or influence from Suncor or other funders, concern was expressed that including dominant regime actors reinforced a market-driven approach to sustainable development. For example, through my observations of the process, it was striking that the idea of "keep [the oil] in the ground,"[45] expressed by environmental NGOs such as 350.org, was not considered a viable option for the EFL to pursue. The EFL instead has adopted an ecomodernist approach that positions nature as a monetizable resource whose exploitation can be maximized through environmentally responsible business.[46] This narrative stance is also embedded within TNSC's core FSSD principles, which assume that there *is* an approach that will allow resources to be developed sustainably. The question of "what if this is not the case with oilsands development?" was not directly addressed within the EFL.

The EFL Design Team immediately latched on to the MLP framing, saying that, although the "Suncor proposal didn't use or explicitly reference [the MLP], nevertheless the design of the Lab reflected the thinking [that we] didn't have the framework to describe." In other words, the MLP helped the team articulate an emergent design idea. This idea was then put into practice in a number of ways. The first was through the recruitment of Fellows, where the MLP "permeates design criteria – e.g. selection criteria of Fellows – influenced thinking about what we conveyed as expectations and who and what type of people to advance along all three levels."[47] For example, a second cohort of Fellows was added in spring 2017.[48] Their selection by the EFL Design Team was partly driven by a desire to include participants who could work at different levels of the MLP.

The second major impact was on the design of the EFL workshop activities and on the three streams of the EFL described above. According to one of the Design Team members, the MLP helped in "thinking through three levels – creating a space for fellowship to innovate. [It] influenced how do we work into existing regime – for example, org engagement strategy – equipping Fellows with tools to engage their orgs, sharing case studies – how to take innovations out of the Lab into the regime that is not ready or receptive [and] challenged us to think about public engagement."[49]

The team also recognized its "tendency to underemphasize the landscape work – others [that is, niche innovations and regime engagement] are important – but landscape [is] often neglected." As a result of this insight, the EFL Design Team put a greater emphasis on landscape-level engagement than originally planned, saying the MLP was "foundational to different activity streams – helping people understand landscape/cultural perspective" and leading to "activities more focused on narrative/outreach and so on." The MLP also affected the EFL's evaluation framework, as the Design Team "decided that 'breakthrough results' are focusing on the MLP levels [and are] using this to map out [EFL] impacts."[50]

The team integrated the MLP into its theory of change "as means of getting to breakthrough results,"[51] stating that "our hypothesis is that systems change happens with a collective focus at the niche, regime and landscape level."[52] The original intent of the EFL of disrupting the energy system for transition did not define an explicit mechanism for how that would happen. The MLP provided this to the Design Team. The following sections detail what design changes were implemented as a result of the introduction of the MLP.

Assessing the System and Developing a Portfolio of Interventions (2016)

The MLP was formally introduced to Fellows at the second EFL workshop in Edmonton in January 2016[53] as a way of thinking about how systems change and about the role of EFL in fostering that transition. This presentation introduced the core concepts of the MLP, and served as an introduction to the backcasting exercise that followed. This exercise was designed to generate a vision of the desired energy system of the future – in other words, to determine what the EFL was trying to transition *to*. The MLP was then used to analyse the current system and look for leverage points that might shift the current system to the desired state. The workshop iterated the first set of portfolio initiatives that were developed in Banff in October 2015 to develop a new portfolio of interventions aligned with the EFL vision and the MLP framework.

After the Edmonton workshop, I mapped the various EFL initiatives against the MLP framework and presented the results of my analysis to the Design Team,[54] and later to the Fellows at large.[55] Questions from this analysis to the Design Team included: How can we support niche activities so they have a better chance of making an impact on the regime? How can we work with the regime to build capacity and receptivity to niche innovations? How can we leverage landscape shifts that are creating windows of opportunity for change in the regime? This portfolio mapping was done again by the EFL team using the MLP framing in late 2017. Mapping activities confirmed for the Design Team that "example projects ideally [cover] the whole spectrum to assess [the portfolio] and challenge the group to think about collaborative work in all three realms." Based on these analyses that showed, in fact, that the projects did not cover the whole spectrum, the portfolio expanded to include a wider range of initiatives than technical solutions, including regime and cultural engagement projects. One of the Design Team members commented that, "without MLP, [it] would be much smaller scope of activities."[56]

Later in 2016 an evolution occurred in how the EFL was understanding its own capacity for shifts at the niche, regime, and landscape levels. Rather than attempting to shift broader cultural narratives through press or other types of public campaigns, the EFL focused on leveraging organizational engagement activities at the regime level.[57] The EFL's strategy was that, by engaging with regime institutions such as Suncor and the National Energy Board, and by delivering workshops that foster conversations about and understanding of energy transitions, systems thinking, collaboration, and innovation, the EFL would build capacity for transitions thinking and action within regime organizations. These workshops are co-hosted by a Fellow from such an organization and EFL staff. As participants gain understanding, they change their behaviour inside and outside the organization. These shifts in behaviour and practice then lead to changes in culture across a broad swath of the system. This type of engagement is now happening with groups of organizations as well. In April 2017 the EFL team facilitated a two-day workshop with six incumbent oil sands producers and an industry trade group concerning an introduction to core EFL activities and concepts. Shifts in groups such as this have the potential to change the "repertoire of possibilities" that Taylor alludes to, and represent an example of leveraging the regime to change the landscape, as Westley et al. discuss.[58]

The Whole Is Greater than the Sum of the Parts (January–May 2017)

At an EFL Design Team meeting in Edmonton in April 2017, I re-emphasized another element of the MLP that I felt had not been adequately addressed in the design: the need to foster mutually reinforcing dynamics between initiatives. These discussions led to the introduction of new exercises in the following workshops in Red Deer and Canmore. In Red Deer an Open Space activity was used with a specific focus on generating collaborations between initiatives, as opposed to moving individual initiatives forward.[59] In Canmore the team introduced an exercise that deliberately mixed Fellows into different groups than they usually worked with in order to develop initiatives that were assemblages of existing and new ideas.[60] Out of that workshop, a number of existing initiatives have explored ways to support one another mutually and a new set of merged initiatives has developed. For example, the Solar Skills initiative (retraining oil sands workers to do solar panel installations) collaborated with the Indigenous Energy Innovation initiative and the Louis Bull Tribe to train sixteen workers (including five members of the Louis Bull Tribe) in Maskwacis to install solar panels on the roof of the daycare centre.[61] Transition theory argues that the alignment of niche innovations such as those described above is one mechanism through with systems transition occurs.

At the Canmore workshop, the EFL Design Team and participants adopted the MLP as a framing device for a "400-day sprint" from June 2017 through to July 2018, when the initial tranche of funding for the EFL would expire.[62] Figure 2.1, developed by the EFL Design Team, provides a visual representation of this strategy. The EFL has focused on developing connections among Fellows and scaling initiatives at the niche level. At the regime level, the team has identified key "regime players" to engage with, and has contributed to policy discussions and social innovation with "major Alberta institutions." Finally, the team has focused on the promotion of "EFL narratives" as a way of influencing the landscape. Specific goals have been set in place for each level of the MLP framework, and the team is tracking progress using the MLP framing.[63]

Signposting (June 2017–January 2018)

By the time of the Waterton workshop in October 2017, the EFL was no longer explicitly using labels (described as "Geels without Geels"),[64] but was still using the three levels of the MLP. These were described as "shifting narratives, alignment of dozens of Canadian institutions, and a platform to initiate and scale hundreds of collaborative initiatives."[65] The MLP has also led to insights in the Design Team's evaluation of the impact of the current portfolio of initiatives: "All the niche innovations require – or seek out – changes at the 'regime' and 'landscape' level. AOSTRA 2.0, an EFL initiative focused on reducing greenhouse gas emissions from oilsands production, requires key government and industry actors to embrace a next generation research and development program; the various worker upskilling programs (e.g., solar) require a variety of policy and regulatory measures to support transition initiatives; the Sustainaville initiative requires a variety of regulatory changes to make development process more efficient."[66] At the time of writing, the EFL Fellows and Design Team are working through the

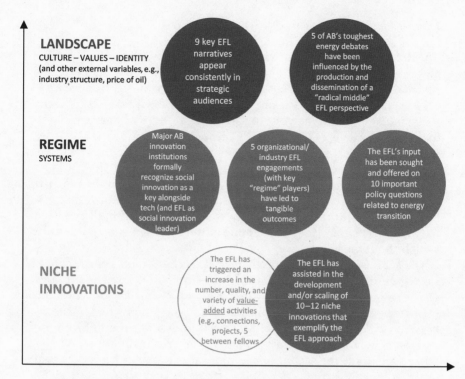

LANDSCAPE
CULTURE – VALUES – IDENTITY
(and other external variables, e.g.,
industry structure, price of oil)

9 key EFL narratives appear consistently in strategic audiences

5 of AB's toughest energy debates have been influenced by the production and dissemination of a "radical middle" EFL perspective

REGIME
SYSTEMS

Major AB innovation institutions formally recognize social innovation as a key alongside tech (and EFL as social innovation leader)

5 organizational/ industry EFL engagements (with key "regime" players) have led to tangible outcomes

The EFL's input has been sought and offered on 10 important policy questions related to energy transition

NICHE INNOVATIONS

The EFL has triggered an increase in the number, quality, and variety of value-added activities (e.g., connections, projects, 5 between fellows

The EFL has assisted in the development and/or scaling of 10–12 niche innovations that exemplify the EFL approach

Figure 2.1 Using the multilevel perspective to frame indicators
Adapted from Frank W. Geels, "The Multilevel Perspective on Sustainability Transitions:
Response to Seven Criticisms," *Environmental Innovation and Societal Transitions* 1, no. 1
(2011): 24–40.

implications of these MLP insights. As described further below, plans
for "EFL 2.0" include a focus on bridging niche and regime to address
the barriers to systems transition highlighted in the above quote.

Finally, at the Waterton workshop, the EFL implemented a "signposting" process to capture landscape shifts. This initiative is designed
to capture qualitative and quantitative indicators of landscape shifts
such as political instability, polarized public discourse, economic pressures, and examples of renewable adoption. Prior workshops had exposed Fellows to energy trend reports from the Alberta government
(Banff EFL Workshop 2015) and government-developed scenarios of
possible energy futures (Canmore EFL Workshop 2017). The signposts
are explicitly designed, however, to act as a context-sensing mechanism that will allow the EFL to respond and adapt to landscape and
regime shifts.

EFL 2.0 and Beyond (January·2018–)

The EFL team has found the MLP sufficiently useful to plan to continue and expand the role of this approach both in the EFL and in other labs that TNSC is managing. The EFL team has "generally introduced the MLP to other teams and team members in TNS[C]" and TNSC sees value in using the framework to "assess best places of intervention"[67] in terms of the level of focus. The EFL team has also found the MLP useful in communicating the value and impact of the EFL to individuals and stakeholders outside the process. The MLP framing "has become one of the core slides in just about any presentation about the EFL. [It] precedes our overview of how the Lab is structured and organized – [and] provides [a] rationale on why we have designed the Lab as we have. In most cases, [the MLP is] one of the core elements in the story we tell about the Lab."[68]

The MLP is also used to frame the EFL's achievements and in fundraising efforts for a potential future iteration: "EFL 2.0" Descriptions of current achievements are mapped to "Geels" in levels of "cultural" (landscape), "existing institutions" (regime), and "innovators/niche innovations."[69] This same mapping is used to describe the EFL's future ambitions in shifting narratives, aligning regime institutions, and creating a platform for scaling niche innovations,[70] with a specific goal of "strengthening connections between niche and regime, especially regime connections."[71] The EFL 2.0 strategy would be to "influence [the energy transition] by niche activities, by practice and policies, influence markets through cultural landscape."[72] The MLP will also be a key element in the final EFL summative report, with plans to "visually show the results on a Geels-like diagram to give people an impression of the overall pattern of outcomes,"[73] and including specific sections on landscape, regime, and niche innovations.

Discussion

The EFL has used the MLP in its analysis of the energy system in Alberta, developed a portfolio of initiatives to engage with the system at all three levels of the MLP, created space for learning and experimentation, facilitated networks between niche and regime actors, supported the alignment of niche innovations, and adapted to the context of a changing landscape. However, the fact that the MLP influenced and was used in the EFL does not answer the question of its usefulness. The EFL Design Team describes the value of the MLP as being "about what to do with innovations – not just about the people coming together, [it] challenged us to ask questions about the regime and how ... we introduce [innovations] to the regime – and culture – how ... we engage at that cultural perspective."[74] The influence and usefulness of the MLP can be clearly seen in the three work streams of the EFL mentioned in the quote: the Fellows, organizational engagement, and public engagement. The Fellows stream shifted from a focus on the Fellows cohort and its innovations to transition dynamics. Because of this, the EFL innovation portfolio strategy now emphasizes how niche innovations can be adopted by, or can shift, the regime and how to provide the support innovators need. Developing and nurturing niche innovations with this goal in mind, through the lens of the MLP, will lead to a greater chance of transition than a random collection of niche innovations.

The organizational engagement stream shifted from a plan to support Fellows in communications to bridging between niche innovations and regime actors. The EFL's engagement with oil and gas companies, extractive industry associations, and provincial and federal government agencies attempts to build adaptive capacity and systems knowledge within regime organizations. Regime actors, even ones participating in transition projects such as the EFL, are not necessarily supporters of transition – in fact, they might actively oppose it.[75] At the regime level, the intention of the EFL is to "engage key actors in the energy system and innovation ecosystem to create opportunities for bridging ideas, initiatives and narratives of the lab with the broader system, in order to help scale and accelerate the adoption of strategies and initiatives to build the energy system that the future requires of us."[76] By creating bridges between niche innovations and regime – through the diversity of participants and direct engagement with regime actors – the EFL has developed a strategy with an explicit focus on fostering transition.

The public engagement stream changed from engaging stakeholders to shifting the landscape through culture and narratives. If successful, a changed narrative will support regime shifts and enhance the resilience of these shifts in the face of political and economic changes. The EFL rationale for this engagement is "to inspire and offer narratives that help depolarize the public conversation about Alberta's energy future in a way that increases cultural acceptance for policy direction [and] innovations that prepare Alberta for a low-carbon future (energy transition)."[77] By emphasizing engagement with cultural narratives at the landscape level, the EFL is effectively investing in insurance that innovations emerging from the EFL have a greater chance of acceptance by the regime and, when adopted, a greater chance at longevity.

Challenges in Using the MLP

Despite the usefulness of the MLP, there were also challenges integrating the framework into the EFL. The MLP was one of a number of frameworks used in design, and participants complained of "framework fatigue." Also unclear to participants was the relationship between the MLP and other frameworks, such as backcasting, Three Horizons (a method for mapping strategy to different time horizons), and scenarios from the Alberta government. Another challenge was that awareness of the implications of the MLP and transitions strategy does not necessarily lead to changes in design. For example, one of the Design Team members reflects that "year 1 of the Lab was very much focused on the innovation side of things, although vision speaks to cultural [shifts]. In hindsight, there might have been value in the distinction."[78] This also led to disengagement by Fellows who were interested in working on landscape and cultural initiatives, as the EFL "defaulted to niche level and others that wanted to work on narrative dropped out."[79] The lack of implementation of landscape initiatives in the early stages of the EFL was due to a combination of factors, including limited resources for large-scale cultural engagement initiatives,[80] time pressures on Fellows that led many to focus on initiatives that were closely related to their day-to-day work,[81] and the time it took for the Design Team to internalize the implications of the MLP.

As the MLP was only one component of the design process, one should not overemphasize its importance in the design of the EFL. For example, the initial "list of criteria [for EFL objectives] included not just technological breakthroughs or policy change but also 'capture imagination of many different stakeholders and the public' and 'altered public narratives.'" This indicates that an interest in cultural shifts preceded the introduction of the MLP, but at that stage of the project the EFL did not engage with mechanisms of systems transition dynamics needed to affect such shifts. That is what the MLP provided.

Evaluating Systems Transition

In this chapter, I have described the Alberta Energy Futures Lab's use of the multilevel perspective to design and deliver a process to facilitate energy systems transition. Further research[82] is needed to develop meaningful measures of whether that transition is actually happening. It is not feasible to track, for example, changes in built form across Alberta, changes in individual electricity consumption, or the adoption of solar technology, and attribute those to the EFL. Nor would it be reasonable to expect the EFL to induce such changes in the short term. It might be more reasonable to assess the EFL's contribution to the energy transition in Alberta. Has the EFL been able to accelerate or steer the transition? Has it been able to lower the bar to innovation or include more people from more diverse groups in the transition? Can the EFL help ensure the transition is more socially just, with an equitable sharing of benefits and costs? These questions will be addressed in forthcoming publications.[83] The EFL process is still ongoing, but the analysis in this chapter suggests that the EFL is on a path to influence and support a sustainable energy transition in Alberta. Further research and assessment is needed to determine the extent to which the adoption of the MLP can help foster a sustainable transition. In other words, do processes designed with MLP principles in mind make a greater contribution to systems transition than otherwise? This is a difficult methodological question, and also one that will be addressed further in forthcoming work.

Value for Participatory Processes

The EFL provides an example of how the MLP can support an engagement process with a focus on systems transition dynamics. Participatory process designers should consider introducing this lens into their design and facilitation processes. In contrast to many participatory processes, the EFL has used the MLP to design a process that works across multiple levels of systems intervention. As one of the EFL Design Team members notes, "most Labs focus on the innovation very heavily and a little bit on the regime and almost nothing on [the] public/cultural level." Public engagement processes that aim to transform the systems of which they are a part can benefit from a theoretical lens on the mechanisms through which that transition happens. The MLP also provides options for broadening the scope of processes such as citizen assemblies or participatory integrated assessments to engage with systems change or transition. Finally, the MLP encourages a social and systems lens, rather than a purely technical one, on change processes. Public engagement processes that are narrowly issue focused can benefit from a wider perspective, since technologies or development projects are embedded in larger sociotechnical systems. Without considering this broader system, engagement processes run the risk of not including critical stakeholders, missing connections of a specific project to other related projects, and, perhaps most important, not contributing to systems change.

Conclusion

The challenges of sustainable energy systems transition in Alberta – indeed, in any jurisdiction – are wide ranging and extend far beyond technological innovations. Public narratives of energy, political considerations, economic factors, employment, technological lock-in, and consumer behaviour all play a role. Public deliberation and deliberative democracy processes – for example, the Alberta Climate Dialogues (ABCD) project – attempt to engage with these factors by determining what the public thinks about an issue such as energy transition and making policy recommendations. Large-scale deliberation projects such the ABCD have the potential to "make a difference to policy responses to climate change in Alberta"[84] and contribute to systemic change. However, a perennial challenge of public deliberation processes is how (and if!) the results of the process will be implemented by policy makers and other stakeholders. The MLP, in addition to being an analytical lens, helps process designers implement activities that can facilitate systems transition. These activities might involve regime actors such as industry and government, but might also take the form of niche innovations or landscape-level cultural engagement with citizens that takes place independent of government. Through the use of the MLP, the Energy Futures Lab has designed a process that engages with the energy system at the levels of niche innovations, regime incumbents, and sociocultural landscapes – a process that focuses on systems transition dynamics, rather than on purely technical and policy innovations. The MLP, while not guaranteeing success for any given process, provides a valuable analytical and design framework for participatory process designers and organizations seeking to support a sustainable systems transition.

Discussion Questions

1   A concern in public engagement processes is that the participation of industry players can lead to *regulatory capture*, defined as when industry advances its own interests in a regulatory or review process. The Energy Futures Lab made a conscious choice to include regime incumbents such as Suncor, Shell, and the government of Alberta in the process. What are the benefits and drawbacks of this decision? Does this affect the legitimacy (or perception thereof) of the EFL? How might the EFL mitigate risks of industry capture of the process?
2   What mechanisms might an engagement process such as the EFL put in place to ensure the resilience of its systems interventions?

How might the EFL prevent "snapback" due to political, economic, or social pressures?

3 Engagement processes such as the EFL always face the challenge of getting the "whole system in the room." After all, it is difficult to get a truly representative sample of four million people – Alberta's population – in one room. What engagement mechanisms might the EFL employ to connect the cohort of EFL Fellows to broader publics? What lessons might the EFL draw from citizen assemblies and deliberative polls that also seek to address this challenge?

ACKNOWLEDGMENTS

I would like to gratefully acknowledge the support of Mitacs Canada, the UBC Public Scholars program, the Social Sciences and Humanities Research Council of Canada, and The Natural Step Canada for my research. In addition, I would particularly like to thank the Energy Futures Lab Fellows and members of the Design Team who were so generous with their time and review of an early draft of this chapter. Feedback from participants at the Symposium canadien sur la transition socioécologique / Canadian Symposium on Sustainability Transitions in Montreal, and the International Sustainability Transitions 2017 Conference in Gothenburg, Sweden, were invaluable in developing my ideas. Finally, I would like to thank my PhD supervisor Dr John Robinson for his insights, critiques, and continuing support.

NOTES

1 Alberta Energy, "Alberta Energy History Prior to 1970," online at http://www.energy.alberta.ca/AU/History/Pages/AEHP1970.aspx., accessed 19 February 2018.

2 Alberta Energy Regulator, "Crude Oil Prices," online at https://www.aer.ca/data-and-publications/statistical-reports/oil-prices, accessed 19 February 2018.

3 US Energy Information Administration, "Oil Imports and Exports," online at https://www.eia.gov/energyexplained/index.cfm?page=oil_imports, accessed 19 February 2018.

4 Frances Westley et al., "Tipping Toward Sustainability: Emerging Pathways of Transformation," *Ambio* 40, no. 7 (2011): 762–80, doi:10.1007/s13280-011-0186-9.

5 Jonathan Salter, John Robinson, and Arnim Wiek, "Participatory Methods of Integrated Assessment – A Review," *Wiley Interdisciplinary Reviews: Climate Change* 1, no. 5 (2010): 697–717, doi:10.1002/wcc.73.
6 John S. Dryzek, André Bächtiger, and Karolina Milewicz, "Toward a Deliberative Global Citizens' Assembly," *Global Policy* 2, no. 1 (5, 2011): |33–42, doi:10.1111/j.1758-5899.2010.00052.x; M.R. Woodford and S. Preston, "Strengthening Citizen Participation in Public Policy-Making: A Canadian Perspective," *Parliamentary Affairs* 66, no. 2 (2013): 345–63, doi:10.1093/pa/gsr065.
7 James S. Fishkin, *When the People Speak: Deliberative Democracy and Public Consultation* (Oxford: Oxford University Press, 2009).
8 Westley et al., "Tipping Toward Sustainability."
9 Julia Abelson et al., "Deliberations about Deliberative Methods: Issues in the Design and Evaluation of Public Participation Processes," *Social Science & Medicine* 57, no. 2 (2003): 239–51, doi:10.1016/S0277-9536(02)00343-X; Laura Black et al., "Methods for Analyzing and Measuring Group Deliberation," in *Sourcebook of Political Communication Research Methods, Measures and Analytical Techniques*, ed. L Holbert (New York: Routledge, 2008), 323–45; Michael X. Della Carpini, Fay Lomax Cook, and Larry Jacobs, "Public Deliberation, Discursive Participation, and Citizen Engagement: A Review of the Empirical Literature," *Annual Review of Political Science* 7, no. 1 (2004): 315–44, doi:10.1146/annurev.polisci.7.121003.091630.
10 Gregory Barrett, Miriam Wyman, and Vera Schattan P. Coehlo, "Assessing the Policy Impacts of Deliberative Civic Engagement," in *Democracy in Motion: Evaluating the Practice and Impact of Deliberative Civic Engagement*, ed. Tina Nabatchi et al. (Oxford: Oxford University Press, 2012), 182–201; Joanne Caddy, *Evaluating Public Participation in Policy Making* (Paris: OECD Publishing, 2005); John Gaventa and Gregory Barrett, "So What Difference Does It Make? Mapping the Outcomes of Citizen Engagement," *IDS Working Papers* 2010, no. 347 (2010): 1–72, doi:10.1111/j.2040-0209.2010.00347 _2.x; Heather Pincock, "Does Deliberation Make Better Citizens?" in Nabatchi et al., *Democracy in Motion*, 135–57.
11 C.J. Lukensmeyer and S. Brigham, "Taking Democracy to Scale: Creating a Town Hall Meeting for the Twenty-First Century," *National Civic Review*, 2002.
12 Archon Fung, "Survey Article: Recipes for Public Spheres: Eight Institutional Design Choices and Their Consequences," *Journal of Political Philosophy* 11, no. 3 (2003): 338–67; Genevieve Fuji Johnson, *Democratic Illusion: Deliberative Democracy in Canadian Public Policy* (Toronto: University of Toronto Press, 2015).
13 Salter, Robinson, and Wiek, "Participatory Methods of Integrated Assessment."

14 Guido Caniglia et al., "Experiments and Evidence in Sustainability Science: A Typology," *Journal of Cleaner Production*, 29 June 2017, 1–10, doi:10.1016/j. jclepro.2017.05.164; Christopher Luederitz et al., "Joint Learning through Evaluation – A Tentative Evaluative Scheme for Sustainability Transition Experiments," Journal of Cleaner Production (2016): 1–42, doi:10.1016/j.jclepro. 2016.09.005; Daniel Rosenbloom et al., "Transition Experiments: Opening Up Low-Carbon Transition Pathways for Canada through Innovation and Learning," *Canadian Public Policy* 44, no. 4 (2018): 368–83.

15 Frank W. Geels, "Technological Transitions as Evolutionary Reconfiguration Processes: A Multi-Level Perspective and a Case-Study," *Research Policy* 31, no. 8 (2002): 1257–74, doi:10.1016/S0048-7333(02)00062-8; idem, "The Multi-Level Perspective on Sustainability Transitions: Responses to Seven Criticisms," *Environmental Innovation and Societal Transitions* 1, no. 1 (2011): 24–40, doi:10.1016/j.eist.2011.02.002.

16 Frans Berkhout, Adrian Smith, and Andy Stirling, "Socio-Technological Regimes and Transition Contexts," in *System Innovation and the Transition to Sustainabilty*, ed. Boelie Elzen, Frank W. Geels, and Kenneth Green (Cheltenham, UK: Edward Elgar, 2004), 48–75; Jan Rotmans and Derk Loorbach, "Complexity and Transition Management," *Journal of Industrial Ecology* 13, no. 2 (2009): 184–96, doi:10.1111/j.1530-9290.2009.00116.x; Adrian Smith, Jan-Peter Voß, and John Grin, "Innovation Studies and Sustainability Transitions: The Allure of the Multi-Level Perspective and Its Challenges," *Research Policy* 39, no. 4 (2010): 435–48, doi:10.1016/j.respol.2010.01.023.

17 Derk Loorbach and Jan Rotmans, "The Practice of Transition Management: Examples and Lessons From Four Distinct Cases," *Futures* 42, no. 3 (April 1, 2010): 238, doi:10.1016/j.futures.2009.11.009.

18 Sarah Burch et al., "Triggering Transformative Change: A Development Path Approach to Climate Change Response in Communities," *Climate Policy* 14, no. 4 (2014): 470, doi:10.1080/14693062.2014.876342.

19 Ibid.

20 Frank W. Geels and Johan Schot, "Typology of Sociotechnical Transition Pathways," *Research Policy* 36, no. 3 (2007): 400, doi:10.1016/j.respol.2007 .01.003.

21 Geels, "Multi-Level Perspective on Sustainability Transitions," 40.

22 Geels, "Technological Transitions as Evolutionary Reconfiguration Processes," 1260.

23 Burch et al., "Triggering Transformative Change," 485.

24 Aidan Davison, *Technology and the Contested Meanings of Sustainability* (Albany: State University of New York Press, 2001), 107.

25 Smith, Voß, and Grin, "Innovation Studies and Sustainability Transitions," 445.

26 Rotmans and Loorbach, "Complexity and Transition Management;" Claes Andersson, "Complexity Science and Sustainability Transitions,"

Environmental Innovation and Societal Transitions 11 (2014): 50–3, doi:10.1016/j.eist
.2014.03.001.

27 Seyedeh Paniz Pajouhesh, "From Theory to Practice: An Analysis of Transformative Social Innovation at the University of British Columbia" (Master's thesis, University of British Columbia, 2016.

28 John Grin, Jan Rotmans, and Johan Schot, "On Patterns and Agency in Transition Dynamics: Some Key Insights from the KSI Programme," *Environmental Innovation and Societal Transitions* 1, no. 1 (2011): 76–81, doi:10.1016 /j.eist.2011.04.008; Darcy Riddell, "Scaling Forest Conservation: Strategic Agency and Systems Change in the Great Bear Rainforest and Canadian Boreal Forest Agreements" (PhD diss., University of Waterloo, 2015).

29 Geels, "Technological Transitions as Evolutionary Reconfiguration Processes," 1272.

30 Jason Chilvers and Matthew Kearnes, "Remaking Participation: Toward Reflexive Engagement," in *Remaking Participation: Science, Environment and Emergent Publics*, ed. Jason Chilvers and Matthew Kearnes (London: Routledge, 2016), 261–88; Caroline W. Lee, *Do-It-Yourself Democracy*, (Oxford: Oxford University Press, 2015); Loorbach and Rotmans, "Practice of Transition Management."

31 Energy Futures Lab, "Funding Partners," online at http://energyfutureslab .com/funding-partners/, accessed 24 February 2018

32 Energy Futures Lab, "About the EFL," online at http://energyfutureslab.com /about-the-efl/, accessed 24 February 2018,

33 Energy Futures Lab. "EFL Design Template," 25 January 2015; emphasis in original.

34 Göran Ingvar Broman and Karl-Henrik Robèrt, "A Framework for Strategic Sustainable Development," *Journal of Cleaner Production* 140, no. 1 (2017): 17–31, doi:10.1016/j.jclepro.2015.10.121.

35 J. Holmberg and K.-H. Robèrt, "Backcasting – A Framework for Strategic Planning," *International Journal of Sustainable Development & World Ecology* 7, no. 4 (2000): 291–308, doi:10.1080/13504500009470049; John Robinson et al., "Envisioning Sustainability: Recent Progress in the Use of Participatory Backcasting Approaches for Sustainability Research," *Technological Forecasting & Social Change* 78, no. 5 (June 1, 2011): 756–68, doi:10.1016 /j.techfore.2010.12.006.

36 Energy Futures Lab, "Vision and Innovation Pathways," online at http:// energyfutureslab.com/vision-and-innovation-pathways, accessed 24 February 2018.

37 Adrian Smith, Andy Stirling, and Frans Berkhout, "The Governance of Sustainable Socio-Technical Transitions," *Research Policy* 34, no. 10 (2005): 1506, doi:10.1016/j.respol.2005.07.005.

38 Interview with EFL Fellow, February 2017.

39 Stephen Williams, "The Splash and the Ripples: Assessing Sustainability Transition Experiments" (PhD diss., University of British Columbia, 2019), online at https://open.library.ubc.ca/cIRcle/collections/ubctheses/24/items/1.0383246.

40 EFL workshops observed: Banff, November 2015; Edmonton, January 2016; Kananaskis, May 2016; Calgary, October 2016; Red Deer, February 2017; Canmore, May 2017; Waterton, October 2017; Olds, February 2018.

41 Patricia Bazeley, *Qualitative Data Analysis: Practical Strategies* (Thousand Oaks, CA: Sage, 2013).

42 Energy Futures Lab, "Strategic Comms and Engagement" (presented at Design workshop, Edmonton, 17 September 2014).

43 Energy Futures Lab, "Narrative ToC Update" (presented at Design workshop, Edmonton, 26 November 2014).

44 Daniel Carpenter, and David. A. Moss, eds., *Preventing Regulatory Capture: Special Interest Influence and How to Limit It* (Cambridge: Cambridge University Press, 2013).

45 Bill McKibben, "Why we need to keep 80% of fossil fuels in the ground," *350.org*, 16 February 2016, online at https://350.org/why-we-need-to-keep-80-percent-of-fossil-fuels-in-the-ground/.

46 Maurie J. Cohen, "Ecological Modernization and Its Discontents: The American Environmental Movement's Resistance to an Innovation-Driven Future," *Futures* 3, no. 8 (2006): 528–47, http://doi.org/10.1016/j.futures.2005.09.002.

47 Interview with EFL Design Team member, March 2017.

48 Energy Futures Lab, "EFL Fellows," online at http://energyfutureslab.com/fellows/, accessed 24 February 2018.

49 Interview with EFL Design Team member, March 2017.

50 Interview with EFL Design Team member, 30 November 2015.

51 Energy Futures Lab, "EFL Simplified Participant TOC," 21 November 2015.

52 Energy Futures Lab, "EFL TOC rev 3," 5 February 2015.

53 Mark Cabaj, "Pathways to Change: Somewhere between a Butterfly & a Blueprint" (presented at Energy Futures Lab workshop, Edmonton, 26 January 2016).

54 Energy Futures Lab, "Mapping the EFL Portfolio," 11 May 2016.

55 Energy Futures Lab, "System Mapping Webinar," 8 March 2017.

56 Interview with EFL Design Team member, March 2017.

57 Energy Futures Lab, "PE & MLP," 31 October 2016.

58 Charles Taylor, *Modern Social Imaginaries* (Durham, NC: Duke University Press, 2004); Westley et al., "Tipping Toward Sustainability."

59 Energy Futures Lab, "EFL February 2017 Fellowship Workshop," 26 February 2017.

60 Energy Futures Lab, "EFL May 2017 Fellow Workshop," 30 May 2017.

61 Brandi Morin, "Partnership between oilsands, Indigenous workers leads to solar panels for daycare," *CBC News*, 20 October 2017, online at http://www.cbc.ca/news/indigenous/partnership-oilsands-indigenous-workers-1.4365202.
62 Energy Futures Lab, "EFL May 2017 Fellowship Workshop," 30 May 2017.
63 Energy Futures Lab, "Draft of Revised Results Framework for EFL_7May1," 5 May 2017.
64 Energy Futures Lab, "EFL Resourcing/Funding Meeting," 4 January 2017.
65 Energy Futures Lab, "300 Day Plan summary for Fellows," 17 October 2017.
66 Energy Futures Lab, "EFL Signature Initiatives_Q 1 Report_Draft," 16 October 2017.
67 Interview with EFL Design Team member, March 2017.
68 Ibid.
69 Energy Futures Lab. EFL Resourcing/Funding Meeting, 4 January 2017.
70 Ibid.
71 Ibid.
72 Ibid.
73 Energy Futures Lab, "EFL Summative Report_4Dec17," 26 January 2018.
74 Interview with EFL Design Team member, March 2017.
75 Sarah Burch et al., "Governing and Accelerating Transformative Entrepreneurship: Exploring the Potential for Small Business Innovation on Urban Sustainability Transitions," *Current Opinion in Environmental Sustainability* 22 (2016): 26–32, doi:10.1016/j.cosust.2017.04.002.
76 Energy Futures Lab, EFL Resourcing/Funding Meeting, 4 January 2017.
77 Ibid.
78 Interview with EFL Design Team member, March 2017.
79 Energy Futures Lab, "EFL 2.0 Design Meeting," 1 February 2018.
80 Energy Futures Lab, "Weekly Team Meeting Minutes," October 2015–February 2017.
81 Interviews with EFL Fellows.
82 Luederitz et al., "Learning Through Evaluation"; Niko Schapke et al., "Linking Transitions to Sustainability: A Study of the Societal Effects of Transition Management," *Sustainability* 9, no. 5, art. 737 (2017): 1–36, doi:10.3390/su9050737; Stephen Williams and John Robinson, "Measuring Sustainability: An Evaluation Framework for Sustainability Transition Experiments," *Environmental Science and Policy* 103 (2020): 58–66.
83 Stephen Williams, "UN Sustainable Development Goals and Sustainability Transition: An Integrated Evaluative Framework" (paper presented at 2018 Summer Institute on Critical Studies of Environmental Governance, Toronto, June 2018); Stephen Williams and Andréanne Doyon, "Justice in Energy Transitions," *Environmental Innovation and Societal Transitions* 31 (2019): 144–53.

84 David Kahane, "Climate Change, Social Change, and Systems Change," in
    Public Deliberation on Climate Change: Lessons from Alberta Climate Dialogue, ed.
    Lorelei L. Hanson (Edmonton: Athabasca University Press, 2018), 197–224.

KEY RESOURCES

Geels, Frank W. "Technological Transitions as Evolutionary Reconfiguration
    Processes: A Multi-Level Perspective and a Case-Study." *Research Policy* 31,
    no. 8 (2002): 1257–74. doi:10.1016/S0048-7333(02)00062-8.
Loorbach, Derk, and Jan Rotmans. "The Practice of Transition Management:
    Examples and Lessons from Four Distinct Cases." *Futures* 42, no. 3 (2010):
    237–46. doi:10.1016/j.futures.2009.11.009.
Westley, Frances, Per Olsson, Carl Folke, Thomas Homer-Dixon, Harrie
    Vredenburg, Derk Loorbach, John Thompson, et al. "Tipping Toward
    Sustainability: Emerging Pathways of Transformation." *Ambio* 40, no. 7
    (2011): 762–80. doi:10.1007/s13280-011-0186-9.

3 Seeing and Believing: Reconciling Shared Outcomes and Shared Participation

ELLEN SZARLETA

Human beings are born into this process of collective action and become individualized by the rules of collective action. Thus an institution is collective action in control, liberation, and expansion of individual action.
— John R. Commons, *The Economics of Collective Action*

Introduction

More than twenty years ago, I moved to the Chicago metropolitan region. As a newcomer, working as a prosecutor, I had many opportunities to interact with attorneys, academics, citizens, and practitioners in all sectors. Our conversations originated in issues related to criminal justice, but quickly expanded to topics related to collective action. Despite overwhelming evidence of urban decay and suburban sprawl, hope, rather than despair, was a tangible sentiment. There was no shortage of ideas for advancing a vision for the future. Many believed that, with sufficient funds and support from public institutions, the challenges of crime, poverty, and environmental degradation could be alleviated, if not eliminated. More than twenty years later, the challenges are mounting, the complexities persist, and hope is waning. Initiatives targeting the policy issues of concern have received funding. Organizations from each sector – public, private, and non-profit – have been engaged in projects related to addressing the perceived obstacles to prosperity, and yet there has been little to no progress.

Appropriately, the public, through the democratic voting process and legal system, places a check on the actions of elected officials and government agencies. Through different forms of citizen action – voting to remove an incumbent, filing a lawsuit, engaging in acts of civil disobedience – government is held accountable for protecting the public interest. In response, the public sector notes insufficient funding and the absence of public will as reasons for the lack of progress on addressing important issues such as climate change and poverty.[1] A narrative once driven by a vision of the future has become a divisive discourse characterized by finger pointing and blame shifting. At the centre of this controversy lie differing views on the roles of public sector institutions in resolving complex issues in society.

The actual and perceived role of the public sector in the United States is grounded in the framework of neoclassical economics. Under this approach, the function of the public sector is largely to correct market failures by providing public goods and responding to externalities.[2] From this perspective, the government's role is to allocate resources not otherwise distributed through markets and to provide services such as infrastructure, income security, and public safety for the benefit of the citizenry. The design and implementation of policies aimed at promoting public welfare vary significantly across levels of government and have done so over time. Today, efforts to promote public welfare are again undergoing review and transformation. One theme that is consistent, however, is that simply laying blame at the feet of the public sector for failures to protect the public welfare has not produced the needed change or improvements for the collective good. As such, alternative models of decision making are necessary for meeting the needs of the public.

In this chapter, I argue that deliberative democratic practices, embedded in collective impact (CI) approaches, offer such an alternative, and I specifically highlight the processes that can emerge in response to challenges facing the public sector. The collective impact model – described in more detail below – responds to market failures while embodying a normative commitment to deliberation, and is of interest because it aims to be inclusive and encourages participation from all sectors as well as from individual citizens. CI initiatives may, but do not necessarily, originate in the public sector. In this sense, thinking about collective impact and deliberative democracy together asks us to consider the emerging and various roles public institutions play in fostering and promoting new and potentially more effective collective action and, thus, policy making.

To advance this argument, I examine two cases where local (city) governments played very different roles in collective impact initiatives aimed at improving public welfare. I draw on the lived experiences of participants and documents associated with these initiatives (such as meeting minutes) to describe the roles played by government, to evaluate how these roles differed, and to consider how these diverging roles contributed differently to CI outcomes. These insights offer new perspectives on how CI initiatives can support authentic engagement and develop shared goals among citizens and across sectors, while contributing to our thinking about deliberative democracy.

Researchers, students, and practitioners should find a connection to this examination of the CI model as a vehicle for improving public outcomes. For researchers, theories of collective impact and deliberative democracy intersect on questions related to power, shared (or disparate) interest, and process. Students will benefit from the success and failure of our theoretical understanding of collective impact and its application. Practitioners will appreciate the context-specific findings and broader analysis of generalized insights. Ultimately it is through the efforts of all three groups that we will achieve a better understanding of the potential importance (or insignificance) of collective impact to deliberative democracy theory and practice.

Background: The Need for New Approaches to Achieving Public Good

Neighbourhoods in the United States have experienced revolutionary changes over the past fifty years.[3] Significant developments in technology and information sharing have changed the ways we connect with one another as well as who participates in social, economic, and political networks. For example, prior to 1994, proposed and final federal regulations were published in the Federal Register and were available in paper form or microfiche in federal depository libraries within the United States. In order to comment on a regulation, a member of the public needed to have access to such a library and/or request a copy of the Federal Register from the government. The interested citizen would also have needed to know the agency that proposed the regulation and when the regulation was published. Those who lacked library access and/or information on the comment process faced significant barriers to participation.[4] With the advent of the federal E-Rulemaking Program in 2002, a cross-agency e-gov initiative was undertaken to improve the breadth and depth of public access to the rule-making process. There is now one central location for all federal regulations. The regulations are available and searchable online, and comments can be submitted online. In fact, today, citizens also can respond to comments submitted by others, thus creating a dialogue on a proposed regulation.[5] Citizens who are interested in tracking regulations related to a particular issue can also sign up for email alerts. In addition, the public policy challenges facing our communities – poverty, racism, income inequality, illiteracy – are increasingly complex and multifaceted. Originally identified by Rittel and Webber as "wicked" problems, these complex policy challenges are both difficult to define and inherently unsolvable.[6] They also call for policy responses across levels of government, including at the local level. Of particular concern to both academics and practitioners are the related negative effects of weakened community ties.[7] For example, evidence suggests that lower levels of social capital are associated with lower levels of civic engagement and participation[8] and higher levels of income and health inequality.[9]

In the face of a range of multifaceted, complex policy problems, developing effective local responses is a significant and pressing challenge. Traditionally, the responsibility for identifying and implementing solutions lay at the feet of local agencies – specifically, local governments. For example, efforts to improve literacy might have originated in a local government unit such as a school district, data were examined to inform policy discussions, and responses developed that could be implemented within the school system. As a result, grade-level teachers might have been encouraged, or required, to refocus learning on reading skills. This sector-specific, government-led approach to what we now understand as a socio-economic issue, however, limited possibilities for collaboration and ignored the increasingly complex, multidimensional nature of the literacy challenge.

Over recent decades, as community awareness of the importance of developing a more integrated approach to solving literacy (and other) problems evolved, various attempts were made by government to broaden the scope of enquiry, explore interconnections, and increase inclusiveness – through, for example, interagency task forces and multisector coalitions such as the Chicago Citywide Literacy Coalition.[10] In a recent study, Katherine Cooper examines literacy programming to gain insight on such integrated approaches, and notes that, at first glance, introducing literacy programming into existing school and community projects might appear to be a straightforward policy initiative. However, stakeholder conversations can easily turn to discussions of racial disparities, learning disabilities, school budget cuts, and cross-agency data-sharing challenges.[11] The complex nature of the policy process is revealed when representatives from local government, non-profits, and business, as well as residents, all come to the table with diverse ideas, knowledge, and expectations. Cooper notes that managing expectations, finding shared interests, and developing solutions requires issue-specific information and knowledge as well as the desire and ability to reach consensus.

This research suggests that past approaches to addressing complex issues – such as illiteracy – are no longer adequate.[12] Relying on local government (for example, the school district) alone to design and deliver effective solutions places an excessive burden on limited human and financial resources. A school district's capacity to design and implement literacy programming might not include the resources to address related issues of poverty, housing, and discrimination.

The collective impact model, developed by John Kania and Mark Kramer, provides an alternative approach to addressing wicked problems.[13] CI works differently than the program-based, discrete solution approach traditionally employed by local governments in the United States. Using the CI model, an emergent process defines the problem and potential solutions. The model views predetermined solutions delivered by discrete programs as inappropriate, given the complexities surrounding socio-economic issues. Kania and Kramer argue that such predetermined solutions rarely work, and that even if they are successful, their adoption spreads very gradually, if at all. The CI model, on the other hand, is as an entirely different model of social progress, drawing its power from a process where multiple organizations look for resources and innovations through the same lens, rapid learning comes from continuous feedback loops, and the immediacy of action arises from a unified and simultaneous response among all participants. According to Kania and Kramer, under conditions of complexity, the CI model leads to changes in behaviour at the individual and organizational levels that promote alignment, discovery, learning, and emergence. This then accelerates the pace of social change. In simple terms, existing organizations find new ways of working together to produce better outcomes.[14]

In this context, government organizations will need to find new ways of working with community stakeholders; therefore, the public sector will assume new and/or modified roles in deliberative processes. These new and emerging roles of government in CI initiatives raise interesting and important questions for deliberative democracy. The CI model asks that all stakeholders look for resources and innovations through the same lens, that they participate in feedback loops, and that there be a unified response. These principles of collective action might not be, in every circumstance, consistent with existing public sector norms and processes. Under CI – a new model of social progress – government would need to determine not only when but also how to participate in the collective decision-making process. It will be important to examine the responses of government and participating stakeholders to these changes to better understand the future direction of deliberative democracy. For instance, CI approaches might have implications for the redistribution of power in the democratic decision-making process. Norm-based deliberative processes might be enhanced or diminished. As changes occur, it will also be important to examine stakeholder perceptions of the changing role of the public sector as it engages in collective impact. The redistribution of power in democratic decision-making processes also is likely to change because of the need to reach a common agenda.

Given the CI model's potential to aid in resolving complex socio-economic policy challenges, in this chapter I take a deeper look at the role of the public sector in collective impact. My focus is on examining how the CI model can enhance the public sector's ability to address wicked problems, including imagining a variety of different roles for the public sector beyond being the central policy-making authority. Specifically, I examine the public sector's role in two CI initiatives to gain insight on emerging forms of deliberative processes within initiatives guided by the CI model and that can advance the public good. In the next section, I provide an overview of the early literature addressing collective decision making, and compare this with the emerging literature on collective action. Following the overview is a discussion of the use of the CI model in policy making and, in turn, the possible roles of government institutions in initiatives guided by the CI model.

Collective Impact and Collective Action: Theoretical Frameworks

Early examinations of collective decision-making processes and their relationship to public policy focused on choices related to externalities and public goods. Francis Bator and Paul Samuelson, among others, specifically identify the existence of public goods as one of the conditions under which markets fail to deliver goods and services efficiently.[15] Specifically, Bator cites the presence of externalities and public goods as limiting the power of markets – where choice is based on maximizing individual benefit – to provide for maximum social benefit. Building on this work, economists James Buchanan and Gordon Tullock focused on developing an economic interpretation of democratic institutions as a framework for better understanding collective decision-making processes.[16]

Throughout the next three decades, the public goods and public management economics literature offered explanations and justification for government action in the face of private sector inefficiencies.[17] These sometimes competing and other times complementary theories of government action (for example, public choice theory) all shared, to some degree, the view that government was an important actor in the sphere of market failures. Yet no single theory offered a complete explanation for all forms of collective action. The later work of Nobel laureate and institutional economist Elinor Ostrom (1990) drew from multiple disciplines to explore the question of collective action.[18] Ostrom's work examined if and when collective action was an effective form of decision making. She suggested that common design principles were responsible for collective success and that collaboration was not an aberration, but rather a construct under which resources could be managed for the good of the collective.

Today, collective action is more widely viewed as a viable process for governing the collective good. The literature has turned from a focus on justifying collective action to examining collective responses to changes in the decision-making environment. Howard Rheingold suggests that new forms of institutional arrangements are evolving in response to developing technology.[19] These new institutional arrangements will not replace government or the public good–focused work of other organizations such as non-profits. They are worthy of study, however, as they offer insights into the ways we view and participate collectively in making decisions, and thus might offer ideas for thinking about the role of government in deliberative democratic processes.

The CI model is a recent application of collective action theory in the context of wicked problems. Wicked problems are viewed by some as the result of market failures, and are complicated by the increasingly interdependent nature of market failures in multiple sectors. Most recently, stakeholders and funders have embraced the CI model as one way to manage resources for the good of the collective by developing what Ostrom would refer to as common design principles. The model, however, should not be confused with the theory of collective action. The CI model is a means of operationalizing basic tenets of the collective action model – for example, developing common design principles – whereas collective action theory outlines the foundation for a deeper understanding of the role of institutions in the distribution of resources for the public good.

Kania and Kramer propose five conditions that are essential to the success of collective efforts focused on addressing complex challenges: (1) a common agenda; (2) shared measurement; (3) mutually reinforcing activities; (4) continuous communication; and (5) backbone support.[20] A brief overview of each of these conditions is presented in table 3.1 and an analysis of their relevance to the cases examined in this chapter follows.

Table 3.1 Conditions for collective impact

Common agenda	A common agenda is the foundation for all collective impact work. At this stage in the process, dialogue among stakeholders focuses on creating a shared vision for change based on a common understanding of the problem and agreement on the approach used to solve it. Participants must agree to the primary goals of the initiative, but do not need to be in complete agreement on all issues.
Shared measurement	When all participants agree on the ways that success is measured and reported, the initiative can move beyond a vision. Common indicators of success provide consistency and transparency, and accountability is introduced. The use of common indicators also provides an opportunity for reflection and continuous learning.
Mutually reinforcing activities	The power of a collective action initiative comes from the coordination of a set of differentiated activities that are mutually reinforcing. The result is a plan that supports differentiated activities that together reinforce the efforts of a diverse set of stakeholders to address and solve a problem.
Continuous communication	In order to achieve consensus and work together to accomplish the common agenda, trust must be built. Building trust is one of the most significant challenges undertaken by stakeholders in a collective action initiative. Frequent and structured open communication will lead to trust and will create a common motivation.
Backbone support	A backbone organization is required to create and manage collective impact initiatives. The organization functions as a backbone for stakeholders engaged in the planning and action stages of collective impact. The staff must possess the skills essential to guiding a diverse set of stakeholders through the initiative, including facilitation, technology, communication, data collection, and data reporting.

Adapted from John Kania and Mark Kramer, "Collective Impact," *Stanford Social Innovation Review* (Winter 2011): 36–41; and Kania and Kramer, "Embracing Emergence: How Collective Impact Addresses Complexity." *Stanford Social Innovation Review* (2013): 1–7.

Theory to Practice: Public Policy and Collective Impact

As noted in the introduction, the limited success of traditional approaches in addressing societal issues inspired the search for alternative models of collective decision making and action, including the CI model. Collective action operationalized through the lens of collective impact has captured the attention of large foundations in the United

States, such as the Knight Foundation, as a viable approach to addressing persistent problems beyond the reach of individual sectors or actors.[21] Where many foundations once believed the best course of action was to fund individualized and local, efforts aimed at correcting market failures today are increasingly embracing the CI model. Interest in the model is not limited to the public and non-profit sector; the private sector is also trying to learn from the experiences of foundations and non-profits as CI implementation takes hold.[22]

The Strive Partnership was one of the first CI initiatives in the country to report successful policy outcomes. The partnership, founded in 2006, focuses on educational cradle-to-career educational outcomes, and is now a nationally recognized model for collective impact.[23] The partnership in Cincinnati and northern Kentucky has documented improvements in 86 per cent of the student outcome indicators, including school readiness and proficiency in reading and maths. In the area of economic development, Memphis Fast Forward has developed a common agenda that includes creating good jobs, a better-educated workforce, a safer community, a healthier citizenry, and fiscally strong and efficient government.[24]

Despite growing interest in the CI model, little attention has focused on the role of government in these initiatives. Instead, much of the research has evaluated outcomes. Evaluating the model's success with respect to outcomes is important, and so is understanding the roles of key stakeholders, including government. Each of the five conditions identified by Kania and Kramer can be supported or limited by the actions of public agencies and policies. For example, some public policies, including restrictive funding models, make it difficult or even impossible to uphold practices needed to promote and sustain collaborative partnerships.[25]

One critical factor influencing public sector participation in, and support for, CI initiatives is a low tolerance for risk. Colin Wood contends that new initiatives can induce fear on the part of public sector leaders. For instance, when failure threatens job security, it can be easier to conduct business as usual than to embrace change. When information beneficial to decision-making processes is guarded, requests for information can be viewed as threats. In the absence of rewards and recognition for collaborative behaviours, there is little incentive for those in the public sector to take a risk and participate in new forms of decision making.[26]

A focus on outcomes and a culture of fear limit the role of the public sector in collective impact and other collaborative initiatives. When the public sector is engaged, however, evidence suggests that it can play both indirect – for example, policies supportive of collaborative decision making – and direct roles in CI initiatives. The consulting firm FSG suggests that the public sector has four important direct (non-policy) roles in CI: providing backbone support, acting as a partner outside of government, collecting data, and championing the need for CI initiatives.[27]

In sum, the literature proposes the collective impact framework as a suitable method for advancing large-scale social change in the face of wicked problems.[28] It also recognizes the potential value of public sector participation in CI,[29] suggests possible roles for its involvement,[30] and explains why its participation can be difficult to secure.[31] The historical importance of the public sector in addressing issues arising from market failure (such as public goods, externalities) and its continued involvement in collective decision making necessitate additional research in this area. The next sections thus examine two CI initiatives by considering their focuses, funding sources, and importantly, interactions with government institutions.

Neighbourhood-Based Collective Impact Case Studies: Background

The cases presented in this chapter emerge from a neighbourhood-based economic development initiative that began in Indiana in 2014. Decades of economic decline had left neighbourhoods struggling socially and economically despite targeted efforts of government agencies and non-profit organizations. Financial and non-financial support from federal, state, and local governments over the decades had resulted in limited improvements in infrastructure (e.g., road maintenance), policing (e.g., drug enforcement), and housing (e.g., low-income housing), yet poverty levels increased and other social problems, such as racism, persisted. Local community foundations had also invested significant resources supporting non-profit organizations in their efforts to address specific issues such as literacy, K–12 performance, diversity, and inclusion. In addition, efforts aimed at improving civic participation were also undertaken. Although successful in part, these varied actions did not create sustainable system-level changes.

Recently, one Lake County, Indiana, community foundation, deeply familiar with the needs of the region and its communities, acknowledged that significant obstacles stand in the way of efforts to address the complex problems facing these communities. As grant makers, community foundations possess the capacity to catalyse connections and lay the foundation for CI initiatives. They can connect non-profits to one another and facilitate partnership conversations and planning. And they can provide the unrestricted long-term support non-profit organizations need to adapt to changing circumstances.[32]

In Indiana, nearly every county is served by a community foundation. Recognizing the need to build capacity for collective action in
Lake County, the community foundation identified and subsequently
implemented a CI model initiative. The initiative was grounded in the
belief that collective action would lead to improvements in the quality
of life for participating neighbourhoods and, ultimately, for the larger
region. Working with CI experts, the foundation designed a pathway
to organize, decide, and act on issues that were most important to the
local communities. The launch of the initiative represented a major
commitment to relational place making, where leaders and citizens
came together to effect positive community change, enabling neighbourhoods to become stronger and more vibrant.[33]

As a convener, the community foundation brought together interested parties from all sectors to learn more about the CI model
through a community-convening/CI-training process. The informa-
tional meetings provided participants the opportunity to develop a
social network and build the social capital needed to move through
the CI process. Residents, businesses, non-profits, and other organizations were encouraged to form "teams," learn, and work together
to collectively identify issues of concern and build a culture of trust
and respect. Interested community stakeholders were encouraged to
foster new and further develop existing relationships to collect local
knowledge and inform discursive dialogue while going through the
training process. Following almost one year of training, the foundation invited the communities that had completed the training to
apply for funding support to advance a CI initiative that would embody the five conditions identified by Kania and Kramer. If selected, a
community would also receive supplemental training and guidance.
Participants would be guided through the CI processes of setting a
common agenda, developing shared measures, designing and implementing mutually reinforcing activities, and advancing continuous
communication. The backbone organization, chosen by the community, would work closely with consultants to empower participants as
they moved through the steps.

In 2014 the foundation issued the first invitation for letters of intent
to participate. The invitation required communities to describe a target area of the proposed initiative, relate the target area initiative to a
set of civic, social, physical, and economic ideals, identify a convening organization, and describe that organization's capacity for serving
as a convener. After a competitive application process, including the
submission of a letter of intent, selection committee review, and an

interview process, two communities were chosen as participants in the program. Their selection was based on an assessment of community readiness and their vision for the future. In 2015 the same communities continued to build their projects, and the process was repeated; two more communities were also added that year, and these communities continued their work through 2016.

The Communities: An Overview

Two of the four communities involved in the CI initiative described above – one from the 2014 cohort and the other from the 2015 cohort – are the focus of this analysis, and are labelled Community A and Community B. These communities were selected for comparison because, as described below, they share many of the same demographic, political, and economic characteristics. Interestingly, despite these similarities, the role of local political institutions in the CI initiative varied in each case. In this section, I describe the communities and the role government played in the CI initiative. In later sections, I consider how those different roles might have contributed differently to the CI outcomes.

Community A and Community B are predominantly white (approximately 70 per cent) and are similarly situated with respect to income levels. The median household income level in both communities is in excess of the state median income ($57,000), and per capita income in both communities is approximately $27,000. The crime rate in Community B slightly exceeds that of the US average for the past decade, with thefts comprising the largest share of recorded crimes (over 80 per cent). Community A experiences a slightly lower rate of crime, also mostly theft (slightly less than 80 per cent of all crimes). Both communities share concerns about infrastructure development and maintenance, as well as economic development. Manufacturing is the most common industry in Community A, while retail trade employs the largest number of workers in Community B.

Both communities also share similar social, economic, and political contexts, given that they are located with five miles of each other. For example, both communities have a long record of voting overwhelmingly for the Democratic candidate in presidential and local elections. Other similarities include a history of shared economic interests, albeit in different sectors. Community A was established in the early 1900s as a town with an economic base in the manufacturing and railroad industries. Community B was incorporated as a town in the late 1800s as a retail and transportation centre. From the late 1930s through the 1960s, growth in Community B continued, with a focus on single-family detached houses. In the 1980s, a moratorium was put in place to halt the population growth that was straining local infrastructure. With major annexations, the one-time town has grown into a city almost four times the physical size of Community A. Throughout the transition, however, residents' strong work ethic and pride in their community remained a hallmark of its identity. A distinguishing characteristic of Community B is the partnership between the citizens and the town – in this community, the town characterizes public sector–citizen relations as growing together.[34]

The Role of the Public Sector in CI Initiatives

As noted above, the public sector is theorized to play four important direct (non-policy) roles in collective impact: providing backbone support, acting as a member of a partnership outside of government, collecting data, and championing the need for CI initiatives.[35] In order to determine the role government played in the instant cases, a review of documents produced through the CI process was conducted. Included in the review was the final output (quality of life plans[36]), as well as supporting documents (project proposals, meeting minutes, agendas), in order to better understand the public sector's role in the initiatives. For instance, to determine if the public sector served as a champion, the public sector's activities were examined throughout the project by looking at the project proposal and subsequent meeting minutes. If the public sector acted to bring stakeholders together early in the application process but did not regularly and actively participate in the planning process, its role was determined to be closer to that of a champion. Alternatively, since creating a common agenda requires true partnership in work, not in name only,[37] the public sector was deemed to be "acting as a member of the partnership" if meeting minutes revealed regular participation. If the public sector provided funding or other support (such as office space) for the initiative, its role was determined to be that of a backbone organization. Finally, if the program documents indicated that the public sector undertook data collection and/or sharing, its role was identified as data collector.

In each case, the public sector partner could be playing anywhere from none to all of these possible roles. Table 3.2 summarizes the major roles played by the public sector in each initiative. In Community A, the public sector served as a champion, participated as a member/partner, and assisted with data collection. In Community B, the public sector's role participated as a backbone organization.

Table 3.2 The role of the public sector in case study communities

Public Sector Role	Community A	Community B
Champion	X	
Backbone organization		X
Member/partner	X	
Data collector	X	

Community A

The public sector's involvement in this community began early in the collective impact process. The director of the community's economic development department took the lead in organizing an effort to learn more about the CI process and actively participated in the pre-grant training. As both a government official and an individual, this person was concerned with crime and racial inequality/relations in the community, and saw the CI process as a potential tool for bringing the community together to address crime and poverty. This commitment continued throughout the process. This individual actively participated in the two-year preparation period preceding the funding award, and continued to engage once funding was awarded. The presence of a local government representative in the CI initiative was leveraged to encourage the participation by other officials, such as council members, with duties and responsibilities related to economic development. These individuals participated in data collection and steering committees, and actively engaged in sharing the results of committee work with the public.

The long-term presence of a local government representative, not only at early stages but throughout the initiative, helped to build the trust needed to establish a common agenda. It was not sufficient, however, to build shared measures of success or mutually reinforcing activities. The effort seemed to stall due in part to local government officials' resistance to change, the perceived threat of the unknown, and the belief that the existing system worked well. Other challenges identified included the belief that elected officials, who engaged at later stages of the initiative, lacked sufficient understanding of the purpose and value of collective impact.

One requirement for the receipt of funds and assistance was that the community create a quality-of-life plan – a document by people and organizations in a specific area that details how to improve quality of life in the area. Quality-of-life plans generally include a vision for the future and issue areas, along with strategies and priorities for action – for example, stabilizing households by creating a path to homeowner-ship. The process of creating quality-of-life plans has been widely used in the United States by communities that wish to engage a wide array of local stakeholders in mapping the assets and challenges stakeholders face as they move to improve the overall quality of life in the commu-nity. The Local Initiatives Support Corporation, founded by the Ford Foundation, is a leader in advancing quality-of-life plans as tools for communities.[38] Upon reviewing the final plan produced by Commu-nity A as part of the CI initiative, it was evident that key stakeholders in the initiative were successful in maintaining existing structures for promoting and supporting community activities and engagement. In other words, even if change was warranted, these long-standing organ-izational structures (e.g., community task forces) were embedded in the plans, and an evaluation and reorganization of community committees did not take place. In fact, in informal conversations with stakehold-ers, it became clear that there was resistance to creating a quality-of-life plan that, in fact, might alter the existing vision of community groups. In this case, it appears that the community's success in connecting with the public sector and participating in government-related or sponsored activities contributed to some resistance to change. The members of the CI initiative noted that bringing together existing efforts to create community, with a new vision for community building that was more inclusive, would take additional time if resistance was to be countered.

Community B

In Community B, the public sector's primary role was one of providing backbone support, in concert with a non-profit organization assigned the "official" role of providing such support. In this case, the non-profit worked to coordinate meetings and monitor finances. A city official, whose regular portfolio included economic development, chaired the CI steering committee and participated in this leadership/coordination role throughout the one-year initiative. Other officials on the thirteen-member steering committee included a council member, the assistant to the mayor, and a representative from a quasi-public organization. In reviewing the initiative's documents, it became clear that the city's role was focused on guiding infrastructure planning. Nevertheless, residents participated in exercises aimed at identifying issues of concern (e.g., traffic patterns, bike lanes). Sufficient num-bers of residents did not participate, however, in the development of shared measures and mutually reinforcing activities. In this instance, the documents reviewed indicate that residents believed the role of the public sector was to address issues, once identified. This CI initiative did not continue, because community members were not willing to assume responsibility for moving the agenda forward. A more detailed analysis of residents' and public sector views of the successes and failures of this initiative is currently underway.

Lessons Learned: Collective Impact and Deliberative Democracy

This case study reveals that the roles assumed by the public sector in the selected collective impact initiatives spanned all four categories identified by FSG. There is a clear need for more detailed and broader examinations of the role of the public sector in CI initiatives. Nevertheless, there also are interesting lessons to draw from these cases that can inform our thinking about deliberative democracy. Public institutions can and do interface with CI initiatives when the market failures accompanying wicked policy problems are recognized. The public sector's long history and tradition of assuming responsibility for addressing these market failures is thus only one approach to addressing these complex issues. When, as is evidenced by this case study, public organizations assume alternate roles (e.g., as champion, partner, or backbone organization), there emerge new opportunities for creating positive change in communities. This raises important questions about the context in which deliberations about policy problems can occur and the role(s) the public sector can play in advancing deliberative democracy. A better understanding of the possible roles for, and consequences of, the public sector's involvement in CI initiatives might further affect our understanding of collaborative processes, data collection, and shared measurement. It might also suggest new ways to create public policies that support collective impact. Both Ferber and White and a study by FSG provide glimpses into the roles public institutions play in such initiatives, given their existing structures and responsibilities.[39] However, emerging CI initiatives also call on institutions to transform their operations and responsibilities to better participate in more collaborative decision-making models. This is in keeping with deliberative democratic commitments as well. Yet, in the face of fear, threats, and lack of incentives, all of which are significant obstacles to institutional change, the capacity for the public sector to develop effective CI initiatives might be limited. Still, the need to change processes, in the face of wicked problems, is critical.

The process of collective impact, as currently envisioned, embraces a deeper understanding of context than more traditional responses to policy problems. Kania and colleagues, for example, assert that culture matters, and must be built intentionally and transparently. A shift in mindset must occur around who is involved, how they work together, and how progress happens, and it must evolve over the course of the initiative.[40] A culture of collaboration is created through shared values, goals, and expectations. Collective impact, by design, can affect the culture of a community by informing the processes, language, and discourse surrounding collective problem solving. In CI processes, the focus shifts from single to multiple issues, and from individual action to collective action. In turn, the culture of decision making changes and communities move closer to defining and accepting a common agenda. Traditional mindsets, based on individualism, change to network mindsets.[41] Sharing underlying common interests and social bonds of friendship, along with promoting substantive and procedural fairness, helps to ensure that all views are heard and trust is engendered. Public institutions can support this process by participating as champions, partners, data collectors, and/or backbone organizations, and perhaps in new ways not yet identified. As evidenced in Community A, the presence of a well-respected government representative provided an opportunity to connect officials not yet engaged to a new model of community development. In Community B, the public institution served the important function of a backbone organization providing a level of support other organizations would not be able to offer.

As processes change, new language emerges. Individuals move from the use of language that describes individual gains and losses to language descriptive of collective impacts. Outputs, outcomes, and shared measures based on individual gains and losses are redefined to reflect common goals. Kania's work informs our understanding of the role of culture in collective impact.[42] The research presented in this chapter, although still in its infancy, suggests that filling the gaps between the collective vision of CI participants and the existing vision and structures of the public sector will be important to ensuring the success of CI initiatives. Public sector officials perceived as keepers of existing practices will not be welcomed into CI practice, since, with a limited understanding of the power or need for collective voice, they will limit the potential for change that can be accomplished through collaboration. When government overlaps with collective action only in the sphere where it is comfortable – creating rules and regulations – the opportunity to reinvent interactions between constituents and government will be missed. This reinvention is similar to what is required in transitions to more deliberative forms of democracy and, as such, CI initiatives can offer sites of deliberation more in keeping with the listening and relationship building called for by other authors in this volume (see, for example, Tungohan, chapter 13; Wiebe, chapter 14).

This chapter has explored the role of the public sector in two local collective impact initiatives aimed at addressing complex, multidimensional social problems. In both cases, local governments played very different roles in collective impact initiatives. In Community B, the public sector engaged in the CI initiative primarily as a backbone organization, helping to bring stakeholders to the table. In Community A, the public sector assumed multiple roles, engaging as a partner, facilitating data collection, and serving as a champion for the CI approach. The case study suggests, perhaps, that the role of the public sector in emerging responses to market failures, such as collective impact, might in fact be flexible. As additional examples unfold, there will be opportunities to further review and classify the different roles public sector institutions play in addressing public concerns and the changing role of citizens in democratic decision-making processes. The question of how deliberative democratic processes will change under alternative models – for example, if these changes are more are less inclusive – will be central to furthering our understanding of emerging collective action models as vehicles of democratic engagement and social change.

Collective impact is notably one model to facilitate consensus building and shared action in the face of wicked problems. The model has limitations, however – namely, that it privileges representatives of stakeholder groups in the name of efficiency. The trade-off between efficiency and inclusiveness is at the heart of the deliberative process. The existing system assigns significant responsibility to the public sector for the correction of market failures. Consequently, government action or inaction is judged in the context of the outcomes realized, despite the fact that wicked problems cannot be solved with sector- or agency-specific actions. In periods when the political system supports advancing the public purpose, both financially and legislatively, resources are more plentiful, obstacles are minimized, and results might seem tangible. When support wanes, the inefficiencies of inaction are perceived as evidence of the public sector's failure to perform.

The cases presented in this chapter provide examples of what a deliberative democratic process might look like when motivated by the need to respond to wicked problems and market failures. The varying roles played by the public sector in the collective impact process suggest that many questions remain. In addition to the need to develop our understanding of the role of the public sector in CI initiatives, other areas of research might include an examination of stakeholder perceptions of the role of the public sector in these initiatives, the effects of the CI approach on norm-based deliberative processes, and the consequences of redistributed power in democratic decision-making processes.

Discussion Questions

1 What roles, other than those mentioned above, could the public sector play in a collective impact process?
2 What incentives could encourage the public sector to move away from existing models of decision making and participation in community revitalization?
3 What public policies, outside of funding, could be developed to support CI initiatives directly?

NOTES

1 Paul C. Light, "A Cascade of Failures: Why Government Fails and How to Stop It" (Washington, DC: Center for Effective Public Management at Brookings, 2014).
2 William Keech, Michael, C. Munger, and Carl Simon, "Market Failure and Government Failure" (paper submitted for presentation to Public Choice World Congress, Miami, 2012). Online at http://michaelmunger.com /papers/keechmungersimon.pdf, accessed 2 June 2018.
3 Marc Dunkelman, "The Transformation of American Community," *National Affairs* 41 (Summer 2011). Online at https://www.nationalaffairs .com/publications/detail/the-transformation-of-american-community.
4 See, for example, the website at https://www.regulations.gov/.
5 Ibid.
6 Horst W.J. Rittel and Melvin M. Webber, "Dilemmas in a General Theory of Planning," *Policy Sciences* 4, no. 2 (1973): 155–69; and John G. Head, *Public Goods and Public Welfare* (Durham, NC: Duke University Press, 1974).
7 Dunkelman, "Transformation of American Community."
8 Carol Hommerich, "Feeling Disconnected: Exploring the Relationship Between Different Forms of Social Capital and Civic Engagement in Japan." *Voluntas* 26, no. 1 (2015): 45–68.
9 I. Kawachi et al., "Social Capital, Income Inequality, and Mortality," *American Journal of Public Health* 87, no. 9 (1997): 1491–8.
10 Chip Donahue, *Family Engagement in the Digital Age* (New York: Routledge, 2017); Margaret Doughty, "Coalition Building: A Tool for Improved Community Literacy" (Washington, DC: US Department of Education, March 2012).
11 Katherine Cooper, "'Wicked Problems': What Are They, and Why Are They of Interest to NNSI Researchers?" (Evanston, IL: Northwestern University, School of Communication, Network for Nonprofit and Social

Impact, 2017). Online at https://nnsi.northwestern.edu/social-impact /wicked-problems-what-are-they-and-why-are-they-of-interest-to-nnsi -researchers/, accessed 12 July 2017.

12 Ibid.

13 John Kania and Mark Kramer, "Embracing Emergence: How Collective Impact Addresses Complexity," *Stanford Social Innovation Review* (2013): 1–7.

14 According to the Center for Community Health and Development at the University of Kansas, successful examples of collective impact can be found across sectors, including efforts related to improving education (e.g., Strive), public health (e.g., LiveWell Colorado), homelessness (e.g., Home Again), youth development (e.g., Project U-turn), and economic development (e.g., Memphis Fast Forward). See University of Kansas, Center for Community Health and Development, "Tools to Change Our World," online at https://ctb.ku.edu/sites/default/files/files/site_files /communitytoolbox-flyer.pdf, accessed 10 January 2018.

15 Francis M. Bator, "The Anatomy of Market Failure," *Quarterly Journal of Economics* 72, no. 3 (1958): 351–71; Paul A. Samuelson, "The Pure Theory of Public Expenditure," *Review of Economics and Statistics* 36, no. 4 (1954): 387–90.

16 James Buchanan and Gordon Tullock, *Calculus of Consent* (Ann Arbor: University of Michigan Press, 1962); see also Norman Schofield, *Collective Decision-Making: Social Choice and Political Economy*. New York: Springer Science & Business Media, 1996.

17 See, for example, Gordon Tullock, "Public Decisions as Public Goods," *Journal of Political Economy* 79, no. 4 (1971): 913–19; and Mancur Olson, *The Logic of Collective Action: Public Goods and the Theory of Groups* (Cambridge, MA: Harvard University Press, 1971).

18 Elinor Ostrom, *Governing the Commons: The Evolution of Institutions for Collective Action* (Cambridge: Cambridge University Press, 1990).

19 Howard Rheingold, *Smart Mobs: The Next Social Revolution* (Cambridge, MA: Perseus Books, 2002).

20 John Kania and Mark Kramer, "Collective Impact," *Stanford Social Innovation Review* (Winter 2011): 36–41.

21 Robertson Adams, "How a Leading Foundation Broke New Ground" (Miami: Knight Foundation, 2011), online at https://knightfoundation.org /articles/leadership-profile-chicago-community-trust/, accessed 3 March 2018.

22 See, for example, Chris Cancialosi, "Collective Impact: A Collaborative Approach to Create Change," *Forbes*, 15 September 2015, online at https:// www.forbes.com/sites/chriscancialosi/2015/09/15/collective-impact-a -collaborative-approach-to-creating-change/, accessed 1 March 2018; Jeff Edmondson, "Using Feedback Loops to Move from Collaboration to Collective Impact," *Forbes*, 31 October 2013, online at https://www.forbes.com/sites

/ashoka/2013/10/31/using-feedback-loops-to-move-from-collaboration
-to-collective-impact/#5188b3fe6018, accessed 22 February 2018.

23 Strive Partnership, "Strive Partnership: About Us," online at www
.strivepartnership.org/about-the-partnership, accessed 4 March 2018.

24 FSG, *Collective Impact Case Study: Memphis Fast Forward* (Boston: FSG, 2013),
online at https://www.fsg.org/publications/memphis-fast-forward.

25 Thaddeus Ferber and Erin White, "Making Public Policy Collective Impact
Friendly," *Stanford Social Innovation Review* (2014): 22–3.

26 Colin Wood, "3 Forces Hindering Public-Sector Collaboration," *Government
Technology*, 4 April 2013, online at https://www.govtech.com/policy
-management/3-Factors-Hindering-Public-Sector-Collaboration.html,
accessed 3 November 2016.

27 Erin White et al., *How Public Policy Can Support Collective Impact* (Boston:
FSG and Collective Impact Forum, November 2014), online at https://www
.fsg.org/publications/how-public-policy-can-support-collective-impact.

28 Kania and Kramer, "Embracing Emergence."

29 White et al., "How Public Policy Can Support Collective Impact."

30 Ibid.

31 Wood, "3 Forces Hindering Public-Sector Collaboration."

32 Lori Bartczak, "The Role of Grantmakers in Collective Impact," *Stanford
Social Innovation Review* (Fall 2014): 8–10.

33 Legacy Foundation, "Neighborhood Spotlight Launch Factsheet" (2014),
online at http://www.legacyfdn.org/neighborhood-spotlight.php,
accessed 6 March 2018.

34 Griffith Diamond Jubilee Corporation, *Seventy-five Years of Growing
Together: Griffith Jubilee, 1904–1979* (Griffith, IN: Griffith Diamond Jubilee
Corporation, 1979).

35 White et al., "How Public Policy Can Support Collective Impact."

36 A plan that details goals and strategies for improving the overall quality
of life in a community as envisioned by residents; see Andy Mooney and
Amanda Carney, *How the New Communities Program Works* (Chicago: Local
Initiatives Support Corporation, 2003).

37 White et al., "How Public Policy Can Support Collective Impact."

38 Local Initiatives Support Corporation, "Sample Quality-of-Life Plans,"
n.d., online at http://archive.instituteccd.org/resources/category/522,
accessed 7 March 2018.

39 Ferber and White, "Making Public Policy Collective Impact Friendly";
White et al., "How Public Policy Can Support Collective Impact."

40 John Kania, Fay Hanleybrown, and Jennifer Splansky Juster, "Essential Mindset Shifts for Collective Impact," *Stanford Social Innovation Review* (2014): 2–5.

41 Ibid.

42 Ibid.

KEY RESOURCES

Foundation for Tacoma Students. "Graduate Tacoma! 2018 Community Impact Report." Tacoma, WA: Foundation for Tacoma Students, 2018). Online at https://graduatetacoma.org/wp-content/uploads/2018/05/ImpactReport18 _040618-lo-res_FNL.pdf.

Kania, John, and Mark Kramer. "Collective Impact." *Stanford Social Innovation Review* (Winter 2011): 36–41.

Spark Policy Institute. *When Collective Impact Has an Impact: A Cross-Site Study of 25 Collective Impact Initiatives*. Denver: Spark Policy Institute, 2018. Online at http://sparkpolicy.com/wp-content/uploads/2018/02/CI-Study-Report _February-2018.pdf.

Strive Together Partnership. "Collective Impact." n.d. Online at https://www .strivetogether.org/our-approach/collective-impact/.

4 Northern Women's Conceptualizations of Well-Being: Engaging in the "Right" Policy Conversations

LEAH LEVAC AND JACQUELINE GILLIS

Introduction

Although Canada's economy continues to rely heavily on natural resources, the policy processes – such as impact assessments (IAs) – that precede resource development and extraction projects are increasingly contested for failing to consider adequately environmental sustainability, Indigenous rights, community well-being, and input from a wide range of citizens, including women and others who historically have been excluded from policy development. This contestation extends to the projects that result, with several ongoing examples of resistance in present-day Canada.

Process and project failures have garnered international attention from organizations such as Amnesty International, which recently found that, "in actively promoting intensive development in the northeast [of British Columbia], federal and provincial officials have emphasized [the] benefits, while largely ignoring serious – and sometimes deadly – unintended consequences for wellness and safety that disproportionately impact the lives of the Indigenous peoples who live there, particularly Indigenous women and girls."[1] These failures raise important questions about whose and which ideas and experiences inform the assessment – and ultimately approval or rejection – of resource projects. Moreover, they point to the critical importance of considering the experiences of women when projects are assessed and approved. Throughout the chapter, "women" should be read as including women from different nations, peoples, and ethnic and cultural backgrounds, and with different abilities, ages, and access to financial and other resources. Where women describe their experiences in relation to their particular identities or social locations, or where we are raising experiences and concerns identified by particular women, it is so noted.

Although there is ample evidence that impact assessment processes in Canada need to better address the heterogeneous needs and concerns of citizens, as one of the authors of this chapter has observed elsewhere, "regulatory mechanisms [in Canada], including environmental assessments (EA) and gender based-analyses provide neither a systematic, comprehensive analysis of the gendered and intersectional impacts of resource development and extraction [on women in the north], nor any guidance on how to mitigate these impacts."[2] Although recent changes to Canadian impact assessment legislation – discussed further below – begin to address these shortcomings, there are still critical gaps in our understanding of how to account fully for women's experiences.

In this chapter, using ideas from the social construction of policy framework,[3] we argue that three dominant social constructions – women as outside the natural resource extraction industry; women as deviant and/or dependent individuals; and natural resource projects as delivering benefits that outweigh burdens – work to silence women's voices in important natural resource-related policy conversations, but also that ample evidence points to women's resistance to these constructions and to their efforts to assert their voices and experiences in resource-related decision making, and in community decision making more broadly. After describing these constructions, we combine the social construction of policy framework's related concept of "feed-forward effects" – defined as the consequences of policy choices and decisions – with an intersectional perspective[4] that examines how social and political structures and systems intersect with an individual's identities to create temporary or sustained experiences of privilege or exclusion. We use this foundation to answer two questions related to how policy problems are defined, which in turn has implications for deliberative democracy: how do women in northern communities conceptualize well-being, and what necessary policy questions related to resource extraction are highlighted through these conceptualizations?

Using data gathered through conversations with over 150 women from across northern Canada, and informed by related literature, we suggest that women's understandings of well-being provide an important foundation for informing policy problems and conversations – and thus the focuses of deliberative democratic processes – not only related to decisions about resource development and extraction projects, but also to decisions about how to mitigate impacts if projects are approved. Keeping with other critical policy scholars,[5] we assert that an important area for further consideration in deliberative democratic scholarship is who decides how policy problems are defined and come to be identified for deliberative focus. We also point out the resonance between our work and environmental justice and reproductive justice literature, highlighting myriad ways women are asserting their voices and bodies in policy conversations despite the risk of their exclusion through dominant social constructions. We close with lessons from this ongoing work and suggestions about how to improve the focuses of deliberative democratic processes in ways that better account for all women's voices.

Background

Our research on this topic has not focused on one policy per se, but Canada's impact assessment (formerly environmental assessment) process – and its shortcomings – is frequently noted as a relevant policy of focus, and so warrants a brief overview. The federal IA process is determined by the Impact Assessment Act, 2019. Based on the results of a series of planning steps,[6] the Impact Assessment Agency of Canada makes a determination as to whether an IA is necessary. An IA can take two forms: either a comprehensive study by a responsible authority (the Canadian Nuclear Safety Commission, the National Energy Board, or the Impact Assessment Agency of Canada) or by a review panel appointed by the minister of the environment and climate change.[7] Regardless of the type, each IA has several essential stages, including a project description review, a public comment period, an analysis of the project, and the release of an IA decision statement.[8] In 2016, after coming under intense scrutiny for, among other things, its failure to engage meaningfully with citizens, the federal government appointed an expert panel to review the assessment process. The panel found that the public's calls for meaningful public participation insist on "the possibility to influence the outcomes of the process, such as the design of proposals, the considerations studied in the assessment, and/or the decision-making itself,"[9] and that such participation should be initiated during project planning and continue throughout.[10] The panel – whose recommendations are reflected in the 2019 legislation – equated this level of public engagement with the "involve" and "collaborate" stages on the five-stage public participation spectrum of the International Association for Public Participation (IAP[2]), which is meant to guide governments, organizations, and others on the goal of any given public engagement initiative. IAP[2]'s spectrum is like Arnstein's ladder of participation,[11] and thus suffers the same limitations, such as treating power as a discrete and fixed entity.[12] It is nevertheless widely used by governments to gauge and guide their public engagement efforts, and so is a useful reference point for thinking about increasing input from diverse citizens.[13]

As already noted, this chapter draws on two ongoing community-initiated and -based research projects with over 150 Indigenous and northern women. Across these communities and nations, the goals have been to better understand and support local responses to, and factors affecting, communities' and women's well-being; to support research capacity building and opportunities for informing policy decisions; and to reflect on and decolonize our own practices and ideas as southern researchers engaging with northern women, including Indigenous women. This process includes recognizing our own histories and locations. Leah Levac's ancestors came from Scotland, Ireland, and France. She grew up on the land of the Huron-Wendat, Mississauga, and Haudenosaunee peoples, and lives today in the treaty lands and territory of the Mississaugas of the Credit, which is also within the Dish with One Spoon territory. Leah has been collaborating with Inuit and Haisla women over the past several years, humbly learning more and more about the strength and resilience of Indigenous and northern women. Jacqueline Gillis, who has worked behind the scenes on different dimensions of these collaborations, is a settler of Scottish and Polish ancestry who lives in Toronto on the traditional territory of many nations, including the Mississaugas of the Credit, the Anishnabeg, the Chippewa, the Haudenosaunee, and the Wendat peoples. Both of us work continuously to deepen our understanding of, and commitment to, anticolonial and decolonial practices. For example, we continuously ask questions about how best to create mutual benefit through our collaborations, and about how to reveal and dismantle power imbalances between university-based and community-based research team members. Each research collaboration is guided by a local advisory group, and employs a local project coordinator and local research assistants whenever possible. This chapter has been reviewed by members of the advisory group in both projects. The research collaborations in each community have been approved by the respective Indigenous nation, organization, or government whose members are involved in the research and by the University of Guelph's Research Ethics Board.

The first project began in the fall of 2012 with a small group of women in Happy Valley-Goose Bay (HV-GB), Labrador, who were (and remain) concerned about the development of a multibillion-dollar hydroelectric dam on the Lower Churchill River. HV-GB sits at the head of Upper Lake Melville, and is home to approximately eight thousand people. Some of the offices of the Nunatsiavut government, as well as of the NunatuKavut Community Council, are in HV-GB. The Innu Nation community of Sheshatshiu is about twenty-five kilometres northwest of HV-GB. Considered the service hub for the region, HV-GB offers the widest range of services of anywhere in Labrador. At the time of the joint environmental assessment review panel's review of the Lower Churchill project, women in the community were acutely aware of the challenges that could result from such large-scale developments but could not find appropriate venues for having their voices heard. Emerging from an existing partnership called FemNorthNet, which was broadly focused on northern Indigenous and settler women's mobility, inclusion, and well-being, we collaborated for over three years on the development of a community vitality index – a framework to describe and monitor the community's well-being from the perspective of women in the community. In spring 2017, under the guidance of a local advisory group comprised of women community members who had been involved in the project since 2012 – some of whom are also affiliated with Indigenous governments and organizations, women's organizations, government agencies, or local academic institutions – we piloted a community-developed well-being survey.[14] The survey serves as one tool for monitoring changes in community well-being, from the perspective of women in the community. Based on the results of the pilot, the survey and recruitment procedures were refined and community well-being data were collected in spring 2018.

On the opposite coast of present-day Canada, the Haisla Nation, whose largest population base lives in Kitamaat Village, and the District of Kitimat (also in Haisla territory) are nestled on the northwest coast of British Columbia at the head of the Douglas Channel. About 700 of the 1,700 members of the Haisla Nation live in Kitamaat Village, which is also home to the Haisla Nation's government offices.[15] Haisla people have lived in the territory that includes present-day Kitimat and stretches across a large section of the northwest coast of British Columbia for over nine thousand years. The District of Kitimat was established officially in 1953, primarily because of the Aluminum Company of Canada's decision to locate a smelter in the area. Today, Kitimat has a population of approximately eight thousand, and continues to be driven economically by ongoing and prospective resource development.[16] In 2015, after learning about our work in HV-GB, the Ending Violence Association of British Columbia contacted us, and connected us to The Tamitik Status of Women Association (TSW) in Kitimat. TSW was (and remains) concerned about increasing instances of gendered violence and racism in the community and, in turn, about the well-being of marginalized community members.[17] Changes in women's well-being, it feared, were connected to the preparatory work underway for the proposed Northern Gateway Pipeline, planned to terminate in Kitimat, and to the Kitimat Aluminum Smelter Modernization project. Although the Northern Gateway project has since been shelved indefinitely and the modernization project is complete, the area has a long history of being affected by the "boom-and-bust" economic cycle that accompanies resource-dependent economies, so concerns about women's voices and experiences being overlooked in resource-related policy decisions persist. As a result, TSW organized a community advisory group, made up of women from Kitimat and the Haisla Nation, to pursue a broad conversation about women's well-being. In spring 2018, the team released an initial report about the well-being of Indigenous and settler women and girls in the area, based on conversations with well over one hundred women across the two communities.[18] It bears mentioning that, in fall 2018, after the data presented in this chapter were collected, LNG Canada and its partners announced they would proceed with the construction of a new multibillion-dollar liquefied natural gas export terminal in the area – a reminder that the well-being of Indigenous and settler women will continue to warrant careful attention.

Although diverse in geography, culture, and proximate resource industry, some women in these communities share a sense that the voices and experiences of women are not always taken seriously in resource-related policy decisions, not only during IA processes, but also during the construction and operation of resource projects. They further sense that a core component of this oversight is the failure to understand and account for women's broad and interconnected conceptualizations of well-being in how policy problems are understood. This aligns with scholars and community organizations who contend that natural resource extraction industries remain masculinized both in terms of the demographic composition of those employed in these sectors and of the prevailing values and assumptions therein.[19] Others have suggested that the heterogeneity of resource-dependent communities means that local context considerably shapes the experiences of men and women, and results in variation in women's experiences.[20] However, our experiences in Kitimat and Kitamaat Village, British Columbia, and Happy Valley-Goose Bay, Labrador, thus far suggest that many experiences are also shared, including that resource projects remain masculinized, that well-being is poorly understood, and that women's considerations frequently remain external to policy conversations, despite extensive and concerted efforts to the contrary.

Theoretical Foundations

The social construction framework provides a way of understanding the broad exclusion of northern women as political actors. Social construction, a critical orientation towards policy analysis, contends that policy formation incorporates not only "the rational and instrumental components of design but also the value-laden components, such as social constructions, rationales, and underlying assumptions."[21] Social construction theorists suggest that people are socially arranged into target populations, which become designated to receive burdens or benefits resulting from policy decisions.[22] These groups are differentiated by their political power and perceived level of deservingness: the advantaged, contenders, dependents, or deviants. The advantaged are politically strong and constructed as deserving, such as the elderly and veterans, while contenders are those who are politically strong but denoted as undeserving, such as the rich and minority peoples. Dependents are constructed as both weak and deserving, and include children, mothers, and people with disabilities, whereas deviants – criminals and drug addicts, for example – are both weak and undeserving.[23] Although these social constructions are understood as being resistant to change, theorists point out some fluidity to them as "new conditions may emerge from unintended consequences of previous policy that alter perceptions of that group's deservedness, the actions of a moral entrepreneur, or a group's power and behavior."[24] This theory helps us think about how and why the experiences of Indigenous and northern women and girls might be considered (or not) in important resource-related policy conversations and decisions.

The theory contends that the characterization of groups as negative or positive has effects on "goals to be achieved or problems to be solved; the tools intended to change behaviour; rules for inclusion, exclusion, and timing; rationales that legitimate the policy and provide an internal cause-and-effect logic connecting means to ends; and the implementation structure."[25] As such, social construction is best seen as an active process, through which powerful characterizations of target populations influence their abilities to participate in policy conversations in terms of shaping the goals, instruments, and related processes of policy development. According to this theory, social constructions of target populations can also have a substantial impact on political attitudes and participation of the populations themselves through feed-forward effects, which include "both material and symbolic (reputational or interpretive) effects on target populations that impact their attitudes and political participation."[26] Research on these impacts has emphasized four major types of feed-forward effects.[27] The one most salient to this discussion is the way in which the rhetoric and logics surrounding a policy are internalized by those in certain target groups. Constructions "discourage the political participation of negatively constructed groups and encourage the participation of positively constructed groups, [and as a result] policy designs come to exert a powerful reinforcement of social constructions, prevailing power relationships, and institutional cultures."[28] As such, the political voices and knowledges of some target populations become minimized and constructed as less reliable, valid, or relevant to the policy conversation, thereby influencing the degree of political voice held by some groups.[29] No studies of which we are aware have sought to examine the impacts of social constructions on women's political participation in policy decisions about natural resource extraction projects, or the implications of this for deliberative democracy.

In sum, the social construction of groups of people affects not only policy decisions, but also approaches to policy development, including in terms of whose voices are considered an important part of the conversation. This has clear implications for deliberative democracy. As Genevieve Fuji Johnson notes in chapter 1 of this volume, "theories of deliberative democracy consist of principles of participatory inclusion, procedural equality, access to information, and respectful exchanges of reasons geared towards a consensus, agreement, or expression of a shared interest, which in turn provides the ethical and democratic justification for a collective decision." Any of these elements of deliberative democracy is easily subjected to social constructions by influencing what constitutes procedural equality, who deserves access to information, and so on. However, we are most interested in which policy problems come to serve as the focuses of deliberations, and how social constructions of Indigenous and northern women shape these focuses.

Adding to the social constructions of target populations is the social construction of the resource sector as (at least primarily) beneficial and masculine. The discourse of benefits[30] surrounding natural resource extraction projects is often central to both proposals and their approval. Promised benefits often take "the form of corporate donations to local communities, preferential procurement and hiring practices, and investments in community infrastructure, [and] are becoming a norm for mineral exploration and mining companies doing business."[31] For example, in the hydroelectric project in HV-GB that sparked this research, Nalcor committed to investing in the community through community donations, providing on-the-job training, and committing to hiring women in trades on its site.[32] Related to the current liquefied natural gas terminal being developed in Haisla territory and Kitimat, similar types of commitments are indicated by LNG Canada in its community charter[33] and through the creation of agreements with several affected First Nations, including the Haisla Nation. These types of agreements, which certainly result in benefits for some women (and others), have also been the subject of criticisms, including that they aim to gain the trust of the community and secure a social licence for the project,[34] in part, we suggest, by constructing the benefits of natural resource extraction as unquestionably outweighing the burdens, a process that may – even if accidentally – have the indirect effect of erasing considerations of women's well-being.

The construction of the resource sector as masculine is clear when considering workers' demographics. For example, in the Lower Churchill hydroelectric project, women make up only 12 per cent of the total workforce and only 6 per cent (34 of 573) of project apprentices.[35] Across Canada, similar trends are notable in forestry, mining, and hydroelectric projects.[36] When women do gain access to typically male-dominated occupations, such as engineering in the oil industry, they describe being inundated by paternalistic discourses in which they "[experience] a masculine value system in their training, in their everyday interactions, in the values of engineering with its focus on technology and in the individualistic, market driven context represented by the frontier myth and the cowboy hero."[37] As a woman in Kitimat explained, "I hear of [women] friends who work ... as engineers and they have an incredibly hard time being taken seriously." For Indigenous women, these experiences can be compounded. Regardless of gender, Indigenous peoples often do not account for a substantial portion of those employed on natural resource extraction projects: "Employment of Indigenous peoples in the mineral/petroleum sector in northern Alberta and Canada has remained relatively steady in the past decade (2007–12) at 5%."[38] Of 4,134 individuals working on the Lower Churchill hydroelectric project at the close of 2016, only 410 self-identified as Indigenous.[39] When Indigenous people do gain employment, they tend to access short-term jobs in construction, rather than long-term jobs in the operations phase – as relevant training for the positions is often unavailable to northerners[40] – or as jobs are outsourced. There are examples of efforts by proponents to respond to these challenges,[41] and some optimism in the community that women's experiences might be receiving more attention now than in the past. However, several Haisla women involved in this research nevertheless spoke of past employment-related challenges. For example, one woman noted that with "the smelter ... there was a real sense that it employed our people, our local people... so you know where at one point in time we looked at the modernization as being something that was giving value back to our community, now it is more a sense of what it is taking out of our community."

The social construction of policy framework allows us to interrogate not only women's possible exclusions from policy-making processes and discourses, but also the framing of the resource sector. Some criticisms, however, have been mounted against the framework. For example, Robert Liberman argues that group identities are subject to substantial contestation and cannot be understood as a unitary phenomenon.[42] In other words, considerations of diversity within these groups might position different subpopulations differently. For example, senior women who are more dependent on public social programs than their male counterparts and who experience higher rates of living in low income[43] might be seen more as dependent because of their gender, than as advantaged because of their age. Liberman also points out that the framework does not account for institutions or shifts in the construction of target populations throughout history.[44] Leading social constructivists have indeed contended that the social construction of groups might shift over time and that public policies themselves are a type of institution.[45] Liberman's critiques, however, are worth bearing in mind.

Our work also aligns with the environmental justice and environmental reproductive justice movements and literatures. Environmental justice is a principle that calls for "the fair treatment and meaningful involvement of all people regardless of race, color, national origin, or income, with respect to the development, implementation, and enforcement of environmental laws, regulations, and policies."[46] The movement has grown from the work of African American waste collection workers responding to unfair treatment and environmental justice concerns to include: "(1) unequal enforcement of environmental, civil rights, and public health laws; (2) differential exposure of some populations to harmful chemicals, ... and (5) exclusionary practices that prevent some individuals and groups from participating in decision-making or limit the extent of their participation."[47] Within the Canadian context, there exist some critical studies and applications of environmental justice, including by community organizations[48] and academics.[49]

The related environmental reproductive justice movement "embeds reproductive rights in an intersectional framework that includes social justice and human rights [and] ... stresses both individual and group rights, since the ability of a woman to determine her reproductive destiny is in many cases directly tied to conditions in her community."[50] As such, the term "environmental reproductive justice" acknowledges and examines how the health of the environment affects a woman's ability to reproduce and raise a healthy child. In addition to this emphasis on physical survival, the concept incorporates aspects of cultural survival, which include the preservation of the earth, language, customs, and community.[51] Several Indigenous scholars similarly have emphasized the need for cultural survival. Jeff Corntassel and Cheryl Bryce, for example, discuss the intimate relationship between

Indigenous resurgence, self-determination, and one's reconnection with the environment, homelands, and cultural practices. Environmental reproductive justice requires us to consider not only corporal injustices, but also the institutional barriers to ameliorating or responding to these inequalities.[52] Within the Canadian context, several scholars have found that Indigenous peoples are systematically more likely to be affected by environmental and environmental reproductive injustices.[53] Our conversations with women echo these concerns and highlight a central tenet of environmental justice and environmental reproductive justice – namely, that many women feel unable to participate equally and effectively in policy discussions related to well-being and resource development and extraction in their communities.

The Broad and Interconnected Nature of Well-Being

Our exploration of women's conceptualizations of well-being includes the following brief synthesis of ideas discussed within and across the communities, peoples, and nation involved in this work.

Happy Valley-Goose Bay. Over several months in 2012 and 2013, and based on ongoing conversations and revisions, approximately twenty Inuit, Labradorian, and settler women in HV-GB developed the following definition of women's well-being:

> The well-being of women in the north depends on having the opportunity to enjoy and develop a healthy and sustainable relationship with the environment. Having the ability to value yourself – both where you have come from and where you are going – is also important. Well-being requires having a sense of safety and security, and having access to appropriate food, housing, resources, finances, and support services. Having a social support network, and being free from violent relationships are critical factors that affect well-being for all women. Food security; having or being able to learn coping mechanisms; being able to make choices about what's best for you and your family; having access to information and resources; and social acceptance of diverse social identities are also critically important factors that affect women's well-being. Having a space to meet to share and learn with other women is also important. Overall well-being is made up of: (1) physical; (2) emotional; (3) mental/intellectual; (4) spiritual; and (5) cultural well-being. (HV-GB workshop participants, 2013)

Participating women represented well-being symbolically with an Inuksuk (see figure 4.1), which they described as representing balance (all stones of our Inuksuk must fit together to form a stable structure),

Figure 4.1 Women's well-being in Happy Valley-Goose Bay, Labrador
Note: This image was imagined by women involved in the research collaboration in Happy Valley-Goose Bay and digitized and refined graphically by Monica Peach of the Nunatsiavut government.

uniqueness (every Inuksuk is different), direction (we all benefit from collective guidance), and connection to the earth. Within the Inuksuk, participants included nets – fishing nets, spider's webs, a woman's womb, dreamcatchers, and snowshoes – because for them, nets symbolized not only the importance of strong social connections to well-being, but also the possibility of having well-being compromised through unhealthy networks (Workshop Notes, 2013).

Kitimat and the Haisla Nation (Kitamaat Village)

In Kitimat and the Haisla Nation's Kitamaat Village, several themes related to well-being emerged in sharing circles held with well over 100 women in summer 2016 and spring 2017. We worked with the Kitimat and Haisla advisory group to create a way of sharing information and stories with each other. We prioritized the safety of participants by hosting sharing circles at the sites of local organizations with feminist mandates and/or that provide judgment-free and culturally relevant services. Women noted strong social infrastructure across their communities, citing many organizations that help to fill service gaps and ameliorate food insecurity for people. Nevertheless, as in Labrador, many service shortages were noted, including inadequate intercommunity transportation – of particular concern for youth and older people – declining educational opportunities, and minimal support for local economic development initiatives. Very limited access to mental health services was repeated here, as in our discussions in HV-GB. Accompanying limited access, women pointed out barriers to accessing services that were available: "I've got to work full time. I work Monday to Friday, 8:00 to 4:30 ... so then those are the same hours as drug and alcohol counsellors, [and] as ... victims services or whatever." Another woman pointed out the barriers "for the women who have children and who are single women, or ... who have children, to have that side care while they're able to [seek counselling]." Women also described fraught relationships with the resource sector, which both provides most of the (albeit precarious) well-paying employment in the region and is a source of fear and sometimes violence: "[the employer was] brutal to the women who were working in there ... The women who are here need to know how to deal with [people] who don't appreciate women's contributions at all."

The cost of living was also a major dividing factor in women's well-being experiences in both Kitimat and the Haisla Nation and in Labrador. The high cost of living in the north is a barrier to accessing recreation and leisure activities in the communities, and means that many families struggle to find affordable housing and go without sufficient food. Food security is an issue for some women in Kitimat, who explained that, until relatively recently, the lack of competition between grocery stores had seemingly led to regular price increases. Food security has also been negatively affected by the decline of important cultural practices in the Haisla Nation. Haisla and Inuit women explained several ways their traditions and cultural practices have become more difficult to uphold, particularly in terms of ensuring that everyone in the community has access to food. As one woman from Haisla told us, "I can't even remember how to catch fish or smoke it. I don't even know how to make a fire." Another noted, "I still remember my mom's smokehouse. She had a big smokehouse, and she put layers of fish in there. She used to fill it up ... the family all worked together just to get the food for the winter. Now you can't do that. Nobody has a smokehouse anymore." Women in Kitimat and the Haisla Nation are also deeply connected to the land – not only for survival, but also for renewal and sense of self. The above quotes help to explain that environmental injustices – which are easily perpetuated by resource development and extraction – threaten not only ecological, but also cultural survival, a point others have highlighted.[54]

Although unique localized realities unquestionably affect northern women's well-being, the women we spoke with share strong connections to the land, lack access to appropriate or sufficient health and social services, and are divided by their economic well-being, a situation one of this chapter's authors has described elsewhere as the competing dynamics of resource development impacts.[55] In other words, women with limited access to resources often benefit from (or survive because of) caring communities, but nevertheless face considerable exclusions. In HV-GB, Kitimat, and the Haisla Nation, women described challenges they (or they, through their partners) have faced working in the resource sector, although some also note benefits that have resulted from resource-related employment. In HV-GB, many Inuit and settler women alike expressed profoundly negative effects from being disconnected from their land base. In Kitimat and the Haisla Nation, the same is true, although the consequences of loss of land access and related traditions seems most acute in the lives of Haisla women. And, as noted above, some women's experiences as workers in the resource sector have been marked by fear and instability.

Social Construction, Women's Well-Being, and Resource Policy

As described above, the social construction of policy framework contends that specific target groups become framed as advantaged, contenders, dependents, or deviants,[56] with women, especially as mothers, generally constructed as dependent. Lack of sufficient childcare in the communities in which we work subtly perpetuates the idea that women ought to be home with their children, and therefore remain dependent on others (primarily male partners) for their economic well-being. Similarly, because policy conversations in the resource sector often focus on employment-related benefits, women's continued limited (or troubled) access to resource-related work reinforces their construction as dependent.

Although not discussed above, it is important to note that Indigenous women might face further exclusion from the policy arena due to social constructions that mark them not only as dependent, but also as deviant. Dating at least as far back as the nineteenth century and the creation of the Indian Act, the construction of the dependence of Indigenous peoples continues, where "territorially concentrated Aboriginal communities are [understood] frequently [as] small, resource starved, and (in some cases) weak in governing capacity, factors that [are denoted as increasing] ... their level of dependence on non-indigenous governments."[57] These colonial and deeply problematic representations remain entrenched. Another example is that the mainstream media coverage of missing and murdered Indigenous women and girls remains limited by the overarching narrative of women as deviant,[58] a point not lost on one of the Haisla women we spoke with, who pointed out the problem of "all this killing of these First Nations ladies. To me I feel that there's not enough done to find out what has happened to these ladies ... It's no closure to the family ... there's not much done to find out what happened, to find their remains, and [instead they] just let it linger on and on and on forever." As a result of these conceptualizations, women's voices often become excluded from key policy discussions, including those related to natural resource extraction.

Including Women in Policy Deliberations

In the broadest sense, our data suggest that resource-related policy processes would have a more sophisticated and wide-ranging way of understanding their impacts if women's voices and well-being experiences were more prominent in informing policy conversations. Short-term economic gains may not figure so centrally, and the current social construction of resource extraction projects as always delivering benefits that exceed burdens would come under question. In this way, it is possible to see how social constructions of women, on the one hand, and of resource projects, on the other, are mutually reinforcing – currently in a way that excludes women, but therefore potentially in a way that invites their knowledge. For example, policy conversations that invite women's voices and well-being experiences would focus much more specifically on the issue of the distribution of risks and benefits highlighted in the environmental justice literature, as well as on issues of physical and cultural survival centred in the environmental reproductive justice literature.

Northern women's conceptualizations of well-being centre on their interconnected relationships with the land – which are clearly disrupted by many resource projects – and highlight the importance of access to robust public social infrastructure, which is often missing prior to project approvals, not to mention becoming seriously overstrained by temporary population influxes that come with resource development. The above conceptualizations of well-being also suggest that efforts to sustain or provide food security and food sovereignty would figure much more centrally into the "goals to be achieved or problems to be solved"[59] by IA processes. In other words, sustaining traditional food access and ensuring universal food security would be a central requirement of obtaining project approval. The idea of a resource development–related policy process, such as the IA process, centring on food sovereignty highlights an interesting paradox. Large-scale resource development and extraction (such as hydroelectric, natural gas) often conflicts with smaller-scale resource work (such as berry picking) that may also employ people and play a role in community sustainability, making it an important part of broader resource policy discussions. As such, whose livelihood is connected to which resources could reasonably be expected to figure into resource-related policy-making processes were women's conceptualizations of well-being considered.

Women as Vigilant

Northern women in HV-GB, Kitimat, and the Haisla Nation (specifically in Kitamaat Village) also challenge the construction of women as dependent and excluded from resource-related conversations, particularly as they assert their claims over land, not only through protest or acting as protectors, but also through their extensive political work as elected leaders. They also exercise power through their work to build solid social infrastructure where governments struggle or have failed to provide adequate health and social services. Although some women we spoke with certainly identified themselves as lacking political agency, many saw themselves as having a role to play in being both active and vigilant. This is pronounced in conversations with women who play an enormous and ongoing role in providing supportive housing, access to education and employment training, culturally appropriate programs and services, and a host of other critical services. As such, although their exclusion from key policy conversations could result in the exclusion of women from the policy process, many women are working to monitor and counter the effects of resource extraction projects, and lead related resistance, response and engagement efforts, rather than be silenced.

Conclusion

Ultimately, what we are learning through our ongoing work with Indigenous and northern women to better understand their well-being is that recognizing the variability and similarities in their experiences is essential to the appropriate formulation of policy problems and solutions, and that these nuances are easily masked if not for intentional efforts to listen to a diverse range of voices and to understand important concepts – such as well-being – from the perspective of people who will be most affected by policy decisions. In other words, the efficacy of deliberative democratic efforts hinges on our ability to recognize and resist dominant social constructions that structure Indigenous and northern women and their experiences out of resource-extraction-related policy conversations. Women in Labrador and northern British Columbia recognize many physical, social, and cultural encroachments associated with the resource industries operating within and near their communities and territories. This can be the case regardless of their support for these same industries, reminding us that the need to better account for women's experiences is not a position limited to opponents of resource projects. They articulate a number of pressing policy needs, including related to mental health services, transportation, food security and sovereignty, and housing. Inadequacies in these and other policy areas are, we suggest, at least partially connected to the construction of women as dependent or deviant, and thus as weak or undeserving of appropriate services. Furthermore, it is clear that women often perceive a lack of opportunity or ability to participate meaningfully in the formulation and implementation of relevant policies, which we suggest is partly the result of feed-forward effects that discourage women's political participation through constructions of their knowledges as less reliable, and even invalid in some circumstances.

At the same time, however, many women in HV-GB, Kitimat, and the Haisla Nation are integral to filling critical service gaps in their communities when policies fail, and some women – both through formal politics and informally – are extremely active in policy conversations, including working on issues related to child care access, housing, violence, employment, economic development, and many other pressing concerns. This is the case despite the fact that the principles of deliberative democracy – such as procedural equality and reasoned dialogue – remain largely unpractised, not only within Canada's IA processes, but in policy conversations related to Indigenous and northern women's well-being in the context of resource development and extraction more generally. While we therefore find resonance with some features of the social construction of policy framework and its related idea of feed-forward effects, we are critical of essentializing women as belonging to a stable "target population," and thus share Liberman's critique that group identities are subject to substantial contestation and fluctuation. Instead, it is critical to capture this variability and nuance, which we suggest is only possible through intentional, time-intensive efforts to engage diverse voices, but essential to better understanding, and subsequently positioning, the well-being experiences of northern women at the core of defining the terms and topics of deliberative policy conversations.

Discussion Questions

1 How could more representative impact assessments be undertaken to capture a wider range of perspectives regarding natural resource extraction projects?
2 Who else is potentially excluded from discussions regarding well-being and natural resource development and extraction in northern Canada?
3 What are some potentially unique barriers to Indigenous women's participation in policy discussions related to well-being and natural resource development and extraction? How might these be similar to, or different from, the barriers facing settler women?

NOTES

Thank you to all of the collaborators in this work for their ongoing efforts to advance northern women's well-being. The research presented in this chapter is supported by a Social Sciences and Humanities Research Council Insight Grant (#435-2015-1493) and an Early Researcher Award from the province of Ontario.

1 Amnesty International, *Out of Sight, Out of Mind: Gender, Indigenous Rights, and Energy Development in Northeast British Columbia, Canada* (London: Amnesty International, 2016), 4, online at https://www.amnesty.ca/sites/amnesty/files/Out%20of%20Sight%20Out%20of%20Mind%20EN%20FINAL%20web.pdf.
2 Deborah Stienstra et al., "Gendered and Intersectional Implications of Energy and Resource Extraction in Resource-Based Communities in Canada's North"{ (n.p.: Feminist Northern Network, 13 May 2016), 5, online at http://fnn.criaw-icref.ca/images/userfiles/files/SSHRC%20KS%20Report.pdf. The newly proposed Impact Assessment Act does recognize the need to consider the gendered implications of resource development and extraction. This is an important step towards recognizing the diversity of citizens' experiences.

3 See Anne Schneider, Helen Ingram and Peter DeLeon, "Democratic Policy Design: Social Construction of Target Populations," in *Theories of the Policy Process*, ed. Paul Sabatier and Christopher Weible (Boulder, CO: Westview Press, 2014), 105–48.

4 See; Kimberlé Crenshaw, "Mapping the Margins: Intersectionality, Identity Politics, and Violence Against Women of Color," *Stanford Law Review* 43, no. 6 (1991): 1241–99, https://doi.org/10.2307/1229039; Rita Kaur Dhamoon, "Considerations on Mainstreaming Intersectionality," *Political Research Quarterly* 64, no. 1 (2010): 230–43, https://doi.org/10.1177 /1065912910379227.

5 See, for example, David R.H. Moscrop and Mark E. Warren, "When Is Deliberation Democratic?" *Journal of Public Deliberation* 12, no. 2 (2016), article 4; Iris Marion Young, *Inclusion and Democracy* (Oxford: Oxford University Press, 2002).

6 Canadian Impact Assessment Agency, "Impact Assessment Process Overview," online at https://www.canada.ca/en/impact-assessment -agency/services/policy-guidance/impact-assessment-process-overview .html, accessed 29 January 2020.

7 Canadian Impact Assessment Act, 2019, S.C. 2019, c. 28, s. 1, online at https://laws-lois.justice.gc.ca/PDF/I-2.75.pdf, accessed 29 January 2020.

8 Canadian Impact Assessment Agency, "Impact Assessment Process Overview," online at https://www.canada.ca/en/impact-assessment -agency/services/policy-guidance/impact-assessment-process-overview .html, accessed 29 January 2020.

9 Canadian Environmental Assessment Agency, *Building Common Ground – A New Vision for Impact Assessment in Canada: The Final Report of the Expert Panel for the Review of Environmental Assessment Processes* (Ottawa: Canadian Environmental Assessment Agency, 2017), 37, online at https://www.canada.ca /content/dam/themes/environment/conservation/environmental-reviews /building-common-ground/building-common-ground.pdf.

10 Ibid., 38. Importantly the resulting legislation calls for the inclusion of a gendered and intersectional analysis.

11 Arnstein's ladder was presented by the author in a 1969 planning article to describe stages of citizen participation from non-involved to citizen-led, with the implicit assumption that engagement 'higher up the ladder' was always preferable.

12 See Jonathan Tritter and Alison McCallum, "The Snakes and Ladders of User Involvement: Moving beyond Arnstein," *Health Policy* 76, no. 2 (2006): 156–68, https://doi.org/10.1016/j.healthpol.2005.05.008.

13 In 2018, following the release of the expert panel's report, the federal government introduced and passed Bill C-69, Part 1 of which repeals the Canadian Environmental Assessment Act and enacts the Impact Assessment Act. At the time of writing this chapter, the Standing Senate

Committee on Energy, the Environment and Natural Resources had finished its review of Bill C-69 and adopted 187 amendments to be put forward for consideration by the full Senate. If these amendments are accepted by the Senate, the bill will need to be revisited by the House of Commons. The legislation as originally passed by the House included new provisions related to public participation – including changes that require public participation in a new planning phase and that provide "for public participation and for funding to allow the public to participate in a meaningful manner" (Bill C-69, ii). Among the amendments put forward by the Senate committee are ones that call for the public's meaningful participation to be qualified with the statement, "in a manner that the Agency considers appropriate."

14 The survey includes sixty-eight questions that reflect five dimensions of well-being: physical, emotional, spiritual, cultural, and mental/intellectual. Questions ask about a wide range of topics, including related to respondents' sense of belonging, ability to access appropriate services, housing and food security, and feelings of safety.

15 Haisla Nation, "Kitamaat Village" (n.d.), online at http://haisla.ca /community-2/kitamaat-village/, accessed 21 December 2017.

16 Haisla Nation, "Kitimat Advantage" (n.d.), online at http://haisla.ca /economic-development/kitimat-advantage/, accessed 21 December 2017.

17 C. Rumley, personal communication, 12 May 2015.

18 Community Vitality Advisory Group and Research Team, "The Wellbeing Experiences of Women in the Haisla Nation and the District of Kitimat" (n.p., May 2018), online at http://haisla.ca/wp-content/uploads/2018/06 /With-Logo-FinalKitimatHaislaCVI-ReportMay-24-2018.pdf, accessed 21 June 2018.

19 See Mokami Status of Women Council, "Out of the Rhetoric and Into the Reality of Local Women's Lives" (submission to Environmental Assessment Panel on the Lower Churchill Hydro Development, 28 March 2011), online at http://fnn.criaw-icref.ca/images/userfiles/files/OutoftheRhetoric.pdf; Gloria Miller, "Frontier Masculinity in the Oil Industry: The Experience of Women Engineers," *Gender, Work, and Organization* 11, no. 1 (2004): 47–73, https://doi.org/10.1111/j.1468-0432.2004.00220.x; David Cox and Suzanne Mills, "Gendering Environmental Assessment: Women's Participation Employment Outcomes at Voisey's Bay." *Arctic* 68, no. 2 (2015): 246–60, https://doi.org/10.14430/arctic4478.

20 Sara O'Shaughnessy and Naomi Krogman, "Gender as Contradiction: From Dichotomies to Diversity in Natural Resource Extraction," *Journal of Rural Studies* 27, no. 2 (2011): 134–43, https://doi.org/10.1016/j.jrurstud .2011.01.001.

21 Anne Schneider and Mara Sidney. "What Is Next for Policy Design and Social Construction Theory?" *Policy Studies Journal* 37, no. 1 (2009): 105, https://doi.org/10.1111/j.1541-0072.2008.00298.x.

22 See Anne Schneider and Helen Ingram, *Policy Design for Democracy* (Lawrence: University Press of Kansas, 1997); idem, "Social Construction of Target Populations: Implications for Politics and Policy," *American Political Science Review*, 87, no. 2 (1993): 334–47, https://doi.org/10.2307/2939044; Anne Schneider, Helen Ingram, and Peter DeLeon, "Democratic Policy Design: Social Construction of Target Populations," in *Theories of the Policy Process*, ed. Paul Sabatier and Christopher Weible (Boulder, CO: Westview Press, 2014), 105–48.

23 Schneider and Ingram, "Social Construction of Target Populations."

24 Schneider, Ingram, and DeLeon, "Democratic Policy Design," 128.

25 Ibid., 107.

26 Ibid., 116.

27 Schneider and Sidney, "What Is Next for Policy Design and Social Construction Theory?"

28 Schneider, Ingram, and DeLeon, "Democratic Policy Design," 106.

29 Schneider and Sidney, "What Is Next for Policy Design and Social Construction Theory?" An example of this is how the experiences of welfare (social assistance) recipients in the United States, a negatively constructed group, affect their perceptions of government as an autonomous actor insulated from citizens' action, resulting in lower inclination to engage in politics. See Joe Soss, "Making Clients and Citizens: Welfare Policy as a Source of Status, Belief, and Action," in *Deserving and Entitled*, ed. Anne Schneider and Helen Ingram (New York: SUNY Press, 2005), 310.

30 This discourse is problematically accompanied by the persistence of the framing of the north as *terra nullius*; see Grace-Edward Galabuzi, "Hegemonies, Continuities, and Discontinuities of Multiculturalism and the Anglo-Franco Conformity Order," in *Home and Native Land: Unsettling Multiculturalism in Canada*, ed. May Chazan, Lisa Helps, Anna Stanley, and Sonali Thakkar (Toronto: Between the Lines, 2011), 61.

31 Karen Heisler and Sean Markey, "Scales of Benefit: Political Leverage in the Negotiation of Corporate Social Responsibility in Mineral Exploration and Mining in Rural British Columbia, Canada," *Society and Natural Resources* 26, no. 4 (2013): 387, https://doi.org/10.1080/08941920.2012.695858.

32 Nalcor Energy, *Muskrat Falls Project: Monthly Report, December 2016* (n.p., February 2017), 7–8, online at http://muskratfalls.nalcorenergy.com/wp-content/uploads/2017/02/Dec-2016-LCP-Monthly-Benefits-Report-final.pdf, accessed 29 January 2020.

33 LNG Canada, *Our Commitment to You*, online at https://www.lngcanada.ca/uploads/subpages/downloads/LNG-Canada_Community-Charter_Mar-11-2019.pdf, accessed 29 January 2020. LNG Canada has also signed a number of agreements with First Nations.

34 Heisler and Markey, "Scales of Benefit."

35 Nalcor Energy, *Muskrat Falls Project*, 7.
36 See Maureen Reed, "Reproducing the Gender Order in Canadian Forestry: The Role of Statistical Representation," *Scandinavian Journal of Forest Research* 23 no. 1 (2008): 78–91, https://doi.org/10.1080/02827580701745778; Adisa Azapagic, "Developing a Framework for Sustainable Development Indicators for the Mining and Minerals Industry," *Journal of Cleaner Production* 12, no. 6 (2004): 639–62. https://doi.org/10.1016/S0959-6526(03)00075-1; Stienstra et al., "Gendered and Intersectional Implications of Energy and Resource Extraction."
37 Miller, "Frontier Masculinity in the Oil Industry," 69.
38 Brenda Parlee, "Avoiding the Resource Curse: Indigenous Communities and Canada's Oil Sands," *World Development* 74 (2015): 431, https://doi.org/10.1016/j.worlddev.2015.03.004
39 Nalcor Energy, *Muskrat Falls Project*, 7.
40 Stienstra et al., 'Gendered and Intersectional Implications of Energy and Resource Extraction," 9.
41 For example, LNG Canada has partnered with Kitimat Valley Institute to subsidize a number of local training programs. See for instance "YOUR PLACE", online at https://yourplace.lngcanada.ca/, accessed 29 January 2020.
42 Robert Liberman, "Social Construction (Continued)," *American Political Science Review* 89, no. 2 (1995): 438, https://doi.org/10.2307/2082436.
43 Deborah Stienstra, "Factsheet: Women and Restructuring in Canada" (Ottawa: Canadian Research Institute for the Advancement of Women, June 2010), online at https://www.criaw-icref.ca/images/userfiles/files/Women%20and%20Restructuring%20Factsheet%20JUNE%204%202010%20.pdf.
44 Liberman, "Social Construction (Continued)," 439.
45 Helen Ingram and Anne Schneider, "Social Construction (Continued): Response," *American Political Science Review* 82, no. 2 (1995): 442, https://doi.org/10.2307/2082437.
46 United States, Environmental Protection Agency, "Environmental Justice" (Washington, DC, 16 November 2017), online at https://www.epa.gov/environmentaljustice.
47 Robert Bullard and Glenn Johnson, "Environmental Justice: Grassroots Activism and Its Impact on Public Policy Decision Making, *Journal of Social Issues* 56, no. 3 (2000): 557, https://doi.org/10.1111/0022-4537.00184.
48 See Native Youth Sexual Health Network, "NYSHN statement to National Energy Board regarding Line 9 pipeline proposal," 18 October 2003, online at http://www.nativeyouthsexualhealth.com/october182013.pdf; Save Lincolnville Campaign, "About the Save Lincolnville Campaign," online at https://www.nspirg.ca/projects/past-projects/save-lincolnville-campaign/.
49 See Sarah Wiebe, *Everyday Exposure: Indigenous Mobilization and Environmental Justice in Canada's Chemical Valley* (Vancouver: UBC Press, 2016);

Christina Dhillon and Michael Young, "Environmental Racism and First Nations: A Call for Socially Just Public Policy Development," *Canadian Journal of Humanities and Social Science* 1, no. 1 (2009): 23–37, doi:10.1289/ehp.1205422; Leith Deacon and Jamie Baxter, "No Opportunity to Say No: A Case Study of Procedural Environmental Injustice in Canada," *Journal of Environmental Planning and Management* 56, no. 5 (2012): 607–23, https://doi.org/10.1080/09640568.2012.692502

50 Elizabeth Hoover et al., "Indigenous Peoples of North America: Environmental Exposures and Reproductive Justice," *Environmental Health Perspectives* 120, no. 12 (2012): 1646, https://doi.org/10.1289/ehp.1205422.

51 Wiebe, *Everyday Exposure*, 118.

52 Ibid., 183.

53 Ibid.; Dhillon and Young, "Environmental Racism and First Nations."

54 Hoover et al., "Indigenous Peoples of North America," 1645–9; Wiebe, *Everyday Exposure*; and idem, in this volume.

55 Deborah Stienstra et al., "Generating Prosperity, Creating Crisis: Impacts of Resource Development on Diverse Groups in Northern Communities," *Community Development Journal* 54, no. 2 (2019): 215–32., https://doi.org/10.1093/cdj/bsx022.

56 Schneider and Ingram, "Social Construction of Target Populations."

57 Michael Murphy, "Representing Indigenous Self-Determination," *University of Toronto Law Journal* 58, no. 2 (2008): 199, https://doi.org/10.1353/tlj.0.0000.

58 See Yasmin Jiwani and Mary Lynn Young, "Missing and Murdered Children: Reproducing Marginality in News Discourse," *Canadian Journal of Communication* 31, no. 4 (2006): 895–917, https://doi.org/10.22230/cjc.2006v31n4a1825; Sherene Razack, "Gendering Disposability," *Canadian Journal of Women and the Law* 28, no. 2 (2016): 285–307, https://doi.org/10.3138/cjwl.28.2.285.

59 Schneider, Ingram, and DeLeon, "Democratic Policy Design," 107.

KEY RESOURCES

Schneider, Anne, Helen Ingram, and Peter DeLeon. "Democratic Policy Design: Social Construction of Target Populations." In *Theories of the Policy Process*, edited by Paul Sabatier and Christopher Weible, 105–48. Boulder, CO: Westview Press, 2014.

Stienstra, Deborah, Leah Levac, Gail Baikie, Jane Stinston, Barbara Clow, and Susan Manning. *Gendered and Intersectional Implications of Energy and Resource Extraction in Resource-Based Communities in Canada's North.* Feminist Northern Network, 2016. http://fnn.criaw-icref.ca/images/userfiles/files/SSHRC%20KS%20Report.pdf.

5 Unsettled Democracy: The Case of the Grandview-Woodland Citizens' Assembly

RACHEL MAGNUSSON

Introduction

Despite their growing popularity, citizens' assemblies are unfamiliar territory for most governments and participants. This means there are inevitably a lot of questions: How exactly do citizens' assemblies represent the broader public? How will members learn enough to make good policy decisions? Who has the final say in the process? Who holds the power? If there is no voting, how are citizens' assemblies democratic? What really goes on in a citizens' assembly, anyway? These are all important questions, and one of the main jobs of an organizer is to have good answers for them. For this purpose, the deliberative tradition is an extremely useful resource; it provides a conceptual framework and a precise language for articulating how exactly citizens' assemblies can be democratic and can help create good policy. Nonetheless, in this chapter, I want to pause, step back, and consider the usefulness of the *unfamiliarity* of citizens' assemblies. Is it possible that this unfamiliarity makes them more democratic? More precisely, is it possible that the unsettledness of our understanding of citizens' assemblies helps instigate a democratic experience for those who participate?[1]

To explore this possibility, I draw on my experience as organizer and chair of the Citizens' Assembly on the Grandview-Woodland Community Plan for the City of Vancouver in 2014–15. I focus on two constellations of concern that emerged for the members of the assembly: first, how can we represent the community? and, second, what do we need to know? I show how these concerns fostered a complex, double experience for members – on the one hand, deep anxiety about their ability to represent the community and a deep humility about their knowledge and understanding of the issues and, on the other, a strong sense of empowerment and of common capacity. Drawing on some of the political thinking of Jacques Rancière, I argue that this complex, double experience is a democratic experience. In doing so, I hope to highlight the upside of the unfamiliarity and unsettledness of citizens' assemblies and the democratic possibilities that lie therein.

Grandview-Woodland Citizens' Assembly: An Overview

In April 2012, the City of Vancouver began a community planning process to develop a thirty-year plan for the much-loved, eclectic neighbourhood of Grandview-Woodland in East Vancouver. Initial public consultations led by the City's planning department were a success, but when the City released an early set of policy directions for the community in June 2013, there was an uproar.[2] To the surprise of those who had been involved in the consultations, the City suddenly proposed as many as a dozen 18–36-storey towers at Broadway and Commercial – an important transportation hub in the region.[3] Suffice to say, many residents in the neighbourhood were furious, and the planning process was derailed. In response, in September 2013 City Council resolved to extend the planning process, and asked the planning department to establish a citizens' assembly to recommend a better direction for the neighbourhood. This was to be Vancouver's first citizens' assembly, as well as the first process of its kind to be used for community planning in North America. After further consultations with the community on how to design the assembly,[4] the City hired my firm, MASS LBP, to organize and host it independently.[5]

In June 2014, over nineteen thousand invitations to volunteer were mailed to every household in the neighbourhood, and additional invitations were available for pickup at community centres. Residents who wished to volunteer were asked to commit to ten full-day, Saturday meetings over the course of eight months. At the end of six weeks, more than five hundred residents had volunteered to sit on the assembly. From this pool, forty-eight members of the assembly were randomly selected through a process that ensured there would be twenty-four men and twenty-four women, a proportional number of residents from four age cohorts, from six areas in the neighbourhood, and from each housing tenure – twenty-eight renters, eighteen owners, and two co-op members. In addition, the selection process held spaces for four members who self-identified as Indigenous, again reflecting the neighbourhood's demographics.[6]

In late September 2014, the Grandview-Woodland Citizens' Assembly met for the first time. The first four Saturdays were dedicated to learning – learning from one another, learning how to work together, and learning about the myriad issues related to community planning: housing, architecture, urban health, transportation, heritage, the arts, food security, reconciliation, local business, social services, sex work, and so on. Members heard from more than forty speakers – some making formal presentations, others participating in informal dialogue sessions with members. Outside the Saturday meetings, there were also walking tours of the seven different subareas in the neighbourhood and a boat tour of the adjacent port. During this phase, members identified and defined the values – such as affordability, wellness, and safety – that should guide future planning in the neighbourhood. They shared these values with the broader community at their first public meeting at the end of November, where upward of 150 people were in attendance. In the second phase of the process, the learning continued – members asked to hear more on certain topics and went on more walking tours of other neighbourhoods in the city – but the primary focus was on developing neighbourhood-wide recommendations. These recommendations ranged from encouraging the city to feature more controversial public art, to pushing the city to provide more supportive and non-market rental housing, to asking the city to try to maintain the current ratio of renters to owners, to calling for more traffic calming and more food trucks.[7] Once these neighbourhood-wide recommendations had been drafted, the assembly hosted another public meeting to get feedback on them. In the final phase of the process, the assembly turned its attention to the most contentious issues: land-use and built form. During the previous phase, the City had hosted its own public workshops – one for each subarea in the neighbourhood – and the reports from these workshops were given to the assembly to help them with their work.[8] The assembly developed recommendations for each of the seven subareas in the neighbourhood – mapping out potential bike paths, where higher buildings might be placed, what public amenities this additional density should fund, where townhouses or small apartment buildings might work well, and what areas of the neighbourhood should be largely preserved.[9] At a final public meeting, members shared their draft land-use maps and recommendations with the broader public. They also received more than eighty written submissions from residents in the neighbourhood. Members wrestled with this community feedback, and used it to help them finalize their recommendations at their last Saturday meeting in May 2015.

In June 2015, the assembly presented its final report, including 268 recommendations, to City Council. The report was well received, and Council asked the planning department to study the assembly's recommendations and respond. The planning department then spent a year reviewing the assembly's recommendations and developing its draft plan for the neighbourhood. According to the City, 92 per cent of the assembly's in-scope recommendations made it into the draft plan.[10] The City also provided a detailed trace document in which it explained how each of the assembly's recommendations was incorporated, and if one was not, a rationale as to why.[11] Before publicly releasing the plan, the City held its own meeting with the assembly to present and explain the draft plan. Of the members in attendance, 95 per cent felt that the draft plan reflected the assembly's values, and 91 per cent reported that they "really liked" or "liked most aspects" of the plan.[12] The one area where the plan significantly diverged from the assembly's recommendations was the one that had originally ignited the controversy: Broadway and Commercial. The assembly recommended a low- to mid-rise vision of transit-oriented density for the transportation hub, also emphasizing the need for a public plaza and a commitment to retaining rental.[13] The tallest buildings the assembly recommended were two twelve-storey buildings at Broadway and Commercial. In the draft plan, however, the City proposed two twenty-four-storey buildings – a significant decrease from the forest of towers originally proposed, but still a significant increase from the assembly's recommendations. The City's justification was primarily one of economic feasibility: we all seem to agree that additional density is desired at this location, and but when we ran the numbers, what you recommended just would not generate the funds for the public amenities you desire. Somewhat surprisingly, most members seemed to think, "OK, fair enough." As one member put it in feedback: "I accept the changes and modifications [to our recommendations] as a reasonable compromise."[14]

With the strong support of the assembly, and more lukewarm support from the broader community residents who attended the City's open houses – 58 per cent reported at open houses that they "really liked" or "liked most aspects" of the draft plan – the City brought its draft plan for the neighbourhood to City Council in July 2016, where it was approved.[15]

Exaggerated Unsettledness

Throughout the process, the questions that preoccupied the members of the Grandview-Woodland Citizens' Assembly were familiar: how can we represent the community? What do we need to know? Do we have real power in this situation? Will we be able to accomplish our task? All citizens' assemblies or reference panels I have been a part of have provoked similar questions and concern from participants.[16] As

I noted in the introduction, this is in part due to the fact that citizens' assemblies are unfamiliar: almost no one has been a part of one before, nor do they know someone who has. This means nobody comes in sure of how they will work or how effective they will be. In the case of the Grandview-Woodland Citizens' Assembly, however, these familiar questions and concerns had more depth and staying power. Official narratives and explanations of the process were not readily accepted, and there was a determination among most members to continue to assess the process for themselves. My sense is that there are three main reasons for this heightened context of unsettledness. First, the Grandview-Woodland Citizens' Assembly got underway in an atmosphere of anger and cynicism. After the city released what one former planner dubbed its "suicidal" *Emerging Directions* in 2013,[17] rallies and petitions were organized, the City held workshops that resembled a "public flogging," and, as one resident put it, there was widespread "hostility and anger... [which] does not make for good planning [and] does not make for good neighbourliness."[18] At this point, any process the city proposed to resurrect the community planning effort was going to be met at minimum with an eye roll, if not with more serious venom.

Second, many of the people who had actively participated in the city's consultations were particularly suspicious of a citizens' assembly. There were concerns about transparency: was the assembly going to be truly independent or would members be schooled into being puppets of the City? There were concerns about diversity: would an English-only process exclude many recent immigrants to the neighbourhood? By far the dominant concern, however, was openness.[19] Here was a process that seemed designed to sideline the participation of those who had been actively involved so far. Random selection meant there was no guarantee of participation; moreover, the guaranteed demographic spread meant more limited odds for older homeowners: "Over the past year, many residents have been meeting, researching, participating in City workshops and speaking at City council meetings. A lottery system will exclude all this effort, and leave out many passionate voices."[20] As a result, a group of residents founded their own group – Our Community, Our Plan (OCOP) – to host their own planning meetings and hold the "faulty" assembly process to account.[21] The organized efforts of OCOP to question and criticize the citizens' assembly process in the media, in the blogosphere, and in the community[22] meant there was continued pressure to examine and re-examine the merits and limitations of the process. Not surprisingly, this pressure was felt acutely by the members of the assembly.[23]

Finally, Grandview-Woodland as a neighbourhood has a sense of itself as counterculture and against the grain. As the assembly put it, the neighbourhood is "quirky and eclectic."[24] To be sure, it has been gentrifying rapidly over the past decade, but it is still home to many artists and progressive types. To offer a caricature of the neighbourhood: there is a near-universal rejection of conservative politicians and a widespread appreciation of the arts, community gardens, and run-down Edwardian mansions with "No pipelines" signs in the windows. This means that even in the best of times there would be plenty of suspicion of government and formal processes, as well as a desire by many to "stick it to the man." Thus, coupled with the political context described above, it is not surprising to hear how assembly members expressed their own initial mood:

> My intentions when I came here were motivated by anger and distrust.

> The sense of betrayal I felt when [*Emerging Directions* was] first released was pretty intense.

> I was overwhelmed by doubts.

> I'm trying to remember what I thought I expected coming into the first meeting. I think I expected voting and someone banging on a gavel saying, "The chair recognizes the gentleman from Cedar Cove." I also have to admit to a bit of scepticism, I didn't see how we were going through all ten meetings without something going terribly wrong.

> I put my name on the ballot as a bit of a whimsical thing ... because a friend told me I should put my money where my mouth is [... and stayed] to sharpen my teeth for the neighbourhood.[25]

Such feelings, I think it is safe to say, were widely held by assembly members and contributed both to a general scepticism and to a commitment to keep asking the difficult questions. Therefore, in the case of the Grandview-Woodland Citizens' Assembly, the political and community context was such that it exaggerated the unsettledness that normally comes with the unfamiliarity of citizens' assemblies.

Two Constellations of Concern: Representation and Knowledge

I want to focus on two constellations of concern that were related to the unsettledness of the Grandview-Woodland Citizens' Assembly. The first constellation revolves around representation: do we have the authority to represent the community? If so, why? What does it mean to represent the community? How do we do this? Who is this community, anyway? The second constellation revolves around knowledge: do we have the information we need to make good recommendations? Are we hearing from all perspectives? Are we getting the full story? What knowledge do we need to make useful and powerful recommendations? How can we possibly make good decisions given all of what we need to know, and all of whom we need to represent?

Of course, representation and knowledge are both constellations of concern for political theorists as well. There are many who have wrestled with how to conceive the representativeness of citizens' assemblies, given members are not elected and thus do not meet our standard account of how political representation works in a liberal democracy. For instance, Mark Warren has argued that citizens' assemblies form "citizen representatives," "not as an alternative but rather as supplements to elected representative bodies or administrative bodies in areas of functional weakness." In an assembly, "a few citizens actively serve as representatives of other citizens ... [and they] have the potential to capture opinions and voices that are not heard [as well as] generate considered opinion."[26] Moreover, they are "authorized" in three ways: "initial constitution by elected representatives, [their] statistically representative makeup (so as to 'look like the people of BC') and [their] submission of [their] final recommendation directly to the people."[27] Similarly, in the context of arguing for a distinction between responsive forms of representation and indicative forms of representation, Philip Pettit highlights citizens' assemblies as a contemporary example of indicative representation. An assembly is a "reliable indicator" of what the citizenry at large might think about the issue if they too had deliberated on it.[28] Building on Pettit's distinction, John Grant argues citizens' assemblies must be understood as "decidedly republican in character," in part because of the form of indicative representation they embody.[29]

Similarly, there is also a lot of discussion among political theorists about "knowledge" in citizens' assemblies. Genevieve Fuji Johnson, for instance, argues that there is often elite control of the agenda.[30] The contention is that those who set the task and control the learning curriculum will influence the outcome. In contrast, in her analysis of the BC Citizens' Assembly on Electoral Reform, Amy Lang claims that citizens engaged in "creative deliberation," whereby "Assembly members developed their own criteria for choosing a new electoral system."[31] In a different vein, much discussion and research has centred on whether deliberation does in fact produce informed citizens and better policy decisions. James Fishkin, for instance, has famously studied how deliberative polls lead to more informed and reflective opinions.[32]

In the context of citizens' assemblies, Dennis Thompson has identified five criteria to assess the competence of citizens' in making their decisions.[33] As Jonathan Rose summarizes: "First, participants should be interested in the project. Second, they need to be able to formulate standards or goals that a system should fulfil. Third, they need to understand basic characteristics, that is, they need sound knowledge. Fourth, citizen-experts should be able to understand the consequences of their goals; in other words, they need to be able to link goals with systems. Finally, they should consider the views of other citizens when making their decision."[34] Using Thompson's criteria, Jonathan Rose maintains that citizens' assembles "are unique because they represent a transformation of citizens into citizen-experts through an in-depth educational programme and remind us about the capacity of citizens to make sound policy."[35]

As organizers, we echo some of these themes throughout the process. During the orientation on the first day, for example, we usually note that members are one of forty-eight selected to consider collectively what is best for the community. We then go on to say, but you are one of 507 people who volunteered for the assembly, all of whom would like to be in your seat today. Moreover, you are one of 33,000 residents currently living in the neighbourhood whose lives will be affected by your recommendations. So, your job is not simply to express your personal views, or what is good for your immediate circle of family and friends, but to endeavour to represent what you think is best for the neighbourhood as a whole. Similarly, on the question of curriculum design, we always emphasize that it is crucial to hear from a range of reasonable perspectives and that the curriculum must pass the "sniff test": it must seem fair and defensible to an outside observer. On the problem of "will you learn enough?" we often quip that members will receive a crash, college-level course in the subject matter. We tell members: "It may feel like drinking from a fire hose, but you'll be provided the information necessary to make smart and thoughtful recommendations."

These explanations are essential – they provide frames for members to understand their role and task, they provide reassurance that this unfamiliar process really can work, and they provide what amounts to rules of thumb that can help members negotiate the complexities of their work. The reality, however, both of the members' work and of the process is inevitably more complicated than the definitions and explanations we provide – especially in an atmosphere of heightened suspicion.

For instance, in the case of the Grandview-Woodland Citizens' Assembly, the political context was such that the assembly's ability to represent the community was a central point of attack and contention. From the beginning, critics such as OCOP dismissed both the assembly's representativeness – it was bound to exclude non-English speakers and people in precarious situations who could not commit to the Saturdays – and its ability to represent the community – they were going to be misled by the city and ignore the voices of the true community.[36] Given this context, assembly members were never going to take for granted their ability to represent the community. At the first meeting of the assembly, for example, one member raised an objection: "When I look around the room, I don't see the full-diversity of the neighbourhood; how are we then supposed to represent the community?"[37] A discussion ensued about diversity and representation. It was clear that the member was concerned about ethnic diversity – to put it bluntly, there were a lot of white-looking people in the room. Another member raised the point that not all kinds of diversity were visible: most obviously, one cannot tell socio-economic status by the colour of a person's skin. As organizers, we pointed out that we did not generally control for ethnicity in the random selection process, except in the case of people who self-identified as Indigenous. We also mentioned that the City was going to lead Chinese-language focus groups, and that the assembly would receive this work. There was also a discussion about how the assembly could never perfectly reflect the full diversity of the neighbourhood, and this was why they had to try to "take a walk in other people's shoes." Nothing, of course, was resolved, but one thing was clear: the assembly was uneasy about its ability to represent the community, and it was not going to easily assume the authority on offer to speak on behalf of the community.

The unease about representation continued, but as the process went on, the concern about representation changed: the emphasis was less about "do we reflect the community's full diversity?" and more about "who counts as 'the community' that we are trying to represent?" This concern manifested itself in a number of ways, and was bound up with the practical challenges of trying to represent the community. Indeed, members began to wrestle with *how* to represent the community. As organizers, we stressed that there were three main channels to hear from people beyond the assembly itself: through informal networks of family, friends, and acquaintances; through submissions to the assembly; and through the public meetings the assembly would host. For many members, however, there was a sense that, no matter how useful these channels might be, they would never give them an adequate sense of what "the community" wanted: "I'm not sure how I would be able to speak on behalf of such a diverse neighbourhood. I could only try to represent the opinions I was hearing as best I could." Or again: "I think most members tried to consider the wishes of the neighbourhood, but at the end of the day we are all still individuals who got feedback from individuals."[38]

For some members of the assembly, the practical difficulties of representation motivated extraordinary outreach efforts. One member organized a series of interviews with various key players in the community, and diligently reported back on each to the assembly. Another visited as many as sixty small businesses along Hastings Street, the commercial and industrial corridor in the north of the neighbourhood, to ask owners and employees about how they felt about the prospect of new development, building heights, likely rent increases, potential new public amenities, and so on. For most, however, the public meetings seemed like the most obvious setting to "hear from the community." Indeed, these meetings provided an important opportunity for face-to-face discussion between assembly members and interested participants from the broader community. Members relied on the public meetings as a testing ground for their recommendations. Not surprisingly, however, these meetings did not provide a magical direct link to "the community." This, in turn, created another practical problem for members: how should they weigh and incorporate the feedback they received from the public at these meetings, or at the City-led workshops?[39] As some members objected in plenary discussions, those in attendance at the meetings were far less "representative" than the assembly itself. For instance, the assembly reflected the housing tenure and age profile of the neighbourhood: 60 per cent renters and 40 per cent homeowners, and in age ranges, 21 per cent from 16 to 29, 35 per cent from 30 to 44, 31 per cent from 45 to 64, and 12 per cent 65 and older. Participants at the public meetings, however, were much less reflective of the community: 20 per cent renters and 73 per cent homeowners, and in age ranges, 11 per cent from 16 to 29, 28 per cent from 30 to 44, 37 per cent from 45 to 64, and 23 per cent 65 and older.[40] As such, these members argued, we need to listen to what we hear, but at the same time take into consideration that we are hearing more from older homeowners. Other members, in contrast, were less worried about the demographic profile of the participants in the public meetings and more suspicious of "outside" voices at the meeting. Were there developers masquerading as community members? Was it appropriate for local advocacy groups – whether the pro-cycling group or the "No towers" coalition – to use the public meetings as a platform?

As one might imagine, debates and discussions about who counted as "the community" were linked to political perspectives: as a general rule, if you were in favour of significantly increasing density in the neighbourhood, you would be suspicious about the dominance of older homeowners at the public meetings; if you were in favour of largely preserving the neighbourhood, you would be on the lookout for developers or realtors gaming the system. The politics of how to represent the community, and who counted as "the community" was intertwined with the politics of the substantive policy choices facing the assembly. Thus, as members deliberated together about what recommendations they wanted to make, questions of representation were always at stake. Indeed, they were unavoidable. As one member remarked on the last day: "I think what I will remember most from this process is how hard it is to find that balance between the community interests as a whole and the community members in that particular spot. It is ... it is a bit hard. And I didn't realize, before, how hard it would be."[41]

In a similar way, concerns about knowledge – do we have the information? Do we know enough? – provoked ongoing discussion and additional efforts from assembly members. One area of worry about knowledge centred around trust. Just as members were not going to assume the authority to speak for the community, neither were they going to trust that they were getting all the information they needed from the formal learning program. As organizers, we always encourage, but never require, members to do their own research, and we pull together additional resources for them as well. Particularly given the broad scope of community planning, many members did their own research on their own time. Some went to extraordinary lengths – developing surveys, conducting official interviews, attending and reporting back on additional community events – and many shared relevant news stories, articles, and policy documents with one another. In addition, the assembly pushed back and asserted its influence over the learning program and the information made available to members – in part to assess the trust they should put in the process and in the City. Members asked, for example, to hear from certain speakers who were famously critical of the City and the assembly. As organizers, these were easy enough requests to accommodate, as we always aim to provide a range of speakers. Where it became slightly more challenging was in relation to the release of information from the City. For instance, a recurring question in community meetings and in the assembly was: do you have population growth targets for the neighbourhood that you would like the community plan to meet? The answer from the City was consistently, "No." Over time, assembly members came to trust that this was, indeed, the truth, but there was nonetheless a consistent effort to keep asking to assess whether they really did have all the information. The most dramatic push for information, however, focused on maps the City had produced during the initial consultation period. Requests for these maps had been heard at public meetings, and the assembly reiterated these requests at their own meeting. The City was reluctant to release them, but after assembly members penned a letter forcefully asking for their release, the City quickly agreed. Once released, the maps themselves were not of much interest, but the assembly had tested the City and the process: how seriously are you taking us? Are you being forthright with all the information?

Beyond the problem of trust, the assembly wrestled more directly with what members needed to know to make a good recommendation. As discussed above, in part this meant deliberations about how best to represent the community. It also involved discussions about what counted as a good recommendation. We encourage members to aim for the right balance – don't get lost in the clouds, don't get lost in the weeds – but to determine what this means is no simple feat. Moreover, many members wanted their recommendations to be as precise and detailed as possible; in their eyes, this would give the City less ability to ignore or circumvent their recommendations. But to make a precise and detailed recommendation, you need to know more. How? Additional research was sometimes the answer; at other points, members relied on experts we had on hand from planning, design, or engineering or on the feedback on their draft recommendations provided by the City. Despite these efforts, however, many members felt a deep sense of anxiety: we simply do not have all the expertise we would like or the time to learn enough, and we cannot possibly figure out all we need to know. As a few members mentioned, it often felt "overwhelming."[42]

At the same time, despite these feelings of anxiety and inadequacy, members also expressed wonder at their collective knowledge and capacity to get things done. Numerous members emphasized how much they learned from each other and how impressed they were with one another's intelligence:

For me the greatest source of learning was from my fellow participants.[43]

What struck me most was the immense amount of collective knowledge in the room. I just couldn't believe it. We make this massive big brain together. I didn't agree with all of you, all the time – probably most of you, most of the time – but I definitely learnt something from every one of you.

My head hurts. I have never been around so many intelligent people in one room before. So, I am humbled by that.

My knowledge has deepened tenfold, a hundredfold ... I am leaving here smarter and stronger, and it is in part because of these amazing people that I worked with at the tables ... you blew my mind. I'm looking at you all. You blew my mind with your depth, your intelligence and your integrity, your vision, and I'm honoured to have worked with you.[44]

What is clear is that members were impressed not only with the collective knowledge and intelligence in the room, but also with their collective capacity to rise to the occasion and accomplish the task. As one member put it: "It is really cool that we were able to apply ourselves to the problems before us, and utilize the skills within us, that maybe we don't use that often, or at all. It was an experience that has made my life richer, and made for, I guess ... a good education."[45] Moreover, this wonder at their own collective intelligence and capacity was not interpreted as a one-off performance, but universalized. Many members concluded that such an exercise of collective intelligence and capacity could be repeated: "I believe that this kind of political process is one that really solves problems, leads to peace, not war, and should be seriously considered as a standard procedure for how we solve problems as a society."[46] Or again, as another member put it: "This should be everywhere. Everyone should be doing this."[47]

How Is Any of This Democratic?

Although the anxiety about the right to represent or the capacity to know enough did not make it easy for members of the assembly, my sense is that it did deepen their democratic experience. To explain how, I want to turn to the writings of Jacques Rancière. It is important to note that Rancière himself is decidedly dismissive of deliberative political theory and practices such as citizens' assemblies,[48] which do not fit his schemas of democratic politics.[49] Nonetheless, Rancière's understanding of politics relies on a rethinking of "emancipation" that bears directly on the experience of members of the Grandview-Woodland Citizens' Assembly.

As I have argued elsewhere,[50] at the heart of Rancière's understanding of politics-as-disagreement are his reflections on emancipation. In *The Ignorant Schoolmaster: Five Lessons of Intellectual Emancipation*, Rancière draws on his archival research into an eccentric teacher and thinker, Joseph Jacotot, to re-examine emancipation and pull it away from our common understanding of the term. Emancipation is not about "seeing the light" and gaining a true understanding of how things are, but rather about assuming and demonstrating one's own intellectual capacity and that of others: to be emancipated is "to learn something and to relate to it all the rest by this principle: all men have equal intelligence."[51] It is about believing in your own intelligence and the intelligence of other people, and then trying to demonstrate this common capacity. Indeed, what is important for Rancière is that emancipation is not just some private moment of enlightenment, but an assumption of capacity that must be practised over and over again to make it felt and to make it real. "The virtue of our intelligence is less in knowing than in doing"; it "is not a given, it is practiced, it is veri-fied."[52] What is important about this for our purposes is that Rancière presents us with an account of emancipation as an exercise of equal-ity that is carried out in uncertain circumstances: we never know for sure that we, or others, are intelligent and capable beings, and we our-selves certainly do not have all the answers. Instead, it is the *practice* of equal capacity that makes its own assumption of equality a reality. What is "emancipatory" about this, according to Rancière, is that it runs counter to our common assumptions and understandings of the world. Whereas we normally assume there is a hierarchy of intelligence that corresponds in some way to the hierarchy of the social order,[53] eman-cipation is the freedom that comes from showing that another reality of common capacity exists. It is also this demonstration of equality that makes emancipation fundamental to any democratic practice. As Rancière writes, democratic politics initiates an "open set of practices driven by the assumption of equality between any and every speaking being and by the concern to test this equality."[54]

Rancière's rethinking of emancipation provides us with a way to understand the complex, double experience of the members of the assembly. Our common understanding of emancipation – the feeling of freedom and power that comes from suddenly apprehending the truth – would not apply to the experience of assembly members. Their experience was not purely positive. If members experienced feelings of freedom, confidence, and power, it was in the context of navigating the anxieties and difficulties of an unsettled and uncertain terrain. What is important here, however, is not simply that the unsettled context gave members the opportunity to rise to the challenge; rather, what Rancière's rethinking of emancipation emphasizes is the democratic nature of this experience.

First, the assembly establishes a situation where members are treated as equals, no matter what degrees or honours they might hold outside the space. And this situation of equality creates an opportunity for members to witness the intelligence and capacity of others. In fact, the capacity of others often comes as a surprise, given that many members come armed, like most of us, with deep suspicions about the intelligence of other people. In the context of the assembly, however, each member sits around a table with others as an equal.

Second, in this context of equality, the uncertainty that members encounter makes room for an even more radical experience of equality. As I have tried to show, at some point the members of the Grandview-Woodland Citizens' Assembly confronted the limits both of their own understanding and that of the experts who were intended to inform and guide them. Not only were organizers unable to provide unshakeable answers about the process, but neither were political theorists, planners, designers, engineers, and community experts about the content of their recommendations. No one had all the answers! This is frustrating, terrifying, *and* liberating. It forces members to assume the responsibility of figuring out a way forward together. It demands that the group take on the roles of political theorist, planner, and community expert. In this way, what members experience is a radical blurring of the hierarchies that exist between themselves in their position in the process as "ordinary citizens" and those whose position is to be the "experts" who know and guide them. With the spread of uncertainty comes a more radical experience of equality. Following Rancière's analysis, I would argue that it is in these moments that the assembly is at its most democratic. Rather than simply staying in their assigned lane, uncertainty ushers assembly members into a world normally reserved for the few thought to be capable of handling complexity. And in the midst of this complexity, members must make decisions with others, in the interests of the "community as a whole."

Arguably, it is also this more radical experience of equality that leads members to the conclusion that others should be doing this, too. Although it is always tempting for some members to interpret their experience as a consequence of their own superior gifts and qualities, many come to the opposite conclusion: if we can do this, so can everyone else. "This should be everywhere. Everyone should be doing this."[55] What uncertainty reveals is that no one has *all the answers* to make the right decision, and what the assembly provides is a context where this uncertainty is negotiated with others who have no particular qualifications or expertise to make a decision. What members of the assembly demonstrate to themselves in this situation, then, is not their own special knowledge or expertise, but rather their common capacity to learn, think, and decide. In fact, knowledge and expertise is most often still admired and valued by the members. What is challenged is the idea that there are only some people who are capable enough to navigate uncertainty and wrestle with difficult and important decisions. Moreover, it is the activity of the members themselves that undermines this myth. They demonstrate to themselves through their own capacity to learn, think, and decide; and, indirectly, they also demonstrate the capacity of all the others who could have been randomly selected to sit in their place. In this way, their own democratic experience is both made real and universalized.

If this is the case, then part of the benefit of a citizens' assembly is its unfamiliarity. The fact that an assembly's role is not settled and that it presents a change from how things are normally done means that it is more likely to provoke a democratic experience. So, although our natural impulse as organizers and political theorists is to want to settle a tense atmosphere, to familiarize the unknown process, and to explain exactly how and why assemblies work, the analysis above should give us pause. In fact, if read through Rancière's understanding of emancipation, one could argue that the great advantage of a citizens' assembly is that the unsettledness it opens can create a testing ground for democracy. As Rancière argues, emancipation is more than an experience of anxiety and empowerment; it is also an activity, a practice wherein we test our capacity and equality with others. What citizens' assemblies might offer, then, is a situation where such a testing of equality can take place.

Discussion Questions

1 Does the "emancipatory" experience of the members of the Grandview-Woodland Citizens' Assembly resonate with anything you have experienced? Witnessed in a public engagement setting? If so, how?
2 If unsettledness and uncertainty can deepen the democratic experience, is this something we can or should plan for in public engagement?
3 If our forms of public engagement discourage participants from challenging their assigned role in the process, can they still be "democratic"?

NOTES

Rachel Magnusson was formerly the director of the western office of MASS LBP and was the chair of the Grandview-Woodland Citizens' Assembly. She now works as a senior public space project manager at the City of Vancouver.

1 In line with the argument that Christopher Holman makes in "Reconsidering the Citizens' Assembly on Electoral Reform Phenomena: Castoriadis and Radical Citizen Democracy," *New Political Science* 35, no. 2 (2013): 203–26,

I assume that assemblies are both representative democratic institutions and forms of participatory or direct democracy. As Holman writes,

> we must reject as a reductive mischaracterization the suggestion that a political phenomenon's institutional non-inclusion of the totality of citizens is in itself a sufficient ground to reject interpreting that phenomenon in direct or participatory terms. Castoriadis writes, for example, that direct democracy today does not mean creating "an ekklesia in which the five billion inhabitants of the Earth would gather together in the Sahara."What it means, rather, is struggling to invent new means of participation, via experiments in decentralization, the self- management of small-scale political units, the utilization of federative principles, the critical redeployment of the technological apparatus, and the establishment of more effective control of centralized institutions. (211)

2 City of Vancouver, *Grandview-Woodland Community Plan: Goals, Objectives & Emerging Policies* (Vancouver, June 2013), online at https://vancouver.ca/files/cov/grandview-woodland-community-plan.pdf, accessed 24 March 2018.

3 Charles Campbell, "At Ground Zero for Vancouver's Towering Debate," *Tyee*, 25 June 2013, online at https://thetyee.ca/Opinion/2013/06/25/Vancouver-Tower-Debate/.

4 Susanna Haas Lyons and City of Vancouver, Planning and Development Services Department, "Summary of Public Input on the Design of the Grandview-Woodland Citizens' Assembly" (Vancouver, April 2014), online at https://vancouver.ca/files/cov/summary-of-public-input-on-the-design-grandview-woodland-2014-april.pdf; and City of Vancouver Planning and Development Services Department, "A Discussion Paper: A Citizens' Assembly for Grandview-Woodland" (Vancouver, January 2014), online at https://vancouver.ca/files/cov/Grandview-Woodlands-Citizens-Assembly-Discussion-Paper-2014-01-23.pdf.

5 Founded by Peter Macleod in 2007, MASS LBP has led some of the country's most original and ambitious efforts to engage citizens in tackling tough policy choices while pioneering the use of citizens' assembly–style processes in Canada. See https://www.masslbp.com/.

6 For more details on the selection process, see Citizens' Assembly on the Grandview-Woodland Community Plan, *Final Report* (Vancouver, June 2015), online at http://www.grandview-woodland.ca/download/final-report-citizens-assembly%e2%80%a8on-the-grandview-woodland-community-plan-low-resolution-2/, accessed 24 March 2018. In 2014, approximately 8 per cent of the residents in the neighbourhood identified

as Aboriginal; see City of Vancouver, "Grandview-Woodland Community Profile – 2014," online at https://vancouver.ca/files/cov/grandview -woodland-community-profile-2014.pdf.

7 Citizens' Assembly on the Grandview-Woodland Community Plan, *Final Report*.

8 For an overview, see ibid. For summary reports of the subarea workshops for Cedar Cove, Britannia-Woodland, Grandview, Hastings, Commercial-Drive, Nanaimo, and Broadway & Commercial, see https://vancouver.ca/files/cov /cedar-cove-workshop-summary.pdf; https://vancouver.ca/files/cov /britannia-woodland-workshop-summary.pdf; https://vancouver.ca/files /cov/grandview-workshop-summary.pdf; https://vancouver.ca/files/cov /nanaimo-workshop-summary.pdf; https://vancouver.ca/files/cov/hastings -workshop-summary.pdf; https://vancouver.ca/files/cov/broadway -commercial-workshop-summary.pdf; https://vancouver.ca/files/cov /commercial-drive-workshop-summary.pdf.

9 Citizens' Assembly on the Grandview-Woodland Community Plan, *Final Report*.

10 The most common reasons recommendations were considered out of scope "were that a recommendation spoke to matters outside of the city's jurisdiction or it was a matter that can be or is more effectively addressed through a citywide policy or program rather than a local area policy." Thirty-two of the assembly's 268 recommendations were considered out of scope. For more details, see City of Vancouver, *Trace Document – How the Plant Responds to the Citizens' Assembly's Recommendations* (June 2016), online at https://vancouver.ca/files/cov/grandview-woodland-community -plan-trace-document.pdf., accessed 24 March 2018.

11 Ibid.

12 City of Vancouver, "Council Report," 18 July 2016, online at https:// vancouver.ca/files/cov/report-grandview-woodland-community-plan -2016-07-26.pdf.

13 Citizens' Assembly on the Grandview-Woodland Community Plan, *Final Report*.

14 City of Vancouver, "Council Report."

15 Ibid.

16 At MASS LBP, terminology is used interchangeably: citizens' assembly, citizens' commission, citizens' reference panel.

17 Frank Ducote, "A stunning transformation is planned for Grandview-Woodlands. Is the community really ready for this?" *State of Vancouver: Frances Bula on City Life and Politics*, 12 June 2013, online at http://www .francesbula.com/uncategorized/guest-post-from-frank-ducote-a -stunning-transformation-is-planned-for-grandview-woodlands-is-the -community-really-ready-for-this/, accessed 24 March 2018.

18 Zakir Suleman, "Rumble on the drive: Broadway and Commercial towers workshop leaves no one happy," *Vancouver Observer*, 16 July 2013, online at http://www.vancouverobserver.com/real-estate/broadway-and-commercial-transit-and-towers-workshop-leaves-no-one-happy, accessed 24 March 2018; Campbell, "At Ground Zero for Vancouver's Towering Debate."

19 Our Community Our Plan, "OCOP! Press release #1," 10 June 2014, online at https://ourcommunityourplan.wordpress.com/2014/06/10/ocop-press-release-1/.

20 Ibid.

21 Our Community Our Plan, "OCOP's 12 Point Program," 12 October 2014, online at https://ourcommunityourplan.wordpress.com/2014/10/12/ocops-12-point-program/, accessed 24 March 2018.

22 For instance, community organizer Jak King posted frequently about the assembly on his blog (see https://jaksview3.wordpress.com/), as did Garth Mullins (http://www.garthmullins.com/). OCOP also organized a "Slice of Democracy" contest to encourage creative alternative uses for invitation letters; see Our Community Our Plan, "Slice of Democracy Contest," 23 July 2014, online at https://ourcommunityourplan.wordpress.com/2014/07/23/slice-of-democracy-contest/. OCOP also asked leafleted the assembly at its final meeting, asking it to hold additional public meetings before submitting its final report to Vancouver City Council.

23 OCOP was invited to speak to the assembly during a "community dialogue" session. One assembly member also sent a list of questions to OCOP for formal response; see Our Community Our Plan, "Citizens' Assembly: Questions & Answers," 3 November 2014, online at https://ourcommunityourplan.wordpress.com/2014/11/03/citizens-assembly-questions-answers/, accessed 24 March 2018.

24 Citizens' Assembly on the Grandview-Woodland Community Plan, *Final Report*.

25 On the last day of the assembly, we recorded the final plenary sessions, at which members discussed their final thoughts and what they would remember most about the process. The above quotes are taken directly from the video. To view the video, please contact the author or MASS LBP.

26 Mark E. Warren and Hilary Pearse, eds., *Designing Deliberative Democracy: The British Columbia Citizens' Assembly* (Cambridge: Cambridge University Press, 2008). For a thorough overview of contemporary debates about representation, see Nadia Urbinati and Mark Warren, "The Concept of Representation in Contemporary Democratic Theory," Annual Review of Political Science 11 (2008): 387–412.

27 Urbinati and Warren, "Concept of Representation," 406.

28 Philip Pettit, "Representation, Responsive and Indicative," *Constellations* 17, no. 3 (2010): 427.

29 John Grant, "Canada's Republican Invention? On the Political Theory and Practice of Citizens' Assemblies," *Political Studies* 62, no. 201: 539–55.

30 Genevieve Fuji Johnson, *Democratic Illusion: Deliberative Democracy in Canadian Public Policy* (Toronto: University of Toronto Press, 2015).

31 Amy Lang, "But Is It Real? The British Columbia Citizens' Assembly as a Model for State-sponsored Citizen Empowerment," *Politics & Society* 35, no. 1 (March 2007): 53.

32 James Fishkin, *When the People Speak: Deliberative Democracy and Public Consultation* (Oxford: Oxford University Press, 2009).

33 Dennis F. Thompson, "Who Should Govern Who Governs? The Role of Citizens in Reforming the Electoral System," in Warren and Pearce, *Designing Deliberative Democracy*, 20–49.

34 Jonathan Rose, "Institutionalizing Participation through Citizens' Assemblies," in *Activating the Citizen: Dilemmas of Participation in Europe and Canada*, ed. Joan DeBardeleben and Jon H. Pammett (Basingstoke, UK: Palgrave Macmillan, 2009), 220.

35 Ibid., 230.

36 Our Community Our Plan, "OCOP! Press release #1."

37 This is a paraphrase of a member's question during a plenary discussion on the first day of the assembly. For a detailed overview of the meetings, see Citizens' Assembly on the Grandview-Woodland Community Plan, "Meeting Summaries for the Citizens' Assembly on the Grandview -Woodland Community Plan."

38 Researchers from the University of British Columbia conducted independent surveys of assembly members midway through and at the end of the process. These comments are from members on the final survey, "May Assembly Member Survey Report" (May 2015).

39 Interestingly, Rose ("Institutionalizing Participation through Citizens' Assemblies," 227) notes a similar tension within the Ontario and BC citizens' assemblies:

> As vehicles of participation, [citizens' assemblies] are caught in an interesting paradox. On the one hand, they are imbued with great authority, independence, and power. On the other hand, they are comprised of citizens who have developed expertise but in many cases are still deferential to the "expert" citizens they hear. Unlike politicians who understand the symbolic and real importance of public consultation, members were often not clear on the competing roles that these public meetings had. [One study describes] these competing functions as expert, official, and public perspectives, which need to be balanced during deliberations. Members

had developed a certain expertise, but as citizens they represented public perspectives. These two roles may have been tough to reconcile. From institutionalizing participation.

40 Citizens' Assembly on the Grandview-Woodland Community Plan, *Final Report*; and results from MASS LBP's feedback surveys at public roundtable meeting #2 on 5 March 2015.

41 From the video of the last day of the assembly.

42 "May Assembly Member Survey Report" (May 2015).

43 Ibid.

44 From the video of the last day of the assembly.

45 Ibid.

46 "May Assembly Member Survey Report" (May 2015).

47 From the video of the last day of the assembly.

48 Jacques Rancière, *Disagreement: Politics and Philosophy*, trans. Julie Rose (Minneapolis: University of Minnesota Press, 1999), 18.

49 Importantly, Rancière himself insists that he is not in the business of developing theories of politics. Thus, his own "definitions" of politics and democracy must be read as polemical interventions directed at certain political and philosophical disputes, rather than as conclusive maps of an intellectual terrain. Quite simply, then, his writings invite readers to do their own work with his ideas. See Jacques Rancière, "A Few Remarks on the Method of Jacques Rancière," *Parallax* 15, no. 3 (2009): 115.

50 Rachel Magnusson, "A Politics in Writing: Jacques Rancière and the Equality of Intelligences," in *Thinking Radical Democracy: The Return to Politics in Post-War France*, ed. Martin Breaugh, Christopher Holman, Devin Penner, Rachel Magnusson, and Paul Mazzocchi (Toronto: University of Toronto Press, 2015), 189–209; Sam Chambers makes a similar argument in *The Lesson of Rancière* (Oxford: Oxford University Press, 2014).

51 Jacques Rancière, *The Ignorant Schoolmaster: Five Lessons in Intellectual Emancipation*, trans. Kristin Ross (Stanford, CA: Stanford University Press, 1991) 18, 17.

52 Ibid., 65, 137.

53 "But the belief in intellectual inequality and in the superiority of one's own intelligence does not belong to scholars and distinguished poets alone. Its force comes from the fact that it embraces the entire population under the guise of humility. I can't, the ignorant one ... declares; I am only a worker. Listen carefully to everything there is in that syllogism: First of all, 'I can't' means 'I don't want to; why would I make the effort?' Which also means: I undoubtedly could, for I am intelligent. But I am a worker:

people like me can't; my neighbor can't. And what use would it be for me, since I have to deal with imbeciles?" Ibid., 39.
54 Rancière, *Disagreement*, 30.
55 From the video of the last day of the assembly.

KEY RESOURCES

Chambers, Sam. *The Lesson of Rancière*. Oxford: Oxford University Press, 2014.
Holman, Chris. "Reconsidering the Citizens' Assembly on Electoral Reform Phenomena: Castoriadis and Radical Citizen Democracy." *New Political Science* 35, no. 2 (2013): 203–26.
Rancière, Jacques. *The Ignorant Schoolmaster: Five Lessons in Intellectual Emancipation*. Translated by Kristin Ross. Stanford, CA: Stanford University Press, 1991.

6 Opening to the Possible: Girls and Women with Disabilities Engaging in Vietnam

DEBORAH STIENSTRA AND XUAN THUY NGUYEN

Introduction

Women and girls with disabilities[1] are among the most invisible members of societies around the world. They face significant barriers to education, employment, and participation in their communities. These come in part from the intersecting negative and stigmatizing assumptions about both gender and disabilities that often lead to lack of access to schools, services, technology, health care, and transport.[2] In addition to the barriers they face, women and girls with disabilities are largely portrayed as vulnerable and as victims, especially in terms of violations of human rights.[3] They are likely to be excluded from or neglected in policy and decision making.[4] Given this, examining the possibilities of deliberative democracy and political engagement among these girls and women poses interesting and challenging insights.

Drawing from an arts-based participatory research project with girls and women with disabilities in Vietnam called Transforming Disability Knowledge, Research, and Activism (TDKRA), we argue that deliberative democracy, as theorized and practised in the global North, has limited capacity to explain the engagement of disabled girls and women in Vietnam. In particular, public or citizen engagement by these Vietnamese girls and women with disabilities is shaped by the historical and political context of the Vietnamese state; the inclusion and exclusion of disabled girls and women because of their differences; and the presence of disabled persons' organizations (DPOs) in Vietnam that are using human rights and transnational collaborations to bring about changes in the lives of girls and women with disabilities in that country.[5] The experiences and relationships of these girls and women enhance their capacities for, and possibilities of, participation in their communities. Their increased participation in TDKRA both challenges and changes their communities, and supports the argument of John Gaventa and Gregory Barrett that engagement can make a positive difference even in less democratic states.[6]

Deliberative Democracy, Participation, and Disability Politics in Vietnam

On the surface, theories of deliberative democracy offer an enticing explanation and normative appeal for participatory inclusion and respectful deliberation across differences in public decision making at all levels. Iris Marion Young provides a sustained consideration of deliberative democracy as a process where participants express and register their interests, beliefs, and judgments, but where these are also transformed through the deliberative process.[7] This understanding of deliberative democracy engages with discussions of democracy as well as inclusion. Young takes what she calls a minimalist understanding of democracy as "a rule of law, promotion of civil and political liberties, [and] free and fair elections of lawmakers."[8] She argues that "inclusive democracy enables participation and voice for all those affected by problems and their proposed solutions."[9] This requires processes that enable inclusive participation and respond to the inequalities and structural differences in societies.

Although Young's description suggests an ideal version of deliberative democracy, her assumptions reflect one stream of thought: a critical approach that focuses on expanding the range of those involved in public discussions and ensuring their capacity to communicate despite structural barriers.[10] This critical approach is in contrast to a more classic liberal approach, which focuses on rational debate among individuals with different opinions.[11] The differences between the two are particularly important for the participation of people with disabilities. The critical approaches offer greater space for the inclusion of people with disabilities through recognition of and support for many different ways of communicating in public deliberations. This reflects key elements of inclusion as valued recognition and meaningful engagement, which, as Melinda Jones argues, requires facilitating the inclusion of people with disabilities through appropriate supports.[12] Harri Raisio and colleagues[13] argue that being present, particularly for those who are non-verbal and therefore cannot take up the communicative opportunities in deliberative democracy, offers a way to widen our understandings of participation and encourage "more attentiveness in listening and more humility in interpretation."[14] Unfortunately, this "politics of presence" often slides towards "benign representation of various differences,"[15] thus eliminating the meaningful engagement of those who embody differences. The challenge to deliberative democracy is effective inclusion and appropriate supports, including for the engagement of people with communications differences.

Neither the classical nor the critical approach, however, addresses how deliberative democratic approaches can ensure access or who is included and excluded. Access is not a word nor a checklist to be completed to enable inclusion; it is a process, perception, and relationship essential to participation. Tanya Titchkosky argues that "access, then, is tied to the social organization of participation, even to belonging. Access not only needs to be sought out and fought for, legally secured, physically measured, and politically protected, it also needs to be understood – as a complex form of perception that organizes socio-political relations between people in social space."[16] This understanding of access is also identified in the United Nations Convention on the Rights of Persons with Disabilities (CRPD), which indicates that having access is a precondition for full and effective participation of people with disabilities.[17]

This transdisciplinary approach to access leads us to ask: who is included and excluded? by whom? and how is that inclusion/exclusion constructed and justified? It also challenges us to recognize that "access initiatives come with the uncomfortable task of needing to ask 'What does inclusion mean?'"[18] Ruth Levitas goes further to suggest that inclusion also requires asking: what do we mean by it?[19] In this chapter, we argue that inclusion efforts illustrate the ways public institutions structure power relations in a particular sociopolitical circumstance and respond to the meaningful participation of marginalized citizens. Taking into account, and responding to, the voices of marginalized populations through diverse modes of communication is essential to the democratic decision-making process.[20] The question of access, then, is central to thinking about and theorizing deliberative democracy because access organizes sociopolitical conditions for the inclusion of disabled people in, and exclusion from, participation in and through public institutions. The relations of access that facilitate inclusion and exclusion have not been made visible, but suggest that the inclusion (or exclusion) of people with disabilities has not (yet) come to the forefront of deliberative democracy initiatives.

Vietnam is a post-colonial, socialist state.[21] Since its emergence from protracted conflicts, it has gone through a process of rapid social and economic change called Đổi Mới (renewal or renovation). Đổi Mới, introduced in 1986, is characterized by liberalization and privatization of the economy, including initiatives to participate in global trade through the World Trade Organization and the Trans-Pacific Partnership; reforms at the central political level that suggest greater openness to some but remain restricted to the Communist Party of Vietnam; and what has been described as a "socialist-oriented" civil society.[22] Some have suggested that these changes are leading towards democratization of Vietnam while it continues to be a one-party state. Nguyen Hai Hong and Pham Minh Quang argue that "continued high-level economic growth, elite competition within the ruling party, the stronger voice of a more assertive and pluralistic parliament, [and] the flourishing association life in society" are evidence of that democratizing process in Vietnam.[23] Together, these changes suggest movement towards a (neo)liberal democratic state.

Although many use Đổi Mới to explain the socio-economic and political struggles in Vietnam, the politics of inclusion of disabled people in that country has a much longer history.[24] Vietnam's colonial history is essential for understanding inclusion and exclusion in the Vietnamese context, and illustrates intersections between global and local conditions. The French established a colony in Vietnam in the 1860s. Its biopolitics of governing Indigenous bodies was institutionalized through colonial policies such as those governing prostitution, public health, and education. The colonial "discovery" of "social diseases" such as leprosy, typhoid, tuberculosis, and tetanus reflected a colonial desire to "civilize" the Indigenous peoples by pathologizing their bodies and minds. Mass campaigns of smallpox vaccination and construction of the first civilian hospitals in the 1860s were some of the ways in which the colonial state exercised its mission civilisatrice. In addition, campaigns for hygiene, policing prostitution, fighting mental health problems, and deformities illustrated how the French colonials used public health to advance their ideology of civilization. Western biomedicine was used to protect the colonials, while Indigenous peoples themselves were constructed as "social diseases" requiring cure and subject to colonial governance.[25] Women and children, including girls, were targeted groups because of their perceived "vulnerable" status. French colonialism in Vietnam both pathologized and infantilized women and girls.[26]

This colonial practice of framing Indigenous peoples as diseases to be cured has had lingering effects on their understanding of their disabilities. In TDKRA discussions, disabled girls and women frequently internalized their disabilities as diseases that required medical intervention. For example, a woman with disabilities from an ethnic minority in A Luoi expressed her fear of passing on her "disease" to her children: "The children are stunted, we don't know how we can cure it." This comment reflects the challenges of deliberative democracy in facilitating inclusion, and might carry an ableist assumption that disability should be cured, which stands in contrast to critical approaches to disability studies.[27] We argue, however, that this politics of cure must be situated within its colonial and post-colonial contexts, where the state has shaped public perceptions of disabilities as diseases, thus illustrating one way difference has been governed in Vietnamese social history.[28]

Participation in normative transnational human rights frameworks offers another example of how the Vietnamese government shapes the inclusion and exclusion of people with disabilities. Vietnam signed the CRPD in 2007 and ratified it in 2015. In that transnational rights context, the government introduced the Law on Persons with Disabilities, which came into effect in 2011. The law draws upon individual rights and applies CRPD principles, including the right "to participate on an equal basis in social activities" and "to live independently and integrate into the community" (Article 4.1). At the same time, the law institutionalizes pathologizing and individualizing disability by enforcing measurement of the degree of disability or impairment as assessed by a committee. Such an approach to determining disability effectively decides who is disabled enough to receive the benefits from the law. This measurement, then, is a way of governing inclusion and exclusion, and justified by using the transnational human rights normative framework of the CRPD. The example also illustrates that, although Vietnam might not fit definitions of a democratic state, it does seek to participate in the rule of law, including through transnational normative human rights frameworks.

Given Vietnam's participation in such transnational frameworks around disability, we believe that citizen or public engagement is a more effective approach within which to discuss disability politics in that country. Drawing from a hundred case studies in twenty countries, Gaventa and Barrett disrupt the link between democracy and citizen engagement often found in the deliberative democracy literature.[29] They suggest that there is no necessary connection between the "level of democratization" and the possibility or success of participation.[30] They argue that civil society associations, in settings in less robust democratic states, can play a significant role in strengthening a sense of citizenship and the practices of participation. This happens largely through local associations, and at what the authors call the first-level impact of citizen engagement: "the development of greater civic and political knowledge, and a greater sense of awareness of rights and empowered self-identity, which serve as a prerequisite to deepen action and participation."[31] These three facets of engagement – civil and political knowledge, awareness of rights, and empowered identity – offer a useful context within which to consider the TDKRA project with girls and women with disabilities in Vietnam.

But we need to probe this framework a bit further in the context of the earlier discussion of access. Titchkosky invites a politics of wonder about access.[32] To wonder is to ask reflexively and politically, to make evident power relations in and among ourselves and the world around us. "Wonder, then, is the political engagement with our own politics regarding disability."[33] Using this approach, we ask: who is part of local associations and why them? Whose and what civic and political knowledge is developed and how? Who gains a greater awareness of rights, when, and which ones? And whose self-identity is empowered, when, and how? These questions can enable us to do three things: to identify whether and how access is a foundational element in citizen engagement; to reflect on and tell some of the stories from the participatory research project with girls and women with disabilities in Vietnam; and to understand intersectional experiences and practices of inclusion and exclusion in communities. The questions help us to frame the work we are doing in this project as engagement and as a necessary foundation for building capacity for deepened action and participation towards more inclusive societies.

Who Participates and Why Them?

TDKRA is a collaborative research project[34] based in Canada with partners in three locations in Vietnam: Can Tho, A Luoi, and Bac Tu Liem. The goal of the four-year project is to engage girls and women with disabilities in the three disadvantaged communities in advocating for their inclusion. It builds on an earlier pilot project to monitor the educational rights of girls with disabilities in Vietnam through visual participatory methodologies.[35] The main purpose of TDKRA is to engage girls and women with disabilities in constructing their perspectives of inclusion and exclusion through critical theory, participatory methodologies, and political activism. The first phase (2016–17) of the project included fieldwork with Canadian researchers, with a five-day workshop in each community in July 2017. The second phase (2017–18) included workshops in each community led by women with disabilities as well as a second round of fieldwork by Canadian researchers, with a four-day workshop in each community in July 2018. During the first phase, the girls (and women) made drawings and cellphilms – short videos made using locally available cellphones – and discussed their experiences of inclusion and exclusion. In the second phase, the girls again used drawing to express themselves, in addition to photovoice[36] and community asset mapping.[37] The girls and women also developed a video about the project through a participatory process. We discuss the results primarily from the first phase of this project in this chapter.

TDKRA partners with DPOs in each community. The partners' involvement is key in making project decisions, organizing the local fieldwork in each location, and reflecting on their activism in addressing disabling issues in their own communities. As a team of researchers and activists, including disabled and non-disabled people in the global North and South, we aim to tackle unequal power relations framed within international development discourses on disability rights, recognizing that such discourses have failed to recognize the politics of impairment in post-colonial contexts.[38] Post-colonial disability scholars argue for the need to engage with the space and social locations in which knowledge about disability and impairment is formed as a consequence of historical struggles.[39] This includes reframing knowledge and power relations through a mutually respectful and engaging process. In nurturing these relationships, the project reaffirms the political call of "nothing about us without us," as well as the decolonizing strategy of "building and constructing" relationships using a politics of solidarity.[40] This politics means learning from the girls and women in Vietnam about their experiences of inclusion and exclusion; building across and honouring those differences; and creating spaces to have often-difficult conversations that might arise from those differences. These commitments also mean working to decolonize traditional power relations between researchers and partner organizations.[41] By establishing the agendas together, giving partners priority when discussing funding matters, meeting regularly together, and co-creating academic articles and other knowledge products, we ensured that our local partners could take ownership of the project and contribute to its intellectual and administrative development. In their evaluation after the first year, partners recognized the project's desire to tackle power relations, while also being aware of the embedded power of those from the global North with primary access to resources. Moving forward, our commitment to decolonizing power relations also might mean seeking out opportunities to leverage the global Northern privileges of the Canadian scholars – recognizing the disparities among us as a result of our racialization, stage of career, age, disability, sexuality, and other differences – for the benefits of our partners.

TDKRA models a unique mentoring and capacity-building process for girls and women with disabilities. In each site, we recruited women with disabilities between the ages of twenty and fifty-three who were interested in becoming trained facilitators, ensuring that they could build on and strengthen their networks through creating relationships with their local DPOs and members of the team. Their experience with disability and gender discrimination was an important factor for shaping relationships with disabled girls. We also recruited sixteen girls with disabilities in each location, chosen from a number of inclusion criteria: they had to be between ten and eighteen years old; have one or more disadvantage associated with her disability, class, gender, and ethnicity; and be interested in advocacy work for educational and disability rights. We recruited women and girls with invisible and visible disabilities, recognizing that they have been historically absent in research relations as well as in their own communities. In each site, the local DPOs, with the international researchers (in person or by Skype), worked with the women with disabilities to share knowledge about themselves, developing their skills in interviewing and leading focus groups, human rights, cellphilm making,[42], media analysis, and advocacy or engagement. The women then worked with the girls in a variety of settings, sometimes in large groups and other times in small groups or one-on-one.

In the 2017 fieldwork, the girls had different ways to share their experiences of being included and excluded through drawing, producing cellphilms in a group, and talking in small or large groups. We began each day with warm-up exercises that were often playful and energetic. Using coloured pencils and paper, the girls were invited to draw pictures of their identities as girls with disabilities and their relationships with their communities, and then to describe their pictures and what they meant. The drawings were displayed at a final public event. The girls played games and ate lunch together. They worked in groups of four or five girls and two women to develop a storyboard and shoot a cellphilm. Cellphilming is a participatory visual method for working with communities through collaboratively planning, filming, and showing videos to an audience. In this project, the girls and women identified a theme for the film and roles for each member of their group, created a storyboard, and shot the film. Some girls were actors, others drew pictures related to the message, while still others directed or shot the film. The groups also identified a message they wanted to share from the cellphilms. For example, many groups used the slogan "don't discriminate against people with disabilities" as a key message they wanted to convey to the audience.

The girls presented what they had drawn, the cellphilms they had developed, and the messages of the drawings and cellphilms to one another in large groups and, at the end, to their parents and local stakeholders in a public display. These multiple spaces for engagement allowed the girls to share what they had done with a larger audience and to identify the meanings of what they had developed. One girl in Bac Tu Liem reflected on her drawing: "The topic of drawing is 'my school.' I want to say that I really want to go to school for studying and I really miss my teachers. I want to go to school for studying and taking part in performance in school, in class. Going to school, to be included, so happy. In school, in class, I meet many teachers. In my old school, I have never forgot my secondary school."

In addition to the girls, women, researchers, and local support team, there were also guests. In Can Tho and Bac Tu Liem, invitations were sent to parents, local government, international organizations, and civil society contacts for a showing of the work produced by the girls. We worked with our local partners to identify key stakeholders, who were invited to join us because they functioned within the local networks with significant effects on the local DPOs and disabled people themselves. The decision-making process regarding who should be invited was primarily taken by our local partners.

In one location, there were also unexpected visitors. Two local police officers came on the first day, and one stayed the entire week. Their purpose appeared to be to monitor the activities. Local women did not appear to find this out of the ordinary, but some of the Canadian researchers were unsettled and resistant to this police presence, in part because of the ethical implications for the research. The Vietnamese women suggested that everyone in the room had been given a role, and perhaps the best way forward was to give the police a role such as providing support to the girls and women. In the following days, the police officer was asked to contribute his time and energy as a support person. His demeanour shifted over the following days from passive observer to active contributor, including sharing meals with the gathering. This experience brought an embodied presence of the Vietnamese state to our gathering, which we reflect on further below.

TDKRA was designed to be an inclusive project, intentionally seeking out girls and women who are often invisible in their own communities and bringing them and their experiences to the front and centre. Our recruitment had the intent of ensuring that a wide variety of girls and women with disabilities could participate. Yet, in practice, it was easier for some girls and women than others to participate. For example, despite having an interpreter to enable her participation, one deaf girl had a hard time working with other girls who were not deaf. Some girls with intellectual disabilities had a difficult time contributing to the development of the storyboard of the cellphilms, especially at first, while others were quick to learn the approaches. Even in a project that brought the girls and women with disabilities to the table, providing many of the necessary supports, TDKRA was unable to ensure full participation by all those who came.

Whose and What Knowledge Is Developed and How?

As academics in the global North who conduct research about the global South, our social positions are challenging. We are mindful of the ways in which this research operates within neoliberal and neocolonial discourses of international development, where we are embodied within colonial structures of knowledge. We found that each of us is both an insider and an outsider of the research locations at the same time. Although one of us (Nguyen) has experience growing up and doing research in Vietnam, she has remained an outsider to some Northern and Southern spaces, as well as to the ethnic minority regions in which we conducted the research. Stienstra had her first experience working in Vietnam with a very different system of thought about disability and gender equality. At the same time, we each brought our personal experiences with disability and chronic illness. This allows us to reflect on and be critical of the ways in which institutional ableism and racism have structured our research practices.

In each location, the teams of women, researchers, and girls shared knowledge about what it was like to live as women or girls with disabilities. As Stienstra notes,[43] we know so little about the lives of girls with disabilities from their own perspectives, and what we do know often sets disability as the most important indicator of a girl's (or woman's) life. We asked the girls (and women) to share any experiences of being included and excluded, without specifically asking about disability, as well as their hopes and dreams.

Many of the girls' stories of exclusion suggested experiences of teasing because of an impairment. One girl said, "when we go to school, we are teased by friends, ignored, and denied to play with." Other girls talked about how they were teased by boys because they were girls and disabled: "In my class, there is also a friend who has problem with her eyes ... She is often teased, but the boys find she is a girl so ... sometimes they are too offensive to her – they say: 'Squint, like this, like that.'"

The girls said that, for them, inclusion was to be cared for, to affirm oneself, and to be included with non-disabled friends. Examples of inclusion were often linked to being accepted or receiving support. One girl said, "I was a person with a disability, the others were without disabilities; they loved me so they didn't tease me." Several girls talked about their friends helping them in school. One girl described how her friends "helped me to go the second floor." For the women, inclusion was often seen in the DPOs in which they participated, including our partner organizations: "Since I joined [the organization], I have had more will to live. I have met many people who have the same condition as me. And I became more confident because I believe that I'm not the only one like that. There are many people like me. There are even people that are more miserable than me. So, I have found a light in my life to help me live until today."

Although the women with disabilities also spoke of their exclusion as a result of their impairments, some spoke of their exclusion in the context of their ethnicity and social class. One woman in A Luoi, a mountainous area with ethnic minorities, said: "When I went to school, no one wanted to sit next to me and study with me because I have no father, no mother ... When I studied in grade 3, the teacher got me discharged; she said: 'You are stupid, you can't learn. Why are you dumber than others?' I said to her that I didn't know how to study, from little until now I hadn't studied anything. Friends laughed at me. They said, 'Don't you go to school anymore?' I didn't have clothes so I always wore one dress. After that, I didn't go to school anymore. I dropped out of school, I didn't dare to come to school anymore because I was scared that friends would tease me." Her comments illustrate the intersections of her ethnicity, poverty, and institutional ableism that constructed her exclusion.

The women described their experiences of inclusion as mothers, daughters, wives, sisters, apprentices, employees, teachers, students, and members of DPOs. Several talked of how their mother's commitment to bringing them to school made them feel more included. Many talked about the importance of the DPO in their community in providing social support, confidence, and work experience. This project offers an opportunity to foster inclusion and activism for disability rights *with* girls and women with disabilities. We see this knowledge as mutually constructed by us – the researchers and our partners – the local disability activists, in collaboration with our participants and research assistants. We see this shared knowledge as belonging to each of these stakeholders, reflecting what Raewyn Connell calls a globally inclusive process that helps to reframe knowledge and power between the global North and South.[44]

Who Gains a Greater Awareness of Rights, When, and Which Ones?

Few of the girls expressed their inclusion or exclusion using the language of rights or discrimination, although they recognized their different treatment and the need for something better. Some of the cellphilms the girls wrote and produced illustrated their claiming their rights. In Bac Tu Liem, one cellphilm had the message: "Girls with disabilities really need to go to school like other students." Another cellphilm expressed: "We want people with disabilities to enjoy like other people. Non-disabled children will be socialized with children with disabilities like us. I hope non-disabled people do not tease people with disabilities, [but] be socialized with them. As for people with disabilities, the most important thing is to be included." Another cellphilm had the message: "Don't discriminate against girls with disabilities. This film represents our hope that we want to be included and need to be protected."

The language of rights was much more familiar to the women, many of whom had taken previous training sessions on human rights and the CRPD. One woman in A Luoi said, "They discriminate against me. Therefore, I have difficulties in life. I feel shy. I am unable to interact with other people." Another woman recognized the effects of discrimination on job opportunities for people with disabilities: "I'm so worried about my children, about the difference of opportunity for having a job between normal people and people with disabilities." While many women used the language of discrimination, they did not identify specific rights. But their comments suggested an appreciation for the principle of rights and fair treatment, even though they did not address a more formal attention to rights or the CRPD.

Most of the comments had to do with the girls' and women's lives, families, schools, and communities. They recognized and articulated situations when they had experienced discrimination or unfair treatment, but they rarely linked these to human rights. In these stages, none of the girls or women spoke of her political life or the possibilities of advocating for change. This suggests a gap between knowledge about human rights and experiences of discrimination and exclusion as well as about advocacy, which was addressed in later stages of the project. DPOs across the world, including in Vietnam, are using the CRPD as a way to claim and monitor their rights, but few have approached this work from the vantage point of girls. Despite the work of UNICEF in Vietnam around both children's rights and the inclusion and participation of all children,[45] there are few resources to promote knowledge of, and engagement with, human rights by girls with disabilities. The comments of the girls and women align with broad understandings of values associated with inclusive citizens,[46] including justice, the right to be treated fairly, and recognition of the intrinsic worth of all humans, including their differences, self-determination and the ability to exercise some control over their lives, and solidarity or to identify with others and act together in their claims.

Whose Self-Identity Is Empowered, When, and How?

Through the process of mentoring and sharing their knowledge, women, girls, researchers, and local leaders learned from one another. In that learning, we each became stronger. One woman with disabilities in Bac Tu Liem talked about how she was changed by watching the girls draw pictures: "It was so touching. I feel like my image is in there. When I was young, I also had dreams like you, a lot of ambition. But at that time I thought I could not do it. But by making efforts, now I have done it. So, I'm very happy when now they always have dreams ... And I hope that they will achieve all the dreams they want."

We observed moments when the girls and women with disabilities felt empowered by their mutual engagement through the workshop activities, including spaces such as community exhibits. The women with disabilities played a key role in mentoring the girls through their facilitation in the groups of girls. The women's experiences with disability and gender discrimination, as well as their struggles to affirm themselves against societal prejudice, became important resources for the girls to build relationships and to become more confident in their participation. When asked about how they felt after participating in this project, some of the girls spoke of their happiness and increased confidence. One girl said she was "very happy ... I feel so happy ... I feel more confident." Her interpreter said "[she] felt so happy when she drew as well as film together with other girls. She didn't feel shy."

As researchers we were also changed in this process. Stienstra learned much about Vietnam's culture, food, and history from the girls and women, including our translators. She was also challenged to reflect on different understandings of disability from her interactions with the girls around disability. In one large group discussion, the facilitator asked specifically about the girls' understandings of disability, and found that many of the girls understood disability as a problem with their bodies that prevented them from doing what they wanted. This echoes our earlier discussion of the effects of colonialism on approaches to disability. It is also in contrast to the understanding of disability as resulting from barriers in the environment that the researchers adopted. This tension gave concrete form to the commitment of this project not to impose a global Northern approach to disability in this particular context.

Most girls with disabilities lacked opportunities to participate in the public sphere, and their contributions can be understood in that context. Of the forty-four girls who participated in the first phase of the project, most contributed to public events for the first time in their lives. Many, including those who used non-verbal communications, experienced challenges in terms of communicating their ideas during the workshops. By using arts-based research, TDKRA hoped not only to provide a more inclusive space for the girls to express their desires as girls with disabilities, but also to counter exclusion.

Additionally, we found that the girls became more confident in telling their stories as they became more involved in the research project. In the second phase, our team, in consultation with the local partners, decided to create more space for women's and girls' engagement, recognizing the importance of such spaces for nurturing their relationships and participation. Both girls and women became more involved in this second stage, where their narratives of inclusion and exclusion were expressed with more depth and insight on their journey to inclusion.

Reflecting on the Possibilities for Engagement for Girls and Women with Disabilities in Vietnam

Nguyen[47] argues that one way to reimagine disability and inclusion is to reconnect the experiences of girls with disabilities within particular social and political contexts of the global South. The politics of location is particularly important for situating their voices and positionality, as well as for creating transformative possibilities. The politics of engagement in this chapter refers to the ways in which "girls with disabilities engaged in constructing their knowledge and negotiating power"[48] through their participation in knowledge production as a method of decolonizing the structure of power in essentializing and pathologizing disabled girls' and women's bodies. At another level, the politics of engagement with disabled women and girls in the globalizing context of neoliberalism means that we must recognize the intersection between global and local politics in exercising inclusion and exclusion through the state and transnational organizations. The engagement of women and girls with disabilities then becomes crucial to the process of speaking back through their stories and activism. A critical understanding of the challenges and possibilities for engaging disabled girls and women in the global South is important because it disrupts the assumption that they are merely vulnerable objects in the face of normative discourses of human rights and development.

Clearly, there are possibilities for the inclusive participation of disabled girls and women in Vietnam through their involvement in the participatory research process. Most saw the workshop spaces as inclusive places that enabled them to connect with one another and to become stronger as an association. At the same time, we recognize and acknowledge the physical and structural barriers some women and girls encountered. Despite our effort to be inclusive of all representations of disability, we found challenges in the lack of accessibility to different types of bodies that our research, despite its inclusive and participatory epistemologies, has continued to face. For example, despite the use of sign language interpretation, some deaf girls found it challenging to understand the questions we asked in the discussion. There remain ethical questions regarding who is doing research, by whom, and for whose benefit, that require us, as hearing researchers, to address. Similarly, some girls with intellectual disabilities also encountered challenges in decoding complex questions. We attempted to involve the women with disabilities in each location to rewrite the research questions in a way that could be understandable to the girls; this, in turn, raised issues related to ableism and adultism – an ideology which assumes that adults know best – and continues to raise political questions regarding who can participate in this research and what it means to be inclusive of difference.

To reiterate what we stated earlier, disabled girls and women were invited to be involved in all stages of the research process. Their voices, perspectives, and subjectivities matter to democratic theory and practice because they challenge us to reframe, reposition, and redebate the ways in which Western theories of deliberative democracy can explain the social contexts of inclusion and exclusion in some particular social locations in the global South.

What These Reflections Teach about Theories and Practices of Deliberative Democracy

Here, we return to the politics of engagement with the voices of women and girls with disabilities as a way of envisioning different vantage points for inclusive policy engagement. The context of Vietnam's participation in the transnational disability rights framework and its broader commitments to development create possibilities and challenges for disabled people to engage in debates over public policy.

The TDKRA project reveals the potential for some women with disabilities to become leaders in the disability movement while others remain in marginal circumstances. Indeed, our project emerged in the context of the disability movement's becoming part of a national discourse embedded with state politics of economic and social liberalization associated with neoliberalism.[49] Clearly, we are not able to interpret the current politics of disability and gender equality in Vietnam without understanding its long struggle against colonialism. The politics of disability and impairment, within the colonial history of Vietnam, reflects more complex and multiple power relations in shaping this research. This further demonstrates the challenges of critical disability studies in relation to theories and practices of deliberative democracy and social justice in the global South. That is, how can we engage participants in a participatory process without imposing or perpetuating the neocolonial assumption that "the West is best" in our politics of engagement? Furthermore, the co-optation of some neoliberal policies in Vietnam in the context of globalization, such as joining the World Trade Organization, has perpetuated some neoliberal and neocolonial ideologies of dependency in local economies. For example, many of our participants are either self-employed or not employed. "Inclusive" development policies, as propagated by the World Bank and other transnational organizations, in effect might perpetuate their exclusion by constructing them as unproductive and therefore as "unfit" for neoliberal economies.[50]

Some women with disabilities, including our partners, have taken leadership roles in their associations, while their organizations have functioned within both the state's policing of disabled bodies and research activities and its neoliberal development initiatives. The state sustains its power in structuring inclusion and exclusion, as the vignette of the policeman who exercised surveillance over our research process illustrates. Although it seems that the disability movement has sought to organize itself within the government's political agenda of liberalization and citizenship restructuring, there is little evidence of the movement's confronting state power, at least in the current context. The movement's active participation in international development programs, however, is well established and in some ways indicative of a distinctive politics of disability in Vietnam.

What we have learned through our work with marginalized communities in Vietnam reflects the ways in which women and girls with disabilities could become powerful constituents in advocating for their rights, with informed knowledge and strategies for political activism for inclusion in the face of institutional policing. In order to do so, the leadership of women and girls with disabilities must be nurtured and strengthened.

Arts-based research produced by both girls and women with disabilities can begin to frame an alternative politics of engagement that challenges exclusive ideologies and practices. Many authors, including some in this volume, suggest that arts-based research offers ways to counter the hegemony of language as the norm for communications.[51] Our earlier work with policy makers,[52] as well as our public display in the first phase of this project, suggests that, for arts-based research to move towards public engagement, we need to create exhibition spaces to showcase the work of disabled girls and invite the larger community, including policy makers, to view and engage with their work. These spaces are particularly useful for making the invisible visible, and for enabling some meaningful conversations between girls and women with disabilities, community stakeholders, and policy makers. By beginning with the representations and voices of girls and women with disabilities, we are reframing where and how public engagement occurs. This allows us to ensure access as well as to understand the intersectional experiences and practices of inclusion and exclusion in communities.

Although we cannot determine how such public engagement will be used in the struggle to be more inclusive of disabled girls and women, we see such public engagement as a necessary foundation for building capacity for deepened action, supporting greater participation, and creating more inclusive dialogues, thus enabling the greater inclusion of girls and women with disabilities in Vietnamese society.

Discussion Questions

1 To what extent is "democracy" required for deliberative democracy? What might deliberative democracy look like in socialist or post-socialist countries?
2 In what ways can disabled people engage in deliberative democracy? What does it take for them to be included? How are they excluded or structured out?
3 How has the Vietnamese state included/excluded people with disabilities, despite its commitment to implement the UN Convention on the Rights of Persons with Disabilities?
4 How do the girls and women participating in TDKRA challenge and change what it means to engage politically?

NOTES

Our thanks go to Shauna Sanvido for her help and keen attention in finalizing this manuscript.

1 We use both women and girls with disabilities and disabled women and girls to reflect the diverse ways women and girls talk about themselves and understand the place of disability in their lives.
2 Deborah Stienstra, "Trumping All? Disability and Girlhood Studies," *Girlhood Studies* 8, no. 2 (2015): 54–70; United Nations, Department of

Economic and Social Affairs, "Situation of Women and Girls with Disabilities and the Status of CRPD," 15 September 2017, online at http://www.un.org/disabilities//documents/gadocs/A_72_227.doc.

3 Xuan Thuy Nguyen, "Girls with Disabilities in the Global South: Rethinking the Politics of Engagement," *Girlhood Studies* 9, no. 1 (2016): 53–71.

4 United Nations, "Situation of Women and Girls with Disabilities."

5 Xuan Thuy Nguyen and Pamela Johnson, "Transnational Conversations in the Context of Disability Rights: Building the Potential for Global Activism," *Third World Thematics: A TWQ Journal* 1, no. 3 (2016): 396–410, https://doi.org/10.1080/23802014.2016.1248232.

6 John Gaventa and Gregory Barrett, "Mapping the Outcomes of Citizen Engagement," *World Development* 40, no. 12 (2012): 2399–10, doi:10.1016/j.worlddev.2012.05.014.

7 Iris Marion Young, *Inclusion and Democracy* (Oxford: Oxford University Press, 2002); and idem, "Communication and the Other: Beyond Deliberative Democracy," in *Democracy and Difference: Contesting the Boundaries of the Political*, ed. Seyla Benhabib (Princeton, NJ: Princeton University Press, 1996), 120–35.

8 Young, *Inclusion and Democracy*, 5.

9 Ibid., 10.

10 Harri Raisio, Katja Valkama, and Elina Peltola, "Disability and Deliberative Democracy: Towards Involving the Whole Human Spectrum in Public Deliberation," *Scandinavian Journal of Disability Research* 16, no. 1 (2014): 77–97, https://doi.org/10.1080/15017419.2013.781957.

11 Daniel Weinstock and David Kahane, "Introduction," in *Deliberative Democracy in Practice*, ed. David Kahane (Vancouver: UBC Press, 2010), 1–18; Raisio, Valkama, and Peltola, "Disability and Deliberative Democracy."

12 Melinda Jones, "Inclusion, Social Inclusion, and Participation," in *Critical Perspectives on Human Rights and Disability Law*, ed. Lee Ann Basser, Melinda Jones, and Marcia H. Rioux (Leiden, Netherlands: Brill, 2011), 57–82, https://doi.org/10.1163/ej.9789004189508.i-552.24.

13 Raisio, Valkama, and Peltola, "Disability and Deliberative Democracy."

14 Stacey Clifford, "Making Disability Public in Deliberative Democracy," *Contemporary Political Theory* 11, no. 2 (2012): 225, doi:10.1057/cpt.2011.11.

15 Chandra Talpade Mohanty, "Transnational Feminist Crossings: On Neoliberalism and Radical Critique," *Signs* 38, no. 4 (2013): 972, https://doi.org/10.1086/669576.

16 Tanya Titchkosky, *The Question of Access: Disability, Space, Meaning* (Toronto: University of Toronto Press, 2011), 4.

17 United Nations, "Situation of Women and Girls with Disabilities."

18 Titchkosky, *Question of Access*, 28.

19 Ruth Levitas, "The Idea of Social Inclusion" (paper presented at the Social Inclusion Research Conference, Bristol, UK, 2003).

20 Young, *Inclusion and Democracy.*
21 Some scholars use the term "post-socialism" to refer to post– *Đổi Mới* in Vietnam and post-1989 in Central and Eastern Europe. The prefix "post" does not refer merely to the departure from state central planning towards the market; it marks a more nuanced understanding of the politics of reform in former communist countries on the path towards "market socialism" in the context of global neoliberalism. See John Pickles, "The Spirit of Post-socialism: Common Spaces and the Production of Diversity," *European Urban and Regional Studies* 17, no. 2 (2010): 127–40; see also Thi Hong Hai Nguyen, Steve Wood, and Neil Wrigley, "The Emerging Food Retail Structure of Vietnam: Phases of Expansion in a Post-socialist Environment," *International Journal of Retail & Distribution Management* 41, no. 8 (2013): 596–626.
22 Nguyen Hai Hong and Pham Minh Quang, "Democratization in Vietnam's Post-Đổi Mới One-Party Rule: Change from Within, Change from the Bottom to the Top, and Possibilities," in *Globalization and Democracy in Southeast Asia*, ed. Chantana Banpasirichote Wungaeo, Boike Rehbein, and Surichai Wun'gaeo (Basingstoke, UK: Palgrave Macmillan, 2016), 148, doi:10.1057/978-1-137-57654-5_7.
23 Ibid.
24 Xuan Thuy Nguyen, *The Journey to Inclusion* (Rotterdam: Sense, 2015).
25 Laurence Monnais, "Preventive Medicine and 'Mission Civilisatrice': Uses of the BCG Vaccine in French Colonial Vietnam between the Two World Wars," *International Journal of Asia-Pacific Studies* 2, no. 1 (2006): 40–66.
26 Frank Proschan, "Eunuch Mandarins, Soldats Mamzelles, Effeminate Boys, and Graceless Women: French Colonial Constructions of Vietnamese Genders," *GLQ: A Journal of Lesbian and Gay Studies* 8, no. 4 (2002): 435–67; Xuan Thuy Nguyen, "Unsettling 'Inclusion' in the Global South: A Post-Colonial and Intersectional Approach to Disability, Gender, and Education," in *SAGE Handbook of Inclusion and Diversity in Education*, ed. Matthew J. Schuelka et al. (London: Sage, 2019), 28–40.
27 Eli Clare, *Brilliant Imperfection: Grappling with Cure* (Durham, NC: Duke University Press, 2017).
28 Nguyen, *Journey to Inclusion.*
29 Gaventa and Barrett, "Mapping the Outcomes of Citizen Engagement."
30 Ibid.
31 Ibid.
32 Titchkosky, *Question of Access.*
33 Ibid., 129.
34 As a research project funded by the Social Sciences and Humanities Research Council of Canada, the team includes researchers primarily in Canada, led by Xuan Thuy Nguyen (Carleton University). Other

contributing researchers are Marnina Gonick (Mount Saint Vincent University), Claudia Mitchell (McGill University) Naydene de Lange (Nelson Mandela University), Marcia Rioux (York University), and Deborah Stienstra (University of Guelph).

35 Nguyen, "Girls with Disabilities in the Global South"; and Xuan Thuy Nguyen et al., "Engaging Girls with Disabilities in Vietnam: Making Their Voices Count," *Disability & Society* 30, no. 5 (2015): 773–87, https://doi.org /10.1080/09687599.2015.1051515.

36 As a research method, photovoice involves participants taking photos of their experiences and sharing them. See Claudia Mitchell, *Doing Visual Research* (London: Sage, 2011); Nguyen et al., "Engaging Girls with Disabilities in Vietnam"; Shan Simmonds, Cornelia Roux, and Ina ter Avest, "Blurring the Boundaries between Photovoice and Narrative Inquiry: A Narrative-Photovoice Methodology for Gender-Based Research," *International Journal of Qualitative Methods* 14, no. 3 (2015): 33–49.

37 Community asset mapping enables participants to identify resources in their communities as well as strengths they bring to making change in their communities. See Falls Brook Centre, "Sustainable Communities: A Guide to Community Asset Mapping" (Knowlesville, NB, 2012), online at https://ccednet-rcdec.ca/en/toolbox/sustainable-communities -guide-community-asset-mapping; Tony Fuller, Denyse Guy, and Carolyn Pletsch, "Asset Mapping: A Handbook" (n.p., 2002), online at https:// ccednet-rcdec.ca/en/toolbox/asset-mapping-handbook; and Dana Griffin and Amy Farris, "School Counselors and Collaboration: Finding Resources through Community Asset Mapping," *Professional School Counseling* 13, no. 5 (2010), https://doi.org/10.1177%2F2156759X1001300501.

38 Helen Meekosha and Karen Soldatic, "Human Rights and the Global South: The Case of Disability," *Third World Quarterly* 32, no. 8 (2011): 1383–97; Karen Soldatic and Shaun Grech, "Transnationalising Disability Studies: Rights, Justice and Impairment," *Disability Studies Quarterly* 34, no. 2 (2014).

39 Raewyn Connell, "Southern Bodies and Disability: Re-thinking Concepts," *Third World Quarterly* 32, no. 8 (2011): 1369–81; Xuan Thuy Nguyen, "Critical Disability Studies at the Edge of Global Development: Why Do We Need to Engage with Southern Theory?" *Canadian Journal of Disability Studies* 7. no. 1 (2018): 1–25; Samantha Wehbi, "Crossing Boundaries: Foreign Funding and Disability Rights Activism in a Context of War," *Disability & Society* 26, no. 5 (2011): 507–20.

40 Helen Meekosha, "Decolonising Disability: Thinking and Acting Globally," *Disability & Society* 26, no. 6 (2011), 678, https://doi.org/10.1080/09687599 .2011.602860.

41 Dan Goodley and Katherine Runswick-Cole, "Decolonizing Methodology: Disabled Children as Research Managers and Participant Ethnographers," in *Inclusive Communities: A Critical Reader*, ed. Shaun Grech and Andrew Azzopardi (Rotterdam: Sense, 2012), 215–32.

42 See Claudia Mitchell, Naydene De Lange, and Relebohile Moletsane, *Participatory Visual Methodologies: Social Change, Community and Policy* (Los Angeles: Sage, 2017).

43 Stienstra, "Trumping All?"

44 Connell, "Southern Bodies and Disability."

45 United Nations International Children's Emergency Fund, *Situation Analysis of Children in Ho Chi Minh City, Viet Nam, 2017* (Hanoi: UNICEF Viet Nam, 2017), online at https://www.unicef.org/vietnam/media/1516/file/Situation %20analysis%20of%20children:%20in%20Ho%20Chi%20Minh%20city%20 -%20Viet%20Nam%202017.pdf; idem, *A Manual on How to Integrate Children's Rights into Social and Economic Development Plans* (Hanoi: UNICEF Viet Nam, 2015), online at https://www.unicef.org/vietnam/media/1386/file/A %20manual%20on%20how%20to%20integrate%20children's%20rights %20into%20socio-economic%20development%20plans.pdf.

46 Naila Kabeer, "Introduction," in *The Search for Inclusive Citizenship: Meanings and Expressions in an Inter-connected World*, ed. Naila Kabeer (New York: Zed Books, 2005), 1–27.

47 Nguyen, "Girls with Disabilities in the Global South."

48 Ibid., 54.

49 Nguyen, *Journey to Inclusion*.

50 Rebecca Dingo, "Making the 'Unfit, Fit': The Rhetoric of Mainstreaming in the World Bank's Commitment to Gender Equality and Disability Rights," *Wagadu* 4, no. 1 (2007): 93–107; Deborah Stienstra, "DisAbling Globalization: Rethinking Global Political Economy with a Disability Lens," *Global Society* 16, 2 (2002): 109–22.

51 Young, *Inclusion and Democracy*.

52 Naydene De Lange, Nguyen Thi Lan Anh, and Nghiem Thi Thu Trang, "Creating Dialogue on Inclusion in Vietnam: Girls with Disabilities Exhibit Their Work," *Girlhood Studies* 9, no. 1 (2016): 104.

KEY RESOURCES

Jones, Melinda. "Inclusion, Social Inclusion and Participation." In *Critical Perspectives on Human Rights and Disability Law*, edited by Lee Ann Basser, Melinda Jones, and Marcia H. Rioux, 57–82. Leiden, Netherlands: Brill, 2011. https://doi.org/10.1163/ej.9789004189508.i-552.24.

Nguyen, Xuan Thuy. "Girls with Disabilities in the Global South: Rethinking the Politics of Engagement." *Girlhood Studies* 9, no. 1 (2016): 53–71. https://doi.org/10.3167/ghs.2016.090105.

Raisio, Harri, Katja Valkama, and Elina Peltola. "Disability and Deliberative Democracy: Towards Involving the Whole Human Spectrum in Public Deliberation." *Scandinavian Journal of Disability Research* 16, no. 1 (2014): 77–97. https://doi.org/10.1080/15017419.2013.781957.

PART TWO

Centring Voices from the Margins: Expanding and Evaluating Engagement Practices

7 Collective Grist: Hacking Telecommunications Policy in Canada

TARA MAHONEY

Introduction

Throughout Western democracies there is a crisis of public confidence in the efficacy of formal, institutionally driven forms of political participation. In neoliberal societies, a major problem for public engagement is the tendency for power to drift away from the formal political system and for market forces to be given much greater rein to allocate resources and define the societal landscape.[1] As mechanisms of neoliberalism such as deregulation, privatization, the contracting out of public services, and the marketization of public goods have come to dominate policy making, policy deliberation is often displaced from the formal political realm into spaces where unaccountable authorities are able to influence decisions behind closed doors and away from public scrutiny. This depoliticization of policy making diminishes the realm of public deliberation, erodes public trust, and alienates people from democratic processes as citizens increasingly feel their voice has no impact in policy-making realms.[2] In order to understand changing forms of public engagement with policy making, we must first understand that political disengagement is a problem not only of personal attitudes and social barriers, but of systemic political inequality that constricts the ability of everyday people to participate effectively in the decision making that affects their daily lives. Although participation in democracy is held up as an idea everyone claims fidelity to, the actual avenues for practising democracy are extremely limited and often without real substance.

As neoliberalism has eroded the efficacy of traditional and institutional forms of political engagement, citizens and publics have been forced to find new ways to express their opinions and shape the conditions that impact their lives and communities.[3] Emerging from this context are new forms of public engagement that draw on communications technologies and social movements to produce citizen-driven policy alternatives. In recent years, "policy hacking"[4] has been taken up by Vancouver-based non-profit OpenMedia as a way to build new roads into the notoriously opaque processes of telecommunications policy making through a combination of widespread digital engagement and collaboration with policy experts. Several OpenMedia campaigns have culminated in crowdsourced policy recommendation reports, submissions, and interventions that have been used as leveraging tools in attempts to democratize decision-making processes at the federal level.

This chapter explores the concept of policy hacking as it relates to the crowdsourcing work of OpenMedia. The notion of "policy hacking" describes a mode of contemporary policy activism that uses digital tools to facilitate citizen-based contributions to concrete policy alternatives. Drawing on Pierre Rosanvallon,[5] I argue that policy hacking operates as a valuable form of counterdemocracy by leveraging public *distrust* to encourage more participatory and robust forms of public engagement. This case study demonstrates how counterdemocracy and participatory politics (or *participatory counterdemocracy*) provide a critical standard against which we might measure current public engagement practices – whereby democratic power can be leveraged through a scepticism of political institutions to conduct public engagement efforts adequately. Through my discussion of policy hacking, we can observe dynamics of *knowledge democracy* and *policy justice* referenced in the introductory chapter to this volume. By leveraging crowdsourcing and digital communication, OpenMedia's campaigns put into practice the idea that public policy knowledge can be generated through an open and collaborative process between the public, advocacy organizations, and policy experts. I argue that this approach provides promising avenues to explore how power relations within administrative decision making can be transformed through novel forms of political engagement.

Neoliberalism

There are numerous ways to interpret what neoliberalism is and how it operates. On the surface, neoliberalism is "the free-market ideology based on individual liberty and limited government that connects human freedom to the actions of the rational, self-interested actor in a competitive marketplace."[6] It gained traction as a counter rationality to the welfare state in the 1970s by promoting principles of competition, efficiency, productivity, profitability, and individual autonomy. Indeed, the goal of early neoliberals was to dismantle the post-war welfare state in which the government played a key role in the protection and promotion of the social and economic well-being of its citizens.[7] From a neoliberalist perspective, the market is imagined as a space of "unconstrained" choices by "autonomous," rationally calculating agents who are simply seeking the best way to satisfy their individual ends, while the actions of the state and state agencies are seen as an imposition of power on the space of individual choice.[8]

David Harvey offers another reading of neoliberalism, describing it as a political project carried out by the corporate capitalist class, which felt threatened both politically and economically by anticorporate social movements and reformists' initiatives that arose towards the end of the 1960s and into the 1970s. Harvey argues that the "ruling class recognized that there were a number of fronts on which they had to struggle: the ideological front, the political front, and above all the struggle to curb the power of labor by whatever means possible. Out of this there emerged a political project which I would call neoliberalism."[9] In other words, neoliberalism manifests as a resistance to state intervention and an intensifying of pressure from the corporate sector to privatize public services. Business interests use their power to push back against the redistributive state in order to assert their own leadership over the economy and society more generally. Embedded in this neoliberalization of society is a critique of democracy. The fear among neoliberals is that an excess of democracy can produce too many collective demands that drive up inefficiency and increase costs. The idea is that democracy is far more efficient if social goods are pursued through principles of consumerism and the free market, rather than state-led economic intervention.[10] This perspective understands capitalism as democratic freedom through the protection of individual rights and property, as opposed to democracy as collective rule. Thomas Frank describes this perspective as "market populism" – the idea that the free market is a more democratic means of articulating the popular will, and much more so than organized politics.[11] Hence, because the market is considered to be efficient at allocating resources, it offers an attractive alternative to the inefficiencies of government bureaucracies.

Colin Crouch[12] argues that neoliberal ideology has transformed democratic systems into "post-democracies" through four key developments: (1) democratic institutions lose influence on the political decision-making process as they become more strongly dominated by a small number of (mostly economic) elites; (2) a "degeneration of political parties" turns political parties into "mere vote catching apparatuses" that are unable to develop meaningful agendas and are mainly steered by information from opinion research; (3) corporate media organizations become victims of marketization and focus on profit instead of political education, which leads to the commodification of political processes; and (4) citizens become passive as a result of widespread disenchantment with formal political participation.[13] Stephen McBride and Heather Whiteside[14] argue that neoliberal societies are in the midst of a "democratic malaise" caused by increasing economic and social inequalities combined with a lack of opportunities for public input into policy decision making. Focusing on the Canadian context, the authors argue that increasing cynicism and mistrust have come to replace political engagement and civic consciousness. They posit that this erosion of trust in government caused by the lack of power people feel in the face of political elites can lead to the rise of behaviours that are destructive for social cohesion and exacerbate the exclusion of already marginalized and disenfranchised groups.

Public Engagement and Telecommunications Policy in Canada

In Canada, communication policy making is divided between the Canadian Radio-television and Telecommunications Commission (CRTC) and the federal government department known as Innovation, Science and Economic Development Canada (ISED, formerly Industry Canada, renamed in 2015). The CRTC is an independent public organization established in 1968 to regulate companies that use the wireless spectrum to provide television, data, and telephone services to Canadians along the objectives later set out in the Broadcasting Act (1991) and the Telecommunications Act (1993). Before being renamed, Industry Canada was the department responsible for the development of a national digital telecommunications infrastructure through the management of wireless spectrum, copyright, and other issues related to internet governance.[15] The CRTC is considered a key institution for opening the door to wider public participation in Canadian telecommunications policy.[16] In some ways, the CRTC has institutionalized public engagement through holding public hearings, roundtable discussions, and informal online discussion forums on communications policy issues.[17] Both the CRTC and the department have also been criticized, however, for effectively sidelining the public from major policy decisions regarding technological development and deployment.[18]

Several scholars have argued that the structure of the CRTC's regulatory processes create significant barriers to participation.[19] For instance, participating in regulatory processes requires considerable resources in terms of time, money, and knowledge. Hearings are generally conducted in Ottawa, and although the commission sometimes reimburses the expenses of interveners, most people or organizations wanting to appear at proceedings must do so at their own expense. In addition, keeping up with the CRTC's regulatory agenda, navigating the bureaucratic online submission system for interventions, and undertaking the research necessary to understand the possible social, political, and economic effects of the issues it addresses is difficult and time consuming. Without considerable time for research, or the benefit of paid staff, participating in proceedings is something few besides major media corporations can afford.[20] As communications researcher Leslie Regan Shade remarks, the federal government's "infrastructure support for capacity building [among advocacy groups] has been negligible."[21] Furthermore, the procedural aesthetics of the hearings themselves, with commissioners at the front of the room on an elevated platform questioning the presenter, creates an intimidating, court-like atmosphere unwelcoming to the average Canadian.[22]

In the context of ISED, decision-making processes are largely closed, and most of the power is bestowed upon the minister, which tends to prevent effective public input into regulatory decisions. As a result, in areas where ISED is the dominant regulator, policy making has been described by scholars as an opaque process with a "pronounced [public interest] advocacy deficit."[23] Communications scholar Darin Barney argues that, since the emergence of information and communications technology (ICT) in the 1990s, telecommunications policy making in Canada has been characterized by "a truncation of opportunities for participation ... and a consistent tendency to respond more readily and decisively to the interests of major commercial and industrial actors than to those of public interest advocates and their constituencies."[24] Particularly, policies concerning ICT have predominantly been concerned with establishing a climate conducive to technological innovation, capital investment, and economic growth, rather than providing a meaningful site for effective democratic participation. Barney demonstrates how the membership of consultative bodies such as CANARIE (formerly the Canadian Network for the Advancement of Research, Industry and Education), the Information Highway Advisory Council, and the National Broadband Task Force have reflected "a consistent overrepresentation of powerful, private actors with vested interests in this policy area, and only token representation of public interest groups and other constituencies."[25] This overrepresentation of industry interests and underrepresentation of public interests has been blamed for the increased concentration of media ownership in Canada, which has risen to among the world's highest.[26] Due to the deregulation of mobile wireless and internet sectors, the Canadian market is now dominated by the "big five" – Bell, Rogers, Telus, Shaw, and Quebecor – which together account for nearly three-quarters (72.1 per cent) of all revenues across Canada's telecom, media, and internet industries.[27]

Therefore, in addition to practical barriers to engagement, ideological barriers to participation have also been erected in recent decades as a neoliberal agenda has come to dominate telecom policy making in Canada. As policy researcher Vanda Rideout argues, because there is a lack of a clearly defined public interest, federal regulators have tended to equate the public interest with the economic interest, where consumers tend to stand in for citizens.[28] This shift from citizen to consumer has been exacerbated by the fact that new technologies are framed as personal media technologies, supporting a focus on individualism in policy practices and ideologies. As a result, collective concerns of social responsibility and public service have often been overtaken by the individualized economic framings of consumer protection.[29]

Communication scholars Robert Hackett and William K. Carroll argue that private media ownership and concentration caused by the deregulating agenda of neoliberalism have a corrosive effect not only on communications policy, but also on democracy itself. They outline key trends that describe a strong link between communication policy and democratic participation. For instance, the exacerbation of the "digital divide" limits access to media services and information – which enable full political and economic participation – to those who can afford it; corporate enclosure puts at risk the public commons of knowledge; and the erosion of privacy and the right of free expression allows governments and the corporate sector to push for growing surveillance, censorship, and sometimes direct repression of content.[30] Indeed, demands for democratic communications policy making are intimately linked to demands for a more democratic society. Therefore, media reform movements such as those led by OpenMedia are not only responding to concentrated media power and the struggle over communications rights; they are also part of a wider challenge to social, political, and economic inequalities. As the media landscape shifts online and as users increasingly access the internet as their primary source for news and information, telecom policy is a site of struggle over both the future of the media and the future of democracy.[31]

Case: OpenMedia

It is within the context of intensifying neoliberalization that OpenMedia emerged in 2008 as a digitally driven advocacy organization focused on facilitating mass public engagement with media reform issues. OpenMedia was originally conceived under the name Canadians for

Democratic Media (CDM), a loose coalition of academics, public interest organizations, and labour groups committed to expanding the public interest voice in communications policy. CDM grew out of a long history of grassroots engagement in media and communications policy in Canada, beginning in the early decades of the twentieth century when Graham Spry and the Canadian Radio League were vocal in encouraging the growth of public ownership and mitigating the effects of market forces on the cost and character of services and products.[32]

In 2010, CDM was rebranded as OpenMedia to reflect its narrowing focus on internet issues such as net neutrality, trade agreements, copyright and intellectual property, spectrum auctions, and internet surveillance. In terms of domestic policy, OpenMedia's campaigns have targeted a variety of decision-making bodies within the federal government, including Industry Canada (now ISED), Heritage Canada, Public Safety Canada, and the CRTC. One of OpenMedia's early and most successful efforts at mass public engagement was the "Stop The Meter" campaign, which used social media, blogs, videos, media appearances, and stakeholder coalitions to intervene in a CRTC decision to allow wholesale internet providers the power to impose "usage-based billing" (pay per byte) on independent internet service providers and, as a consequence, many Canadian internet users. The online petition garnered over 300,000 signatures and flooded the CRTC offices with over 100,000 comments, an unprecedented level of public engagement in telecommunications.[33] Several scholars have suggested that this pressure led the CRTC to change its decision to reflect more consideration of the public interest;[34] the campaign was described by a representative of Library and Archives Canada as the "most significant online movement in Canadian history."[35] Since the "Stop the Meter" campaign, several of OpenMedia's petition campaigns have drawn over 100,000 signatures, and the organization is now regularly consulted as a public interest group by regulators, policy makers and the media, leading some to claim that OpenMedia has set a new benchmark for online organizing in Canada.[36]

Methodology

The data that form the basis for my analysis were collected from interviews with six past and present OpenMedia staff members, one expert in Canadian telecommunications policy, OpenMedia's crowdsourced reports, and news stories associated with its campaigns and crowdsourcing efforts. The interviews were conducted over a two-month period (August–September 2017), and aimed to understand OpenMedia's processes of policy hacking and the ideology guiding its public engagement work. The analysis I report here is limited to two crowdsourcing campaigns ("Time for an Upgrade" and "Our Privacy Plan") that arguably were the crowdsourcing efforts with the highest profile. I did not examine all OpenMedia campaigns in which crowd-sourcing was used, nor did I investigate the effects of participation on those who participated. The key aim of gathering these data was to present evidence of how OpenMedia's approach to public engage-ment offers a compelling way to think about how deliberation can be used in new ways to influence public policy in the era of neoliberalism. My hope is that this analysis will serve as an instructive case of how unconventional forms of engagement are being used as a type of coun-terdemocracy to intervene in policy discourse.

Crowdsourcing is a media-based engagement process centred on the idea that knowledge is most accurate when it consists of inputs from a distributed population. A crowdsourcing process often manifests as an open call to participate in a task online by sharing an opinion or submitting information, knowledge, or talent.[37] Over the past decade, improved communications technologies have enabled crowdsourc-ing to act as a method of harnessing collective intelligence in public engagement processes ranging from urban planning[38] to open source journalism,[39] and, more recently, public policy development.[40]

OpenMedia has produced five crowdsourced policy recommenda-tions that each address a key communications policy issue: "Canada's Privacy Plan" (government surveillance); "Time for an Upgrade" (wireless spectrum); "Casting an Open Net" (net neutrality); "Our Digital Future" (copyright); and "Reimagine CBC" (public media). OpenMedia's process for producing crowdsourced policy recommen-dation reports is multiphased, and can last anywhere from six to eight-een months. It can include some combination of targeted in-person consultations with specific stakeholder groups; broad online actions, where participants can indicate their support for a specific idea or prin-ciple or produce media in support of an idea; a "drag and drop" inter-active survey, where participants answer questions about their views on the policy; and "internet town halls," where participants can submit questions and comments regarding the policy and discuss the policy with OpenMedia staff and policy experts.

Once significant data have been gathered, OpenMedia staff work with policy experts, scholars, and legal professionals to identify themes and core concerns. As a senior campaigner at OpenMedia remarked when describing the crowdsourced policy recommendation reports in an interview with the author, "We don't just come up with policy ourselves. First, we reach out to find out what the community thinks and wants at a high level. Then we work with policy experts to translate the high-level desires into a formal set of recommendations ... either in the form of a crowdsourced report or an official submission to the government."

This comment reflects how OpenMedia's crowdsourcing model operates as a process of two-way translation between the public and political institutions. The first translation is from policy language to clear, jargon-free language so the public can understand what is being decided. The second translation is from everyday language back to policy language so the recommendation can have resonance with the institution and have weight in official processes. As one senior staff member remarked, "the trick is to work with experts in the field to articulate [in clear language] what the big problems are, then to figure out how to translate what everyday people want into specific policy asks at the institutional level."

Example 1: "Time for an Upgrade"

The first example is the "Time for an Upgrade" report. The engagement process began in January 2012 when OpenMedia launched the "Stop the Squeeze" campaign to stop cellphone providers Bell, Rogers, and Telus from blocking the ability of independent competitors to acquire places on the wireless spectrum. OpenMedia argued that because the big three providers controlled the vast majority of the wireless market, blocking independent providers from the wireless spectrum auction would result in longer-term contracts, bad customer service, and new fees. This came at a time when Canadians were already paying some of the highest prices in the industrialized world for wireless services.[41]

The campaign encouraged public engagement by providing supporters with digital media tools – petitions, videos, posters, and viral share images – to pressure Prime Minister Stephen Harper and industry minister Christian Paradis to intervene. Over 65,000 Canadians signed the "Stop the Squeeze" petition, and in October 2012 the CRTC announced a public proceeding on national rules for wireless services. After the announcement, OpenMedia repurposed the thirteen-page official "notice of consultation" from the CRTC into a digital tool that enabled Canadians to share their "horror stories" of high wireless prices and poor service.[42] Over three thousand submissions were received, some of which consisted of multiple pages detailing mistreatment customers received from the Big Three.[43]

The submissions formed the basis of a presentation OpenMedia made to the CRTC at a public hearing in February 2013; the lead OpenMedia campaigner also offered live updates via social media during the hearing. The "horror stories" were then combined with advice from experts to create a crowdsourced report that reflected how the participants wanted to see the wireless market reformed.[44] In June 2013, the CRTC announced a new Code of Conduct that, despite its shortcomings, addressed complaints stressed in the campaign, including capping data roaming rates, shortening contracts, and making it easier to switch to a new provider.[45]

Example 2: Canada's Privacy Plan

The second example concerns the struggle to defeat two attempts made by the federal government to expand its cybersurveillance capabilities: Bill C-30 and Bill C-51. Bill C-30, commonly referred to as the Lawful Access Bill, was an attempt to expand the search and seizure, interception, surveillance, collection, and decryption capabilities of Canadian law enforcement. The primary goal was to remove legal and technical barriers inhibiting seamless access to information held in private internet and mobile accounts.[46] OpenMedia played a leadership role in the public outcry against C-30, which brought together numerous civil society organizations and thousands of individuals in the "Stop Online Spying" campaign. In their discussion of the campaign, Jonathan Obar and Leslie Shade describe how it created "a digitally mediated Fifth Estate" that reinvigorated the public as a watchdog of government accountability by drawing on the communicative power of online petitions, digital letters-to-the-editor, internet townhalls, films, volunteer-made videos, and powerful hashtag campaigns. As the authors argue, these efforts operated outside the framework of traditional civic engagement, drawing on three key strategies: (1) building an online community of networked individuals; (2) shaping pre-existing digital platforms to enable members of the public to contribute focused and pointed user-generated content; and (3) developing targeted content to be shared and distributed. Over the course of several months of mounting public pressure, the government eventually cancelled Bill-30, with justice minister Rob Nicholson remarking, "we've listened to the concerns of Canadians who have been very clear on this."[47] As Obar and Shade point out, however, this was not the result of government consultations, as there were no public hearings, formal calls for public comment, and or reports by Members of Parliament. Although traditional methods of public consultation were not pursued, a clear message of public dissent was advanced by leveraging practices of social and digital media.[48]

Following the defeat of Bill-30, the Conservative government brought forward Bill C-51 in 2015, which extended the measures put forward in

Bill-30 and would give government institutions unprecedented powers to monitor and profile Canadians through the internet. Again, there was widespread opposition to the bill, with a petition of more 300,000 signatures and over fifty protest events in cities across Canada.[49] As a result of these and other actions, Bill C-51 became a central issue of the 2015 federal election, with the Liberals campaigning on a promise to reform the proposed legislation if elected.[50]

Leading up to the election, OpenMedia produced "Canada's Privacy Plan," a comprehensive policy plan that was crowdsourced from the comments and survey responses of over 125,000 Canadians who responded to questions such as: What is most important to you when it comes to privacy? What will it take to tackle our privacy deficit? What safeguards do you think are necessary to protect our human rights in a digital age?[51]

One senior staff member describes the impetus for the report: "When you're faced with a really hostile government that's pushing very extreme surveillance legislation and [that] is not interested in hearing from citizens, it really puts an onus on us as an organization to learn from crowdsourcing what it is that citizens want. We need to make sure that the process actually distils what exactly the people want the government to do rather than just say 'no' ... the trick is to work with experts to translate what people want into policy language to argue for institutional change."

Shortly after the Liberals won the election, the government began public consultations on Bill C-51 reforms. However, the government-led online consultation process was marred with concerns over bias and one-sided language,[52] and the in-person consultations were described by some as "utterly demoralizing."[53] In response, OpenMedia and Canadian internet Policy and Public Interest Clinic launched a crowdsourcing tool that translated the survey into accessible language and fed participants' answers into the official government consultation online survey. Over 15,000 of the 50,000 submissions to the government survey were made using the tool provided by OpenMedia.[54]

After the consultation process was over, the government initially refused to make the consultation submissions public, instead promising a "summary" of results. An open letter was published in the online publication *National Observer* from over thirty civil society organizations and experts urging the government to release the results of the consultation; eventually it did so. Not trusting the government to analyse the public feedback in good faith, OpenMedia built another online tool that enabled the public to assess the consultation submissions. Funded by grassroots donations, the tool asked each participant to read submissions and answer a few simple questions about them. This crowdsourced analysis showed that the vast majority of submissions that mentioned Bill C-51 called for the repeal of the bill, and expressed strong support for the protection of privacy and deep concern about the sharing of personal information with Canadian agencies or foreign governments. OpenMedia then used this analysis as evidence to increase pressure on the government to adopt the policy positions put forward in the crowdsourced "Canada's Privacy Plan."

Policy Hacking + Participatory Politics

"Policy hacking" describes a mode of contemporary activism based on the "citizen-based DIY creation of concrete policy alternatives."[55] It connects the dynamics of "policy windows" and "consensus mobilization"[56] with a do-it-yourself ethos that improves, upgrades, and repackages policy. Just as computer hackers change and upgrade code, so policy hackers revise, upgrade, and change policies to better serve the public interest. In his discussion of policy hacking, Arne Hintz points out that, typically, policy interventions carried out by traditional non-governmental organizations are too limited in their responses to policy windows and policy challenges because of the limited range of actors involved in policy advocacy, and the limited range of tactics and approaches used. As a result, "new informal connections, loose collaborations, and temporary alliances among engaged individuals ... have had little opportunity to be involved in the process, even though they are increasingly recognized as complementing 'organized civil society.'"[57]

By putting the public at the centre of proposing and developing policy changes, policy hacking challenges us to think differently about how to establish new norms of public engagement that allow for more robust and participatory engagement with policy making. This shift could have profound implications. As Hintz describes, policy hacking is a "prefigurative action that interacts with the policy environment neither inside nor outside institutional or governmental processes, but beyond those processes by creating alternatives to hegemonic structures and procedures and by adopting a tactical repertoire of circumvention."[58] What is unique about OpenMedia's approach, and what differentiates its activities from Hintz's original conception of policy hacking, is that it combines policy hacking with *participatory politics* to facilitate widespread engagement by significantly lowering the barriers to participation. The concept of participatory politics has been used by contemporary media researchers to designate digitally mediated forms of political engagement that are not guided by formal institutions and that encompass a wide range of mediated activities, including video production, web design, mobile apps, digital activism, and peer production.[59] Rather than engaging only a small group of well-informed citizens and experts, OpenMedia's approach to policy hacking uses participatory politics to open the process to as many people as possible through multiple entry points that help citizens speak out strategically against proposed legislation, circulate and analyse information related to policy issues, and produce original content that contributes to campaigns. Participation can range from writing a comment on social media, filling out a survey, creating an image or a video, telling the participant's story, or proposing a fully fleshed out policy idea. OpenMedia then uses these diverse forms of engagement to build people power behind a position and develop crowdsourced policy plans in collaboration with experts.

Policy Hacking as Deliberative Counterdemocracy

In recent decades, the theory and practice of deliberative democracy has gained traction as a way to enable publics to authorize and contribute to policy decisions. Although representative democracies traditionally have practised *elitist deliberative democracy* through decision-making bodies such as legislatures and courts, forms of *populist deliberative democracy* – such as citizens' assemblies, deliberative polling, and participatory budgeting – increasingly have been employed to facilitate citizen engagement with policy initiatives. In Canada and other Western democracies, populist deliberative approaches have been used in a diversity of policy areas from education, policing, and urban planning to resource management, waste management, language protection, and climate change adaptation.[60] Indeed, the hope of these procedures is that they work to educate and empower individuals by providing opportunities for direct contribution to policy making. However, as Genevieve Fuji Johnson points out in her detailed study of deliberative processes in Canada, deliberative democracy initiatives often serve to "uphold dominant interest, pre-existing power structures, hierarchical subcultures and elites approaches to policy."[61] As she describes, deliberative procedures "may have been empowering for participants in moments when they were discussing issues, exchanging reasons, and coming to conclusions, and they may have appeared empowering in providing institutionalized opportunities to contribute to collective decision-making, but they turned out to be non-empowering in terms of outcomes that did not significantly challenge the status quo approach to formulating and implementing policy."[62] Indeed, other sceptics argue that governments can use deliberative forms of participation as "pseudoparticipation" – a form of "window dressing" that disguises forgone policy conclusions.[63] These forms of *faux* participation do not meet the real demand for engagement among concerned publics, but rather operate to create the illusion of meaningful participation and therefore risk becoming processes that undermine, rather than strengthen, democracy.

As discussed earlier, unaccountable interests have a disproportionate influence over telecommunications policy decisions in Canada. As such, the values and practices of deliberative democracy, on their own, are not adequate to address the democratic inequality inherent in neoliberalism. As Chantal Mouffe points out, "in their attempt to reconcile the liberal tradition with the democratic one, deliberative democrats tend to erase the tensions that exist between liberalism and democracy and they are therefore unable to come to terms with the conflictual nature of democratic politics."[64] To strengthen the efficacy of and build trust in democratic institutions, processes of deliberative democracy must be accompanied by a "countervailing power"[65] that demands more consequential and transparent public engagement. Indeed, political deliberation without political struggle is effectively limited to established institutions and processes that embody and secure prevailing distributions of power and resources.[66] As such, deliberative democracy and collective action should not be positioned as conflicting forms of public engagement, with cooperative discussion on the one hand and adversarial protest and negotiation on the other.[67] Rather, they should be understood as two parts of the same process, two sides of the same coin. The most important innovations in deliberative democracy, such as citizens' assemblies, participatory budgeting, and even democracy itself, stem from populist demands for greater inclusiveness in public decision making.[68] Therefore, deliberative democracy initiatives ought simultaneously to engage the public in policy deliberation *and* facilitate collective action that holds public authorities accountable for the outputs of participation.

The OpenMedia case demonstrates how critical actors are key to innovation in deliberative democracy and how participatory politics can build power behind deliberative processes. Although OpenMedia does appear to have had some influence on the outcome of several internet-related policy issues, I do not claim causality between OpenMedia's campaigns and policy decisions. It is extremely difficult to determine the impact of one group's actions on public policy processes, and other contextual factors have an influence on these outcomes. Nor am I claiming that counterdemocracy is without problems. Indeed, counterdemocracy risks its own kind of elitism in that it can appeal to a certain type of citizen with a specific set of interests. There are also valid questions as to whom OpenMedia represents and with what legitimacy. Although OpenMedia has over 600,000 people in its online community, it cannot claim to represent all Canadians. My argument, rather, is that counterdemocracy and participatory politics (or *participatory counter-democracy*) provide a critical standard against which we might measure current public engagement practices.

The concept of counterdemocracy was developed by Pierre Rosanvallon to describe how democracy has been changing (and in some respects improving), in ways that do not involve electoral competition between political parties or the formation of a government by the winners. He traces manifestations of counterdemocracy as far back as ancient Greece, but argues that it is the contemporary erosion of trust in politics that makes the need for counterdemocracy pressing. By counterdemocracy, I do not mean the opposite of democracy, but rather a form of democracy that reinforces the usual electoral democracy as a kind of buttress, a democracy of indirect powers disseminated throughout society – in other words, a durable democracy of distrust, which complements the episodic democracy of the usual electoral representative system. Thus counterdemocracy is part of a larger system that also includes legal democratic institutions. It seeks to complement those institutions and extend their influence – to shore them up.[69]

As an approach to political engagement, counterdemocracy does not try to avoid the politics of distrust, but instead to organize it as a positive force for improving democracy. Importantly, Rosanvallon sees counterdemocracy as a new form of political engagement that offers productive strategies for handling distrust and improving existing institutionalized forms of political participation. In Canada, counterdemocracy has emerged most consistently in the Indigenous sovereignty movement, which has combined the distrust of government decisions with direct action and strategic use of legal precedents to demand the fulfilment of treaty promises and stronger recognition of Indigenous land rights.[70] This form of counterdemocracy has been remarkably effective in allowing disenfranchised people to force powerful settler democracies to reckon with Indigenous demands, and thereby open a new space for post-colonial politics.[71]

OpenMedia's facilitation of participatory counterdemocracy lays bare the reality that, within the context of neoliberalism, participation is a site of democratic struggle between minimalist and maximalist forms of public engagement. Indeed, public policy decisions pivot precisely on power relations, and the struggle over what type of public participation will inform policy making is a struggle over power. Nico Carpentier[72] explains how minimalist forms of participation are congruent with elite models of democracy that tend to emphasize representation, where the role of citizens is largely limited to the selection of their representatives. Maximalist forms of participation are consistent with participatory models of democracy, and underscore more extensive forms of participation. Carpentier argues that the overemphasis on the minimalist forms of electoral representative democracy is ideological and reinforces depoliticized versions of participation. The hegemonic position of representative democracy means that alternatives are often deemed as either impractical or undesirable, even while digital communication makes these approaches increasingly viable. Contrary to approaches that centre bureaucrats and elected representatives as the primary sources of democratic legitimacy in the policy-making process, participatory counterdemocracy positions the public as the most legitimate and qualified actor to determine public policy. By positioning the public as the protagonist in the empowering roles of storyteller (example 1) and watchdog (example 2), we can observe how OpenMedia's practice of participatory counterdemocracy functions as a form of what Andrew Feenberg calls "democratic rationalization,"[73] where emergent political practices use technology in ways not envisaged within the rationality of political and technological elites.

On its own, digital engagement or innovations in political participation are not inherently good, democratic, or progressive; they are ambivalent and contingent, their power derived from the ends served in any given context.[74] Indeed, to live in a neoliberal society is to confront the "participation paradox" where new forms of participation are immensely promising and, simultaneously, "knit to the accumulation of capital through forms of social production in which immaterial labour, communication, and affect are central."[75] What remains to be seen, however, is the extent to which emerging publics are able to use participatory politics in critical ways that counter depoliticization and mitigate the structural inequalities associated with neoliberalism.

Conclusion

At a time when information communications technology increasingly mediates social, political, cultural, and economic life, telecommunications policy is arguably one of the most important public policy areas in Canadian society. As such, addressing the democratic deficit of telecommunications policy is essential for moving towards policy justice and addressing the wider erosion of democracy across political institutions. It also reminds us that the internet as we know it is partly a result of policies pursued by various stakeholders with specific interests – and thus could be politically altered to reflect a different set of interests.[76] In a context of cynicism, distrust, and retreat from political institutions, OpenMedia's practice of participatory counterdemocracy demonstrates how public engagement can be put at the centre of the struggle to democratize telecommunications policy making.

We are currently in the midst of a paradigm shift in telecommunications policy. In the United States, the marked turn towards the more authoritarian tendencies of the Trump administration and recent regulatory changes to repeal net neutrality threaten the core of democracy – citizens' ability to have the information they need to hold their leaders accountable and to affect the decisions that shape their lives. In Canada, promises by the federal government to "review and modernize" the Broadcasting Act and Telecommunications Act means that the laws governing television, telecommunications, and the internet will soon be overhauled.[77] This case study offers a number of important insights for those interested in the praxis of public engagement with public policy. The first is the need for public engagement praxis to confront the reality that existing political institutions are rooted in systems that often perpetuate political inequality by favouring industry voices over those of the public. Actors that lead processes of deliberative democracy ought to be willing to leverage counterdemocracy in order to confront practices of inadequate public engagement and build power behind policy proposals that are supported by widespread digital participation. Second, further attention needs to be paid to how digital technology can be used to facilitate, aggregate, and translate informal and unconventional forms of deliberation by large and dispersed populations into coherent and workable policy alternatives. Ultimately, this case study supports the argument that too little attention has been paid to examining the initiatives, ideas, and techniques involved in leveraging the conditions of neoliberalism in order to go beyond it.[78] In a political environment increasingly marked by the individualization of choice, the dissipation of established solidarities, and an entrepreneurial mode of engagement,[79] we need to understand better how personalized, network-based communications can be leveraged to influence public policy and, ultimately, to rethink how power is leveraged within neoliberal societies.

Discussion Questions

1 How should the success of crowdsourced policy efforts be measured – by the volume of participation, the diversity or quality of participation, or the quality of outcome?
2 How can we define "quality," "access," and "public interest" in the context new forms of participation with policy making?
3 Given the character of the media landscape, how do we situate the role of participatory media in public engagement with policy making?

NOTES

1 David Harvey, *A Brief History of Neoliberalism* (Oxford: Oxford University Press, 2007).
2 Colin Hay, *Why We Hate Politics* (Cambridge: Polity Press, 2007); Mark Fisher, *Capitalist Realism: Is There No Alternative?* (Winchester, UK: O Books, 2009); John Gray, *False Dawn: The Delusions of Global Capitalism* (London: Granta Books, 2015).
3 Donatella Della Porta, "Communication in Movement: Social Movements as Agents of Participatory Democracy," *Information, Communication & Society* 14, no. 6 (2011): 800–19; Russell J. Dalton, *The Good Citizen: How a Younger Generation Is Reshaping American Politics* (Thousand Oaks, CA: SAGE, 2008); Pippa Norris, *Democratic Phoenix: Reinventing Political Activism* (Cambridge: Cambridge University Press, 2002); Howard Ramos and Kathleen Rodgers, eds. *Protest and Politics: The Promise of Social Movement Societies* (Vancouver: UBC Press, 2015).
4 Arne Hintz, "Policy Hacking: Citizen-based Policymaking and Media Reform," in *Strategies for Media Reform*, ed. Des Freedman et al. (New York: Fordham University Press, 2016), 223–38.
5 Pierre Rosanvallon, *Counter-Democracy: Politics in an Age of Distrust*, trans. Arthur Goldhammer (Cambridge: Cambridge University Press, 2008).
6 Daniel Jones Stedman, *Masters of the Universe: Hayek, Friedman, and the Birth of Neoliberal Politics*, updated ed. (Princeton, NJ: Princeton University Press, 2014), 2.
7 David M. Kotz, "Neoliberalism, Globalization, Financialization: Understanding Post-1980 Capitalism" (University of Massachusetts, Department of Economics, 2015), online at https://www.umass.edu/economics/sites/default/files/Kotz.pdf.
8 Nick Couldry, *Why Voice Matters: Culture and Politics after Neoliberalism* (Thousand Oaks, CA: SAGE, 2010), 53.
9 Harvey, *Brief History of Neoliberalism*.

10 Thomas Biebricher, "Neoliberalism and Democracy," *Constellations* 22, no. 2 (2015): 255–66.

11 Thomas Frank, *One Market under God: Extreme Capitalism, Market Populism, and the End of Economic Democracy* (Toronto: Anchor Canada, 2001).

12 Colin Crouch, *Post-Democracy* (Cambridge: Polity Press, 2004), 70.

13 Claudia Ritzi, "Neoliberal Hegemony and the Post-Democratization of the Public Sphere: An Analytical Framework to Evaluate the Democratic Quality of Political Discourse," *IC Revista Científica de Información y Comunicación* 11 (2015): 167–87.

14 Stephen McBride and Heather Whiteside, *Private Affluence, Public Austerity: Economic Crisis and Democratic Malaise in Canada* (Black Point, NS: Fernwood, 2011).

15 Darin Barney, *Communication Technology* (Vancouver: UBC Press, 2011), 42.

16 Tamara Shepherd, Gregory Taylor, and Catherine Middleton, "A Tale of Two Regulators: Telecom Policy Participation in Canada," *Journal of Information Policy* 4 (2014): 1–22; Marc Raboy, "The Role of Public Consultation in Shaping the Canadian Broadcasting System," *Canadian Journal of Political Science* 28, no. 3 (1995): 455–77.

17 Canadian Radio-television and Telecommunications Commission, "Our Mandate, Mission and What We Do" (Ottawa, 11 May 2018), online at https://crtc.gc.ca/eng/acrtc/acrtc.htm.

18 Shepherd, Taylor, and Middleton, "Tale of Two Regulators."

19 Leslie Regan Shade, "Media Reform in the United States and Canada: Activism and Advocacy for Media Policies in the Public Interest," in *The Handbook of Global Media and Communication Policy*, ed. Robin Mansell and Marc Raboy (New York: John Wiley, 2011), 147–65; Shepherd, Taylor, and Middleton, "Tale of Two Regulators."

20 David Skinner and Kathleen Cross, "Media Activism in Canada: The Cases of Media Democracy Day, OpenMedia, and ReImagine CBC," in Freedman et al., *Strategies for Media Reform*, 167–81.

21 Shade, "Media Reform in the United States and Canada," 157.

22 Shepherd, Taylor, and Middleton, "Tale of Two Regulators," 7.

23 Ibid., 6.

24 Barney, *Communication Technology*, 39.

25 Ibid., 64.

26 Marita Moll and Leslie Regan Shade, *For Sale to the Highest Bidder: Telecom Policy in Canada* (Ottawa: Canadian Centre for Policy Alternatives, 2008).

27 Dwyane Winseck, "Poster: Mapping Canada's Top Telecoms, Internet and Media Companies by Revenue and Market Share (2016)," Canadian Media Concentration Research Project, 22 November 2016, online at https://www.cmcrp.org/poster-2016-mapping-canadas-top-telecoms-internet-media-companies-by-revenue-and-market-share/, accessed 6 January 2018.

28 Vanda Rideout, *Continentalizing Canadian Telecommunications: The Politics of Regulatory Reform* (Montreal; Kingston, ON: McGill-Queen's University Press, 2003), 44.

29 Jan Van Cuilenburg and Denis McQuail, "Media Policy Paradigm Shifts: Towards a New Communications Policy Paradigm," *European Journal of Communication* 18, no. 2 (2003): 200.

30 Robert Hackett and William Carroll, *Remaking Media: The Struggle to Democratize Public Communication* (New York: Routledge, 2006).

31 Des Freedman, and Jonathan Obar, "Media Reform: An Overview," in Freedman et al., *Strategies for Media Reform*, 3–18.

32 Skinner and Cross, "Media Activism in Canada."

33 Ibid.

34 David Skinner, Robert Hackett, and Stuart Poyntz, "Media Activism and the Academy, Three Cases: Media Democracy Day, Open Media, and Newswatch Canada," *Studies in Social Justice* 9, no. 1 (2015): 86–101; Kate Milberry, "Freeing the Net: On-line Mobilizations in Defence of Democracy," in *Alternative Media in Canada*, ed. Kirsten Kozolanka, Patricia Mazepa, and David Skinner (Vancouver: UBC Press, 2010), 226–43.

35 Nicholas Charney, "The Future of Documentary Heritage," GovCamp Canada, 8 June 2011.

36 Skinner and Cross, "Media Activism in Canada."

37 Daren C. Brabham, "Crowdsourcing as a Model for Problem Solving: An Introduction and Cases," *Convergence* 14, no. 1 (2008): 75–90; Jeff Howe, *Crowdsourcing: How the Power of the Crowd Is Driving the Future of Business* (New York: Random House, 2008).

38 Howe, *Crowdsourcing*, 242–62.

39 Katherine Fink and Christopher W. Anderson, "Data Journalism in the United States: Beyond the "Usual Suspects," *Journalism Studies* 16, no. 4 (2015): 467–81.

40 Tanja Aitamurto, "Crowdsourcing for Democracy: A New Era in Policy-Making" (Helsinki: Parliament of Finland, Committee for the Future, 2015).

41 "Confirmed: Canadians pay some of the highest prices for some of the worst telecom service in the world," *OpenMedia*, 16 July 2013, online at https://openmedia.org/article/item/confirmed-canadians-pay-some -highest-prices-some-worst-telecom-service-industrialized-world, accessed 20 December 2017.

42 Gillian Shaw, "Cell phone horror stories: OpenMedia.ca report," *Vancouver Sun*, 7 March 2013, online at https://vancouversun.com/news/staff-blogs /cell-phone-horror-stories-openmedia-ca-report, accessed 20 December 2017; "Your cell phone horror stories," *OpenMedia*, 19 October 2012, online

at https://openmedia.org/en/your-cell-phone-horror-stories, accessed 23 November 2017.

43 David Christopher, "OpenMedia: Working toward an Open Connected Future," in Freedman et al., *Strategies for Media Reform*, 115–207.

44 "Your cell phone horror stories," *OpenMedia*; "Time for an upgrade: Demanding choice for Canada's cell phone market," *OpenMedia*, 9 November 2012, online at https://openmedia.org/article/item/telling-your-cell-phone -horror-stories, accessed 23 November 2017.

45 Gillian Shaw, "CRTC axes three-year contracts in new wireless code of con- duct," *Vancouver Sun*, 4 June 2013, online at http://www.vancouversun .com/news/crtc+axes+three+year+contracts+wireless+code+conduct +with+video/8470344/story.html, accessed 20 December 2017.

46 Jonathan Obar and Leslie Regan Shade, "Activating the Fifth Estate: Bill C-30 and the Digitally-Mediated Public Watchdog," in Freedman et al., *Strategies for Media Reform*, 39–57.

47 Laura Payton, "Government killing online surveillance bill," *CBC News*, 11 February 2013, online at https://www.cbc.ca/news/politics/government -killing-online-surveillance-bill-1.1336384. accessed 15 December 2017.

48 Obar and Shade, "Activating the Fifth Estate."

49 Katie O'Malley, "Bill C-1 'Day of Action' protests denounce new policing powers," *CBC News*, 14 March 2015, online at https://www.cbc.ca/news /politics/bill-c-51-day-of-action-protests-denounce-new-policing-powers -1.2994226., accessed 18 December 2017.

50 Chris Hall, "Bill C-51: Political battle lines drawn over anti-terror bill as election nears," *CBC News*, 19 February 2015, online at https://www.cbc .ca/news/politics/bill-c-51-political-battle-lines-drawn-over-anti-terror -bill-as-election-nears-1.2962764, accessed 1 December 2017.

51 OpenMedia, "Canada's Privacy Plan: A Crowdsourced Agenda for Tackling Canada's Privacy Deficit" (2015), online at https://www.scribd.com /document/266021264/Open-Media-Canada-s-Privacy-Plan-A -Crowdsourced-Agenda-for-Tackling-Canada-s-Privacy-Deficit., accessed 23 November 2017.

52 Justin Ling, "National Security Consultation: Leading Questions?" *National Magazine*, September 2016; idem, "Ottawa drafted plans to allow war- rantless access of your data while still 'consulting' the public," *Vice News Canada*, 24 March 2017, online at https://www.vice.com/en_ca/article /evaw3z/ottawa-began-writing-plans-to-allow-warrantless-access-of -canadians-data-while-they-were-still-consulting-with-the-public., accessed 16 December 2017.

53 Jordan Pearson, "Toronto's public hearing on Bill C-51 was utterly demor- alizing," *Vice*, 20 October 2016, online at https://www.vice.com/en_us

/article/ezpkd4/torontos-public-hearing-on-bill-c-51-was-utterly
-demoralizing, accessed 15 December 2017.

54 Meghan Sali, "We're calling for transparency on Bill C-51," *OpenMedia*,
15 December 2016, online at https://openmedia.org/article/item/were
-calling-transparency-bill-c-51, accessed 16 December 2017.

55 Hintz, "Policy Hacking," 234.

56 Sanjeev Khagram, James V. Riker, and Kathryn Sikkink, "From Santiago to
Seattle: Transnational Advocacy Groups Restructuring World Politics," in
*Restructuring World Politics: Transnational Social Movements, Networks, and
Norms*, ed. Sanjeev Khagram, James V. Riker, and Kathryn Sikkink (Minne-
apolis: University of Minnesota Press, 2002), 11.

57 Hintz, "Policy Hacking," 226.

58 Ibid., 227; Arne Hintz and Stefania Milan, "Media Activists and the Commu-
nication Policy Process," in *Encyclopaedia of Social Movement Media*, ed. John
D. Downing (Thousand Oaks, CA: SAGE, 2010), 317–19; Milan, Stefania,
Social movements and their technologies: Wiring social change, Springer, 2013.

59 Cathy J. Cohen and Joseph Kahne, *Participatory Politics: New Media and
Youth Political Action* (Oakland, CA: YPP Research Network, 31 May 2012),
online at https://ypp.dmlcentral.net/publications/107.html.

60 Genevieve Fuji Johnson, *Democratic Illusion: Deliberative Democracy in
Canadian Public Policy* (Toronto: University of Toronto Press, 2015), 6.

61 Ibid., 5.

62 Ibid.

63 Sidney Verba, *Small Groups and Political Behavior: A Study of Leadership*
(Princeton, NJ: Princeton University Press, 2015).

64 Chantal Mouffe, "Deliberative Democracy or Agonistic Pluralism," IHS
Political Science Series Working Paper 72 (Vienna: Institute for Advanced
Studies, December 2000), online at http://irihs.ihs.ac.at/1312/1/pw_72
.pdf, accessed 11 January 2018.

65 Archon Fung and Erik Olin Wright, "Countervailing Power in Empowered
Participatory Governance," in *Deepening Democracy: Institutional Innova-
tions in Empowered Participatory Governance*, ed. Archon Fung and Erik Olin
Wright (London: Verso, 2003), 259–80.

66 Darin Barney, "Politics and Emerging Media: The Revenge of Publicity,"
Global Media Journal 1, no. 1 (2008): 89.

67 Mouffe, "Deliberative Democracy or Agonistic Pluralism"; Iris Marion
Young, "Activist Challenges to Deliberative Democracy," *Political theory* 29,
no. 5 (2001): 670–90.

68 Julien Talpin, "Democratic Innovations," in *The Oxford Handbook of Social
Movements*, ed. Donatella della Porta and Mario Diani (Oxford: Oxford
University Press, 2015), 781–92.

69 Rosanvallon and Goldhammer, *Counter-democracy*, 8.

70 For instance, the Ipperwash standoff in 1995; the 2006 reclamation of land by activists from Six Nations Reserve slated to be used for a suburban housing development near Caledonia, Ontario; and the withdrawal of Gitxsan and Wet'suwet'en people from their treaty negotiations and the occupation of treaty offices in response to deals relating to the Enbridge pipeline project. For an overview see Adam J. Barker, "'A direct act of re-surgence, a direct act of sovereignty': Reflections on Idle No More, Indigenous Activism, and Canadian Settler Colonialism," *Globalizations* 12, no. 1 (2015): 43–65.

71 Miranda Johnson, *The Land Is Our History: Indigeneity, Law, and the Settler State* (New York: Oxford University Press, 2016).

72 Nico Carpentier, *Media and Participation: A Site of Ideological-Democratic Struggle* (Bristol: Intellect Books, 2011), 17.

73 Andrew Feenberg, "Critical Theory of Communication Technology: Introduction to the Special Section," *Information Society* 25, no. 2 (2009): 77–83.

74 Darin Barney, "Excuse us if we don't give a fuck: The (Anti-) Political Career of Participation," *Jeunesse: Young People, Texts, Cultures* 2, no. 2 (2010): 143.

75 Stuart R. Poyntz, "The Participation Paradox, or Agency and Sociality in Contemporary Youth Cultures," *Jeunesse: Young People, Texts, Cultures* 2, no. 2 (2010): 114.

76 Stephen Coleman and Jay G. Blumler, *The internet and Democratic Citizenship: Theory, Practice and Policy* (Cambridge: Cambridge University Press, 2009); Andrew Feenberg and Norm Friesen, eds., *(Re) Inventing the internet* (Berlin: Springer Science+Business Media, 2012).

77 Greg O'Brian, "Budget 2017: Review of Broadcasting Act, Telecommunications Act is on the way," *CARTT.ca*, 23 March 2017, online at https://cartt.ca/budget-2017-review-of-broadcasting-act-telecommunications-act-is-on-the-way/, accessed 15 January 2018.

78 Wendy Larner, "The Limits of Post-Politics: Rethinking Radical Social Enterprise," in *The Post-Political and Its Discontents: Spaces of Depoliticisation, Spectres of Radical Politics*, ed. Japhy Wilson and Erik Swyngedouw (Edinburgh: Edinburgh University Press, 2014), 189–207.

79 W. Lance Bennett and Alexandra Segerberg, "The Logic of Connective Action: Digital Media and the Personalization of Contentious Politics," *Information, Communication & Society* 15, no. 5 (2012): 739–68; Bruce Bimber, Cynthia Stohl, and Andrew J. Flanagin, "Technological Change and the Shifting Nature of Political Organization," in *Routledge Handbook of internet Politics*, ed. Andrew Chadwick and Philip N. Howard (Abingdon, UK: Routledge, 2009), 72–85.

KEY RESOURCES

Allen, Danielle, and Jennifer S. Light, eds. *From Voice to Influence: Understanding Citizenship in a Digital Age.* Chicago: University of Chicago Press, 2015.
Barney, Darin. *Communication Technology.* Vancouver: UBC Press, 2011.
Dahlgren, Peter. *The Political Web: Media, Participation and Alternative Democracy.* Basingstoke, UK: Palgrave Macmillan, 2013.
OpenMedia. "OpenMedia's Crowdsourcing Principles." n.d. Online at https://openmedia.org/article/item/crowdsource.

8 Engaging the "Heart and Mind": Building Community Capacity for Culturally Grounded Approaches to Substance Use on Post-Secondary Campuses

CATRIONA REMOCKER, TIM DYCK, AND DAN REIST

Introduction

Policy responses to psychoactive substance use have become increasingly contentious across various societies and communities. The Canadian campus context is no exception. Academics and student groups are among those calling for change at national, municipal, and institutional levels. This chapter discusses one regional attempt to incorporate deliberative democratic approaches to addressing the challenges around developing appropriate substance use policies in the post-secondary setting.

Evidence, including feedback from members of campus communities, suggests that policies at post-secondary institutions are often inattentive to the complexities of substance use and too frequently endorse overly simplistic and blunt approaches to managing use.[1] This can result in policies that are, at best, ineffectual and, at worst, detrimental to the health and welfare of community members. For instance, in most cases, campus policies neglect to account for the notion that substance use is both an individual and collective phenomenon that includes the potential for harms and for significant social benefits.[2] Further, post-secondary institutions typically underappreciate the elemental role that ongoing and intensive engagement can play in creating nuanced and thoughtful policies that reflect the democratic will of the collective.

Compounding the issue, post-secondary campus communities also face special challenges when it comes to policy engagement around divisive issues such as substance use. For example, post-secondary institutions generally embody a conventional hierarchical and divisional structure that often results in significant "silo effects."[3] These silo effects are often reinforced by a competitive organizational culture that lacks the capacity for the information sharing essential to community ownership and integration.[4] Further, the transient nature of the campus community – with ongoing inflows and outflows of students, faculty, staff, and senior-level administration – can create complications for ensuring that policies reflect the will of the current collective, maintain stability, and still not become relics of past thinking and outdated organizational processes. Finally, post-secondary institutions must balance the political tensions involved in being recipients of public funding while remaining attentive to educational ideals and mandates.[5] These structures and tensions often result in policies that are made by, and reflect the motivations of, some individuals and groups within the organization, without input from those who have to live with the repercussions of those policies. This, in turn, can lead to significant gaps between the institutional policies and actual practices in the campus community.

In 2012, the British Columbia Ministry of Health, impressed with the direction and potential of an existing initiative in the province's post-secondary domain, granted special funding to stewards of the Healthy Minds | Healthy Campuses initiative to enhance their efforts to promote healthier relationships with substances. The supported project, called *Changing the Culture of Substance Use*, aimed to build capacity in and between campuses to develop sustained and appropriate responses to the challenges around substance use, including sounder policy approaches.

This chapter, authored by members of the project's support team, reflects on the theoretical underpinnings of the project, and – in the spirit of the project's emphasis on phenomenology and embodiment – offers an accompanying first-hand account of our experience of trying to put that theory into practice with our campus colleagues from participating institutions. The concepts of phenomenology and embodiment speak to the co-penetration between subject and world.[6] We are all part of the cultures in which we live and through which we experience the world. Yet those cultures are themselves shaped by our interconnectedness with one another and with the objects of our world. After exploring our theoretical grounding at some length in this chapter, we offer readers the opportunity to see inside the actors, as it were, as they experience being in the project as both subject and object. In addition, we provide some more descriptive summaries of processes and outcomes from the project to date. We invite readers to reflect on this perspective and story, and to contemplate its utility for their own settings, particularly for the possibilities it highlights for creating more participatory forms of policy development.

A Complex Confluence of Theory

The *Changing the Culture of Substance Use* project is conceptualized under, and buoyed up by, a complex confluence of theoretical streams, including socio-ecological health promotion, culture as being in the world, and deliberative dialogue. These streams originate in a variety of disciplines, but can all be seen as part of the broad humanistic tradition with its focus on understanding the meaning of the human condition. This grounding in the humanistic tradition harkens back to the very emergence of the university as a social institution, yet stands in contrast to current approaches to substance use policy on most campuses.

A Focus on Health Promotion

The vision of the Ottawa Charter on Health Promotion, drawing on the World Health Organization's ideal of health as more than simply the absence of disease, was, "enabling people to increase control over, and to improve, their health."[7] This vision is well summarized by Emory Cowen,[8] who suggests that "allocations of our energies and resources must go increasingly toward building wellness rather than toward struggling, however compassionately, to contain troubles." This was clearly understood by Jake Epp, Canada's minister of health at the time of the Charter, whose report documented the need to strategically foster public participation to help citizens "assert control over factors that affect their health" and to develop healthy public policy that supports self-care, mutual aid, and healthy environments.[9]

Unfortunately, health promotion efforts, at least in North America, have tended to focus on influencing individual lifestyle choices. This has resulted in a heavy dependence on social marketing strategies targeting selected potential adverse consequences of using substances. Any attention to influencing environmental factors has concentrated primarily on external controls that regulate choices in ways that maximize physically defined goods – for example, controlling price and access to alcohol with the intention of reducing injury and property damage.

The broader vision of health promotion calls on us to recognize the tension between the need for community and the importance of individual rights. This requires us to avoid overemphasizing the individual's freedom of choice while not embracing the determinism of the science of behaviour control.[10] This vision of health promotion offers a framework for a challenge facing post-secondary institutions today: how to influence student behaviour while respecting student independence. Ernest Boyer has argued that institutions of higher learning "should help students become independent, self-reliant human beings, yet they should also give priority to community ... To serve private priorities while neglecting social obligations is, ultimately, to undermine self-interest."[11] Health promotion, à la the Ottawa Charter, provides a framework for institutions to address the well-being of students that is not separate from their educational mandate.[12]

An Ecological Understanding

A focus on social ecology asks us to consider how the social system itself affects individuals and their behaviours. This is in sharp contrast to most efforts to address substance use on campus to date. Current policies and programs focus almost exclusively on changing individuals.[13] A socio-ecological understanding takes a much broader view of the campus community. In developing the socio-ecological model, Urie Bronfenbrenner[14] drew attention to multiple nested structures that affect individuals' development and well-being, from direct interpersonal relationships to complex interconnected processes. This directs attention well beyond individuals and their specific lifestyle choices related to health. This ecological approach requires consideration of an array of influencers that both shape and are shaped by the actions of individuals.

An emphasis on social ecology encourages a focus on structural interventions that "locate, often implicitly, the cause of public health problems in contextual or environmental factors that influence risk behavior ... rather than in characteristics of individuals who engage in risk behaviors."[15] This follows naturally from the Ottawa Charter's attention to the social determinants of health, which draw from Durkheim's insight into the relationship between social factors and health[16] or what others have termed "the fundamental causes,"[17] rather than the behavioural or proximate risk factors that are the focus of so much research and programming. Addressing these proximate causes alone does little, in the long term, to promote health. When it comes to substance use, Bruce Alexander's "rat park" experiments in the 1970s[18] demonstrated the importance of social ecology. He went on to document how drug use and its consequences among human populations are related to social factors. Just as Durkheim argued that suicide rates were linked to a lack of congruence between social integration and social regulation,[19] Alexander has argued that psychosocial dislocation is at the heart of the increases in all kinds of addiction. Ultimately, he links the growing epidemic of addiction to cultural factors in Western free market societies.[20]

In recommending an ecological approach, William Hansen points out that, among college-age adults, social factors are the best predictors of substance use. Furthermore, he suggests that within this theoretical perspective "variables like culture, traditions, rituals, interpersonal relationships (including power relationships), group value systems, and social norms" are of particular importance.[21] Richard Eckersley sees culture as "a system of meanings and symbols that shape how people see the world and their place in it and give meaning to personal and collective experience," and that this, in turn, has a powerful influence on health and well-being.[22] Edmund Leach, in his classic discussion of culture, acknowledges this influence, but also recognizes the influence of the individual on culture – that we are actors in a complex ecosystem of culture, society, and environment.[23]

Culture as Being in the World

This interconnection of actor and ecosystem underpins Heidegger's notion of being-in-the-world. Being-in-the-world involves a more immediate focus on being in the experience itself rather than some abstract articulation of the issues. As he points out, "hammering a nail" is not explained by thinking about ideal forms of "nail" and "hammer."[24] Merleau-Ponty helps us connect Heidegger's emphasis with the above discussion of social ecology or culture by drawing attention to our experience as that of a body immersed "in the world" or "intermingled with things."[25] Thus, attention to the embodied social experiences of pleasure, insecurity, and so forth is critical to understanding the social phenomena around substance use. The environment is far more than structural factors, but must encompass the full scope of subtle cultural elements that define the interconnectedness of individuals in the community. Focusing on the behaviours of the actor apart from the cultural realities makes no sense.

The definition of culture has long been a topic of debate. For our purposes, culture is seen as everything in human society that is socially rather than biologically transmitted. This includes the symbolic and learned aspects of human society, such as learned patterns of behaviour, patterns of thought and perception, belief systems, values, ideologies, myths, and language.[26] This social world is broadly constituted through systems of shared meanings, and influences the behaviour, including drug use behaviour, of individuals within cultural communities. Culture is constantly evolving, recreated, and reinterpreted. We often think of it as the result of shared traditional understandings, but increasingly it is influenced through the media.[27] Yet Jürgen Habermas, in his theory of communicative action, holds out the possibility that culture can still be based on a consensus achieved through reasoned discourse in the public sphere.[28] This suggests that, by raising intentionality and encouraging conversations among members of a community, we might affect the evolution of culture within that community.

It is also important to note that culture is not a single entity; rather, it functions at various nested levels from global and national through institutional and down to the group and individual.[29] Furthermore, the direction of influence is both top down (from the macro level to the micro) and bottom up (from the micro to the macro).[30] When considering the culture of substance use on campuses, we need to think far beyond the norms and practices on an individual campus. We need to consider the macro cultures that associate student life with alcohol, and even more broadly the global culture that emphasizes values related to individualism and consumerism. We should also look at the micro cultures of departments and groups on campus. The fact is that we are all part of various overlapping cultures, and many of us move back and forth between them in the course of our daily lives.

Cowen sets out two clusters of indicators of wellness that fit well with Alexander's psychological discussion of psychosocial integration and the phenomenologists' emphasis on the body bound up with the world. The first cluster consists of what Cowen calls "earthy indicators," and includes eating well, sleeping well, and doing one's mandated life tasks well. The second, more "ethereal" cluster includes having a sense of control over one's life, a feeling of purpose and belonging, and a basic satisfaction with oneself and one's existence.[31] Post-secondary institutions seeking to develop policy related to substance use would do well to pay attention to both aspects of being-in-the-world. Substance use is a phenomenon of campus life grounded in those matters of space and time that are often the focus of policy, but it is also deeply connected to matters of meaning and power. This has implications not only for the nature of the policies developed, but also for the policy-making process itself.

Dialogue within the Humanistic Tradition

All of the above streams of thought share a concern for understanding the meaning of the human condition. Dialogue, within this broad humanistic tradition, provides an opportunity for participants to listen to one another and, as a result, gain further understanding of the different perspectives that make up a community. A number of thinkers from a variety of disciplines have contributed to the theoretical foundation for dialogue.[32] Aristotle's musings on practical reason and ethics recognize the need for constructive conversations that enable decision making and that move people to act.[33] Buber saw in dialogue the possibility of opening a space between the subjective and objective domains of human experience within the attitude held by the word pair I-You.[34] Dialogue is a participatory encounter "in which we are not playing a game against each other, but with each other."[35] Through authentic communication, mutual curiosity, and the suspension of judgment, while critically examining presuppositions, the I-You seeks to imagine and realize the possibilities of life together.

Habermas's[36] theory of communicative action that underpins his discussion of deliberative democracy calls for widespread participation in public conversation to achieve good outcomes in public discourses.[37] This acknowledges the helpful input ordinary thoughtful citizens can offer from their varied experiences, rather than simply privileging the technical expertise of formally trained specialists and established elites.[38] There is no pretension that dialogue will yield full consensus and complete collaboration, but a realization that it can engender respect for divergent persuasions alongside an increased capacity for cooperative efforts. This is seen in Hans-Georg Gadamer's discussion of philosophical hermeneutics,[39] where he emphasizes the need for openness to others, with their differing insights – a receptivity that allows for the possibility of attaining expanded horizons of understanding. In exploring this openness that leads to possibility, Gadamer unpacks both the relationships in Buber's I-You word pair and the essence of questions in the Socratic dialogues to articulate the nature of authentic conversation. Fundamental to dialogue is an awareness of fallibility – as Gadamer puts it, "one must want to know, and that means knowing that one does not know."[40] Not only is dialogue essential to the realization of possibility, it "comprises our being-in-the-world and serves the ends of being and action."[41] Furthermore, dialogue is fundamental to identity formation and self-understanding. We view ourselves through interactions with how others communicate their recognition of us in our encounters with them.[42]

Dialogue, as the bridge between the I and the You (the self and the other), is grounded in caring. Caring requires treating the other with respect and engaging through empathy. Both of these concepts are complex and reflexive. When this complexity is not recognized, both notions are easily misused. To say that we respect someone is more than a declaration of non-infringement (a respect for rights); it is to stand in a relationship of mutual dignity, without which it can become alternately paternalism or hero worship.[43] Likewise, empathy might provide "a bridge between differences, the affective reason for engaging in democratic dialogue with the other."[44] But passive empathy, according to Megan Boler, deceives us into believing we can imagine the unimaginable. She contrasts passive empathy with "testimonial reading," in which "the reader accepts a commitment to rethink her own assumptions, and to confront the internal obstacles encountered as one's views are challenged."[45] Within the hermeneutic circle, to engage in dialogue is to remain open, and to submit to that which is beyond us, acknowledging the dignity of the other and accepting the possibility of being changed and of being challenged to bring about change.

Implications for Policy

We can think of policy as a normative course of action that a collective body typically follows to manage operations. How it emerges and is practised is of particular interest. In its least ethical forms, policy can be used by powerful elites to control populations. Policy, however, can also be used as a tool to empower a group's members to achieve shared ambitions. These different goals align with Michael Sandel's distinction between the "procedural republic" that prioritizes fair procedures over substantive ends and "civic republicanism" in which liberty depends on sharing in self-government.[46] Charles Taylor draws attention to related distinctions in his discussion of "morality" with its narrow focus on obligatory action versus "ethics" that considers broader questions about ways of being.[47] This is reflected in discussions about the "ethics of justice" versus the "ethics of caring,"[48] but both Taylor and Annatjie Botes caution us against thinking there is any one-sided resolution to these tensions.[49] We might argue that policy should create the conditions that help people work together to achieve the kind of community they want to live in together. Policy can only take on this more aspirational tenor when it nurtures a healthy public sphere[50] and ensures the engagement of the multiplicity of publics within the community.[51] However we conceive it, policy is a cultural phenomenon and a part of the complex phenomenological ecosystem.

All of the above commentators on dialogue acknowledge the difficulty of engaging in genuine dialogue, and these challenges are made even more difficult in the presence of significant power inequalities between the partners in the dialogue.[52] The means to successful dialogue are both social and personal. They involve practice in calling "into the space of questions" the assumptions embedded within one's own sense of identity and tradition, awareness of the multiple axes of diversity, engagement in deep listening, and the evolution of a new shared language.[53] Policies that emerge from a broad dialogic process are more likely to represent the community's consistent interpersonal expression of its commitments, and community members are more likely to be motivated to uphold those particular policies.

The post-secondary context is particularly befitting for practising healthy policy processes. The public role for institutions of advanced education is to equip members – faculty, staff, and students alike – to be strong citizens and leaders in enabling the other communities they will be a part of to be inclusive and cohesive, supportive and empowering, and skilled and engaged in the pursuit of collective well-being.[54] Modelling wholesome policy approaches on campus that actively involve members is a crucial component of fulfilling that social educational mandate.

Breaking In: Exploring Cultural Change

As a young, newly graduated public health student, when first asked to take on a facilitating role within the *Changing the Culture of Substance Use* project, I (Catriona) was both honoured and daunted. My educational background included a strong emphasis on the role of social "determinants" in shaping health, with a great deal of importance placed on the policies, programs, and practices by which public health aimed to mitigate health risks in the population and/or promote healthier communities. However, the goals of this project pushed my thinking into places it had never gone before. The premise of the project – that culture plays an important role in influencing how people relate to substances (and potentially how they experience benefits and/or harms from use) – challenged me to consider the less concrete ways in which communities come to shape their own health. A further challenge was considering what our role as public health professionals might be in affecting community cultures, with each community holding its own unique norms, traditions, and values, and, moreover, what it was possible to do *ethically* in guiding communities towards healthier culture.

A great deal of what influenced my thinking at the outset came from my knowledge of community-based participatory research (CBPR), an approach rooted in Kurt Lewin's[55] and Orlando Fals-Borda's[56] participatory action research and Paulo Freire's[57] critical pedagogy movement. CBPR asks a researcher to suspend the academic research agenda and simply engage in curiosity and relationship building with the community in trying to develop a community-generated research agenda. Although our project was not conducting research per se, we were using many of CBPR's tools, such as appreciative enquiry and dialogue, to better understand each community's culture. CBPR is notoriously slow and patient work; however, it is also an ethical way to ensure that the research conducted is of benefit to and empowers the community towards its own ways of knowing and practical ends.[58] It has seen particular success in its uses with historically underrepresented and marginalized populations such as racial minorities,[59] men who have sex with men[60] and other sexual minority groups,[61] migrant farm workers,[62] and sex workers.[63]

Taking this approach was not without tension. We had been tasked with "changing the culture of substance use" by our funders, who wanted to see an action plan. Furthermore, there was pressure from community members, who often expressed, explicitly or implicitly, an expectation that we were "the experts" and we should be "providing answers." An initial task, therefore, was to try to facilitate a general education in the process of how we might consider this idea of "changing the culture." This process of education was relevant not only for the campus-based participants in our budding community, but also for ourselves and our funders. The latter ultimately would become supportive and integral members of the learning community. Somehow, amid the swirling winds, we all had to find a calm place together in the "not knowing."

The Project Unfolds

Prior to reaching out to potential participants, the support team (including all authors) had engaged in several in-depth discussions about how to proceed with the project in a thoughtful and purposeful way. Following this deliberation, we issued an open invitation to all post-secondary institutions in British Columbia involved in the Healthy Minds | Healthy Campuses community to express interest in participating. Campuses were asked to answer a few key questions to help us assess their level of readiness for involvement in the project. The questions allowed us to gauge an understanding of their current concerns, what resources they currently had at their disposal, and what approaches had been tried already. We hoped this would give us a better picture of their thinking about the "problem" on their campuses and what they viewed as potential "solutions." We then used our theoretical foundations to help us inform the conversation around these expressions of interest, working with the campuses to develop their thinking and building the foundation for respectful, open dialogue that we would all come to rely upon as the project progressed. Campus-based members often voiced their appreciation of our openness in these conversations and our balanced view on substance use, which resonated well with many of their experiences of the complexity of these issues on their campuses.

Following this recruitment effort, six campuses became the founding members of the project. Diverse stakeholder teams representing each campus were invited to gather at a retreat centre for three days of intensive, immersive, theory-informed social learning and dialogue about culture, the nature of substance use in the campus environment, and what it might mean to build a learning community together. A concerted effort was made on the organizers' part to suspend the roles of expert and participant during this event. For instance, rather than offer a series of expert-led workshops around substance use and culture change, we opted for allowing the group to shape the learning agenda throughout the retreat. As we moved through the event, we responded to their interests and inquiries, but also called on the group to act as resources for one another. The intention was to create a group that could work together to share collective expertise as we explored the topics together. Through this experience, campuses formed new relationships with one another, and project areas of focused enquiry began to emerge. Many of the participants in the retreat talked about finding the experience transformational, both for themselves and for the group. They would continue to mention its impact for years to come when discussing their experiences of the project.

Following this initial event, the support team facilitated an ongoing consultation process with the community of participants to assess their needs and refine the team's thinking around how to proceed. This effort involved a lot of encouragement, as campuses came up against institutional barriers, honed in on project ideas, and built relationships with other stakeholders on campus. We offered small grants to the campuses to support them in developing their focused areas of learning and in forming strategic partnerships among themselves. These mini-grants also served the purpose of justifying many of our campus-based members' time on the project, and lent some clout to the project's status within their institutions. Through the mini-grants, we were able to help the campuses take a broader approach to substance use (informed by health promotion and the socio-ecological model) and integrate elements of dialogue into their efforts. This allowed them to explore alternatives to the traditional approaches of social marketing, regulation, and didactic health education.

Simultaneously, we actively developed various means by which the campuses could engage in a more ongoing way with one another and which would allow them to easily access resources that emerged from the community. This involved providing opportunities for community social learning in the form of webinars, teleconference dialogues, face-to-face workshops and meetings, and facilitated consultations. These various forms emerged in response to requests from the community. We also developed an online social engagement platform with a public community website meant to house our most refined and well developed resources. Ongoing feedback from the community throughout the development process ensured the online space met members' needs.

Our understanding was that policy and action were interconnected, and that any one-size-fits-all approach was likely to be too blunt to be effective. This meant encouraging campus-based partners to remain cognizant of the diversity on their own campuses and between campuses. They often found this challenging, as many were encouraged by their institutions to use tools that were "evidence based." An early example of an innovative effort came from Selkirk College, nestled in the folds of the West Kootenay mountains. A member of the Selkirk team (a counsellor) became very interested in the idea of sharing a meal as a means of encouraging dialogue on her campus. After ongoing conversations with her colleagues and our team, they created a tool by which students could gather, cook a meal together, and openly discuss their thoughts and feelings on substance use. After several years, this approach became so popular at the institution that faculty, staff, and senior leadership became involved in the conversations. These conversations slowly led to wider institutional engagement and support for the work they were doing. Eventually, a new health promotion position in the institution was created, one of whose main priority areas was the continued use of these "Dinner Dialogues." The approach is now used throughout the institution to engage people on a much wider variety of topics. It has also been adapted and used by several other institutions across the province. As an institutional mainstay, it has encouraged greater openness, with many of the conversations turning to how to create better policies and practices to support students using substances on- and off-campus.

A second example came from Thompson Rivers University, which was experiencing significant challenges within its residence environment around a "party culture." Rather than simply implement and enforce a policy, the university chose to engage students and residence advisors in seeking a solution. Led by the head of the residence staff, a program was developed to educate students about the role of hosts in having a successful party. This involved promoting a positive message, "Drink with Class," and supportive conversations with party hosts before, during, and following parties. What they found was that empowering students as hosts gave them the agency to speak up when fellow students were stepping out of line at their parties. As such, the residence environment saw a significant shift in the party culture within a single school year. Ongoing feedback suggests this has held through subsequent years.

This change in culture facilitated changes in residence policies that now better support students in their roles as positive party hosts.

These two cases exemplify some of the ways institutions involved in the *Changing the Culture of Substance Use* project were able to build community capacity and develop a culture of open, thoughtful dialogue, which ultimately supports the democratic engagement necessary for effective substance use policy development.

Discussion

At the outset, it is important to note that changing a culture takes time, and that any intentional process with that goal in mind must be prepared to engage for the long haul. Although it might be difficult enough to change a micro-culture, mezzo- and macro-cultures represent greater levels of diversity and complexity that make change processes even more uncertain and faltering. The push for "evidence-based programs" and even "evidence-based policies" along the model set by "evidence-based medicine" often does not sit well with this reality of diversity and complexity.[64]

Within our project, it has been important to provide one another regular support to look routinely beyond the conventional pathogenic framing of the issue of substance use on campus. This problem-focused framing does not accurately represent the complex roles psychoactive substances play within campus cultures. Replacing that default way of seeing the world within health care systems with a more positive health promotion frame focused on well-being rather than on disease is challenging. Nonetheless, it opens up new opportunities for dialogue about the complex cultural considerations that underpin substance use behaviours and patterns of harm. It also makes possible a democratization of the policy-making process.

A deep respect for diversity sits at the heart of the cultural perspective. Cultures are made up of diverse networks of complex relationships. Recognizing how these networks and relationships are organized and structured is at least as important as analysing causal chains of action and consequence.[65] In the traditional frame, those in positions of power and authority bear responsibility for protecting individuals in the community and the community itself from those individuals and, ultimately, individuals from themselves. There is a growing awareness of the unreasonableness of this model.[66] A cultural perspective recognizes the need for integrated, egalitarian participation from diverse groupings and stakeholders. Campus-based teams in the project sought to include a broad cross-section of students, staff, faculty, and administrators in understanding their environments and in constructing initiatives to influence those environments positively from within.

Informed as it is by a phenomenological understanding of the relationship of subject and world, the cultural approach appears to allow for deeper reflection by students and other members of the community, leading to a greater sense of intentionality. Traditional interventions that seek to market particular social norms and simple health-related messages encourage students to receive the messages passively and conform to them. The dialogic emphasis in this project, however, saw students gain new and unpredicted insights into their own and others' behaviours and unique situations. For example, one discussion at Selkirk College of what "a good night of drinking" might look like led to an epiphany about the importance of social connectedness and the ability to draw on resources within one's social network and the need for the social network to make itself accessible. In another example, at Thompson Rivers University, students expressed how increased open dialogue provided new tools to act on what they already "kind of knew." Finally, it is important to note that the democratization of policy making through culture-focused dialogue has at least two major benefits. First, it ensures that the emergent policy better reflects the diversity and complexity of issues within the community. Second, it creates buy-in that lessens the need for external enforcement. This is not about manipulating the community to internalize rules set by some external authority; rather, it reflects the phenomenological reality by which the community understands and defines itself by articulating rules that reflect the functioning of the community consistent with broadly endorsed values.

Conclusion

The *Changing the Culture of Substance Use* project challenged everyone involved to rethink assumptions about substance use and the means for addressing it on campus. Seeking to apply consistently an approach grounded in health promotion, an ecological and phenomenological understanding, and a commitment to humanistic values bumps up against many current defaults in the areas of policy making and action. The impulse to control – either by compelling compliance with top-down policies and regulations or through the influence of social marketing – has been an attractive option for campuses. Nonetheless, this project demonstrated that, in resisting the inclination to control, campuses need not be left with a relativistic free-for-all. Engaging diverse voices in dialogic processes to examine campus cultures critically – this intermingling of social and personal – often led instead to greater understanding, new insights about agency, and increased social commitment. Within the project, changes in policies or practices tended to emerge out of this changed context and to reflect broad pro-social values.

In the course of the project, it became clear that the processes being used are well suited to adaptation in addressing many other areas of interest beyond that of substance use. It is our contention that complex social issues facing the community generally are best navigated by engaged processes involving diverse stakeholders. It is our experience that such processes enable the development of policy that better reflects the mind of the community and is broadly accepted and culturally reinforced. In other words, the benefits of policy-making efforts that uphold deliberative democratic commitments are compelling. Since we sometimes come up against significant barriers in this very complex work, patience and flexibility are critical. Iterative processes allow for strength in the community to build through the engagement. The exact nature of culture change can never be predicted *a priori*, but a positive outcome can be expected from processes that create positive interactions among committed community members. We hope that others will consider the utility of such a culturally attentive approach to policy making in their own areas of interest. We believe that the more we can encourage critical, democratic processes, the more we will strengthen society as a whole.

Discussion Questions

1 The chapter presents particular understandings of health, community, and health promotion. What benefits and challenges do you see in those perspectives?
2 The chapter draws attention to the phenomenological reality of individuals' being embodied in the world, inextricably intermingled with things and other beings in complex relationships. What do you see as implications of this insight for power relations, policy-making processes, and goals?
3 How do you see culture, dialogue, and policy as variously intersecting with and affecting one another?
4 What do you see as promising pathways for promoting participatory policy-making initiatives on your campus?
5 In applying a culturally attentive, dialogical approach to policy formulation and implementation (for example, in relation to substance use) what sorts of indicators might we use to evaluate success or measure progress?

NOTES

1 William David Burns and Margaret Klawunn, "The Web of Caring: An
   Approach to Accountability in Alcohol Policy," in *Designing Alcohol and Other
   Drug Prevention Programs in Higher Education: Bringing Theory into Practice*
   (Newton, MA: Higher Education Development Center for Alcohol and Other
   Drug Prevention, 1997), 58–62, online at https://safesupportivelearning
   .ed.gov/sites/default/files/hec/product/designing-theory.pdf.
2 Dwight B. Heath, *Drinking Occasions: Comparative Perspectives on Alcohol
   and Culture* (Philadelphia: Brunner/Mazel, 2000); Stanton Peele and
   Archie Brodsky, "Exploring Psychological Benefits Associated with
   Moderate Alcohol Use: A Necessary Corrective to Assessments of Drinking
   Outcomes?" *Drug and Alcohol Dependence* 60, no. 3 (2000): 221–47; Antonia
   Trichopoulou and Pagona Lagiou, "Healthy Traditional Mediterranean
   Diet: An Expression of Culture, History, and Lifestyle," *Nutrition Reviews*
   55, no. 11 (2009): 383–9.
3 Jason L. Pontius and Shaun R. Harper, "Principles for Good Practice in
   Graduate and Professional Student Engagement," *New Directions for Student
   Services* 115 (2006): 47–58.
4 Tony Becher and Paul R. Trowler, *Academic Tribes and Territories: Intellectual
   Enquiry and the Culture of Disciplines*, 2nd ed. (Buckingham, UK: SRHE &
   Open University Press, 2001), https://doi.org/10.1306/74D70B87-2B21
   -11D7-8648000102C1865D.
5 Sheila Slaughter and Gary Rhoades, *Academic Capitalism and the New Economy:
   Markets, State, and Higher Education* (Baltimore: Johns Hopkins University
   Press, 2009).
6 Maurice Merleau-Ponty, *Phenomenology of Perception*, trans. Donald A. Landes.
   (New York: Routledge, 2012), 27–64.
7 World Health Organization, "Ottawa Charter for Health Promotion" (Geneva:
   World Health Organization Europe, 1986); idem, "Constitution of the World
   Health Organization" (Geneva: World Health Organization, 1946).
8 Emory L. Cowen, "In Pursuit of Wellness," *American Psychologist* 46, no. 4
   (1991): 404.
9 Jake Epp, "Achieving Health for All: A Framework for Health Promotion"
   (Ottawa: Health and Welfare Canada, 1986).
10 Burns and Klawunn, "Web of Caring"; David R. Buchanan, "Perspective:
   A New Ethic for Health Promotion: Reflections on a Philosophy of Health
   Education for the 21st Century," *Health Education & Behavior* 33, no. 3
   (2006): 290–304, https://doi.org/10.1177/1090198105276221.
11 Ernest L. Boyer, *College: The Undergraduate Experience in America* (New
   York: Harper & Row, 1987).

12 See "Okanagan Charter: An International Charter for Health Promoting
    Universities and Colleges," (Kelowna, BC, 2015), online at https://open
    .library.ubc.ca/cIRcle/collections/53926/items/1.0132754.
13 William B. Hansen, "A Social Ecology Theory of Alcohol and Drug Use
    Prevention among College and University Students," in *Designing Alcohol
    and Other Drug Prevention Programs in Higher Education*, 155–75.
14 Urie Bronfenbrenner, *The Ecology of Human Development: Experiments by
    Nature and Design* (Cambridge, MA: Harvard University Press, 1979).
15 K.M. Blankenship et al., "Structural Interventions: Concepts, Challenges
    and Opportunities for Research," *Journal of Urban Health* 83, no. 1 (2006):
    59, https://doi.org/10.1007/s11524-005-9007-4.
16 Dennis Raphael, ed., *Social Determinants of Health: Canadian Perspectives*,
    3rd ed. (Toronto: Canadian Scholars Press, 2016); Lisa F. Berkman et al.,
    "From Social Integration to Health: Durkheim in the New Millennium,"
    Social Science & Medicine 51, no. 6 (2000): 843–57.
17 For example, Jo C. Phelan et al., "'Fundamental Causes' of Social Inequalities
    in Mortality: A Test of the Theory," *Journal of Health and Social Behavior* 45,
    no. 3 (2004): 265–85; see also Nancy Fraser, "From Redistribution to Recog-
    nition? Dilemmas of Justice in a 'Postsocialist' Age," in *Justice Interruptus:
    Critical Reflections on the "Postsocialist" Condition* (New York: Routledge,
    1997), 11–40, https://doi.org/10.1002/9780470756119.ch54.
18 Bruce K. Alexander, Robert B. Coambs, and Patricia F. Hadaway, "The
    Effect of Housing and Gender on Morphine Self-Administration in Rats,"
    Psychopharmacology 58, no. 2 (1978): 175–9; Bruce K. Alexander et al., "Effect
    of Early and Later Colony Housing on Oral Ingestion of Morphine in Rats,"
    Pharmacology Biochemistry and Behavior 15 (1981): 571–6.
19 Emile Durkheim, *Suicide: A Study in Sociology*, ed. George Simpson, trans.
    John A. Spalding (New York: Simon and Schuster, 1951).
20 Bruce K. Alexander, "Dislocation Theory of Addiction," 26 December 2010,
    online at http://www.brucekalexander.com/articles-speeches/dislocation
    -theory-addiction/250-change-of-venue-3; idem, "Replacing the Official
    View of Addiction," in *To Fix or to Heal: Patient Care, Public Health, and the
    Limits of Biomedicine*, ed. Joseph E. Davis and Ana Marta Gonzalez, Kindle
    ed. (New York: New York University Press, 2016), Loc 4528–5180; idem,
    The Globalization of Addiction: A Study in Poverty of the Spirit (New York:
    Oxford University Press, 2008); idem, "The Globalization of Addiction,"
    Addiction Research 8, no. 6 (2001): 501–26.
21 Hansen, "Social Ecology Theory of Alcohol and Drug Use Prevention,"
    157.
22 Richard M. Eckersley, "'Cultural Fraud': The Role of Culture in Drug Abuse,"
    Drug and Alcohol Review 24, no. 2 (2005): 158.

23 Edmund R. Leach, "Culture and Social Cohesion: An Anthropologist's View," *Daedalus* 94, no. 1 (1965): 24–38.
24 Martin Heidegger, *Being and Time*, trans. John Macquarrie and Edward Robinson (New York: Harper & Row, 1962), 49–55.
25 Merleau-Ponty, *Phenomenology of Perception*, 466.
26 David M. DeJoy, "Behavior Change versus Culture Change: Divergent Approaches to Managing Workplace Safety," *Safety Science* 43, no. 2 (2005): 107, https://doi.org/10.1016/j.ssci.2005.02.001; Jennifer B. Unger et al., "A Cultural Psychology Approach to 'Drug Abuse' Prevention," *Substance Use & Misuse* 39, nos. 10–12 (2004): 1782, https://doi.org/10.1081/JA-200033224.
27 Sonia Livingstone and Peter Lunt, "The Mass Media, Democracy and the Public Sphere," in *Talk on Television: Audience Participation and Public Debate* (London: Routledge, 1994), 9–35.
28 Graham Scambler, "Class, Power and the Durability of Health Inequalities," in *Habermas, Critical Theory and Health*, ed. Graham Scambler (New York: Routledge, 2001), 86–119.
29 Miriam Erez and Efra Gati, "A Dynamic, Multi-Level Model of Culture: From the Micro-Level of the Individual to the Macro-Level of a Global Culture," *Applied Psychology: An International Review* 53, no. 4 (2004): 583–98, https://doi.org/10.1111/j.1464-0597.2004.00190.x.
30 Ibid., 589–91.
31 Cowen, "In Pursuit of Wellness," 404.
32 See William N. Isaacs, "Toward an Action Theory of Dialogue," *International Journal of Public Administration* 24, nos. 7–8 (2001): 713.
33 R. Jay Wallace, "Practical Reason," in *The Stanford Encyclopedia of Philosophy Archive*, 2014, online at https://plato.stanford.edu/archives/sum2014/entries/practical-reason/.
34 Martin Buber, *I and Thou*, trans. Walter Kaufmann (New York : Charles Scribner's Sons, 1970), 53–4.
35 David Bohm, *On Dialogue*, ed. Lee Nichol, e-Library (London: Routledge, 1996), 6.
36 Jürgen Habermas, *The Theory of Communicative Action*, vol. 1, *Reason and Rationalization of Society*, trans. Thomas McCarthy (Boston: Beacon, 1984); idem, *Between Facts and Norms: Contributions to a Discourse Theory of Law and Democracy*, trans. William Rehg (Cambridge, MA: MIT Press, 1996).
37 Cf. Tomas Englund, "Rethinking Democracy and Education: Towards an Education of Deliberative Citizens," *Journal of Curriculum Studies* 32, no. 2 (2000): 305–13, https://doi.org/10.1080/002202700182772.
38 Cf. Paulo Freire, *Pedagogy of the Oppressed*, trans. Myra Bergman Ramos (New York: Bloomsbury Academic, 2000).
39 Hans-Georg Gadamer, *Truth and Method*, trans. Joel Weinsheimer and Donald G. Marshall, rev. 2nd ed. (London: Bloomsbury Publishing, 2004), 369.

40 Ibid., 371.

41 Scherto Gill, "'Holding Oneself Open in a Conversation' – Gadamer's Philosophical Hermeneutics and the Ethics of Dialogue," *Journal of Dialogue Studies* 3, no. 1 (2015): 24.

42 Charles Taylor, "The Politics of Recognition," in *Multiculturalism and "The Politics of Recognition,"* ed. Amy Gutman (Princeton, NJ: Princeton University Press, 1994), 32–4; Margaret McKee, "Excavating Our Frames of Mind: The Key to Dialogue and Collaboration," *Social Work* 48, no. 3 (2003): 403.

43 Charles Taylor, *Sources of the Self: The Making of the Modern Identity* (Cambridge, MA: Harvard University Press, 1989), 14–16; David R. Buchanan, *An Ethic for Health Promotion: Rethinking the Sources of Human Well-Being* (New York: Oxford University Press, 2000), 162–5.

44 Megan Boler, "The Risks of Empathy: Interrogating Multiculturalism's Gaze," *Cultural Studies* 11, no. 2 (1997): 254.

45 Ibid., 262.

46 Cited in Buchanan, *Ethic for Health Promotion*, 120–4.

47 Charles Taylor, "Iris Murdoch and Moral Philosophy," in *Dilemmas and Connections: Selected Essays* (Cambridge, MA: Belknap Press, 2011), 3–23.

48 Annatjie Botes, "A Comparison between the Ethics of Justice and the Ethics of Care," *Journal of Advanced Nursing* 32, no. 5 (2000): 1071–5.

49 Taylor, "Iris Murdoch and Moral Philosophy," 22; Botes, "Comparison between the Ethics of Justice and the Ethics of Care," 1074.

50 Habermas, *Theory of Communicative Action*, vol. 1.

51 Nancy Fraser, "Rethinking the Public Sphere: A Contribution to the Critique of Actually Existing Democracy," *Social Text* 25/26 (1990): 56–80; James Tully, "Deparochializing Political Theory and Beyond: A Dialogue Approach to Comparative Political Thought," *Journal of World Philosophies* 1, no. 5 (2016): 51–74, online at https://www.researchgate.net/publication/312909208 _Deparochializing_Political_Theory_and_Beyond_A_dialogue_approach_to _comparative_political_thought.

52 Michel Foucault, *Power/Knowledge: Selected Interviews and Other Writings 1972–1977*, ed. Colin Gordon, trans. Colin Gordon et al. (New York: Pantheon Books, 1980).

53 Tully, "Deparochializing Political Theory and Beyond."

54 Boyer, *College*; "Okanagan Charter."

55 Kurt Lewin, "Action Research and Minority Problems," *Journal of Social Issues* 2, no. 4 (1946): 34–46.

56 Orlando Fals-Borda, "The Application of Participatory Action-Research in Latin America," *International Sociology* 2, no. 4 (1987): 329–47.

57 Paulo Freire, *Pedagogy of the City* (New York: Continuum International, 1993).

58 Barbara A. Israel et al., "Review of Community-Based Research: Assessing Partnership Approaches to Improve Public Health," *Annual Review of*

Public Health 19, no. 1 (1998): 173–202; idem, "Critical Issues in Developing and Following CBPR Principles," in *Community-Based Participatory Research for Health: From Process to Outcomes*, 2nd ed., ed. Meredith Minkler and Nina Wallerstein (San Francisco: Jossey-Bass, 2008), 47–66.

59 Scott D. Rhodes et al., "Depressive Symptoms among Immigrant Latino Sexual Minorities," *American Journal of Health Behavior* 37, no. 3 (2013): 404–13.

60 Cathy Maulsby et al., "HIV among Black Men Who Have Sex with Men (MSM) in the United States: A Review of the Literature," *AIDS and Behavior* 18, no. 1 (2014): 10–25, https://doi.org/10.1007/s10461-013-0476-2.

61 Michelle Marie Johns et al., "Butch Tops and Femme Bottoms? Sexual Positioning, Sexual Decision Making, and Gender Roles among Young Gay Men," *American Journal of Men's Health* 6, no. 6 (2012): 505–18, https://doi.org/10.1177/1557988312455214.

62 Scott D. Rhodes et al., "HIV and Sexually Transmitted Disease Risk among Male Hispanic/Latino Migrant Farmworkers in the Southeast: Findings from a Pilot CBPR Study," *American Journal of Industrial Medicine* 53, no. 10 (2010): 976–83.

63 Zhang Youchun et al., "Sexual Health Knowledge and Health Practices of Female Sex Workers in Liuzhou, China, Differ by Size of Venue," *AIDS and Behavior* 18, no. 2 (2014): 162–70.

64 Jonathan Lomas, "Using Research to Inform Healthcare Managers' and Policy-Makers' Questions: From Summative to Interpretive Synthesis," *Healthcare Policy* 1, no. 1 (2005): 55–71; Deborah Stone, *Policy Paradox: The Art of Political Decision Making*, 3rd ed. (New York: W.W. Norton, 2012), 311–30.

65 Buchanan, "Perspective."

66 Peter Marsh, "In Praise of Bad Habits," ICR Lecture (London: Institute for Cultural Research at the King's Fund, 17 November 2001), online at http://www.sirc.org/publik/bad_habits.shtml.

KEY RESOURCES

Buchanan, David R. "Perspective: A New Ethic for Health Promotion: Reflections on a Philosophy of Health Education for the 21st Century." *Health Education & Behavior* 33, no. 3 (2006): 290–304. https://doi.org/10.1177/1090198105276221.

Burns, William David, and Margaret Klawunn. "The Web of Caring: An Approach to Accountability in Alcohol Policy." In *Designing Alcohol and Other Drug Prevention Programs in Higher Education: Bringing Theory into Practice*, 49–124. Newton, MA: Higher Education Development Center for Alcohol and Other Drug Prevention, 1997. Online at https://safesupportivelearning.ed.gov/sites/default/files/hec/product/designing-theory.pdf.

Canadian Institute for Substance Use Research. "A Framework for Thought and Action: Substance Use Policy on Campus." Victoria: University of Victoria, 2017. Online at https://healthycampuses.ca/wp-content/uploads /2018/05/A-Framework-for-Thought-and-Action.pdf.

Canadian Institute for Substance Use Research. "Understanding Substance Use: A Health Promotion Perspective." Victoria: University of Victoria, 2013. Online at http://www.heretohelp.bc.ca/sites/default/files/understanding -substance-use-a-health-promotion-perspective.pdf.

Hallam, Christopher, and Dave Bewley-Taylor. "Drug Use: Knowledge, Culture and Context." London: Beckley Foundation, 2010. Online at http:// beckleyfoundation.org/wp-content/uploads/2016/04/paper_21.pdf.

9 Art-ful Methods of Democratic Participation: Listening, Engagement, and Connection

JOANNA ASHWORTH

Introduction

This chapter explores the role of art practices in supporting meaningful citizen participation in democratic life. Democratic participation refers to the engagement of citizens in one or all phases of public policy formation: problem finding, solutions generation, and/or decision making. In the analysis of a variety of civic engagement processes that I have led, I reflect here on the significance of using artistic tools – such as simple visual art projects involving drawing with pen, ink, chalk, or paint, and using collage techniques – in these processes to amplify diverse voices, including those of children. I suggest that art making in civic dialogue adds value to the mutualistic act of expressing and listening respectfully to different viewpoints – activities that are central to public policy making. Having facilitated numerous dialogic engagement projects focused on issues such as early childhood education, public safety, sustainability, ecological restoration, and multiculturalism, I have come to recognize that basic forms of visual art making can be powerful mechanisms for evoking voice, story, and legitimacy, and for bridging varied and often conflicting viewpoints on complex issues. But it is not sufficient simply to amplify the speech acts of the citizen. Art-based forms of participation are further legitimized when they are linked with political listening that is responsive to the public work of citizens in public policy formation. While unpacking these ideas and practices, I invite readers to interrogate their own experience with art making in public engagement as an innovation in democratic participation, and to reflect on the contribution these practices might make to enhancing their own convening.

For example, if we were talking together about participatory democracy face-to-face in real time, we might begin with an exercise that allows us to discover something about what participatory democracy means to each of us. The instructions might include the following: "Using the paper and pens provided, create an image of what participation means to you. Then introduce yourself, and tell us what your image can teach us about participation." This is how we began a recent workshop at a summer institute on democratic participation hosted by Participedia.net and the Université de Montréal.[1] The images of participation (see figure 9.1) and stories that emerged springboarded us into a deep discussion about the variety of ways to define and understand participation, from identifying issues to finding solutions to collaborative decision making and action. Graduate students, faculty, and professional practitioners who attended the week-long session suddenly came to know one another in new and unexpected ways through this exercise.

This kind of purposeful art making allows for unique, complex, and, at times, shared stories to emerge, stories that potentially break down social barriers and hierarchies so often present when citizens from diverse backgrounds (such as graduate students in class with their professors and professionals) convene around social or political issues. The image does not care what social or economic status a person has; it could not care less if the artist is the mayor or the local barista. The image captures lived experience, and in the telling of the story arising from the image the art maker finds her voice and the listener finds a pathway to connection.

Artists and Art-ful Methods

Over many years of civic engagement and dialogue convening, I have worked with several talented artists. I particularly want to acknowledge the spoken word and visual artist Nadia Chaney, whom I met when I was director of dialogue programs at Simon Fraser University in Vancouver from 2002 to 2010. Working with Nadia on several civic engagement dialogue projects, I learned what becomes possible when visual art making, poetry, theatre games, and music are brought into these convening spaces to welcome participants, to facilitate the contribution of their ideas in personal ways, and to create a shared identity and a shared language within a short period of time.

For example, quite often, when citizens were invited to meetings I convened at Simon Fraser University's Morris J. Wosk Centre for Dialogue, many were strangers to one another. Whether the topic was global health, multiculturalism, or sustainable cities, some people had never stepped into a university meeting room or attended a community meeting, and were shy and uncertain about what would happen. On many occasions, we turned the awkward time before the meeting

began into an opportunity for connection. As participants registered and claimed their "Hello My Name Is" name tag, they were invited to decorate their name tags artfully with ink or to glue on feathers and stickers and an image or word that described who they are, thus providing a way for them to ease into the public space, make something, and then talk with other strangers about the meaning of what they had created. And when they were done, as Nadia says, these mini works of art "allow the wearer to bring their whole selves into the room, somehow safer and more willing to risk something because their name is now a piece of art"[2] (see figure 9.2). These art-making moments change the atmosphere. They bind a group together beyond the cognitive and the verbal. Creating human connection by engaging with strangers to fashion a colourful name tag with feathers, jewels, and bright colours eases people into friendly conversation. Even before the program begins, they are ready to meet and be present with one another.

Art making at times can be more transcendent than words alone. Nadia thinks it is because "words seem to be distant from the thing itself. Art making connects the knowledge, the knower and the things that are known closely. Art making creates a wrapping of coherence – emotional energy – that runs through the space. Through this process, I know people better and this knowing is a bridge. There is no distance between us. Art making among strangers is a spiritual experience; the

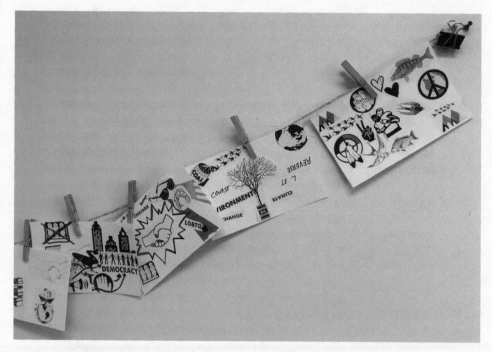

Figure 9.1 (this page and opposite) Examples of visual representations of "participation"
Source: Photos by author.

ego boundaries blur, and in that instance, we recognize that we are temporary blips, time is suspended, we are decentred."[3]

Art disrupts our routine ways of thinking and knowing. Decentred, we might be willing to bring a fresh presence of mind to our thinking together in real time, and more openness to the uncertainty and the suspension of ordinary reality that comes with a truly transformative, generative dialogue. Art making can also be playful and fun. Fun has a place in evoking meaningful dialogue, by allowing participants to reveal themselves in non-threatening ways, by being the authors of their own experience, and by playing with viewpoints. Fun begins to set the container for trust, for openness, and for more challenging work together. In *Making Democracy Fun*, Josh Lerner says that, aside from the usual critiques of democratic institutions, such as changing voter expectations, cynicism, and lack of trust in public officials, for most people "democratic participation is relatively unappealing. It is boring, painful, and pointless."[4] Typically, town hall meetings, council chambers, or public hearings tend to lack intrinsic pleasure or concrete

Figure 9.2 Nadia Chaney at the art table, Wosk Centre for Dialogue, 2010
Source: Photo by author.

outcomes. Ask any experienced convenor of citizen engagement, and they will tell you that food, fun, and day care are all essential. But as challenging as it can be to convene for dialogue and engagement, the purpose of these practices must be clear, intentional, and transparent. Playful art making is serious work.

Clarity of Purpose

"Why engage?" is a question that must be asked before we rush to engage citizens and to offer them art-ful materials for so doing. Context matters. In a democracy, we vote for our representatives, based on their political platforms, and we expect them to govern accordingly for the most part. Why engage further? There are two sides to this question: the supply side and the demand side. On the supply side of engagement, there is often an enlightened public official or a city councillor who suggests that constituents might have something valuable or useful to offer about policy issues such as early childhood education, public safety, housing, or how to support new immigrants. On the demand side, participatory democracy does have appeal – one survey suggests that 83 per cent of young people, racial minorities, and people in low in-come are interested in participation in a deliberative political meeting.[5]

Lerner's research supports this idea, and suggests that fun is a fundamental ingredient. Fun is about pleasure, enjoyment, fellowship, and discovery – all stimulants that release endorphins in the body. I suggest that, aside from doing serious work, art-ful methods are fun in the way Lerner describes and a necessary part of a robust and engaged citizenry. They can set the stage for more difficult and complex work together by establishing a human connection, surfacing values and priorities. In this participatory democracy moment, where many citizens are carving their way into public life in a manner that resonates with their values, public officials are learning to change their approaches to inviting citizens to participate and what they are aiming for as a result of their participation. As Dave Knapp, city manager from Cupertino, says:

> It used to be that if you did something, you had to tell the public about it. And then it became, if you are planning to do something, you have to tell them about it. And then it became, if you are planning to do something, you have to offer them an opportunity to come in and say what they want to say. You don't have to do anything about it, but you have to give them the opportunity to come and have input. The model now is when you have an issue, you are better off to have the community weigh in on the definition of the problem, the possible solutions of the problem, and to actually affect the outcome of the decisions process.[6]

As citizens, students, workers, leaders, or politicians, do we all not want to have our fingerprints on plans that affect our lives? When we gather in the public sphere,[7] we know that, if others set the agenda for us, write the plan for us, do not listen to the meaning behind our images or stories, and do not involve us in the deliberations, we are in essence handing over our destiny to others. Theories of direct democracy include participatory democracy and deliberative democracy. Both refer to the way citizens relate to their governments. Participatory democracy empowers citizens to bring their local knowledge to identify problems, frame solutions, and define policies. Deliberative democracy emphasizes the process of citizens engaging in deliberation on public issues as equals regardless of their status and standing in life to arrive at a decision. In my work with communities, the emphasis is on participatory democracy and the importance of involving citizens (even children, I suggest). Participation takes many forms, from building a community garden to cleaning up a neighbourhood to providing local knowledge on public safety or the accessibility of health care services to the local health authority – activities that extend well beyond the "thin democracy" that assumes voting is a sufficient form of participation. Frances Moore Lappé, in *Democracy's Edge*, suggests that dialogue, negotiation, conflict resolution, and deliberative decision making are the capacities necessary for strong, full-bodied democracy.[8] I have observed and tested many forms of art making that support the practice of these capacities, and suggest that at the core of what is fundamental to participatory democracy is dialogue.

Dialogue

Dialogue is the respectful, relational back and forth in which values, priorities, and dreams are uncovered and expressed; it is a form of communication at the heart of civic engagement. There are many ways to define and practice dialogue in the public sphere. Daniel Yankelovich says that "dialogue is a conversation among peers, one in which everyone is equally responsible. Distinct from discussion or negotiation, dialogue is a form of talk that is not intended to reach agreement, but to reach new understanding. Genuine dialogue reaches deeper than conversation. In dialogue, I take in your viewpoint and engage with it fully. You do the same. In dialogue, we penetrate behind the polite superficialities and defenses in which we habitually armor ourselves."[9]

What does it mean to engage in genuine dialogue, and what are the conditions? Dialogue offers opportunities for participants to respond genuinely to the issues at hand and to learn about each other's assumptions and priorities. Such thinking together can move a group from individual intelligence to collective wisdom. And such thinking together requires attention to the particular conditions, which Yankelovich refers to as the "three E's" for creating the climate for dialogue:

- Equality: Approach the conversation as individuals, not positions.
- Empathy: Listen attentively to understand the other person's perspective and demonstrate empathy (gestures of empathy may include a touch of the hand, a smile, or a nod).
- Examine assumptions: Clarify underlying beliefs and expectations.

Participants are asked to view each other as colleagues or peers and to let go of job titles and organizational hierarchies, to listen with empathy even when you don't agree with or understand the speaker, and to suspend your assumptions and bring them into the open.[10] Dialogue involves openness to exploring your most deeply rooted assumptions about who you are and what you deem to be important. Attendant skills include reflection, transparency, and enquiry. Art-ful methods of engagement, I suggest, make this enquiry more possible.

The ink drawings in figure 9.3 are examples of art created in a community project that invited artists, new immigrants, and other

Figure 9.3 Ink drawings by participants in the Finding Home Project, Cowichan Valley, British Columbia.
First panel: To know one another, all voices are heard. Equality (in a non-argumentative atmosphere) allows you to reach new understandings.
Second panel: We all put our meanings into the pot.
Third panel: We celebrate moving from individuals to the collective.

interested citizens to explore one another's interests and concerns in the Cowichan Valley, on Vancouver Island. Participants, many of whom spoke English as their second language, were invited to paint their interpretation of what "dialogue" meant to them – and, as the sequence of images shows, there are multiple ways to define this concept. The painted images allowed a new kind of voice to emerge, one not circumscribed by one's English-speaking skills or confidence to speak in public. All voices were expressed and legitimate.

More Stories of Art-ful Methods

The photos in figure 9.4 come from a place-based planning project that I directed, funded by the United Way, in the Guildford neighbourhood of Surrey, British Columbia, a fast-growing suburban municipality outside Vancouver.

In this placed-based engagement process, which unfolded over four months, we began with art. Hanging out in local parks and malls and connecting with parents and children from early childhood programs in libraries and health centres, we asked parents of young children to draw the answer to this question: "What makes this place a good neighbourhood for families?" We invited the children to draw their answers as well. From these images and from other data collected, we learned a great deal about the assets of this neighbourhood – what people value, what is working, and what would make the lives of children under six years old and those of their caregivers better. From their stories about issues and problems that emerged from the art and from their later deliberations on solutions, we formulated a set of interventions that included peer-led health promotion, neighbourhood leadership programs, a health arts festival, an early literacy writing program, and a mental health outreach program at the library, as well as a number of sharing projects, all supporting a theory of change. Art making gave the diverse people of this neighbourhood an avenue to tell their stories, in their own way, on their own terms, and in their own voices.

In another engagement project, a series of public conversations on safety, again in the growing city of Surrey, we convened fourteen public meetings with over a thousand citizens who shared their experiences, their knowledge, and their innovative ideas that would inform a public safety strategy. The process began with the question, "What makes a safe city?" The participants included seniors, business leaders, health professionals, frontline responders, youth, and many diverse members of the community. In their own way, they each answered this question with drawings. These images were then used as a springboard to stories of lived experience.

Figure 9.4 Photographs from "My Neighbourhood My Future" place-based engagement, Simon Fraser University.
First panel: Autocartography by students in Surrey, British Columbia, park
Second panel: Grandfather with grandchildren responding to the question: What makes you happy about your neighbourhood?
Source: Photos by Lani Brunn, with permission.

Figure 9.5 Safety imagined.
This is what safety looks and feels like. It locates problem areas where safety
is absent, and imagines a world where smokers on the corner do not make
it scary or difficult to walk down the block. It imagines a safe community
where neighbours know one another, take care of their properties, and keep
an eye out for one another. It is a place where people are mobile and safe on
the streets, on wide, evenly paved sidewalks free from racing cars, and where
children and mobility-challenged people can make their way. It is a beautiful
utopia full of colour and connection.
Source: City of Surrey, "Public Safety Strategy" (2019), online at http://www.surrey.ca
/community/19149.aspx.

The conversation unfolded to dialogue about the current state, the desired future, and the actions that are needed to create this future.

Citizen-centred adherents stress that, although deliberation, dialogue, and discussion are important to citizen-centred public work, they are not enough to enhance and sustain healthy civic cultures. If people do not see the results of all this deliberation at one time or another, it will be difficult to sustain any kind of civic renewal. If people are just engaged in process, not results, it is an empty promise – the process and outcomes must be linked.[11] And this linking requires political listening. Listening to the unfamiliar, not to defend or seek weakness in the other, but to listen for meaning and for values, rather than just facts or arguments. This kind of political listening, as we see from the research done by Bickford, Arendt, and others, is what makes a dialogic engagement process valuable to all involved. Art-ful methods enhance this experience as tools of expression that draw on lived experience.

Listening

> Listening involves an active willingness to construct certain relations of attention, to form a "Gestalt" in which neither of us, as parts of a whole structure, has meaning without the other. Listening to another person cannot mean abnegating oneself; we cannot but hear as ourselves, against the background of who we are. But without moving ourselves to the background, we cannot hear another at all. This interdependence, in which speaker and listener are different-but-equal participants, seems particularly apt for describing listening as a practice of citizenship. It makes listening, and not simply speaking, a matter of agency.
>
> – Susan Bickford, *The Dissonance of Democracy*[12]

For Bickford, listening is communicative engagement that takes into account conflict and differences and allows for joint action. Listening is central to our political lives – and yet how often is listening included in a theory of participatory democracy?[13] Listening requires an openness of being, which requires a form of "not knowing" that can seem too risky to many policy makers and leaders. And yet this element of surprise, which occurs when listening to the "strange and unfamiliar," is what I have observed to be the most satisfying part of citizen engagement. The surprise or learning that arises from the discovery of emergent ideas and possibilities for action demonstrates to all involved that new solutions to old and complex problems might be possible. And this involves an active form of reception.

Bickford suggests that listening involves two simultaneous procedures: making oneself the background, and placing the other in the foreground. In other words, listening is not a process of identifying with the other, or of hearing from the other's perspective, or even of having compassion or sympathy. Additionally, she says that one must become the horizon against which the other becomes legible and where *difference must be retained*. In fact, as Bickford convincingly shows, the easy (and non-listening) thing to do is simply to erase difference. Retaining difference in the act of listening defamiliarizes our own positions and thus challenges our own identity. Furthermore, the reversibility and interactivity of the figure in the foreground and what is in the background requires us to acknowledge the other's capacity for creative listening. This, for Bickford, is the basis of taking responsibility for listening.[14] But if this dialectic describes a general practice of listening, at what point does that practice become a form of political listening?

Bickford argues that political listening requires a kind of multiplicity of perspectives on a shared event, problem, or issue. Using Aristotle's distinction between the social and the political, she argues that the political requires some form of action. Such active listening not only retains difference; it considers that its varying perspectives are crucial to dialogue and action and, by extension, solidarity. She argues that listening is a deliberative act that makes meaning, rather than excavating it. The making of meaning becomes political once it enters the realm of dialogue, collectivity, and the call to action. In other words, this form of listening to citizens takes on a commitment to action.

This next story of art making and civic engagement is about the power of listening to a neglected river, a public initiative that led to the restoration of a neighbourhood ravine on the east side of Vancouver. For over seventy years, Still Creek, at one time a vibrant urban stream running from the regional watershed, was choked by sewage, garbage, and industrial waste, and struggled to survive. Thanks to an intergovernmental adaptive management process, the buried creek was uncovered and, through tireless public and private efforts, restored to its natural state. The ecosystem restoration practices began in early 2000 with a simple "Clean up!" invitation extended by Carmen Rosen, a local artist. Her organization, The Still Moon Society, went on to bring national attention to Still Creek by creating an annual lantern festival with local citizens crafting small (biodegradable) paper lantern boats and then launching these beautiful figures into the stream. Salmon returned in healthy numbers to the stream some years ago, and now swim mightily through these waters. But it was art making that lit the way forward, quite literally. A story of place is richly told in this neighbourhood – a story of a creek rejuvenated and a community bonded through shared purpose. All levels of government eventually stepped in and played their part, but it was the amplified telling of the story

Figure 9.6 Imagine BC delegates deliberating on the future of British Columbia.
Source: Photographer unknown.

of place, through art-ful methods, that brought the parties together to plan, negotiate, restore, and continue to steward what the community had come to value.

Telling and listening to stories, particularly stories of place, are powerful ways to connect political listening with action. I highlighted the use of storytelling as a method when leading "Imagine BC," a series of community-based dialogues about the future of British Columbia from 2004 to 2009. This project brought political, social, business, and cultural leaders together to investigate the question: "What should BC be 30 years from now?" We began the process by inviting stories of place, asking participants: "What is it about BC that defines it?" and "What particular place holds special meaning for you?" Delegates, strangers to one another, shared their stories of place as the starting point of the multiday dialogues, revealing their cultural, social, environmental, and economic values (figure 9.6). As the conversation deepened over days and months – and the inevitable conflicts about joint action arose – we found our connections and common ground through these values. Narrative storytelling was the art-ful method that became central to the exploration of meaning in this engagement, and was foundational for collaborative action.

The final art-ful practice discussed here is that of collective singing, which can also be a medium for building and sustaining community and a metaphor for the collectivity of dialogic engagement. The choir is one of the most powerful and inclusive art-ful methods of engagement, joyfully teaching participants about collaboration, resilience, and collective action. Vanessa Richards is the remarkable conductor of Woodward's Community Singers in Vancouver's Downtown Eastside. Vanessa's work involves cultivating participation, teamwork, and the civic imagination through music. As a community-engagement facilitator, arts programmer, and teaching artist, she also works with organizations to increase their social capital and relevancy.

Vanessa was once a member of another choir called the Cultural Medicine Cabinet, which I invited to open a public dialogue at Simon Fraser University on The Future of Multiculturalism, an event funded by the provincial government. The day was a meaningful examination of the lived experiences of immigrant settlement agency staff arising from the province's multiculturalism policy and the changes needed to address the needs of newcomers. We began the dialogue with a performance by the choir, itself a living example of socio-economic, cultural, and musical diversity. The singers' gospel and pop call-and-response songs immediately brought the participants to their feet. The dialogue about what policies make a city welcoming for new immigrants was off to a promising beginning. We discovered a shared language, and we began to see ourselves not as strangers but as recognizable citizens with an important shared purpose.

Woodward's Community Singers meet every week and come from all parts of the city. Wherever they perform, they are a living and breathing testament to the power of art to create resilience in the community. It is not an overstatement to claim that the singers are enriching the community, overcoming social isolation, and even saving lives. Filmmaker and activist Michael Moore considers participation in a choir to be an excellent example of what is needed to encourage and sustain participatory democracy:

> This morning I have been pondering a nearly forgotten lesson I learned in high school music. Sometimes in band or choir, music requires players or singers to hold a note longer than they actually can hold a note. In those cases, we were taught to mindfully stagger when we took a breath so the sound appeared uninterrupted. Everyone got to breathe, and the music

stayed strong and vibrant. Yesterday, I read an article that suggested the administration's litany of bad executive orders is a way of giving us "protest fatigue" – we will literally lose our will to continue the fight in the face of the onslaught of negative action. Let's remember MUSIC. Take a breath. The rest of the chorus will sing. The rest of the band will play. Rejoin so others can breathe. Together, we can sustain a very long, beautiful song for a very, very long time. You don't have to do it all, but you must add your voice to the song. With special love to all the musicians and music teachers in my life.[15]

Conclusion

What do creating stick figures, chalk drawing on the sidewalk, launching lanterns in a ravine, decorating name tags, telling stories of place, and community choirs have in common? These simple art-ful approaches begin to frame the problems that we seek to address, make space for diverse voices to be heard, and help make sense of the differences we hold in our ways of seeing and knowing. These art-ful forms also help bring to the surface the assumptions we have about the nature of the problem, usually well before we determine what solutions are required. John Forester, the urban planning scholar, suggests that "[m]essiness teaches us that before problems are solved, they have to be constructed ... the challenge we face, as planners and policy analysts more broadly, is to do more: to listen carefully to the practice stories we hear and to understand who is attempting what, why and how, in what situation and what really matters."[16] Art-ful methods help to articulate this messiness, and give us – convenors, policy makers, and elected officials – a foundation for building partnerships and collaborations that move us forward and sustain us in long-term commitments to change.

Art-ful engagement not only helps marginal voices develop their capacity to participate in policy dialogues; it also demands political listeners commit to listening from an open-minded, collaborative stance, as opposed to a closed-minded, adversarial one. Rebalancing our attention on political listening means not simply articulating, but also attending to, cognition *and* affect, to agenda setting *and* issue reformulation, and to mutual enquiry.[17] Bringing art-ful methods to engage citizens opens up possibilities of expression and listening that would make our public policy process richer and more meaningful for participants and elected officials alike. It forms a strong bridge between policy makers and the experiences, knowledges, and values of citizens, thereby informing public policy while creating meaningful encounters in which citizens have voice, respect, and legitimacy.

Discussion Questions

1 What art-ful methods of participation have you experienced?
2 What are the barriers to and opportunities for using art making for citizen engagement?
3 How does art making build a bridge between citizens' voices and public policy makers?
4 Can you cite examples of art-ful methods that could be part of a more robust and engaged citizenry and set the stage for more difficult and complex framing of issues and -identification of solutions?

NOTES

1 "Artful Engagement: Innovations in Civic Participation Workshop," Participedia summer school, Université de Montréal, Centre for International Studies and Research (CERIUM), co-led by Joanna Ashworth and Tara Mahoney, PhD Candidate, School of Communications and Participedia Researcher.
2 Personal conversation with Nadia Chaney, January 2017
3 Ibid.
4 Josh Lerner, *Making Democracy Fun: How Game Design Can Empower Citizens and Transform Politics* (Cambridge, MA: MIT Press, 2014), 330.
5 Michael A. Neblo et al., "Who Wants to Deliberate – and Why?" *American Political Science Review* 104, no. 3 (2010): 566.
6 Quoted in W. Barnett Pearce and Kimberly A. Pearce, "Aligning the Work of Government to Strengthen the Work of Citizens: A Study of Public Administrators in Local and Regional Government" ([Dayton, OH]: Kettering Foundation, February 2010), 2, online at http://ncdd.org/rc/wp-content/uploads/2010/06/Pearces-Aligning_Work_of_Govt.pdf.
7 "By 'public sphere,' we mean first of all a domain of our social life in which such a thing as public opinion can be formed. Access to the public sphere is open in principle to all citizens. A portion of the public sphere is constituted in every conversation in which private persons come together to form a public. They are then acting neither as business or professional people conducting their private affairs, nor as legal consociates subject to the legal regulations of a state bureaucracy and obligated to obedience. Citizens act as a public when they deal with matters of general interest without being subject to coercion; thus with the guarantee that they may assemble and unite freely, and express and publicize their opinions freely." See Jürgen Habermas, "The Public Sphere," in *Rethinking Popular Culture: Contemporary Perspectives in Cultural Studies*, ed. Chandra Mukerji and Michael Schudson (Berkeley: University of California Press, 1991), 398–404.

8 Frances Moore Lappé, *Democracy's Edge: Choosing to Save Our Country by Bringing Democracy to Life* (San Francisco: Jossey-Bass, 2006).

9 Daniel Yankelovich, *The Magic of Dialogue: Transforming Conflict into Cooperation* (New York: Touchstone Press, 1999), 45.

10 Ibid.

11 Peter Levine, "Civic Renewal in America," *Philosophy and Public Policy Quarterly* 26, no. 1 (2006), 3.

12 Susan Bickford, *The Dissonance of Democracy: Listening, Conflict, and Citizenship* (Ithaca, NY: Cornell University Press, 1996), 5.

13 Ibid.

14 Ibid.

15 Courtland School of Performing Arts, "Quote from Michael Moore," 13 February 2017, online at http://cortarts.com/cspa-blog/2017/2/13/quote-from-michael-moore.

16 Andrew Dobson, *Listening for Democracy: Recognition, Representation, Reconciliation* (New York: Oxford University Press, 2014), 55.

17 Hannah Arendt, *The Human Condition* (Chicago: University of Chicago Press, 1958).

KEY RESOURCES

Hersey, Leigh Nanney, and Bryna Bobick, eds. *Handbook of Research on the Facilitation of Civic Engagement through Community Art*. Hershey, PA: IGI Global, 2017.

Taylor, Peggy, and Charlie Murphy. *Catch the Fire: An Art-ful Guide to Unleashing the Creative Power of Youth, Adults and Communities*. Gabriola, BC: New Society Publishers, 2014.

10 Power, Privilege, and Policy Making: Reflections on "Changing Public Engagement from the Ground Up"

ALANA CATTAPAN, ALEXANDRA DOBROWOLSKY,
TAMMY FINDLAY, AND APRIL MANDRONA

Introduction

In 1967, the Royal Commission on the Status of Women launched an innovative public engagement strategy that informed a sweeping policy agenda for women's equality. Supported by public hearings and participation guides distributed in grocery stores, libraries, and churches, the Royal Commission's consultation process made clear that, if effectively engaged, Canadian women had a lot to say about policy making. Today, over fifty years later, we are involved in research inspired by the Royal Commission's approach to creating spaces for women to inform policy making by telling their own stories. Entitled "Changing Public Engagement from the Ground Up," this project interrogates the starting points of public engagement by seeking out communities that are often under- or misrepresented in policy debates in Nova Scotia, and inviting them to participate in policy-related conversations without a predetermined agenda. These conversations feature collaborative and creative approaches to the formats used and the topics explored.[1]

This chapter details both the successes and the limitations of our project, which aims to engage women where they are situated and on their own terms. We ask: What would it look like to engage in policy making (and research on policy making) that is generated by communities from the outset? And we argue that, while the answer remains unclear, addressing the limits of "ground-up" policy making is an important step in public engagement processes that take social justice seriously.[2] Further, through a discussion of our experiences working with communities to pilot experimental, experiential, and community-centred methods of engagement,[3] we identify how missteps and discomfort have been productive in highlighting how far conventional public engagement strategies still have to go.

We begin with a review of relevant scholarship that explores the opportunities and constraints of public policy theorizing of "public engagement" and of innovation in public engagement exercises. In particular, we outline the contributions of critical feminist scholars in identifying the shortcomings of conventional approaches to public engagement, drawing attention to concerns about reflexivity, ethics, and multiple power differentials. Our commitment to principles of feminist research and intersectionality also make clear the implications of our own identities and situatedness. We then consider lessons learned by providing an overview of our project's context and methodology and by reflecting on our experiences of privilege as white settler, able-bodied academics conducting, and committed to, this research. In turn, this interpretation demonstrates how and why even intentionally "ground-up" policy consultations are rife with challenges and contradictions – from our initiation of the exercises to the communication of the findings. In the end, although we document a number of fundamental challenges, our objective is not to dissuade researchers from acting on feminist commitments and/or to deter those who wish to devise creative, consultative policy mechanisms. Rather, our intent is to encourage and enhance community-based policy research on public engagement by contributing to the advancement of progressive policy justice approaches that seek to build and maintain trust with communities typically on the margins of policy development.

This chapter thus aligns with the themes of this volume not only by interrogating all too common "tick box" and/or transactional forms of public consultation, but also by sharing our lessons learned. The latter include: our efforts to reach out to various "publics"; our explorations of different access points to public engagement and alternative public engagement efforts; and our considerations of cause, effect, and affect. And again, all of this is done with the hope of framing and implementing meaningful public engagement and enacting policy justice.

Feminist Policy Analysis and Public Engagement

Apathy, cynicism, and scepticism directed towards formal democratic processes and traditional forms of political engagement are widespread – attested to by low voting rates and the citizenry's rising distrust of many political figures and standard avenues of representation.[4] In communities that are often excluded from policy making and/or that have experienced long-standing and systemic discrimination, this distrust, not surprisingly, is likely to be intensified. For us, public engagement processes[5] – variously referred to as "public participation" or "citizen engagement" – offer ways for citizens to participate directly in policy processes, bypassing more conventional forms of political participation. Rather than vote for a representative who might speak on their behalf or join an interest group – or engage in more contentious politics through social movements in unconventional or informal ways – individual members of the public are able to partake in policy making that evokes deliberative democracy.[6] This allows for "interactive, deliberative dialogue between citizens (and/or their organizations) and government officials that contributes meaningfully to specific policy decisions in a transparent and accountable manner."[7]

The structure and form of these engagements vary widely, from town halls to online surveys, but broadly speaking they aim to serve as a means of letting the public into the policy process. Ideally, then, this could provide a more open doorway between government and citizens, through which diverse forms of knowledge and experience can pass. For government, however, this occurs largely at the stage of policy design – rather than at problem definition, agenda setting, implementation, or evaluation – where the public provides input on an already-conceived policy direction.

Nonetheless, interest in public engagement processes – scholarly and otherwise – has been increasing steadily since the 1990s.[8] At that time, public consultation processes started expanding to new domains of public policy, used as a means to demonstrate that a "broad representation of the Canadian public had been consulted, as both a means of obtaining input into policy and legitimizing policy decisions."[9] By the 1990s, the effects of neoliberalism and an increasing emphasis on the interests of individuals brought with it a mistrust of "special interest" groups.[10] Public engagement processes sought out "ordinary Canadians," and thereby served to displace collective actors in civil society with other methods of consultation. The various committees, commissions, and conferences leading up to the Charlottetown Accord constitutional amendment process of the early 1990s provide prime examples. This push to engage with "ordinary Canadians" favoured individualized over organized input, systematically serving to edge out feminist organizations and many other groups based on collective identity (with some exceptions, such as major male-led Indigenous organizations).[11] A smaller public service and the growing centralization of executive power also meant a decreased commitment to bureaucrats developing expertise and relationships in particular policy domains. In Tammy Findlay's study of the Ontario Women's Directorate, interview participants spoke of a "bureaucratization of the bureau," in which specific policy expertise was being replaced by "multitasking" and demands simply to "know about everything."[12] Traditional links developed between "femocrats" and the community have been lost.[13] Initiatives with the intent of improving connections between governments and non-profit and voluntary organizations,[14] as well as intensified public engagement processes, have worked to fill the void.

Feminist scholars – as demonstrated throughout this volume[15] – have raised additional concerns about the nature of public engagement and its seeming importance to contemporary policy making. Feminist critiques of mainstream (often malestream)[16] public policy that emphasize neglect of gender differences and broader forms of diversity are important here, insofar as these absences in public engagement processes, as elsewhere, produce "partial and perverse understandings" of how women experience the impacts of policy making.[17] And so, critical feminist policy analysis in general has pointed to the contradictions between the interests of women (in all their diversity), the purported interests of the state, and the need for sustained questioning of each stage of the policy process. This interrogation has included the turn to public engagement, drawing attention to how deliberative processes might work to replicate hierarchies of power.[18]

More specifically, feminist critical policy analysis offers several overarching critiques of civic engagement, four of which dovetail with the concerns of our study. First, public engagement processes are still "lopsided" – informed by top-down power structures – requiring citizens to provide input on a predetermined policy direction with the problem defined and the agenda already set.[19] Although the language of engagement (rather than consultation) has long signified an attempt to move towards two-way dialogues and information exchange between the public and the state,[20] in practice this has not typically occurred. Instead, public consultations and engagement processes become sites where a policy process is granted legitimacy, rather than forums for problem definition and agenda setting.

The failure to engage relevant communities and individuals at the beginning of the process has a long history. For example, Shannon Walsh describes the ways that the National Film Board of Canada's Challenge for Change initiative in the 1960s used participatory video projects to facilitate "dialogue between marginalized communities (the poor, Indigenous people, etc.) and government agencies, social workers, and the 'poor themselves'" operating on assumptions about what communities might need, and assuming that certain kinds of changes were in order.[21] Walsh depicts the role of filmmakers in this context as would-be missionaries aiming to facilitate the self-expression of communities, assuming that "individual voice" and "empowerment" were ends in themselves, rather than means to substantive, material change. This perspective underscores why the meaningful inclusion of relevant communities is critical from the outset in identifying problems and setting policy agendas to enable effective public engagement and responsive policy outcomes.

Second, not only are problems pre-identified and agendas pre-set, so, too, are the ways people are engaged, with the recurring use of what have become all-too-familiar protocols, among them surveys, questionnaires, town halls, and now, increasingly, web-based technologies.[22] These standard methods of public engagement can fail to accommodate the different experiences, knowledges, and capacities of relevant groups and individuals. As one study acknowledges, "[c]ommunity partners who may have little or no formal higher education, no credit card, or no former related experience may, in fact, become the most informed and central knowledge holders within a community project,"[23] and yet their contributions remain overlooked and untapped with conventional public engagement mechanisms. Katherine Graham and Susan Phillips have suggested a number of principles for effective, responsive public engagement, including that "the process of engagement should be sensitive to differences in the ability of different groups to access government and in their preferred methods of engagement."[24]

Although public engagement enables individuals to tell their stories to government – adding experiential knowledge to technical and too-broad understandings of the implications of policy decisions for people's lives – consideration should be given to the ways this process must reflect social, cultural, and communication norms and differences across groups, gendered public/private dichotomies, and geographic exclusions. In this way, "sensing policy," the "affective framework for analysis," developed by Sarah Marie Wiebe[25] might provide guidance. Bringing together critical, intersectional, and decolonizing approaches, sensing policy involves *"multilayered analysis, lived experience, geopolitical location, and situated bodies of knowledge."*[26]

Arts-based engagement models have the potential to engage those "who want to take an active part in democracy, but cannot due to their education, culture, status, or gender,"[27] and a number of scholars have identified the benefits of other innovative approaches to public engagement that move past conventional engagement practices.[28] But these kinds of community-driven creative engagement exercises tend to be "messy, contingent and full of tensions," and while feminist approaches recognize that incorporating the experiential in policy making requires "moving from a notion of policy as knowable and rational, to policy as having a broad range of illusory effects and constraints that are unreliable and unpredictable,"[29] experiences of policy in the real world are not easily reconciled with government agendas. Nonetheless, more realistic and effective public engagement might necessitate bringing this messiness to light.

A third and related problem is the ongoing exclusion of those who are difficult to reach (or who are perceived of as such), including women and other marginalized groups, because they are rarely thought of as the "public" or are defined out of public engagement processes through selective categorization and even discursive dismissal. For example, Leah Levac's work demonstrates that young women's absence from processes of public engagement is attributable both to political discourses that construct young women as at once unwitting victims and agentic subjects who choose not to engage, as well as to public engagement processes that are not amenable to their participation. Young women are left out of constructions of the public precisely because "they are assumed to be undesirable and/or incapable participants, or able but disinterested in participating."[30] Further, the ways that problem definition and agenda setting define the public relevant to an engagement process – the affected constituency[31] – is critical to the inclusion of those often left out. A limited and/or highly circumscribed "public" was apparent in public consultations on the Assisted Human Reproduction Act in 2016 and 2017, when specific feedback was requested on a discussion document imbued with technical language and distributed largely through Health Canada's website. This process ultimately involved few, if any, attempts to reach out to those critically implicated in the processes being regulated who might be difficult to reach – namely, egg donors and surrogates. The failure to consider egg donors and surrogates as a "public" that could and should be consulted worked to perpetuate the ongoing exclusion of their interests from the relevant legislation.[32]

Feminist scholars and researchers thus draw attention to who is excluded from conventional processes of public engagement, but they also consider how alternative theorizations and approaches might be possible to create greater inclusion. Here, a final feminist contribution comes with the recognition that effective public engagement processes must rest on relationships of trust between the state and the groups and individuals being engaged. But trust is not a given; it might be tenuous, partial, inconsistent, and even unattainable, especially for historically marginalized groups. It is more likely to develop, however, when there is meaningful engagement that involves reflexive understanding of the power relations between the state and those being "engaged" – often developed through co-creation of engagement exercises – as well as a genuine, demonstrated commitment to ensuring that the engagement will result in change to benefit the participating groups or individuals. Relationships of trust also require clear and effective communication and follow-through.

A prime illustration of these shortfalls came with the backlash against the Trudeau Liberal government's National Inquiry into Missing and Murdered Indigenous Women and Girls.[33] This inquiry – a process long called for by Indigenous women and their communities – was the subject of a great deal of criticism by families and Indigenous organizations for its narrow process of engagement, and lack of communication and consultation. These critiques not only pointed to insufficient inclusion of key stakeholders in the design of the inquiry and a breakdown in communications throughout the process, but also the state's failure to build and maintain relationships of trust.

As feminist researchers, we are sceptical of mainstream political preoccupations with public engagement, particularly those that see public engagement as an end in itself.[34] Our commitments to social justice, reflexivity, and feminist praxis require us to recognize the need to examine critically our own situations of privilege and power, and to interrogate how, when, and why we include relevant communities in the development of pilot engagement exercises. As a result, the lines between public engagement and community-engaged research were blurred in our efforts[35] as we sought out communities to help us design and test potential models for public engagement. Indeed, the principles of community-engaged research served "as another foundational concept for informing the context of public engagement initiatives," insofar as the role of the community is critical to both, as is the role of the researcher and the state in shaping involvement.[36]

We proceeded with our efforts by weighing the merits and shortcomings of a range of potential practices, such as storytelling, creative writing, social media platforms, and visual methodologies including participatory games and the use of various art forms from drawing to dance. To be sure, there still can be "hidden politics" with respect to these creative mechanisms, as Shannon Walsh shows, which can come into play even among those who are committed to a progressive social change agenda. She points out that "the asymmetry of the research reality, no matter the good intentions of the researcher, cannot be overlooked.[37]

With these struggles and caveats in mind, our approach to public engagement represents an attempt to speak to feminist and other creative, community-based policy research commitments, and is geared towards building ongoing trust with communities. As such, rather than identifying a problem, then conducting research and analysis, and building legitimacy through public consultations, we started from the "ground up" – by asking participants initially what was important to them, and then building a research response to address their concerns. We now turn to a more detailed examination of our efforts and their limitations.

Changing Public Engagement from the Ground Up

In an effort to revive public conversations about women and public policy by building research-community networks and capacity and using innovative engagement strategies, we embarked on a project we called "Changing Public Engagement from the Ground Up" (CPE). It constitutes a regional pilot that is part of a larger pan-Canadian research collaboration[38] marking the fiftieth anniversary of the Royal Commission on the Status of Women. Situated in Halifax, Nova Scotia, the goal of CPE (in the spirit of the Royal Commission) is to develop accessible models of public engagement that mobilize academic, practitioner, and experiential knowledge, with a view to the potential application of these models across Canada, "scaling up" their use for application in other locations or through the use of information and communications technologies. To do so, CPE began investigating how women could initiate policy consultations with and from their own communities, what supports they might need to do so, and what kinds of approaches, events, and exercises might work best to engage them. Moreover, we agreed to pay close attention to communities that are often underrepresented or misrepresented in policy engagement processes.

CPE was launched in October 2016 at an event marking the closing of another community-based research project.[39] The event, the Women's Research and Action Forum, was held at Mount Saint Vincent University (MSVU), and designed as a means to report back to the community about the completed research and to introduce CPE to relevant community members. After presenting the overarching objectives of the new research, we started conversations to discuss public engagement processes, brainstorming with participants around the questions: what does real public engagement look like? And how can we engage others in exciting and creative ways? (see figure 10.1)

The brainstorming session was a critical starting point for identifying ways in which community groups and members might want to think and talk about public policy and challenge conventional models of engagement. Suggestions included film screenings, art shows, kitchen table discussions, panels, and hashtag campaigns, among others. We committed to organizing "a variety of creative community-led public

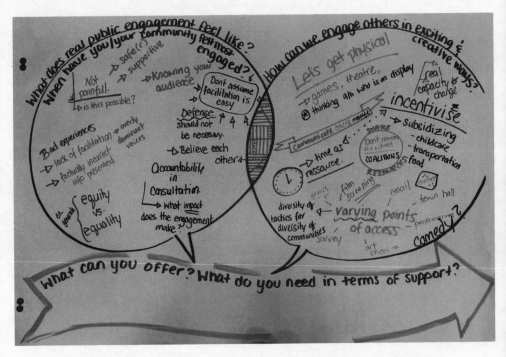

Figure 10.1 Ideas generated by some of the participants in the brainstorming session

engagement exercises where we would look to communities themselves to deliberate on and help solve policy issues."[40] Participants filled out contact forms and were added to our mailing list.

In response, we started reaching out to community members to design several "non-traditional" engagement exercises, with the goal of explicitly working with and including marginalized communities, particularly building on relationships developed through the previous research project and considering the engagement of those it was unable to reach.[41] The following groups were identified as initial priorities: Indigenous women, young women and girls, immigrant women, and rural women, although overlap and intersections between these groups certainly exist. The engagement exercises were to be designed in conjunction with interested community groups (in part as a means of redistributing and reallocating resources), and the topic of engagement as well as the format would emerge from the groups' self-identified needs. After much discussion, we decided that data collection and evaluation would occur through observation and note taking, as well as through participants' formal evaluations. By September 2017, we had facilitated two "engagement exercises"; since then, two others have taken place.[42] Here, we reflect on the promises and pitfalls of these first two efforts.

The Sharing Circle

The first engagement exercise was conducted with Indigenous women in the format of a Sharing Circle following the opening of the *Walking with Our Sisters* memorial at MSVU. *Walking with Our Sisters* featured more than 1,800 pairs of women's moccasin vamps and more than 100 pairs of children's vamps, providing a means to commemorate the lives of missing and murdered Indigenous women and girls. Sometimes called "uppers," vamps are the top, often beaded portion of moccasins. The vamps included in the memorial were not sewn into completed moccasins, signifying "the unfinished lives of murdered or missing Indigenous women."[43] Our Sharing Circle exercise was designed in collaboration with Catherine Martin, a Mi'kmaw filmmaker and activist and, at the time, the Nancy's Chair in Women's Studies at MSVU, and two Indigenous students. The guiding questions for the conversation were largely generated by our research group, in discussion with Martin and her team.

There were seven Indigenous participants in the Sharing Circle, who had been involved with the memorial as part of its board, as organizing committee members, and/or as volunteers. They were provided five questions that gave them the opportunity to reflect and engage on their experiences before, during, and after the memorial, as well as their views broadly on public policy.[44] The Sharing Circle was held at the Aboriginal Student Centre on the MSVU campus, and began with food and socializing. Eventually, we all proceeded to sit in a circle to begin the "sharing" process. We began with a smudging ceremony and a "drumming in," with a song performed by the facilitator, Catherine Martin, who would also serve as a counsellor if required. Each person was asked to introduce themselves. Martin then described the Sharing Circle protocols, which included the use of a talking stick to guide the conversation, to be passed to each of the seven participants in turn, moving in a clockwise direction. Participants were informed that they could speak as much or as little as they wished when they held the talking stick. There would be no interruptions or questions, and the other participants were encouraged to listen without reacting or anticipating or formulating what they were going to say when it came to their turn to speak. The circle gave each participant the opportunity to share personal stories and feelings about their experiences with the memorial and about this method of public engagement. One participant visually recorded the conversation on a flip chart, and all participants were given markers and papers to write or draw if they desired.

The process allowed for deep reflection on what was involved in staging as well as participating in the *Walking with Our Sisters* memorial in Halifax and its broadly felt community impact and repercussions. Although we examine the complexity and nuance of the discussion in more detail below, it is important to note that the participants (and the researchers) concurred that the Sharing Circle was a very effective (and indeed affective)[45] mode of public engagement. In particular, it gave the participants the space to debrief and collectively consider their experiences with the memorial and its relationship to broader social and political change.

The Girls Conference

The second engagement exercise was conducted with girls and young women in March 2017 and created as part of the 2017 Girls Conference.[46] This is an annual event held at MSVU with diverse junior and senior high school girls and young women from across Nova Scotia, in conjunction with participants from colleges, universities, and community organizations. The workshop that occurred as part of CPE aimed to involve girls and young women in conversations about the systemic barriers in society that can cause persistent inequality among social classes. It was developed and led by our project assistant, Jennifer O'Keefe, who was at the time a public policy student at MSVU.

The participants were not told what the exercise represented until after it was completed. They were asked to line up shoulder-to-shoulder from one end of the room to the other. Once in line, each was handed a coloured card (blue, yellow, or red) representing a social class (upper, middle, and lower). Every second card had a X marked on it representing a cisgender female identity (cards without an X represented a cisgender male identity for the card holder). The facilitator then asked the participants holding cards of a specific colour either to step forward, stay in the same place, or step backwards, depending on scenarios that typically led to prosperity or disparity, depending on the card's group category. For example, participants holding a blue card were asked to step forward if they grew up speaking English as a first language, while others remained in the same spot.

At the end of the exercise, the participants were asked to share their views and opinions through a series of questions posed by Jennifer O'Keefe. They generally articulated that the method of engagement gave them an opportunity to express their views and exchange ideas about these social issues and public policy, and provided a visual enactment of the "policy problem." For example, one participant did not realize that transportation would have an impact on someone's social mobility. Another spoke about how it would be "hard to catch up" as they moved further back in comparison to their peers. Many stated that they had never thought about the issues discussed before, and that this engagement had started a conversation for them to take back to their schools, homes, and communities on how they could make a difference.

In sum, both the Sharing Circle and the workshop at the Girls Conference were powerful experiences for the participants and the researchers. At the Sharing Circle, the memorial was a critical starting point for discussions about the experiences of Indigenous women and their communities with public policy. The form of the circle itself and the use of a talking stick both encouraged active listening and enabled frank and nuanced discussion. At the Girls Conference, the workshop served as a way to both educate and facilitate conversation about socio-economic difference, with the cards and physical space standing as a visual, embodied representation of the social, political, and economic implications of class and gender distinctions. The workshop had added value for our student facilitator, also a young woman, in developing her own leadership and facilitation skills.

Challenges and Contradictions

As these engagement exercises were planned and carried out, we tried to practise reflexivity about our identities and responsibilities in initiating and supporting the participating groups, considering our "own social position[s], role[s], and power."[47] We were, and are, simultaneously researchers committed to the feminist and intersectional critical study of public policy and initiators of (pilot) public engagement exercises.

For clarity, feminist policy is rooted in collective struggle, typically involves bottom-up praxis, and "is assessed by whether it makes the policy process more open to feminist actors and issues ... in the pre-formulation, formulation, implementation, and evaluation of a specific policy and whether the policy generates institutional feedback in the state and society."[48] Feminist critical policy brings together feminism and critical theory, problematizing traditional mainstream approaches to policy analysis.[49] Intersectionality is also a means of collective struggle and an alternative critique that encompasses multiple marginal communities. In so doing, an "intersectional prism can inform connections across privilege as well as subordination to better facilitate meaningful collaboration and political action."[50]

The confluence of these two roles (both researcher and initiator), as well as the limits to our operationalization of these perspectives (particularly in relation to intersectionality), led to a range of insights about how effective, reflexive, feminist public engagement might occur, focused on the four previously mentioned critiques of historic and conventional approaches to public engagement. In the end, then, while developing and carrying out these engagement exercises, we also experienced some of the challenges identified above that governments typically face in conducting public consultations. We also received some serious critiques (from within and outside the project) about the extent to which we, as privileged white women, were succeeding in working across intersecting inequalities, not only in theory but also in practice.

The "Lopsided" Nature of Public Engagement

In the case of both the Sharing Circle and the Girls Conference, the power dynamics were somewhat "lopsided." To be sure, the Sharing Circle was created through partnership, as the initial idea emerged from a conversation between Catherine Martin and Tammy Findlay in which the former suggested that the public engagement project provided a potential opportunity to connect with the *Walking with Our Sisters* memorial that was coming to MSVU. The format and content for the Sharing Circle was negotiated over multiple meetings that included some combination of our research team (including our undergraduate and graduate assistants), Catherine Martin, and her students and colleagues involved with the memorial and with the Aboriginal Student Centre at MSVU. Without these relationships, things could have gone very wrong. And we must acknowledge that our positions as white settler academics have enabled us to benefit by reporting on it in the context of our scholarly careers – an unequal process of risk and reward.

Yet, the core research team, with the help of two students working with us, Meva Learmond and Jennifer O'Keefe – graduate and undergraduate student assistants, respectively – largely formulated the questions that would be used in the Sharing Circle,[51] with some interesting results. Consequently, we took for granted conventional political concepts that we use regularly. One guiding question was about reflecting on public policy, and the reaction from the participants was very telling. We heard that: politics is the problem, not the solution; government is equated with colonialism, oppression, and violence; Indigenous people are unsafe with government; "public policy created residential schools"; policy is not protection; public policy is made from a European perspective; governments renege on policy promises; "we call it public policy but it has always been about money"; Indigenous people are forgotten in policy; policy is made by "white government"; policy is a "cover-up"; "policy makers just aren't with us"; and "the policy question is not for Indigenous people!" References to "policy," indeed, were heavily loaded and alienating for our participants. In some ways, we, largely white settler women,[52] had entered the Sharing Circle with questions too naively conceived, failing to account for the ongoing illegitimacy of the settler state in offering solutions through public policy to problems it created. It was an important lesson.

In the case of the Girls Conference, the nature of the event required our research team to put in a workshop proposal that would then be carried out. Undergraduate student Jennifer O'Keefe, our project assistant and the youngest member of our team, designed the workshop to reflect some of the concerns she had and issues we collectively thought would be of interest to young women and girls in generating discussion about public policy. While our intentions were good, both the content and form of the engagement exercise were generated by our research team. We were attentive to the ways the various ages of the research team informed our experiences and to the kind of engagement (and content) we thought might be useful, but the exercise took a relatively one-way approach, providing us participants' input on issues and ideas that we brought to them. The workshop clearly served as a starting point to get young women and girls talking about issues of social policy that might affect their day-to-day lives. This amounted, however, to a starting point for potential future engagement, rather than a substantive, "ground-up" process. On the one hand, the process could be critiqued for its "lopsided" approach to power, which did not go far enough in the theorization of intersectionality and held too strictly to our preconceived policy frames. For instance, it problematized and privileged particular identities – namely, gender and class – which in turn meant less consideration of other identities, such as race, ability, sexuality, and Indigeneity. On the other hand, the feedback we received from participants and from our project assistant was very positive, and suggested some potential for working across generational divides.

Taken together, the experience of these two engagement exercises reveals the importance and difficulty of working together with communities in the initial stages of public engagement and the power differentials at play. Public engagement exercises must be initiated by someone, somewhere, sometime, and it is most often policy makers or other actors of the state who will have the mandate and resources to do so. Genuine two-way dialogue is difficult to achieve and, at the very least, requires a commitment to integrating the groups or individuals involved at the beginning of the process to design the questions and workshop format from the outset. A more expansive approach could encompass James Tully's concept of "reciprocal elucidation," which involves multidialogues. For Tully, participants "learn their way around the places and connecting paths and the labyrinth becomes full of meaning to them. Thus ... [the] 'dia' in 'dialogue' does not mean 'two.' It means to partake in and of *logos* (meaning) with others."[53] A feminist, critical, and intersectional approach would affirm that these multidialogues need to be embraced not only by the participants but by the researchers as well.

Failure to Accommodate Difference in the Form of the Engagement

Both the Sharing Circle and the workshop at the Girls Conference "broke the mould" of conventional public engagement exercises. The latter used movement through space to ask young women and girls to identify their social locations and biases and to think critically about privilege. In the case of the Sharing Circle, the original plan was for women (Indigenous and settler) to attend the art "exhibit," and then meet immediately after for a dialogue about their reactions. It was only through several intense conversations that we came to understand the numerous problems with this proposal.

First, we learned that *Walking with Our Sisters* should not have been referred to as an "exhibit"; it is a memorial. Second, this would have required the researchers to observe participants and take notes as they moved through the memorial, essentially invading a sacred space of mourning. Finally, we would have been asking women who might have just had a traumatic experience to talk immediately about it in a group setting that included both Indigenous and settler women. After all of these realizations, we collectively decided that a more appropriate and productive approach would be to create a space for Indigenous women to reflect on the memorial after they had some time to process their thoughts, so we turned our attention to working with our partners to come up with a suitable format. As noted above, the Sharing Circle and its focus on listening and creating space for people to speak frankly proved to be an extraordinary model for engagement. In fact, a useful distinction can be made between "hearing," which can connote a lack dialogue, and "listening" – especially "deep listening"[54] – which in this context involves not only conversation but ultimately and ideally transformation for all concerned.[55]

One of the most significant challenges we faced in designing the Sharing Circle was identifying how "data" might be generated. Since this was both a public engagement exercise and a research project, how should information be gathered? The power dynamic of white settler academics' observing Indigenous women talking about their experiences was not lost on us, particularly given that they were being asked to share sensitive and intimate details about themselves. This was addressed by recognizing that we would not be able to formalize all details in advance, and that we would have to work out how we would observe, where we would sit, how notes could/should be taken, on site with the participants, according to their comfort level. At one point, participants invited Meva Learmond, the only woman of colour on our research team, to share her experiences with Indigeneity, racism, and immigration in Canada in ways that helpfully upended the roles of researcher and participant. Her deeply moving response affected everyone involved, and contributed important and different insights. The flexibility of the Sharing Circle did raise challenges for understandings of objectivity," "observation," and "data collection." At the same time, it clearly helped the research team reflect on our own assumptions, subjectivities, and identities, thereby allowing us to rethink the utility of the Sharing Circle not only for participants, but also for us as participant researchers.

Recognizing Diverse Publics

The engagement exercises we have conducted to date – the two discussed in this chapter, along with two subsequent efforts – involved "publics" that were considered to be priorities, given historic practices of exclusion, or that were identified as not sufficiently reached in a previous research initiative. We sought out groups (namely, Indigenous women and young women and girls) to address long-standing failures to include these groups in public engagement processes. In both cases, we were relatively successful. The collaboration with Catherine Martin and her colleagues and students facilitated the engagement of Indigenous women involved with *Walking with Our Sisters*, and the pre-established Girls Conference provided a space where young women and girls could participate in the workshop.

At the same time, the convenience of these collaborations could have hindered our broader goal of engaging women and girls who might not otherwise be engaged in public policy making. Participants in the Sharing Circle had played a significant role in the *Walking with Our Sisters* memorial and were previously catalysed to action. Their activism and participation in the memorial were already ways of engaging on policy issues, and although the Sharing Circle was an effective exercise, it is not clear that we were successful in reaching out to Indigenous women who might not already have been engaged or who would be more likely to engage through alternative/non-conventional engagement exercises. Further, the workshop at the Girls Conference occurred within the preorganized space of the conference, in which particularly enthusiastic, motivated young women and girls typically participate. The reliance on individuals and groups with whom we had some connections and/or on those who were already engaged was not only expedient; it also served to legitimize our efforts somewhat, and helped build a modicum of trust (as we discuss below). Nonetheless, it might not have contributed sufficiently to an expansion of those included in the theorization of the "public."

Further, the decision to host both events at MSVU might have excluded those who could have otherwise engaged. The Sharing Circle did take place in the MSVU Aboriginal Student Centre, and we did make provisions for support for transportation and child care. Despite our efforts at accessibility, however, we also recognize that the university can be an intimidating and unwelcoming space for many. Consequently, we intend for future exercises to occur in other kinds of spaces – including, for example, coffee shops, public libraries, museums, online, and even retail store parking lots.[56] Our intention is, and has always been, to meet women where they are, and to minimize potential obstacles to engagement.

Building Relationships of Trust

The capacity of these engagement exercises to effect change is a matter of establishing and building long-term relationships. It was possible to create and carry out relatively focused events that genuinely involved members of the communities we had identified as priorities where strong relationships of trust already existed. This was particularly true of the Sharing Circle, as Catherine Martin's experience as a Mi'kmaw filmmaker and activist and simultaneously as the Nancy's Chair in Women's Studies at MSVU led to her involvement in the project. Although the Sharing Circle was created through partnership, the research team still missed opportunities to take the perspectives of potential participants to heart in designing and carrying out the exercise. This was clear in the concern expressed by participants about our questions on public policy and strategies for change. If we had started with their interests and perspectives in mind, and if more extensive relationship building had occurred prior to the event, we might have been better positioned to ask the kinds of questions that would convey more of an understanding that, for our participants, "policy is violence." And although the relationship between the research team and participants was strong enough to enable us to discuss their reactions openly and thoughtfully, our design of the questions should have been more attuned to these power dynamics.

Moreover, as both events were pilot exercises for a broader research endeavour, we provided only limited benefits to those who participated, beyond the opportunity to reflect on their experiences in their respective engagement exercises. As we move forward, therefore, we need not only to factor in, but also to act on our obligation to our participants and their communities to ensure we are doing our part in offering our research findings and continuing to communicate openly and effectively about how our work is progressing.

Ethics, Intersectionality, and Capacity

Our capacity to engage effectively through these exercises has, in some ways, been hampered by our position as university faculty. To be sure, this bestows us with privilege and locates us within powerful institutional structures. At the same time, however, our positions also subject us to rigid rules and procedures. One of our goals with this project was to co-produce creative methods of engagement with the communities themselves, offering resources wherever possible to help them facilitate their work in ways that might also offer sites for public engagement. And yet, we are limited in what we can do by funding limitations, the regulations of funding agencies, and restrictions governing university-based research.

As one example, we require approval from our respective University Research Ethics Boards (UREBs) before we can work with communities – approval that necessitates the clear, specific discussion of research plans. The responsive, reflexive goals of this project – including, for example, deciding how observation/data collection would occur on the day of the Sharing Circle – were not well aligned with the research ethics process at our respective universities, and it was difficult to get approval for a flexible, "open-ended" research design in which different engagement exercises would emerge depending on the needs and interests of our community partners. This was compounded by our engagement with two so-called vulnerable communities: Indigenous people and girls and young women.

Ethics procedures are in place for good reason, as UREBs guard against harmful research practices by seeking to mitigate risks to participants and their communities. Still, Natalie Clark and colleagues point to the ways in which university ethics procedures give precedence to protection over inclusion.[57] They suggest a reversal in the order of accountability, maintaining that "[e]thics is not something that we obtain from our funder or university REB and then proceed to the research. Rather, we centralize the power of the community stakeholders by first engaging in a meaningful dialogue about the research ethics at a community level, and then move onto obtaining institutional approval. Through this process, we can better account for community-institutional power dynamics and consider ethical dilemmas that are apparent to community members but may be invisible within the institutional ethics process."[58] Even though, in the end, we were able to navigate through the ethics process across several universities, the systemic tension remains.

As would be expected, time and capacity are constant issues for community-engaged research, as they are for public engagement exercises, limiting the ability of those conducting either to do so in ways that advance the feminist principles of engagement listed above. It is not always a matter of a lack of knowledge or desire, but rather a lack of capacity. The latter includes resource constraints such as the limited and/or circumscribed funding available for experimental projects of this kind, as well as temporal restrictions. Time was an issue for our research team and our participants. Competing schedules and time poverty proved to be major challenges in the engagement experiments examined in this chapter, as well as in the two exercises that followed.

Conclusion: Towards Radical Policy Futures

The intent of the "Changing Public Engagement from the Ground Up" project is to identify how public engagement processes might disrupt hierarchies of power, with women from marginalized communities identifying the issues to be discussed and the form engagement should take. We started out trying to develop, design, and conduct engagement processes that worked to overcome the critiques of public engagement raised by feminist critical policy analysis. More specifically, we aimed to pilot engagement processes that (1) avoided the lopsidedness of "top-down" power arrangements; (2) truly engaged people using non-conventional methods; (3) involved difficult-to-reach publics; and (4) ensured that people were participating in the context of well-established relationships of trust.

What occurred were two exercises that revealed the significant challenges of designing reflective, meaningful public engagement "from the ground up." The examples illustrate that, especially in the context of structural constraints (both temporal and resource-based), committed feminist, "ground-up" public engagement processes might be desirable, but also might be constrained and, in some instances, not even entirely possible. Ironically, some of the challenges and contradictions we faced in developing and carrying out our pilot exercises were not as far removed from more conventional consultations and engagement processes as we would have hoped.

In the end, our experience points to the need for a fundamental shift in the conceptualization of consultation in relation to public engagement and civic participation. It is particularly critical to tease apart the distinctions between research participants' potential modes of policy engagement and social activism, and to recognize how diverse young women and diverse Indigenous women might resist or engage policy in subtle ways in their daily lives. A more nuanced understanding would also take up notions of Indigenous sovereignty and self-determination that reject the insertion of state structures – and, by extension, academic researchers with government funding – into community concerns.[59] Thus, feminist policy research must identify and develop methodologies that are built on more collaboration and greater practices of solidarity.

Ultimately, we hope that our critical reflections on highly contested efforts at, and forms of, public engagement shed light on both the merits and limits of the state's purported attempts at responsiveness, as well as well-intentioned but nonetheless fraught, feminist efforts to engage from the "ground up." We conclude with one scenario for a possible way forward. We turn to examples of collaborative art initiatives, as these practices might serve to strengthen existing epistemological links between feminist policy engagement and creative research methods. Like other forms of unconventional public engagement, collaborative art involves researchers (and/or artists) working directly with more diverse "publics" to address issues of concern in their lives. Such practices recognize the "necessary interdependence between 'cultural' and 'political' action, and a more complex understanding of cause and effect in the production of social change."[60] Successful collaborative art projects require a deep knowledge of participants developed through years of interaction and co-existence. Vernacular methods of cultural production are harnessed, transformed, and remixed in order to subvert conventional bureaucratic pathways of public consultation.

Discussion Questions

1 How might public engagement from "the ground up" be possible?
2 What can feminist critical policy scholars do to avoid replicating the hierarchical power relations associated with traditional government-led public engagement efforts?

3 What could the authors have done differently? What did they do well?
4 What challenges are associated with "unconventional" public engagement methods?
5 Should alternative engagement models be embedded in government processes or replace them completely?

NOTES

Note that the authors contributed equally to this work, and their names appear in alphabetical order.

This project is supported by a Social Sciences and Humanities Research Council Partnership Development Grant (#890-2015-0024), led by Dr Barbara Cameron at York University. We thank María José Yax-Fraser for taking the time to provide feedback on an earlier version of this chapter and our students, Meva Learmond and Jennifer O'Keefe, for their invaluable assistance on this project.

1 Claudia Mitchell, Naydene de Lange, and Relebohile Moletsane, *Participatory Visual Methodologies: Social Change, Community and Policy* (Los Angeles: SAGE, 2017).
2 Lucio Baccaro and Konstantinos Papadakis, *The Promise and Perils of Participatory Policy-Making* (Geneva: International Institute for Labour Studies and International Labour Organization, 2008); Lindsay Cattell et al., *Participatory Policymaking: A Toolkit For Social Change* (Berkeley: University of California, Berkeley, Goldman School of Public Policy, 2015), online at https://gspp.berkeley.edu/assets/uploads/page/ GSPP_Participatory _Policy_Toolkit_Version_1.pdf; Yea-Wen Chen, "Public Engagement Exercises with Racial and Cultural 'Others': Some Thoughts, Questions, and Considerations," *Journal of Public Deliberation* 10, no. 1 (2014), online at https://www.publicdeliberation.net/jpd/vol10/iss1/art14.
3 See, for example, the tools described in *Effective Engagement: Building Relationships with Community and Other Stakeholders*, an engagement guide developed in 2015 by the Victoria (Australia) Department of Environment, Land, Water, and Planning. The tools described range from more conventional models of public engagement, including expert panels and surveys, to photovoice, "speakouts," and shopfronts. Online at https:// sustainingcommunity.wordpress.com/2018/05/14/effective-engagement/.
4 Shaun Bowler, Todd Donovan, and Jeffrey A. Karp, "Enraged or Engaged? Preferences for Direct Citizen Participation in Affluent Democracies," *Political Research Quarterly* 60, no. 3 (2007): 351–62, https://doi.org/10.1177 /1065912907304108; Mark Chou, Jean-Paul Gagnon, and Lesley Pruitt,

"Putting Participation on Stage: Examining Participatory Theatre as an Alternative Site for Political Participation," *Policy Studies* 36, no. 6 (2015): 607–22, https://doi.org/10.1080/01442872.2015.1095281; Katherine A. Graham and Susan D. Phillips, "Citizen Engagement: Beyond the Customer Revolution," *Canadian Public Administration* 40, no. 2 (1997): 255–73, https://doi.org/10.1111/j.1754-7121.1997.tb01509.x; and Kathleen McNutt, "Public Engagement in the Web 2.0 Era: Social Collaborative Technologies in a Public Sector Context," *Canadian Public Administration* 57, no. 1 (2014): 56, https://doi.org/10.1111/capa.12058.

5 Our definition of public engagement requires that ordinary people be involved directly in the practices of policy making, particularly as a means of addressing complex and pressing issues that affect their lives in nuanced ways. Engagement is enacted through various mechanisms that position members of the public as knowledge producers, and that encourage debate, the development of recommendations, and the articulation of alternative relationships between individuals and the state.

6 For deliberative democracy, we adopt the following definition: "a) a process that involves the careful weighing of information and views, b) an egalitarian process with adequate speaking opportunities and attentive listening by participants, and c) dialogue that bridges differences among participants' diverse ways of speaking and knowing." See Stephanie Burkhalter, John Gastil, and Todd Kelshaw, "A Conceptual Definition and Theoretical Model of Public Deliberation in Small Face-to-Face Groups," *Communication Theory* 12, no. 4 (2002): 398–422, https://doi.org/10.1111/j.1468-2885.2002.tb00276.x.

7 Susan D. Phillips, "SUFA and Citizen Engagement: Fake or Genuine Masterpiece?" *IRPP Policy Matters* 2, no. 7 (2001): 10.

8 Graham and Phillips, "Citizen Engagement"; Susan D. Phillips and Michael Orsini, "Mapping the Links: Citizen Involvement in the Policy Process" (Ottawa: Canadian Policy Research Networks, 2002); Julia Abelson and François-Pierre Gauvin, *Transparency, Trust, and Citizen Engagement* (Ottawa: Canadian Policy Research Networks, 2004); Keith Culver and Paul Howe, "Calling All Citizens: The Challenges of Public Consultation," *Canadian Public Administration* 47, no. 1 (2004): 52–75, https://doi.org/10.1111/j.1754-7121.2004.tb01970.x; Rachel Laforest and Susan D. Phillips, "Citizen Engagement: Rewiring the Policy Process," in *Critical Policy Studies*, ed. Michael Orsini and Miriam Smith (Vancouver: UBC Press, 2007), 68–90; Chris Aulich, "From Citizen Participation to Participatory Governance in Australian Local Governance," *Commonwealth Journal of Local Governance* 1, no. 2 (2009): 44–60; Pamela Attree et al., "The Experience of Community Engagement for Individuals: A Rapid Review of Evidence," *Health & Social Care in the Community* 19, no. 3 (2011): 250–60, https://doi.org/10.1111/j.1365-2524.2010.00976.x.

9   Laforest and Phillips, "Citizen Engagement," 74.
10 Miriam Smith, *A Civil Society? Collective Actors in Canadian Political Life* (Toronto: University of Toronto Press, 2005).
11 See Alexandra Dobrowolsky, "Of 'Special Interest': Interest, Identity and Feminist Constitutional Activism in Canada," *Canadian Journal of Political Science* 31, no. 4 (1998): 707–42, https://doi.org/10.1017/S0008423900009616.
12 Tammy Findlay, *Femocratic Administration: Gender, Governance, and Democracy in Ontario* (University of Toronto Press, 2015), 162.
13 Ibid.
14 Kathy Brock. *Improving Connections between Governments and Nonprofit and Voluntary Organizations: Public Policy and the Third Sector* (Montreal; Kingston, ON: McGill-Queen's University Press, 2002), online at https://catalog.hathitrust.org/Record/004252478.
15 See, for example, Levac (chapter 11 in this volume); and Pérez and Piñán (chapter 16 in this volume).
16 Toni Schofield and Susan Goodwin, "Gender Politics and Public Policy Making: Prospects for Advancing Gender Equality," *Policy and Society* 24, no. 4 (2005): 26.
17 Sandra G. Harding, *The Science Question in Feminism* (Ithaca, NY: Cornell University Press, 1986).
18 Kathleen M. Shaw, "Using Feminist Critical Policy Analysis in the Realm of Higher Education," *Journal of Higher Education* 75, no. 1 (2004): 58–9, https://doi.org/10.1080/00221546.2004.11778896; see also Johnson (chapter 1 in this volume).
19 Phillips, "SUFA and Citizen Engagement?" 10.
20 Susan Phillips and Michael Orsini identify eight positive dimensions of public engagement, including, among others, the mobilization of interests, the potential for claims making, and the potential to challenge convention notions of expertise; see Phillips and Orsini, "Mapping the Links."
21 Shannon Walsh, "Critiquing the Politics of Participatory Video and the Dangerous Romance of Liberalism," *Area* 48, no. 4 (2016): 406, https://doi.org/10.1111/area.12104.
22 In her work on digital party politics, Tamara Small concludes that, "[o]n several dimensions examined, online politics has done little to transform the quality of political communication in this country"; see Tamara Small, "Two Decades of Digital Party Politics in Canada: An Assessment," in *Canadian Parties in Transition*, 4th ed., ed. Alain-G. Gagnon and Brian Tanguay (Toronto: University of Toronto Press, 2017), 402.
23 Lisa J. Hardy et al., "Hiring the Experts: Best Practices for Community-Engaged Research," *Qualitative Research* 16, no. 5 (2016): 593, https://doi.org/10.1177/1468794115579474.
24 Graham and Phillips, "Citizen Engagement," 269.

25 Sarah Marie Wiebe, *Everyday Exposure: Indigenous Mobilization and Environmental Justice in Canada's Chemical Valley* (Vancouver: UBC Press, 2016), 188.
26 Sarah Marie Wiebe, "Decolonizing Engagement? Creating a Sense of Community through Collaborative Filmmaking," *Studies in Social Justice* 9, no. 2 (2016): 15, https://doi.org/10.26522/ssj.v9i2.1141; author's emphasis.
27 Chou, Gagnon, and Pruitt, "Putting Participation on Stage," 609.
28 Ibid.; Carolyn Kagan and Karen Duggan, "Creating Community Cohesion: The Power of Using Innovative Methods to Facilitate Engagement and Genuine Partnership," *Social Policy and Society* 10, no. 3 (2011): 393–404, https://doi.org/10.1017/S147474641100011X; Walsh, "Critiquing the Politics of Participatory Video"; Wiebe, "Decolonizing Engagement?"
29 Sara M. Childers, "Getting in Trouble: Feminist Postcritical Policy Ethnography in an Urban School," *Qualitative Inquiry* 17, no. 4 (2011): 347, https://doi.org/10.1177/1077800411401197.
30 Leah Levac, "Complicating the Public: Enabling Young Women's Participation in Public Engagement Initiatives," *Journal of Youth Studies* 16, no. 3 (2013): 336, https://doi.org/10.1080/13676261.2012.710742.
31 David R.H. Moscrop and Mark E. Warren, "When Is Deliberation Democratic?" *Journal of Public Deliberation* 12, no. 2 (2016), article 4, https://www.publicdeliberation.net/jpd/vol12/iss2/art4.
32 Alana Cattapan and Françoise Baylis, "Egg Donors and Surrogates Need High-Quality Care," *The Conversation* (blog), 27 September 2017, online at http://theconversation.com/egg-donors-and-surrogates-need-high-quality-care-84664.
33 Nancy Macdonald and Meagan Campbell, "Lost and Broken," *Macleans*, 13 September 2017, online at http://www.macleans.ca/lost-and-broken/.
34 These concerns are addressed extensively in Genevieve Fuji Johnson, *Democratic Illusion: Deliberative Democracy in Canadian Public Policy* (Toronto: University of Toronto Press, 2015).
35 Hardy et al., "Hiring the Experts"; Lisa Mikesell, Elizabeth Bromley, and Dmitry Khodyakov, "Ethical Community-Engaged Research: A Literature Review," *American Journal of Public Health* 103, no. 12 (2013): e7–14, https://doi.org/10.2105/AJPH.2013.301605.
36 Levac, "Complicating the Public," 348.
37 Walsh, "Critiquing the Politics of Participatory Video," 4.
38 There are five regional pilot projects, each testing new methods to engage diverse communities of women across Canada in conversations about the public policy challenges facing us in the decades ahead. In addition to CPE (Halifax), the other pilot projects are "Engaging with CEDAW" (Vancouver), "Measuring Violence" (Ottawa), "Surveying Priorities" (Saskatchewan), and "Gender Equality Plan" (national). These projects are described on the

Engendering Public Engagement project website (http://policy4women.
com). The larger project, entitled *Engendering Public Engagement, Democratizing Public Space*, is led by Barbara Cameron, a feminist political scientist
at York University, and is a partnership among a number of universities
and community organizations, including (important for our purposes) the
Canadian Research Institute for the Advancement of Women.

39 "Changing Public Services: Women and Intersectional Analysis" was a
research project funded by the Social Sciences and Humanities Research
Council of Canada that interrogated the ways reductions to publicly funded
service provision have impacted the lives of women, both as public sector employees and as those using the services in question. Through a pan-Canadian
research network, the research occurred in four different regional clusters
(Vancouver, Saskatoon, Ottawa, and Halifax), and explored the "barriers and
opportunities" faced by different groups of women. See http://www
.criaw-icref.ca/en/page/changing-public-services for more information.

40 Jennifer O'Keefe, "CPS Women's Research and Action Forum – Nova Scotia"
(Ottawa: Canadian Research Institute for the Advancement of Women,
September 2017).

41 The previous research project, "Changing Public Services," in Halifax
included "Indigenous, non-Indigenous/settler, Canadian citizen, permanent
resident immigrant, from a racialized group, from a non-racialized group,
heterosexual, LGBTQ, female, transgender, with a disability, and without a
disability"; see Tammy Findlay and Mary-Dan Johnston, "Public Services –
Who Does What?" (Canadian Research Institute for the Advancement of
Women, August 2017), 4.

42 In addition to the two public engagement experiments described in this
chapter, we have since engaged in two more: one with rural women, and
another with women with disabilities and deaf women.

43 See the website of Walking With Our Sisters, at http://
walkingwithoursisters.ca.

44 The five questions were: (1) What was your expectation before you went
into the memorial? (2) Do you remember your reaction when you went
through the memorial for the first time? (3) You've had some time since
visiting the memorial. Do you feel any differently now? (4) Has the memorial had an impact on your thinking about public policy? (5) What change
would you like to see come out of the memorial?

45 See Wiebe, *Everyday Exposure*.

46 The Girls Conference, held at Mount Saint Vincent University and supported by the Alexa McDonough Institute for Women, Gender and Social
Justice, aims to engage junior and senior high school girls and young
women to "participate in various workshops and activity sessions which
include confidence building, leadership skills, personal and professional

growth, and developing stronger minds and bodies. They [are] also be able to share their ideas and opinions while learning effective strategies for expressing themselves and new ways to explore making a difference in their communities." For more information, see the Alexa McDonough Institute for Women, Gender and Social Justice website at https://www .msvu.ca/research-at-the-mount/research-chairs/centres-and-institutes /the-alexa-mcdonough-institute-for-women-gender-and-social-justice /projects-events/girls-2020-conference/.

47 Olena Hankivsky, "Intersectionality 101" (Victoria, BC: Institute for Inter-sectionality Research and Public Policy, April 2014), 3, online at https:// studylib.net/doc/10714281/intersectionality-101-olena-hankivsky--phd.

48 Amy G. Mazur, *Theorizing Feminist Policy* (Oxford: Oxford University Press, 2002), 4.

49 Catherine Marshall, "Researching the Margins: Feminist Critical Policy Analysis," *Educational Policy* 13, no. 1 (1999): 59–76, https://doi.org/10.1177 /0895904899131006.

50 Sumi Cho, Kimberlé Williams Crenshaw, and Leslie McCall, "Toward a Field of Intersectionality Studies: Theory, Applications, and Praxis," *Signs* 38, no. 4 (2013): 785–810, https://doi.org/10.1086/669608.

51 We took on some of the organizing of the Sharing Circle to use our resources – time and money – to put fewer demands on Martin and her team than might otherwise be the case. This included drafting the questions, which was in some ways a trade-off between the need for participant-informed questions to guide the talking circle and requiring more time and effort from participants.

52 As noted above, we are white settler women, with the exception of one stu-dent on the team.

53 James Tully, "Deparochializing Political Theory and Beyond: A Dialogue Approach to Comparative Political Thought," *Journal of World Philosophies* 1, no. 1 (2016): 67, https://scholarworks.iu.edu/iupjournals/index.php /jwp/article/view/623.

54 Emily Beausoleil, "Responsibility as Responsiveness: Enacting a Dispositional Ethics of Encounter," *Political Theory* 45, no. 3 (2017): 291–318, https://doi.org /10.1177/0090591716651109.

55 Sincere thanks to the editors for making this point stronger and clarifying this distinction.

56 Indeed, since we wrote this chapter, one of our subsequent engagement efforts took the form of two podcasts that drew attention to the policy shortfalls faced by rural women in Nova Scotia.

57 Natalie Clark et al., "Ethical Dilemmas in Community-Based Research: Working with Vulnerable Youth in Rural Communities," *Journal of Academic Ethics* 8, no. 4 (2010): 243–52, https://doi.org/10.1007/s10805-010-9123-y.

58 Ibid., 248.
59 Consider, for instance, Kim Anderson and Bonita Lawrence, *Strong Women Stories: Native Vision and Community Survival* (Toronto: Sumach Press, 2003); Carolyn Kenny and Tina Ngaroimata Fraser, *Living Indigenous Leadership: Native Narratives on Building Strong Communities* (Vancouver: UBC Press, 2012); Kino-nda-niimi Collective, *The Winter We Danced: Voices from the Past, the Future, and the Idle No More Movement* (Winnipeg: ARP Books, 2014); and Audra Simpson, *Mohawk Interruptus: Political Life Across the Borders of Settler States* (Durham, NC: Duke University Press, 2014) . See also the activism work of the Native Youth Sexual Health Network, online at http://www.nativeyouthsexualhealth.com/index.html.
60 Grant H. Kester, *The One and the Many: Contemporary Collaborative Art in a Global Context* (Durham, NC: Duke University Press, 2011), 207.

KEY RESOURCES

Cattell, Lindsay, Sarah Chevalier, Trinetta Chong, Nicole Danna, Sasha Feldstein, Nereida Heller, Bryan Klickstein, Anna Maier, Terra Rose, and Sarah Steele Wilson. *Participatory Policymaking: A Toolkit for Social Change.* Berkeley: University of California, Berkeley, Goldman School of Public Policy, 2015. Online at https://gspp.berkeley.edu/assets/uploads/page/GSPP_Participatory_Policy_Toolkit_Version_1.pdf.
Chen, Yea-Wen. "Public Engagement Exercises with Racial and Cultural 'Others': Some Thoughts, Questions, and Considerations." *Journal of Public Deliberation* 10, no. 1 (2014), online at https://www.publicdeliberation.net/jpd/vol10/iss1/art14.
Laforest, Rachel, and Susan D. Phillips. "Citizen Engagement: Rewiring the Policy Process." In *Critical Policy Studies*, edited by Michael Orsini and Miriam Smith, 68–90. Vancouver: UBC Press, 2007.
Marshall, Catherine. "Researching the Margins: Feminist Critical Policy Analysis." *Educational Policy* 13, no. 1 (1999): 59–76.
Policy4Women. "Policy4Women." Online at http://policy4women.com/.

11 Engaging with Women in Low Income: Implications for Government-Convened Public Engagement Initiatives and Deliberative Democracy

LEAH LEVAC

Introduction

Between 2008 and 2010, the province of New Brunswick on Canada's east coast convened a public engagement initiative called *Bringing the Pieces Together* (BPT).[1] Led by the Department of Social Development, its primary goal was to develop a poverty-reduction plan for the province. BPT was lauded in public engagement literature[2] and by prominent private, public, and community sector leaders[3] as an innovation in public policy development. The initiative was meant to serve as a flagship model of public engagement in the province. Since then, public participation in policy development has continued to garner attention in New Brunswick and across other Canadian jurisdictions. For example, and as noted below, New Brunswick employed a subsequent public engagement initiative to update the original results of BPT. Elsewhere, Rachel Magnusson (chapter 5, in this volume) describes the use of a citizens' assembly in local neighbourhood planning, an approach similar to what has been used in electoral reform efforts in both British Columbia and Ontario.[4] However, meaningful inclusion of diverse and historically marginalized citizens remains elusive. Immigrants often face barriers to participation, and as Frances Ravensbergen and Madine VanderPlaat[5] point out, trauma and lack of access to public places and networks can prevent the participation of people living in poverty. Of importance in BPT, then, was the explicit intention to include people living in low income in all stages of the process. In this chapter, I draw on gender-based and intersectional policy analysis frameworks, combined with public engagement evaluation literature, to examine BPT from the perspective of women – including women living in low income – who participated in the initiative as members of the public. In so doing, I address the questions: What do women identify as important to their participation in public policy development? And what implications does this have for deliberative democratic theory?

Public engagement in policy development receives both supportive and critical attention in a variety of policy areas in Canada, including health policy development and priority setting,[6] resource extraction,[7] environmental planning,[8] electoral reform,[9] housing,[10] and poverty reduction.[11] The surge in attention aligns with a broad and increasing focus on public engagement around the world.[12] Often, the "public" is treated as a homogenous group, even though a useful definition of public engagement initiatives is that they involve *diverse members* of the public in collective agenda setting, dialogue and/or deliberation, decision making, and policy-forming activities sponsored, convened, or led by organizations/institutions responsible for policy development.[13] Efforts to involve diverse citizens – particularly those who historically have been marginalized or excluded – in policy development are essential to the realization of a more inclusive democracy, and warrant attention to both "*equality* in opportunities for participation, and *equity* in processes and outcomes."[14] Efforts to involve diverse citizens in policy development are supported by the principle of affected interests[15] – the claim that those most affected by policy decisions should be involved in their development, and which grounds *policy justice.* Such efforts are also supported by principles of deliberative democracy, which include not only valuing reasoned debate and including citizens in binding decisions, but also important precursors of deliberation such as "popular participation (how individuals come to have standing and voice *as participants*) and agenda setting (how concerns come to be defined *as issues*)."[16]

Deliberative democracy, which grounds public engagement practice, is a theoretical conception of democracy that aims to make governments more accountable to differentiated and unequal publics[17] and to disrupt systems of power and their effects on individuals' and communities' access to political decision making. Deliberative democracy scholars suggest that the "first and most important characteristic [of deliberative democracy] is its *reason-giving* requirement,"[18] which demands that reasons given to justify positions be widely accessible and "accepted by free and equal persons seeking fair terms of cooperation."[19] Amy Gutmann and Dennis Thompson also suggest that the process should be reasonably expected to lead to binding decisions for some time, and should be considered dynamic, because "we ... cannot be sure that the decisions we make today will be correct tomorrow."[20] The study of deliberative democracy has evolved from a focus on normative arguments about the benefits of inclusion and deliberation to an empirical focus on institutionalization and on making deliberative democracy work in practice.[21]

Contemporary deliberative democratic scholarship includes the study of participatory mechanisms such as mini-publics,[22] as well as citizens' engagement in both macro (public sphere) and micro (specific institutionalized mechanisms) forms of deliberative democracy,[23] a notion taken up by Genevieve Fuji Johnson (chapter 1, in this volume). It is within this empirical domain that the case of BPT is most interesting because it offers insight into how a state-led effort to engage with diverse citizens and residents, including women and women living in low income, can inform aspirations of a more deliberative and inclusive society.

Despite ongoing interest in public engagement, several challenges are associated with the ideals of deliberative democracy, including limitations posed by unequal deliberative capacities and deliberative biases,[24] the possibility of suppression of differences,[25] and the failure of even genuinely deliberative exercises to inform related policy decisions, a paradox discussed by Johnson[26] and Sarah Marie Wiebe.[27] In essence, even though public engagement is normatively important and is premised on the notion of broad inclusion, we know relatively little about the participation experiences of the public, including women in general and women living in low income specifically, who are often excluded from public policy development. As Peter John notes, there is a wide body of research pointing to the persistently negative impact that low socioeconomic status has on political participation.[28] However, in his study on England and Wales comparing participation in citizen governance activities (decision-making community boards, tenant committees, etc.) and civic participation (attending public meetings, participating in protest, signing petitions, etc.), he finds that income is not a predictor of participation and that, overall, citizen governance offers more opportunities for representativeness in participation. He concludes that "the aim is to make participation less reliant on conventional forms of political engagement so that it better represents the population through more direct connection to service users and attention to populations normally excluded from direct involvement."[29] These findings are important for the research presented in this chapter because they point to the possibility that public engagement initiatives make small contributions to dismantling status quo power distributions. Indeed, it is possible that inclusive forms of citizen governance offer the most promise for including the voices of people living in low income. In Canada, because unequal access to representative democratic institutions persists for women and people living in low income, and because women living in low income might face additional or unique barriers to participation, their explicit inclusion in the democratic institutions that represent them requires more careful consideration. One way to offer such consideration is to conceive and evaluate public engagement initiatives from diverse women's perspectives.

In this chapter, I contribute to closing this gap by examining data collected with women participants in New Brunswick's BPT initiative. I also draw on observations made by members of the research team and interviews with public servants who were instrumental in designing and implementing BPT. After describing the provincial context and its outcomes, I use an evaluative framework to examine the initiative from the perspective of participating women. The framework draws on Julia Abelson and François-Pierre Gauvin's[30] contextual factors affecting citizen engagement, and Florence Larocque's[31] criteria for evaluating public engagement processes, both of which offer important considerations for evaluating the process and context of public engagement initiatives. My analysis is further informed by gender-based and intersectional policy analysis frameworks. New Brunswick's Women's Equality Branch explains that gender-based analyses "make [policies and practices] more inclusive and responsive to the needs of all concerned citizens and ... reduce inequalities between the sexes and between other groups in society."[32] In addition to focusing on sex and gender as affecting peoples' experiences with policies and programs, the ending of the province's description ("between other groups in society") implies an understanding of intersectionality, an idea that helps to reveal how "social identities such as race, class, gender, ability, geography, and age interact to form unique meanings and complex experiences within and between groups in society."[33]

New Brunswick and *Bringing the Pieces Together*

New Brunswick is in the territory of the Mi'kmaq, Wolastoqiyik, and Passamaquoddy Nations. As of 2011, the Indigenous population of New Brunswick numbered approximately 22,500, or just over 3 per cent of the population.[34] Today, approximately 747,000 people call New Brunswick home. The third-smallest province by land area and population, New Brunswick is the only officially bilingual (French and English) province. According to the most recent census data, it is also the only province (or territory) in the country to have posted a gross population decline between 2011 and 2016.[35] In 2008, faced with troubling rates of low income, an aging population, and a stagnating tax base, New Brunswick launched *Bringing the Pieces Together*. BPT's primary goal was to develop a poverty-reduction plan for New Brunswick, but it was also lauded as an innovation in public policy development and was meant to serve as a flagship model of public engagement in the province. The initiative unfolded in three phases: (1) a series of public dialogues; (2) an invitation-only deliberative dialogue with approximately twenty-five people that took place over eight facilitated roundtable sessions; and (3) a two-day final forum chaired by the premier with forty-eight participants from the public, private, and non-profit sectors, as well as residents living in poverty.

A key outcome of BPT was *Overcoming Poverty Together: The New Brunswick Economic and Social Inclusion Plan*. It contained several action items, including the creation of a provincial Crown corporation, the Economic and Social Inclusion Corporation (ESIC), whose mandate is "to develop, oversee, coordinate and implement strategic initiatives and plans to reduce poverty and assist thousands of New Brunswickers to become more self-sufficient."[36] Its board of directors is co-chaired by representatives from the public, private, non-profit, and citizen sectors.[37] The work of the ESIC is facilitated through twelve regional Community Inclusion Networks (CINs), which "identify regional issues and priorities, and develop and implement [regional plans] in line with the provincial plan. The CINs develop revised regional plans every two years which reflect the movement of regional priorities regarding economic and social inclusion."[38] In 2014, the ESIC released an updated economic and social inclusion plan to guide its efforts through 2019. Like the first plan, this plan's development was grounded by a province-wide public engagement process. Its twenty-eight priority actions offer limited detail, but they include initiatives ranging from "[considering] the creation of comprehensive pay equity legislation"[39] to "[developing] a comprehensive rural and urban transportation strategy."[40] The replication of parts of the original public engagement process to produce the updated report signify some entrenchment of the commitment to pursuing more meaningful citizen inclusion in policy development. The public engagement process to create the next five-year plan concluded in spring 2019. The process boasted participation by over 2,300 New Brunswickers and full participation from all four sectors: citizens and residents, businesses, non-profits, and government.[41]

Over the same period, reviews on progress towards poverty reduction in the province have been mixed. An information document prepared to guide the 2019 renewal process highlights, among other things, improvements to health, dental, and vision coverage; minimum wage increases; and improvements to school breakfast programs.[42] According to a 2013 report issued by Canada Without Poverty,

> Progress has been made in reducing poverty in New Brunswick including a re-evaluation of the social assistance program and 4% rise in rates, as well

as a health benefits [program] for children from low-income households and a proposed Drug Plan for the uninsured. This has been supported by a commitment to community engagement with individuals in poverty which has remained central ... However, the number of citizens living in poverty has not decreased significantly, the level of income for most of these individuals is still well below the poverty line, the unemployment rate is one of the highest in Canada and the private sector, one of the foundations of the poverty strategy, demonstrates wavering commitment.[43]

The 2016 and 2017 reports by the same organization highlight similarly mixed results, noting increases to social assistance and the minimum wage, and modest improvements to community transportation, alongside increases in food bank usage, persistent concentrations of poverty in the lives of Indigenous people, lone mothers, and children, and a lack of clear goals and metrics for charting progress.[44]

Assessing Public Engagement: Context and Process

John Gaventa and Gregory Barrett note that "a large gap still exists between normative positions promoting citizen engagement and the empirical evidence and understanding of what difference citizen engagement makes."[45] Evaluations from the perspective of historically marginalized citizens and residents – such as women living in low income – are more limited still. Although there are several methodological tensions raised related to evaluation criteria,[46] overall, scholars note the need to evaluate processes,[47] outcomes,[48] and contexts[49] of public engagement initiatives. Because of my focus on the participation experiences of women, including those living in low income, the findings in this chapter focus on the process and context of BPT.

Broadly, process evaluations consider the process's representativeness, quality of communication or deliberation, procedural rules, and information exchange.[50] In a study focused explicitly on the participation of people living in poverty, Larocque[51] draws on the work of John Dryzek[52] to identify and operationalize three criteria with corresponding indicators to evaluate process – namely, franchise, quality, and accountability.[53] Larocque offers evaluative questions for each criterion, focused on: participation and experiences of people living in poverty (franchise); style of dialogue and role in framing the subject (quality); and ongoing and "locked-in" (institutionalized) opportunities for participation (accountability). Using these criteria, she finds that institutionalized processes are better at ensuring the participation of people living in poverty than are politicized processes. She notes, however, that "the impact of democratic innovations on the participation of low-income or poor people remains uncertain."[54]

Tulia Falleti and Julia Lynch[55] argue persuasively that the hope of determining causality of outcomes in a public engagement initiative rests on careful attention to the context in which the initiative takes place. Abelson and colleagues explore five different contextual elements that can affect public engagement initiatives: political, decision making, community, researcher–decision maker relationships, and organizational factors. They conclude that contextual factors do influence the outcomes of public engagement initiatives, and that there is consistency across cases, including that "leadership and commitment at all levels of the organization clearly plays a crucial role in facilitating successful implementation."[56] Building on their work, I have argued elsewhere[57] that participants' identity is another important contextual factor to consider, particularly in the case of attempts to include the voices of young mothers, who frequently live in low income. Engagement context cannot necessarily be decoupled from process as easily as this breakdown implies. Christopher Karpowitz, Tali Mendelberg, and Lee Shaker suggest that "deliberative design may thus need to concern itself both with the equal opportunity to speak and with the equal use of that opportunity,"[58] which implies the need to consider process and context concurrently. They find that women are most likely to participate equally when they are in the majority in majority-rule decision-making arrangements and when they are in the minority in unanimous-rule decision-making arrangements.

Women, Poverty Reduction, and Public Engagement

The analysis in this chapter draws on short questionnaires completed by 324 women who attended a public dialogue during the first phase of BPT, 44 of whom self-identified as living in poverty; observations of the same public dialogue sessions; and interviews with five of the public servants responsible for designing and implementing all phases of BPT. The first phase of BPT took place in fall 2008 and winter 2009. Surveys and interviews were completed during the same period. Almost all participants who completed questionnaires identified as connected to the subject of poverty, either because they self-identified as living in poverty, worked to support those living in poverty, or both. Fourteen per cent of participants self-identified as living in poverty; they were not given, nor asked to provide, a definition of poverty. This is higher than the provincial average of 8.2 per cent falling below Statistics Canada's after-tax "low income cut-off" threshold at that time.[59]

Questionnaires were distributed at the beginning of each of sixteen public dialogue sessions. Participants were informed that they were under no obligation to complete a questionnaire, and that participation in the dialogue was not dependent on participation in the research. Questionnaires were created in collaboration with the public servants who designed BPT, available in English and French, and designed for ease of readability. Questionnaires asked for non-identifying demographic information, including, gender, age range, marital/familial status, and current education and employment status (see table 11.1). Participants were also asked what they liked best about the session and what they would have changed. Both English and French responses are included in this analysis; quotes that have been translated from French to English are so noted. Session observations focused on logistics and space – for example, room set-up, number of participants, space accessibility – and interactions among participants and between participants and others, including volunteer facilitators at each table. Interviews with public servants gathered descriptive data about the process, and were guided by questions about process development and modifications, and strategies used to promote broad engagement.

Participant demographics: Based on the research team's observations and discussions with participants and public servants involved in implementing the dialogues, of 774[60] public dialogue participants, approximately 65 per cent were female, 65 to 70 per cent were over age forty, and 60 to 65 per cent participated in English. Less than 2 per cent of the participants were under age twenty, and there was a near absence of racialized and Indigenous participants[61] – so much so that, in the case of the latter, the province subsequently commissioned a First Nations consultant to hear more about the experiences of poverty of First Nations people in New Brunswick. These figures align closely with the demographic information gathered from survey respondents presented in table 11.1.

What is important to engaging women, including women living in low income, in policy development? Women's written comments emphasized the value of participant diversity and the need for space for personal stories and diverse ideas to emerge and inform the process. Women participants also commented on the benefits of particular design features, including the use of facilitators at table dialogues. Public servants who designed and implemented BPT talked extensively about their efforts to design an inclusive process.

Diversity and acceptance: Many women mentioned the diversity of participants as a highlight of the process. One woman highlighted the value of hearing "feedback from various individuals – corporate, NGO

Table 11.1 Demographics of survey respondents

		Female	Male	Total (%)
	Total Respondents (%)	324 (66.3)	165 (33.7)	489 (100)
Age	< 40 (%)	76 (15.5)	27 (5.5)	103 (21)
	40–59 (%)	159 (32.5)	74 (15.1)	233 (48)
	60+ (%)	89 (18.2)	64 (13.1)	153 (31)
Family status	couple with children	157	97	254 (52)
	couple without children	34	26	60 (12)
	single with children	42	10	52 (11)
	single without children	71	29	100 (20)
Employment status	employed full time	157	85	242 (49)
	employed part time (including seasonally)	65	20	85 (17)
	not employed/retired	78	45	123 (25)
Education status	studying full time	32	7	39 (8)
	studying part time	9	6	15 (3)
	not attending school	230	129	359 (73)
Economic status	living in poverty	44	24	68 (14)
Home community size	< 10,000	161	94	255 (52)
	10,000–50,000	35	14	49 (10)
	> 50,000	128	57	185 (38)
Personal benefit from session	learned some or a lot	284	137	421 (86)

Note: Not all totals add up to total sample size due to missing responses.
Source: Adapted from Leah Levac, "Complicating the Public in Public Engagement: Young Mothers' and Young Women's Engagement in Policy-Making" (PhD diss., University of New Brunswick, 2011).

[non-governmental organization], et cetera." Another noted that she enjoyed "bilingual multilingual table discussions because conversations can be richer when perspectives are more diverse culturally." Some respondents referenced participants' economic diversity as an important feature of representativeness. One mentioned the "great mixture of people; [including] people living in poverty and people who work with people in poverty." Several participating women commented specifically on the need for more representation of people living in poverty. Young people were also identified as an underrepresented group. One young woman participant stated simply: "Invite more young people." Another noted that "there were very few young people. We could be missing out on some important insights/opinions," while a third asked that youth "be more involved, either included in the current dialogue or as separate dialogue sessions." Besides people living in poverty and young people, three women referenced the need for greater participation of political representatives, through the presence either of various government departments or of elected officials.

Beyond the importance of hearing from diverse voices, women noted the importance of "equal weight [being] given to all who participated." Questionnaire responses suggested that the dialogue sessions, where participants were divided into discussion groups according to their birth month as a randomizing tool, helped to "ensure a broad range of experiences and backgrounds discussing the issue" at each table. Participants also described the sessions as being "very comfortable and encouraging everyone's ideas" and as promoting an "atmosphere of mutual respect" where "the voices of everyone counted" [translated from French]. The rich, open conversations and diversity of ideas were frequently complimented by participating women. Participants noted that this allowed them "the ability to share their own opinions and build on others'" and to "voice their own opinion no matter what it was." Women connected this openness to participants' being able to "contribute different skills and backgrounds"; women participants mentioned the exchange of ideas and the opportunity to communicate their own thoughts as highlights of the dialogue sessions. Women's descriptions of the importance of idea sharing were connected to the group's diversity. For example, women commented that "having a cross section of individuals speaking and sharing was very positive," and that having "diverse backgrounds at the table was so interesting and educational." Several respondents explicitly identified the experiences of people living in poverty as having contributed important information to the process.

This is not to say that women were uncritically supportive of the process. A participant who prefaced her comments by saying, "I don't want to sound cynical, but ... ," was one of thirty-one women who wondered whether the results of BPT would translate into meaningful change. Women referenced past government reports that were completed and then not implemented, and wondered why another discussion or report was even necessary. For example, one woman asked: "So many reports and consultations have been done ... My concern is that nothing critical will change. Is the political will to make major changes there?" Another stated: "We have everything we need to reduce poverty. It's time to act!" [translated from French]. Some women suggested that their evaluation of the process was dependent on future action: "To improve the whole process, ensure there is real action taken on people's input."

Designing for inclusion: Many women mentioned the importance of the facilitators to the process. Of the thirty-five women who commented that personal learning was a highlight of their engagement, twenty-seven attributed their learning to the use of facilitators. Facilitators were complimented for being fair, "supportive [without interfering] with conversation," and "great at allowing everyone to speak." Women participants' comments about facilitators were overwhelmingly positive. The few negative comments focused on instances of facilitators' not including everyone at the table and not remaining impartial. Two women felt that facilitators should have been "more informed on social and economic issues." A primary criticism of the BPT dialogues came from older women, who noted that the noise level during the dialogues "made hearing a challenge" and hindered group conversations. This small observation provides an excellent reminder of the wide range of considerations necessary when designing for inclusion.

Some of the steps that were taken to facilitate the involvement of people living in low income included training dialogue facilitators to be aware of power dynamics in conversations, paying careful attention to inclusion details, hiring an outreach worker, and partnering with community-based organizations to facilitate involvement. The initiative's outreach worker discussed soliciting the involvement of people living in low income by connecting with shelters, community kitchens, and municipalities: "Basically, my job was to travel the province and build connections and stir up support for the process ... I worked to open doors with mayors across the province ... The feedback from a lot of people was that it was the first time government had reached out to them ... in some cases, the first time anyone [from government] had stepped foot in their office." One of the public servants involved gave an example of the careful attention to detail: "What do you do when you have [dialogue participants] who can't read or write? ... I was writing [one participant's name on a nametag] and his buddy ... whispered to him, 'can you write my name?' and the guys turned to me and [casually] I said, 'oh, it's okay, I can write it.' And [the first guy] says to me, 'that's good, [because] he can't do it' ... If you want to bring [a diverse group of] participants in, you have to be ready for it. You have to make it so that people aren't singled out."

Trained facilitators were critical for hosting inclusive conversations during the public dialogues. BPT facilitators were volunteers who received one day of training and then attended one or more public dialogue sessions to facilitate conversations among participants. As discussed above, many participants mentioned the importance of the facilitators to the process in their survey responses. Observers also noted facilitators' efforts to ensure different perspectives were invited and respected. Observation notes pointed out that facilitators enhanced the quality of inclusion by making frequent eye contact with all participants, summarizing key points made by participants, and asking non-judgmental clarifying questions: "People seemed to speak at a high comfort level and input from others often showed that everyone listened to one another by repeating their comments back" (Observation Notes, January 2009).

Designing for uptake: To demonstrate and enhance both the political and decision-making contexts in which BPT occurred, the public servants who designed BPT simultaneously implemented a process with elected and senior government officials. It consisted primarily of an interdepartmental steering committee of deputy ministers and a series of meetings with cabinet. The purposes were to work on breaking down interdepartmental silos, a noted challenge to public engagement,[62] to engage the departments that were most likely to be affected by the final poverty-reduction plan, and to encourage members of the steering committee to help their own departments learn about the public engagement process. The public servants who designed BPT noted the need for this because of the tension between the desired iterative nature of quality public engagement on the one hand, and the more typical formal, secretive, and somewhat linear nature of policy making on the other. Public servants understood and designed this internal process as a means of resolving this tension, particularly by highlighting decisions that elected officials were going to have to make, given alternatives that were emerging in the public dialogues. One public servant described the importance of this component as follows:

The [participating] ministers need to know what they are allowed to do because [decision making within the legislature is] a legal framework ... [Elected officials] don't have the legal authority or the democratic authority to [make agreements on the spot], so we have to figure out how to set up boundaries. So, if, for example ... people say that the [social assistance] system needs to change [because] it's too punitive ... When we go to [cabinet], we're going to say to them "people are telling us that we need to change the social assistance system to be more developmental rather than punitive. And here are the things that will need to be changed to be able to do that ... You have to change the wage exemption, you have to change the asset policy, you have to not pay as last resort, which means this, this, and this." And so we'll give [cabinet] all the things that need to change, and we'll have to tell them how much it's going to cost: "Look, to make this change, it's going to cost $20 million," for example, and they'll have to say, "okay, yeah," or "no," or "not now," or ...

What Matters for Women? For Democracy?

Women's evaluations of the BPT dialogue sessions, combined with information from public servants who designed and implemented BPT, focused on two procedural dimensions as important to the inclusion of women, including women living in low income: participants' diversity and experiences as a source of information (diversity and acceptance), and the importance of facilitators (designing for inclusion). Overall, women's evaluations of the process design were positive, even though some expressed cynicism about the likelihood of change resulting from the process. Such cynicism was expressed using non-agentic language, implying a limited trust of political will, as opposed to a lack of trust in the procedural design. Given the importance of political will in enacting meaningful policy change[63] and the importance of sociopolitical factors in informing the context of public engagement experiments,[64] participating women were making an astute distinction. Women commented on the importance of participants' diversity, and their evaluations made explicit reference to participants' stories as providing information that was essential to the process. Women's reliance on first-hand experience and personal stories responds to the absence of their perspectives in many bodies of research and public discourses,[65] affirms the need to acknowledge information that is created in every day gendered settings, and reinforces the value of using gender and intersectional policy analyses to reveal the diverse experiences of women and women living in poverty.

In their research to identify strategies for facilitating the participation of people living in poverty, Ravensbergen and VanderPlaat call for "(i) an increase in local learning and action opportunities for people living in poverty; (ii) more supportive front-line interactions between governmental and non-governmental agencies,"[66] and efforts related to reducing stigma. That women participants in BPT specifically referenced the important information contributed by participants who lived in low income, combined with the fact, as noted, that 14 per cent of participants self-identified as living in low income, could be indicative of some success with reducing stigma. Still, women's comments in the surveys noted an underrepresentation, or absence, of people living in poverty.

Women's calls for greater participation of people living in poverty seem slightly incongruous with the relatively high percentage of actual participants who self-described as living in poverty. This could be due, however, to participants' random assignment to tables, leaving some tables without participants who were living in low income, or to the particularly high participation of those living in low income at one dialogue session that was held in a low-income neighbourhood.

Although there were people at every session who self-identified as living in poverty, at some sessions there were very few. It is also possible that some participants had inaccurate perceptions of people living in poverty, or were using inaccurate indicators to determine the presence of people living in poverty. For example, 36 per cent of participants who self-identified as living in poverty were employed, full time or part time, whereas participants might have assumed that all participants who referred to having a job at some point during the dialogue were not living in poverty. Finally, calls for greater participation of people living in poverty might point to women's beliefs that those living in poverty should have accounted for an even larger proportion of participants overall. Evaluating the representativeness of an experiment involves "carefully considering whose input should be considered."[67] Women's evaluations might suggest that people whose ideas are least likely to be considered in current policy-making processes are those who are most critical in public engagement processes.

The value women placed on sharing experiences and opinions might help to explain the importance they gave to having a facilitator guide the discussion and ensure that all voices were heard. Most facilitators had past experience with facilitation, and were trained to ensure equal participation among dialogue participants and to intervene when people's experiences or opinions were being discredited or discouraged by other participants. Given the barriers to women's participation – such as pre-existing inequalities,[68] the discord between societal messages and women's experiences that results in silencing women,[69] and the historical exclusion of women's perspectives – participants' reliance on facilitators suggests that facilitators enabled more inclusive discussion and even that facilitators were necessary to ensuring that women could participate meaningfully in the dialogue.

As noted above, understanding the context of public engagement initiatives is essential to understanding the outcomes of such initiatives.[70] Several contextual factors – including those relating to politics, decision making, organization, and identity – are important.[71] Although scholars argue that context influences public engagement processes and their outcomes, these findings suggest that processes can also influence the context. This is evidenced through public servants' efforts to include the voices of people living in low income, and through their attempts to foster a political and decision-making environment open to participants' ideas and knowledge. The above description of efforts to engage both politicians and senior public servants in the process exemplifies how public servants negotiated between "democratizing" and "bureaucratizing" logics,[72] and highlights efforts to influence the initiative's context, which includes the issue under consideration and the timeframe of the decision-making process.[73] In their framework, Abelson and colleagues suggest that the political context accounts for the historical relationship between the public and the government.[74] Public engagement initiatives – and by extension their participants – thus have the potential to influence the context in which future engagement initiatives take place. Although not revealed by the data presented in this chapter, related evidence that this might be the case comes from the fact that ESIC's enabling legislation – which emerged from *Bringing the Pieces Together* – requires that the plan be updated at least every five years using a public engagement approach.[75] As such and as noted above, three years after the conclusion of BPT and the release of New Brunswick's poverty-reduction plan, the province undertook another public engagement initiative to update the poverty-reduction plan and chart the next five-year plan. What is interesting about this, and about the original process, is that the provincial government has changed twice over the same period. In other words, even though the formal political context has changed, the political will towards public engagement has remained strong enough that this legislative requirement has not been altered. This finding contributes to deliberative democracy theory, and supports the argument put forward by David Moscrop and Mark Warren[76] that suggests engagement processes can influence the context that frames public engagement initiatives, and that the context of public engagement initiatives is dynamic, whereas existing scholarship typically examines the relationship in the other direction – that is, the importance of context to possibilities for engagement.[77]

Still, and not surprisingly, previous experiences with inauthentic engagement – where reports were written and shelved, or issues were explored but not addressed – created cynicism among some participants and dissuaded participation, suggesting caution over too much optimism about how influential public engagement initiatives can hope to be in the future context of public participation. Certainly, one initiative cannot repair a long history of exclusion. However, the findings from this study do suggest that public engagement initiatives that are explicit about engaging with historically marginalized citizens and residents, such as women – including women living in low income – can help to shape the context in which future public engagement initiatives unfold. This finding aligns with those by others, such as Alana Cattapan and colleagues (chapter 10, in this volume), who explore "approach[es] to public engagement ... [that] speak to feminist and other creative, community-based policy research commitments, and [that are] geared towards building ongoing trust with communities."

268   Leah Levac

Conclusion

Women, including those living in low income, who participated in the dialogue phase of *Bringing the Pieces Together*, a public engagement initiative in New Brunswick designed to inform the development of a provincial poverty-reduction plan, spoke to the importance of participants' diversity and of space for personal stories and diverse ideas to emerge. Participants' comments seemed to suggest that an overrepresentation of the voices of people living in low income would have been warranted to ensure ample opportunities for their experiences and ideas to be heard. Despite the usual emphasis on contextual factors informing public engagement initiatives, my analysis suggests that, because contexts are dynamic, the reverse might also be true. In other words, there might be benefit in evaluating public engagement initiatives based on the extent to which they contribute to successful public engagement contexts. It is impossible to say with certainty what New Brunswick's poverty-reduction strategy would have looked like had there not been explicit efforts to engage with people living in low income, including women. However, the high participation rates in the most recent renewal process for updating the strategy suggest that citizens and residents remain willing to participate. This might signal that their experiences and knowledges are being meaningfully taken up in the resulting decisions, which in turn might make their continuing participation more likely. Although there is widespread acceptance of the normative value of public engagement, debate remains about how best to design and evaluate meaningful public engagement initiatives. The evaluation of BPT by participating women, including women living in low income, offers some important insights on design features that matter for inclusion.

Discussion Questions

1 Based on your knowledge of public administration, what other strategies, such as the one described above in the "designing for inclusion" section, could help to shift the political context in greater favour of public engagement?
2 Very few young, racialized, or Indigenous people – who have all been excluded historically from public policy development – participated in the public dialogues of BPT. What design features could have been added to address these persistent exclusions?
3 Jurisdictions across Canada use a variety of public engagement initiatives as part of their policy-making processes. These initiatives are greeted with varying degrees of cynicism. Have you ever

participated in such an initiative as a member of the public? In some other capacity? What was your experience?

NOTES

1 A detailed overview of this initiative is laid out by Jocelyne Bourgon, "NS Live Case Series 2017: Overcoming Poverty Together, New Brunswick Citizen-centric Perspectives" (Ottawa: Public Governance International, November 2017), online at https://www.pgionline.com/wp-content /uploads/2017/12/OvercomingPovertyNB.ebook_1.pdf.

2 Don Lenihan, *Rescuing Policy: The Case for Public Engagement* (Ottawa: Public Policy Forum, 2012).

3 The clearest evidence of this was that the process and resulting implementation plan were co-chaired by prominent NB businessperson Gerry Pond, widely recognized anti-poverty advocate and community organizer Léo-Paul Pinet, and then Premier Shawn Graham.

4 Amy Lang, "But Is It for Real? The British Columbia Citizens' Assembly as a Model of State-Sponsored Citizen Empowerment," *Politics & Society* 35, no. 1 (2007): 35–69; Jonathan Rose, "Putting the Public Back in Public Policy: The Ontario Citizens' Assembly on Electoral Reform," *Canadian Parliamentary Review* 30, no. 3 (2007): 9–16.

5 Frances Ravensbergen, and Madine VanderPlaat, "Barriers to Citizen Participation: The Missing Voice of People Living in Low Income," *Community Development Journal* 45, no. 4 (2009): 389–403.

6 Julia Abelson et al., "Will It Make a Difference if I Show Up and Share? A Citizens' Perspective on Improving Public Involvement Processes for Health System Decision-Making," *Journal of Health Services Research and Policy* 9, no. 4 (2004): 205–12; Julia Abelson et al., "Examining the Role of Context in the Implementation of a Deliberative Public Participation Experiment: Results from a Canadian Comparative Study," *Social Science and Medicine* 64 (2007): 2115–28.

7 D.J. Gamble, "The Berger Inquiry: An Impact Assessment Process," *Science* 199, no. 4332 (1978): 946–52.

8 Jeffrey Masuda, Tara K. McGee, and Theresa D. Garvin, "Power, Knowledge, and Public Engagement: Constructing 'Citizenship' in Alberta's Industrial Heartland," *Journal of Environmental Policy and Planning* 10, no. 4 (2008): 359–80; Genevieve Fuji Johnson, "The Limits of Deliberative Democracy and Empowerment: Elite Motivation in Three Canadian Cases," *Canadian Journal of Political Science* 44, no. 1 (2011): 137–59; Sarah Marie Wiebe, *Everyday Exposure: Indigenous Mobilization and Environmental Justice in Canada's Chemical Valley* (Vancouver: UBC Press, 2016).

9 Lang, "But Is It for Real?"

10 Johnson, "Limits of Deliberative Democracy."

11 Florence Larocque, "The Impact of Institutionalization, Politicization and Mobilization on the Direct Participation of Citizens Experiencing Poverty," *Canadian Journal of Political Science* 44, no. 4 (2011): 883–902.

12 Brian W. Head, "Community Engagement: Participation on Whose Terms?" *Australian Journal of Political Science* 42, no. 3 (2007): 441–54.

13 Adapted from Gene Rowe and Lynn J. Frewer, "A Typology of Public Engagement Mechanisms," *Science, Technology and Human Values* 30, no. 2 (2005): 253.

14 David Moscrop and Mark E. Warren, "When Is Deliberation Democratic?" *Journal of Public Deliberation* 12, no. 2 (2016): article 4, emphasis in original.

15 Robert Goodin, "Enfranchising All Affected Interests, and Its Alternatives," *Philosophy and Public Affairs* 35, no. 1 (2007): 40–68.

16 Moscrop and Warren, "When Is Deliberation Democratic?" emphasis in original.

17 Emma Jones and John Gaventa, *Concepts of Citizenship: A Review*, IDS Development Bibliography 19 (Brighton, UK: Institute of Development Studies, 2002), online at https://www.ids.ac.uk/files/dmfile/Db19.pdf.

18 Amy Gutmann and Dennis F. Thompson, *Why Deliberative Democracy?* (Princeton, NJ: Princeton University Press, 2009), 3, italics in original.

19 Ibid., 3.

20 Ibid., 6.

21 Stephen Elstub and Peter McLaverty, eds., *Deliberative Democracy: Issues and Cases* (Edinburgh: Edinburgh University Press, 2014).

22 Mini-publics are widely discussed as a tool of deliberative democracy. Contemporary discussions of mini-publics often reference the ideas of Robert Dahl, *Democracy and Its Critics* (New Haven, CT: Yale University Press, 1989).

23 Carolyn Hendriks, "Integrated Deliberation: Reconciling Civil Society's Dual Role in Deliberative Democracy," *Political Studies* 54, no. 3 (2006): 486–508.

24 Gutmann and Thompson, *Why Deliberative Democracy*.

25 Iris Marion Young, "Polity and Group Difference: A Critique of the Ideal of Universal Citizenship," *Ethics* 99, no. 2 (1989): 250–74.

26 Johnson, "Limits of Deliberative Democracy."

27 Wiebe, *Everyday Exposure*.

28 Peter John, "Can Citizen Governance Redress the Representative Bias of Political Participation?" *Public Administration Review* 69, no. 3 (2009): 494–503.

29 Ibid., 500.

30 Julia Abelson and François-Pierre Gauvin, *Assessing the Impacts of Public Participation: Concepts, Evidence and Policy Implications* (Ottawa: Canadian Policy Research Network, 2006).

31 Larocque, "Impact of Institutionalization."

32 New Brunswick, Executive Council Office, "Gender-Based Analysis," n.d.,
    online at http://www2.gnb.ca/content/gnb/en/services/services_renderer
    .201259.Gender-Based_Analysis.html.
33 Olena Hankivsky and Renee Cormier, "Intersectionality and Public Policy:
    Some Lessons from Existing Models," *Political Research Quarterly* 64, no. 1
    (2011): 217.
34 Elena Chernikova, "Aboriginal Peoples: Fact Sheet for New Brunswick"
    (Ottawa: Statistics Canada, 2016), online at https://www150.statcan.gc.ca
    /n1/en/pub/89-656-x/89-656-x2016005-eng.pdf?st=9fxadm59.
35 Statistics Canada, "Population and Dwelling Count Highlight Tables, 2016
    Census," online at: http://www12.statcan.gc.ca/census-recensement
    /2016/dp-pd/hlt-fst/pd-pl/Table.cfm?Lang=Eng&T=101&S=50&O=A.
36 Economic and Social Inclusion Corporation, "Overcoming Poverty Together:
    The New Brunswick Economic and Social Inclusion Plan 2014–2019"
    (Fredericton: ESIC, 2014), online at http://www2.gnb.ca/content/dam
    /gnb/Departments/esic/pdf/NBEconomicSocialInclusionPlan2014-2019.pdf.
37 The addition of a fourth co-chair, representing the experiences of people
    living in poverty, was the result of pressure from community members.
38 Economic and Social Inclusion Corporation, "Overcoming Poverty
    Together," 7.
39 Ibid., 16.
40 Ibid., 19.
41 Economic and Social Inclusion Corporation, "Public engagement process
    concludes for renewed poverty reduction plan," News Release, 10 May
    2019, online at https://www2.gnb.ca/content/gnb/en/departments/esic
    /news/news_release.2019.05.0310.html.
42 Economic and Social Inclusion Corporation, "Looking Back to Move Forward:
    Renewal of Overcoming Poverty Together: The New Brunswick Economic
    and Social Inclusion Plan" (Fredericton, [2019]), online at https://nbtogether
    .ca/wp-content/uploads/2019/03/LookingBack2019_WEB_ENG.pdf.
43 Canada Without Poverty, "New Brunswick Provincial Poverty Profile,"
    2013, online at https://www.cwp-csp.ca/resources/sites/default/files
    /resources/NB_Provincial_Profile.pdf (link no longer active).
44 Canada Without Poverty, "New Brunswick Provincial Poverty Profile,"
    2016, online at https://cwp-csp.ca/wp-content/uploads/2016/12/NB
    -Report-Fixed.pdf; idem, *2017 Poverty Progress Profiles*, online at https://
    cwp-csp.ca/wp-content/uploads/2018/03/2017-Poverty-Progress
    -Profiles-318.pdf.
45 John Gaventa and Gregory Barrett, "Mapping the Outcomes of Citizen
    Engagement," *World Development* 40, no. 12 (2012): 2399.
46 Paul Burton, "Conceptual, Theoretical and Practical Issues in Measuring
    the Benefits of Public Participation," *Evaluation* 15, no. 3 (2009): 263–84.

47　Larocque, "Impact of Institutionalization"; Abelson and Gauvin, *Assessing the Impacts of Public Participation*; Abelson et al., "Will It Make a Difference if I Show Up and Share?"

48　Gaventa and Barrett, "Mapping the Outcomes"; Larocque, "Impact of Institutionalization."

49　Abelson et al., "Examining the Role of Context"; Tulia Falleti and Julia Lynch, "Context and Causal Mechanisms in Political Analysis," *Comparative Political Studies* 42, no. 9 (2009): 1143–66.

50　Abelson and Gauvin, *Assessing the Impacts of Public Participation*; Abelson et al., "Will It Make a Difference if I Show Up and Share?"

51　Larocque, "Impact of Institutionalization."

52　John Dryzek, *Deliberative Democracy and Beyond: Liberals, Critics, and Contestations* (New York: Oxford University Press, 2000; idem, *Democracy in Capitalist Times: Ideals, Limits, and Struggles* (New York: Oxford University Press, 1996).

53　Larocque, "Impact of Institutionalization," 888.

54　Ibid., 887–8.

55　Falleti and Lynch, "Context and Causal Mechanisms."

56　Abelson et al., "Examining the Role of Context," 2125.

57　Leah Levac, "Complicating the Public: Enabling Young Women's Participation in Public Engagement Initiatives," *Journal of Youth Studies* 16, no. 3 (2013): 334–57.

58　Christopher F. Karpowitz, Tali Mendelberg, and Lee Shaker, "Gender Inequality in Deliberative Participation." *American Political Science Review* 106, no. 3 (2012): 553.

59　Statistics Canada, *Income in Canada, 2007*, cat. no. 75-202-X (Ottawa, June 2009), online at https://www150.statcan.gc.ca/n1/en/pub/75-202-x/75-202-x2007000-eng.pdf?st=Hyls2RKa.

60　Participants' occupations were not collected, but based on the research team's observations, the collection of participants' organizational affiliations, and conversations with participants and with the project team, we concluded that most Phase I participants had a personal connection to the subject of poverty (worked in a community service organization) beyond interest as an average citizen.

61　This limitation, despite considerable effort, serves as a reminder of the current limits of diversity inclusion in institutionalized public engagement initiatives.

62　Head, "Community Engagement."

63　Carmen Malena, *From Political Won't to Political Will: Building Support for Participatory Governance* (Sterling, VA: Kumarian Press, 2009).

64　Abelson and Gauvin, *Assessing the Impacts of Public Participation*.

65 Patricia A. Gouthro, "Active and Inclusive Citizenship for Women: Democratic Considerations for Fostering Lifelong Education," *International Journal of Lifelong Education* 26, no. 2 (2007): 143–54.

66 Ravensbergen and VanderPlaat, "Barriers to Citizen Participation," 389.

67 Abelson et al., "Will It Make a Difference if I Show Up and Share?" 211.

68 Kara Dillard, "Assessing the Problem of Gender Inequality in Deliberative Democracy" (PhD diss., Kansas State University, 2011), online at http://krex.k-state.edu/dspace/bitstream/handle/2097/12005/KaraDillard2011.pdf?sequence=3&isAllowed=y.

69 Carol Gilligan, *In a Different Voice: Psychological Theory and Women's Development* (Cambridge, MA: Harvard University Press, 1982).

70 Falleti and Lynch, "Context and Causal Mechanisms."

71 Abelson et al., "Examining the Role of Context"; Levac, "Complicating the Public."

72 Caroline Lee, "Walking the Talk: The Performance of Authenticity in Public Engagement Work," *Sociological Quarterly* 55, no. 3 (2014): 493–513.

73 Abelson et al., "Examining the Role of Context."

74 Ibid., 2119.

75 Economic and Social Inclusion Act, (2010) s. 41(1), online at http://laws.gnb.ca/en/showfulldoc/cs/E-1.105//20200212?command=search&caller=SI&fragment=economic%20and%20social%20inclusion&search_type=all&day=12&month=2&year=2020&search_domain=cs&length=5#idhit1.

76 Moscrop and Warren, "When Is Deliberation Democratic?"

77 See, for example, Falleti and Lynch, "Context and Causal Mechanisms"; Abelson et al., "Examining the Role of Context."

KEY RESOURCES

Gutmann, Amy, and Dennis F. Thompson. *Why Deliberative Democracy?* Princeton, NJ: Princeton University Press, 2009.

Institute for Development Studies. "Governance, Power and Participation." Online at https://www.ids.ac.uk/research/governance-power-and-participation/.

International Association for Public Participation. Website at https://www.iap2.org/.

PART THREE

Effective and Affective Spaces
of Deliberation

12 The HeART of Engagement: Experiences of a Community-Created Mobile Art Gallery in Brazil

BRUNO DE OLIVEIRA JAYME

Introduction

It's 10:00 in the morning on 22 June 2012 in a metropolis where rush hour is every hour. There are people everywhere rushing to get to places, being shoved into public transportation. The air traffic with its helicopters is chaotic. Cars and motorcycles honk their way onto the pavement. Street vendors try to sell anything they can to make a living. An audience contemplates a preacher who loudly announces: "Jesus is coming." Sirens of police cars and ambulances are heard from kilometres away. Although it is not summer in this city, the heat is unbearable, the air pollution is heavy, and green space is lacking. The heat accentuates the stench of garbage that has not yet been collected. A group of executive men sweating inside their suit jackets ignore a panhandler begging for food.

This could be just an ordinary day in the city of São Paulo, Brazil, except that, at this moment, a van drives through the crowd onto the main public square and parks in front of City Hall. I am confused. Is it a riot? Some kind of terrorist act? A strike? Suddenly, five people arrive and begin unloading art supplies. A set of twelve easels is unfolded, and artworks are carefully hung on them. On the other side of the square, an old bus parks, its door opens, and a young crowd jumps out, hip-hop music blasting. Each one grabs a can of spray paint and starts to graffiti the bus. In between two light poles, a big banner is strung, titled in bold letters: *Recycling Stories – A Community-Created Art Gallery*. At that moment the chaos in the public square seems to stop, transformed now into an open-air art exhibit. The police and security guards approach abruptly, pointing their truncheons at the young people while loudly talking on their walkie-talkies and cell phones. Why did the police react so violently against that art gallery and these artists?

How can we create meaningful spaces of engagement for citizens who work in the recycling industry in Brazil but suffer marginalization? What can we learn from the Brazilian experience of opening spaces of engagement? Seeking answers to these questions, I embarked upon a journey of participatory action and arts-based research, and developed a series of visual arts workshops and public exhibits in São Paulo. In this context, the objective of this chapter is to explore the diverse role of the arts, not just in creating spaces for engagement that are inherently deliberatively democratic, but also in holding the space for dialogue, knowledge construction and mobilization, and civic engagement. Deliberative democracy advances the idea that inclusive public decision making emerges through dialogical and dialectical spaces and interactions between the oppressed and the oppressor. In this sense, deliberative democracy sustained the art workshops and the exhibit and represented the core value of the community art gallery that was established during this project. Civic engagement, in the context of this study, refers to the complex and ever-changing construction of knowledge and its mobilization, through collaboration between participants and the general public. With this in mind, the ultimate goal of civic engagement is to empower participants to take leading roles in the art-making process and, later on in their lives, as subjects of their own history, not mere objects of it. This process of *conscientização* is what Paulo Freire[1] eloquently defines as "the pedagogy of possible dreams," which I articulate later on.

In this chapter, I welcome my readers into four different spaces of engagement we co-constructed during an arts-based research project that was developed collaboratively in São Paulo with workers from the recycling industry, the so-called *recyclers*. These spaces are represented and illustrated here by three arts workshops (on abstract painting, expressionism painting, and mosaics) and one art exhibit that travelled the country. These spaces of engagement were constructed and secured through extensive and intensive work and hours of conversation on effective listening and talking, mutual respect, community building, and trust among participants. The recyclers who participated in this project work in different recycling cooperatives in the city, and these cooperatives in turn are involved with a very politically engaged Brazilian environmental adult education organization and social movement called Movimento Nacional de Catadores de Materiais Recicláveis (MNCR, National Recycling Social Movement). The main goals of this organization are to make visible to the public recyclers' reality of poverty and to help recyclers find their own voices so they can fight for the development of their community. The episodes I describe in this chapter are a reflection not just of the artworks produced by the recyclers, but also of the experience of publicly exhibiting their artworks and how the art-making process and exhibit constructed important visual meaning, created opportunities for civic engagement, opened dialogical and dialectical political spaces, and even provided income generation for those involved in the recycling industry. By sharing these episodes, I suggest that community-created art galleries are deliberately democratic pedagogical sites in and for environmental adult education because they indeed are spaces of engagement, where knowledge around environmental issues regarding the Brazilian recycling industry is co-constructed and mobilized. Although these episodes unfolded in a Brazilian context, they should not be taken as isolated phenomena. They emerged from ordinary situations among real people and their environment, and these situations are daily co-constructed and continuously reproduced in different scenarios and with different actors. Although set on a different stage, the stories I present fall under the same umbrella of a very complex system of power that produces and reproduces poverty, perpetuating uneven development. These stories, however, illustrate how participants, through an art-making process and art exhibit, can experience a different reality for themselves and their community. Once this imaginary is produced, recyclers are left with two routes to choose from: they either can stay where they are, tied to a system of power and oppression, or they can pursue this alternative reality, and enhance the spaces of engagement they create themselves and make it real. The stories I tell in this chapter are the stories of those recyclers who chose the second route.

I begin by noting the polarization of art galleries, which on one side perpetuate hegemonic power through their exhibit, and on the other represent political and pedagogical spaces. I then explain how environmental adult education[2] and arts-based research[3] are important frameworks for exploring the role of art exhibits in the context of adult education. Then, through sharing two stories that happened with recyclers during the workshops and exhibits, I illustrate their realities of marginalization and how they negotiate their presence in the Brazilian political realm as strong and powerful community leaders and environmental agents.

Art Galleries

Worldwide, the arts have been applied to help marginalized populations fight for community development, because the arts create and mobilize new knowledge, resist oppression, and speak truth to power.[4] Such

powerful aspects of the arts are achieved by engaging citizens in dialogues about social and political issues. When it comes to displaying artwork, art galleries play a very important role in education because these
spaces trouble identity and share hidden, or even provide alternative,
narratives to misrepresented stories. This is because art galleries are not
neutral, apolitical spaces that represent cultural and social knowledge. In
fact, art galleries always tell a story, and the way they tell it, through their
exhibits, is necessarily positional. Museum educators for example, outline the potential of museums to construct "new narratives that reflect
demographic, social, and cultural diversity, and represent a plurality of
lived experiences, histories, and identities."[5] Others suggest that art galleries contain "some of the necessary spaces for renegotiating hegemonic
relations."[6] Darlene Clover goes further, arguing that not only is there
potential, but in the face of widespread oppression it is absolutely necessary, for art galleries to "magnify injustices and indignities and capture
the fury and anger felt against the sharp edge of imperialism and neo
conservative capitalism."[7] Carmel Borg and Perter Mayo also see art galleries as sites of "cultural politics and public pedagogy and repositories
of what counts as official knowledge."[8] They draw on critical pedagogy
to question the way culture and power are legitimized in art galleries.
Moreover, art galleries have the potential to create democratic spaces
where knowledge is co-constructed not by Eurocentric academic work,
but rather through the eyes of the viewers, who bring their own prior
knowledge and previous experiences about and with art itself.

As pedagogical sites, one can expect that art galleries can be spaces of
engagement and knowledge construction and knowledge mobilization
(KM). This is important because KM opens opportunities for people
to perceive their world(s) through different lenses, hoping that they
can make more conscious decisions on issues that affect their environment. For L. Ardra Cole and Maura McIntyre, art galleries are powerful spaces for KM because of their innate ability to "evoke emotional,
cultural, social, and political complexities"; as well, art galleries have a
"unique and creative way of engaging the audience in meaning-making
and KM."[9] Making an art gallery more accessible to the general public,
especially those living on the margins, was the reason we created a mobile art gallery called "Recycling Stories." As our art gallery travelled to
different cities in Brazil, it displayed and sold the artwork produced by
the recyclers. I describe below how "Recycling Stories" came about and
how it unfolded throughout this project. But first, I explain the theoretical frameworks (arts-based research and environmental adult education) that support these art explorations, followed by a brief description
of the MNCR.

The Role of Arts-Based Research and Environmental Adult Education in Community Development

One way of learning about the politics that goes on in a particular community is through arts-based research, which can "uncover or create new knowledge, highlight experience, pose questions, or tackle problems."[10] Arts-based research also generates trust, builds community, and inspires individual and collective empowerment and emancipation. Furthermore, artistic approaches to research mediate communication – and therefore spaces of engagement – among participants because the arts bring together verbal, behavioural, and visual modes of expression, drawing from what people have to say, which might not be accessible in certain situations.[11] In addition, as Clover, Joyce Stalker, and Laurie McGauley argue, these discourses bring forth (and challenge) bias and show us "things that we might not want to see."[12]

Along with arts-based research, another important framework for theorizing spaces of knowledge mobilization such as art galleries is environmental adult education (EAE). This framework engages recyclers and the public in critical discourses around environmental issues such as the collection and separation of recyclable materials. EAE also, through dialogue, problematizes hegemonic standpoints with the ultimate goal of promoting social change. Essentially, EAE is a community-oriented and participatory process of political and sociological learning that goes beyond individual behavioural change and the transmission of information. EAE processes start from individuals' personal knowledge by bringing this knowledge forth through dialogue to create new understandings about people's world(s).

The debate on EAE in Brazil has been strengthened throughout the years by conferences, capacity building, community meetings, and engagement, as well as research by non-governmental organizations and social movements.[13] Such initiatives have been opening spaces for sharing experiences, critical dialogue, construction of new knowledge, and knowledge mobilization. These dialogues open opportunities for a collective positioning of the public regarding environmental education and public policies. A paramount concept in EAE is its emancipatory character, which is critical and context bound. This concept invites participants to engage in deliberative democracy through respectful dialogue among those involved, and questions behaviourist and reductionist approaches to environmental education.[14] Deliberative democracy in the context of EAE is so important, especially within the Brazilian recycling cooperatives and social movement, because it helps to improve collective decisions about the politics that go on within the cooperatives. Within this concept, by focusing on individual emancipation, EAE is a critical element for social change because citizenship is the main focus of discussion.[15]

In Brazil, most environmental education organizations and networks sprang up in the 1970s, and became stronger with the end of the military dictatorship in 1980, when people's participation and emancipation became the core of learning processes.[16] These environmental organizations, through participatory actions, question consumerism and mediate the public's *conscientização* regarding social and environmental issues. For Freire, *conscientização* refers to individuals learning to recognize social, political, and economic constraints, and acting against these constraints. This is an important framework because it is through *conscientização* that people can achieve a "truly liberating education and emancipation," opening windows for individuals to be part of their "historical process as responsible subjects"[17] – in other words, history is a possibility, not deterministic. This is evident within the MNCR, a social movement that creates learning spaces where power structures are more democratic and shared among participants.

The Brazilian Recycling Social Movement

Working in the recycling industry represents an important livelihood for many of the world's poor and excluded populations. This activity includes collecting recyclable materials on the streets, and then separating, classifying, and selling them as a means of subsistence. Those engaged in recycling often remain socially and economically marginalized, face harassment, and experience disempowerment, even though they play an important role in overall environmental health. In Brazil, there are approximately 60,000 recyclers organized in recycling cooperatives,[18] which provide employment, improve working conditions, and increase environmental education.[19] These cooperatives are affiliated with the MNCR, which helps recyclers with capacity building and networking with government and non-governmental sectors, creating inclusive solutions to recycling management.[20] The MNCR also plays an important role in KM and political advocacy for Brazilian recyclers, and aims to improve the quality of life of recyclers by recognizing their work and by playing a strong political and leadership role in the sector.

The Art Workshops

Once a week, from March to September of 2012, I facilitated three art workshops with fifty recyclers affiliated with the MNCR. The duration of each workshop depended on its nature, location, and date, but they ranged from a day to a weekend long. The goals of these workshops were the same and twofold. Since none of the recyclers had previous formal art training, my first goal was to teach three art techniques to those interested in learning how to express themselves through an artistic form. The second goal was to explore the potential of the visual arts to help recyclers voice their stories under the theme, "what it means to be a recycler." This theme, which was collectively decided by the recyclers, aimed to create dialogue among recyclers, the general public, and policy makers, making visible to the public the importance of the work the recyclers perform as environmental agents.

The first workshop was on abstract painting. This technique incorporated an assemblage of recyclable materials, modelling paste, and acrylic painting to create unique images that illustrated recyclers' experiences working in their cooperatives. Throughout the workshop, as their images started to emerge onto the canvas, I kept asking questions such as: "What does this object represent to you? Why did you decide to assemble those objects in that way? What do those images mean to you?" These questions kept our conversation flowing and mediated recyclers' thinking about what they were creating, while helping them to explore their personal stories more deeply. The final artworks were absolutely powerful because they all embodied their stories of poverty, oppression, racism, stigmatization, and, above all, stories of their fight for a better life. Finally, I asked recyclers to describe their artworks and to reflect on the process of creating them. The second workshop was on impressionist painting. In this workshop, participants brought photographs they found in magazines, newspapers, or personal family photo albums to which they felt emotionally connected. The images were spread on a table, and participants were asked to choose one image as a reference for their artwork and to explain their choice. Once again, the artworks were powerful and visually voiced participants' stories. The third workshop was on mosaics. Here, each recycler received one square of canvas and was asked to paint symbols or words that responded to the overall theme of "what it means to be a recycler." Once painted, the squares were assembled together forming a unified image. Later, during the art exhibits, the recyclers reproduced the mosaic technique with gallery visitors by asking attendees to paint their impressions about the art show.

All the art workshops were recorded on video and audio because I was interested in the free discourse that emerged among participants to explore further what could be learned from such interaction. Over 221 hours of video and sound material were produced, serving as my data corpus. Recorded sections that illustrated my claims were fully transcribed and translated verbatim. I used discourse analysis as an analytical tool for interpreting the transcripts.[21]

Over 100 paintings were created during the workshops. Each participant then chose one painting to be part of the art gallery; in the end, fifty paintings representing the fifty participants composed a mobile art exhibit that recyclers titled "Recycling Stories: A Community-Created Mobile Art Gallery." Below, I explore this art show through two different stories that were collected during the workshops and exhibit. The first story illustrates the ways in which participants constructed their own visual thought (meaning making through artistic expression). Visual thought awakens a higher level of consciousness, which is critical in environmental adult education processes. The second story is an example of how this art gallery became not just a space of engagement, but also an alternative space for income generation for the recyclers.

"Recycling Stories: A Community-Created Mobile Art Gallery"

Seven art shows were set up outside the boundaries of traditional art galleries and institutions and travelled to three different cities: São Paulo (one public library, two city halls in two municipalities, one public square, and one public elementary school); Rio de Janeiro (one exhibit during the Rio+20 Conference); and Londrina (one exhibit during the MNCR Women's Conference). During the art shows, which often happened in open air – for example, on Copacabana beach in Rio de Janeiro – the paintings were hung on easels or carefully laid on the floor, enabling visitors to mingle among them. A mosaic-making station was set up during these events with paint, brushes, and pens, so visitors could visually express their impressions about the artworks. At least one recycler was present at all times during the shows to talk to the public about their experiences in the art-making process and to engage visitors in conversation around the themes presented in the paintings. The recyclers also facilitated mosaic workshops during the art shows. In total, seven mosaics were created, representing the seven cities visited by the gallery.

Since visitors were able to walk freely around the artworks and interact with the recyclers, one can expect that much was talked about during the art shows. Most of the conversations regarded the politics around the works the recyclers created. The recyclers explained to visitors the ways in which they could cooperate with each other when it comes to domestic recyclable materials. From these dialogues, new recycling networks for cooperation were established. From these free conversations, many unique stories emerged during the workshops and exhibits. One is that of Luzia, a fifty-five-year-old recycler associated with the MNCR. According to Luzia, the MNCR, through capacity building, empowers her to be a strong and active community leader as well as a skilful environmental agent, because she helps this social movement to organize community events and promote environmental education programs in the city.

The First Story: Community-Created Art Galleries Construct People's Visual Thoughts

The following episode unfolded upon Luzia's return from Rio de Janeiro and Londrina, where she participated in the Rio+20 Summit and the MNCR Women's Conference, respectively. Her role in these two events was to host the "Recycling Stories" gallery and to facilitate mosaic workshops with visitors: "Today, I perceive that there are different ways of seeing things. My views have expanded after we went to Rio+20 and to Londrina. It was cool. Now, let's create our mosaic. And then we called everybody to paint. So, we started to perceive that there are other universes that we can work together to help those who are trying to discover their own values. And that makes me feel with a more open mind."

When Luzia starts her discourse using the noun "today," followed by her own perception of how she sees things, she is in fact suggesting that whatever she perceives in the present is not the same as what she perceived in the past. In other words, something has changed for Luzia that shifts the ways she looks at things. Later on, she explains that this shift was mediated by her participation in two events – the Rio+20 Summit and the MNCR Women's Conference – where she hosted the mobile gallery and facilitated mosaic workshops. Luzia neither explains the things she sees differently nor how she used to see them before. However, she indicates that her points of view have changed. This is evident in her next sentence, where she affirms that her views have expanded.

Luzia affirms that her participation in the two events was impressive ("it was cool"). Then, through her discourse, she revisits what she might have said to gallery visitors when she invited them to engage with the mosaic activity: "Now, let's create a mosaic. And then we invited everybody to paint." Luzia had never facilitated an arts workshop before – she gained such skill through the previous workshop in which she participated. The fact that Luzia facilitated the workshop on her own is a sign of her learning process about mosaic construction and how it can be used as a methodology to share people's stories. What happened cognitively with Luzia – learning how to create mosaics and later teaching it to peers – is what both Margaret Brooks and Lev Vygotsky identify as "visual thought": the combination of meaning-making and art-making processes. In other words, visual thought refers to the process by which individuals make sense of their surroundings through the artistic process.[22] Such visual thought awakens a higher level of consciousness[23] – Freire's *conscientização*. This is evident when Luzia utters that she was able to see another universe. Thus, *conscientização* is critical in EAE, because it initiates individuals' learning to recognize social, political, and economic constraints and contradictions, and to act against them. The fact that Luzia was able to facilitate a mosaics workshop during the two events she participated in is evidence of her visual thought construction, which was mediated during the workshops as both learner and facilitator.

Moreover, according to Luzia, producing the mosaic along with visitors helped them to perceive that there are other universes of possibilities for them to explore their own values. For her, working as a group mediated ways for people to find their own values. Luzia does not articulate what those values are, but we can infer that she is referring to visitors' perceptions about the important work recyclers perform as environmental agents, since that was the theme of their artworks. Luzia concludes by stating that her experience of hosting the "Recycling Stories" and facilitating the mosaic workshops made her feel "more open minded," which reaffirms how this experience helped her perceive her surroundings differently.

Luzia's episode is important because it is evidence of three potential contributions of community-created mobile art galleries as spaces of engagement. First, alternative art galleries can empower participants to move out of their comfort zones by experiencing art in an authentic way, meaning that they can create their own artworks without previous formal art training. Second, since recyclers created their art and curated their art show, they had ownership of the stories they wanted to tell, rather than leaving it to someone else to share their stories, which might be disconnected from their own world(s). In so doing, the mobile art gallery represented recyclers' realities of daily struggles for better working conditions. Third, Luzia's episode is an indication of the potential of community-created art galleries to help visitors find their own values, with the aim of decreasing stigma around marginalized communities.

The Second Story: Community-Created Art Galleries as Alternative Sites for Income Generation

Selma is a fifty-six-year-old recycler and a community leader in her low-income neighbourhood. She is also an active MNCR spokesperson. The following discourse emerged during one of the "Recycling Stories" exhibits in São Paulo: "We didn't think about it. We just thought about sustainability. I will collect, separate, and sell. So this became such an absurd vicious cycle that we couldn't see other horizons. We couldn't imagine that our mobile art gallery could be an event that would generate income for the recyclers."

Selma starts her discourse by saying that they (the recyclers) had not yet reflected upon the potential of a mobile art gallery as an income generator. When she says they had thought only about sustainability, she is in fact referring to the sustainability of their work as recyclers – that is, working at the cooperative, recyclers are in charge of collecting, separating, and selling recyclable materials. For Selma and other recyclers, the activity became so embodied, or what she calls an "absurd vicious cycle," that they were not able to perceive other alternatives for income generation – or to "see other horizons," as she states poetically. Selma concludes that recyclers did not anticipate that they would be able to sell their artworks through their art gallery.

When I designed this project collaboratively with the recyclers, my intention was to explore the potential of the visual arts in sharing their stories, with the ultimate goal of decreasing the prejudice suffered by the recyclers. Once "Recycling Stories" started travelling to different communities, however, visitors showed interest in the artworks and shared their desire to purchase some of the pieces. This was a remarkable moment for the recyclers because it added value to their work, not just as environmental agents, but also as artists.[24] When the recyclers started receiving monetary offers for their artworks, it sparked confidence in their art-making process. At the beginning of the project, they were unsure about producing art because they did not have previous formal art training. That lack of confidence shifted throughout the project, however; as one recycler said at the end, "I did not know I could do this." Most of the artworks were sold during the exhibits. The price depended on negotiations between recyclers and their clients, but the average was around $100. Having monetary value added to their artworks empowered them to break through what Selma refers to as a "vicious cycle." That is, instead of just working in the recycling cooperative, the mobile art gallery became an alternative site for income generation.

Discussion

Historically, in cases of extreme oppression, people have found ways of using community art to resist dominant forces because the arts empower people to understand and commit to their own ideologies.[25] Moreover, community art highlights values and ideological messages that are opposed to hegemonic standpoints and bystanders, crossing boundaries of age, gender, class, and geography. A community-created mobile gallery is what Gilles Deleuze and Félix Guattari describe as a "minor" art form. For them, "minor" refers to art created by minorities or marginalized people and is characterized by "deterritorializations" – that is, art that disrupts territories once taken by traditional art institutions. In this case, minor arts are political and collectively produced. When an art exhibit takes place within the community – that is, away from elitist areas – it challenges sociogeographical spaces,[26] and these artful demonstrations uncover an ensemble of highly engaged citizens who are externalizing their deep passion and compassion for the other and for the work they perform as environmental agents.

Additionally, community-created art galleries break taboos when people's personal experiences are shared, bringing forth a community's social identities. This aspect of an art exhibit was evident throughout this study because "Recycling Stories" was created by the community for the community, and presented in a way that challenged the confined walls of traditional art institutions. Moreover, our mobile gallery generated dialogue among visitors and recyclers around environmental issues. "Recycling Stories" indeed "deterritorialized" traditional art standpoints by challenging peoples' views of who can produce art and where art can be displayed. More specifically, it made art more democratic by trekking into territory once occupied by formally trained artists. Such democracy of the arts welcomed ordinary people from different backgrounds to express themselves through artistic forms. This is not to say that everybody is an artist – just as not everybody is a lawyer, for example – but it reinforces the idea that we all have the ability and the right to produce art. As well, due to its mobility, "Recycling Stories" created alternative and affective spaces within everyday life. This was evident when our gallery disrupted a public space in front of São Paulo City Hall, getting the attention of politicians, media, and the public. At that moment, in that public square, conventional public spaces were challenged, power was questioned, alternative social dynamics were established, and a hopeful atmosphere was created.

As pedagogical sites and spaces of engagement, art galleries should invite viewers to see their environment through different lenses by helping them to situate themselves within their own culture and history. This aligns with Freire's *conscientização*. Furthermore, as Eithne Nightingale and Richard Sandell claim, art exhibits mediate an individual's *conscientização* because exhibits construct "new narratives that reflect demographic, social and cultural diversity, and represent a plurality of lived experiences, histories and identities."[27] This is not always the case, however; art galleries constitute inaccessible sites that still exclude marginalized populations, and do not reflect their realities. For instance, Carmel Borg, Bernard Cauchi, and Peter Mayo examine how the National Maritime Museum in Malta reproduced a colonial representation of history, where the local fishing community could not identify with the story being told because it lacked social and cultural context. They point out that, in disregarding the local tradition of oral history, the museum affirmed Eurocentric epistemology.[28] Similarly, Borg and Mayo[29] discuss the white corporate male representations of New York's Museum of Modern Art, and Carol Duncan[30] speaks of the "civilizing rituals" of modern art galleries.

Through civic engagement, art galleries become important spaces for knowledge construction and mobilization. As opposed to reading academic reports, which present static final results and define authors as producers and owners of the knowledge, community-created galleries enable a more democratic, creative, and interactive knowledge construction and knowledge mobilization, thus reaching a wider public. In my study, knowledge mobilization unfolded between various actors (recyclers and the public), and thus dispersed the voices defining the outcomes and future inquiries. In other words, "Recycling Stories" de-hierarchized knowledge production and knowledge mobilization.

During one of the mobile exhibits, viewers expressed their opinions about "Recycling Stories." According to one visitor, it is "something you don't see every day, everywhere," while another uttered: "you always see traditional paintings." In other words, viewers found "Recycling Stories" amusing because the exhibit was innovative, an event out of their ordinary lives. Visitors' reviews provided a counternarrative to the current state of art galleries, which, according to them, display only traditional paintings. These two visitors did not explain what they meant by "traditional painting," but one can infer that they intended artwork that has been long established, which quite often does not reflect local community realities. From this perspective, there is a disconnect between the "real world" and what is commonly displayed in galleries. "Recycling Stories," in contrast, shared with the general public contemporary and relevant stories about the recyclers, including their daily struggles working on the streets and living on the edge of extreme poverty.

One remarkable action-oriented result from "Recycling Stories" emerged after the exhibit at a public school where Selma talked to students and teachers about the importance of recycling. During her presentation, a few students felt connected to her story because they either knew or had a family member who worked as a recycler. Selma's story also got attention from the principal, who decided that day to save recyclable materials from the school and donate them to Selma's cooperative. The partnership continues to this day.

Additionally, "Recycling Stories," as a deliberative and democratic process, allowed the community to choose which stories they were willing to share. This helped recyclers create their own identity and make their reality visible, inviting the public to reflect critically about social justice. This aspect of our community-created art gallery is important because, when the community creates its own artworks and curates their exhibit, we do not take the risk of hiding or misrepresenting stories, and thus of perpetuating the "status quo." The process of creating the mosaics perhaps moved people out of their comfort zones by inviting them to experiment and play with materials that might not be part of their daily lives. Such experimentation at first might have sparked anxiety, fear, shyness, weirdness, and "discomfort" in some participants. After its completion, however, these same participants verbally expressed their joy, happiness, peace, sense of belonging, warmth, empowerment, and, most important, love, because it was a collective effort.

In the same way that Deleuze and Guattari[31] use the metaphor of a patchwork quilt as a gathering of disjointed elements, our mosaics are indeed the gathering of disjointed individual stories. Each symbol, chosen by participants, is a separate and unique element, but these same symbols are combined to form a whole, a collective message. Similar to a rhizome, the mosaics grow in multiple directions, while defying traditional, linear, male, Eurocentric "status quo" representations of beauty, because they are a co-construction of a post-modern self-narrative. That is, rather than describing the self as a linear being evolving along a single narrative, the mosaics describe the self as collective identities, just like Deleuze and Guattari's patchwork quilt, acknowledging the disparate elements that combine to form what is experienced as a unified identity.

Conclusion

In this study I have challenged the notion of art galleries as elitist sites, and formal art training as the only alternative way to produce art, while reinforcing the idea of community-created art galleries as spaces for critical reflection and valuable sites in environmental adult education. The findings suggest that, although art galleries can be spaces for reflection about our world(s) by mirroring our different realities, they tend to remain inaccessible. Elitist control of the arts and the stories they tell are often still Western oriented. When it comes to the display of community art, it is rarely part of a permanent collection, and the works are often displayed as a "sideshow" away from the main elitist exhibit. From this perspective, artworks are created and curated by those who "possess" the talent and formal training, and imposed upon those without such status. "Recycling Stories" challenged this context by magnifying social injustice and indignity while (re)conceptualizing legitimate knowledge and art practices. With the occupation of public spaces, the exhibit confronted the public, challenged hegemonic use of the arts, and empowered the voices and stories of participants. Since "Recycling Stories" was mobile, it was able to travel to unexpected places, inviting people to engage in critical dialogue regarding recyclers' well-being.

Due to the playfulness of the arts-making environment, safe places were created where participants felt comfortable sharing their deepest fears, frustrations, and hopes for a different reality. This might not be possible in traditional ways of doing qualitative research, such as questionnaires. Even though the art workshops presented here did not require any previous art experience on the part of participants or facilitators, the workshops still moved people out of their comfort zones and helped them to situate themselves in historical context and to dream and fight for a different reality. I hope these stories will inspire art galleries to meet their potential by challenging the kind of social exclusion the Brazilian recyclers experience, and invite social movement organizers to include art and art galleries as strategic spaces of contestation and empowerment.

Discussion Questions

1 What is the relationship between environmental adult education and popular education?
2 What is the difference between dialogic and dialectical spaces?
3 How can Vygotsky's sociocultural theory help us to understand civic engagement?
4 How can museums and art galleries foster meaningful dialogue regarding policies on environmental issues?
5 How can social movements promote civic engagement?

NOTES

1 Paulo Freire, *Pedagogia dos sonhos possíveis* [The pedagogy of possible dreams] (São Paulo: Unesp, 2001).
2 Carlos Rodrigues Brandão, *Pesquisa participant* [Participatory research] (São Paulo: Brasilience, 1982).

3 Darlene Clover, "Successes and Challenges of Feminist Arts-Based Participatory Methodologies with Homeless/Street-Involved Women in Victoria,"
   Action Research 11, no. 9 (2011): 12–26.
4 Ibid.
5 Darlene Nightingale and Richard Sandell, "Introduction," in *Museums,
   Equality, and Social Justice,* ed. Richard Sandell and Eithne Nightingale (New
   York: Routledge, 2012), 1–9.
6 Carmel Borg and Peter Mayo, "Adult Education as Cultural Politics," *New
   Directions in Adult and Continuing Learning* 127 (2010): 37.
7 Clover, "Successes and Challenges."
8 Borg and Mayo, "Adult Education as Cultural Politics," 35.
9 L. Ardra Cole and Maura McIntyre, *Arts-Informed Research for Public
   Education: The Alzheimer's Project, Proceedings of the Canadian Association for the
   Study of Adult Education (CASAE)* (Halifax: Dalhousie University/University
   of King's College, 2003).
10 Clover, "Successes and Challenges," 13.
11 David Silverman, *Doing Qualitative Research: A Practical Handbook* (London:
   SAGE, 2000).
12 Darlene E. Clover, Joyce Stalker, and Laurie McGauley, *Feminist Popular
   Education and Community Arts/Crafts: The Case for New Directions* (Quebec:
   CSSE, 2004).
13 Angela Martins Baeder, *Educação ambiental e mobilização social: Formação de catadores na grande São Paulo* [Environmental education and social mobilization:
   Recyclers formation in greater São Paulo] (PhD diss., Universidade de São
   Paulo–São Paulo, 2009).
14 Brandão, *Pesquisa participante.*
15 Ibid.
16 Rede Paulita de Educação Ambiental (REPEA), online at http://www.repea
   .org.br/, accessed 1 November 2011.
17 Freire, *Pedagogia dos sonhos possíveis.*
18 Jutta Gutberlet, *Recovering Resources – Recycling Citizenship: Urban Poverty
   Reduction in Latin America* (Aldershot, UK: Ashgate, 2008).
19 Ibid.
20 Crystal Tremblay, "Towards Inclusive Waste Management: Participatory
   Video as a Communication Tool," *ICE Journal of Waste and Resource
   Management* 4, no. 66 (2012): 177–86.
21 Wolff-Michael Roth, "The Interaction of Students' Scientific and Religious
   Discourses: Two Case Studies," *International Journal of Science Education* 2,
   no. 19 (1998): 125–46.
22 Margaret Brooks, "Drawing, Thinking, Meaning" (Loughborough, UK:
   University of Loughborough, September 2003), online at https://www
   .lboro.ac.uk/microsites/sota/tracey/journal/thin/brooks.html.

23 Lev Semyonovich Vygotsky, *Mind in Society: The Development of Higher Psychological Processes* (Cambridge, MA: Harvard University Press, 1978).
24 I use the term "artist" not in the sense of a professionally trained artist, but to refer to our research participants who actively engaged in our art classes.
25 Melody Milbrandt, "Understanding the Role of Art in Social Movements and Transformation," *Journal of Art for Life* 1, no. 1 (2010), 7–18.
26 Jonathan Mandell, "They're Not Actors, But They're Playing Themselves," *TDF Stages*, 12 October 2012, online at https://www.tdf.org/articles/746/Theyre-Not-Actors-But-Theyre-Playing-Themselves.
27 Nightingale and Sandell, "Introduction."
28 Carmel Borg, Bernard Cauchi, and Peter Mayo, "Museums Education and Cultural Contestation," *Journal of Mediterranean Studies* 13, no. 1 (2013): 89–108.
29 Borg and Mayo, "Adult Education as Cultural Politics."
30 Carol Duncan, *Civilizing Rituals* (London: Routledge, 2005).
31 Gilles Deleuze and Félix Guattari, *A Thousand Plateaus: Capitalism and Schizophrenia* (Minneapolis: University of Minnesota Press, 1987).

KEY RESOURCES

Clover, Darlene E., Bruno de Oliveira Jayme, Bud L. Hall, and Shirley Follen. *The Nature of Transformation: Environmental Adult Education*. Rotterdam: Sense Publishers, 2013.
Clover, Darlene E., and Joyce Stalker, eds. *The Arts and Social Justice: Re-crafting Adult Education and Community Cultural Leadership*. Leicester, UK: National Institute of Adult Continuing Education, 2007.
Gutberlet, Jutta. *Recovering Resources – Recycling Citizenship: Urban Poverty Reduction in Latin America*. Aldershot, UK: Ashgate, 2008.
Sandell, Richard. *Museums, Moralities and Human Rights*. Abingdon, UK: Routledge, 2017.
Stringer, Ernest T. *Action Research*. Thousand Oaks, CA: SAGE, 2014.

13 Temporary Migrant Workers' Engagement and (Dis)engagement with the Policy Process

ETHEL TUNGOHAN

On 17 May 2014, in a packed auditorium at the University of Alberta, dozens of temporary foreign workers under the "low-skilled" Temporary Foreign Workers Program (TFWP) gathered to listen to representatives from the grassroots migrants' rights organization Migrante Alberta discuss the Canadian government's changes to the TFWP. These changes included limiting the numbers of temporary foreign workers that employers could employ, prohibiting the hiring of temporary foreign workers in the restaurant and hospitality industries, and increasing the fees of Labour Market Impact Assessments (LMIAs) that employers would have to pay before they could hire temporary foreign workers. All these changes would effectively limit temporary foreign workers' presence in the country, compelling many either to find new employment or to live with irregular status.

As such, during this forum, most of those who gathered together were afraid of what the future would bring. One of those who attended was a man in his forties I will call Raul. Raul had lived and worked in Edmonton since 2008 as a food-counter attendant, and thought of Edmonton as "home." He attended the forum because he was worried about the pending expiration of his work permit and whether his employer's plan to nominate him for permanent residency under the Provincial Nominee Program (PNP) would be affected. Another audience member who attended was a teenage girl I will call Sandra, whose parents worked as temporary foreign workers in Edmonton. Sandra expressed concern that the changes being implemented would affect her plans to graduate from high school. Since their work permits would expire in the middle of the school year, did the proposed policy changes mean that she would have to leave school?

Stories like Raul's and Sandra's were commonplace. Because I was living in Alberta from 2013 to 2016 for my postdoctoral research on temporary foreign workers' lived experiences under the TFWP, I became well acquainted with communities of temporary foreign workers, and observed first-hand temporary foreign workers' fear in the summer of 2014 as a direct result of the Canadian government's decision to cut back on the numbers who were present in the country.[1] In that forum, and in subsequent community gatherings throughout 2014 and 2015, I noticed a visible increase in stress and trepidation among the communities of temporary foreign workers.

Specifically, in March and April 2013, the Canadian government announced the aforementioned changes to the TFWP in response to an enormous public outcry against the program, which emerged in part because of a media exposé that revealed how the Royal Bank of Canada fired Canadian workers and replaced them with temporary foreign workers.[2] Even though many more stories were circulating about the abuse of temporary foreign workers under the TFWP,[3] public scrutiny was placed on the program's displacement of Canadian workers and, relatedly, on temporary foreign workers' "theft" of Canadians' jobs. That the workers who supposedly replaced Canadian workers entered the country not through the low-skilled TFWP but through a *different* program that allowed "high-skilled" "immigrants-in-waiting" to apply for permanent residency after two years was conveniently neglected in these media accounts.[4]

As a result of the public outcry that "propelled a massive Canada-wide uproar against immigrant workers,"[5] the Canadian government stated it would now "put Canadians first."[6] When taken in conjunction with the passage of the cumulative-duration or four-year-in, four-year-out rule in 2011, which mandated that temporary foreign workers could live and work in the country for four years and would then have to wait another four years before being allowed back into Canada, temporary foreign workers felt targeted. Because of the sudden reversal in the Canadian government's policies on temporary foreign work, temporary foreign workers found they were at risk of losing status "just like that."[7]

Although measures restricting temporary foreign workers' presence in Canada might at first appear to be reasonable – if not necessary – correctives to policies that supposedly worked to the disadvantage of Canadian workers, upon further reflection several questions emerge. First, is it accurate to see the issue as one where migrant workers are "stealing" jobs from Canadians? What is the history of migrant labour in Canada? How have different stakeholders, such as the Canadian government, employers, and temporary foreign workers themselves, framed the issue of "temporary foreign work"? And, more crucially, what are the effects of these policies on temporary foreign workers? Second, how have temporary foreign workers reacted to these policies? How have they attempted to shift public policies to take into account their specific needs? And finally, what are the competing considerations at stake when thinking about the broader issues of migrant labour in Canada?

I address these questions in three sections, responding sequentially to the questions raised. I begin by contextualizing the TFWP within the history of migrant labour in Canada and address the issues of precariousness facing temporary foreign workers. Like Paul Pierson,[8] who advocates for the importance of policy history, I believe that policy changes cannot be understood as providing a particular "snapshot" of a given period in history, but are best assessed as part of a "specific moment within a larger dynamic process."[9] Studying the specific policy area in question – in this case, temporary foreign work – as it has evolved over time makes clear the "factors that provide the 'glue' for a particular arrangement."[10]

Second, I look at academic theories on the engagement and (dis) engagement of migrant non-citizens in public policies. I discuss academics who see migrants as being uninvolved in the policy process because of theories of "political quiescence," which attribute migrants' so-called reticence to the fact that many come from authoritarian countries where democratic engagement is uncommon. I then contrast these academics' approaches with those who argue that migrants *do* become politically involved, depending on the types of institutional mechanisms that states create to encourage their participation. I analyse the rich literature on migrant community organizing to show that notions of migrants' political engagement should go beyond conventional understandings of political participation – which see such participation as primarily encompassing voting or running for public office, neither of which is an activity that temporary foreign workers can undertake – to include social movement activism. I highlight how temporary foreign workers have attempted to be included in policy deliberations concerning the TFWP, even when policy makers chose not to consult them because they were not Canadian citizens. I show that, despite lacking citizenship status, temporary foreign workers are political agents who use a variety of tactics to ensure their voices are heard.

Finally, I discuss how a quickly shifting political landscape in Canada and in other countries is placing temporary labour migrants in a vulnerable position. Not only must they adapt to policy changes that are seemingly implemented without much advance notice; they also increasingly have to contend with anti-migrant, xenophobic, and racist ideologies. What questions, then, can we ask about the limitations to temporary foreign workers' attempts to insert themselves in the policy-making process? Ultimately, I argue that temporary labour migrants and their allies have to be flexible when responding to sudden policy changes, and form alliances with different social movements to ensure that their needs are listened to and taken into account by policy makers.

Migrant Labour in Canada

Historically, Canada recruited migrant workers from countries in the global South to come into the country on a restricted basis.[11] The most prominent example of the racialized nature of Canadian immigration policy is the situation of Chinese railroad workers in the early twentieth century. Despite Chinese workers' contributions to the settlement of Western Canada, the Canadian government strove to limit their presence by instituting a head tax and by creating policies that made it hard for Chinese labourers to bring their families with them. Canada's white settler policy prioritized the settlement of European immigrants to the exclusion of migrants from the global South, who were deemed unassimilable to Canadian cultural norms.[12]

Moreover, many immigration scholars have observed that Canada's immigration policies were marked by racial double standards.[13] People who were working in the same occupations but who were from different countries did not receive the same entitlements. For example, from the early to mid-1900s, British and Western European women who worked as "nannies" and "nursemaids" were immediately allowed to immigrate permanently to Canada, yet women from the Caribbean who entered the country through the Caribbean Domestics Scheme and also worked as nannies were prevented from enjoying the same privilege of Canadian citizenship. The Foreign Domestics Movement, established in 1981 and replaced by the Live-in Caregiver Program in 1992 and the Caregiver Program in 2014, offered conditional and limited pathways to citizenship that required women from the global South to finish their two-year employment contracts and to meet other criteria *before* being allowed to apply for citizenship. Double standards are in effect when caregivers who are mostly women from developing countries such as the Philippines have to wait before being allowed to apply for Canadian citizenship, whereas in the past their British and European counterparts automatically obtained citizenship.

To use another example, Caribbean and, later, Mexican and Central American farmers have been allowed to enter Canada only on a temporary basis through the Seasonal Agricultural Workers Program, yet Mennonite farmers who helped settle the prairies in the nineteenth and early twentieth centuries automatically accessed Canadian citizenship.

The decision to prevent Caribbean migrant farm workers from settling permanently in Canada had a clear racial basis: Adam Perry notes how immigration officials saw Caribbean workers as inferior to white Canadians.[14] Citing Vic Satzewitch, Perry further underscores how "the ideology of racism structured the decision to exclude these people from entry into the country and subsequently allocate them to positions as unfree migrant labour."[15]

Immigration scholars make the same observations about the TFWP. Its predecessor was the Non-Immigrant Employment Authorization Program (NIEAP), which the federal government established in 1973 to allow employers to bring in workers from overseas on time-limited contracts. Under NIEAP, migrants with different skill levels were accepted. "High-skilled" migrants from the United States and European countries were placed in professional and managerial jobs, while "low-skilled" migrants from Central and South America were placed in menial occupations.[16] "High-skilled" American and European migrants received more opportunities for permanent residency and had more labour rights, whereas "low-skilled" migrants from the global South had fewer entitlements and were prevented from applying for permanent residency,[17] leading Nandita Sharma to observe trenchantly that NIEAP enforced a form of "apartheid," with differential treatment on the basis of race.[18]

Similar to NIEAP, Canada's "low-skilled" TFWP was established as a Pilot Project in 2002 as a "last and limited resort" to relieve labour shortages in Canada.[19] The TFWP is an employer-driven program that enables employers owning businesses as diverse as fast-food chains to construction sites to food-processing plants to hire workers from abroad whose job responsibilities are classified under the Canadian government's "National Occupation Classification" program as either requiring a high school diploma (NOC C) or only on-the-job training (NOC D). The TFWP was meant to be only temporary, but it soon rapidly expanded because there were no limits to the numbers of workers who could be brought into the country under the program. Employers only had to prove through submission of a Labour Market Opinion (LMO) – later called a Labour Market Impact Assessment – that they tried and failed to hire Canadian workers in the specific occupations the Canadian government deemed "under pressure."[20] From 2002 to 2013, the number of temporary foreign workers who entered the country rose rapidly, with such entries soon exceeding the number of permanent immigrants entering the country.[21] Instead of prioritizing long-term settlement through permanent immigration, the Canadian government "favours the flexibility that temporary programs offer."[22] That the Canadian government supported the growth of the TFWP is without question. In 2009, then immigration minister Jason Kenney described the TFWP as "the motor of tens of thousands of businesses that are growing and succeeding."[23] A briefing note addressed to Kenney's successor, immigration minister Chris Alexander, in 2013 stated that the "Canadian government is committed to creating a *fast, flexible* immigration system that serves Canada's economic interests."[24] Consequently, the Canadian government passed policies that made it easier for employers to hire temporary foreign workers without concurrently considering policies that would protect such workers from abuse. In 2012, for example, the government made processing times of LMOs much faster,[25] leading to charges by migrant activists that faster processing made it difficult to vet a potential workplace adequately as safe for temporary foreign workers.

Between 2006 and 2013, migrant activists repeatedly charged that the government was not responding seriously to criticisms about the lack of oversight concerning the TFWP's rapid expansion. The government saw the TFWP as a program that brought multiple benefits for everyone involved: it helped Canada retain its economic advantage, while giving employers the opportunity to hire workers at lower wages who they saw as having "a stronger work ethic" than Canadian workers.[26] As a Canadian labour consultant said in an interview with Geraldina Polanco, "here come these bright university graduate foreign workers that are delighted to be here, are happy for what you are paying them, they are not whining about their salary all the time or expecting you to pay them double because they are charming ... [Employers] put up with a lot, they really do, a lot, and when they get these foreign workers, it's a treat."[27] For temporary foreign workers, the possibility of being able to transition out of the TFWP and be nominated for permanent residency under the Provincial Nominee Program made the program a huge draw.[28]

Indeed, Canada's "two-step" immigration program enabling temporary foreign workers to "transition" to permanent residency through the PNP is a source of much abuse.[29] Rather than alienating their employers, whom they hoped would sponsor their applications for permanent residency, temporary foreign workers were reluctant to voice their opposition to violations of their employment contract, a situation that employers exploited.[30] The fact that temporary foreign workers' work permits are tied to their employers only exacerbates situations of abuse. Temporary foreign workers who leave their jobs risk being unable to land another, since that would require finding another employer, paying the funds to file another LMO/LMIA, and being sent home if putting new work requirements in place is not possible.

Investigative reports highlighting how the TFWP was supposedly affecting Canadian workers negatively played a huge role in instigating the 2011 and 2014 policy changes discussed at the beginning of this chapter. These changes heightened temporary foreign workers' precariousness by constraining their opportunities for continued employment. With policies limiting employers' ability to hire them, temporary foreign workers faced even more pressure to remain in their employers' good graces.

To be clear, the 2014 policy changes were accompanied by measures to help abused temporary foreign workers, and were more detailed than previous measures in discussing how their rights would be protected. For example, the policies included an increase in the scope and number of inspections of workplaces employing temporary foreign workers, regular interviews with employers and temporary foreign workers during these inspections, and the creation of a confidential tip-line and a website to report abuse.[31] However, the fact that these measures led in extreme cases to abusive employers being barred from employing temporary foreign workers reduced the incentive for such workers to be forthcoming – put differently, if complaining about abuse results in being out of a job and sent home, most would opt to stay silent.

Seeing the TFWP as part of Canada's long history of differential treatment of migrant workers on the basis of country of origin, race, and "skill" level makes clear that double standards are still at play – as always, racialized migrants who are considered to have "low skills" are deemed unworthy of permanent settlement in Canada. Thus, rather than accusing migrant workers of stealing Canadians' jobs, it is perhaps more instructive to see such accusations as part of the larger history of the depiction of racialized migrant workers as the "other" in Canadian society. Migrant workers today are subjected to the same exclusions their predecessors faced. Taking a historical perspective unearths patterns of unequal treatment that make Chinese railroad workers, seasonal agricultural workers, migrant domestic workers, and temporary foreign workers "unfree" – "in effect, the migrant worker program in Canada has legalized the re-subordination of many non-whites by creating a divide based on citizenship rights."[32] Overcoming this divide is, in fact, one of the driving forces behind migrant organizing, as I now discuss.

Temporary Foreign Workers Fight Back

Migrant Political Quiescence versus Migrant Political Involvement

Temporary foreign workers face various impediments that make it difficult for them to participate politically in Canada, not least of which is the Canadian government's efforts to portray them as outsiders.

The government's stance towards temporary foreign workers can best be seen in a briefing note circulated among Citizenship and Immigration Canada (CIC) bureaucrats in 2011 that emphasized that the cumulative-duration rule was instituted because the Canadian government wanted to ensure that temporary foreign workers "do not lose ties with their country of origin due to their prolonged stay in Canada."[33] This attitude can also be seen in the virtual absence of government funding for settlement service organizations to provide services for temporary foreign workers – including seasonal agricultural workers and caregivers. The logic is that temporary foreign workers do not need settlement and integration services because they are not permanent members of Canadian society. As a settlement service worker told me in an interview, "this doesn't make sense because temporary foreign workers have been here for years. Some have been here for almost a decade."[34]

As such, whether and how migrant workers can be engaged in the policy process is up for debate among scholars. The aforementioned conditions limiting migrant workers' political participation ring true for migrant workers in other countries as well. Initially, immigration and social movement scholars unanimously upheld the theory of migrant workers' "political quiescence," which characterized such workers as "apolitical and characterized by political apathy" and as following existing policies without much dissent.[35] Because migrant workers were barred from voting or running for office in receiving states and might have come from politically repressive countries that did not have a culture of democratic political participation, these scholars believed that examining migrant workers' political involvement was a waste of time.[36]

Yet later scholars have questioned the theory of "political quiescence." On the one hand, there are scholars who consider the institutional apparatus that exists in sending and receiving states that actively enables migrants' political participation. Steven Vertovec, for example, discusses the various institutional mechanisms that western European states have established to foster migrant inclusion, such as municipal councils that allow representatives of migrant communities to provide their input into municipal policies.[37] Robyn Rodriguez looks at the various institutions established by the Philippines as a "labour brokerage" state in order to encourage migrants' political and economic ties to the country, and finds that, although migrant workers might be barred from electoral modes of political participation, some states have designed institutions that allow for their input into public policies.[38]

On the other hand, other scholars have considered political participation outside state institutions by focusing on community organizing. There is a rich literature on migrant activism that successfully
illustrates how migrants use community organizing as a way to make
their voices heard.[39] While these scholars examine different forms of
migrant activism in different countries, and while they do not agree
on their understanding of the extent, scope, and normative implications of such activism, they are united in their belief that "movements
matter."[40] Patricia Landolt and Luin Goldring, however, caution immigration scholars not to assume there is a "linear relationship between
civic engagement and ... electoral politics."[41] They argue that seeing
migrant political involvement as an "ongoing and mutually constitu-
tive process" enables consideration of the varied layers of organizing
work that migrant communities undertake.[42] For example, in their longitudinal analysis of Latin American organizing in Toronto, they find
that different "layers" of migrant organizing take place, with ethnicity
being the initial starting point for organizing, followed by "pan-ethnic"
forms of mobilization, which then culminate in intersectional forms
of organizing where migrants' multiple and overlapping social locations are key.[43] By explicitly bringing in a social justice agenda, such
intersectional forms of organizing allow activists to surpass previous
partisan models of advocacy whereby shared ethnicity and country of
origin became the basis for supporting political causes "back home."
Landolt and Goldring find, for instance, that Latin American feminist
organizers put at the forefront their intersecting social locations as
immigrant and/or refugee women who have experienced domestic
violence in their advocacy work. In contrast to political opportunity
structure (POS) theorists, who assume that existing state policies and
state institutions determine the types of activism that movements
engage in, the authors conclude that activists themselves influence
POS, as seen when considering how "Latin American modes and bases
of organizing entered the vocabulary of local politics."[44]

Landolt and Goldring's observations certainly ring true for the
Filipino temporary foreign workers in my study. In the course of my
research, I repeatedly observed temporary foreign workers' diverse
tactics when attempting to shift policies and when challenging mainstream narratives that they do not belong in Canada. As I show in the
following section, temporary foreign workers engage in different forms
of resistance, from "everyday" forms that allow them to carve spaces of
inclusion for themselves to organizational forms that lead to the building of multiple alliances that strengthen the persuasiveness of their critiques of temporary foreign worker policies.

Temporary Foreign Workers' Different Forms of Resistance

All of the temporary foreign workers whom I met in the course of my research are part of social networks as varied as churches, sports leagues, arts collectives, and grassroots migrant organizations that show they are present in their communities.[45] In addition, these organizations enable temporary foreign workers to form affective communities of support. Although such organizations initially might be a way for different individuals to gather together because of shared beliefs and shared interests, in practice they encourage the formation of friendships that allow their members to feel supported. Deriving strength from community – in "being there" for one another – becomes a political act, especially for temporary foreign workers who, in the aftermath of the Royal Bank scandal, have felt scapegoated.

I observed just how much courage it took for temporary foreign workers to gather together when participating in Migrante Alberta's community forum in May 2014. Although Migrante Alberta advocates for the rights and welfare of migrant workers and has undertaken several campaigns to support migrant workers, this gathering was meant to share information on recent policy changes – no overtly political actions such as protesting or lobbying policy makers were planned. A few days before the event, I received a phone call from a university administrator, who helped me book the room for the event. She had received information that notice of Migrante Alberta's forum had reached a group called the "End the Temporary Foreign Worker Program" coalition, which consisted of people who were opposed to the presence of temporary foreign workers. Some members of this group were outraged that temporary foreign workers were gathering, and planned to attend the forum to intimidate them. Upon hearing about this plan, I alerted the leaders of Migrante Alberta, who then alerted members of labour unions that supported their work. Because of the advance notice, Migrante Alberta was able to ensure that there were enough Canadian allies present at the forum to provide support for temporary foreign workers. The presence of allies was helpful during the event, when one member of the "End the Temporary Foreign Worker Program" coalition disrupted the proceedings. To ensure temporary foreign workers' safety, allies from the labour unions confronted the man and escorted him outside the classroom.

As a witness, I was flummoxed that someone would be so upset by the idea of temporary foreign workers' gathering together to share information with one another that he would attempt to disrupt the proceedings. The incident made clear to me that, for temporary foreign workers, participating in community organizations was an act of everyday resistance. When such workers take up space in a political landscape that is hostile to their presence, they flout tacit societal expectations that they minimize their visibility.

Indeed, forcing the Canadian government to acknowledge the harms wrought by its policies on temporary foreign work was a key intervention for temporary foreign workers who are part of grassroots migrant organizations. Migrante Alberta, which included temporary foreign workers in important leadership roles in its organization, held numerous press conferences in 2014 and 2015 outlining the harms of the changes to the TFWP and offering testimonies from temporary foreign workers who were directly affected. The organization took a "united front" approach to activism, whereby different and at times contradictory tactics were used in order to get support. They lobbied officials from the municipal, provincial, and federal levels of government, while temporary foreign workers themselves called government representatives directly to seek changes, and gathered to protest in front of their constituency offices. On 16 July 2014, Migrante Alberta chartered a bus to drive to then federal employment minister Jason Kenney's constituency office in Calgary, where temporary foreign workers and their allies unfurled banners with slogans such as "Scrap the 4-year Cap," "Lift the Moratorium," and "Rights and Full Status for All Workers," and handed Kenney's representatives a list of demands. The mood during the bus ride and the rally was festive, with many of the temporary foreign workers there excited to take an active part in an event to draw attention to their issues. "Since they did not even talk to any of us about the changes, it is time that we forced them to listen," one temporary foreign worker who attended the rally told me.

It is notable that temporary foreign workers who were part of Migrante Alberta worked in alliance with different organizations supporting ethnic communities (both Filipino and non-Filipino), labour unions, social justice organizations, and even churches to disseminate their message about the precariousness they faced. From 2014 to 2016, Migrante Alberta organized monthly meetings of a "Temporary Foreign Worker Support Group" at the headquarters of the trade union Unifor in Edmonton to discuss strategies to assist temporary foreign workers, which they and their allies attended regularly. Migrante Alberta joined national coalitions for migrants' rights, such as the Migrant Workers Alliance for Change (MWAC), taking part in regular conference calls to plan actions.

When attending sessions in Edmonton and listening to MWAC conference calls, it was clear to me how being part of this alliance enabled temporary foreign workers' issues to have a wider political reach. This ensured that different stakeholders, such as members of various labour unions, settlement service workers, academics, and even members of the public who became interested in the plight of temporary foreign workers, felt a shared commitment to shifting unfair policies. Consequently, there was national coordination on migrant justice campaigns, with MWAC member groups organizing in cities and towns across Canada. This meant that even though temporary foreign workers were barred from electoral participation, being part of community organizations allowed them to broadcast their demands.

Temporary foreign workers were also successful in forcing themselves into policy spaces that initially excluded them. For example, in May 2016, they were able to provide testimonies to the House of Commons Standing Committee on Human Resources, Skills, and Social Development and the Status of Persons with Disabilities (HUMA) when the committee was considering changes to Canada's temporary foreign worker programs.[46] The original speakers list included only members of employer groups and professional associations, yet MWAC organizations' interventions gave five temporary foreign workers the ability to provide their testimonies. The ultimate irony – that the parliamentary committee was considering policy changes to the TFWP without consulting the very workers who arguably would be the most affected by shifts in policy – was not lost on the temporary foreign workers who were there.

Through these various activities, temporary foreign workers clearly have not allowed their lack of Canadian citizenship to prevent them from publicizing their concerns. Spaces for citizen engagement in public policies were closed to temporary foreign workers because they were not Canadian citizens, yet they forced policy makers to acknowledge their demands. Even though political institutions are structured such that temporary foreign workers do not have easy access to policy makers, the very acts of protesting, lobbying, and strategic alliance building gave temporary foreign workers' openings to share their concerns.

It was also clear that temporary foreign workers had to be flexible and adaptable when taking advantage of these openings. Openings for temporary foreign workers on the HUMA speakers list, for example, were announced only five days prior to the meeting in Ottawa. This left temporary foreign workers and their allies very little time to get prepared. In addition, that these openings resulted from relationships temporary foreign workers had developed with sympathetic policy makers showed the importance of strategic alliance building and of taking part in different "layers" of community organizing. Similar to Landolt and Goldring's findings,[47] I noticed that the contours of migrant mobilization had different layers, with temporary foreign workers participating in ethnic organizations, pan-ethnic organizations, and organizations representing different individuals from intersecting social locations. By being part of all of these networks, temporary foreign workers are more likely to get their voices heard by a bigger audience and thus make an impact on public policies.

I close this section by emphasizing that temporary foreign workers' activism takes place at different scales, thereby embodying what Olena Hankivsky and colleagues describe as a key component of intersectionality-based policy analysis, where attention is given to the various "levels" of power. Temporary foreign workers engage in macro ("global and national level"), meso ("provincial and regional level"), and micro ("community level") forms of organizing.[48] I have already covered temporary foreign workers' campaigns at the micro, individual, and macro levels. At the global, macro level, too, temporary foreign workers are participating in grassroots transnational migrants' assemblies such as the International Migrants Alliance. In addition, members of Migrante Alberta are also automatically part of Migrante International, the transnational coordinating body that oversees the activities of different Migrante chapters worldwide and wages transnational campaigns in support of migrants' rights. Although space constraints preclude a detailed discussion of these global efforts, suffice it to say that they are crucial in entrenching a deeper consciousness among migrant workers of their distinct needs and concerns. Being part of a "global" migrants movement engenders feelings of solidarity, thereby fostering the belief that migrants' issues are part of a broader global struggle for migrant justice.[49]

Changing Activist Tactics: How to Confront Global Antimigrant Discourses and Policies

In December 2016, then immigration minister John McCallum announced the end of the cumulative-duration or four-year-in, four-year-out rule,[50] arguing that its abolition was necessary because of evidence that the rule exacerbated temporary foreign workers' experiences of abuse. Since temporary foreign workers had long called for the rule's abolition, it would appear that their efforts at mobilizing against the rule led to this policy shift. Similar to the case of migrant domestic workers in the 1970s whose activism led to the establishment of the Foreign Domestics Movement, which granted migrant domestic workers pathways to permanent residency,[51] temporary foreign workers' mobilization persuaded policy makers to review their policy. Migrant activism thus matters. When looking at migrant labour in

Canada through the lens of "policy history,"[52] which draws attention to how policies have developed over time, it becomes evident that improvements to Canada's policies on temporary foreign work have come about only as a result of migrant workers' advocacy efforts.

To return to the stories of Raul and Sandra, what will happen to precarious temporary foreign workers and their children? Although the cumulative-duration rule was abolished, this does not cover those whose permits have expired. What can temporary foreign workers like Raul and migrant children like Sandra justifiably ask the Canadian government to do on their behalf? And how will they compel the government to listen, to hear, and to act on the concerns of temporary foreign workers and their families? When considering the historic maltreatment of racialized migrant workers in Canada, would refusing to give Raul and Sandra access to Canadian permanent residency mean that Canada is continuing with its policies of preferring the settlement of "desirable" migrants over others?

The history of migrant activism in Canada shows that migrant workers and their allies have been active in mobilizing the government to enact policy improvements even when they were prevented from accessing formal spaces of engagement due to their lack of Canadian citizenship. Being unable to vote or run for office were not barriers to migrant workers' engagement in the policy process. Participating in migrant social movements provided a crucial space for migrants' concerns to be broadcast. Yet new political realities might compel a reconsideration of activist strategies: migrant activists might have to create different spaces for public engagement, spaces that directly confront global antimigrant discourses and policies.

Discussion Questions

1 How might temporary foreign workers and their allies fight effectively against larger systemic global trends that have seen the rise of antimigrant policies in the United States and in the United Kingdom and other western European countries?

2 Canada's policies towards temporary foreign workers might not appear to be as bad as, for instance, the United Kingdom's proposal to expel foreign workers from the European Union following Brexit or the United States' intensifying efforts to deport migrants without papers through the increased surveillance of spaces such as schools and churches by agents from Immigration and Customs Enforcement. How, then, might temporary foreign workers and their allies modify their tactics to persuade reluctant policy makers to improve

Canadian policies that already compare favourably to those of other countries?

3 As a result of these global trends, does it continue to be tenable for temporary foreign workers and their allies to seek permanent Canadian residency for all temporary foreign workers?

NOTES

1 Ethel Tungohan, "From Encountering Confederate Flags to Finding Refuge in Spaces of Solidarity: Filipino Temporary Foreign Workers' Experiences of the Public in Alberta," *Space & Polity* 21, no. 1 (2017): 11–26.
2 Kathy Tomlinson, "RBC replaces Canadian staff with foreign workers," *CBC News*, 6 April 2013, online at http://www.cbc.ca/news/canada/british-columbia/rbc-replaces-canadian-staff-with-foreign-workers-1.1315008.
3 See, for example, Carlito Pablo, "Foreign workers file class-action lawsuit against Denny's Restaurants in BC," *Georgia Straight*, 11 January 2011, online at https://www.straight.com/article-367835/vancouver/foreign-workers-file-classaction-lawsuit-against-dennys-restaurants-bc." See also Lori Waller, "Union helps migrants counter worst abuses of Temporary Foreign Worker Program," *Rabble.ca*, 20 November 2012, online at http://rabble.ca/news/2012/11/union-helps-migrants-counter-worst-abuses-foreign-temporary-worker-program.
4 Syed Hussan, "What's missing from the coverage of the Amanda Lang-RBC saga?" *Rabble.ca*, 13 January 2015, online at http://rabble.ca/blogs/bloggers/hussan.
5 Ibid.
6 Canada, "Temporary Foreign Worker Program and Live-in Caregiver Program (Worker Protection)" (Ottawa: Citizenship and Immigration Canada, 2013), 8–11.
7 Audrey Macklin, "And just like that, you're an illegal immigrant," *National Post*, 19 March 2015, online at http://news.nationalpost.com/full-comment/audreymacklin-poof-now-youre-an-illegal-immigrant.
8 Paul Pierson, "The Study of Policy Development," *Journal of Policy History* 17, no. 1 (2005): 34–51.
9 Ibid., 48.
10 Ibid.
11 Phil Triadafilopoulous, *Becoming Multicultural: Immigration and the Politics of Membership in Canada and Germany* (Vancouver: UBC Press, 2012).
12 Similar to other liberal immigrant receiving states, Canada historically prioritized the immigration of people from western European countries because it saw such immigrants as subscribing to Canada's cultural

values, thereby supposedly making it easier for them to assimilate. The pervasiveness of human rights discourses following the Second World War – which put into question the merits of such policies – led to the removal of these policies. Put in their place were race-blind immigration policies that do not consider culture, race, or country of origin. For a trenchant assessment of Canada's immigration history, see ibid. See also Lisa Jakubowski and Elizabeth Comack, "Managing Canadian Immigration: Racism, Racialiization and the Law," in *Gender, Race and Canadian Law*, ed. Wayne Antony et al. (Halifax, NS: Fernwood, 2016), 88–115.

13 Jakubowski and Comack, "Managing Canadian Immigration"; Nandita Sharma, *Home Economics: Nationalism and the Making of Migrant Workers in Canada* (Toronto: University of Toronto Press, 2006).
14 J. Adam Perry, "Barely Legal: Racism and Migrant Farm Labour in the Context of Canadian Multiculturalism," *Citizenship Studies* 16, no. 2 (2012): 189–201.
15 Ibid., 192.
16 Alison Taylor and Jason Foster, "Migrant Workers and the Problems of Social Cohesion in Canada," *International Migration and Integration* 16, no. 1 (2015): 153–72.
17 Ibid.
18 Sharma, *Home Economics*.
19 Canada, "Overhauling the Temporary Foreign Workers Program: Putting Canadians First" (Ottawa: Government of Canada, 2014).
20 Bob Barnetson and Jason Foster, "The Political Justification of Migrant Workers in Alberta, Canada," *International Migration and Integration* 15 (2014): 349–70.
21 Taylor and Foster, "Migrant Workers and the Problems of Social Cohesion in Canada."
22 Perry, "Barely Legal," 191.
23 Canada, Parliament, House of Commons, Standing Committee on Citizenship and Immigration, *Minutes of Proceedings*, 40th Parliament, 2nd Session, Meeting 37 (Ottawa, 2009), online at https://www.ourcommons.ca/DocumentViewer/en/42-1/CIMM/meeting-106/minutes.
24 Canada, "Temporary Foreign Worker Program," emphasis mine.
25 Barnetson and Foster, "Political Justification of Migrant Workers in Alberta," 351.
26 Geraldina Polanco, "Consent Behind the Counter: Aspiring Citizens and Labour Control under Precarious Immigration Schemes," *Third World Quarterly* 37 no. 8 (2016): 1340.
27 Ibid., 1343.
28 Ibid.

29 Jenna Hennebry, "Who Has Their Eye on the Ball? 'Jurisdictional Fútbol' and Canada's Temporary Foreign Worker Program," *Policy Options* 63 (July/August 2010): 62–7.
30 Ibid.
31 Canada, "Overhauling the Temporary Foreign Workers Program," 17–19.
32 Taylor and Foster, "Migrant Workers and the Problems of Social Cohesion in Canada," 9.
33 Canada, "The Canadian Media Production Association and Cumulative Duration in the Temporary Foreign Workers Program (F-7363)" (Ottawa: Citizenship and Immigration Canada, 2011).
34 Anonymous, personal communication with the author, 14 March 2014. This interview was part of my postdoctoral research on Filipino temporary labour migrants' experiences in Edmonton, Alberta. As part of this project, I interviewed advocates, who included settlement service workers. Overall, I spoke to four settlement service providers.
35 Martin Martinello, "Political Participation, Mobilization, and Representation of Immigrants and their Offspring in Europe," Willy Brandt Series of Working Papers in International Migration and Ethnic Relation (Malmo, Sweden: Malmo University, 2005), 4.
36 Ibid.
37 Steven Vertovec, "Minority Associations, Networks, and Public Policies: Re-assessing Relationships," *Journal of Ethnic and Migration Studies* 25, no. 1 (1999): 26.
38 Robyn Rodriguez, *Migrants for Export: How the Philippine State Brokers Labour to the World* (Minneapolis: University of Minnesota Press, 2010).
39 See, for example, Nicole Constable, "Migrant Workers and the Many States of Protest in Hong Kong," *Critical Asian Studies* 41, no. 1 (2009): 143–64; Salina Abji, "Post-nationalism Reconsidered: A Case Study of the No One Is Illegal Movement in Canada," *Citizenship Studies* 17, nos. 3–4 (2013): 322–38; Leah Briones, "Rights with Capabilities: A New Paradigm for Social Justice in Migrant Activism," *Studies in Social Justice* 5, no. 1 (2011): 127–43; and Harsha Walia, *Undoing Border Imperialism* (Oakland, CA: AK Press, 2013).
40 Jennifer Fish, *Domestic Workers of the World Unite!* (New York: NYU Press, 2017), 10.
41 Patricia Landolt and Luin Goldring, "Immigrant Political Socialization as Bridging and Boundary Work: Mapping the Multi-Layered Incorporation of Latin American Immigrants in Toronto," *Ethnic and Racial Studies* 32, no. 7 (2009): 1230.
42 Ibid.
43 Ibid., 1242–3.
44 Ibid., 1244.

45 Tungohan, "From Encountering Confederate Flags to Finding Refuge in Spaces of Solidarity."
46 Canada, Parliament, House of Commons, Standing Committee on Human Resources, Skills and Social Development and the Status of Persons with Disabilities, *Minutes of Proceedings*, 42nd Parliament, 1st Session, Meeting 11 (Ottawa, 2016), online at https://www.ourcommons.ca/Committees /en/HUMA/StudyActivity?studyActivityId=8845433.
47 Landolt and Goldring, "Immigrant Political Socialization."
48 Olena Hankivsky, "Intersectionality-Based Policy Analysis," in *An Intersectionality-Based Policy Analysis Framework*, ed. Olena Hankivsky (Vancouver: Simon Fraser University, Institute for Intersectionality Research & Policy, 2012), 35.
49 Ethel Tungohan, "Intersectionality and Social Justice: Assessing Activists' Use of Intersectionality through Grassroots Migrants' Organizations in Canada," *Politics, Groups, and Identities* 4, no. 3 (2016): 347–62.
50 Nicholas Keung, "Ottawa ends '4-in-4-out' rule for migrant workers," *Toronto Star*, 13 December 2016, online at https://www.thestar.com/news /immigration/2016/12/13/ottawa-ends-4-in-4-out-rule-for-migrant -workers.html.
51 Ethel Tungohan, "The Transformative and Radical Feminism of Grassroots Migrant Women's Movements in Canada," *Canadian Journal of Political Science* 50, no. 2 (2017): 479–94.
52 Pierson, "Study of Policy Development."

KEY RESOURCES

Bindra, Tanya Kaur. "In Pictures: The Misery of Migrant Workers." *Al Jazeera*, 18 December 2012. Online at https://www.aljazeera.com/indepth/inpictures /2012/12/20121217981786357.html.
Boti, Mari, and Malcolm Guy, dir. *End of Immigration*. Montreal: Diffusion Multi-Monde, 2013. DVD.
Canadian Council for Refugees. "Migrant Workers Provincial and Federal Government Report Cards." Ottawa: Canadian Council for Refugees, 2013. Online at http://ccrweb.ca/files/migrant-worker-report-cards.pdf, accessed 10 May 2018.
Faraday, Fay. *Made in Canada: How the Law Constructs Migrant Workers' Insecurity*. Toronto: Metcalf Foundation, 2012. Online at http://metcalffoundation.com /wp-content/uploads/2012/09/Made-in-Canada-Full-Report.pdf, accessed 10 May 2018.
Lee, Min Sook, dir. *Migrant Dreams*. Toronto: Cinema Politica, 2016. DVD.

14 Storytelling as Engagement: Learning from Youth Voices in Attawapiskat

SARAH MARIE WIEBE

My message to you, if you're having a hard time, look to the trees, as it shows you to stand tall and proud. Look to the rock, as it shows you the strength you need. Look to the river, as it shows you to keep moving forward in life, as it flows, and to never give up. To the flowers, as it shows you the love you need. The colours. The grass, as it teaches you forgiveness as it always grows and grows no matter if you keep stepping on it, it's there to show you to forgive. We matter. Every little thing matters. The trees. The rocks. The flowers. You matter. Stay strong.

– Jack Linklater Jr, We Matter campaign message[1]

Speaking from the James Bay shoreline in the Mushkegowuk territory of Attawapiskat, via a YouTube video published online in the fall of 2016, youth leader Jack Linklater Jr's message invites viewers to listen to stories of strength that are grounded in the lands and waters of his community. On 11 April 2016, Attawapiskat leadership declared a State of Emergency due to an escalating rate of youth suicide attempts in the community.[2] The April 2016 declaration followed a similar declaration in October 2011 due to inadequate housing conditions, a situation that led then Attawapiskat chief Theresa Spence to commence a ceremonial fast, framed by the media and public officials as a "hunger strike," in December 2012.[3] For six weeks over the winter of 2012–13, in the shadow of Canada's Parliament, Spence engaged her body in this way to draw attention to the lack of respect for treaty relations between Canadians and the Attawapiskat Nation, while seeking to cultivate dialogue about systemic inequality between Indigenous peoples and Canadians.[4] Tired of living in a normalized State of Emergency where conditions of crisis had become the norm, as a last resort her efforts spoke to the heart of settler colonial relations in Canada, and contributed to igniting the Idle No

More movement, which urged Canadians to cease turning a blind eye to the issues facing Indigenous communities across the country.[5] Indeed, each State of Emergency signals the need for Canadians to enter a robust dialogue about what it means to engage, responsibly, respectfully, and reciprocally, in treaty *relations* in our colonial present, and pushes the boundaries of how we come to think about deliberative democracy.

How can we engage in meaningful decolonial dialogue in order to imagine Canadian-Indigenous relations beyond the oppressive colonial status quo? To answer this question, I draw from community perspectives while centring youth voices from Attawapiskat. In doing so, I argue that creative and collaborative mixed media storytelling methodologies with Indigenous youth have the potential to interrupt the predominant crisis narrative that frames Attawapiskat as vulnerable and in need of intervention and protection from external experts. Reframing and changing the narrative aligns with recent "Wise Practices" scholarship and policy efforts to centre purpose, hope, belonging, and meaning in order to connect communities to culturally appropriate care.[6] I contend that understanding what it means to be in a treaty relationship requires creativity, humility, and imagination. For researchers, it necessitates listening to community voices and not assuming that outsiders have all the answers. I further discuss how, through community engagement, researchers can co-create narratives to cultivate dialogue about how to treat and relate to one another better and enhance understanding about Indigenous peoples, cultures, and perspectives.

Weaving together theoretical tools from feminist cinematics, Indigenous storytelling methodologies, and deliberative democracy scholarship, this chapter highlights the myriad ways in which the situated knowledges of Indigenous youth in Attawapiskat offer counternarratives that critique, problematize, and (re)frame stories about community health and wellness.[7] This creative and collaborative research methodology aims to counteract the making of crisis stories.[8] As Jaskiran Dhillon advises, scholars have much to learn from the life stories of Indigenous youth who encounter, engage with, and resist a "constellation of contextual factors" that produce crises narratives that are bound up in settler-colonial governmentalities.[9] I begin by examining the emergence and expressions of crisis framing in Attawapiskat. I next explain the mixed media storytelling methodology that our team of artists and researchers undertook to generate counternarratives: a series of storytelling workshops meant to interrupt the predominant crisis narrative. I then examine the youths' digital stories to centre their voices and recalibrate the conversation about youth wellness beyond the need for intervention from outside authorities and experts. I conclude with some lessons learned and reflections for academic activists and policy makers who might benefit from employing creative arts-based methodologies while working with Indigenous communities to promote justice and deepen the practice of deliberative democracy in pursuit of policy justice.

Reframing Attawapiskat: More than a Community "in Crisis"

In the wake of an escalating number of suicide attempts in Attawapiskat, on 9 April 2016, then chief Bruce Shisheesh declared a State of Emergency.[10] Official reports revealed that, on a single night, eleven youth attempted to take their own lives. Twenty-eight attempts were made the previous month.[11] Declaring a State of Emergency meant that public officials beyond the community would be compelled to respond. Regional, provincial, and federal health authorities, including the Weeneebayko Health Authority, based in Moose Factory, Ontario, and Health Canada, were called to action. Provincial and federal health authorities immediately announced support, and a mental health team soon flew into the community. Provincial officials committed to deploy Ontario's Emergency Medical Assistance Team and to work with Attawapiskat authorities to determine appropriate avenues to resolve this issue. Although these emergency efforts cultivated consciousness about systemic and interrelated issues of government neglect, they failed to provide long-term solutions for overall community health and wellness. Responses such as these offer a band-aid approach to addressing a legacy of settler colonialism and its felt, lived, and visceral effects in Indigenous communities in Attawapiskat, in Canada, and globally.[12]

As the resources from outside experts began to trickle in, along with donations and letters from Canadians across the country, the opinions of thought leaders also began to flow. The term "crisis" dominated headlines.[13] In response, several journalists called for the relocation of community members away from reserves and into urban centres, suggesting that "moving is the only hope for communities like Attawapiskat."[14] News about the April 2016 State of Emergency declaration reached an international audience.[15] While this coverage raised awareness about the slow-moving violence and systemic oppression confronting Indigenous peoples in Canada, it also overlooked the community's strengths, including long-standing connections that many Attawapiskat citizens have to the lands and waters that make up their home.

In an effort to mobilize, shortly after the 2016 State of Emergency declaration the Pahsahwaytagwan "Sounding Echo" Youth Committee formed, with the intention of bringing Attawapiskat youth together to support one another, engage with outside officials on their own terms, and challenge the narratives of crisis and hopelessness.[16] The youth organized to make their voices heard. Several representatives flew to Ottawa in June 2016 to meet with Prime Minister Justin Trudeau, who announced additional funding for Indigenous mental health services.[17] During their visit, they attended a special performance and fundraiser featuring Indigenous artists and musicians, including A Tribe Called Red.[18] Many returned to Attawapiskat feeling invigorated and ready to enact change. Youth led healing marches and engaged in environmental clean-up efforts to come together.[19] Others mobilized by walking from community to community along the shore of James Bay in an effort to build connections and raise awareness.

In October that year, some youth from the community participated in the We Matter campaign to speak their truths and share them with a wider audience. Attawapiskat youth Jack Linklater Jr and Tyra Hookimaw participated in the campaign, which began to receive widespread attention.[20] As one of the We Matter founders, Tunchai Redvers, shared during an interview, the events in Attawapiskat were the impetus behind starting the campaign in the spring of 2016, which was grounded in youth community voices as well as those of role models and supporters.[21] The We Matter campaign is Indigenous driven, and employs a video messaging model to reshape the narrative around Indigenous youth mental health. The founders started their work by holding focus group workshops in Vancouver, the Northwest Territories, and Attawapiskat.[22] Jack Linklater Jr was one of the youth participants who shared a message to launch the national campaign in October 2016 as part of the video series. As Tunchai confirmed, Jack's video was one of the most widely screened. His message is directly rooted in land-based healing. It forms the basis for educational content, workshops, and resources further developed by the We Matter campaign team. Through social media, the campaign has continued to grow ever since, with over two hundred messages from youth, prominent role models, and allies from across the country.[23] The We Matter campaign emphasizes life promotion, and centres youth voices by reconfiguring the community health narrative beyond one of constant crisis, focusing instead on hope and strength. The Reimagining Attawapiskat project team and participants also share this vision.

Prior to the April 2016 State of Emergency declaration, several youth leaders and art students from Attawapiskat began a Reimagining Attawapiskat project to celebrate culture and to tell stories about the community that challenge its framing as hopeless, as in a constant state of crisis, and as in consistent need of outside intervention. The April 2016 State of Emergency declaration strengthened their resolve.

Under the leadership of Keisha PaulMartin, who met with the project team through a series of workshops in the Vezina Secondary School's art class, the Reimagining Attawapiskat project emerged to support youth as they spoke their truths and shed light on what life is like in Attawapiskat. The project does not aim to gloss over the haunting realities of ongoing colonization, but rather to acknowledge this history with the intention of honouring culture and co-creating ideas between Indigenous and non-Indigenous peoples about how to move towards a brighter, shared, healthy, and sustainable future. As such, the project follows youth direction while connecting past, present, and future.

To interrupt the crisis conditions, which discursively and materially affect Attawapiskat, the Reimagining Attawapiskat project is a collaborative research project that celebrates youth voices, articulated through the arts ranging from painting, poetry, and photography to film, music, and performance. These counternarratives are curated and collected by a team of academic and artist collaborators within and external to the community, and published on the Reimagining Attawapiskat website (www.reimaginingattawapiskat.com). My role in the project is the academic project director, while Keisha serves as the community project director. The publicly available website seeks to cultivate dialogue while centring youth voices in shaping the narrative about suicide prevention and community well-being.

Mixed Media Storytelling: A Prism to Engage and Enact Relational Research

Emergency declarations expose the edges of democratic societies. The pivotal decision to declare a state of emergency presents an opportunity to flip the gaze from the need for outside intervention to solve a community's problems to the need to intervene more broadly on the underlying systemic relations that produce conditions of inequality in the first place. As political theorist Bonnie Honig highlights, the context of emergency politics reveals the need for an important intervention into the conversation about democratic theory and practice.[24] Aligned with Honig, in this chapter I seek to contribute to a necessary dialogue about how to live well in contemporary democratic societies – especially salient during times of "crisis." States of emergency are exceptional modes of governance that present opportunities for imagination about how democratic and political engagement might be enacted beyond the colonial status quo. Engagement through the arts offers an avenue for this (re)imagination by centring community stories and voices in this process.

Mixed media storytelling is an applied research approach informed by Indigenous methodologies, deliberative democracy, and emergent literature in feminist cinematics. Through the prism of post-positivist feminist cinematics, this lens underscores the idea that all truth claims are contextual and perspectival. Combining feminism, post-positivism, and media studies under the umbrella of "feminist cinematics," it raises questions about the production of knowledge, power, and difference in order to challenge and interrupt a socially and environmentally unjust, gendered, settler-colonial status quo. Not only does a post-positivist feminist cinematic orientation examine and interrogate the social production of power through language; it is equally committed to co-creating opportunities for interruptions and interventions through creative avenues.[25] The post-positivist prism of feminist cinematics interrogates how certain discourses are sanctioned, and how they influence institutions and individuals. Sanctioning can occur through how media present or represent certain realities. This lens thus focuses on the power relations between hegemonic and subjugated discourses, which are produced by sanctioning processes such as the circulation and valuing of certain concepts, ideas, and words.[26] This orientation motivates the methodology of mixed media storytelling.

As a post-positivist prism, mixed media storytelling centres situated bodies of knowledge, and imagines possibilities for counternarratives that contend with the predominant accounts, representations, and portrayals of community experiences. This methodology is of particular interest to feminist, intersectional, and critical race scholars, as it seeks to interrupt the ways in which dominant discourses rationalize asymmetrical relations between women and racialized communities.[27] Feminist scholarship has long looked to women's lived experiences in particular, and experiential knowledge in general, as sources of knowledge in order to raise awareness and shift consciousness. Mixed media storytelling is thus about shifting the gaze of how we come to know what we know and see what we see in order to change these uneven relations. By design, it is action oriented, and aims for social, environmental, and policy justice.

Mixed media storytelling is community engaged and collaborative. This approach has the potential to enhance deliberative dialogue by engaging with decision makers and officials at multiple sites of authority. As Crystal Tremblay and Bruno de Oliveira Jayme demonstrate based on their research with recycling cooperatives in Brazil, methodologies such as participatory video serve as powerful tools to promote dialogue among diverse parties, including policy makers and those affected by compromised environments.[28] These creative and participatory methods mobilize collective, community knowledge for social and environmental change. Similar to participatory video, digital storytelling (and mixed media storytelling broadly) can be understood as an applied research tool that can release the imaginations of research participants and create a sense of community while cultivating dialogue between multiple parties affected by policy decisions and various levels of authority.[29]

Mixed media storytelling is a relational approach to research that invites a conversation about the power of meaning making. Reimagining Attawapiskat is a collaborative mixed media approach to community engagement that aims to co-create knowledge through the practice of "research as resistance."[30] In Attawapiskat, predominant media narratives initially pushed the voices of community members to the margins. Although some accounts did endeavour to circulate the perspectives of community members generally, and Indigenous youth specifically, the majority of mainstream media coverage framed Attawapiskat as constantly in crisis and as needing outside intervention. As an attempt to engage compassionately and creatively with a community experiencing the effects and affects of emergency politics, mixed media storytelling offers a prismatic lens through which academic activists can engage in democratic renewal through "alternative angles of vision."[31] This lens is a prism insofar as it casts light beyond one singular, linear, unidirectional beam to draw into focus a multiplicity of ways of seeing, from a diverse range of vantage points, situated knowledges and lived experiences.

As a multilayered lens, mixed media storytelling not only sheds light on the voices and lived experiences of those directly affected by discourses and "sensing policy" in their daily lives; it also interrogates broader socio-economic and geopolitical contexts that both shape and inform the systemic and underlying conditions that affect how certain communities come to live within compromised environments.[32] *Sensing policy* is an embodied approach to policy making that examines how policies affect people's everyday lives: how they are sensed and felt on the ground and in communities. This includes an emphasis on four central elements: *lived experience, geopolitical location, bodies of knowledge,* and *multilayered analysis*. To flesh out sensing policy in practice, as tool for deliberative scholars and policy makers, mixed media storytelling aims to be an iterative methodology that aligns with recent scholarship in deliberative democratic theory by seeking to engage the perspectives of those most directly affected by political decisions to generate ideas about how to imagine relations otherwise.[33] This iterative, collaborative, and dialogical process requires constant communication, reflexivity about one's own positionality, a willingness to revise the terms of collaboration based on the input of those affected, and follow-up on findings and the dissemination of results.

Mixed media storytelling is a multilayered transmedia prism for engaging communities in a relational research practice; in the process, mixed media storytelling creates a "sense of community" for all involved.[34] With respect to centring youth voices in the Reimagining Attawapiskat project, mixed media storytelling involves the following features: (a) an interrogation of predominant portrayals of the community when faced with a time of duress; (b) dialogue with those directly affected by the predominant portrayals to incite a conversation about what these portraits capture and what remains invisible; and (c) an opportunity to intervene on these outside portrayals to speak back to asymmetrical narratives through the situated voices, perspectives, and stories of those experiencing duress in their everyday lives. Mixed media storytelling operates from the assumption that those most affected by complex policies and political decisions are well placed to provide insight to decision makers and can better inform policy processes through a democratic process that gives voice to those who have conventionally been pushed to the margins.

With an emphasis on storytelling, the mixed media storytelling approach draws inspiration from Indigenous and participatory research methodologies. As Margaret Kovach has discussed, Indigenous research methodologies align with anti-oppressive methodologies and offer an alternative to positivist approaches, which have a tendency to "reproduce the epistemic privilege of the scientific paradigm."[35] Decolonizing research methodologies aim to replace knowledge extraction with relationships. The 1996 Royal Commission on Aboriginal Peoples recommended guidelines for ethical considerations that articulate the importance of *ownership, control, access, and possession*, and emphasized collaborative research, access to results, and benefit to community.[36] Researchers who aim to conduct decolonial research must be in service to community and centre Indigenous voices and practices. This necessarily entails creating opportunities for self-determination in the research process, which means supporting communities as they tell their stories in their words on their own terms.

Concepts of discourse and language are central to decolonizing research methodologies. As Margaret Kovach eloquently states, drawing upon post-modern scholarship, "the language that we use shapes the way we think" – thus, researchers working within a decolonial framework have an obligation to interrogate how a dominant society uses language to silence voices, and to challenge the ways in which "metanarratives" construct the parameters of "truth" and "normalcy."[37] Instead, researchers who are committed to a decolonial framework and to working in solidarity with Indigenous communities must find ways to encourage community members to share their own stories while respecting the wisdom of the storyteller. This is what mixed media storytelling aims to facilitate.

Decolonial research grounds itself in Indigenous epistemology. According to Kovach, this means it is "fluid, nonlinear, and relational."[38] Not only does this approach emphasize building relationships between researchers and the research team; it also encourages reflexivity, inviting all participants to consider carefully what they think and how they feel, and to pay attention to tensions, frictions, and discomforts during the process. Kovach articulates so well how "research, like life, is about relationships."[39] Indigenous methodologies aim to be holistic, relational, reciprocal, and storied. They entail protocols and ethics of care, accountability, and reciprocity. Contrary to liberal individualism, Indigenous methodologies "[are] a way of life that creates a sense of belonging, place and home."[40] This is in stark contrast to Western positivist orientations, where external experts come into contact with research subjects, gather data, leave and publish findings, with limited involvement of the researched along the way. There exists a long tradition in interpretive and qualitative research that fundamentally challenges this methodology.[41]

As a relational, storied approach, mixed media storytelling encourages reciprocity, gift exchange, laughter, and humour. Our research team thus spent considerable time getting to know the community and learning their protocols.[42] Mixed media storytelling also requires humility about the entire research process, from design to dissemination. Putting this humility into practice means having multiple conversations with knowledge holders from a range of perspectives and backgrounds while developing research goals and objectives. During my visit in February 2016, the senior art students attending Vezina Secondary School in Attawapiskat gathered materials for a postcard project.[43] Contributing images ranged from dancers to wolves, sunsets to boat rides. The young people involved in Reimagining Attawapiskat brought together their materials to reframe how the community is portrayed and seen by outsiders. As a researcher committed to relational research, I facilitated workshops with the art students and participated in community events and gatherings, including cross-country skiing on the river and feasting with community members. I committed to returning the following June to see the involved youths' final projects and to discuss where to circulate them. It was between these visits in February and June 2016 that the community leadership declared a State of Emergency. During this time, media coverage of Attawapiskat as a place constantly in crisis poured over the community. In June, it was an honour to attend the high school graduation and dance with Keisha and others to lift our spirits, be in ceremony, and collaboratively imagine where to exhibit and feature the project.

While I was visiting Attawapiskat in June 2016, I received confirmation from the Social Sciences and Research Humanities Council of Canada that we would be able to continue this research, supported through an Insight Development Grant. This meant I would be able to return to Attawapiskat with a team of artists, including Indigenous and non-Indigenous collaborators, to continue the creative storytelling process. Many stories centring youth voices are available on our Reimagining Attawapiskat website;[44] in them, participating youth sing, dance, and drum, sharing messages about the challenges they face while also celebrating their community and their culture. Each story is a mixture of light and shadows.

Light and Shadows: Celebrating Culture, Critiquing Colonialism

Youths' digital stories created as part of Reimagining Attawapiskat aim to reframe the discussion of how their home is represented. In her video, "This is Home," Keisha PaulMartin talks about the beauty of her surroundings, the scenery, the greenery, and the enjoyment of campfires with her family and friends.[45] These colourful qualities of her community appear in stark contrast to the bland, muted images circulated by media coverage of her community, which often shows the unpaved dirt roads. In her video, Keisha speaks about her interest in photography, and how taking photographs is a popular activity for her and her peers. In her comments, she mentions the various seasons, the colours of fall, and sunsets amid a backdrop of snow.

All of these images challenge the conventional understanding of her community as a wasteland, devoid of colour, life, and meaning. In Keisha's words, "it shows outsiders how it's not all ugly here."[46] She discusses the healing power of photography by explaining that "it makes people feel better" and offers a language, a form of communication, and a way to heal.[47] Keisha loves several activities that connect her to the lands and waters in her community and are another source of connection, health, and wellness, including tea picking – especially tundra tea – berry picking, and fishing.[48] She mentions her favourite spots, walking to the rapids and around the community. As her story reveals, she is not someone who is idle, stuck, and waiting for outside intervention. While she acknowledges the difficulties and challenges with the suicide crisis, she sums her reality up well in her concluding reflection: "it's home."[49]

For his digital story, another community leader, Jack Linklater Jr, took us to the rapids. His video opens with images of the water at the rapids and his voice, singing to the water in Cree. Then the sounds of the flowing water and his song fade into his narrative: "you need water to live. Without water, it's like you're nothing."[50] The camera follows Jack, who explains in his own words: "I love this place. It's where I find myself. It's where I truly am. The trees, the water, the rocks, the grass, the branches, the grass. Everything. The animals. This is where I be myself."[51] Jack discusses the significance of the elements to him: it's not just the water, but also "the trees, the wind; they can tell you many things. All you gotta do is just listen carefully. There are many teachings behind them."[52] His story emphasizes the importance of the connections between human and the more-than-human environment. The elements and surroundings Jack talks about are not passive; like him and his community, they are vibrant and full of life. According to Jack, "Just like the grass, it teaches me forgiveness. No matter if you cut it, you step on it, it would still grow. The trees, they teach me how to stand together and stick together."[53]

Jack's narrative speaks to themes of healing, resilience, and abundance. With reference to a fallen tree, he articulates how "other trees will grow around it."[54] The fallen tree can be used for firewood, which keeps one warm. The fire, too, teaches many things. As Jack highlights so affectionately, "it teaches me to love. 'Cause my heart's so warm."[55] With humility, he concludes with a reflection on his knowledge. Humble, yet wise beyond his years, he states: "I only know a little. But I know there's more. Many stories behind these, but it will take a lifetime for me to understand. I'm only seventeen and have many years ahead of me."[56]

Jack demonstrates similar humility in another digital story, in which he speaks about hitting a drum every day as a way to relax and as an emotional release.[57] In this video, he sings in Cree while drumming. As our research team learned during our visit, the drum is the heartbeat of the earth, and connects humans to their environments. It puts humans in relation to all living beings, and with these relations come responsibilities to care for others beyond the individual self in a wider interconnected ecosystem of relations.

Other youth videos draw the viewer's attention to themes of community, care for future generations, and healing. In her video, Marlen PaulMartin speaks about her own personal healing journey while raising her son, and how this experience changed her, as she wanted to "break the cycle."[58] She speaks about her hopes and dreams in the story. This includes an image of her son dancing, demonstrating his potential to grow up to be a grass or traditional dancer. She notes that her son loves to dance, and that each dance has a meaning.[59] She concludes by saying that she wants to graduate so that she can show him "he has a future." Fighting through tears while presenting with me in Vancouver at the annual Native American and Indigenous Studies Association conference in June 2017, Keisha told the audience that her sister Marlen was graduating that very same day. Making space for and honouring these emotions, connections, and relationships are critical for interpretive, Indigenous, and mixed media storytelling research methodologies.

The Reimagining Attawapiskat project began to generate widespread interest from journalists and academics. Youth voices became the subject of an article in *Maclean's*, a national magazine in Canada with a broad readership. In the April 2017 article, the authors refer to the Reimagining Attawapiskat project as a way for youth to "fight back" with their own stories in response to the mainstream media's coverage of the suicide crisis.[60] In visceral detail, drawing upon youth voices, including Keisha's, the journalists (one raised in, and one external to, the community) document the mental health struggles that many Attawapiskat youth face in their community. At the same time, the article points to the efforts of youth who are reframing the narrative on their own terms. This chimes with the message advanced by Indigenous activists and youth leaders Kelvin and Tunchai Redvers that Indigenous youth "are their own heroes," and it is time for others not to speak on behalf of youth, but to listen.[61] There is increasing agreement that youth themselves are in the best position to identify the root causes of feelings of hopelessness and to develop strategies to respond to these emergent mental health concerns. Indigenous youth are well placed to generate alternatives to the intervention-based model of mental health care and to suggest ideas for culturally appropriate healing. This is part of what the Pahsahwaytagwan Sounding Echo Youth Council aims to achieve – a sense of community rooted in land, culture, and ceremony, while respecting their home and connections to one another, to animals, and to ancestors. As both the *Maclean's* article and the digital stories from the Reimagining Attawapiskat project reveal, a healthy environment is inextricably connected to these young people's sense of overall well-being. Tunchai Redvers also articulates this grounding of health in land and culture as a key frame of reference for improving Indigenous mental wellness.[62]

In this spirit of listening, during Keisha's visit to Coast Salish territory (Vancouver), she had an opportunity to meet with researchers who were developing youth-led solutions to suicide prevention in partnership with Health Canada. Our team sat together and explained the Reimagining Attawapiskat project to the researchers. They expressed their intention to develop "Wise Practices" based on culturally grounded strategies for suicide prevention and health promotion. Turning to Keisha for advice was their starting point; you can see the coverage of the initiative on their website.[63] This collaborative effort demonstrates the ways in which academics, researchers, and eventually policy makers and practitioners – and potentially the general public – cannot just "hear" the voices of youth, but *listen* meaningfully to their stories and their strategies for social, political, and environmental change. As I have discussed in this chapter, mixed media storytelling is one avenue for advancing policy dialogue about tough, messy, and multilayered policy problems by creating space for engagement among a range of diverse perspectives, such as between youth and decision makers.

The Reimagining Attawapiskat project and the We Matter campaign are examples of youth-driven and Indigenous-led initiatives that intend to address multilayered issues such as Indigenous mental health and wellness.[64] These initiatives take direct aim at narratives that paint communities with a bleak brush, highlighting stories of despair while eclipsing counternarratives from youth themselves. Both the Reimagining Attawapiskat project and the We Matter campaign are examples of mixed media storytelling platforms that offer a venue for Indigenous youth to share messages with the world, rather than passively serving as a mirror for outside projections and representations. These initiatives are publicly accessible, create connections between people, and provide a platform to bring forward voices that traditionally have been left out of important conversations and policy decisions that shape their lives. For instance, Health Canada provided funding for the We Matter campaign, including to develop a public service announcement called #strongertogether, filmed in partnership with Facebook, a video produced by over twenty Indigenous youth talking about healing in a way that makes sense for them. Health Canada also provides funding to We Matter for the campaign's educational resources.[65] One next step for We Matter was a gathering in Ottawa in January 2018 that brought together partners from across Canada to discuss Indigenous youth and mental wellness, as well as Indigenous youth speaking about their own solutions to the issue of youth suicide. No leadership or politicians were invited to speak, but they were invited to *listen* to the youth leaders.[66] The gathering engaged youth voices and supported their agency as drivers of change. In these ways, youth themselves became active agents in a movement for radical representational change. The onus is on the rest of us to develop our capacities to listen to and learn from their stories.

Concluding Reflections: Lessons for Deliberative Democracy Scholars and Practitioners Enacting the Arts of Engagement

We learned a few lessons for the theory and practice of deliberative democracy along the way that are worth sharing here. First, creative collaborations require an investment. This refers not just to the financial resources for travel to and from the research setting or funding for a local research assistant with community expertise, but also to an investment in relationships. In accordance with Indigenous methodologies oriented to envisioning possibilities for decolonial futures, researchers must be humble, willing to revisit their aims and expectations, and continue the dialogue beyond the project's end date. Second, mixed media storytelling is multifaceted, which means that it can be difficult to hone a message or control stories for a coherent narrative. At times, this can lead to hurt feelings, dislocation, or discomfort around the identification of one spokesperson. With a mixed media approach such as this, there is no one, singular central storyteller. The website becomes a prism casting light on the spectrum of stories and voices from youth themselves. Third, with mixed media storytelling, one has to expect the unexpected. Related to the first lesson about building relationships and investing in people, our research team made a judgment call to stay in the community longer than initially expected in order to publicly exhibit their artworks and present youth participants in the project with certificates of completion. It was important for the team to be able to honour the youth voices through ceremony and to have a community screening to feature their hard work, rather than quickly departing the field with youth stories as "data" for extractive academic inquiry and analysis.

Mixed media storytelling projects in particular, and community-engaged research broadly speaking, require an ongoing ethic and practice of reflexivity. This means not entering community spaces with a fixed agenda, but approaching communities as places of learning. When you enter and leave community, you engage in a relationship with the people, lands, waters, plants, and animals you encounter. Researchers can do good work in service to community when they acknowledge and recognize that they are not the experts but have much to learn from community. By engaging in the practice of storytelling, you become a witness and must be held accountable. Community-engaged research and mixed media storytelling are practices of relational research that touch peoples' lives. As such, you affect those you come into dialogue with and leave community forever affected. With this affectedness comes not necessarily a neat and tidy conclusion, or the tight packaging of a formal strategy or recommendation for immediate social, political, or environmental change, but a necessary commitment to engage in an ongoing and unfinished conversation beyond the foreseeable future. In sum, mixed media storytelling is a collaborative research methodology that has the potential to critique the colonial status quo, cultivate community connections, and create conditions for ongoing democratic conversations among diverse groups of participants into the future.

Discussion Questions

1 How can mixed media storytelling complement Indigenous research methodologies?
2 What are some avenues for public officials and policy makers to listen to youth voices?
3 In what ways can policy-making processes engage with voices through mixed media storytelling?
4 How can we evaluate the impact of mixed media storytelling?
5 Does mixed media storytelling create space for conversations about difficult topics? What are some opportunities and challenges with this approach to research?

NOTES

1 For more about the We Matter campaign, see https://wemattercampaign .org/, and Jack Linklater Jr's video at https://www.youtube.com/watch?v =kZ5bBq63U7g.
2 "Attawapiskat: Four things to help understand the suicide crisis," *Globe and Mail*, 11 April 2016, online at https://beta.theglobeandmail.com/news /national/attawapiskat-four-things-to-help-understand-the-suicidecrisis /article29583059/?ref=http://www.theglobeandmail.com&, accessed 20 October 2017.
3 When Theresa Spence began her ceremonial fast on Victoria Island in the heart of a cold Ottawa winter in December 2012, the general Canadian public was largely confused, intrigued, and indifferent. Her action revealed the need for a vibrant conversation about Canada's responsibilities and treaty relationships with Indigenous peoples. In 1905, Cree leaders from present day Attawapiskat territories signed the James Bay Treaty, Treaty 9, with Crown representatives, including the federal and provincial governments. Reluctantly putting her body into the media spotlight, Chief Spence's political engagement aimed to reignite a conversation about what it means to be part of a treaty relationship today.
4 Sarah Barmak, "Attawapiskat First Nation Chief Theresa Spence ends hunger strike," *Toronto Star*, 25 January 2013, online at https://www.thestar.com /news/insight/2013/01/25/attawapiskat_first_nation_chief_theresa_spence _ends_hunger_strike.html, accessed 20 October 2017.

5 "Timeline: States of Emergency Attawapiskat has declared in recent years," *CBC News*, 11 April 2016, online at http://www.cbc.ca/news/canada/sudbury/attawapiskat-states-of-emergency-1.3530222, accessed 20 October 2017. See also Glen Coulthard, *Red Skin, White Masks: Rejecting the Colonial Politics of Recognition* (Minneapolis: University of Minnesota Press, 2014).

6 Wise Practices, "Action Guide for Communities: Bringing Wise Practices to Life," n.d., online at https://wisepractices.ca/wp-content/uploads/2018/10/WisePractices_ActionGuide_v13.pdf. See also Canada, Health Canada, *First Nations Mental Wellness Continuum Framework* (Ottawa: Health Canada, January 2015), online at: http://www.thunderbirdpf.org/wp-content/uploads/2015/01/24-14-1273-FN-Mental-Wellness-Framework-EN05_low.pdf.

7 See Bonnie Honig and Lori J. Marso, eds., *Politics, Theory, and Film* (Oxford: Oxford University Press, 2016); Krista Lynes, *Prismatic Media, Transnational Circuits: Feminism in a Globalized Present* (Basingstoke, UK: Palgrave-Macmillan, 2012); Gillian Rose, *Visual Methodologies: An Introduction to Researching with Visual Materials*, 4th ed. (Thousand Oaks, CA: SAGE, 2016); Margaret Kovach, *Indigenous Methodologies* (Toronto: University of Toronto Press, 2014); idem, "Emerging from the Margins: Indigenous Methodologies," in *Research as Resistance*, ed. Susan Strega and Leslie Brown (Toronto: Canadian Scholars Press, 2015), 43–64; David Kahane et al., eds., *Deliberative Democracy in Practice* (Vancouver: UBC Press, 2010); Genevieve Fuji Johnson, *Democratic Illusion: Deliberative Democracy in Canadian Public Policy* (Toronto: University of Toronto Press, 2015); John Dryzek, *Deliberative Democracy and Beyond: Liberals, Critics, Contestations* (New York: Oxford University Press, 2000); and Iris Marion Young, *Inclusion and Democracy* (Oxford: Oxford University Press, 2000).

8 For more on this topic, see Jaskiran Dhillon, *Prairie Rising: Indigenous Youth, Decolonization and the Politics of Intervention* (Toronto: University of Toronto Press, 2017).

9 Ibid., 11.

10 Kate Rutherford, "Attawapiskat declares state of emergency over spate of suicide attempts," *CBC News Sudbury*, 9 April 2016, online at http://www.cbc.ca/news/canada/sudbury/attawapiskat-suicide-first-nations-emergency-1.3528747, accessed 20 October 2017.

11 Ibid.

12 For an in-depth discussion of settler-colonialism, see Coulthard, *Red Skin, White Masks*.

13 Ben Spurr, "How the Attawapiskat suicide crisis unfolded," *Toronto Star*, 18 April 2016, online at https://www.thestar.com/news/canada/2016/04/18/how-the-attawapiskat-suicide-crisis-unfolded.html, accessed 20 October 2017; "Attawapiskat: Four things to help understand the suicide crisis"; "Attawapiskat suicide emergency: Health Canada, province

send in crisis teams," *CBC News Sudbury*, 11 April 2016, online at https://
www.cbc.ca/news/canada/sudbury/attawapiskat-suicide-emergency
-help-1.3529750, accessed 20 October 2017; "'Shocked the world': Suicide
crisis at Attawapiskat reverberates in rare emergency debate," *National
Post*, 13 April 2017, online at http://nationalpost.com/news/politics
/shocked-the-world-suicide-crisis-at-attawapiskat-reverberates-in-rare
-emergency-debate, accessed 20 October 2017; "Attawapiskat suicide
crisis: Police break up suicide pact between 13 youths," *Huffington Post*,
12 April 2016, online at http://www.huffingtonpost.ca/2016/04/12
/attawapiskat-suicide-pact_n_9671298.html, accessed 20 October 2017.

14 Jonathan Kay, "Moving is the only hope for communities like Attawapiskat," *National Post*, 16 April 2016, online at http://nationalpost.com
/opinion/jonathan-kay-little-hope-for-attawapiskat-as-long-as-its-people
-stay-put, accessed 20 October 2017; Scott Gilmore, "The unasked question
about Attawapiskat," *Maclean's*, 13 April 2016, online at http://www
.macleans.ca/news/canada/the-unasked-question-about-attawapiskat/,
accessed 20 October 2017.

15 Laurence Mathieu-Léger and Ashifa Kassam, "First Nations community grappling with suicide crisis: 'We're crying out for help,'" *Guardian*,
16 April 2014, online at https://www.theguardian.com/world/2016/apr
/16/canada-first-nations-suicide-crisis-attawapiskat-history, accessed
20 October 2017; Camila Domonoske, "Canadian First Nation declares
state of emergency over suicide attempts," *NPR News*, 11 April 2016, online
at http://www.npr.org/sections/thetwo-way/2016/04/11/473784919
/canadian-first-nation-declares-state-of-emergency-over-suicide-attempts,
accessed 20 October 2017; "Canadian Attawapiskat First Nation suicide
emergency," *BBC News*, 11 April 2016, online at http://www.bbc.com
/news/world-us-canada-36012578, accessed 20 October 2017.

16 Amitha Kalaichandran and Chelsea Jane Edwards, "A youth-driven movement remakes Attawapiskat," *Maclean's*, 5 April 2017, online at http://
www.macleans.ca/news/canada/a-youth-driven-movement-remakes
-attawapiskat/, accessed 20 October 2017.

17 Susana Mas, "Trudeau announces nearly $70M over 3 years for Indigenous
mental health services," *CBC News*, 13 June 2016, online at http://www.cbc
.ca/news/politics/trudeau-attawapiskat-youth-chief-meeting-1.3629960,
accessed 20 October 2017.

18 As announced on A Tribe Called Red's Twitter feed, 13 June 2016, online
at https://twitter.com/atribecalledred/status/742357562746667009.,
accessed 20 October 2017.

19 Angela Gemmill, "Attawapiskat youth group cleans up community to
cope during suicide crisis," *CBC News Sudbury*, 19 May 2016, online at
http://www.cbc.ca/news/canada/sudbury/attawapiskat-youth-cleanup
-litter-1.3589138, accessed 20 October 2017.

20 Mark Hume, "'I want to speak to you from the heart,'" *Globe and Mail*, 21 October 2016, online at https://beta.theglobeandmail.com/news /british-columbia/we-matter-videos-speak-to-aboriginal-youth-incrisis /article32483265/?ref=http://www.theglobeandmail.com, accessed 20 October 2017.

21 Author's interview with Tunchai Redvers, 3 October 2017.

22 Ibid.

23 Ibid.

24 Bonnie Honig, *Emergency Politics: Paradox, Law, Democracy* (Princeton, NJ: Princeton University Press, 2009).

25 Honig and Marso, *Politics, Theory, and Film.*

26 In their edited volume, *Politics, Theory, and Film: Critical Encounters with Lars von Trier,* Bonnie Honig and Lori J. Marso and the contributing authors interrogate gender, race, and power relations with a biopolitical engagement of predominant cinematic portrayals to shatter monolithic perspectives and cultivate radical conversations. On post-modern and post-positive approaches, see also Susan Strega, "The View from the Poststructural Margins: Epistemology and Methodology Reconsidered," in Strega and Brown, *Research as Resistance*, 120–52.

27 Strega, "View from the Poststructural Margins," 137.

28 Crystal Tremblay and Bruno de Oliveira Jayme, "Community Knowledge Co-creation through Participatory Video," *Action Research* 13, no. 3 (2015): 298–314.

29 For a range of literature about arts-based research, visual methodologies, and digital storytelling, see Maxine Greene, *Releasing the Imagination: Essays on Education, the Arts and Social Change* (San Francisco: Jossey-Bass, 1995); Simone Chambers and Anne Costain, eds., *Deliberation, Democracy, and the Media* (Lanham, MD: Rowman & Littlefield, 2000); Joe Lambert, *Digital Storytelling: Capturing Lives, Creating Community* (Berkeley, CA: Digital Diner Press, 2002); Gillian Rose, *Visual Methodologies: An Introduction to Researching with Visual Materials*, 3rd ed. (Thousand Oaks, CA: SAGE, 2012).

30 Strega and Brown, *Research as Resistance.*

31 Honig, *Emergency Politics*, xv.

32 For a more complete discussion of "sensing policy," see Sarah Marie Wiebe, *Everyday Exposure: Indigenous Mobilization and Environmental Justice in Canada's Chemical Valley* (Vancouver: UBC Press, 2016).

33 David R.H. Moscrop and Mark E. Warren, "When Is Deliberation Democratic?" *Journal of Public Deliberation* 12, no. 2 (2016): article 4.

34 I discuss this concept at length in Sarah Marie Wiebe, "Decolonizing Engagement? Creating a Sense of Community through Collaborative Filmmaking," *Studies in Social Justice* 9, no. 2 (2015): 244–57.

35 Kovach, "Emerging from the Margins," 47.

36 Ibid., 48.
37 Ibid., 51.
38 Ibid., 53.
39 Ibid., 55.
40 Ibid.
41 See, for example, Peregrine Schwartz-Shea and Dvora Yanow, *Interpretive Research Design: Concepts and Processes* (New York: Routledge, 2012); and contributors to Dvora Yanow and Peregrine Schwartz-Shea, eds., *Interpretation and Method: Empirical Research Methods and the Interpretive Turn* (Armonk, NY: M.E. Sharpe, 2006).
42 For instance, my entry point to the community took place as a volunteer during the annual summer pow wow in August 2015. At that time, as a postdoctoral researcher, I used some of my funds to travel to the community and stay in the local White Wolf Inn. Prior to the visit, I spoke on the phone with one of the pow wow organizers, who recommended that I first come to witness and to listen, then to develop my project in close collaboration with the community. During the days of, and following, the pow wow, I met with the newly elected chief, as well as educators, artists, and health care staff. One of the high school teachers invited me to put together a proposal to work with art students on a digital storytelling initiative, which received approval from the local education board. I returned in the winter to speak with the high school students about media coverage of the community, and we began brainstorming how to create and circulate alternative narratives. With the leadership of Keisha PaulMartin, the Reimagining Attawapiskat project came into being in February 2016.
43 See these images online at www.reimaginingattawapiskat.com.
44 See the digital stories under "Youth Voices," online at www.reimaginingattawapiskat.com.
45 See "This is Home," Youth Digital Story by Keisha PaulMartin, online at https://www.reimaginingattawapiskat.com/youth-digital-stories.
46 Ibid.
47 Ibid.
48 Ibid.
49 Ibid.
50 See "Water Is Life," Youth Digital Story by Jack Linklater Jr, online at https://www.reimaginingattawapiskat.com/youth-digital-stories.
51 Ibid.
52 Ibid.
53 Ibid.
54 Ibid.
55 Ibid.
56 Ibid.

57 Ibid.
58 See Marlen PaulMartin's digital story, online at https://www
    .reimaginingattawapiskat.com/youth-digital-stories.
59 Ibid.
60 Kalaichandran and Edwards, "Youth-driven movement remakes
    Attawapiskat."
61 Kelvin Redvers and Tunchai Redvers, "Indigenous youth are their own
    heroes – it's time we listened," *Globe and Mail*, 10 September 2017, online at
    https://beta.theglobeandmail.com/opinion/indigenous-youth-are-their
    -own-heroes-its-time-we-listened/article36217830/?ref=http://www
    .theglobeandmail.com&, accessed 27 September 2017.
62 Author's interview with Tunchai Redvers, 3 October 2017.
63 See Wise Practices, "Reimagining Attawapiskat," n.d., online at http://
    wisepractices.thunderbirdpf.org/practices/reimagining-attawapiskat/,
    accessed 27 September 2017.
64 For more on the We Matter campaign, see https://wemattercampaign.
    org/, accessed 27 September 2017; note that Jack Linklater Jr is one of the
    featured youth.
65 Author's interview with Tunchai Redvers, 3 October 2017.
66 Ibid.

KEY RESOURCES

Coulthard, Glen. *Red Skin, White Masks: Rejecting the Colonial Politics of
   Recognition*. Minneapolis: University of Minnesota Press, 2014.
Dhillon, Jaskiran. *Prairie Rising: Indigenous Youth, Decolonization and the Politics
   of Intervention*. Toronto: University of Toronto Press, 2017.
Kovach, Margaret. *Indigenous Methodologies*. Toronto: University of Toronto
   Press, 2014.
Lynes, Krista. *Prismatic Media, Transnational Circuits: Feminism in a Globalized
   Present*. Basingstoke, UK: Palgrave-Macmillan, 2012.
"Reimagining Attawapiskat." n.d. Online at http://wisepractices.
   thunderbirdpf.org/practices/reimagining-attawapiskat/, and at https://
   www.reimaginingattawapiskat.com/.
Wiebe, Sarah Marie. *Everyday Exposure: Indigenous Mobilization and
   Environmental Justice in Canada's Chemical Valley*. Vancouver: UBC Press, 2016.

15 Making Spaces for Truth: Deliberating Reconciliation in Post-Secondary Education

DEREK TANNIS

Not Shutting Up

> A member at the retreat reports from his group. He says, "We think community engagement is good, because we'll get more donors and we'll commercialize more stuff. Instead of ignoring community, we should ask them, 'Do you think this is a good thing?' But you wouldn't want productive or new faculty members to do it." So, you can imagine my face. I cannot let that go. I get chills. My heart starts pounding. I briefly consider, "Just shut up." But I think, "No way I'm shutting up." So, I ask to speak. I get up, thank my colleague, and everyone beams at me. I say, "But, where to start?" Smiles drop. My voice rises. I'm talking fast and I feel heat in my face. Then my colleague says, "You know what we used to do with First Nations? We used to go in there and take their blood and never see them again. Now we're asking permission." We're asking permission? That's community engagement? I grind to a halt. I say thank you and sit down.

Across Canada, universities are recognizing they must adapt to a growing population of Aboriginal students.[1] The Calls to Action of the Truth and Reconciliation Commission of Canada (TRC)[2] have led organizations such as Universities Canada to develop *Principles on Indigenous Education*.[3] Proponents of such principled engagement stress that institutional initiatives should "be led by Indigenous people, supported by non-Indigenous allies, with everyone sharing and learning from the exchange."[4] Sceptics are concerned, however, that the rush to Indigenize institutions, narrowly framed as a matter of expanding notions of inclusion, leads to haphazard and symbolic initiatives that ultimately sustain the status quo.[5] Lasting change, it is argued, involves educational institutions in deliberating reconciliation as a commitment to decolonizing institutional policies and practices.[6] It might not be a surprise, then, that deliberating reconciliation in post-secondary education can be controversial. In the opening quote, as Melinda describes her efforts to overcome her hesitation to speak at a senior leadership session, she scratches beneath the surface and exposes institutional rifts. As the leader of a faculty dedicated to community-engaged scholarship, Melinda speaks for the ethical, Indigenous engagement in research that Sarah Marie Wiebe describes in chapter 14. As an ally, she reveals the necessity of forming political alliances in pursuing reconciliation, a concept that Ethel Tungohan explores in chapter 13. Reconciliation, as Melinda's intervention illustrates, includes the necessary, institutionally and personally implicating, practical, and systemic changes needed to develop respectful relations with Aboriginal peoples and to atone for past injustices inflicted on them.[7] Unfortunately, however, as Melinda reminds us, "we are not there yet," for the "relationship between Aboriginal and non-Aboriginal peoples is not a mutually respectful one."[8]

This chapter explores faculty, staff, and student lived experiences, such as Melinda's, of multidimensional deliberations of reconciliation strategies and related policy matters at a Canadian post-secondary institution. As such, this exploration delves into the lived tensions and potentialities of taking a policy justice orientation to deliberation within one's own institution, an orientation that often challenges institutional policy norms and deliberative practices. The following pages describe such tension and potentiality, in the context of reconciliation, as involving a revealing of known and hidden practices and structures that perpetuate exclusionary policies, strategies, and processes that, in order to be reframed, require Aboriginal and non-Aboriginal faculty, staff, and students to listen to and learn from one another. In such spaces of inclusive engagement, the practice of kindness emerges as a crucial disposition of allowing and attending to deliberative spaces of transformative learning and ethical relations that resist certainties and closure.

The chapter is organized in three sections. First, I situate myself within, and provide an overview of, the phenomenological approach of my research, including how it relates to deliberative democracy. Second, I explore the experiences shared by participants in the research. The subtitles I use in this section are meant to represent the variable meanings of the lived experiences explored. By this, I mean that all variations of each subtitle, with and without parenthesis, are in some way reflective of the lived experiences shared by the participants in this study. These variations open to the ways in which we make and do not make connections between what we believe to be the truths or facts of our deliberations on reconciliation, and how participants describe such deliberations as an evolving of their certainties and expectations. In the final section, I explore how participants describe what might be called the dispositions they take on in relation to their day-to-day practice as they seek to create and engage in such conflicting and connective spaces of deliberating reconciliation within their institutions.

Situating Self in/and Study

As Catriona Remocker, Tim Dyck, and Dan Reist explore in chapter 8, in the quasi-governmental context of post-secondary education, campuses are sites of citizen engagement on complex societal issues. As such, campuses offer a rich context for exploring the deliberation of reconciliation. In a competitive policy context, an "aspiration" such as reconciliation can galvanize faculty, staff, and students "to imagine the meaning of a common goal."[9] In a deliberative democratic context, however, associated deliberations can rest on weak assumptions that common goals are identifiable and implementable among diverse faculty, staff, and students.[10] In pursuing reconciliation, we must ultimately "include some things and exclude others";[11] as such, reconciliation might be viewed as a set of interrelated problems associated with multiple strategies and policies.[12] As a means of Indigenization, the scope of this interrelationship is vast, spanning from curriculum and teaching to research ethics and student affairs.[13] In all cases, we must, as Dale Turner argues, "engage colonialism in its physical and intellectual contexts and in the process strive to overcome the colonial mindset in both Indigenous and non-Indigenous communities."[14] This chapter explores such faculty, student, and staff engagement and striving for policy justice, wherein "indigenous ways of knowing the world are not devalued, marginalized, or ridiculed in the marketplace of ideas" that constitute institutional strategy and policy in post-secondary education.[15]

Impossible Pretence

Before going further, I must position myself as a settler in relation to my research and work. For over twenty-five years, I have sought to become an ally of Aboriginal peoples. Since moving west, however, I have come to recognize fully the implications of my ancestry. I grew up in Ottawa, in a mixed Arab-European family, but my maternal grandparents met in the city in which I now live. My cousin once showed me a land certificate, dated 1913, of my great-grandparents' homestead in southeast Saskatchewan. At that moment, I realized my connection with the greatest wave of settlement in Canadian history, an intentional act to displace Aboriginal people from their homelands.[16] In this place I call home, my family and I have benefited from the Treaty Six relationship established over 140 years ago, signed under the auspices that, as settlers, "we have not come here to deceive you, ... we have not come here to take away anything that belongs to you."[17]

I now work in institutions that struggle with and seek to overcome the legacies of colonialism. I have worked for the majority of my career in the field of international education, wherein a majority of international students intend to immigrate to Canada.[18] As such, I have been implicated in the continuing settlement of this land. In tandem, institutional efforts at developing faculty, staff, and students' intercultural competencies can conceal biased conceptions of what constitutes inclusion.[19] The paradoxical nature of such struggles does not escape me. I recognize this paradox as a faithful starting point at how I engage with reconciliation personally, professionally, and politically, including the manner in which I have approached the research and the writing of this chapter.

Incumbent Noticing

This chapter explores the phenomenological insights from a larger doctoral research project on the deliberation and enactment of Indigenization and internationalization in post-secondary education. From my participant interviews with twenty-four Indigenous and non-Indigenous faculty, staff, and students, reconciliation emerged as an area of shared praxis across student affairs, teaching, advising, human resources, research, and leadership. As phenomenology, the lived experience of deliberating reconciliation might be viewed as a case, in and of itself, worthy of "analysis, description, and interpretation ... an exemplary nodal point of meanings."[20]

Reflecting on lived experience might enable the examination of the "taken-for-granted" in higher education,[21] and demand that we "consider not only the consequential outcomes of planning, not only the general principles of planning practice, but the demands, the vulnerable and precarious virtues required of a politically attentive, participatory professional practice."[22] Through such an exploration, we might, as Max van Manen explains, gain "an intuitive or inspirited grasp of the ethics and ethos of life commitments and practices,"[23] including the "formative relations between being and acting, between who we are and how we act, between thoughtfulness and tact" in how we deliberate strategies and policies associated with reconciliation in our roles in our own institutions and in the public spaces of deliberation we enter into and co-create.[24]

I approached this study as a process of "noticing," a recognition that one is usually looking for what one expects to see, and, at the same time, as method – as a sustained effort to look for "what doesn't seem to fit."[25] According to Shawn Wilson, such self-location and noticing is a matter of establishing relationality with others in a voice that declares one's unique perspective based in one's experience in and knowledge of the world.[26] In this manner, in the following pages, I seek to "make new connections to ideas" in such a way that readers may "come to their own decisions on the shape that the new ideas will take and to make their own conclusions" regarding the implications of interpretive policy analysis for reconciliation and deliberative democracy.[27] It is to this offering to "make new connections to ideas" that I now turn.

Day-to-Day Reconciliation

In post-secondary education, deliberating matters related to reconciliation can reveal "hidden emotional and symbolic issues," such that "a small concern" might reflect deeper issues of "identity, cultural history, and social injustice."[28] In revealing such concerns, we might find substantive spaces of meaning making. In the next section, I explore such day-to-day acts of deliberating reconciliation as experienced by the participants in my study.

(Un)Expected (Dis)Connections

I begin with Kendra, who leads first-year Aboriginal student transition programming at her campus.

> When I started, I went into one of the family houses. I was thinking, "As long as I could see myself living here, then it's great for the student." The carpet was so gross, I didn't want to take off my shoes. And so, my mission was, "That carpet has to get changed." Everyone was responding, "No. That's not going to happen." At that time, we also only had two family houses. But I stayed on top of that situation. I was just, at any meeting we were at: "We need more space." And yet, it didn't seem like there was much we could do besides protect the little space everyone was fighting for.

In advocating for adequate Aboriginal student housing, Kendra finds herself as one voice among many in a competition for limited resources. Kendra persists by making the connection, at countless meetings, between Aboriginal student success and on-campus housing, until new carpets are laid and more space is provided. Her experience mirrors

Leslie's, who recounts contacting a professor regarding an Aboriginal student's request for a deferred exam.

> For this student, there is an ill family member and the student feels responsible to go home. Even though it doesn't meet the conditions for a deferred exam, I have a conversation with the student's professor, who is strict. I tell him we know the student is not trying to get away with something. I explain that I'm willing to go out on the line for this student and ask this. That authenticity moves things along, much more than the student asking himself, which is frustrating. It is a real-life situation to the professor when I make it personal. All the professor sees is the piece of paper. The professor doesn't have to look that student in the face and say "No, I don't believe you. This is not important enough to me."

In speaking with this professor, Leslie cannot draw from existing rationales, but must inform the professor as to why, for this student, and for Aboriginal students generally, this type of situation warrants consideration. As Kendra's and Leslie's reflections illustrate, deliberating policies and related procedures that intersect with reconciliation might require patient, persistent attention to matters that might not resonate with, or worse, be ignored by our colleagues. In our work, we might find ourselves reiterating how seemingly disparate issues are linked, from first-year programming and course assessment to campus safety and cultural gathering spaces.

Diane, a faculty member, expects this disconnect. She states that dominant, Western approaches to education policy and practice neither reflect, nor respect, traditional practices of education held by Indigenous students and faculty. This disconnect requires her and her colleagues constantly to "rationalize and justify what they're doing" in relation to their teaching and research. Sophie notes that, when her institution tries to address underlying barriers to reconciliation, it can feel "like walking through a field of landmines."

> My colleague showed our survey to some key people and one of them said, "I think you have to rephrase these questions about racism." I feel deflated and frustrated. I think, "This is why these things never change. Because people are afraid to ask hard questions. How are we going to do a survey about this topic and not use the word for it?"

Sophie describes a dispute over language in a survey on racism. She senses denial, and is left feeling despair and confusion. Her feeling is similar to that of another interview participant, Daniela, when she hears "push back about the TRC" and "some really mean-spirited things." She says it feels "like a knife cuts through" her, and she is left wondering if reconciliation is possible. For Dominic, another interview participant, avoiding the issue of campus racism can be experienced as a form of silencing, forcing us to ask, "what is wrong with our system" that makes it so we "cannot have these difficult conversations?"

We might have asked similar questions. We might wonder why faculty and staff are not fully engaging in reconciliation. We might look at first-year completion rates and shake our heads at the number of Aboriginal students who withdraw. Such concerns were raised in my interviews. Participants spoke of feeling outside policy influence, regardless of the level of authority, even for those who succeeded in making important, quietly achieved changes. We must ask ourselves what it is about our environment that makes us feel we are not a constructive part of reconciliation, even when, as Genevieve Fuji Johnson describes in chapter 1, in our micro-level, day-to-day deliberations we might be shaping how, as an institution, we approach its macro-level deliberation and framing.

(Un)Ravelling (Un)Truths

We might sense our ineffectiveness when we come up against systemic barriers, grounded in issues associated with "who has the authority to define the key terms and issues" under deliberation.[29] We might also find, as Paulette Regan writes, that, in many cases, our approaches to reconciliation are rendered "no different from settler practices of the past – a new colonial tool of oppression" when they do not involve a "peeling back" of the "layers of myth" confronting "our own repressed and unscrutinized past" as Canadians.[30] For Diane, lack of representation and what Rauna Kuokkanen describes as a "stance of studied ignorance"[31] persist through bias and misleading, misinformed understandings of history.

> Policy stymied our growth, stymied change, and stymied everything. I don't have time in my life to navigate and fight this system that says, "This privileged knowledge is better than Indigenous knowledge. There's no rigour. There's nothing in it." When this knowledge has been here for thousands of years.

As Diane relates, policies and strategies related to reconciliation might be held in deep suspicion. Policy can be experienced as a subterfuge that presumes superiority over, and undermines the value of, Indigenous knowledges, experiences, and self-determination. Deliberating reconciliation can be experienced as a waste of time or an imposition demanding self-legitimation, subtly sliding towards further assimilation. What can matter most, then, is how we ravel and unravel what we understand, individually and collectively, to be the truths and untruths associated with our understandings of Canada's colonial past and present.

I am training a group of staff and I say to them, "If you have always wanted to know how to refer to Aboriginal people, ask. This is your chance." I see some of them thinking, "He's going to put me on a list of racists if I ask that question." But, it's the opposite. I want them to be engaged in this topic. I say, "You've got someone in front of you now who you can ask the uncomfortable question. Why can't I use the word Indian anymore? Good question. Why do I hear people self-refer as Indian but I was told not to do that?"

As Dominic reflects, our baseline intention in our work may, at times, simply be to recognize how our (lack of) knowledge and our prejudices, viewed as "the initial directedness of our whole ability to experience," form the "biases of our openness" to reconciliation.[32] Although deliberation can open up to improved understanding, it can also lead to confusion, even aversion.

I am at a forum on reconciliation and feel appalled and helpless. I am in a panic. The leader hosting the forum is challenged by students and Elders. He's being asked, "Why aren't we ...? And why aren't we ...? And why aren't we ...?" He keeps a smile on his face and says, "I have less power than people think." It's "Okay. Speak. Everybody speak. Whether it's true or not. But we're not going to do anything meaningful with it right now. We're not going to say 'Let's stop for a minute. Let's consider that. Let's talk about these things.'" We're not going to do that. I can't imagine a less safe space for anybody.

Melinda speaks of entering an overwhelming policy space, a space ostensibly meant to instantiate her institution's social licence on issues related to reconciliation. Multiple people speak, yet she gets the impression that no one is heard. As Leah Levac and Sarah Marie Wiebe explain in the Introduction of this book, the "securing" of social licence to address policy matters related to reconciliation cannot be achieved simply by appearing to be consultative. In such deliberative spaces involving vast differences in understanding and perspective, it might be that we must first "say how [we] feel before the discussion turns to specific plans or programs."[33] We might find that, in the examination of the truths and untruths that underlie deliberations on reconciliation, "pushing for solutions too soon – before affected parties have been able to listen to one another – can end up taking far more time"[34] than if we create space for us "to speak the unspeakable – no matter how unpleasant or how painful it might be for the others to hear."[35]

And yet, at the same time, if, as deliberative policy practitioners within our institutions, we constantly point out each other's lack of knowledge or prejudice, we can find ourselves perceived as "paid agitators," in Dominic's words, and not receive the "call backs" that, for Daniela, form long-term relations and influence. In creating space for deliberation, we might find ourselves, as Daniela describes, taking a subtler, relational approach.

> In the discussion around who is going to be nominated for an award, someone states, "I don't know if that person fits." I'm waiting for them to talk about what "fit" means, because I've alerted them to that language and what it produces. I'm thinking "OK. Pretty soon I will be stepping in." But the external member of the committee is appalled. She says, "I can't believe you're talking about personalities. She looks at me and darts off. I want to say to her, "Too bad you have to leave. We are going to get to that point." But I am waiting to see if the leader will step in, to see what is going to unfold.

Daniela describes how she handles potential underlying prejudice in a selection committee. In not speaking immediately, Daniela risks seeming to be in agreement. In speaking too quickly, she risks appearing domineering. Daniela senses success if, as the process unfolds, her colleagues speak to the issues at stake, in their own ways, in their own time. Such interactions might be "unpredictable and uncontrollable moments" that "may yield insights and clarity but are often brought on by pain, agony and feelings of frustration and desperation."[36] Gordon, a student leader, speaks to such a moment.

> In my first term on a council for Aboriginal issues, I ask to be put on the agenda. I give the presentation and the entire room is not on board. I can feel it in the atmosphere. I get emotional because I am presenting about racism. There are individuals who agree. They acknowledge gaps, that we aren't dealing with our mandate. I feel I bring in a change of attitude. I feel a shift to safety. I have achieved something. Convincing non-Indigenous people that Indigenous students and faculty and staff matter is emotional.

When you don't have to focus solely on your humanity, it changes the conversation.

At this meeting, Gordon experiences moving from hesitation and resistance to safety and achievement. He desires to have his thinking heard and acknowledged, his criticisms taken seriously. It is as if he senses being "absolutely present" in "the meaning and significance"[37] of reconciliation. In unravelling assumed truths held by committee members, he reframes the issues at stake. He opens the space of deliberation to uncertainty.

(Un)Framing (Un)Certainties

Dialogical spaces where shared truths emerge as "insight" and "clarity" are not to be taken for granted. The participants in this study describe such spaces of "truth telling" as being intentionally structured into training or teaching, or as unfolding naturally in policy forums or through collective projects. However, such spaces also might have roots in the creation of informal interactions without specific "outcomes."

> We invite bookstore staff to an event because they're dealing with our students with third party billing, but they don't know anything about our students. We invite international staff, registrars. They're sometimes quick to say, "You're Aboriginal? Go over there. We can't help you." It's panic. We want to make staff comfortable to ask questions, to come to our space, to feel comfortable with and understand our students. We want to create an environment where we're all Treaty people. We're all in this relationship together.

To help her non-Aboriginal colleagues question assumptions and develop connections with Aboriginal students, staff, and faculty, Leslie makes the centre she works in a space of shared intention.[38] Such dialogue across difference in relation to Indigenization in post-secondary education must include listening carefully to the "professionals who work closely with Native students and are truly concerned about their welfare," as it is "campus-wide efforts and commitments," extending into the Indigenous communities the institution serves, that ultimately will bring about positive change. For all participants in this study, this invitational, listening-oriented focus in relation to deliberating reconciliation is central to their experience, from informal phone calls to discussions with students after class to social interactions or "participatory rituals" before, between, and after meetings with colleagues.[39] At times, however, we might have to step away from our institutions to experience and learn from Aboriginal ceremonies and the wisdom of Elders.

> I ask a university leader to come with me to an Aboriginal traditional ceremony. She has to break out her calendar, give meetings to somebody else, or change the meetings to come into this space. And she does it. I invite her on a road trip. She sees Indigenous professors who are engaged in that process. For these professors to invite her is a profound moment of trusting her. The Elders invite her into that space and, in that space, she converses with them, with me, and others.

In Diane's invitation to a senior university leader to travel together and participate in a traditional Aboriginal ceremony, she has clear intent. The invitation is an offering, an opening to a sacred space. We might say that, as reconciliation, invitation circulates through relationships, grounding knowledge through learning from each other, in the earning and sharing of trust. In the process, we might say that we disturb our unquestioned certainties and/or overcome some of our underlying uncertainties. Such an invitation can also require compromise. Diane recalls being approached at a conference where issues of representation arose.

> After the panel, two Indigenous women ask me how I feel about a Caucasian woman who had spoken in a demanding way that there had to be change. I am comfortable with what she did, because I've known her for a while and believe she is an ally. Maybe the Indigenous women's interpretation is coming out of the feeling that, "Here we go again. White people speaking for us." I interpret anger but look at it from a relational base around partnerships, collaborations, teamwork, and Elder teachings. Interestingly, the Indigenous women also thank me. At a meeting before the panel, somebody stated there should be Indigenous people on the board. There is an Indigenous woman who is part of the association. The allies felt it would be disrespectful to have just one Indigenous person on the board. The board asked the panel members, "What do you think?" I thought, "If our Elder was here, he would say, 'We take the one spot, even if they think it's disrespectful.'" So I replied, "She should take the spot, because one is better than nothing." Those ladies thank me because they feel the same way.

In this recollection, Diane responds to her peers' frustration with a Caucasian woman's interjections. Diane looks into and through interpretations, considering how her actions might be guided by the wisdom of her Elders. She says simply, "it is complex work," to describe how, in one moment, she defends a white woman who speaks self-assuredly as an ally, and then defends the assignment of what she describes as a "tokenistic" board position. The demonstration of alliance, for Diane, demands recognition, a reasoned response within what Levac and Wiebe describe in the Introduction as the "power-infused contexts" of "sticky, tricky, multilayered policy problems" related to such critical matters as reconciliation. As Diane describes, such acts of multicultural recognition ultimately might require a "political and ethical stance" of "refusal" that "comes with the requirement of having one's *political* sovereignty acknowledged and upheld."[40]

> Years ago, when I was an international student during the time of the Meech Lake Accord, there was an Aboriginal activist giving a talk. Several of us went to her and said, "What could we, as newcomers, do?" I remember her looking at me and saying, "You have negotiated with an illegal government for your place here. You don't have a right in this conversation." I was frozen in the moment. I had to think about that.

This recollection has sat with Sarina for years, and she still wonders how she can be engaged in reconciliation on her campus. In my interviews, non-Aboriginal participants shared similar hesitation to engage in reconciliation for fear of doing something inappropriate. And yet, participants also spoke of having a responsibility to act and that, in acting, they wanted to be certain their speech and actions did not perpetuate oppressive relations. Daniela describes how being "adopted" into communities of her Aboriginal colleagues is a "gift of trust." When she feels she has been "more outspoken" at meetings, she "checks back" with her colleagues to be sure she has not overreached. She reflects:

> I had a conversation once with an Indigenous faculty member when I was struggling with self-questioning, "I'm a white woman. Who am I to be in this role?" The faculty member said, "But you're at the table. I'm not at the table. I'm excluded. You're not, so you have an important role." That stays with me. I have a responsibility. If I want to see change then I have to do whatever I can.

In the inward and outward movements of retreat and advance, we can find ourselves, like Daniela, making "deep epistemological shifts, informed by notions of relationality, respect and responsibility," such that we aim to "avoid reproducing contemporary versions of coloniality, despite what may be very good intentions."[41] As Melinda describes in her experiences in both a closed forum of institutional leaders and an

open forum of faculty, staff, and students, the deliberation of reconciliation, as a mini-public, can be unsettling for us, serving as the kind of
democratic experience that Rachel Magnusson describes in chapter 5.
Sophie reflects how being open to such unsettled uncertainty can lead
to us to new questions and critically aware intentions.

> We identify Canada as a colonial project with a genocidal past whose
> effects continue in the present, and then say, "What are we supposed to
> do about it?" We talk about what it means to be an ally, but it's up to all
> of us to approach Indigenous people and say, "What does a decolonized
> Canada look like, feel like, act like for you?" Sometimes we feel like we
> can't speak, nor should we speak, about what reconciliation is. In the uni-
> versity, where everybody's a know-it-all, nobody wants to say, "What a
> mess. We don't know what to do."

Deliberating (in) Kin(dness)

When we commit together, as Sophie describes, to overcome colonial
patterns, we must be prepared for diverse reactions. I have learned
through this research and personal experience that allowing for and
attending to these reactions is of critical importance. Deliberating
reconciliation, as many of us are aware, is "neither straightforward nor
easy" and, as such, "has to be carefully organized, facilitated – even
cultivated and nurtured."[42]

> Having experienced oppression, I know how that feels. How do we do
> our work without oppressing somebody else? We nurture that person. We
> nurture them to become a part of a bigger system of people who have
> good relationships. People who have relationships based on what we
> would consider natural law around kindness, caring, sharing, strength,
> and determination. These are the foundational laws that the Elders have
> passed onto us. How we work together comes from that space and place.

Diane speaks of creating relationships among students, staff, and
faculty based on natural laws passed on by her Elders. One of these
is kindness, a word that, "while 'out of place' in talk about higher
education," fits with an approach to deliberating reconciliation as transformative learning.[43] Kindness in our deliberations could be considered
both "interaction to which [we] bring an intention to critically explore
avenues of thinking and action,"[44] and "communicative" deliberation
that acts as "deference and conciliatory caring" in the face of our own
and others' "disagreement, anger, counterargument, and criticism."[45]

At moments when we make unexpected connections between issues that might not seem self-evident to colleagues, when we challenge established truths that our colleagues hold close, or when we feel ourselves shifting into uncomfortable spaces of uncertainty, it might be kindness that enables us to "view one another in light of values that allow the abilities and traits of the other to appear for shared praxis."[46] This relationship involves "felt concern for what is individual and particular about the other person," whereby we might "actively care about the development of the other's characteristics," even if those characteristics "seem foreign" to us.[47] Will Hamrick provides a depiction that captures the significance of such a conception of kindness in deliberating reconciliation.

> The totalizer, the colonizer, and the officious do-gooder all provide clear and familiar examples of an inappropriate presence of self, and the uninvolved, coldhearted egoist illustrates the inappropriate absence of self. In contrast, the truly kind person offers us a model of intervening into the lives of others while at the same time refusing to transfer her own mental baggage. Kindness is a way of knowing the other as other, because it requires both closeness and distance, proximity and tactful differentiation, compassionate intervention and appropriate withdrawal.[48]

Kindness, as portrayed by Hamrick, is a learned disposition, but he warns that kindness can be misconstrued with niceness, or obligation, subservience, or manipulation, and that its veneer can mask superficiality or oppressive, self-serving intentions. If, however, kindness is viewed as a dialectic "instantiated" through ethical decision making over time, it might be seen as an embodied practice that grounds "beliefs about [our] own capabilities for kind interventions in the lives of others" through our socialization within our institutions and broader sociocultural environments.[49] Kindness might be viewed as a commitment to developing our capacities to engage in the difficult, often strained interpersonal situations that can include, but extend far beyond, formal policy and strategy processes and forums related to reconciliation.

In reflecting on kindness, I have come to understand the necessity of acknowledging our own and our students' and colleagues' struggles to come to terms with responsibility in relation to reconciliation. We can learn from such struggles by allowing our students and colleagues to express themselves, even if their understandings, at times, have racist undertones, are enmeshed in privilege, or are intermixed with seemingly unrelated issues. We must also be capable, as Frank Fischer writes, to attend to "confrontation and dialogue across the divide of cultural differences" through being "knowledgeable and fluent in various modes of communication, from storytelling and listening to interpreting visual and body language."[50] In this sense, to be kind, as a practice of allowing and attending in our work, requires of us what Max van Manen terms "pedagogical tactfulness."

> Tact implies sensitivity, a sensitive and mindful or aesthetic perception. Tact is defined as a keen sense of what to do or say in order to maintain good relations with others or avoid offense. But the essence of tact does not inhere in the simple desire to get on well with others or establish good social relations ... We speak of tact as an instant knowing what to do, an improvisational skill in dealing with others ... [T]act does not necessarily connote a soft, meek or acquiescent sensitivity. One can be sensitive and strong. A tactful person must be strong, as tact may require frankness, directness, and candor when the situation calls for it.[51]

Kindness, as a form of deliberative tact, requires us to be attentive to language, such as when Sophie recognizes a student's referencing to her childhood in the north and gradual revelation of her confusion from feeling disliked by Aboriginal people. We might step in, as Cassandra does, when an Aboriginal student abruptly leaves the talking circle. We might, as Elsie does, help her student reflect on colonialism through her personal reckoning with the sexism she endures as a female athlete. At the same time, we can resist being swept up in the moment, such as when Daniela poses broader questions to nudge dialogue with a colleague who disparages hiring equity.

Kindness, in this manner, might be attributed to how we tactfully direct our own and our students' and colleagues' attention without breaking what Diane and Nadine describe as the "circle" where we "teach together ... as human beings in a relationship." This circle presents us with what Eva Mackey describes as the making of "treaty" together.

> Therefore, instead of seeing treaty as an object – a noun – I think one way to begin to decolonize is to learn to conceptualize and experience treaty-making as a verb. It is a historical and ongoing, exploratory and often uncertain process of building relationships for which non-Indigenous people must also take responsibility and in which they must engage. In other words, we need to think about how "we treaty," and how to behave responsibly if "we treaty together" or "make treaty" together. It is a relationship we build over time. Like all good relationships, there are rules of respect and autonomy, but there can be no pre-planned and decided trajectory because a treaty is relational and interactive. Relationships are

by their nature uncertain: they require seeing, listening and responding creatively to an "other" who is autonomous and also connected to us.[52]

When "we treaty together," using Mackey's words, we may, as the participants in this study describe, form bonds associated with kinship (mother, sister, grandmother), collegiality (teamwork, collaboration, trust), and friendship or solidarity ("holding each other up," support, care). Such bonds may form a strong foundation upon which we can enter into the more politicized deliberations of reconciliation on our campuses.

"Pushing (Re)Start"

Mary's reflection on teaching a seminar on residential schools evokes the personal and professional demands of nurturing and sustaining kindness in the deliberation of reconciliation.

> I am ready to break down and cry. Should I do that? I could. I just can't get over how much it is moving me to tears. I ask myself, "Why am I so emotional? Why, in the years that I've been here, I could just walk in like a turtle with a hard shell?" When I listen to that short clip, that's my pride. My Dad and what they went through. I went and saw a play recently and I cried quite a bit. It's okay because it's theatre. You go for that. But when I'm teaching a class ... Put on the video. Push "Start."

Mary presents a video of a residential school survivor that reminds her of her own father. It is a video she has shown before, and yet, this time, she feels she is shedding self-protection. The "short clip" acts as a catalyst. She knows that, once she pushes "start," there is no going back from desire, rejection, guilt, potentiality, and connection. Deliberation, in this sense, may be experienced as a weaving of new threads of truth and shared intention. In these threads, and in their interweaving, we may move between inviting and attending, between weaving and unravelling. At times, as Mary describes, we may experience both simultaneously.

In the interweavings of our deliberations, we might say that we enact our "willingness to reconcile (care-for-the-world)" in a manner that enables us to ethically take risks in the simultaneous "willingness to politicise (agonistic striving)" that "postpones the moment of positive-affirmative closure that reconciliation inevitably tends towards."[53] In resisting closure, we must, as Mary states, be prepared to "push 'Start.'" In offering our stories, knowledge, experience, questions, and ways of teaching, leading, and helping faculty, staff, and students in the service of reconciliation, we must push "(re)start" with every class, meeting, and advising session, term after term, year after year. Each time we push "start," we might come closer to what Marie Battiste describes as an "ethical, trans-systemic" approach that does not "infringe on another's space or standards, codes of conduct, or the community ethos in each community."[54] Each time we push "(re)start," we might (re)orient to what Willie Ermine describes as a "cooperative spirit between Indigenous peoples and Western institutions" that could "create new currents of thought that flow in different directions and overrun old ways of thinking."[55] In making of spaces for truth in the deliberation of reconciliation in post-secondary education, we must have such courage and trust, and seek strength and understanding with one another as colleagues and as friends, and in the spirit of kinship that binds us together in our ongoing making of treaty. In the closing words of Daniela's interview:

> How can we start disrupting spaces that are rigid and longstanding and not hospitable? Are there other ways to approach our educational system that's not Western-based? And then, you're no longer in power. That brings me back to my belief in courage and bravery. When you shift everything and the ground is uneven or there's some holes in it, trusting that, "I have to take this leap and if I fall through it, I'll manage."

Discussion Questions

1 How does reconciliation between settler and Aboriginal peoples relate to your work, relationships, and deliberations in your day-to-day interactions? How can such day-to-day acts of deliberation on reconciliation be applied in larger spaces of public engagement?
2 How do you face uncertainty, hardened disagreement, or another's confusion or suffering when you create and engage in spaces of deliberation on matters as complex as reconciliation?
3 (How) does a disposition of kindness relate to the creation of spaces of public engagement on deeply divisive matters? (How) do/can you practise kindness in your work as a deliberative practitioner?

NOTES

1 Association of Universities and Colleges of Canada, *Creating Opportunities in Education for Aboriginal Students* (Ottawa, 2013), online at https://www.univcan.ca/wp-content/uploads/2015/07/aboriginal-students-report-2013.pdf.

2 Truth and Reconciliation Commission of Canada (hereafter TRC), *Truth and Reconciliation Commission of Canada: Calls to Action* (Winnipeg, 2015), online at http://trc.ca/assets/pdf/Calls_to_Action_English2.pdf.
3 Universities Canada, *Principles on Indigenous Education* (Ottawa, 2015), online at https://www.univcan.ca/wp-content/uploads/2015/11/principles-on-indigenous-education-universities-canada-june-2015.pdf.
4 Moira MacDonald, "Indigenizing the Academy: What Some Universities Are Doing to Weave Indigenous Peoples, Cultures and Knowledge into the Fabric of the Campuses," *University Affairs*, 6 April 2016, 4, online at http://www.universityaffairs.ca/features/feature-article/Indigenizing-the-academy/.
5 Adam Gaudry and Danielle Lorenz, "Indigenization as Inclusion, Reconciliation and Decolonization: Navigating the Different Visions for Indigenizing the Academy," *AlterNative* 14, no. 3 (2018): 218–27.
6 Marie Battiste, *Decolonizing Education: Nourishing the Learning Spirit* (Saskatoon: Purich, 2013); Eve Tuck and Wayne Wang, "Decolonization Is Not a Metaphor," *Decolonization, Indigeneity, Education & Society* 1, no. 1 (2012): 1–40; Jason Warick, "It's not just add Indigenous and stir: U of S' Indigenization approach raises questions," *CBC News*, 23 September 2017, online at http://www.cbc.ca/news/canada/saskatoon/indigenous-education-university-saskatchewan-1.4299551.
7 TRC, *Honouring the Truth, Reconciling the Future: Summary of the Final Report of the Truth and Reconciliation Commission of Canada* (Winnipeg, 2015), 6, online at https://web-trc.ca/.
   For the purposes of this chapter, I use the terms Aboriginal and Indigenous in accordance with the Association of Canadian Deans of Education, "Accord on Indigenous Education," wherein Aboriginal is inclusive of Aboriginal, First Nations, Métis, and Inuit peoples, and Indigenous is inclusive of the term Aboriginal as well as "the more global context of First Peoples' epistemologies, ways of knowing, knowledge systems, and lived experience." For more detail, see Association of Canadian Deans of Education, "Accord on Indigenous Education," (2010), 1, online at https://www.trentu.ca/education/sites/trentu.ca.education/files/ACDE%20Accord%20on%20Indigenous%20Education.pdf. I acknowledge that, in taking this approach, the term Aboriginal has colonial roots in the Canadian Constitution. I also acknowledge, however, from the research undertaken in this study, that collapsing all Indigenous peoples together can be problematic. In particular, within our institutions, there are Indigenous faculty, staff, and students who are not Aboriginal, and thus also experience deliberating reconciliation within the Canadian context from their unique positions as settlers themselves.
8 TRC, *Honouring the Truth*, 6.

9 Deborah Stone, *Policy Paradox: The Art of Decision Making* (New York: W.W. Norton, 2002), 383.

10 Ryan Knowles and Christopher Clark, "How Common Is the Common Good? Moving beyond Idealistic Notions of Deliberative Democracy in Education," *Teaching and Teacher Education* 71 (April 2018): 12–23.

11 Stone, *Policy Paradox*, 378.

12 Leslie Pal, *Beyond Policy Analysis: Public Issue Management in Turbulent Times*, (Toronto: Nelson Education, 2014).

13 See Jacqueline Ottman, "Indigenizing the Academy: Confronting 'Contentious' Ground," *Morning Watch: Education and Social Analysis* 40, nos. 3–4 (2013): 8–24, online at http://www.mun.ca/educ/faculty/mwatch/vol40/winter2013/indigenizingAcademy.pdf. Ottman presents the breadth of what Indigenization entails in post-secondary education, citing curriculum content, teaching practices, research methodologies and methods, research funding, community engagement, practices of faculty and staff hiring, recognition and professional development, student recruitment, advising, and policies and procedures associated with reasonable accommodation, discrimination and harassment, and student conduct. For further reading, see Heather J. Shotton, Shelley C. Lowe, and Stephanie J. Waterman, eds., *Beyond the Asterisk: Understanding Native Students in Higher Education* (Sterling, VA: Stylus, 2013); and Dean A. Mihesua and Angela C. Wilson, eds., *Indigenizing the Academy: Transforming Scholarship and Empowering Communities* (Lincoln: University of Nebraska Press, 2004).

14 Dale Turner, *This Is Not a Peace Pipe: Towards a Critical Indigenous Philosophy* (Toronto: University of Toronto Press, 2006), 113.

15 Ibid.

16 Bill Waiser, *Saskatchewan: A New History* (Calgary: Fifth House, 2005).

17 Alexander Morris, *The Treaties of Canada with the Indians* (1880; repr., Toronto: Prospero, 2000).

18 Yuqian Lu and Feng Hou, "International Students Who Become Permanent Residents in Canada," *Insights on Canadian Society*, cat. no. 75-006-X (Ottawa: Statistics Canada, 2015), online at http://www.statcan.gc.ca/pub/75-006-x/2015001/article/14299-eng.pdf.

19 D'Arcy Vermette, "Inclusion Is Killing Us," *Teaching Perspective* 17 (Fall 2012): 18–20, online at https://moodle.stu.ca/pluginfile.php?file=/6082/mod_page/content/4/Issue%2019%20-%20Fall%202013.pdf; Sarah Ahmed, *On Being Included: Racism and Diversity in Institutional Life* (Durham, NC: Duke University Press, 2012); Simon Marginson and Erlenwati Sawir, *Ideas for Intercultural Education* (New York: Palgrave Macmillan, 2011).

20 Max van Manen, *Researching Lived Experience: Human Science for an Action Sensitive Pedagogy* (London: Althouse Press, 1997).

21 Cecily Scutt and Julia Hobson, "The Stories We Need: Anthropology, Philosophy, Narrative and Post-secondary Education Research," *Higher Education Research and Development*, 31, no. 1 (2013): 17–29.
22 John Forester, *The Deliberative Practitioner: Encouraging Participatory Planning Processes*, (Cambridge, MA: MIT Press, 1999).
23 Max van Manen, *Phenomenology of Practice: Meaning-Giving Methods in Phenomenological Research and Writing* (Walnut Creek, CA: Left Coast Press, 2014), 355.
24 Ibid., 70.
25 Mark Vagle, *Crafting Phenomenological Research* (Walnut Creek, CA: Left Coast Press, 2014).
26 Shawn Wilson, *Research Is Ceremony: Indigenous Research Methods* (Winnipeg: Fernwood, 2008).
27 Ibid., 94.
28 Frank Fischer, *Democracy and Expertise: Discursive Politics and Deliberative Practices* (New York, Oxford University Press, 2009), 287.
29 Eva Mackey, *Unsettled Expectations: Uncertainty, Land and Settler Decolonization* (Winnipeg: Fernwood, 2016), 183.
30 Paulette Regan, *Unsettling the Settler Within: Indian Residential Schools, Truth Telling, and Reconciliation in Canada* (Vancouver: UBC Press, 2010), 66.
31 Rauna Kuokkanen, *Reshaping the University: Responsibility, Indigenous Epistemes, and the Logic of the Gift* (Vancouver: UBC Press, 2007), 115.
32 Hans-Georg Gadamer, *Philosophical Hermeneutics*, trans. and ed. David Linge (Los Angeles: University of California Press, 1977), 9.
33 Fischer, *Democracy and Expertise*, 291.
34 Forester, *Deliberative Practitioner*, 132.
35 Fischer, *Democracy and Expertise*, 291.
36 Van Manen, *Phenomenology of Practice*, 52.
37 Ibid.
38 Joshua Mihesuah, "Graduating Students by Confronting the Academic Environment," in *Indigenizing the Academy: Transforming Scholarship and Empowering Communities*, ed. Devon Mihesua and Angela Wilson (Lincoln: University of Nebraska Press, 2004), 199.
39 Forester terms "participatory rituals" as interactions "that enable participants to develop more familiar relationships or to learn about one another before solving the problem they face"; Forester, *Deliberative Practitioner*, 131.
40 Audra Simpson, *Mohawk Interruptus: Political Life across the Borders of Settler States* (Durham, NC: Duke University Press, 2014), 11.
41 Mackey, *Unsettled Expectations*, 176.
42 Fischer, *Democracy and Expertise*, 75.
43 Sue Clegg and Stephen Rowland, "Kindness in Pedagogical Practice and Academic Life," *British Journal of Sociology of Education* 31, no. 6 (2010):

722. See also Fischer, *Democracy and Expertise*, and Forester, *Deliberative Practitioner* for an account of democratic deliberation as transformative learning.

44 Lisa Bedinger, "Let's Talk: Dialogue and Deliberation in Higher Education," in *Resolving Community Conflicts and Problems: Public Deliberation and Sustained Dialogue*, ed. Roger Lohmann and Jon Van Til (New York: Columbia University Press, 2011), 60.

45 Iris Marion Young, "Communication and the Other: Beyond Deliberative Democracy," in *Democracy and Difference: Contesting the Boundaries of the Political*, ed. Seyla Benhabib (Princeton, NJ: Princeton University Press, 1996), 129–30.

46 Axel Honneth, *The Struggle for Recognition: The Moral Grammar of Social Conflicts* (Cambridge, MA: MIT Press, 1995), 129–30.

47 Ibid.

48 William Hamrick, *Kindness and the Good Society: Connections of the Heart* (Albany: State University of New York Press, 2002), 68–9.

49 Ibid., 197.

50 Fischer, *Democracy and Expertise*, 291.

51 Van Manen, *Pedagogical Tactfulness*, 104.

52 Mackey, *Unsettled Expectations*, 141.

53 Andrew Schaap, *Political Reconciliation* (New York: Routledge, 2005), 74.

54 Battiste, *Decolonizing Education*, 105.

55 Willie Ermine, "The Ethical Space of Engagement," *Indigenous Law Journal* 6, no. 1 (1989): 203.

KEY RESOURCES

Kuokkanen, Rauna. *Reshaping the University: Responsibility, Indigenous Epistemes, and the Logic of the Gift*. Vancouver: UBC Press, 2007.

Regan, Paulette. *Unsettling the Settler Within: Indian Residential Schools, Truth Telling, and Reconciliation in Canada*. Vancouver: UBC Press, 2010.

Turner, Dale. *This Is Not a Peace Pipe: Towards a Critical Indigenous Philosophy*. Toronto: University of Toronto Press, 2006.

16 Global Goals with Local Relevance? "Glocal" Approaches, Tensions, and Lessons on Measuring Aid Effectiveness

ASTRID V. PÉREZ PIÑÁN

Introduction

There is a paradox in the global aid effectiveness agenda with regard to gender equality and citizen engagement. Instead of promoting the fulfilment of development goals, the push towards measuring effectiveness itself undermines the ability of women's organizations to carry out their work effectively. To illustrate this paradox, I begin this chapter by offering a brief overview of the global landscape in development cooperation, which has been shaped by the attempts of international civil society organizations (CSOs) to claim democratic spaces within which to exercise their "response-ability" towards the imperial problem of inequality, exploitation, and poverty of the global South.[1] I then seek to trace how global commitments guiding aid effectiveness efforts are translated into country-specific actions. Drawing on feminist political economy, with a critical focus on gender and development, I provide a case study based on Nicaragua to discuss how the new global framework on aid effectiveness is enacted, experienced, resisted, and (re)interpreted by local civil society feminist organizations in support of womxn's[2] human rights. The use of the term "womxn" is intentional to avoid the suffix "-men" as a way to decentre patriarchal linguistic forms while simultaneously highlighting diversity among women, and people outside the binary. I pay particular attention to complexities that manifest in their struggles to comply with the requirements to measure the effectiveness of gender and human rights-based aid programs. The case looks back to three relatively successful international development aid projects and programs on womxn's rights from 2005 to 2014, and is geared towards interrogating and identifying good practices of measuring aid effectiveness – that is, practices that are gender responsive, use participatory approaches to engage people in the policy process, and focus on human development outcomes. Based on the lessons learned from this case, I conclude the chapter by offering some insights for those intending to develop gender-responsive indicators regarding social and economic development at the local level, and for those interested in advancing such work in line with more deliberative democratic practices.

Background

Since the start of the new millennium, the development cooperation landscape has been undergoing dramatic changes. The official story is that both donor and aid beneficiary countries determined that development aid was not achieving its goal of poverty reduction. They recognized that aid management requirements varying from donor to donor placed enormous bureaucratic burdens on beneficiaries. Further, donor governments continued to pursue "tied aid" and "aid conditionality" policies that created long-term heavy burdens for aid beneficiary countries,[3] preventing them from executing their own development plans.

In 2005, under the auspices of the Organisation for Economic Development and Co-operation (OECD), the Paris Declaration on Aid Effectiveness was signed with the aim of instituting a new, partnership approach to a more coherent way of delivering and managing aid.[4] Guided by five principles – ownership, alignment, harmonization, managing for results, and mutual accountability – the Paris Declaration was, at least rhetorically, intended to support efforts towards the achievement of the United Nations Millennium Development Goals (MDGs), now succeeded by the Sustainable Development Goals. A key milestone of the "new aid architecture,"[5] the Paris Declaration was meant to respond to the long-term issues mentioned above, which impinged on the ability of aid beneficiary countries from making progress towards the overall goal of poverty eradication.

But in direct contradiction to the partnership approach said to underpin the Paris Declaration, the agreement was created using a closed, top-down process that caused outrage among international CSOs, which were invited to the signing ceremony without any prior opportunity to provide input into what would have been expected to be a democratic, participatory process.[6] CSOs had formerly expressed scepticism over the OECD's Development Assistance Committee's legitimacy and capacity to lead the aid effectiveness process, and contended that the organization represented a "donors club" of mainly industrialized countries that follow an increasingly neoliberal approach to promoting economic development.[7] With only thirty-four members, the OECD is not considered representative of developing countries' interests.[8]

Citizen Engagement: Democratic Participation Demanded by Civil Society

The top-down approach to, and content of, the Paris Declaration were both denounced by more than a thousand international CSOs globally for being undemocratic, too technical, and gender blind, and for imposing most of the responsibilities on aid recipient countries.[9] The declaration's focus on the efficiency of aid management neglected matters of aid impact and the achievement of goals such as poverty reduction, gender equality, and the elimination of social discrimination and disparities.[10] International CSOs subsequently self-organized into coalitions to continue demanding that their participation and demands be heard in formal global forums. These events provided important precedents for the creation of the Global Partnership for Effective Development, intended to support the realization of the MDGs (and now the Sustainable Development Goals). The creation of the Global Partnership is largely the result of the process of participation started by international CSOs in response to the exclusionary Paris Declaration process. The work of the Global Partnership and its predecessors represents a change of paradigm from a narrow emphasis on aid effectiveness to a more comprehensive process of development effectiveness.[11]

From Global Agreement to Local Realities

Despite the now-recognized shortcomings – both procedural and substantive – of the Paris Declaration, its framework remains a guiding document for national governments and other donors. Given the declaration's shortcomings, how can countries go about implementing the aid effectiveness agenda in their respective localities? How do donor governments work through their local partners to ensure the aid is effective in issue areas neglected by the Paris Declaration – such as gender equality – that are complex and difficult to measure? How do local actors go about facilitating democratic engagement with aid beneficiaries in measuring this effectiveness? I turn to the Nicaraguan case to explore these questions.

Introduction to the Nicaraguan Case Study

Among aid recipient countries, Nicaragua has followed a dual track in its development policy, at least rhetorically. As a beneficiary of aid, Nicaragua is part of the OECD – an organization that follows a neoliberal economic approach to development – while simultaneously being a member of the (anti-neoliberal) Alianza Bolivariana para los Pueblos de Nuestra América (ALBA, or Bolivarian Alliance for the Peoples of Our America). ALBA is a regional platform of social, political, and economic integration comprising eight Latin American and Caribbean countries.[12] Its main priority has been to break away from the capitalist logic of competition, profit, and gain. ALBA is described as a popular construction, with people's participation having an important role in the task of regional integration in Latin America. Its main values are complementary action, cooperation, solidarity, and respect for the sovereignty of nations.[13]

In Nicaragua, the Consejos de Poder Ciudadano (CPCs, or Citizen Power Councils) are the main government mechanisms to promote citizen participation and the implementation of important pro-poor programs. But, while proclaiming to be anti-neoliberal, people centred, and committed to fostering a participatory democracy, President Daniel Ortega's government has had uneasy and mainly antagonistic relations with some key areas of civil society, including feminist and womxn's rights groups. As such, it is unclear whether or how local womxn's organizations can work with the government to benefit from aid resources (whether from the OECD or ALBA) for gender equality projects or programs. If, as gender and development theory suggests,[14] democratic participatory approaches to development involving womxn are so important to the co-production of gender-responsive policies, how legitimate or reliable are gender measurements in Nicaragua, considering this antagonistic relationship?

Although the new aid agenda has an increased focus on channelling aid money through governments, it is also common for donor countries to work through their own CSOs in partnership with CSOs in the aid recipient country. This is the case in the projects presented here, which were selected due to their success and thus their potential to offer practical examples of gender-responsive approaches to measuring aid effectiveness.

Project One: Indigenous and Womxn's Rights on Nicaragua's Atlantic Coast, March 2012–February 2014

The first project I wish to cover is Gender Equality and Violence Against Women, led by Horizons of Friendship, a non-governmental organization based in Canada. Funded by the Canadian government, Horizons of Friendship works through a partnership with the Association of Indigenous Women of the Atlantic (AMICA), based in Puerto Cabezas, Nicaragua. The project aimed at building capacity in local communities among both men and womxn to prevent interfamily, sexual, and gender-based violence.

Project Two: Civil and Economic Rights in Nicaragua, April 2005–March 2008

The second project was funded by the UK government and managed by the London-based Central America Women's Network (CAWN), in collaboration with Maria Elena Cuadra (MEC), its partner organization in Nicaragua. The project promoted economic literacy and womxn's labour rights.

Project Three: From Rhetoric to Reality: Promoting Womxn's Participation and Gender Budgeting, August 2008–August 2011

The third project was an MDG Achievement Fund program involving nine UN agencies and ten Nicaraguan government institutions operating in fifteen municipalities. As is explicit in the title, the joint program aimed to promote womxn's participation in decision making (at various levels) and gender budgeting.

Theory to Inform Practice: Feminist Political Economy

The gendered impact of economic development policies has been known for decades in development practice.[15] Drawing on critical gender and development scholarship, international relations, feminist economics, and more, a feminist political economy framework[16] provides insights into the gendered effects of the "new" aid architecture and, more important for this essay, into participatory democratic engagement approaches that can create gender-responsive policy engagement processes. Feminist political economy helps to expose and clarify how gender determines or influences social and political relationships and structures of power, as well as the uneven economic effects that flow from these relationships and structures. Feminist political economy focuses on the well-being of all people, not just on the market economy, and employs gender as a defining category of analysis.[17] Included in this approach is an intersectional lens that captures the various dimensions of people's identities, such as sexual orientation, ability/disability, ethnic background, religion, citizenship status, language, and more. When combined, these identities produce unique lived experiences that need to be revealed in order to overcome discriminations and advance human rights.[18]

Case Findings and Analysis

In search of answers to conceptual and practical questions about the implementation of the aid effectiveness agenda at the local level, I conducted an analysis based on document reviews and interviews with aid recipient organizations from the projects/programs described above. My goal was to identify exemplary practices of measuring effectiveness that could serve as guidance for those seeking to develop gender-responsive indicators and practices. Additionally, I asked participants about their own definitions of aid effectiveness in the context of their specific work and how they went about measuring it. Rather than direct answers to these questions, I found that difficult "contextual conditions" undermine transformative, long-term approaches to gender equality and weaken feminist organizations, and that, under these conditions, womxn's full deliberative democratic participation through the development process is unlikely.

Difficult "contextual conditions" undermine transformative, long-term approaches to gender equality and weaken feminist organizations: One of the ironies of the new approach to aid used by donor and aid recipient governments alike to fund CSOs is that it has resulted in the weakening of human rights–related gender equality work, such as violence against women, including jeopardizing the very existence of womxn's and feminist organizations.[19] At the heart of this irony lie two underestimated aspects of Nicaragua's unique sociopolitical landscape: first, the political context framing the divide between government and civil society/feminist organizations and the politicization of gender equality by religious groups; and, second, the way in which funding for CSOs, including womxn's organizations, is managed. In feminist political economy terms, these are "influencing factors" that press upon, shape, and change gender relations in a given society.[20]

The politization of gender equality by religious groups: Back in the 1980s, during the structural adjustment era, some aid donors intentionally set out to support the creation of an independent civil society in Nicaragua. According to Sarah Hunt,[21] donors pressured the government to carry out consultations with civil society in order to comply with World Bank and International Monetary Fund criteria for a satisfactory poverty reduction strategy process. But donors unduly influenced the selection of participants to favour selected organizations. Besides fomenting a divisive environment and alienating key areas of society – government representatives and CSOs – from each other, this selective approach to "creating an independent civil society" highly influenced the climate of distrust on the part of the Nicaraguan government towards CSOs that are still seen as representing foreign (neoliberal) agendas.

Another key event that affected the government's relations with civil society – feminist organizations, in particular – took place in the late 1990s, when feminist organizations publicly supported the president's stepdaughter, who accused him of rape. This aggravated existing animosities between the president and womxn's groups that had felt betrayed by the revolution's disappointing record on bringing about womxn's emancipation.

The power of religious institutions constitutes a further factor in shaping government policies on womxn. This influence is visible in recent legal setbacks on reproductive rights and violence against womxn (where foreign donor funding has become vital). Although abortion had been illegal in Nicaragua for many years, therapeutic abortion was normally allowed in cases where the mother's life was at risk. But after President Ortega's strategic move to side with pro-life Christians to obtain much-needed votes to win the 2006 elections, his government implemented a total ban on abortion. Since then, foreign funding for sexual health and reproductive rights in Nicaragua has been controversial, and organizations working on such rights have faced intense hostility from the state and are at risk.[22]

The exercise of power of religious institutions over state matters related to womxn's human rights extends to legal reforms with respect to violence against womxn. Notoriously, a Catholic bishop labelled a new law that protected womxn in cases of domestic violence as "Law 666," alluding to the "anti-Christ," claiming it would destroy families and undermine Christian values. The law, largely the product of the long-term work of womxn's organizations, was reformed to satisfy the Church's demands. Since the government did not feel compelled to look at these issues from a rights and entitlements perspective, such religious considerations influenced the likelihood of accounting for (and funding) CSOs that seek to continue working on violence against womxn and also on sexual health and reproductive rights (including through input in the national development plans). This case illustrates what Patricia Muñoz Cabrera[23] calls "entangled ideologies," referring to the interactions among patriarchy, masculinity, religious fundamentalism, and the perpetuation of violence against womxn.

The funding and aid management framework for CSOs does not promote sustainable, effective, people-centred development: The new competitive bidding processes donors use to allocate funds to local organizations mean that only those working on the issues or geographical areas considered priorities for funders are eligible to apply. Prior to the Paris Declaration, organizations used a bottom-up approach to propose projects and programs based on the needs of the communities they served. Since the Paris Declaration, this no longer has been the case. Largely influenced by the financial crisis of 2008, many donor countries, including Canada, have made significant cutbacks in their aid budgets, which now go to carefully selected "priority countries." A new system based on "calls for proposals" has been enacted, whereby budgets are distributed on the basis of thematic areas established by donor countries. The interviews carried out by both Horizons of Friendship and CAWN revealed that it is the competitive bidding framework that is hurting womxn's organizations the most.[24] The short-term timeframes afforded by the calls for proposals, both in terms of when these calls are announced and the length of time for which funding is provided, pose serious difficulties for carrying out meaningful gender planning with communities. For AMICA, constantly applying for funding became a new reality as it was, at the time of the interview, on a "year-to-year" project cycle with Horizons of Friendship. The organization spent a disproportionate amount of time on administrative tasks, which robbed it of its focus on actual development work. Further, the changing nature of each individual call meant that project or program sustainability was not guaranteed. For its part, CAWN found itself applying for hard-to-get lottery funds in order to survive and continue its support for its Nicaraguan partners. Funding from the European Union was practically unmanageable for such a small organization considering the large amounts of money involved and the lengthy and onerous application process.

Two relevant points emerge from this area of difficulty. One relates to the expectations of funders regarding the use of specific aid management techniques and reporting. The other point relates to the way in which aid money is being used to further[25] entrench mainstream neoliberal activities that produce and reproduce current gender inequalities. On the first point, the new aid landscape requires organizations to use "results-based management" frameworks in their operations. According to the Canadian Department of Foreign Affairs, Trade and Development (Global Affairs Canada), results-based management is defined as "a life-cycle approach to management that integrates strategy, people, resources, processes, and measurements to improve decision-making, transparency, and accountability. The approach focuses on achieving outcomes, implementing performance measurement, learning and adapting, as well as reporting performance."[26]

Global Affairs Canada and other donors use three main results-based management working tools: the logic model, the performance measurement framework, and the risk register. The logic model is meant to show the *causal relationships* among inputs, activities, outputs, and the outcomes of a given policy or program. All three tools are intended to be used following participatory processes. The logic model comprises six levels: inputs, activities, outputs, immediate outcomes, intermediate outcomes, and ultimate outcomes. According to the model, a result is defined as "a describable or measurable *change* that is derived from a cause and effect relationship."[27] This linear cause-and-effect approach can help establish links between certain results as direct consequence of specific planned actions, but it also assumes that change occurs in a linear fashion. This assumption, however, leaves out the role of context or the possibility that change can take place in non-linear manners. This way of measuring change also postulates that change is necessarily positive, leaving behind the possibility that maintaining past gains (that is, no change) can be a sign of the success of an intervention.[28] For instance, if respect for the right to access therapeutic abortion had been maintained in Nicaragua, it could be considered a positive result in the midst of such a challenging political environment with respect to sexual health and reproductive rights. As an organizational approach to aid management, results-based management has been criticized for being inadequate for monitoring and measuring complex interventions and issues because of its tendency towards simplification and quantification.[29] Following Brooke Ackerly, it should be pointed out here that much of the work that addresses gender injustices (such as violence against womxn) is difficult to measure or to fit into results-based management tools because of the nature of these injustices: "They are patterned, but often happen as the aggregate result of individual interactions, each of which may seem insignificant; they are forms of injustice that are linked to others such as poverty and environment; and they often take place 'back-stage' out of public view."[30]

Further, the various types of gender injustices, and the interactions between them, can be very context specific and in continual change. In addition, monitoring frameworks such as results-based management are reported to be "inappropriate for multi-layered, complex organisations, transnational and regional networks, coalitions, membership-based organisations, and re-granting organisations such as women's funds."[31] When working in these types of collectivities and reporting back to funders, one of the organizations has to collate and summarize information coming from multiple levels and actors and make it fit into the established framework to make it appear as part of a single change or intervention. For the organization receiving the funding, this also means that it needs to spell out its own contribution to the process "using tools that are simply not designed to handle this level of complexity."[32] A further challenge for these types of collective work arrangements is tied to the use of participatory processes for planning, monitoring, and evaluation embedded in results-based management. Even though participative processes are highly valued and desirable in development work, how such multiple processes conducted by each individual member organization of a collective are captured and condensed in final reporting to the funding agency is a highly complex and challenging task.[33]

CAWN offered a further angle on results-based management, referring to organizations that sought a politically transformative agenda through advocacy. Under the new approach to aid, CAWN found it impossible to align advocacy work with its effectiveness, as one cannot say whether advocacy is going to result in a change of legislation or an effect on policy. CAWN asserted that there was little or no support for advocacy on the part of the UK government, so here, the new aid effectiveness approach weakened the possibility of a transformative approach to gender equality work. The emphasis on quickly demonstrable, quantifiable, short-term, easy-to-measure initiatives in the context of the above-mentioned difficult framework conditions demonstrates at least three main shortcomings of the new aid effectiveness approach: (1) how unsuitable results-based management is for gender-based approaches to gender equality work; (2) that results-based management falls short in attempts to capture complex, non-linear, hard-to-measure, long-term issues of gender inequality that are often inextricably interlinked; and (3) that the emphasis on technocratic and management approaches that ignore country and local politics can have harmful consequences for womxn and for womxn's organizations and their ability to pursue a transformative gender equality agenda of action. Further, such emphasis signals that deliberative democratic approaches to policy development that are insensitive to these gendered contextual issues might well result in the very perpetuation of gender inequality, a human rights violation.

Womxn's participation in the (deliberative democratic) development process is unlikely: As the first principle of the Paris Declaration, "ownership" plays a central role in a country's national development plans. The expectation is that a participative process involving civil society will shape the national development plans—also known as poverty-reduction strategies. At the global level, gender equality advocates engaging with the aid effectiveness agenda have advocated for womxn's groups and voices to be part of the process in a true gender-sensitive approach. But the expectation that Nicaragua is going to launch itself into a series of consultations with its citizens to this end ignores the significance of the country's recent history. As a result of this history, foreign-funded civil society organizations have been deemed "subversive" and even labelled by the presidential couple as "vile" – using a play of words in Spanish: *sociedad civil* (civil society) and *sociedad sí vil*. It would be naive to assume that the existing CPCs – the main mechanism the government uses to promote citizen participation and implementation of important government pro-poor programs in the country – can be the actual sites of citizens' engagement[34] with the development process. Evidence from the academic literature and newspapers shows that these CPCs are viewed with great scepticism, if not outright hostility, by many in civil society. This perception is due to deeply rooted political animosities surrounding the CPCs, which are often accused of clientelism and corruption and of serving the (increasingly authoritarian) interests of President Ortega – much like the old Sandinista Defence Committees.[35] Thus, the CPCs have not, and cannot be expected to, promote the demands of CSOs – feminist and womxn's organizations, in particular, whose conflicting relationship with the government, and with the CPCs themselves, continues to this day.[36] This political scenario also poses a challenge for gender and development theory, which promotes the participation of people of all genders in decision making. Such a polarized political context raises questions about what constitutes "participation," where the sites and mechanisms exist for translating participation into concrete actions for a transformative approach to gender equality, and whose participation counts, under what conditions, and at what price.

The case of the MDG Achievement Fund offers a unique picture. The promotion of womxn's participation in gender budgets was the stated goal of this joint program between the Nicaraguan government (institutions and municipalities) and UN agencies. The collaborative fashion of the joint program and the involvement of the UN agencies as a "third party" provided a unique set of platforms for womxn. Contrary to the previous cases, where organizations rely heavily on foreign government funding and are often excluded from national government funding and initiatives, this joint program received plentiful resources, and had the "buy in" of the relevant government ministries and municipalities. Working with a combination of local and state-wide government actors led by the Instituto Nicaraguense de la Mujer (INIM, the main Nicaraguan agency for womxn) and the United Nations Fund for Population

Activities, the joint program's reach was expanded in terms of participants and beneficiaries. Although the process of selection of municipalities remains unclear in the documentation I reviewed, the open nature of the program and the mechanisms for participation devised allowed for people's involvement through CPCs and municipalities. In light of the previous discussion regarding claims of the CPCs' record, it is logical to assume that the beneficiaries of the program were friendly to the Sandinista party, although this cannot be verified. The joint program focused on working with people from the CPCs and staff at the various participating government ministries. However, despite the program's aim to include "women's participation in gender budgets," there is no mention in the reports about the involvement of feminist or womxn's CSOs of any sort. Again, context comes into play here to reveal the political parameters within which gender equality work takes place in Nicaragua. It should be further noted that INIM now operates under the Ministry of the Family, Youth and Children, which has governed the National Program on Gender Equality since 2007 and whose mission, according to its website, is to safeguard the family institution "from a rights and values perspective, using gender practices ... with the direct participation of the population in the recuperation of human dignity."[37] The family unit, and thus womxn in their roles as mothers, spouses, and family members, are at the centre of the gender equality program (as opposed to a focus on womxn as individuals in their own right). Seen from this perspective, one cannot ignore the extent to which political ideology and religion insert themselves into every aspect of gender equality initiatives, including seemingly progressive aid funded programs such as the MDG Achievement Fund.

Possibilities through Womxn's Agency

In the midst of the political alienation of feminists in Nicaragua, and considering the pressures brought by the new aid agenda, one should ask: how do womxn manage to participate in the official development process? What forms of agency are manifested in this difficult context? Here I refer to agency in its positive sense, as defined by Naila Kabeer as people's power and ability to make and act on their own life choices, even in the face of others' opposition.[38]

Organizations like AMICA and MEC are able to conduct their work in service of womxn's human rights largely due to solidarity-based relationships with like-minded organizations and with beneficiaries who often remain involved with them as volunteers. Indeed, both AMICA and MEC rely heavily on the voluntary work of local community actors. MEC, which experienced a significant loss of staff due to reduced funding, relies on a network of voluntary *promotoras* who identify issues of importance to MEC's membership, follow up with existing cases, and support members at the community level. The *promotoras* often serve as direct links for dialogue between the community and local municipalities, and boast a high status (in terms of respect) with the authorities for their effective work. Similarly, AMICA uses volunteers to escort womxn in legal processes, and relies on their work to support beneficiaries in the process of seeking justice in cases of violence against womxn. Because of their close links to their communities, volunteers' local knowledge about effective strategies for mobilizing and supporting womxn, and the solidarity aspects of their work – especially that of volunteers – both MEC and AMICA are able to carry on with their operations. They do so despite insufficient support from the government and the imminent threat of the discontinuation of foreign government funding that, ironically, is partly a consequence of the new aid effectiveness agenda.

The effectiveness of aid here is invisible by Paris Declaration indicators, as is the economic vulnerability these organizations and their beneficiaries face. Also invisible to the wider world through indicators is the significance of womxn's particular ways of knowing and shaping their own political engagement amid these difficult funding and political circumstances. Their strategies are based on their "situated knowledges" about which Donna Haraway famously theorized.[39] It is through those same situated knowledges that AMICA's staff knows the importance of working with local men and community judges in their understanding of gender equality issues. In the case of the judges, it is they who have the power to refer cases to the higher authorities at the state level (to which womxn would not have easy access by themselves).

Through the three case examples of citizen engagement, womxn can be seen as reconceptualizing the dominant discourse on effectiveness in three areas that Cathy McIlwaine and Kavita Datta identify as relatively recent transformations in gender and development theory.[40] The first is recognition of the diversity among womxn. The work of Horizons of Friendship through AMICA and the MDG Achievement Fund joint program are examples of a relatively new movement towards engagement with Indigenous and Afrodescendant womxn, in addition to working with "majority group" womxn in Nicaragua. But this move means there is plenty to be learned about culturally appropriate interventions, and about ways to support the strategic and practical needs of Indigenous and Afrodescendant peoples. Horizons of Friendship recognizes the limits of its engagement as an organization – remote and hard-to-reach locations do not allow for a consistent presence there. In the case of the MDG Achievement Fund, reports speak of the limits of the joint program to understand fully and address the needs of these groups, which have been shaped by distinct cosmologies, paradigms, and cultural attributes.

The second area attesting to the recent shifts and transformations within gender and development theory is the explicit integration of men and masculinities in the three cases. Such integration is meant to address the culture of *machismo* that permeates Nicaraguan (and most of Latin American) society, in recognition that womxn cannot change the aggressive behaviours of men.[41] AMICA had a violence against womxn education strategy focused on working with men as a way to subvert the possibility of retaliation against womxn who seek the services of the organization.[42] AMICA also worked with male community judges to help their understanding of the gender dimensions of violence against womxn and, thus, on their decisions to refer cases to locally based state justice authorities. Further, AMICA reported that, following the organization's training, the communal judges who participated attended *directly* to cases of violence against womxn by ensuring that due process was followed for victims seeking justice. Working with men proved so popular and successful that a national network called "Men Allied with Women's Health" was created – an example to other countries in the region.

The third area in which womxn can be seen as transforming the gender and development discourse through aid effectiveness is the shift from a needs-based to a rights-based approach to development.[43] All three cases are explicit about womxn's engagement as a goal, and are centred on human rights: Indigenous rights (Horizons/AMICA); civil and economic rights (CAWN/MEC); and a range of civil, economic, sexual health, and reproductive rights (MDG Achievement Fund). Interestingly, in all three cases womxn's engagement is being undermined, but womxn reclaim their rights by appropriating the language of effectiveness on feminist lines in resistance to the technocratic approach. For instance, contrary to the predominant short-term approach of donors, the interviewees emphasized that effectiveness in gender equality is about achieving development results and that this was a long-term process. Horizons of Friendship, which used the terms "efficiency," "effectiveness," and "results" interchangeably, considered effectiveness to be taking place when positive results were seen in three interlinked areas – service to the community, knowledge production, and citizen engagement – pointing at a more elaborate and complex interpretation of what is involved in obtaining an "effective" result. This more complex understanding of what constitutes effective results speaks directly to an interpretation of issues of gender equality as multilayered and requiring a multifaceted approach. For CAWN, "effectiveness is about transformation, about empowering women."[44] According to CAWN, this entails many small and big steps with short- and long-term strategies. It is not a linear progressive process, and requires steady support to deal with the usual setbacks typical of any process of change.

Results-based management tools make it virtually impossible to account for the non-linear changes described above or to prevent non-linear ways of knowing from being used in reporting results. Such transformation and empowerment are often a collective experience, but rooted in individual (equally empowering) experiences that lead to relationships of solidarity. Such solidarity comes closest to a form of power described as "relationships of mutual enablement."[45] It is this type of empowerment that effective aid should seek to support *as well as* individual empowerment.

Conclusion: Lessons from the Case Studies to Engender Effectiveness

The above examples highlight womxn's insistence on appropriating the language of effectiveness and on forming part of the alternative discourse that Latin American feminists encourage us to chart in order to reveal the asymmetry of positions in the rhetoric of equality and universality – and, in this case, of aid effectiveness and womxn's empowerment. Their intention is not to reject such rhetoric completely, but to own it using their own terms. As Maria Luisa Femenías argues, "Nuestros discursos alternativos favorecen la ruptura político-epistemológica de los contextos naturalizados y abren espacios de comprensión y de re significación. Al hacerlo, generan espacios diversos para pensar, explicar y dar voz propia a las múltiples fuerzas étnicas, sexuales, económicas, culturales que se precipitan en el lugar de lo nuevo" [Our alternative discourses favour the political and epistemological rupture of the naturalized contexts and open spaces of understanding and redefinition. By doing so, our discourses generate diverse spaces to think, to explain, and to give voice to the multiple ethnic, sexual, economic, and cultural forces that advance to the place of the new].[46]

Speaking about the kind of epistemological rupture that Femenías promotes, I follow various Latin American feminists who also argue for a break from the assumptions and epistemologies based on Western notions of universalism that were brought by colonialism and

368 Astrid V. Pérez Piñán

that structure modern Latin American states.[47] They remind us of the specific colonial context and pluralistic identities that shape the experiences of Latin American peoples. In order to counter this colonial legacy, and what is often referred to as the resulting "epistemic injustice,"[48] it is necessary to engage situated knowledges through processes that value the participation of those benefiting from aid – Afrodescendants and Indigenous womxn and men, in particular, as well as people of all genders. Accounting for situated knowledges allows for practices and indicators of aid effectiveness to be informed by the particular perspectives of those who receive the aid, in all their diversity, according to their particular contexts (economic, spiritual, cultural, and so on) and social locations. This further allows the collection of place- and context-specific data, responsive to gender and other identities, that shape the development of indicators and foster knowledge democracy. The practice would allow for the kind of "strong objectivity" that Harding speaks of, which recognizes that multiple perspectives, problems, and methods are context specific and value laden.[49] Locally produced gender-responsive indicators of aid effectiveness can emphasize and allow people's agency to shape their own conceptions of what effective interventions should be supported by foreign aid. This is not to say, however, that we should "fetishize the local" as a pure and innocent space.[50] The Nicaraguan example clearly shows that local spaces are fraught with power struggles that perpetuate the favouring of some to the detriment of others. Any attempt to develop gender-responsive indicators of aid effectiveness should take into consideration such realities and avoid reproducing or exacerbating existing negative power dynamics and discrimination.

In closing, I want to reiterate the need for further exploration of the epistemologies emerging from Indigenous and Afrodescendant womxn's resistance to the neoliberal aid effectiveness paradigm. The cases explored here illustrate the paradox of the broader aid effectiveness agenda within which womxn's rights organizations are situated. Making aid more effective presents setbacks and poses serious challenges for the deliberative democratic policy process, and for the measurement and continuation of gender equality work. Yet, womxn's agency has enriched conceptualizations of effectiveness by their use of new strategies to demand effectiveness in their own terms. Finally, as it would be counterproductive to prescribe yet another list of recipes in a "one-size-fits-all" approach to engendering effectiveness, I would like to point to some questions that emerged from this research as important in the development of gender-responsive indicators of aid and development effectiveness.

Discussion Questions

1 To what extent have the beneficiaries and mediators of aid money been involved in the creation of indicators? What is the (power) history between them and how might differences be worked through?
2 What are the experiences/histories of the country or locality in question with participative processes? What lessons were learned, and what culturally responsive approaches can be developed to capitalize on the existing networks and structures to ensure a fruitful process of indicator development?
3 To what extent are those involved in the management and facilitation of aid money, men and womxn, representative of a variety of voices in their community?
4 How does the process of indicator development allow or hinder local womxn's and men's ways of knowing in shaping the planning, monitoring and evaluation of aid initiatives?

NOTES

1 James Tully, "The Crisis of Global Citizenship," *Radical Politics Today*, 2009, online at https://core.ac.uk/download/pdf/14527443.pdf.
2 The term womxn is commonly used by feminists to avoid the suffix "-men" as a way to decentre patriarchal linguistic forms.
3 Aid conditionality refers to a common practice of many donors whereby they place conditions on how and when countries receiving aid are supposed to spend the aid received. The conditions usually advantage donors' own interests and priorities. Tied aid refers to yet another practice of donors whereby they stipulate that aid money must be spent on products and services from the country providing the aid or from a selected group of countries.
4 Organisation for Economic Co-operation and Development, "The Paris Declaration on Aid Effectiveness" (Paris, 2005), online at http://www.oecd.org/dac/effectiveness/34428351.pdf.
5 The term "new aid architecture" refers to the policies and structures that make up the new approach to aid effectiveness.
6 Cecilia Alemany, Fernanda Hopenhaym, and Nerea Craviotto, "Implementing the Paris Declaration: Implications for the Promotion of Women's Rights and Gender Equality" (paper commissioned by the Canadian Council on International Cooperation, January 2008), online at https://www.awid.org/sites/default/files/atoms/files/implementing_the_paris_declaration_implications_for_the_promotion_of_womens_rights.pdf.

7 Rosalind Eyben, "Struggles in Paris: The DAC and the Purposes of Development Aid," *European Journal of Development Research* 25, no. 1 (2013): 78–91, https://doi.org/10.1057/ejdr.2012.49.

8 Stephen Brown and Bill Morton, "Reforming Aid and Development Cooperation: Accra, Doha and Beyond," Policy Note (Ottawa: North-South Institute, August 2008), online at http://www.nsi-ins.ca/content/download /DAW_policy.pdf.

9 Alemany, Hopenhaym, and Craviotto, "Implementing the Paris Declaration."

10 Ibid.; Roberto Bissio, "Application of the Criteria for Periodic Evalua-tion of Global Development Partnerships – as Defined in Millennium Development Goal 8 – from the Right to Development Perspective: The Paris Declaration on Aid Effectiveness" (Geneva: Working Group on the Right to Development, 2008); Better Aid, "Development Effectiveness in Development Cooperation: A Rights-Based Perspective," October 2010, online at https://www.ituc-csi.org/IMG/pdf/betteraid_development _effectiveness_dev_cooperation_1_.pdf.

11 Emma Mawdsley, Laura Savage, and Sung-Mi Kim, "A 'Post-Aid World'? Paradigm Shift in Foreign Aid and Development Cooperation at the 2011 Bisan High Level Forum," *Geographical Journal* 180, no. 1 (2014): 27–38, https://doi.org/10.1111/j.1475-4959.2012.00490.x; Eyben, "Struggles in Paris"; Busan Partnership for Effective Development Cooperation, "Busan Outcome Document" (Busan, South Korea, 29 December 2011), online at http://www.oecd.org/dac/effectiveness/49650173.pdf. It should be noted that the Global Partnership emphasized the participation of the private sec-tor, which was met with scepticism by many CSOs working in human rights.

12 ALBA members are Antigua and Barbuda, Bolivia, Cuba, Dominica, Ecuador, Nicaragua, Saint Lucia, Saint Vincent and the Grenadines, and Venezuela.

13 Alianza Bolivariana para los Pueblos de Nuestra América, "Portal ALBA," 13 November 2013, online at http://www.portalalba.org/; Thomas Muhr, "Nicaragua Re-visited: From Neo-liberal 'Ungovernability' to the Bolivarian Alternative for the Peoples of Our America (ALBA)," *Globalisation, Societies and Education* 6, no. 2 (2008): 147–61, https://doi .org/10.1080/14767720802061447.

14 Nalini Visvanathan et al., *The Women, Gender and Development Reader*, 2nd ed. (London: Zed Books, 2011); Andrea Cornwall, "Revisiting the 'Gender Agenda,'" *IDS Bulletin* 38, no. 2 (2009): 69–78, https://onlinelibrary.wiley. com/doi/abs/10.1111/j.1759-5436.2007.tb00353.x; Janet Henshall Momsen, *Gender and Development*, Routledge Perspectives on Development (London: Routledge, 2004); Jane L. Parpart, Patricia M, Connelly, and V. Eudine Barriteau, *Theoretical Perspectives on Gender and Development* (Ottawa: International Development Research Centre, 2000), 51, online at https:// www.idrc.ca/en/book/theoretical-perspectives-gender-and-development.

15 Esther Boserup, *Women's Role in Economic Development* (London: George Allen & Unwin, 1970); Caroline O.N. Moser, "Gender Planning in the Third World: Meeting Practical and Strategic Gender Needs," *World Development* 17, no. 11 (1989): 1799–825, https://doi.org/10.1016/0305 -750X(89)90201-5; Lourdes Beneria, "Globalization, Gender and the Davos Man," *Feminist Economics* 5, no. 3 (1999): 61–83; Shirin Rai, *Gender and the Political Economy of Development* (Oxford: Polity Press, 2002).

16 Kate Bedford and Shirin M. Rai, "Feminists Theorize International Political Economy," *Signs: Journal of Women in Culture and Society* 36, no. 1 (2010): 1–18, https://doi.org/10.1086/652910; Maria Riley, "A Feminist Political Economic Framework," (n.p.: Center of Concern, 2008), online at https:// pdfs.semanticscholar.org/752a/93623d25ab857f420645631d8d2bc38a2cb7 .pdf?_ga=2.188500587.218309311.1578315338-753571327.1578315338; Spike V. Peterson, "How (the Meaning of) Gender Matters in the Political Economy," *New Political Economy* 10, no. 4 (2005): 499–521; Suzanne Bergeron, "Political Economy Discourses of Globalization and Feminist Politics," *Signs* 26, no. 4 (2001): 983–1006.

17 Riley, "Feminist Political Economic Framework."

18 Mary Hawkesworth, "Intersectionality: Diagnosing Conceptual Practices of Power," *New Political Science* 37, no. 4 (2015): 628–36; Association for Women's Rights in Development, "Intersectionality: A Tool for Gender and Economic Justice," *Women's Rights and Economic Change* 9 (August 2004): 1–8.

19 Angelika Arutyunova and Cindy Clark, "Watering the Leaves, Starving the Roots: The Status of Financing for Women's Rights Organizing and Gender Equality" (Toronto: Association for Women's Rights in Development, 2013); Rosalind Eyben, "What Is Happening to Donor Support for Women's Rights?" *Contestations: Dialogues on Women's Empowerment* 4 (11 March 2011), online at https://www.contestations.net/issues/issue-4 /what-is-happening-to-donor-support-for-womens-rights-response-to -rosalind-eyben-2/; idem, "Hiding Relations: The Irony of 'Effective Aid,'" *European Journal of Development Research* 22, no. 3 (2010): 382–97.

20 Parpart, Connelly, and Barriteau, *Theoretical Perspectives on Gender and Development*.

21 Sarah Hunt, "Civil Society Participation: Poverty Reduction in Bolivia, Honduras and Nicaragua," in *Civil Society and the State in Left-Led Latin America: Challenges and Limitations to Democratization*, ed. Barry Cannon and Peadar Kirby (London: Zed Books, 2012), 161–72.

22 Gilles Bataillon, "Caza de brujas en Managua," *Letras Libres* (31 December 2008): 72–5; Barry Cannon and Mo Hume, "Civil Society-State Relations in Left-Led El Salvador, Honduras and Nicaragua," in Cannon and Kirby, *Civil Society and the State in Left-Led Latin America*, 3–16.

23 For a review of these debates in the context of Latin America, see Patricia
    Muñoz Cabrera, *Intersecting Inequalities: A Review of Feminist Theories and
    Debates on Violence Against Women and Poverty in Latin America* (London:
    Central America Women's Network, 2010).

24 Author's interview with Central America Women's Network representative,
    17 February 2014; author's interview with Horizons of Friendship represent-
    ative, November 2013.

25 In my PhD thesis, I provide a full discussion of how the aid effectiveness
    agenda, and its indicators of effectiveness in particular, are used by donors
    to gear countries towards a neoliberal economic order detrimental to
    gender and human rights-based development goals. See Astrid Pérez
    Piñán, "Engendering Effectiveness: A Feminist Critique of the New Aid
    Architecture" (PhD diss., Trinity College, Dublin, 2015).

26 Canada, Department of Foreign Affairs, Trade and Development, "Results-
    Based Management for International Assistance: A How-to Guide" (Ottawa,
    2018), online at http://www.international.gc.ca/world-monde/funding
    -financement/results_based_management-gestion_axee_resultats-guide
    .aspx?lang=eng.

27 Ibid., emphasis mine.

28 Srilatha Batliwala and Alexandra Pittman, "Capturing Change in Women's
    Realities: A Critical Overview of Current Monitoring & Evaluation
    Frameworks and Approaches" (Toronto: Association for Women's Rights
    in Development, 2010), online at https://www.awid.org/sites/default
    /files/atoms/files/capturing_change_in_womens_realities.pdf.

29 Debra J. Liebowitz and Susanne Zwingel, "Gender Equality Oversimplified:
    Using CEDAW to Counter the Measurement Obsession," *International
    Studies Review* 16, no. 3 (2014): 362–89; Sally Engle Merry, "Measuring the
    World," *Current Anthropology* 52, no. S3 (2011): S83–95; Alnoor Ebrahim,
    "Accountability in Practice: Mechanisms for NGOs," *World Development* 31,
    no. 5 (2003): 813–29.

30 Brooke A. Ackerly, "Feminist Theory, Global Gender Justice, and the
    Evaluation of Grant-Making," *SSRN Electronic Journal* 37, no. 2 (2009), online
    at http://ssrn.com/paper=1348902.

31 Batliwala and Pittman, "Capturing Change in Women's Realities."

32 Ibid., 11.

33 Ibid.

34 Citizen engagement here means the meaningful involvement of citizens in
    the development of policies or program initiated by government

35 Cannon and Kirby, *Civil Society and the State in Left-Led Latin America*;
    Nils-Sjard Schulz, "Nicaragua: A Rude Awakening for the Paris
    Declaration," *FRIDE*, November 2007, online at https://eulacfoundation
    .org/en/system/files/Nicaragua%20a%20rude%20awakening%20for

%20the%20Paris%20Declaration.pdf; Názere Habed Lopez, "Por qué y para qué los consejos del poder ciudadano?" *El Nuevo Diario*, 28 August 2007, online at http://impreso.elnuevodiario.com.ni/2007/08/28/opinion/57372.

36 In 2007, over twenty CSOs petitioned the opposition to revoke the CPCs. See "Demandan ley para anular consejos de poder ciudadano," *El Nuevo Diario*, 17 July 2007, online at http://impreso.elnuevodiario.com.ni/2007/07/17/politica/54013.

37 See the Nicaragua Ministry of the Family, Youth and Children website at http://www.mifamilia.gob.ni, accessed 30 January 2020.

38 Naila Kabeer, "Gender Equality and Women's Empowerment: A Critical Analysis of the Third Millennium Development Goal," *Gender and Development* 13, no. 1 (2005): 13–24, online at http://www.visionaryvalues.com/wiki/images/Gender_Equality_and_Empowerment_MDG_Kabeer.pdf.

39 Donna Haraway, "Situated Knowledges: The Science Question in Feminism and the Privilege of Partial Perspective," *Feminist Studies* 14, no. 3 (1988): 575–99, https://doi.org/10.2307/3178066.

40 Cathy McIlwaine, and Kavita Datta, "From Feminising to Engendering Development," *Gender, Place and Culture* 10, no. 4 (2003): 369–82.

41 Muñoz Cabrera, *Intersecting Inequalities*.

42 Author's interview with AMICA representative, 14 November 2013.

43 McIlwaine and Datta, "From Feminising to Engendering Development."

44 Author's interview with Central America Women's Network representative, 17 February 2014.

45 J. Ann Tickner, *A Feminist Voyage through International Relations* (Oxford: Oxford University Press, 2014), 12.

46 María Luisa Femenías, "Esbozo de un feminismo latinoamericano," *Revista Estudios Feministas* 15, no. 1 (2007).

47 Ibid.; Karina Bidaseca and Vanesa Vázquez Laba, "Feminismos y (des) colonialidad: las voces de las mujeres indigenas del sur," *Tema de Mujeres* 7, no. 7 (2011): 24–42, online at http://ojs.filo.unt.edu.ar/index.php/temasdemujeres/article/view/44/44; Berny Mendoza, "La epistemología del sur, la colonialidad del género y el feminismo latinoamericano," Centro de Estudios e Investigación Simón Rodríguez, n.d., online at http://funceisimonrodriguez.blogspot.ca/2012/10/la-epistemologia-del-sur-la.html.

48 Boaventura de Sousa Santos, *Epistemologies of the South: Justice against Epistemicide* (Boulder, CO: Paradigm, 2014).

49 Sandra Harding, "'Strong Objectivity': A Response to the New Objectivity Question," *Synthese* 104, no. 3 (1995): 331–49; Ann Sisson Runyan and V. Spike Peterson, *Global Gender Issues in the New Millennium*, Dilemmas in World Politics (Boulder, CO: Westview Press, 2014), 69.

50 Runyan and Peterson, *Global Gender Issues in the New Millennium*, 244.

374   Astrid V. Pérez Piñán

KEY RESOURCES

Liebowitz, Debra J., and Susanne Zwingel. "Gender Equality Oversimplified: Using CEDAW to Counter the Measurement Obsession." *International Studies Review* 16, no. 3 (2014): 362–89.
Merry, Sally Engle. "Measuring the World." *Current Anthropology* 52, no. S3 (2011): S83–95.
Pérez Piñán, Astrid. "Engendering Effectiveness: A Feminist Critique of the New Aid Architecture." PhD diss., Trinity College, Dublin, 2015.
Pérez Piñán, Astrid. "Gender Responsive Approaches to Measuring Aid Effectiveness: Options and Issues." *Social Politics* 22, no. 3 (2015): 432–55.
Tully, James. "The Crisis of Global Citizenship." *Radical Politics Today*, 2009. Online at https://core.ac.uk/download/pdf/14527443.pdf.

Conclusion: Reflections on Deliberative Democracy, Public Participation, and the Future of Policy Making

LEAH LEVAC and SARAH MARIE WIEBE

These are challenging times for *policy justice*. In early 2018, seventeen people – mostly youth – were shot and killed at a Florida high school. CNN reported that, in the first twenty-one weeks of the same year, "there [had] already been 23 school shootings [in the United States] where someone was hurt or killed."[1] Despite enormous and disproportionate rates of school violence compared to those of other member countries of the Organisation for Economic Co-operation and Development and compelling engagement by tens of thousands of citizens, the United States cannot get a grip on its gun policies. In two Canadian provinces, less than five months apart, jurors acquitted two white men who shot and killed – at close range – young, unarmed Indigenous men. Yet Canada cannot get a handle on the tangled web of colonial criminal justice policies – including those related to jury selection, property rights, and policing – that allow these unjust outcomes to persist. Also in Canada, rates of food insecurity are persistent and outrageously high. Nearly 50 per cent of households in parts of the North, and 12 to 15 per cent of households in the rest of the country, do not have enough and/or healthy food to eat, yet we cannot seem to resolve food – and related income – insecurity.[2] As of mid-2018, more than 776,000 children across the country did not have access to licensed child care spots. Despite vast and long-standing knowledge about the importance of child care access for a range of public goals of liberal democracies (such as labour market access, especially for women, and public health),[3] Canada cannot seem to create appropriate child care policy. From the more sensationalized to the more mundane, gross policy failures are not difficult to uncover.

At the same time, it is easy to uncover persistent and varied engagement efforts[4] to rectify these injustices. The March For Our Lives, sparked by the Parklands shooting, attracted hundreds of thousands of protestors in cities around the world.[5] Failures of the criminal justice system related to the experiences of Indigenous people are well documented, and many citizens, residents, and organizations have worked, and continue to work, diligently to address these failures.[6] While progress towards zero hunger is elusive,[7] the creation of local food policy councils and efforts to promote a national food policy, combined with research on food insecurity, suggest there is broad agreement that food insecurity is both unacceptable and actionable. Unions and advocacy groups have been working for universal child care for decades.[8]

Beyond the challenges presented by persistent policy injustices, there remain considerable challenges in attributing specific citizen engagement processes with particular policy outcomes, including in the area of reducing inequalities.[9] In other words, even if there were equitable outcomes in these or myriad other areas, to what would we attribute success? What difference then, will *Creating Spaces of Engagement* make if our broad goal is to contribute to the pursuit of *policy justice*? As we detailed in the Introduction, *policy justice* is grounded in a commitment to anti-oppressive and social justice–oriented aims, demands dedication to pursuing inclusive practices, and requires a sustained critique of power – which, as we note in the Introduction, keeps not only with the ideas of critical, intersectional, and interpretive policy scholars,[10] but also with the ideas and practices of transdisciplinarity and reciprocal and ethical forms of participatory and community-engaged research.[11] Although we focus heavily on procedural dimensions of *policy justice* in this collection, we also see *policy justice* as characterized by substantive policy outcomes that ultimately reduce inequities. Our argument is in keeping with recent work by Patricia Hill Collins, who notes that, "[for intersectionality and participatory democracy], achieving [equality, fairness, inclusion, and social justice] requires building equitable communities of enquiry and praxis that can survive within yet challenge intersecting oppressions. Stated differently, both [intersectionality and participatory democracy] confront the thorny question of building intellectual and political solidarities across differences in power."[12] It is for this reason that this anthology highlights various ways the voices of citizens – particularly those who have historically been marginalized – can be listened to, not simply heard, and can help develop and guide public engagement deliberations. The chapters in this collection were not intended to present concrete empirical claims of the relationship between policy processes and their outcomes. Nevertheless, we think the cases they examine could contribute substantially to such an argument, in that they support the idea that more just processes lead to more just outcomes. For instance, if people who are often rendered invisible – such as girls with disabilities in Vietnam, Indigenous youth, and women living in low income – are truly listened to, their experiences seem much more likely to be reflected in corresponding policy decisions. Further, our authors closely examine site-specific examples and vignettes that address how public engagement processes might be envisioned as more inclusive. In doing so, they suggest that enhancing policy makers' toolkits – especially to create pathways for the voices of those most directly affected by policy decisions to have input into all stages of the process – bears direct influence on possible policy outcomes.

On this foundation, we contend that the arguments and analyses laid out in this collection matter for at least three reasons. First, as we noted in the introduction, our goal was to document public engagement initiatives locally and globally, to expose their edges as part of evaluating their inclusiveness, and to contribute to a broader dialogue about how public engagement processes can be improved to advance democracy, decolonization, and justice. Theoretically and practically, the book's contributors have succeeded in reaching this goal by using examples from across policy areas and around the globe to expand our ideas about, and applications of, participatory and deliberative democracy in ways that help us to better understand and resist exclusions and to practise anti-oppression. The authors in part 1 do this by drawing on examples and theories from within and beyond political science to push for more careful theoretical consideration of who gets included and excluded, and how and why this happens. Some authors, including Stephen Williams (chapter 2) and Ellen Szarleta (chapter 3), ask us to consider the role of governments as participants in, rather than conveners of, public engagement initiatives. Ultimately, the book's first contribution is to offer guidance on how to think about and practise deliberative democracy – as a particular form of participatory democracy – in more transdisciplinary and inclusive ways.

Second, it is painfully clear – if one is seeking *policy justice* – that our current policy mechanisms are inadequate for dealing with the sticky and tricky (complex, interrelated, striated, and power-laden) policy problems we face. Indeed, as authors such as Vera Schattan Ruas Pereira Coelho and Laura Waisbich have noted, the limits of specific public engagement mechanisms for ensuring substantive justice-oriented policy outcomes highlight the importance of analysing participatory experiences "as political mechanisms that can, even when operating outside the standards deemed appropriate by deliberative theory, enjoy the necessary vitality to foster policies capable of reducing inequalities."[13] It is therefore critical that we continue to ask ourselves how to change the dynamics of the systems and conversations in which policy decisions are imbedded. We opted not to explore these dynamics through a single policy field or from the perspective of one state, one sphere, one actor, or one theory of the policy process. Instead, the collection argues for the need to consider the striated[14] spaces of policy making, which we described in the Introduction as defined yet malleable, nuanced, power-full, and "hitched to rigid statist hierarchies of governance." This argument keeps with, and extends, Genevieve Fuji Johnson's argument (in chapter 1) that "[f]ormal mechanisms of deliberative democracy in the political/juridical-institutional (micro) sphere need to be better connected to the activities of the broader civil society (macro) sphere." In other words, the book's second contribution is to take up and advance more seriously the commitments of interpretive, intersectional, and critical policy works and scholars, who have already made important contributions to our understandings of how systems and structures of power organize experiences of inclusion and exclusion.[15] One way we advance this broad body of policy work is by thinking through conceptualizations of space as they relate to policy making. These commitments are reflected by contributors who note that deliberative democracy can be expanded by looking outside of democracies (Deborah Stienstra and Xuan Thuy Nguyen, chapter 6), outside of formal governance mechanisms (Ethel Tungohan, chapter 13), and inside and across large institutions, including post-secondary institutions (Catriona Remocker, Tim Dyck, and Dan Reist, chapter 8; Derek Tannis, chapter 15).

Third, and related, this book contributes practical ideas about how to create and work within these spaces of engagement, a contribution that necessarily reveals the paradox of transforming while resisting state power; of interacting with the colonial state while rejecting colonialism. Of course, we do not offer complete answers, but we do offer some glimmers of light that we hope will spark conversations about the work of achieving *policy justice*. For example, contributors highlight ways of shifting all stages of the policy-making process – including problem definition (Leah Levac and Jacqueline Gillis, chapter 4) and decision making (Stephen Williams, chapter 2) – to become more inclusive. Contributors also emphasize the importance of balancing reason and emotion by engaging the affective dimensions of human experience through creative forms of artistic expression. In other words, beyond fostering reasoned debate, there is a need to embrace mind/body/spirit connections using practices such as storytelling (Sarah Marie Wiebe, chapter 14), arts-based approaches (Joanna Ashworth, chapter 9; Bruno de Oliveira Jayme, chapter 12), online forums (Tara Mahoney, chapter 7), and sharing circles (Alana Cattapan, Alexandra Dobrowolsky, Tammy Findlay, and April Mandrona, chapter 10). Broadly, these analyses suggest that the context in which public policies develop is critical, and that, accordingly, unique consideration of the design, and commitments, of public engagement is – to a large extent – both place based and essential. Simply, practise is critical. In other words, we highlight a range of multidimensional examples as a way of arguing against one monolithic approach to public engagement. This accords with the underlying orientation of this collection towards interpretive and critical forms of policy analysis, which Dvora Yanow describes as focusing "not only on figuring out what policy-relevant elements carry or convey meaning, what these meanings are, who is making them, and how they are being communicated, but also on the methods through which the analyst-researcher accesses and generates these meanings and analyzes them."[16] Fischer[17] also contributes to our thinking about critical policy analysis, including through a lengthy discussion of the importance of citizen participation in policy analysis, a commitment that rests on deliberative practices, inquiry, and the Freirean idea of "problematization."[18]

Together, these three contributions – thinking about deliberative democracy using a transdisciplinary approach; advancing critical, interpretive, and intersectional policy scholarship; and offering practical ideas about more inclusive, relational, and radical public engagement practices – have the effect of highlighting exciting opportunities and formidable challenges. This is not to say that all the contributors agree on the sites or sources of exclusion or on their remedies. What the chapters have in common, though, is a recognition that listening to the lives and experiences of citizens matters deeply as we strive for *policy justice* – see, in particular, Ashworth (chapter 9) Tungohan (chapter 13), and Wiebe (chapter 14) for discussions about the importance of listening. Besides the contributions detailed above, which imply the need to accept citizens' experiences as valid sources of policy information, it is also important to acknowledge that people are impacted by their participation and inclusion (or not) in public policy development, and moreover, that these effects and affects transcend formal politics, and even democracy. In other words, thinking about creating and working in spaces of engagement for publics – especially those whose voices continue to be marginalized by policy processes and dominant interpretations of policy problems – is about quite a lot more than changing public policy. It is also about changing society. As David Moscrop and Mark Warren point out in a 2016 special issue of the *Journal of Public Deliberation* that focused on equality, equity, and deliberation, if we take both equality and equity as commitments of democracies, deliberations that are democratic (and democracies that are deliberative) need to be concerned about the answer to the question, "who gets to deliberate, and about what?"[19] This, they suggest, is fundamentally a question about equity. And it speaks to what they describe as two "pre-deliberative democratic features [that] stand out as particularly important ... : popular participation – how individuals come to have standing and voice *as participants*, and agenda-setting – how concerns come to be defined *as issues*."[20] It is in keeping with both of these points that Levac and Gillis (chapter 4) use the social construction of policy framework to raise a flag about the persistent exclusion of Indigenous and Northern women as policy participants, and of their ideas about defining policy problems related to resource extraction.

(Im)possibilities and Policy Solidarities for *Policy Justice*

Building on the book's three main contributions, we close by thinking about ways forward in the face of the formidable challenges and paradoxes highlighted by the contributors. There are myriad institutional challenges associated with pursuing *policy justice*, including some mentioned in this volume – for example, Johnson (chapter 1) discusses explicit disconnects between institutions and broader civil society, and Levac (chapter 11) discusses how public servants had to help navigate the legal decision-making framework while pursuing citizens' policy feedback. Other such challenges include the pressures of balancing full participation and decision-making timelines, the lack of political will to uphold both rhetorical and legal commitments to Indigenous peoples, the possibility of significant disconnects between policy intent and implementation, and the habitual enactment of public consultation as a one-way communications exercise, rather than a relational and iterative process. Despite our insistence on careful reflection about public engagement, we hope to offer more than a cautionary tale. We are measured yet optimistic about meaningful forms of deliberative democracy in theory and in practice in Canada and around the globe. In closing, however, our focus is oriented to more general commitments that we can pursue. Since participants – who can face multiple and interlocking barriers to participation – matter for policy outcomes, the creation of, and practices within, spaces of engagement are deeply important. There is no getting around the fact that present-day Canada is a colonial state whose policies (one need not look further than the Indian Act) continue to displace, subjugate, and disrupt Indigenous peoples and their knowledge systems, land relationships, and forms of governance. It is clear why some Indigenous peoples, First Nations, governments, and organizations reject colonial public policy processes and outcomes altogether, and determine that efforts within such a system do not have the capacity to advance justice. It is also clear why others choose the path of trying to build working relationships and solidarities, even across enormous power imbalances, fraught histories, and ongoing dislocations. It is further the case that racism – including anti-Black racism – is alive and well across the Western world, including in Canada, and that the physical safety of racialized peoples is disproportionately in question, often at the hands of state actors.[21] As Tungohan (chapter 13) details, racialized migrant workers in Canada exercise political courage simply by choosing to attend community forums. Again, in this context, it is not difficult to understand that some efforts focus on resisting state power while others focus on its transformation.

Given this context, we do not romanticize the ease of the work of *policy justice*, nor do we overlook the tensions inherent. Levac and Gillis (chapter 4), Cattapan and colleagues (chapter 10), Wiebe (chapter 14), and Tannis (chapter 15) grapple with their settler privilege and their own histories of migration, and what these mean for trying to create and work within spaces of engagement. In his recent exploration of the need for reciprocity for transforming Canada's sociopolitical terrain, Elliott calls for Indigenous-settler engagement in pursuit of decolonization. This, he argues, will require addressing "barriers to reciprocity [which] are found not only in the ways that settlers imagine and speak about the social world but also how they typically behave and orient themselves within it."[22] We share the conviction – as editors, and with many of the contributors – that transforming state policy development is one, albeit small, component of a much broader political commitment to *policy justice*. Our dedication to this work stems from a deep desire to build bridges across difference, and is demonstrated in part through a commitment to knowledge democracy, which is imbedded in the transdisciplinary approaches explored in this anthology.

In chapter 10, Cattapan and colleagues argue that, to move towards "radical policy futures," we must strive to ."[avoid] the lopsidedness of 'top-down' power arrangements; ... [engage] people using non-conventional methods; ... [reach] difficult-to-reach publics; and ... [invite engagement] in the context of well-established relationships of trust." This call is certainly in keeping with a commitment to transdisciplinary and more collaborative policy-making processes, and is in line with how we imagine the work of building policy solidarities. Still, there is more work to be done in imagining transdisciplinary approaches to public policy – especially with respect to informing how policy problems come to be defined and how decisions are made. The point at which policy decisions are made is often the most exclusive – ultimately limited to elected officials and, further, in many cases, to the governing majority. How policy agendas are defined and set in a society striving for *policy justice* is thus an important area for further exploration. So, too, is the question of how to transform representative democracies' decision-making processes so that they are better informed by trans-disciplinarity. To this end, we hope that the contributions in this book encourage others to take further efforts to assess the creation of radical policy futures that move beyond top-down processes and instead place affected parties' perspectives and experiences at the centre. Such an emotive and relational orientation is not a call to replace technical expertise in policy, but to *complement* it with a commitment to knowledge democracy and to the artful expressions and experiential expertise that emerge from situated bodies of knowledge. Creating spaces of engagement is not a finite endeavour. It requires a long-term iterative commitment to building and struggling through the challenges of policy solidarities in pursuit of *policy justice*. This radical lens creatively illuminates the dark edges of public engagement, while finding light in the shadows to incite imagination about the enactment of alternative policy futures.

NOTES

1 Saeed Ahmed and Christina Walker, "There has been, on average, 1 school shooting every week this year," *CNN*, 25 May 2018, online at https://www.cnn.com/2018/03/02/us/school-shootings-2018-list-trnd/index.html.

2 Statistics Canada measures food security in the Canadian Community Health Survey using the Household Food Security Survey Module. The module is not always mandatory, so some provinces do not regularly monitor food insecurity. Rates since 2007–8, however – including in two years when monitoring was required and in other years when several provinces and territories monitored voluntarily – are virtually unchanged. Lack of income is a major cause of food insecurity; see, for example, Valerie Tarasuk, Naomi Dachner, and Rachel Loopstra, "Food Banks, Welfare, and Food Insecurity in Canada," *British Food Journal* 116, no. 9 (2014): 1405–17. In Food Banks Canada's HungerCount 2019 Report, the five main policy recommendations put forward are: "support the creation of affordable early learning and childcare across the country," "increase supports for single adults living with low incomes," "immediately implement the Canada housing benefit," "develop pilot projects towards a basic income for all Canadians," and "reduce northern food insecurity"; online

at https://hungercount.foodbankscanada.ca/assets/docs/FoodBanks
_HungerCount_EN_2019.pdf.

3 For documentation of the wide-ranging knowledge of, and support for,
universal approaches to child care provision, see Lynell Anderson, Morna
Ballantyne, and Martha Friendly, "Child Care for All of Us: Universal
Child Care for Canadians by 2020" (Ottawa: Canadian Centre for Policy
Alternatives, 2016), online at https://www.policyalternatives.ca/sites
/default/files/uploads/publications/National%20Office/2016/12/Child
_Care_AFB2017_technical_paper.pdf.

4 Including by citizens, neighbourhood groups, community researchers and
organizations, university researchers, think tanks, public servants, unions,
subjugated Nations, and others, in these and myriad other policy areas.

5 These events were covered extensively by news media. See, for example,
Amanda Holpuch and Paul Owen, "March for Our Lives: hundreds of
thousands demand end to gun violence – as it happened," *Guardian*, 5 June
2019, online at https://www.theguardian.com/us-news/live/2018/mar
/24/march-for-our-lives-protest-gun-violence-washington; Sarah Gray,
"The March for Our Lives Protest Is This Saturday. Here's Everything to
Know," *Time*, 23 March 2018, online at http://time.com/5167102/march
-for-our-lives-parkland-school-shooting-protest/; and Dakine Andone,
"What you should know about the March for Our Lives," *CNN*, 21 March
2018, online at https://www.cnn.com/2018/03/21/us/march-for-our
-lives-explainer/index.html.

6 Two examples are IndiGenius, retrieved from http://indigeniusandassociates
.com/#services, and the Elizabeth Fry Society (including past national executive director and current independent Senator Kim Pate). Governments have
also commissioned reports, including, for example, the work of Justice Frank
Iacobucci, *First Nations Representation on Ontario Juries* (Toronto: Ministry of the
Attorney General, February 2013), online at https://www.attorneygeneral.jus
.gov.on.ca/english/about/pubs/iacobucci/First_Nations_Representation
_Ontario_Juries.html.

7 Lynn McIntyre, Patrick B. Patterson, and Catherine L. Mah, "A Framing
Analysis of Canadian Household Food Insecurity Policy Illustrates
Co-construction of an Intractable Problem," *Critical Policy Studies* 12, no. 2
(2016): 149–68.

8 Examples of organizations and unions working on this issue include Child
Care Now (https://timeforchildcare.ca/about-us/) and the Canadian
Union of Postal Workers through their creation of a *Child Care Action
Toolkit* (https://www.cupw.ca/en/child-care-action-toolkit).

9 John Gaventa, "Can Participation 'Fix' Inequality? Unpacking the
Relationship between the Economic and Political Citizenship" Innovation

Series 5 (Antigonish, NS: St Francis Xavier University, Coady International Institute, April 2016), online at https://www.participatorymethods.org /sites/participatorymethods.org/files/Gaventa%20Coady%20Innovation %20series5%20Can%20participation%20fix%20inequality.pdf.

10 Chantal Mouffe, "Deliberative Democracy or Agonistic Pluralism," IHS Political Science Series Working Paper 72 (Vienna: Institute for Advanced Studies, December 2000), online at http://irihs.ihs.ac.at/1312/1/pw_72 .pdf, accessed 11 January 2018; Dvora Yanow, "Interpretation in Policy Analysis: On Methods and Practice," *Critical Policy Analysis* 1, no. 1 (2007): 111; Iris Marion Young, *Inclusion and Democracy* (Oxford: Oxford University Press, 2002).

11 Contributions to this discussion are wide ranging, including from community organization such as the Community Research Ethics Office (http:// www.communityresearchethics.com/), and from scholars including Danielle Alcock et al., "Developing Ethical Research Practices between Institutional and Community Partners: A Look at the Current Base of Literature Surrounding Memorandums of Understanding in Canada," *International Indigenous Policy Journal* 8, no. 4 (2017), article 3; Budd Hall et al., eds., *Knowledge, Democracy and Action: Community-University Research Partnerships* (Manchester: Manchester University Press); and Meredith Minkler and Nina Wallerstein, eds., *Community-Based Participatory Research for Health: From Process to Outcomes* (San Francisco: Jossey-Bass, 2011).

12 Patricia Hill Collins, "The Difference that Power Makes: Intersectionality and Participatory Democracy," *Investigaciones Feministas* 8, no. 1 (2017): 34–5.

13 Vera Schattan Ruas Pereira Coelho and Laura Waisbich, "Participatory Mechanisms and Inequality Reduction: Searching for Plausible Relations," *Journal of Public Deliberation* 12, no. 2 (2016): article 13, 13.

14 This term draws upon the distinction between "smooth" and "striated" space as discussed in Gilles Deleuze and Félix Guattari, *A Thousand Plateaus: Capitalism and Schizophrenia* (Minneapolis: University of Minnesota Press, 1987). See also, Flora Lysen and Patricia Pisters, "Introduction: The Smooth and the Striated," *Deleuze Studies* 6, no. 1 (2012): 1–5.

15 We include in here works by Iris Marion Young; see, for example, *Inclusion and Democracy*; and "Polity and Group Difference: A Critique of the Ideal of Universal Citizenship," *Ethics* 99, no. 2 (1989): 250–74. We also include Michel Foucault's thinking about governmentality, as well as that of scholars such as Natalie Clark, who proposes Red intersectionality to inform our thinking about relationships between public policy and violence in the lives of Indigenous girls. In particular, she highlights the importance of "[centring] the knowledge of Indigenous girls and affected Indigenous communities and [supporting] Indigenous researchers and policy

processes grounded in Indigenous epistemologies"; see Natalie Clark, "Red Intersectionality and Violence-informed Witnessing Praxis with Indigenous Girls," *Girlhood Studies* 9, no. 2 (2016): 50, 46–64. doi:10.3167 /ghs.2016.090205.

16 Yanow, "Interpretation in Policy Analysis," 111.

17 Frank Fischer, 2007, "Policy Analysis in the Critical Perspective: The Epistemics of Discursive Practices," *Critical Policy Analysis* 1, no. 1 (2007): 97–109.

18 Paolo Freire, *Education for Critical Consciousness* (New York: Seabury Press, 1973).

19 David R.H. Moscrop and Mark E. Warren, "When Is Deliberation Democratic?" *Journal of Public Deliberation* 12, no. 2 (2016): article 4, 3.

20 Ibid., 1.

21 See, for example, Robyn Maynard, *Policing Black Lives: State Violence in Canada from Slavery to the Present* (Black Point, NS: Fernwood, 2017).

22 Michael Elliott, "Indigenous Resurgence: The Drive for Renewed Engagement and Reciprocity in the Turn Away from the State," *Canadian Journal of Political Science* 51, no. 1, 61–81.

Bibliography

Abelson, Julia, and François-Pierre Gauvin. *Transparency, Trust, and Citizen Engagement*. Ottawa: Canadian Policy Research Networks, 2004.

Abelson, Julia, Pierre-Gerlier Forest, Ann Casebeer, and Gail Mackean. "Will It Make a Difference if I Show Up and Share? A Citizens' Perspective on Improving Public Involvement Processes for Health System Decision-Making." *Journal of Health Services Research and Policy* 9, no. 4 (2004): 205–12.

Abelson, Julia, Pierre-Gerlier Forest, John Eyles, Ann Casebeer, Elisabeth Martin, and Gail Mackean. "Examining the Role of Context in the Implementation of a Deliberative Public Participation Experiment: Results from a Canadian Comparative Study." *Social Science and Medicine* 64 (2007): 2115–28.

Abelson, Julia, Pierre-Gerlier Forest, John Eyles, Patricia Smith, Elisabeth Martin, and Francois-Pierre Gauvin. "Deliberations about Deliberative Methods: Issues in the Design and Evaluation of Public Participation Processes." *Social Science & Medicine* 57, no. 2 (2003): 239–51. doi:10.1016 /S0277-9536(02)00343-X.

Abji, Salina. "Post-nationalism Reconsidered: A Case Study of the No One Is Illegal Movement in Canada." *Citizenship Studies* 17, no. 3–4 (2013): 322–38.

Ackerly, Brooke A. "Feminist Theory, Global Gender Justice, and the Evaluation of Grant-Making." *SSRN Electronic Journal* 37, no. 2 (2009). Online at http://ssrn.com/paper=1348902.

Ahmed, Saeed, and Christina Walker. "There has been, on average, 1 school shooting every week this year." *CNN*, 25 May 2018. Online at https://www .cnn.com/2018/03/02/us/school-shootings-2018-list-trnd/index.html.

Ahmed, Sarah. *On Being Included: Racism and Diversity in Institutional Life*. Durham, NC: Duke University Press, 2012.

Aitamurto, Tanja. "Crowdsourcing for Democracy: A New Era in Policy-Making." Helsinki: Parliament of Finland, Committee for the Future, 2015.

Alcock, Danielle, Jennifer Elgie, Chantelle Richmond, and Jerry White. "Developing Ethical Research Practices between Institutional and

Community Partners: A Look at the Current Base of Literature Surrounding Memorandums of Understanding in Canada." *International Indigenous Policy Journal* 8, no. 4 (2017).

Alemany, Cecilia, Fernanda Hopenhaym, and Nerea Craviotto, "Implementing the Paris Declaration: Implications for the Promotion of Women's Rights and Gender Equality." Paper commissioned by the Canadian Council on International Cooperation, January 2008. Online at https://www.awid .org/sites/default/files/atoms/files/implementing_the_paris_declaration _implications_for_the_promotion_of_womens_rights.pdf.

Alexander, Bruce K. "Dislocation Theory of Addiction." 26 December 2010. Online at http://www.brucekalexander.com/articles-speeches/dislocation -theory-addiction/250-change-of-venue-3.

Alexander, Bruce K. "The Globalization of Addiction." *Addiction Research* 8, no. 6 (2001): 501–26.

Alexander, Bruce K. *The Globalization of Addiction: A Study in Poverty of the Spirit*. New York: Oxford University Press, 2008.

Alexander, Bruce K. "Replacing the Official View of Addiction." In *To Fix or to Heal: Patient Care, Public Health, and the Limits of Biomedicine*, edited by Joseph E. Davis and Ana Marta Gonzalez, Kindle., Loc 4528–5180. New York: New York University Press, 2016.

Alexander, Bruce K., Barry L. Beyerstein, Patricia F. Hadaway, and Robert B. Coambs. "Effect of Early and Later Colony Housing on Oral Ingestion of Morphine in Rats." *Pharmacology Biochemistry and Behavior* 15 (1981): 571–6.

Alexander, Bruce K., Robert B. Coambs, and Patricia F. Hadaway. "The Effect of Housing and Gender on Morphine Self-Administration in Rats." *Psychopharmacology* 58, no. 2 (1978): 175–9. https://doi.org/10.1007/BF00426903.

Alfred, Taiaiake. *Wasáse: Indigenous Pathways of Action and Freedom*. Toronto: University of Toronto Press, 2005.

Allen, Danielle, and Jennifer S. Light, eds. *From Voice to Influence: Understanding Citizenship in a Digital Age*. Chicago: University of Chicago Press, 2015.

Amnesty International. *Out of Sight, Out of Mind: Gender, Indigenous Rights, and Energy Development in Northeast British Columbia*. London: Amnesty International, 2016. Online at https://www.amnesty.ca/sites/amnesty /files/Out%20of%20Sight%20Out%20of%20Mind%20EN%20FINAL_0.pdf

Amnesty International. *Stolen Sisters: A Human Rights Response to Discrimination and Violence against Indigenous Women in Canada*. Ottawa: Amnesty International Canada, October 2004. Online at https://www.amnesty.ca /news/stolen-sisters-human-rights-response-discrimination-and-violence -against-indigenous-women.

Anderson, Kim, and Bonita Lawrence. *Strong Women Stories: Native Vision and Community Survival*. Toronto: Sumach Press, 2003.

Anderson, Lynell, Morna Ballantyne, and Martha Friendly. "Child Care for All of Us: Universal Child Care for Canadians by 2020." Ottawa: Canadian Centre for Policy Alternatives, 2016. Online at https://www.policyalternatives.ca/sites /default/files/uploads/publications/National%20Office/2016/12/Child_Care _AFB2017_technical_paper.pdf.

Andersson, Claes. "Complexity Science and Sustainability Transitions." *Environmental Innovation and Societal Transitions* 11 (2014): 50–3. doi:10.1016/ j.eist.2014.03.001.

Andone, Dakine . "What you should know about the March for Our Lives," *CNN*, 21 March 2018. Online at https://www.cnn.com/2018/03/21/us/ march-for-our-lives-explainer/index.html.

Arendt, Hannah. *The Human Condition.* Chicago: University of Chicago Press, 1958.

Arthur, Joyce. "Honouring the Truth for Vancouver's Missing and Murdered Women." *Rabble.ca.* Vancouver, 2 November, 2012.

Arutyunova, Angelika, and Cindy Clark. *Watering the Leaves, Starving the Roots: The Status of Financing for Women's Rights Organizing and Gender Equality.* Toronto: Association for Women's Rights in Development, 2013.

Ashforth, Adam. "Reckoning Schemes of Legitimation: On Commissions of Inquiry as Power/Knowledge Forms." *Journal of Historical Sociology* 3, no. 1 (1990): 1–22.

Association for Women's Rights in Development. "Intersectionality: A Tool for Gender and Economic Justice." *Women's Rights and Economic Change* 9 (August 2004): 1–8.

Association of Universities and Colleges of Canada. *Creating Opportunities in Education for Aboriginal Students.* 2013. Online at https://www.univcan.ca /media-room/publications/creating-opportunities-in-education-for -aboriginal-students/.

Attree, Pamela, Beverley French, Beth Milton, Susan Povall, Margaret Whitehead, and Jennie Popay. "The Experience of Community Engagement for Individuals: A Rapid Review of Evidence." *Health & Social Care in the Community* 19, no. 3 (2011): 250–60.

Aulich, Chris. "From Citizen Participation to Participatory Governance in Australian Local Governance." *Commonwealth Journal of Local Governance* 1, no. 2 (2009): 44–60.

Azapagic, Adisa. "Developing a Framework for Sustainable Development Indicators for the Mining and Minerals Industry." *Journal of Cleaner Production* 12, no. 6 (2004): 639–62. https://doi.org/10.1016/S0959-6526(03)00075-1.

Baccaro, Lucio, and Konstantinos Papadakis. *The Promise and Perils of Participatory Policy-Making.* Geneva: International Institute for Labour Studies and International Labour Organization, 2008.

Baeder, Angela Martins. "Educação ambiental e mobilização social: formação de catadores na grande São Paulo" [Environmental education and social mobilization: Recyclers formation in greater São Paulo]. PhD diss., Universidade de São Paulo–São Paulo. 2009.

Ball, David. "Amnesty International and Native groups release scathing open letter about Pickton inquiry." *Vancouver Observer*, 10 April 2012.

Ball, David. "Missing women: Dave Pickton among 20 outstanding witness requests ignored since 2011." *Vancouver Observer*, 19 April 2012.

Ball, David. "Missing women inquiry ends in outrage: 'We need more answers, what really happened?" *Rabble.ca*, 8 June 2012.

Barker, Adam J. "'A direct act of resurgence, a direct act of sovereignty': Reflections on Idle No More, Indigenous Activism, and Canadian Settler Colonialism." *Globalizations* 12, no. 1 (2015): 43–65.

Barmak, Sarah. "Attawapiskat First Nation Chief Theresa Spence ends hunger strike." *Toronto Star*, 25 January 2013. Online at https://www.thestar.com /news/insight/2013/01/25/attawapiskat_first_nation_chief_theresa _spence_ends_hunger_strike.html, accessed 20 October 2017.

Barnetson, Bob, and Jason Foster. "The Political Justification of Migrant Workers in Alberta, Canada." *International Migration and Integration* 15 (2014): 349–70.

Barney, Darin. *Communication Technology*. Vancouver: UBC Press, 2011.

Barney, Darin. ""Excuse us if we don't give a fuck": The (Anti-) Political Career of Participation." *Jeunesse: Young People, Texts, Cultures* 2, no. 2 (2010): 138146.

Barney, Darin. "Politics and Emerging Media: The Revenge of Publicity." *Global Media Journal* 1, no. 1 (2008): 89–106.

Barrett, Gregory, Miriam Wyman, and Vera Schattan P. Coehlo. "Assessing the Policy Impacts of Deliberative Civic Engagement." In *Democracy in Motion: Evaluating the Practice and Impact of Deliberative Civic Engagement*, edited by Tina Nabatchi, John Gastil, Matt Leighninger, and G. Michael Weiksner, 182–201. Oxford: Oxford University Press, 2012.

Bartczak, Lori. "The Role of Grantmakers in Collective Impact." *Stanford Social Innovation Review* (Fall 2014): 8–10.

Bataillon, Gilles. "Caza de brujas en Managua." *Letras Libres* (31 December 2008): 72–5.

Batliwala, Srilatha, and Alexandra Pittman. "Capturing Change in Women's Realities: A Critical Overview of Current Monitoring & Evaluation Frameworks and Approaches." Toronto: Association for Women's Rights in Development, 2010. Online at https://www.awid.org/sites/default/files /atoms/files/capturing_change_in_womens_realities.pdf.

Bator, Francis M. "The Anatomy of Market Failure." *Quarterly Journal of Economics* 72, no. 3 (1958): 351–71.

Battiste, Marie. *Decolonizing Education: Nourishing the Learning Spirit*. Saskatoon: Purich, 2013.

Bazeley, Patricia. *Qualitative Data Analysis: Practical Strategies*. Thousand Oaks, CA: SAGE, 2013.

Beausoleil, Emily. "Responsibility as Responsiveness: Enacting a Dispositional Ethics of Encounter." *Political Theory* 45, no. 3 (2017): 291–318.

Becher, Tony, and Paul R. Trowler. *Academic Tribes and Territories: Intellectual Enquiry and the Culture of Disciplines.* 2nd ed. Buckingham, UK: SRHE & Open University Press, 2001. https://doi.org/10.1306/74D70B87-2B21-11D7 -8648000102C1865D.

Bedford, Kate, and Shirin M. Rai. "Feminists Theorize International Political Economy." *Signs: Journal of Women in Culture and Society* 36, no. 1 (2010): 1–18. https://doi.org/10.1086/652910.

Bedinger, Lisa. "Let's Talk: Dialogue and Deliberation in Higher Education." In *Resolving Community Conflicts and Problems: Public Deliberation and Sustained Dialogue,* edited by Roger Lohmann and Jon Van Til, 59–76. New York: Columbia University Press, 2011.

Beneria, Lourdes. "Globalization, Gender and the Davos Man." *Feminist Economics* 5, no. 3 (1999): 61–83.

Benhabib, Seyla. "Toward a Deliberative Model of Democratic Legitimacy." In *Democracy and Difference: Contesting the Boundaries of the Political,* edited by Seyla Benhabib, 67–94. Princeton, NJ: Princeton University Press, 1996.

Bennett, D., D. Eby, K. Govender, and K. Pacey. *Blueprint for an Inquiry: Learning from the Failures of the Missing Women Commission of Inquiry.* Vancouver: B.C. Civil Liberties Association, West Coast LEAF, & Pivot Legal Society, 2012.

Bennett, W. Lance, and Alexandra Segerberg. "The Logic of Connective Action: Digital Media and the Personalization of Contentious Politics." *Information, Communication & Society* 15, no. 5 (2012): 739–68.

Bergeron, Suzanne. "Political Economy Discourses of Globalization and Feminist Politics." *Signs* 26, no. 4 (2001): 983–1006.

Berkhout, Frans, Adrian Smith, and Andy Stirling. "Socio-Technological Regimes and Transition Contexts." In *System Innovation and the Transition to Sustainability,* edited by Boelie Elzen, Frank W Geels, and Kenneth Green, 48–75. Cheltenham, UK: Edward Elgar, 2004.

Berkman, Lisa F., Thomas Glass, Ian Brissette, and Teresa E. Seeman. "From Social Integration to Health: Durkheim in the New Millennium." *Social Science & Medicine* 51, no. 6 (2000): 843–57. https://doi.org/10.1016/S0277 -9536(00)00065-4.

Better Aid. "Development Effectiveness in Development Cooperation: A Rights-Based Perspective." October 2010. Online at https://www.ituc-csi.org/IMG /pdf/betteraid_development_effectiveness_dev_cooperation_1_.pdf.

Bickford, Susan. *The Dissonance of Democracy: Listening, Conflict, and Citizenship.* Utica, NY: Cornell University Press, 1996.

Bidaseca, Karina, and Vanesa Vázquez Laba. "Feminismos y (des) colonialidad: las voces de las mujeres indigenas del sur." *Tema de Mujeres* 7, no. 7 (2011): 24–42. Online at http://ojs.filo.unt.edu.ar/index.php /temasdemujeres/article/view/44/44.

Biebricher, Thomas. "Neoliberalism and Democracy." *Constellations* 22, no. 2 (2015): 255–66.

Bimber, Bruce, Cynthia Stohl, and Andrew J. Flanagin. "Technological Change and the Shifting Nature of Political Organization." In *Routledge Handbook of Internet Politics*, edited by Andrew Chadwick and Philip N. Howard, 72–85. Abingdon, UK: Routledge, 2009.

Bindra, Tanya Kaur. "In Pictures: The Misery of Migrant Workers." *Al Jazeera*, 18 December 2012. Online at https://www.aljazeera.com/indepth/inpictures /2012/12/20121217981786357.html.

Bissio, Roberto. "Application of the Criteria for Periodic Evaluation of Global Development Partnerships – as Defined in Millennium Development Goal 8 – from the Right to Development Perspective: The Paris Declaration on Aid Effectiveness." Geneva: Working Group on the Right to Development, 2008.

Bivens, Felix, Johanna Haffenden, and Budd L. Hall, "Knowledge, Higher Education, and the Institutionalization of Community-University Research Partnerships." In *Strengthening Community University Research Partnerships: Global Perspectives*, edited by Budd Hall, Rajesh Tandon, and Crystal Tremblay, 5–30. Victoria: University of Victoria, 2015.

Black, Laura, Stephanie Burkhalter, John Gastil, and Jennifer Stromer-Galley. "Methods for Analyzing and Measuring Group Deliberation." In *Sourcebook of Political Communication Research Methods, Measures and Analytical Techniques*, edited by L. Holbert, 323–45. New York: Routledge, 2008.

Blankenship, K.M., S.R. Friedman, S. Dworkin, and J.E. Mantell. "Structural Interventions: Concepts, Challenges and Opportunities for Research." *Journal of Urban Health* 83, no. 1 (2006): 59–72. https://doi.org/10.1007/s11524-005 -9007-4.

Bohm, David. *On Dialogue*, edited by Lee Nichol. E-Library. London: Routledge, 1996.

Boler, Megan. "The Risks of Empathy: Interrogating Multiculturalism's Gaze." *Cultural Studies* 11, no. 2 (1997): 253–73.

Borg, Carmel, Bernard Cauchi, and Peter Mayo. "Museums Education and Cultural Contestation." *Journal of Mediterranean Studies* 13, no. 1 (2013): 89–108.

Borg, Carmel, and Peter Mayo. "Adult Education as Cultural Politics." *New Directions in Adult and Continuing Learning* 127 (2010): 35–44.

Boserup, Esther. *Women's Role in Economic Development*. London: George Allen & Unwin, 1970.

Botes, Annatjie. "A Comparison between the Ethics of Justice and the Ethics of Care." *Journal of Advanced Nursing* 32, no. 5 (2000): 1071–5. https://doi.org /10.1046/j.1365-2648.2000.01576.x.

Boti, Mari, and Malcolm Guy, dir. *End of Immigration*. Montreal: Diffusion Multi-Monde, 2013. DVD.

Bourgon, Jocelyne. "NS Live Case Series 2017: Overcoming Poverty Together, New Brunswick Citizen-centric Perspectives." Ottawa: Public Governance International, November 2017. Online at http://www.pgionline.com/wp-content/uploads/2017/12/OvercomingPovertyNB.ebook_1.pdf.

Bowler, Shaun, Todd Donovan, and Jeffrey A. Karp. "Enraged or Engaged? Preferences for Direct Citizen Participation in Affluent Democracies." *Political Research Quarterly* 60, no. 3 (2007): 351–62.

Boyer, Ernest L. *College: The Undergraduate Experience in America*. New York: Harper & Row, 1987.

Brabham, Daren C. "Crowdsourcing as a Model for Problem Solving: An Introduction and Cases." *Convergence* 14, no. 1 (2008): 75–90.

Brady, M. "Researching Governmentality Studies through Ethnography: The Case of Australian Welfare Reforms and Programs for Single Parents." *Critical Policy Studies* 5, no. 3 (2011): 264–82.

Brandão, Carlos Rodrigues. *Pesquisa participante*. São Paulo: Brasilience, 1982.

Briones, Leah. "Rights with Capabilities: A New Paradigm for Social Justice in Migrant Activism." *Studies in Social Justice* 5, no. 1 (2011): 127–43.

Brock, Kathy. *Improving Connections between Governments and Nonprofit and Voluntary Organizations: Public Policy and the Third Sector*. Montreal; Kingston, ON: McGill-Queen's University Press, 2002.

Broman, Göran Ingvar, and Karl-Henrik Robèrt. "A Framework for Strategic Sustainable Development." *Journal of Cleaner Production* 140, no. 1 (2017): 17–31. doi:10.1016/j.jclepro.2015.10.121.

Bronfenbrenner, Urie. *The Ecology of Human Development: Experiments by Nature and Design*. Cambridge, MA: Harvard University Press, 1979.

Brooks, Margaret. "Drawing, Thinking, Meaning." Loughborough, UK: University of Loughborough, September 2003. Online at https://www.lboro.ac.uk/microsites/sota/tracey/journal/thin/brooks.html.

Brown, Stephen, and Morton, Bill. "Reforming Aid and Development Cooperation: Accra, Doha and Beyond." Policy Note. Ottawa: North-South Institute, August 2008. Online at http://www.nsi-ins.ca/content/download/DAW_policy.pdf.

Buber, Martin. *I and Thou*. Translated by Walter Kaufmann. New York: Charles Scribner's Sons, 1970.

Buchanan, David R. *An Ethic for Health Promotion: Rethinking the Sources of Human Well-Being*. New York: Oxford University Press, 2000.

Buchanan, David R. "Perspective: A New Ethic for Health Promotion: Reflections on a Philosophy of Health Education for the 21st Century." *Health Education & Behavior* 33, no. 3 (2006): 290–304. https://doi.org/10.1177/1090198105276221.

Buchanan, James, and Gordon Tullock. *Calculus of Consent*. Ann Arbor: University of Michigan Press, 1962.

Bullard, Robert, and Glenn Johnson. "Environmental Justice: Grassroots Activism and Its Impact on Public Policy Decision Making." *Journal of Social Issues* 56, no. 3 (2000): 556–78. https://doi.org/10.1111/0022-4537.00184.

Burch, Sarah, Mark Andrachuk, Dustin Carey, Niki Frantzeskaki, Heike Schroeder, Niklas Mischkowski, and Derk Loorbach. "Governing and Accelerating Transformative Entrepreneurship: Exploring the Potential for Small Business Innovation on Urban Sustainability Transitions." *Current Opinion in Environmental Sustainability* 22 (2016): 26–32. doi:10.1016/j.cosust .2017.04.002.

Burch, Sarah, Alison Shaw, Ann Dale, and John Robinson. "Triggering Transformative Change: A Development Path Approach to Climate Change Response in Communities." *Climate Policy* 14, no. 4 (2014): 467–87. doi:10.1080 /14693062.2014.876342.

Burkhalter, Stephanie, John Gastil, and Todd Kelshaw. "A Conceptual Definition and Theoretical Model of Public Deliberation in Small Face-to-Face Groups." *Communication Theory* 12, no. 4 (2002): 398–422.

Burns, William David, and Margaret Klawunn. "The Web of Caring: An Approach to Accountability in Alcohol Policy." In *Designing Alcohol and Other Drug Prevention Programs in Higher Education: Bringing Theory into Practice*, 49–124. Newton, MA: Higher Education Development Center for Alcohol and Other Drug Prevention, 1997. Online at https://safesupportivelearning .ed.gov/sites/default/files/hec/product/designing-theory.pdf.

Burton, Paul. "Conceptual, Theoretical and Practical Issues in Measuring the Benefits of Public Participation." *Evaluation* 15, no. 3 (2009): 263–84.

Busan Partnership for Effective Development Cooperation. "Busan Outcome Document. Busan, South Korea, 29 December 2011. Online at http://www .oecd.org/dac/effectiveness/49650173.pdf.

Cabaj, Mark. "Pathways to Change: Somewhere between a Butterfly & a Blueprint." Presented at Energy Futures Lab workshop, Edmonton, 26 January 2016.

Caddy, Joanne. *Evaluating Public Participation in Policy-Making*. Paris: OECD Publishing, 2005.

Campbell, Charles. "At Ground Zero for Vancouver's Towering Debate." *Tyee*, 25 June 2013. Online at https://thetyee.ca/Opinion/2013/06/25/Vancouver -Tower-Debate/.

Canada. "The Canadian Media Production Association and Cumulative Duration in the Temporary Foreign Workers Program (F-7363)." Ottawa: Citizenship and Immigration Canada, 2011.

Canada. "Overhauling the Temporary Foreign Workers Program: Putting Canadians First." Ottawa: Government of Canada, 2014.

Canada. "Temporary Foreign Worker Program and Live-in Caregiver Program (Worker Protection)." Ottawa: Citizenship and Immigration Canada, 2013.

Canada. Department of Foreign Affairs, Trade and Development. "Results-Based Management for International Assistance: A How-to Guide." Ottawa, 2018. Online at http://www.international.gc.ca/world-monde/funding-financement/results_based_management-gestion_axee_resultats-guide.aspx?lang=eng.

Canada. Health Canada. *First Nations Mental Wellness Continuum Framework.* Ottawa: Health Canada, January 2015. Online at: http://www.thunderbirdpf.org/wp-content/uploads/2015/01/24-14-1273-FN-Mental-Wellness-Framework-EN05_low.pdf.

Canada. Parliament. House of Commons. Standing Committee on Citizenship and Immigration. *Minutes of Proceedings,* 40th Parliament, 2nd Session, Meeting 37. Ottawa, 2009. Online at https://www.ourcommons.ca/DocumentViewer/en/42-1/CIMM/meeting-106/minutes.

Canada. Parliament. House of Commons. Standing Committee on Human Resources, Skills and Social Development and the Status of Persons with Disabilities. *Minutes of Proceedings,* 42nd Parliament, 1st Session, Meeting 11. Ottawa, 2016. Online at https://www.ourcommons.ca/Committees/en/HUMA/StudyActivity?studyActivityId=8845433.

Canada Without Poverty. *2017 Poverty Progress Profiles.* Online at http://www.cwp-csp.ca/wp-content/uploads/2018/03/2017-Poverty-Progress-Profiles-318.pdf.

Canadian Council for Refugees. "Migrant Workers Provincial and Federal Government Report Cards." Ottawa: Canadian Council for Refugees, 2013. Online at http://ccrweb.ca/files/migrant-worker-report-cards.pdf, accessed 10 May 2018.

Canadian Environmental Assessment Agency. *Building Common Ground – A New Vision for Impact Assessment in Canada: The Final Report of the Expert Panel for the Review of Environmental Assessment Processes.* Ottawa: Canadian Environmental Assessment Agency, 2017. Online at https://www.canada.ca/content/dam/themes/environment/conservation/environmental-reviews/building-common-ground/building-common-ground.pdf.

Canadian Environmental Assessment Agency. "Environmental Assessment Process Managed by the Agency." Ottawa: Canadian Environmental Assessment Agency, May 2013. Online at https://www.canada.ca/content/dam/ceaa-acee/documents/environmental-assessments/basics-environmental-assessment/environmental-assessment-process.pdf, accessed 5 November 2017.

Canadian Institute for Substance Use Research. "A Framework for Thought and Action: Substance Use Policy on Campus." Victoria: University of Victoria, 2017. Online at https://healthycampuses.ca/wp-content/uploads/2017/05/Substance-Use-Policy-on-Campus.pdf.

Canadian Institute for Substance Use Research. "Understanding Substance Use: A Health Promotion Perspective." Victoria: University of Victoria, 2013. Online at http://www.heretohelp.bc.ca/sites/default/files/understanding -substance-use-a-health-promotion-perspective.pdf.

Cancialosi, Chris. "Collective Impact: A Collaborative Approach to Create Change." Forbes, 15 September 2015. Online at https://www.forbes.com /sites/chriscancialosi/2015/09/15/collective-impact-a-collaborative -approach-to-creating-change/, accessed 1 March 2018.

Caniglia, Guido, Niko Schapke, Daniel J Lang, David J Abson, Christopher Luederitz, Arnim Wiek, Manfred D Laubichler, Fabienne Gralla, and Henrik von Wehrden. "Experiments and Evidence in Sustainability Science: A Typology." Journal of Cleaner Production (29 June 2017): 1–10. doi:10.1016 /j.jclepro.2017.05.164.

Cannon, Barry, and Mo Hume. "Civil Society-State Relations in Left-Led El Salvador, Honduras and Nicaragua." In Civil Society and the State in Left-Led Latin America: Challenges and Limitations to Democratization, edited by Barry Cannon and Peadar Kirby, 3–16. London: Zed Books, 2012.

Carpenter, Daniel, and David. A. Moss, eds. Preventing Regulatory Capture: Special Interest Influence and How to Limit It. Cambridge: Cambridge University Press, 2013.

Carpentier, Nico. Media and Participation: A Site of Ideological-Democratic Struggle. Bristol, UK: Intellect Books, 2011.

Cattapan, Alana, and Françoise Baylis. "Egg Donors and Surrogates Need High-Quality Care." Conversation (blog), 27 September 2017. Online at http://theconversation.com/egg-donors-and-surrogates-need-high-quality -care-84664.

Cattell, Lindsay, Sarah Chevalier, Trinetta Chong, Nicole Danna, Sasha Feldstein, Nereida Heller, Bryan Klickstein, Anna Maier, Terra Rose, and Sarah Steele Wilson. Participatory Policymaking: A Toolkit for Social Change. Berkeley: University of California, Berkeley, Goldman School of Public Policy, 2015. Online at https://gspp.berkeley.edu/assets/uploads/page /GSPP_Participatory_Policy_Toolkit_Version_1.pdf.

Chambers, Sam. The Lesson of Rancière. Oxford: Oxford University Press, 2014.

Chambers, Simone. "Deliberative Democratic Theory." Annual Review of Political Science 6 (2003): 307–26.

Chambers, Simone, and Anne Costain. Deliberation, Democracy, and the Media. Lanham, MD: Rowman & Littlefield, 2000.

Charney, Nicholas. "The future of documentary heritage GovCamp Canada." GovCamp Canada. 2011.

Chen, Yea-Wen. "Public Engagement Exercises with Racial and Cultural 'Others': Some Thoughts, Questions, and Considerations." Journal of Public Deliberation 10, no. 1 (2014).

Chernikova, Elena. "Aboriginal Peoples: Fact Sheet for New Brunswick." Ottawa: Statistics Canada, 2016. Online at https://www150.statcan.gc.ca /n1/en/pub/89-656-x/89-656-x2016005-eng.pdf?st=9fxadm59.

Childers, Sara M. "Getting in Trouble: Feminist Postcritical Policy Ethnography in an Urban School." *Qualitative Inquiry* 17, no. 4 (2011): 345–54.

Chilvers, Jason, and Matthew Kearnes. "Remaking Participation: Toward Reflexive Engagement." In *Remaking Participation: Science, Environment and Emergent Publics*, edited by Jason Chilvers and Matthew Kearnes, 261–88. London: Routledge, 2016.

Cho, Sumi, Kimberlé Williams Crenshaw, and Leslie McCall. "Toward a Field of Intersectionality Studies: Theory, Applications, and Praxis." *Signs* 38, no. 4 (2013): 785–810.

Chou, Mark, Jean-Paul Gagnon, and Lesley Pruitt. "Putting Participation on Stage: Examining Participatory Theatre as an Alternative Site for Political Participation." *Policy Studies* 36, no. 6 (2015): 607–22.

Christopher, David. "OpenMedia: Working toward an Open Connected Future." In *Strategies for Media Reform: International Perspectives*, edited by Des Freedman, Jonathan Obar, Cheryl Martens, and Robert W. McChesney, 115–207. New York: Fordham University Press, 2016.

Citizens' Assembly on the Grandview-Woodland Community Plan. *Final Report*. Vancouver, June 2015. Online at http://www.grandview-woodland .ca/download/final-report-citizens-assembly%e2%80%a8on-th e-grandview-woodland-community-plan-low-resolution-2/, accessed 24 March 2018.

City of Vancouver. *Grandview-Woodland Community Plan: Goals, Objectives & Emerging Policies*. June 2013. Online at https://vancouver.ca/files/cov /grandview-woodland-community-plan.pdf, accessed 24 March 2018.

City of Vancouver. "Grandview-Woodland Community Profile – 2014." Online at https://studylib.net/doc/8097196/grandview-woodland-community -profile-2014.

City of Vancouver. *Trace Document – How the Plant Responds to the Citizens' Assembly's Recommendations*. June 2016. Online at https://vancouver.ca /files/cov/grandview-woodland-community-plan-trace-document.pdf., accessed 24 March 2018.

City of Vancouver Community Services and City of Vancouver Planning and Development Services. *Local Area Profile 2013*. November 2013.

City of Vancouver Planning and Development Services. "A Discussion Paper: A Citizens' Assembly for Grandview-Woodland." January 2014. Online at https://vancouver.ca/files/cov/Grandview-Woodlands-Citizens-Assembly -Discussion-Paper-2014-01-23.pdf, accessed 24 March 2018.

Clare, Eli. *Brilliant Imperfection: Grappling with Cure*. Durham, NC: Duke University Press, 2017.

Clark, Natalie. "Red Intersectionality and Violence-informed Witnessing Praxis with Indigenous Girls." *Girlhood Studies* 9, no. 2 (2016): 46–64. doi:10.3167 /ghs.2016.090205.

Clark, Natalie, Sarah Hunt, Georgia Jules, and Trevor Good. "Ethical Dilemmas in Community-Based Research: Working with Vulnerable Youth in Rural Communities." *Journal of Academic Ethics* 8, no. 4 (2010): 243–52.

Clegg, Sue, and Stephen Rowland. "Kindness in Pedagogical Practice and Academic Life." *British Journal of Sociology of Education* 31, no. 6. (2010): 719–35.

Clifford, Stacy. "Making Disability Public in Deliberative Democracy." *Contemporary Political Theory* 11, No. 2 (2012): 211–28.

Clover, Darlene. "Successes and Challenges of Feminist Arts-Based Participatory Methodologies with Homeless/Street-Involved Women in Victoria." *Action Research* 11, no. 9 (2011): 12–26.

Clover, Darlene E., Bruno de Oliveira Jayme, Bud L. Hall, and Shirley Follen. *The Nature of Transformation: Environmental Adult Education*. Rotterdam: Sense Publishers, 2013.

Clover, Darlene E., and Joyce Stalker, eds. *The Arts and Social Justice: Re-crafting Adult Education and Community Cultural Leadership*. Leicester, UK: National Institute of Adult Continuing Education, 2007.

Clover, Darlene, Joyce Stalker, and Laurie McGauley. *Feminist Popular Education and Community Arts/Crafts: The Case for New Directions*. Quebec City: CSSE, 2004.

Cohen, Cathy J., and Joseph Kahne. *Participatory Politics: New Media and Youth Political Action*. Oakland, CA: YPP Research Network, 31 May 2012. Online at https://dmlhub.net/wp-content/uploads/files/YPP_Survey_Report _FULL(1).pdf.

Cohen, Joshua. "Procedure and Substance in Deliberative Democracy." In *Democracy and Difference: Contesting the Boundaries of the Political*, edited by Seyla Benhabib, 95–119. Princeton, NJ: Princeton University Press, 1996.

Cohen, Maurie J. "Ecological Modernization and Its Discontents: The American Environmental Movement's Resistance to an Innovation-Driven Future," *Futures* 3, no. 8 (2006): 528–47. http://doi.org/10.1016/j.futures .2005.09.002.

Cole, Ardra. L., and Maura McIntyre. *Arts-Informed Research for Public Education: The Alzheimer's Project*. Proceedings of the Canadian Association for the Study of Adult Education, Dalhousie University/University of King's College, Halifax, NS, 2003.

Coleman, Stephen, and Jay G. Blumler. *The Internet and Democratic Citizenship: Theory, Practice and Policy*. Cambridge: Cambridge University Press, 2009.

Collins, Patricia Hill. "The Difference that Power Makes: Intersectionality and Participatory Democracy." *Investigaciones Feministas* 8, no. 1 (2017), 34–5.

Community Vitality Advisory Group and Research Team. "The Wellbeing Experiences of Women in the Haisla Nation and the District of Kitimat." n.p., May 2018. Online at http://haisla.ca/wp-content/uploads/2018/06/With -Logo-FinalKitimatHaislaCVI-ReportMay-24-2018.pdf, accessed 21 June 2018.

Connell, Raewyn. "Southern Bodies and Disability: Re-thinking Concepts." *Third World Quarterly* 32 (2011): 1369–81.

Constable, Nicole. "Migrant Workers and the Many States of Protest in Hong Kong." *Critical Asian Studies* 41, no. 1 (2009): 143–64.

Cooper, Katherine. "'Wicked Problems': What Are They, and Why Are They of Interest to NNSI Researchers?" Evanston, IL: Northwestern University, School of Communication, Network for Nonprofit and Social Impact, 2017. Online at https://nnsi.northwestern.edu/social-impact/wicked-problems -what-are-they-and-why-are-they-of-interest-to-nnsi-researchers/, accessed 12 July 2017.

Cornwall, Andrea. "Revisiting the Gender Agenda." *IDS Bulletin* 38, no. 2 (2007): 69–78. Online at https://onlinelibrary.wiley.com/doi/abs/10.1111 /j.1759-5436.2007.tb00353.x.

Couldry, Nick. *Why Voice Matters: Culture and Politics after Neoliberalism*. Thousand Oaks, CA: SAGE, 2010.

Coulthard, Glen S. *Red Skin, White Masks: Rejecting the Colonial Politics of Recognition*. Minneapolis: University of Minnesota Press, 2014.

Coulthard, Glen S. "Subjects of Empire: Indigenous Peoples and the 'Politics of Recognization' in Canada." *Contemporary Political Theory* 6 (2007): 437–60.

Cowen, Emory L. "In Pursuit of Wellness." *American Psychologist* 46, no. 4 (1991): 404–8.

Cox, David, and Suzanne Mills. "Gendering Environmental Assessment: Women's Participation Employment Outcomes at Voisey's Bay." *Arctic* 68, no. 2 (2015): 246–60. https://doi.org/10.14430/arctic4478.

Crenshaw, Kimberlé. "Mapping the Margins: Intersectionality, Identity Politics, and Violence Against Women of Color." *Stanford Law Review* 43, no. 6 (1991): 1241–99. https://doi.org/10.2307/1229039.

Crouch, Colin. *Post-Democracy*. Cambridge, UK: Polity Press, 2004.

Culhane, Dara. "Their Spirits Live within Us: Aboriginal Women in Downtown Eastside Vancouver Emerging into Visibility." *American Indian Quarterly* 27, nos. 3-4 (2003): 593–606.

Culver, Keith, and Paul Howe. "Calling All Citizens: The Challenges of Public Consultation." *Canadian Public Administration* 47, no. 1 (2004): 52–75.

Dahl, Robert. *Democracy and Its Critics*. New Haven, CT: Yale University Press, 1989.

Dahlgren, Peter. *The Political Web: Media, Participation and Alternative Democracy*. Basingstoke, UK: Palgrave Macmillan, 2013.

Dalton, Russell J. *The Good Citizen: How a Younger Generation Is Reshaping American Politics*. Thousand Oaks, CA: SAGE, 2008.

Davison, Aidan. *Technology and the Contested Meanings of Sustainability*. Albany: State University of New York Press, 2001.

Deacon, Leith, and Jamie Baxter. "No Opportunity to Say No: A Case Study of Procedural Environmental Injustice in Canada." *Journal of Environmental Planning and Management* 56, no. 5 (2012): 607–23. https://doi.org/10.1080/09640568.2012.692502

DeJoy, David M. "Behavior Change versus Culture Change: Divergent Approaches to Managing Workplace Safety." *Safety Science* 43, no. 2 (2005): 105–29. https://doi.org/10.1081/JA-200033224.

De Lange, Naydene, Thi Lan Anh Nguyen, and Thi Thu Trang Nghiem. "Creating Dialogue on Inclusion in Vietnam." *Disability and Girlhood: Transnational Perspectives* 9, no. 1 (2016).

Deleuze, Gilles, and Felix Guattari. *A Thousand Plateaus: Capitalism and Schizophrenia*. Minneapolis: University of Minnesota Press, 1987.

Della Carpini, Michael X., Fay Lomax Cook, and Larry Jacobs. "Public Deliberation, Discursive Participation, and Citizen Engagement: A Review of the Empirical Literature." *Annual Review of Political Science* 7, no. 1 (2004): 315–44. doi:10.1146/annurev.polisci.7.121003.091630.

Della Porta, Donatella. "Communication in Movement: Social Movements as Agents of Participatory Democracy." *Information, Communication & Society* 14, no. 6 (2011): 800–19.

Dhamoon, Rita Kaur. "Considerations on Mainstreaming Intersectionality." *Political Research Quarterly* 64, no. 1 (2010): 230–43. https://doi.org/10.1177/1065912910379227

Dhillon, Christina, and Michael Young. "Environmental Racism and First Nations: A Call for Socially Just Public Policy Development." *Canadian Journal of Humanities and Social Science* 1, no. 1 (2009): 23–37. doi:10.1289/ehp.1205422

Dhillon, Jaskiran. *Prairie Rising: Indigenous Youth, Decolonization and the Politics of Intervention*. Toronto: University of Toronto Press, 2017.

Dillard, Kara. "Assessing the Problem of Gender Inequality in Deliberative Democracy." PhD. diss., Kansas State University, 2011. Online at http://krex.k-state.edu/dspace/bitstream/handle/2097/12005/KaraDillard2011.pdf?sequence=3&isAllowed=y.

Dingo, Rebecca. "Making the Unfit Fit: The Rhetoric of Mainstreaming in the World Bank's Commitment to Gender Equality and Disability Rights." *Wagadu* 4, no. 1 (2007): 93–107.

Dobrowolsky, Alexandra. "Of 'Special Interest': Interest, Identity and Feminist Constitutional Activism in Canada." *Canadian Journal of Political Science* 31, no. 4 (1998): 707–42.

Dobson, Andrew. *Listening for Democracy: Recognition, Representation, Reconciliation*. New York: Oxford University Press, 2014.

Domonoske, Camila. "Canadian First Nation declares state of emergency over suicide attempts," *NPR News*, 11 April 2016. Online at http://www.npr.org /sections/thetwo-way/2016/04/11/473784919/canadian-first-nation -declares-state-of-emergency-over-suicide-attempts, accessed 20 October 2017.

Donahue, Chip. *Family Engagement in the Digital Age*. New York: Routledge, 2017.

Doughty, Margaret. "Coalition Building: A Tool for Improved Community Literacy." Washington, DC: US Department of Education, March 2012.

Dryzek, John. *Deliberative Democracy and Beyond: Liberals, Critics, Contestations*. New York: Oxford University Press, 2000.

Dryzek, John. *Democracy in Capitalist Times: Ideals, Limits, and Struggles*. New York: Oxford University Press, 1996.

Dryzek, John. "Democratization as Deliberative Capacity Building," *Comparative Political Studies* 42, no. 11 (2009): 1379–402.

Dryzek, John S., André Bächtiger, and Karolina Milewicz. "Toward a Deliberative Global Citizens' Assembly." *Global Policy* 2, no. 1 (2011): 33–42. doi:10.1111 /j.1758-5899.2010.00052.x.

Ducote, Frank. "A stunning transformation is planned for Grandview-Woodlands. Is the community really ready for this?" *State of Vancouver: Frances Bula on City Life and Politics*, 12 June 2013. Online at http://www.francesbula.com /uncategorized/guest-post-from-frank-ducote-a-stunning-transformation-is -planned-for-grandview-woodlands-is-the-community-really-ready-for-this/, accessed 24 March 2018.

Duncan, Carol. *Civilizing Rituals*. London: Routledge, 2005.

Dunkelman, Marc. "The Transformation of American Community." *National Affairs* 41 (Summer 2011). Online at https://www.nationalaffairs.com /publications/detail/the-transformation-of-american-community., accessed 11 July 2019.

Dupuis-Déri, Francis. "Global Protesters versus Global Elites: Are Direct Action and Deliberative Politics Compatible?" *New Political Science* 29, no. 2 (2007): 167–89.

Durkheim, Emile. *Suicide: A Study in Sociology*. Translated by John A Spalding. New York: Simon & Schuster, 1951.

Ebrahim, Alnoor. "Accountability in Practice: Mechanisms for NGOs." *World Development* 31, no. 5 (2003): 813–29.

Eckersley, Richard M. "'Cultural Fraud': The Role of Culture in Drug Abuse." *Drug and Alcohol Review* 24, no. 2 (2005): 157–63. https://doi.org/10.1080 /09595230500102590.

Economic and Social Inclusion Corporation. "Looking Back to Move Forward: Renewal of Overcoming Poverty Together: The New Brunswick Economic and Social Inclusion Plan." Fredericton, [2019]. Online at https://nbtogether. ca/wp-content/uploads/2019/03/LookingBack2019_WEB_ENG.pdf.

Economic and Social Inclusion Corporation. "Overcoming Poverty Together: The New Brunswick Economic and Social Inclusion Plan 2014–2019."

Fredericton: ESIC, 2014. Online at http://www2.gnb.ca/content/dam/gnb
/Departments/esic/pdf/NBEconomicSocialInclusionPlan2014-2019.pdf.

Economic and Social Inclusion Corporation. "Public engagement process
concludes for renewed poverty reduction plan." News Release, 10 May 2019.
Online at https://www2.gnb.ca/content/gnb/en/departments/esic/news
/news_release.2019.05.0310.html

Edmondson, Jeff. "Using Feedback Loops to Move from Collaboration to
Collective Impact." *Forbes*, 31 October 2013. Online at https://www.forbes
.com/sites/ashoka/2013/10/31/using-feedback-loops-to-move-from
-collaboration-to-collective-impact/#5188b3fe6018, accessed 22 February 2018.

Elliott, Michael. "Indigenous Resurgence: The Drive for Renewed Engagement
and Reciprocity in the Turn Away from the State." *Canadian Journal of Political
Science* 51, no. 1 (2018): 61–81.

Elstub, Stephen, and Peter McIaverty. *Deliberative Democracy: Issues and Cases.*
Edinburgh: Edinburgh University Press, 2014.

Englund, Tomas. "Rethinking Democracy and Education: Towards an Education
of Deliberative Citizens." *Journal of Curriculum Studies* 32, no. 2 (2000): 305–13.
https://doi.org/10.1080/002202700182772.

Epp, Jake. "Achieving Health for All: A Framework for Health Promotion."
Ottawa: Health and Welfare Canada, 1986.

Erez, Miriam, and Efra Gati. "A Dynamic, Multi-Level Model of Culture: From
the Micro-Level of the Individual to the Macro-Level of a Global Culture."
Applied Psychology: An International Review 53, no. 4 (2004): 583–98. https://
doi.org/10.1111/j.1464-0597.2004.00190.x.

Ermine, Willie. "The Ethical Space of Engagement." *Indigenous Law Journal* 6,
no. 1 (2007): 193–203.

Eyben, Rosalind. "Hiding Relations: The Irony of 'Effective Aid.'" *European
Journal of Development Research* 22, no. 3 (2010): 382–97.

Eyben, Rosalind. "Struggles in Paris: The DAC and the Purposes of Development
Aid." *European Journal of Development Research* 25, no. 1 (2013): 78–91. https://
doi.org/10.1057/ejdr.2012.49.

Eyben, Rosalind. "What Is Happening to Donor Support for Women's Rights?"
Contestations: Dialogues on Women's Empowerment 4 (11 March 2011). Online
at https://www.contestations.net/issues/issue-4/what-is-happening-to-
donor-support-for-womens-rights-response-to-rosalind-eyben-2/.

Falleti, Tulia, and Julia Lynch. "Context and Causal Mechanisms in Political
Analysis." *Comparative Political Studies* 42, no. 9 (2009): 1143–66.

Falls Brook Centre. "Sustainable Communities: A Guide to Community Asset
Mapping." Knowlesville, NB, 2012. Online at https://ccednet-rcdec.ca/en
/toolbox/sustainable-communities-guide-community-asset-mapping.

Fals-Borda, Orlando. "The Application of Participatory Action-Research in
Latin America." *International Sociology* 2, no. 4 (1987): 329–47.

Faraday, Fay. *Made in Canada: How the Law Constructs Migrant Workers' Insecurity.* Toronto: Metcalf Foundation, 2012. Online at http://metcalffoundation.com /wp-content/uploads/2012/09/Made-in-Canada-Full-Report.pdf, accessed 10 May 2018.

Feenberg, Andrew. "Critical Theory of Communication Technology: Introduction to the Special Section." *Information Society* 25, no. 2 (2009): 77–83.

Feenberg, Andrew, and Norm Friesen. *(Re) Inventing the Internet.* Berlin: Springer Science + Business Media, 2012.

Femenías, María Luisa. "Esbozo de un feminismo latinoamericano." *Revista Estudios Feministas* 15, no. 1 (2007).

Ferber, Thaddeus, and Erin White. "Making Public Policy Collective Impact Friendly." *Stanford Social Innovation Review* 2014: 22–3.

Findlay, Tammy. *Femocratic Administration: Gender, Governance, and Democracy in Ontario.* Toronto: University of Toronto Press, 2015.

Findlay, Tammy, and Mary-Dan Johnston. "Public Services – Who Does What?" Ottawa: Canadian Research Institute for the Advancement of Women, August 2017.

Fink, Katherine, and Christopher W. Anderson. "Data Journalism in the United States: Beyond the 'Usual Suspects.'" *Journalism Studies* 16, no. 4 (2015): 467–81.

Fischer, Frank. *Democracy and Expertise: Reorienting Policy Inquiry.* New York: Oxford University Press, 2009.

Fischer, Frank. "Policy Analysis in the Critical Perspective: The Epistemics of Discursive Practices." *Critical Policy Analysis* 1, no. 1 (2007): 97–109.

Fish, Jennifer. *Domestic Workers of the World Unite!* New York: NYU Press, 2016.

Fisher, Mark. *Capitalist Realism: Is There No Alternative?* Winchester, UK: O Books, 2009.

Fishkin, James S. *When the People Speak: Deliberative Democracy and Public Consultation.* Oxford: Oxford University Press, 2009.

Floridia, Antonio. *From Participation to Deliberation: A Critical Genealogy of Deliberative Democracy.* Colchester, UK: ECPR Press, 2017.

Forester, John. *The Deliberative Practitioner: Encouraging Participatory Planning Processes.* Cambridge, MA: MIT Press, 1999.

Foucault, Michel. *Power/Knowledge: Selected Interviews and Other Writings 1972–1977.* Edited by Colin Gordon. Translated by Colin Gordon, Leo Marshall, John Mepham, and Kate Soper. New York: Pantheon Books, 1980.

Foundation for Tacoma Students. "Graduate Tacoma! 2018 Community Impact Report." Tacoma, WA: Foundation for Tacoma Students, 2018). Online at https://graduatetacoma.org/wp-content/uploads/2018/05/ImpactReport18 _040618-lo-res_FNL.pdf.

Frank, Thomas. *One Market under God: Extreme Capitalism, Market Populism, and the End of Economic Democracy.* Toronto: Anchor Canada, 2001.

Fraser, Nancy. "From Redistribution to Recognition? Dilemmas of Justice in a 'Postsocialist' Age." In *Justice Interruptus: Critical Reflections on the "Postsocialist" Condition*, 11–40. New York: Routledge, 1997. https://doi.org/10.1002/9780470756119.ch54.

Fraser, Nancy. "Rethinking the Public Sphere: A Contribution to the Critique of Actually Existing Democracy." *Social Text* 25/26 (1990): 56–80.

Friere, Paolo. *Education for Critical Consciousness*. New York: Seabury Press, 1973.

Friere, Paolo. *Pedagogia dos sonhos possíveis*. São Paulo: Unesp, 2001.

Friere, Paolo. *Pedagogy of the City*. New York: Continuum International, 1993.

Friere, Paolo. *The Pedagogy of the Oppressed*. New York: Continuum Press, 1997.

FSG. *Collective Impact Case Study: Memphis Fast Forward*. Case Study, Boston: FSG, 2013. Online at https://www.fsg.org/publications/memphis-fast-forward.

Fuller, Tony, Denyse Guy, and Carolyn Pletsch. "Asset Mapping: A Handbook." n.p., 2002.

Fung, Archon. "Deliberation before the Revolution: Toward an Ethics of Deliberative Democracy in an Unjust World." *Political Theory* 33, no. 2 (2005). 397–419.

Fung, Archon. "Recipes for Public Spheres: Eight Institutional Design Choices and Their Consequences." *Journal of Political Philosophy* 11, no. 3 (2003): 338–67.

Fung, Archon. "Varieties of Participation in Complex Governance." *Public Administration Review* 66, (2006): 66–75.

Fung, Archon, and Erik Olin Wright. "Countervailing Power in Empowered Participatory Governanace." In *Deepening Democracy: Institutional Innovations in Empowered Participatory Governance*, edited by Archon Fung and Erik Olin Wright, 259–80. London: Verso, 2003.

Gadamer, Hans-Georg. *Philosophical Hermeneutics*. Translated and Edited by David Linge. Los Angeles: University of California Press, 1977.

Gadamer, Hans-Georg. *Truth and Method*. Translated by Joel Weinsheimer and Donald G. Marshall. London: Bloomsbury Publishing, 2004.

Galabuzi, Grace-Edward. "Hegemonies, Continuities, and Discontinuities of Multiculturalism and the Anglo-Franco Conformity Order." In *Home and Native Land: Unsettling Multiculturalism in Canada*, edited by May Chazan, Lisa Helps, Anna Stanley and Sonali Thakkar, 105–48. Toronto: Between the Lines, 2011.

Gamble, D.J. "The Berger Inquiry: An Impact Assessment Process." *Science* 199, no. 4332 (1978): 946–52.

Gastil, John. *Political Communication and Deliberation*. Thousand Oaks, CA: SAGE, 2008

Gastil, John, and Peter Levine. *The Deliberative Democracy Handbook: Strategies for Effective Civic Engagement in the 21st Century*. San Francisco: Jossey-Bass, 2005.

Gaudry, Adam, and Danielle Lorenz. "Indigenization as Inclusion, Reconciliation, and Decolonization: Navigating the Different Visions for Indigenizing the Canadian Academy." *AlterNative*, 14, no. 3. (2018): 218–27.

Gaventa, John. "Can Participation 'Fix' Inequality? Unpacking the Relationship between the Economic and Political Citizenship." Innovation Series 5. Antigonish, NS: St Francis Xavier University, Coady International Institute, April 2016. Online at https://www.participatorymethods.org/sites /participatorymethods.org/files/Gaventa%20Coady%20Innovation %20series5%20Can%20participation%20fix%20inequality.pdf.

Gaventa, John, and Gregory Barrett. "Mapping the Outcomes of Citizen Engagement." *World Development* 40, no. 12 (2012): 2399–410.

Gaventa, John, and Gregory Barrett. "So What Difference Does It Make? Mapping the Outcomes of Citizen Engagement." IDS Working Papers 347 (1 October 2010): 1–72. doi:10.1111/j.2040-0209.2010.00347_2.x.

Geels, Frank W. "The Multi-Level Perspective on Sustainability Transitions: Responses to Seven Criticisms." *Environmental Innovation and Societal Transitions* 1, no. 1 (2011): 24–40. doi:10.1016/j.eist.2011.02.002.

Geels, Frank W. "Technological Transitions as Evolutionary Reconfiguration Processes: A Multi-Level Perspective and a Case-Study." *Research Policy* 31, no. 8 (2002): 1257–74. doi:10.1016/S0048-7333(02)00062-8.

Geels, Frank W., and Johan Schot. "Typology of Sociotechnical Transition Pathways." *Research Policy* 36, no. 3 (2007): 399–417. doi:10.1016/j.respol.2007 .01.003.

Gemmill, Angela. "Attawapiskat youth group cleans up community to cope during suicide crisis." *CBC News Sudbury*, 19 May 2016. Online at http:// www.cbc.ca/news/canada/sudbury/attawapiskat-youth-cleanup-litter-1 .3589138, accessed 20 October 2017.

Gill, Scherto. "'Holding Oneself Open in a Conversation' – Gadamer's Philosophical Hermeneutics and the Ethics of Dialogue." *Journal of Dialogue Studies* 3, no. 1 (2015): 9–28.

Gilligan, Carol. *In a Different Voice: Psychological Theory and Women's Development*. Cambridge, MA: Harvard University Press, 1982.

Gilmore, Scott. "The unasked question about Attawapiskat." *Maclean's*, 13 April 2016. Online at http://www.macleans.ca/news/canada/the-unasked -question-about-attawapiskat/, accessed 20 October 2017.

Goodin, Robert E. "Enfranchising All Affected Interests, and Its Alternatives." *Philosophy and Public Affairs* 35, no. 1 (2007): 40–68.

Goodley, Dan, and Katherine Runswick-Cole. "Decolonizing Methodology: Disabled Children as Research Managers and Participant Ethnographers." *In Inclusive Communities: A Critical Reader*, edited by Shaun Grech and Andrew Azzopardi, 215–32. Rotterdam: Sense, 2012.

Gouthro, Patricia A. "Active and Inclusive Citizenship for Women: Democratic Considerations for Fostering Lifelong Education." *International Journal of Lifelong Education* 26, no. 2 (2007): 143–54.

Graham, Katherine A., and Susan D. Phillips. "Citizen Engagement: Beyond the Customer Revolution." *Canadian Public Administration* 40, no. 2 (1997): 255–73.

Grant, John. "Canada's Republican Invention? On the Political Theory and Practice of Citizens' Assemblies." *Political Studies* 62 (2014): 539–55.

Gratl, J. *"Wouldn't Piss on Them if They Were on Fire": How Discrimination Against Sex Workers, Drug Users, and Aboriginal Women Enabled a Serial Killer*. Report of Independent Counsel to Commissioner of the B.C. Missing Women Commission of Inquiry. Vancouver, 25 June, 2012.

Gray, John. *False Dawn: The Delusions of Global Capitalism*. London: Granta Books, 2015.

Gray, Sarah. "The March for Our Lives Protest Is This Saturday. Here's Everything to Know." *Time*, 23 March 2018. Online at http://time.com /5167102/march-for-our-lives-parkland-school-shooting-protest/.

Green, Joyce. *Making Space for Indigenous Feminism*. Black Point, NS: Fernwood, 2007.

Green, Joyce. "Taking Account of Aboriginal Feminism." In *Making Space for Indigenous Feminism*, edited by Joyce Green, 20–32. Black Point, NS: Fernwood, 2007.

Greene, Maxine. *Releasing the Imagination: Essays on Education, the Arts and Social Change*. San Francisco: Jossey-Bass, 1995.

Griffin, Dana, and Amy Farris. "School Counselors and Collaboration: Finding Resources through Community Asset Mapping." *Professional School Counseling* 13, no. 5 (2010). https://doi.org/10.1177%2F2156759X1001300501.

Griffith Diamond Jubilee Corporation. *Seventy-five Years of Growing Together: Griffith Jubilee, 1904–1979*. Griffith, IN: Griffith Diamond Jubilee Corporation, 1979.

Grin, John, Jan Rotmans, and Johan Schot. "On Patterns and Agency in Transition Dynamics: Some Key Insights from the KSI Programme." *Environmental Innovation and Societal Transitions* 1, no. 1 (2011): 76–81. doi:10.1016/j.eist.2011 .04.008.

Gutberlet, Jutta. *Recovering Resources – Recycling Citizenship: Urban Poverty Reduction in Latin America*. Aldershot, UK: Ashgate, 2008.

Gutmann, Amy, and Dennis Thompson. *Democracy and Disagreement*. Cambridge, MA: Belknap Press of Harvard University Press, 1996.

Guttman, Amy, and Dennis Thompson. *Why Deliberative Democracy?* Princeton, NJ: Princeton University Press, 2009.

Habed Lopez, Názere. "¿Por qué y para qué los consejos del poder ciudadano?" *El Nuevo Diario* (Managua, Nicaragua), 28 August 2007. Online at http:// impreso.elnuevodiario.com.ni/2007/08/28/opinion/57372.

Habermas, Jürgen. *Between Facts and Norms: Contributions to a Discourse Theory of Law and Democracy*. Translated by William Rehg. Cambridge, MA: MIT Press, 1996.

Habermas, Jürgen. "The Public Sphere." In *Rethinking Popular Culture: Contemporary Perspectives in Cultural Studies*, edited by Chandra Mukerji and Michael Schudson, 398–404. Berkeley: University of California Press, 1991.

Habermas, Jürgen. *The Theory of Communicative Action*, vol. 1, *Reason and Rationalization of Society*. Translated by Thomas McCarthy. Boston: Beacon, 1984.

Habermas, Jürgen. *The Theory of Communicative Action*, vol. 2, *Lifeworld and Systems*. Translated by Thomas McCarthy. Boston: Beacon, 1987.

Hackett, Robert, and William Carroll. *Remaking Media: The Struggle to Democratize Public Communication*. New York: Routledge, 2006.

Hall, Budd L., Edward T. Jackson, Rajesh Tandon, Jean-Marc Fontan, and Nirmala Lall. *Knowledge, Democracy and Action: Community-University Research Partnerships in Global Perspectives*. Manchester: Manchester University Press, 2016.

Hall, Chris. "Bill C-51: Political battle lines drawn over anti-terror bill as election nears." *CBC News*, 19 February 2015. Online at http://www.cbc.ca /news/politics/bill-c-51-political-battle-lines-drawn-over-anti-terror-bill -as-election-nears-1.2962764, accessed 1 December 2017.

Hallam, Christopher, and Dave Bewley-Taylor. "Drug Use: Knowledge, Culture and Context." London: Beckley Foundation, 2010. Online at http:// beckleyfoundation.org/wp-content/uploads/2016/04/paper_21.pdf.

Hamrick, William. *Kindness and the Good Society: Connections of the Heart*. Albany: State University of New York Press, 2002.

Hankivsky, Olena. "Intersectionality 101." Vancouver: Simon Fraser University, Institute for Intersectionality Research and Public Policy, 2014. Online at http://vawforum-cwr.ca/sites/default/files/attachments/intersectionallity _101.pdf.

Hankivsky, Olena, ed. *An Intersectionality-Based Policy Analysis Framework*. Vancouver: Simon Fraser University, Institute for Intersectionality Research and Public Policy, 2012.

Hankivsky, Olena, et al. "Intersectionality-Based Policy Analysis." In *An Intersectionality-Based Policy Analysis Framework*, edited by Olena Hankivsky. Vancouver: Simon Fraser University, Institute for Intersectionality Research and Policy, 2012.

Hankivsky, Olena, and Renee Cormier. "Intersectionality and Public Policy: Some Lessons from Existing Models." *Political Research Quarterly* 64, no.1 (2011): 217–29.

Hansen, William B. "A Social Ecology Theory of Alcohol and Drug Use Prevention among College and University Students." In *Designing Alcohol and Other Drug Prevention Programs in Higher Education: Bringing Theory into*

Practice, 155–75. Newton, MA: Education Development Center, Inc., 1997. https://doi.org/10.4018/978-1-5225-1744-3.ch010.

Haraway, Donna. "Situated Knowledges: The Science Question in Feminism and the Privilege of Partial Perspective." *Feminist Studies* 14, no. 3 (1988): 575–99. https://doi.org/10.2307/3178066.

Harding, Sandra G. *The Science Question in Feminism*. Ithaca, NY: Cornell University Press, 1986.

Harding, Sandra G. "'Strong Objectivity': A Response to the New Objectivity Question." *Synthese* 104, no. 3 (1995): 331–49.

Hardy, Lisa J., Amy Hughes, Elizabeth Hulen, Alejandra Figueroa, Coral Evans, and R. Cruz Begay. "Hiring the Experts: Best Practices for Community -Engaged Research." *Qualitative Research* 16, no. 5 (2016): 592–600.

Harvey, David. *A Brief History of Neoliberalism*. Oxford: Oxford University Press, 2007.

Hawkesworth, Mary. "Intersectionality: Diagnosing Conceptual Practices of Power." *New Political Science* 37, no. 4 (2015): 628–36.

Hay, Colin. *Why We Hate Politics*. Cambridge: Polity Press, 2007.

Head, Brian W. "Community Engagement: Participation on Whose Terms?" *Australian Journal of Political Science* 42, no. 3 (2007): 441–54.

Head, John G. *Public Goods and Public Welfare*. Durham, NC: Duke University Press, 1974.

Heath, Dwight B. *Drinking Occasions: Comparative Perspectives on Alcohol and Culture*. Philadelphia: Brunner/Mazel, 2000.

Heidegger, Martin. *Being and Time*. Translated by John Macquarrie and Edward Robinson. New York: Harper & Row, 1962.

Heisler, Karen, and Sean Markey. "Scales of Benefit: Political Leverage in the Negotiation of Corporate Social Responsibility in Mineral Exploration and Mining in Rural British Columbia, Canada." *Society and Natural Resources* 26, no. 4 (2013): 386–401. https://doi.org/10.1080/08941920.2012 .695858.

Hendriks, Carolyn. "Integrated Deliberation: Reconciling Civil Society's Dual Role in Deliberative Democracy." *Political Studies* 54, no. 3 (2006): 486–508.

Hennebry, Jenna. "Who Has Their Eye on the Ball? 'Jurisdictional Fútbol' and Canada's Temporary Foreign Worker Program." *Policy Options* 63 (July/August 2010): 62–7.

Hersey, Leigh Nanney, and Bryna Bobick, eds. *Handbook of Research on the Facilitation of Civic Engagement through Community Art*. Hershey, PA: IGI Global, 2017.

Hintz, Arne. "Policy Hacking: Citizen-Based Policymaking and Media Reform." In *Strategies for Media Reform*, edited by Des Freedman, Jonathan Obar, Cheryl Martens, and Robert W. McChesney, 223–38. New York: Fordham University Press, 2016.

Hintz, Arne, and Stefania Milan. "Media Activists and the Communication Policy Process." In *Encyclopaedia of Social Movement Media*, edited by John D. Downing, 317–19. Thousand Oaks, CA: SAGE, 2010.

Holman, Chris. "Reconsidering the Citizens' Assembly on Electoral Reform Phenomena: Castoriadis and Radical Citizen Democracy." *New Political Science* 35, no. 2 (2013): 203–26.

Holmberg, J., and K.-H. Robèrt. "Backcasting — a Framework for Strategic Planning." *International Journal of Sustainable Development & World Ecology* 7, no. 4 (2000): 291–308. doi:10.1080/13504500009470049.

Holpuch, Amanda, and Paul Owen. "March for Our Lives: Hundreds of thousands demand end to gun violence – as it happened." *Guardian*, 5 June 2019. Online at https://www.theguardian.com/us-news/live/2018/mar /24/march-for-our-lives-protest-gun-violence-washington.

Hommerich, Carol. "Feeling Disconnected: Exploring the Relationship Between Different Forms of Social Capital and Civic Engagement in Japan." *Voluntas* 26, no. 1 (2015): 45–68.

Honig, Bonnie. *Emergency Politics: Paradox, Law, Democracy*. Princeton, NJ: Princeton University Press, 2009.

Honig, Bonnie, and Lori J. Marso, eds. *Politics, Theory, and Film*. Oxford: Oxford University Press, 2016.

Honneth, Axel. *The Struggle for Recognition: The Moral Grammar of Social Conflicts*. Cambridge, MA: MIT Press, 1995.

Hoover, Elizabeth, Katsi Cook, Ron Plain, Kathy Sanchez, Vi Waghiyi, Pamela Miller, Renee Dufault, Caitlin Sislin, and David Carpenter. "Indigenous Peoples of North America: Environmental Exposures and Reproductive Justice." *Environmental Health Perspectives* 120, no. 12 (2012): 1645–9. https:// doi.org/10.1289/ehp.1205422

Howe, Jeff. *Crowdsourcing: How the Power of the Crowd Is Driving the Future of Business*. New York: Random House, 2008.

Hume, Mark. "I want to speak to you from the heart." *Globe and* Mail, 21 October 2016. Online at https://beta.theglobeandmail.com/news/british-columbia /we-matter-videos-speak-to-aboriginal-youth-incrisis/article32483265/?ref =http://www.theglobeandmail.com&, accessed 20 October 2017.

Hunt, Sarah. "Civil Society Participation: Poverty Reduction in Bolivia, Honduras and Nicaragua." In *Civil Society and the State in Left-Led Latin America: Challenges and Limitations to Democratization*, edited by Barry Cannon and Peader Kirby, 161–72. London: Zed Books, 2012.

Hussan, Syed. "What's Missing from the Coverage of the Amanda Lang-RBC Saga?" *Rabble.ca*, 13 January 2015. Online at http://rabble.ca/blogs/bloggers /hussan.

Iacobucci, Frank. *First Nations Representation on Ontario Juries*. Toronto: Ministry of the Attorney General, February 2013. Online at https://www.attorneygeneral

.jus.gov.on.ca/english/about/pubs/iacobucci/First_Nations_Representation
_Ontario_Juries.html.

Ingram, Helen, and Anne Schneider. "Social Construction (Continued): Response." *American Political Science Review* 82, no. 2 (1995): 441–6. https://doi.org/10.2307/2082437.

Isaacs, William N. "Toward an Action Theory of Dialogue." *International Journal of Public Administration* 24, nos. 7–8 (2001): 709–48. https://doi.org/10.1081/PAD-100104771.

Israel, B.A., A.J. Schulz, E.A. Parker, A.B. Becker, A.J. Allen, and R. Guzman. "Critical Issues in Developing and Following CBPR Principles." In *Community-Based Participatory Research for Health: From Process to Outcomes*. 2nd ed., edited by Meredith Minkler and Nina Wallerstein, 47–66. San Francisco: Jossey-Bass, 2008.

Israel, Barbara A., Amy J. Schulz, Edith A. Parker, and Adam B. Becker. "Review of Community-Based Research: Assessing Partnership Approaches to Improve Public Health." *Annual Review of Public Health* 19, no. 1 (1998): 173–202. https://doi.org/10.1146/annurev.publhealth.19.1.173.

Jakubowski, Lisa, and Elizabeth Comack. "Managing Canadian Immigration: Racism, Racialiization and the Law." In *Gender, Race and Canadian Law*, edited by Wayne Antony et al., 88–115. Halifax: Fernwood, 2016.

Jiwani, Yasmin, and Mary Lynn Young. "Missing and Murdered Children: Reproducing Marginality in News Discourse." *Canadian Journal of Communication* 31, no. 4: (2006) 895–917. https://doi.org/10.22230/cjc.2006v31n4a1825.

John, Peter. "Can Citizen Governance Redress the Representative Bias of Political Participation?" *Public Administration Review* 69, no. 3 (2009): 494–503.

Johns, Michelle Marie, Emily Pingel, Anna Eisenberg, Matthew Leslie Santana, and José Bauermeister. "Butch Tops and Femme Bottoms? Sexual Positioning, Sexual Decision Making, and Gender Roles Among Young Gay Men." *American Journal of Men's Health* 6, no. 6 (2012): 505–18. https://doi.org/10.1177/1557988312455214.

Johnson, Genevieve Fuji. *Democratic Illusion: Deliberative Democracy in Canadian Public Policy*. Toronto: University of Toronto Press, 2015.

Johnson, Genevieve Fuji. "The Limits of Deliberative Democracy and Empowerment: Elite Motivation in Three Canadian Cases." *Canadian Journal of Political Science* 44, no. 1 (2011): 137–59.

Johnson, Holly. *Measuring Violence against Women: Statistical Trends 2006*. Ottawa: Statistics Canada, 2006.

Johnson, Miranda. *The Land Is Our History: Indigeneity, Law, and the Settler State*. New York: Oxford University Press, 2016.

Jones, Emma, and John Gaventa. *Concepts of Citizenship: A Review*, IDS Development Bibliography 19. Brighton, UK: Institute of Development Studies, 2002. Online at https://www.ids.ac.uk/files/dmfile/Db19.pdf.

Jones, Melinda. "Inclusion, Social Inclusion and Participation." In *Critical Perspectives on Human Rights and Disability Law*, edited by Lee Ann Basser, Melinda Jones, and Marcia H. Rioux, 57–82. Leiden, Netherlands: Brill, 2011. https://doi.org/10.1163/ej.9789004189508.i-552.24.

Kabeer, Naila. "Gender Equality and Women's Empowerment: A Critical Analysis of the Third Millennium Development Goal." *Gender and Development* 13, no. 1 (2005): 13–24. Online at http://www.visionaryvalues.com/wiki /images/Gender_Equality_and_Empowerment_MDG_Kabeer.pdf.

Kabeer, Naila. "Introduction." In *The Search for Inclusive Citizenship: Meanings and Expressions in an Inter-connected World*, edited by Naila Kabeer, 1–27. New York: Zed Books, 2005.

Kagan, Carolyn, and Karen Duggan. "Creating Community Cohesion: The Power of Using Innovative Methods to Facilitate Engagement and Genuine Partnership." *Social Policy and Society* 10, no. 3 (2011): 393–404.

Kahane, David. "Climate Change, Social Change, and Systems Change." In *Public Deliberation on Climate Change: Lessons from Alberta Climate Dialogue*, edited by Lorelei L. Hanson, 197–224. Edmonton: Athabasca University Press, 2018.

Kahane, David, Daniel Weinstock, Dominique Leydet, and Melissa Williams, eds. *Deliberative Democracy in Practice*. Vancouver: UBC Press, 2010.

Kalaichandran, Amitha, and Chelsea Jane Edwards. "A youth-driven movement remakes Attawapiskat." *Maclean's*, 5 April 2017. Online at http://www.macleans.ca/news/canada/a-youth-driven-movement-remakes-attawapiskat/., accessed 20 October 2017.

Kania, John, Fay Hanleybrown, and Jennifer Splansky Juster. "Essential Mindset Shifts for Collective Impact." *Stanford Social Innovation Review* (Fall 2014): 2–5.

Kania, John, and Mark Kramer. "Collective Impact." *Stanford Social Innovation Review* (Winter 2011): 36–41.

Kania, John, and Mark Kramer. "Embracing Emergence: How Collective Impact Addresses Complexity." *Stanford Social Innovation Review* (January 2013): 1–7.

Karpowitz, Christopher F., Tali Mendelberg, and Lee Shaker. "Gender Inequality in Deliberative Participation." *American Political Science Review* 106, no. 3 (2012): 533–47.

Kassam, Ashifa. "Canada: Trudeau vows to push ahead with pipeline plans in spite of protests." *Guardian*, 16 April 2018. Online at https://www .theguardian.com/world/2018/apr/16/canada-trudeau-transcanada-pipeline, accessed 30 June 2018.

Kawachi, I., B.P. Kennedy, K, Lochner, and D. Prothrow-Stith, "Social Capital, Income Inequality, and Mortality." *American Journal of Public Health* 87, no. 9 (1997): 1491–8.

Kay, Jonathan. "Moving is the only hope for communities like Attawapiskat." *National Post* 16 April 2016. Online at http://nationalpost.com/opinion

/jonathan-kay-little-hope-for-attawapiskat-as-long-as-its-people-stay-put, accessed 20 October 2017s.

Keech, William, Michael C. Munger, and Carl Simon. "Market Failure and Government Failure." Paper submitted to Public Choice World Congress, Miami, 2012. Online at http://michaelmunger.com/papers /keechmungersimon.pdf, accessed 2 June 2018.

Kenny, Carolyn, and Tina Ngaroimata Fraser. *Living Indigenous Leadership: Native Narratives on Building Strong Communities.* Vancouver: UBC Press, 2012.

Kester, Grant H. *The One and the Many: Contemporary Collaborative Art in a Global Context.* Durham, NC: Duke University Press, 2011.

Keung, Nicholas. "Ottawa ends '4-in-4-out' rule for migrant workers." *Toronto Star*, 13 December 2016. Online at https://www.thestar.com/news /immigration/2016/12/13/ottawa-ends-4-in-4-out-rule-for-migrant -workers.html.

Khagram, Sanjeev, James V. Riker, and Kathryn Sikkink. "From Santiago to Seattle: Transnational Advocacy Groups Restructuring World Politics." In *Restructuring World Politics: Transnational Social Movements, Networks, and Norms*, edited by Sanjeev Khagram, James V. Riker, and Kathryn Sikkink, 3–23. Minneapolis: University of Minnesota Press, 2002.

Kino-nda-niimi Collective. *The Winter We Danced: Voices from the Past, the Future, and the Idle No More Movement.* Winnipeg: ARP Books, 2014.

Knowles, Ryan, and Christopher Clark. "How Common Is the Common Good? Moving beyond Idealistic Notions of Deliberative Democracy in Education." *Teaching and Teacher Education* 71 (April 2018): 12–23.

Koch, P. "Bringing Power Back in: Collective and Distributive Forms of Power in Public Participation." *Urban Studies* 50, no.14 (2013): 2976–92.

Kotz, David M. "Neoliberalism, Globalization, Financialization: Understanding Post-1980 Capitalism." University of Massachusetts, Department of Economics, 2015. Online at https://www.umass.edu/economics/sites/default /files/Kotz.pdf.

Kovach, Margaret. "Emerging from the Margins: Indigenous Methodologies." In *Research as Resistance*, edited by Susan Strega and Leslie. Brown, 43–64. Toronto: Canadian Scholars Press, 2015.

Kovach, Margaret. *Indigenous Methodologies.* Toronto: University of Toronto Press, 2014.

Kuokkanen, Rauna. "Globalization as Racialized, Sexualized Violence: The Case of Indigenous Women." *International Feminist Journal of Politics* 10, no. 2 (2008): 216–33.

Kuokkanen, Rauna. *Reshaping the University: Responsibility, Indigenous Epistemes, and the Logic of the Gift.* Vancouver: UBC Press, 2007.

Laforest, Rachel, and Susan D. Phillips. "Citizen Engagement: Rewiring the Policy Process." In *Critical Policy Studies*, edited by Michael Orsini and Miriam Smith, 68–90. Vancouver: UBC Press, 2007.

Lambert, Joe. *Digital Storytelling: Capturing Lives, Creating Community.* Berkeley, CA: Digital Diner Press, 2002.

Landolt, Patricia, and Luin Goldring. "Immigrant Political Socialization as Bridging and Boundary Work: Mapping the Multi-Layered Incorporation of Latin American Immigrants in Toronto." *Ethnic and Racial Studies* 32, no. 7 (2009): 1226–47.

Lane, Temryss MacLean. "The Frontline of Refusal: Indigenous Women Warriors of Standing Rock." *International Journal of Qualitative Studies in Education* 31, no. 3 (2018): 197–214.

Lang, Amy. "But Is It for Real? The British Columbia Citizens' Assembly as a Model of State-Sponsored Citizen Empowerment." *Politics & Society* 35, no. 1 (2007): 35–69.

Lappé, Frances Moore. *Democracy's Edge: Choosing to Save Our Country by Bringing Democracy to Life.* San Francisco: Jossey-Bass, 2006.

Larner, Wendy. "The Limits of Post-Politics: Rethinking Radical Social Enterprise." In *The Post-Political and Its Discontents: Spaces of Depoliticisation, Spectres of Radical Politics,* edited by Japhy Wilson and Erik Swyngedouw, 189–207. Edinburgh: Edinburgh University Press, 2014.

Larocque, Florence. "The Impact of Institutionalization, Politicization and Mobilization on the Direct Participation of Citizens Experiencing Poverty." *Canadian Journal of Political Science* 44, no. 4 (2011): 883–902.

Leach, Edmund R. "Culture and Social Cohesion: An Anthropologist's View." *Daedalus* 94, no. 1 (1965): 24–38.

Lee, Caroline W. *Do-It-Yourself Democracy,* Oxford: Oxford University Press, 2015.

Lee, Caroline W. "Walking the Talk: The Performance of Authenticity in Public Engagement Work." *Sociological Quarterly* 55, no. 3 (2014): 493–513.

Lee, Min Sook, dir. *Migrant Dreams.* Toronto: Cinema Politica, 2016. DVD.

Legacy Foundation. "Neighborhood Spotlight Launch Factsheet." *Legacy Foundation.* January 2014. www.legacyfdnl.org/neighborhood-spotlight.php (accessed March 6, 2018).

Lenihan, Don. *Rescuing Policy: The Case for Public Engagement.* Ottawa: Public Policy Forum, 2012. Online at http://www.politicipublice.ro/uploads /rescuing_policy_ebook.pdf.

Lepard, D. *Missing Women Investigation Review.* Vancouver: Vancouver Police Department, August 2010.

Lerner, Josh. *Making Democracy Fun: How Game Design Can Empower Citizens and Transform Politics.* Cambridge, MA: MIT Press, 2014.

Levac, Leah. "Complicating the Public: Enabling Young Women's Participation in Public Engagement Initiatives." *Journal of Youth Studies* 16, no. 3 (2013): 334–57.

Levac, Leah, Lisa McMurtry, Deborah Stienstra, Cindy Hanson, Gail Baikie, and Devi Mucina. "Learning across Indigenous and Western Knowledge Systems

and Intersectionality: Reconciling Social Science Research Approaches."
May 2018. Online at https://www.criaw-icref.ca/images/userfiles/files
/Learning%20Across%20Indigenous%20and%20Western%20Knowledges
FINAL.pdf.

Levinas, Emmanuel. *Otherwise than Being or Beyond Essence.* Translated by
Alphonso Lingis. Pittsburg: Duquesne University Press, 1998. First published
1974.

Levine, Peter. "Civic Renewal in America." *Philosophy and Public Policy Quarterly*
26 (2006): 2–12.

Levitas, Ruth. "The Idea of Social Inclusion." Paper presented at the Social
Inclusion Research Conference, Bristol, UK, 2003.

Lewin, Kurt. "Action Research and Minority Problems." *Journal of Social Issues*
2, no. 4 (1946): 34–46.

Liberal Party of Canada. "Environmental Assessments." n.d. Online at https://
www.liberal.ca/realchange/environmental-assessments/, accessed 30 June
2018.

Liberman, Robert. "Social Construction (Continued)." *American Political
Science Review* 89, no. 2 (1995): 437–41. https://doi.org/10.2307/2082436.

Liebowitz, Debra J., and Susanne Zwingel. "Gender Equality Oversimplified:
Using CEDAW to Counter the Measurement Obsession." *International
Studies Review* 16, no. 3 (2014): 362–89.

Light, Paul C. "A Cascade of Failures: Why Government Fails and How to Stop
It." Washington, DC: Center for Effective Public Management at Brookings,
2014.

Ling, Justin. "Ottawa drafted plans to allow warrantless access of your data
while still 'consulting' the public." *Vice News Canada*, 24 March 2017. Online
at https://news.vice.com/story/ottawa-began-writing-plans-to-allow
-warrantless-access-of-canadians-data-while-they-were-still-consulting-with
-the-public, accessed 16 December 2017.

Livingstone, Sonia, and Peter Lunt. "The Mass Media, Democracy and the
Public Sphere." In *Talk on Television: Audience Participation and Public Debate,*
9–35. London: Routledge, 1994.

Lomas, Jonathan. "Using Research to Inform Healthcare Managers' and Policy
Makers' Questions: From Summative to Interpretive Synthesis." *Healthcare
Policy* 1, no. 1 (2005): 55–71.

Loorbach, Derk, and Jan Rotmans. "The Practice of Transition Management:
Examples and Lessons from Four Distinct Cases." *Futures* 42, no. 3 (2010):
237–46. doi:10.1016/j.futures.2009.11.009.

Lu, Yuqian, and Feng Hou. "International Students Who Become Permanent
Residents in Canada." *Insights on Canadian Society,* cat. no. 75-006-X. Ottawa:
Statistics Canada, 2015. Online at http://www.statcan.gc.ca/pub/75-006
-x/2015001/article/14299-eng.pdf.

Luederitz, Christopher, Niko Schapke, Arnim Wiek, Daniel J. Lang, Matthias
Bergmann, Joannette J. Bos, Sarah Burch, et al. "Learning through Evaluation –
A Tentative Evaluative Scheme for Sustainability Transition Experiments."
Journal of Cleaner Production (2016): 1–42. doi:10.1016/j.jclepro.2016.09.005.

Lukensmeyer, C.J., and S. Brigham. "Taking Democracy to Scale: Creating a
Town Hall Meeting for the Twenty-First Century." *National Civic Review*,
2002.

Lynes, Krista. *Prismatic Media, Transnational Circuits: Feminism in a Globalized
Present.* Basingstoke, UK: Palgrave Macmillan, 2012

Lysen, Flora, and Patricia Pisters. "Introduction: The Smooth and the
Striated." *Deleuze Studies* 6, no. 1 (2012): 1–5.

MacDonald, Moira. "Indigenizing the Academy: What Some Universities
Are Doing to Weave Indigenous Peoples, Cultures and Knowledge into
the Fabric of Their Campuses." *University Affairs*, 6 April 2016. Online at
http://www.universityaffairs.ca/features/feature-article/Indigenizing-the
-academy/.

Macdonald, Nancy, and Meagan Campbell. "Lost and Broken." *Maclean's*,
13 September 2017. Online at http://www.macleans.ca/lost-and-broken/.

Mackey, Eva. *Unsettled Expectations: Uncertainty, Land and Settler Decolonization.*
Winnipeg: Fernwood, 2016.

Macklin, Audrey. "And just like that, you're an illegal immigrant." *National
Post*, 19 March 2015. Online at http://news.nationalpost.com/full-comment
/audreymacklin-poof-now-youre-an-illegal-immigrant.

Magnusson, Rachel. "A Politics in Writing: Jacques Rancière and the Equality
of Intelligences." In *Thinking Radical Democracy*, edited by Martin Breaugh,
Christopher Holman, Devin Penner, Rachel Magnusson and Paul Mazzocchi,
189–209. Toronto: University of Toronto Press, 2015.

Malena, Carmen. *From Political Won't to Political Will: Building Support for
Participatory Governance.* Sterling, VA: Kumarian Press, 2009.

Mandell, Jonathan. "They're Not Actors, But They're Playing Themselves."
TDF Stages, 12 October 2012. Online at https://www.tdf.org/articles/746
/Theyre-Not-Actors-But-Theyre-Playing-Themselves.

Mansbridge, Jane, James Bohman, Simone Chambers, Thomas Christiano,
Archon Fung, John Parkinson, Dennis F. Thompson, and Mark E. Warren.
"A Systematic Approach to Deliberative Democracy." In *Deliberative
Systems: Deliberative Democracy at the Large Scale*, edited by J. Parkinson and
J. Mansbridge, 1–26. New York: Cambridge University Press, 2012.

Marginson, Eva, and Erlenwati Sawir. *Ideas for Intercultural Education.* New York:
Palgrave Macmillan, 2011.

Marsh, Peter. "In Praise of Bad Habits." ICR Lecture. London: Institute for
Cultural Research at the King's Fund, 17 November 2001. Online at http://
www.sirc.org/publik/bad_habits.shtml.

Marshall, Catherine. "Researching the Margins: Feminist Critical Policy Analysis." *Educational Policy* 13, no. 1 (1999): 59–76.

Martin, Carol Muree, and Harsha Walia. *Red Women Rising*. Vancouver: Downtown Eastside Women's Centre, 2019.

Martiniello, Martin. "Political Participation, Mobilization, and Representation of Immigrants and their Offspring in Europe." Willy Brandt Series of Working Papers in Internatiomal Migration and Ethnic Relations. Malmö, Sweden: Malmö University, 2005.

Mas, Susana. "Trudeau announces nearly $70M over 3 years for Indigenous mental health services." *CBC News*, 13 June 2016. Online at http://www.cbc.ca/news/politics/trudeau-attawapiskat-youth-chief-meeting-1.3629960, accessed 20 October 2017.

Masuda, Jeffrey, Tara K. McGee, and Theresa D. Garvin. "Power, Knowledge, and Public Engagement: Constructing 'Citizenship' in Alberta's Industrial Heartland." *Journal of Environmental Policy and Planning* 10, no. 4 (2008): 359–80.

Mathieu-Léger, Laurence, and Ashifa Kassam. "First Nations community grappling with suicide crisis: 'We're crying out for help.'" *Guardian*, 16 April 2014. Online at https://www.theguardian.com/world/2016/apr/16/canada-first-nations-suicide-crisis-attawapiskat-history, accessed 20 October 2017.

Maulsby, Cathy, Greg Millett, Kali Lindsey, Robin Kelley, Kim Johnson, Daniel Montoya, and David Holtgrave. "HIV among Black Men Who Have Sex with Men (MSM) in the United States: A Review of the Literature." *AIDS and Behavior* 18, no. 1 (2014): 10–25. https://doi.org/10.1007/s10461-013-0476-2.

Mawdsley, Emma, Laura Savage, and Sung-Mi Kim. "A 'Post-Aid' World? Paradigm Shift in Foreign Aid and Development Cooperation at the 2011 Bisan HIgh Level Forum." *Geographical Journal* 180, no. 1 (2014): 27–38. https://doi.org/10.1111/j.1475-4959.2012.00490.x.

Maynard, Robyn. *Policing Black Lives: State Violence in Canada from Slavery to the Present*. Black Point, NS: Fernwood, 2017.

Mazur, Amy G. *Theorizing Feminist Policy*. Oxford: Oxford University Press, 2002.

McBride, Stephen, and Heather Whiteside. *Private Affluence, Public Austerity: Economic Crisis and Democratic Malaise in Canada*. Black Point, NS: Fernwood, 2011.

McIlwaine, Cathy, and Datta, Kavita. "From Feminising to Engendering Development." *Gender, Place and Culture* 10, no. 4 (2003): 369–82.

McIntyre, Lynn, Patrick B. Patterson, and Catherine L. Mah. "A Framing Analysis of Canadian Household Food Insecurity Policy Illustrates Co-construction of an Intractable Problem." *Critical Policy Studies* 12, no. 2 (2016): 149–68.

McKee, L. "Post-Foucauldian Governmentality: What Does It Offer Critical Social Policy Analysis?" *Critical Social Policy* 29, no. 3 (2009): 465–86.

McKee, Margaret. "Excavating Our Frames of Mind: The Key to Dialogue and Collaboration." *Social Work* 48, no. 3 (2003): 401–8.

McKibben, Bill. "Why we need to keep 80% of fossil fuels in the ground." *350. org*, 16 February 2016. Online at https://350.org/why-we-need-to-keep-80 -percent-of-fossil-fuels-in-the-ground/.

McNutt, Kathleen. "Public Engagement in the Web 2.0 Era: Social Collaborative Technologies in a Public Sector Context." *Canadian Public Administration* 57, no. 1 (2014): 49–70.

Meekosha, Helen. "Decolonising Disability: Thinking and Acting Globally." *Disability & Society* 26, no. 6 (2011): 667–82. https://doi.org/10.1080/09687599 .2011.602860.

Meekosha, Helen, and Karen Soldatic. "Human Rights and the Global South: The Case of Disability." *Third World Quarterly* 32, no. 8 (2011): 1383–97.

Mendoza, Berny. "La epistemología del sur, la colonialidad del género y el feminismo latinoamericano." Bogotá: Centro de Estudios e Investigación Simón Rodríguez, n.d. Online at http://funceisimonrodriguez.blogspot.ca /2012/10/la-epistemologia-del-sur-la.html.

Merleau-Ponty, Maurice. *Phenomenology of Perception*. Translated by Donald A. Landes. New York: Routledge, 2012.

Merry, Sally Engle. "Measuring the World." *Current Anthropology* 52, no. S3 (2011): S83–95.

Mihesua, Dean A., and Angela C. Wilson, eds. *Indigenizing the Academy: Transforming Scholarship and Empowering Communities*. Lincoln: University of Nebraska Press, 2004.

Mihesua, Joshua. "Graduating Indigenous Students by Confronting the Academic Environment." In *Indigenizing the Academy: Transforming Scholarship and Empowering Communities*, edited by Devon Mihesua and Angela Wilson, 191–9. Lincoln: University of Nebraska Press, 2014.

Mikesell, Lisa, Elizabeth Bromley, and Dmitry Khodyakov. "Ethical Community-Engaged Research: A Literature Review." *American Journal of Public Health* 103, no. 12 (2013): e7–14.

Milberry, Kate. "Freeing the Net: On-line Mobilizations in Defense of Democracy." In *Alternative Media in Canada*, edited by Kristen Kozolanka, Patricia Mazepa, and David Skinner, 226–43. Vancouver: UBC Press, 2010.

Milbrandt, Melody. "Understanding the Role of Art in Social Movements and Transformation." *Journal of Art for Life* 1, no. 1 (2010): 7–18.

Miller, Gloria. "Frontier Masculinity in the Oil Industry: The Experience of Women Engineers." *Gender, Work, and Organization* 11, no. 1 (2004): 47–73. https://doi.org/10.1111/j.1468-0432.2004.00220.x.

Million, Dian. *Therapeutic Nations: Healing in an Age of Indigenous Human Rights*. Tuscon: University of Arizona Press, 2014.

Minkler, Meredith, and Nina Wallerstein. *Community-Based Participatory Research for Health: From Process to Outcomes*. San Francisco: Jossey-Bass, 2011.

Mitchell, Claudia. *Doing Visual Research*. Los Angeles: SAGE, 2011.

Mitchell, Claudia, Naydene De Lange, and Relebohile Moletsane. *Participatory Visual Methodologies: Social Change, Community and Policy*. Los Angeles: SAGE, 2017.

Mohanty, Chandra Talpade. "Transnational Feminist Crossings: On Neoliberalism and Radical Critique." *Signs* 38, no. 4 (2013): 967–91. https://doi.org/10.1086/669576.

Mokami Status of Women Council, "Out of the Rhetoric and Into the Reality of Local Women's Lives." Submission to Environmental Assessment Panel on the Lower Churchill Hydro Development, 28 March 2011. Online at http://fnn.criaw-icref.ca/images/userfiles/files/OutoftheRhetoric.pdf

Moll, Marita, and Leslie Regan Shade. *For Sale to the Highest Bidder: Telecom Policy in Canada*. Ottawa: Canadian Centre for Policy Alternatives, 2008.

Momsen, Janet Henshall. *Gender and Development*. Routledge Perspectives on Development. London: Routledge, 2004.

Monnais, Laurence. "Preventive Medicine and 'Mission civilisatrice': Uses of the BCG Vaccine in French Colonial Vietnam between the Two World Wars." *International Journal of Asia-Pacific Studies* 2, no. 1 (2006): 40–66.

Mooney, Andy, and Amanda Carney. *How the New Communities Program Works*. Chicago: Local Initiatives Support Corporation, 2003.

Morin, Brandi. "Partnership between oilsands, Indigenous workers leads to solar panels for daycare." *CBC News*, 20 October 2017, online at http://www.cbc.ca/news/indigenous/partnership-oilsands-indigenous-workers-1.4365202.

Morris, Alexander. *The Treaties of Canada with the Indians*. 1880. Reprint, Toronto: Prospero, 2000.

Moscrop, David R.H., and Mark E. Warren. "When Is Deliberation Democratic?" *Journal of Public Deliberation* 12, no. 2 (2016): article 4.

Moser, Caroline O.N. "Gender Planning in the Third World: Meeting Practical and Strategic Gender Needs." *World Development* 17, no. 11 (1989): 1799–825. https://doi.org/10.1016/0305-750X(89)90201-5.

Mouffe, Chantal. "Deliberative Democracy or Agonistic Pluralism." IHS Political Science Series Working Paper 72. Vienna: Institute for Advanced Studies, December 2000. Online at http://irihs.ihs.ac.at/1312/1/pw_72.pdf, accessed 11 January 2018.

Mouffe, Chantal. *The Democratic Paradox*. London: Verso, 2000.

Muhr, Thomas. "Nicaragua Re-visited: From Neo-liberal 'Ungovernability' to the Bolivarian Alternative for the Peoples of Our America (ALBA)." *Globalisation, Societies and Education* 6, no. 2 (2008): 147–61. https://doi.org/10.1080/14767720802061447.

Muñoz Cabrera, Patricia. *Intersecting Inequalities: A Review of Feminist Theories and Debates on Violence Against Women and Poverty in Latin America.* London: Central America Women's Network, 2010.

Murphy, Michael. "Representing Indigenous Self-Determination." *University of Toronto Law Journal* 58, no. 2, (2008): 185–216. https://doi.org/10.1353/tlj.0.0000.

Murray, K. "Governmentality and the Shifting Winds of Policy Studies." In *Critical Policy Studies,* edited by M. Orsini and M. Smith, 161–84. Vancouver: UBC Press, 2007.

Nalcor Energy. *Muskrat Falls Project: Monthly Report, December 2016.* n.p., February 2017. Online at http://muskratfalls.nalcorenergy.com/wp-content/uploads/2017/02/Dec-2016-LCP-Monthly-Benefits-Report-final.pdf.

National Energy Board. *Trans Mountain Expansion Project: Final Report, May 2016.* OH-001-2014. Ottawa, 2016.

National Inquiry into Missing and Murdered Indigenous Women and Girls. *Reclaiming Power and Place: The Final Report of the National Inquiry into Missing and Murdered Indigenous Women and Girls,* vol. 1a. n.p.: National Inquiry into Missing and Murdered Indigenous Women and Girls, 2019. Online at https://www.mmiwg-ffada.ca/.

Native Youth Sexual Health Network. "NYSHN statement to National Energy Board regarding Line 9 pipeline proposal." Press release, 18 October 2003. Online at http://www.nativeyouthsexualhealth.com/october182013.pdf.

Neblo, Michael A., Kevin M. Esterling, Ryan P. Kennedy, David M.J. Lazer, and Anand E. Sokhey. "Who Wants to Deliberate – and Why?" *American Political Science Review* 104, no. 3 (2010): 566–83.

New Brunswick. Executive Council Office. "Gender-Based Analysis." n.d. Online at http://www2.gnb.ca/content/gnb/en/services/services_renderer.201259.Gender-Based_Analysis.html.

Nguyen, Hai Hong, and Minh Quang Pham. "Democratization in Vietnam's Post-Đổi Mới One-Party Rule: Change from Within, Change from the Bottom to the Top, and Possibilities." In *Globalization and Democracy in Southeast Asia,* edited by Chantana Banpasirichote Wungaeo, Boike Rehbein, and Surichai Wun'gaeo, 131–55. Basingstoke, UK: Palgrave Macmillan, 2016.

Nguyen, Thi Hong Hai, Steve Wood, and Neil Wrigley. "The Emerging Food Retail Structure of Vietnam: Phases of Expansion in a Post-Socialist Environment." *International Journal of Retail & Distribution Management* 41, no. 8 (2013): 596–626.

Nguyen, Xuan Thuy. "Critical Disability Studies at the Edge of Global Development: Why Do We Need to Engage with Southern Theory?" *Canadian Journal of Disability Studies* 7, no. 1 (2018): 1–25.

Nguyen, Xuan Thuy. "Girls with Disabilities in the Global South: Rethinking the Politics of Engagement." *Girlhood Studies* 9, no. 1 (2016): 53–71. https:// doi.org/10.3167/ghs.2016.090105.

Nguyen, Xuan Thuy. *The Journey to Inclusion*. Rotterdam: Sense Publishers, 2015.

Nguyen, Xuan Thuy. "Unsettling 'Inclusion' in the Global South: A Post-colonial and Intersectional Approach to Disability, Gender, and Education." In *SAGE Handbook of Inclusion and Diversity in Education*, edited by Matthew J. Schuelka, Christopher J. Johnstone, Gary Thomas, and Alfredo J. Artiles. London: SAGE, 2019.

Nguyen, Xuan Thuy, and Pamela Johnson. 2016. "Transnational Conversations in the Context of Disability Rights: Building the Potential for Global Activism." *Third World Thematics: A TWQ Journal* 1 (3): 396–410. https://doi .org/10.1080/23802014.2016.1248232.

Nguyen, Xuan Thuy, Claudia Mitchell, Naydene de Lange, and Kelly Fritsch. "Engaging Girls with Disabilities in Vietnam: Making Their Voices Count." *Disability & Society* 30, no. 5 (2015): 773–87. https://doi.org/10.1080/09687599 .2015.10515155.

Nightingale, Eithne, and Richard Sandell. "Introduction." In *Museums, Equality and Social Justice*, edited by Richard Sandell and Eithne Nightingale, 1–9. New York: Routledge, 2012.

Norris, Pippa. *Democratic Phoenix: Reinventing Political Activism*. Cambridge: Cambridge University Press, 2002.

NWAC (Native Women's Association of Canada). "Fact Sheet: Missing and Murdered Aboriginal Women and Girls in British Columbia." Ottawa: NWAC, 2010.

NWAC and Canadian Feminist Alliance for International Action. *Murders and Disappearances of Aboriginal Women and Girls in Canada: Information Update for the United Nations Committee on the Elimination of Discrimination Against Women*. 25 June, 2013.

O'Donnell, Vivian, and Susan Wallace. "First Nations, Métis and Inuit Women." *Women in Canada: A Gender-Based Statistical Report*. Ottawa: Statistics Canada, 2011.

O'Keefe, Jennifer. "CPS Women's Research and Action Forum – Nova Scotia." Ottawa: Canadian Research Institute for the Advancement of Women, September 2017.

O'Malley, Katie. "Bill C-1 'Day of Action' protests denounce new policing powers." *CBC News*, 14 March 2015. Online at http://www.cbc.ca /news/politics/bill-c-51-day-of-action-protests-denounce-new-policing -powers-1.2994226, accessed 18 December 2017.

O'Shaughnessy, Sara, and Naomi Krogman. "Gender as Contradiction: From Dichotomies to Diversity in Natural Resource Extraction." *Journal of Rural Studies* 27, no. 2 (2011): 134–43. https://doi.org/10.1016/j.jrurstud.2011.01.001

Olson, Mancur. *The Logic of Collective Action: Public Goods and the Theory of Groups.* Cambridge, MA: Harvard University Press, 1971.

Oppal, Wallace. *Forsaken: The Report of the Missing Women Commission of Inquiry,* 4 v. Vancouver: Missing Women Commission of Inquiry, 2012.

Oppal, Wallace. "Missing Women Commission of Inquiry: Ruling on Participant Funding." Vancouver, 2 May, 2011.

Organisation for Economic Co-operation and Development. "The Paris Declaration on Aid Effectiveness." Paris: OECD, 2005. Online at http://www.oecd.org/dac/effectiveness/34428351.pdf.

Orsini, Michael, and Miriam Smith. *Critical Policy Studies.* Vancouver: UBC Press, 2007.

Ostrom, Elinor. *Governing the Commons: The Evolution of Institutions for Collective Action.* Cambridge: Cambridge University Press, 1990.

Ottman, Jacqueline. "Indigenizing the Academy: Confronting 'Contentious' Ground." *Morning Watch: Education and Social Analysis* 40, nos. 3–4 (2013): 8–24. Online at http://www.mun.ca/educ/faculty/mwatch/vol40/winter2013/indigenizingAcademy.pdf

Our Community Our Plan. "Citizens' Assembly: Questions & Answers." 3 November 2014. Online at https://ourcommunityourplan.wordpress.com/2014/11/03/citizens-assembly-questions-answers/, accessed 24 March 2018.

Our Community Our Plan. "OCOP! Press release #1." 10 June 2014. Online at https://ourcommunityourplan.wordpress.com/2014/06/10/ocop-press-release-1/. Online at https://ourcommunityourplan.wordpress.com/2014/06/10/ocop-press-release-1/, accessed 24 March 2018.

Our Community Our Plan. "OCOP's 12 Point Program." 12 October 2014. Online at https://ourcommunityourplan.wordpress.com/2014/10/12/ocops-12-point-program/, accessed 24 March 2018.

Our Community Our Plan. "Slice of Democracy Contest." 23 July 2014. Online at https://ourcommunityourplan.wordpress.com/2014/07/23/slice-of-democracy-contest/.

Pablo, Carlito. "Foreign workers file class-action lawsuit against Denny's Restaurants in BC." *Georgia Straight,* 11 January 2011. Online at https://www.straight.com/article-367835/vancouver/foreign-workers-file-classaction-lawsuit-against-dennys-restaurants-bc.

Pajouhesh, Seyedeh Paniz. "From Theory to Practice: An Analysis of Transformative Social Innovation at the University of British Columbia." Master's thesis, University of British Columbia, 2016.

Pal, Leslie. *Beyond Policy Analysis: Public Issue Management in Turbulent Times.* Toronto: Nelson Education, 2014.

Parkinson, John. *Deliberating in the Real World: Problems of Legitimacy in Deliberative Democracy.* Oxford: Oxford University Press, 2006.

Parkinson, John, and Jane Mansbridge. *Deliberative Systems: Deliberative Democracy at the Large Scale*. New York: Cambridge University Press, 2012.

Parlee, Brenda. "Avoiding the Resource Curse: Indigenous Communities and Canada's Oil Sands." *World Development* 74 (2015): 426–36. https://doi.org /10.1016/j.worlddev.2015.03.004

Parpart, Jane L., Patricia M. Connelly, and V. Eudine Barriteau. *Theoretical Perspectives on Gender and Development*. Ottawa: International Development Research Centre, 2000. Online at https://www.idrc.ca/en/book/theoretical -perspectives-gender-and-development.

Pateman, Carole. "APSA Presidential Address: Participatory Democracy Revisited." *Perspectives on Politics* 10, no. 1 (2012): 7–19.

Payton, Laura. "Government killing online surveillance bill." *CBC News*, 11 February 2013. Online at https://www.cbc.ca/news/politics/government -killing-online-surveillance-bill-1.1336384, accessed 15 December 2017.

Pearce, W. Barnett, and Kimberly A. Pearce. "Aligning the Work of Government to Strengthen the Work of Citizens: A Study of Public Administrators in Local and Regional Government." [Dayton, OH]: Kettering Foundation, February 2010. Online at http://ncdd.org/rc/wp-content/uploads/2010/06/Pearces -Aligning_Work_of_Govt.pdf.

Pearson, Jordan. "Toronto's public hearing on Bill C-51 was utterly demoralizing." *Vice*, 20 October 2016. Online at https://motherboard.vice.com/en_us/article /ezpkd4/torontos-public-hearing-on-bill-c-51-was-utterly-demoralizing, accessed 15 December 2017.

Peele, Stanton, and Archie Brodsky. "Exploring Psychological Benefits Associated with Moderate Alcohol Use: A Necessary Corrective to Assessments of Drinking Outcomes?" *Drug and Alcohol Dependence* 60, no. 3 (2000): 221–47.

Pérez Piñán, Astrid. "Engendering Effectiveness: A Feminist Critique of the New Aid Architecture." PhD diss., Trinity College, Dublin, 2015.

Pérez Piñán, Astrid. "Gender Responsive Approaches to Measuring Aid Effectiveness: Options and Issues." *Social Politics* 22, no. 3 (2015): 432–55.

Perry, J. Adam. "Barely Legal: Racism and Migrant Farm Labour in the Context of Canadian Multiculturalism." *Citizenship Studies* 16, no. 2 (2012): 189–201.

Peterson, Spike V. "How (the Meaning of) Gender Matters in the Political Economy." *New Political Economy* 10, no. 4 (2005): 499–521.

Pettit, Philip. "Representation, Responsive and Indicative." *Constellations* 17, no. 3 (2010): 426–34.

Phelan, Jo C., Bruce G. Link, Ana Diez-Roux, Ichiro Kawachi, and Bruce Levin. "'Fundamental Causes' of Social Inequalities in Mortality: A Test of the Theory." *Journal of Health and Social Behavior* 45, no. 3 (2004): 265–85.

Phillips, Susan D. "SUFA and Citizen Engagement: Fake or Genuine Masterpiece?" *IRPP Policy Matters* 2, no. 7 (2001): 15–19.

Phillips, Susan D., and Michael Orsini. "Mapping the Links: Citizen Involvement in the Policy Process." Ottawa: Canadian Policy Research Networks, 2002.

Pickles, John. "The Spirit of Post-Socialism: Common Spaces and the Production of Diversity." *European Urban and Regional Studies* 17, no. 2 (2010): 127–40.

Pierson, Paul. "The Study of Policy Development." *Journal of Policy History* 17, no. 1 (2005): 34–51.

Pincock, Heather. "Does Deliberation Make Better Citizens?" In *Democracy in Motion: Evaluating the Practice and Impact of Deliberative Civic Engagement,* edited by Tina Nabatchi, John Gastil, Matt Leighninger, and G. Michael Weiksner, 135–57. Oxford: Oxford University Press, 2012.

Pohl, Christian, and Gertrude Hirsch-Hadorn. "Principles for Designing Transdisciplinary Research." In *Handbook of Transdisciplinary Research.* Munich: Oekom Verlag, 2007.

Polanco, Geraldina. "Consent Behind the Counter: Aspiring Citizens and Labour Control under Precarious Immigration Schemes." *Third World Quarterly* 37 no. 8 (2016): 1332–50.

Pontius, Jason L., and Shaun R. Harper. "Principles for Good Practice in Graduate and Professional Student Engagement." *New Directions for Student Services* 115 (2006): 47–58.

Poyntz, Stuart R. "The Participation Paradox, or Agency and Sociality in Contemporary Youth Cultures." *Jeunesse: Young People, Texts, Cultures* 2, no. 2 (2010): 110–19.

Proschan, Frank. "Eunuch Mandarins, Soldats Mamzelles, Effeminate Boys, and Graceless Women: French Colonial Constructions of Vietnamese Genders." *GLQ: A Journal of Lesbian and Gay Studies* 8, no. 4 (2002): 435–67.

Raboy, Marc. "The Role of Public Consultation in Shaping the Canadian Broadcasting System." *Canadian Journal of Political Science* 28, no. 3 (1995): 455–77.

Rai, Shirin. *Gender and the Political Economy of Development.* Oxford: Polity Press, 2002.

Ramos, Howard, and Kathleen Rodgers, eds. *Protest and Politics: The Promise of Social Movement Societies.* Vancouver: UBC Press, 2015.

Rancière, Jacques. "A Few Remarks on the Method of Jacques Rancière." *Parallax* 15, no. 3 (2009): 114–23.

Rancière, Jacques. *Disagreement: Politics and Philosophy.* Translated by Julie Rose. Minneapolis: University of Minnesota Press, 1999.

Rancière, Jacques. *The Ignorant Schoolmaster: Five Lessons in Intellectual Emancipation.* Translated by Kristin Ross. Stanford, CA: Stanford University Press, 1991.

Raphael, Dennis, ed. *Social Determinants of Health: Canadian Perspectives.* 3rd ed. Toronto: Canadian Scholars Press, 2016.

Ravensbergen, Frances, and Madine VanderPlaat. "Barriers to Citizen Participation: The Missing Voices of People Living in Low Income." *Community Development Journal* 45, no. 4 (2009): 389–403.

Razack, Sherene H. "Gendered Racial Violence and Spatialized Justice: The Murder of Pamela George." In *Race, Space and the Law: Unmapping a White Settler Society*, edited by Sherene H. Razack, 121–56. Toronto: Between the Lines, 2002.

Razack, Sherene H. "Gendering Disposability." *Canadian Journal of Women and the Law* 28, no. 2 (2016): 285–307, https://doi.org/10.3138/cjwl.28.2.285.

RCMP (Royal Canadian Mounted Police). *Missing and Murdered Aboriginal Women: A National Operational Overview*. Ottawa, 2014.

Redvers, Kelvin, and Tunchai Redvers. "Indigenous youth are their own heroes – it's time we listened." *Globe and Mail*, 10 September 2017. Online at https://beta.theglobeandmail.com/opinion/indigenous-youth-are-their -own-heroes-its-time-we-listened/article36217830/?ref=http://www .theglobeandmail.com&, accessed 27 September 2017.

Reed, Maureen. "Reproducing the Gender Order in Canadian Forestry: The Role of Statistical Representation." *Scandinavian Journal of Forest Research* 23 no. 1 (2008): 78–91. https://doi.org/10.1080/02827580701745778.

Regan, Paulette. *Unsettling the Settler Within: Indian Residential Schools, Truth Telling, and Reconciliation in Canada*. Vancouver: UBC Press, 2010.

Rheingold, Howard. *Smart Mobs: The Next Social Revolution*. Cambridge, MA: Perseus Books, 2002.

Rhodes, Scott D., Werner E. Bischoff, Jacqueline M. Burnell, Joseph G. Grzywacz, Haiying Chen, and Thomas A. Arcury. "HIV and Sexually Transmitted Disease Risk among Male Hispanic/Latino Migrant Farmworkers in the Southeast: Findings from a Pilot CBPR Study." *American Journal of Industrial Medicine* 53, no. 10 (2010): 976–83.

Rhodes, Scott D., Omar Martinez, Eun-Young Song, Jason Daniel, Jorge Alonzo, Eugenia Eng, Stacey Duck, et al. "Depressive Symptoms among Immigrant Latino Sexual Minorities." *American Journal of Health Behavior* 37, no. 3 (2013): 404–13.

Riddell, Darcy. "Scaling Forest Conservation: Strategic Agency and Systems Change in the Great Bear Rainforest and Canadian Boreal Forest Agreements." PhD diss., University of Waterloo, 2015.

Rideout, Vanda. *Continentalizing Canadian Telecommunications: The Politics of Regulatory Reform*. Montreal; Kingston, ON: McGill-Queen's University Press, 2003.

Riley, Maria. "A Feminist Political Economic Framework." n.p.: Center of Concern, 2008. Online at https://pdfs.semanticscholar.org/752a/93623d25ab 857f420645631d8d2bc38a2cb7.pdf?_ga=2.188500587.218309311.1578315338 -753571327.1578315338.

Rittle, Horst W.J., and Melvin M. Webber. "Dilemmas in a General Theory of Planning." *Policy Sciences* 4, no. 2 (1973): 155–69.

Ritzi, Claudia. "Neoliberal Hegemony and the Post-Democratization of the Public Sphere: An Analytical Framework to Evaluate the Democratic Quality of Political Discourse," *IC Revista Científica de Información y Comunicación* 11 (2015): 167–87.

Rodriguez, Robyn. *Migrants for Export: How the Philippine State Brokers Labour to the World*. Minneapolos: University of Minnesota Press, 2010.

Roper Greyell. "Missing Women Commission of Inquiry Workplace Investigation," 29 May 2012. Online at https://missingwomen.library.uvic.ca/wp-content/uploads/2012/06/Independent-Investigation-Report.pdf.

Rosanvallon, Pierre. *Counter-Democracy: Politics in an Age of Distrust*. Translated by Arthur Goldhammer. Cambridge: Cambridge University Press, 2008.

Rose, Gillian. *Visual Methodologies: An Introduction to Researching with Visual Materials*. 4th ed. Thousand Oaks, CA: SAGE, 2016.

Rose, Jonathan. "Institutionalizing Participation through Citizens' Assemblies." In *Activating the Citizen: Dilemmas of Participation in Europe and Canada*, edited by Joan DeBardeleben and Jon H. Pammett, 214–32. Basingstoke, UK: Palgrave Macmillan, 2009.

Rose, Jonathan. "Putting the Public Back in Public Policy: The Ontario Citizens' Assembly on Electoral Reform." *Canadian Parliamentary Review* 30, no. 3 (2007): 9–16.

Roth, Wolff-Michael. "The Interaction of Students' Scientific and Religious Discourses: Two Case Studies." *International Journal of Science Education* 2, no. 19 (1998): 125–46.

Rotmans, Jan, and Derk Loorbach. "Complexity and Transition Management." *Journal of Industrial Ecology* 13, no. 2 (2009): 184–96. doi:10.1111/j.1530-9290.2009.00116.x.

Rowe, Gene, and Lynn J. Frewer. "A Typology of Public Engagement Mechanisms." *Science, Technology and Human Values* 30, no. 2 (2005): 51–290.

Runyan, Ann Sisson, and V. Spike Peterson. *Global Gender Issues in the New Millennium*. Boulder, CO: Westview Press, 2014.

Rutherford, Kate. "Attawapiskat declares state of emergency over spate of suicide attempts." *CBC News Sudbury*, 9 April 2016. Online at http://www.cbc.ca/news/canada/sudbury/attawapiskat-suicide-first-nations-emergency-1.3528747., accessed 20 October 2017.

Sali, Meghan. "We're calling for transparency on Bill C-51." *OpenMedia*, 15 December 2016. Online at https://openmedia.org/en/were-calling-transparency-bill-c-51, accessed 16 December 2017.

Salter, Jonathan, John Robinson, and Arnim Wiek. "Participatory Methods of Integrated Assessment – A Review." *Wiley Interdisciplinary Reviews: Climate Change* 1, no. 5 (2010): 697–717. doi:10.1002/wcc.73.

Samuelson, Paul A. "The Pure Theory of Public Expenditure." *Review of Economics and Statistics* 36, no. 4 (1954): 387–90.

Sandel, Richard. *Museums, Moralities and Human Rights*. Abingdon, UK: Routledge, 2017.

Santos, Boaventura de Sousa. *Epistemologies of the South: Justice against Epistemicide*. Boulder, CO: Paradigm, 2014.

Save Lincolnville Campaign. "About the Save Lincolnville Campaign." Online at https://www.nspirg.ca/projects/past-projects/save-lincolnville-campaign/, accessed 22 December 2017.

Scambler, Graham. "Class, Power and the Durability of Health Inequalities." In *Habermas, Critical Theory and Health*, edited by Graham Scambler, 86–119. New York: Routledge, 2001.

Schaap, Andrew. *Political Reconciliation*. New York: Routledge, 2005.

Schapke, Niko, Ines Omann, Julia Wittmayer, Frank van Steenbergen, and Mirijam Mock. "Linking Transitions to Sustainability: A Study of the Societal Effects of Transition Management." *Sustainability* 9, no. 5, art. 737 (2017): 1–36. doi:10.3390/su9050737.

Schneider, Anne, and Helen Ingram. *Policy Design for Democracy*. Lawrence: University Press of Kansas, 1997.

Schneider, Anne, and Helen Ingram. "Social Construction of Target Populations: Implications for Politics and Policy." *American Political Science Review* 87, no. 2 (1993): 334–47. https://doi.org/10.2307/2939044.

Schneider, Anne, Helen Ingram, and Peter DeLeon. "Democratic Policy Design: Social Construction of Target Populations." In *Theories of the Policy Process*, edited by Paul Sabatier and Christopher Weible, 105–48. Boulder, CO: Westview Press, 2014.

Schneider, Anne, and Mara Sidney. "What Is Next for Policy Design and Social Construction Theory?" *Policy Studies Journal* 37, no. 1 (2009): 103–19. https://doi.org/10.1111/j.1541-0072.2008.00298.x.

Schofield, Norman. *Collective Decision-Making: Social Choice and Political Economy*. New York: Springer Science & Business Media, 1996.

Schofield, Toni, and Susan Goodwin. "Gender Politics and Public Policy Making: Prospects for Advancing Gender Equality." *Policy and Society* 24, no. 4 (2005): 25–44.

Schulz, Nils-Sjard. "Nicaragua: A Rude Awakening for the Paris Declaration." *FRIDE*, November 2007. Online at https://eulacfoundation.org/en/system/files/Nicaragua%20a%20rude%20awakening%20for%20the%20Paris%20Declaration.pdf.

Schwartz-Shea, Peregrine, and Dvora Yanow. *Interpretive Research Design: Concepts and Processes*. New York: Routledge, 2012.

Scutt, Cecily, and Julia Hobson. "The Stories We Need: Anthropology, Philosophy, Narrative and Higher Education Research." *Post-secondary Education Research and Development* 32, no. 1 (2013): 17–29. https://doi.org/10.1080/07294360.2012.751088.

Shade, Leslie Regan. "Media Reform in the United States and Canada: Activism and Advocacy for Media Policies in the Public Interest." In *The*

Handbook of Global Media and Communication Policy, edited by Robin Mansell and Marc Raboy, 147–65. New York: John Wiley, 2011.

Sharma, Nandita. *Home Economics: Nationalism and the Making of Migrant Workers in Canada.* Toronto: University of Toronto Press, 2006.

Shaw, Gillian. "Cell phone horror stories: OpenMedia.ca report." *Vancouver Sun*, 7 March 2013. Online at http://vancouversun.com/news/staff-blogs/cell-phone-horror-stories-openmedia-ca-report, accessed 20 December 2017.

Shaw, Gillian. "CRTC axes three-year contracts in new wireless code of conduct." *Vancouver Sun*, 4 June 2013. Online at http://www.vancouversun.com/news/crtc+axes+three+year+contracts+wireless+code+conduct+with+video/8470344/story.html, accessed 20 December 2017.

Shaw, Kathleen M. "Using Feminist Critical Policy Analysis in the Realm of Higher Education." *Journal of Higher Education* 75, no. 1 (2004): 56–79.

Shepherd, Tamara, Gregory Taylor, and Catherine Middleton. "A Tale of Two Regulators: Telecom Policy Participation in Canada." *Journal of Information Policy* 4 (2014): 1–22.

Shotton, Heather, Shelley Lowe, and Stephanie Waterman. *Beyond the Asterisk: Understanding Native Students in Higher Education.* Sterling, VA: Stylus, 2013.

Silverman, David. *Doing Qualitative Research: A Practical Handbook.* London: SAGE, 2000.

Simmonds, Shan, Cornelia Roux, and Ina ter Avest. "Blurring the Boundaries between Photovoice and Narrative Inquiry: A Narrative-Photovoice Methodology for Gender-Based Research." *International Journal of Qualitative Methods* 14, no. 3 (2015): 33–49.

Simpson, Audra. *Mohawk Interruptus: Political Life across the Borders of Settler States.* Durham, NC: Duke University Press, 2014.

Skinner, David, and Kathleen Cross. "Media Activism in Canada: The Cases of Media Democracy Day, OpenMedia, and, ReImagine CBC." In *Strategies for Media Reform: International Perspectives*, edited by Des Freedman, Jonathan Obar, Cheryl Martens, and Robert W. McChesney, 167–81. New York: Fordham University Press, 2016.

Skinner, David, Robert Hackett, and Stuart Poyntz. "Media Activism and the Academy, Three Cases: Media Democracy Day, Open Media, and Newswatch Canada." *Studies in Social Justice* 9, no. 1 (2015): 86–101.

Slaughter, Sheila, and Gary Rhoades. *Academic Capitalism and the New Economy: Markets, State, and Higher Education.* Baltimore: Johns Hopkins University Press, 2009.

Small, Tamara. "Two Decades of Digital Party Politics in Canada: An Assessment." In *Canadian Parties in Transition*. 4th ed., edited by Alain-G. Gagnon and Brian Tanguay, 388–408. Toronto: University of Toronto Press, 2017.

Smith, Adrian, Andy Stirling, and Frans Berkhout. "The Governance of Sustainable Socio-Technical Transitions." *Research Policy* 34, no. 10 (2005): 1491–510. doi:10.1016/j.respol.2005.07.005.

Smith, Adrian, Jan-Peter Voß, and John Grin. "Innovation Studies and Sustainability Transitions: The Allure of the Multi-Level Perspective and Its Challenges." *Research Policy* 39, no. 4 (2010): 435–48. doi:10.1016/j.respol .2010.01.023.

Smith, Graham. *Democratic Innovations: Designing Institutions for Citizen Participation.* New York: Cambridge University Press, 2009.

Smith, Miriam. *A Civil Society? Collective Actors in Canadian Political Life.* Toronto: University of Toronto Press, 2005.

Smith, William. "Democracy, Deliberation, and Disobedience." *Res Publica* 10, no. 4 (2004): 353–77.

Soldatic, Karen, and Shaun Grech. "Transnationalising Disability Studies: Rights, Justice and Impairment." *Disability Studies Quarterly* 34, no. 2 (2014).

Soss, Joe. "Making Clients and Citizens: Welfare Policy as a Source of Status, Belief, and Action." In *Deserving and Entitled*, edited by Anne Schneider and Helen Ingram, 291–328. New York: SUNY Press, 2005.

Spark Policy Institute. *When Collective Impact Has an Impact: A Cross-Site Study of 25 Collective Impact Initiatives.* Denver: Spark Policy Institute, 2018. Online at http://sparkpolicy.com/wp-content/uploads/2018/02/CI-Study-Report _February-2018.pdf.

Spurr, Ben. "How the Attawapiskat suicide crisis unfolded." *Toronto Star*, 18 April 2016. Online at https://www.thestar.com/news/canada/2016/04 /18/how-the-attawapiskat-suicide-crisis-unfolded.html, accessed 20 October 2017.

Statistics Canada. *Income in Canada, 2007.* Cat. no. 75-202-X. Ottawa, June 2009. Online at https://www150.statcan.gc.ca/n1/en/pub/75-202-x/75-202 -x2007000-eng.pdf?st=Hyls2RKa.

Stedman, Daniel Jones. *Masters of the Universe: Hayek, Friedman, and the Birth of Neoliberal Politics.* Updated ed. Princeton, NJ: Princeton University Press, 2014.

Stienstra, Deborah. "DisAbling Globalization: Rethinking Global Political Economy with a Disability Lens." *Global Society* 16, no. 2 (2002): 109–22.

Stienstra, Deborah. "Factsheet: Women and Restructuring in Canada." Ottawa: Canadian Research Institute for the Advancement of Women, June 2010. Online at https://www.criaw-icref.ca/images/userfiles/files/Women%20 and%20Restructuring%20Factsheet%20JUNE%204%202010%20.pdf.

Stienstra, Deborah. "Trumping All? Disability and Girlhood Studies." *Girlhood Studies* 8, no. 2 (2015): 54–70. https://doi.org/10.3167/ghs.2015.080205.

Stienstra, Deborah, Leah Levac, Gail Baikie, Jane Stinson, Barbara Clow, and Susan Manning. "Gendered and Intersectional Implications of Energy and

Resource Extraction in Resource-Based Communities in Canada's North."
Feminist Northern Network, 2016. Online at http://fnn.criaw-icref.ca
/images/userfiles/files/SSHRC%20KS%20Report.pdf.

Stienstra, Deborah, Susan Manning, Leah Levac, and Gail Baikie. "Generating
Prosperity, Creating Crisis: Impacts of Resource Development on Diverse
Groups in Northern Communities." *Community Development Journal* 54,
no. 2 (2019): 215–32. https://doi.org/10.1093/cdj/bsx022.

Stone, Deborah. *Policy Paradox: The Art of Political Decision Making*. New York:
W.W. Norton, 2002.

Strega, Susan. "The View from the Poststructural Margins: Epistemology and
Methodology Reconsidered." In *Research as Resistance: Revisiting Critical,
Indigenous and Anti-Oppressive Approaches*. 2nd ed., edited by Susan Strega
and Leslie Brown, 120–52. Toronto: Canadian Scholars Press, 2015.

Stringer, Ernest T. *Action Research*. Thousand Oaks, CA: SAGE, 2014.

Suleman, Zakir. "Rumble on the drive: Broadway and Commercial towers
workshop leaves no one happy." *Vancouver Observer*, 16 July 2013. Online at
http://www.vancouverobserver.com/real-estate/broadway-and-commercial
-transit-and-towers-workshop-leaves-no-one-happy, accessed 24 March 2018.

Talpin, Julien. "Democratic Innovations." In *The Oxford Handbook of Social
Movements*, edited by Donatella della Porta and Mario Diani, 781–92.
Oxford: Oxford University Press: 2015.

Tarasuk, Valerie, Naomi Dachner, and Rachel Loopstra. "Food Banks, Welfare,
and Food Insecurity in Canada." *British Food Journal* 116, no. 4 (2014): 1405–17.

Taylor, Alison, and Jason Foster. "Migrant Workers and the Problems of Social
Cohesion in Canada." *International Migration and Integration* 16, no. 1 (2015):
153–72.

Taylor, Charles. "Iris Murdoch and Moral Philosophy." In *Dilemmas and
Connections: Selected Essays*, 3–23. Cambridge, MA: Belknap Press, 2011.

Taylor, Charles. *Modern Social Imaginaries*. Durham, NC: Duke University
Press, 2004.

Taylor, Charles. "The Politics of Recognition." In *Multiculturalism and "The
Politics of Recognition,"* edited by Amy Gutman, 25–73. Princeton, NJ: Princeton
University Press, 1994.

Taylor, Charles. *Sources of the Self: The Making of the Modern Identity*. Cambridge,
MA: Harvard University Press, 1989.

Taylor, Peggy, and Charlie Murphy. *Catch the Fire: An Art-ful Guide to Unleashing
the Creative Power of Youth, Adults and Communities*. Gabriola, BC: New Society
Publishers, 2014.

Thompson, Dennis F. "Deliberative Democratic Theory and Empirical Political
Science." *Annual Review of Political Science* 11 (2008): 497–520.

Thompson, Dennis F. "Who Should Govern Who Governs? The Role of
Citizens in Reforming the Electoral System." In *Designing Deliberative*

Democracy: The British Columbia Citizens' Assembly, edited by Mark E. Warren and Hilary Pearse, 20–49. Cambridge: Cambridge University Press, 2008.

Tickner, J. Ann. *A Feminist Voyage through International Relations*. Oxford: Oxford University Press, 2014.

Titchkosky, Tanya. *The Question of Access: Disability, Space, Meaning*. Toronto: University of Toronto Press, 2011.

Tomlinson, Kathy. "RBC replaces Canadian staff with foreign workers." *CBC News*, 6 April 2013. Online at http://www.cbc.ca/news/canada/british -columbia/rbc-replaces-canadian-staff-with-foreign-workers-1.1315008.

Tremblay, Crystal. "Towards Inclusive Waste Management: Participatory Video as a Communication Tool." *ICE Journal of Waste and Resource Management* 4, no. 66 (2012): 177–86.

Tremblay, Crystal, and Bruno de Oliveira Jayme. "Community Knowledge Co-creation through Participatory Video." *Action Research* 13, no. 3 (2015): 298–314.

Triadafilopoulus, Phil. *Becoming Multicultural: Immigration and the Politics of Membership in Canada and Germany*. Vancouver: UBC Press, 2012.

Trichopoulou, Antonia, and Pagona Lagiou. "Healthy Traditional Mediterranean Diet: An Expression of Culture, History, and Lifestyle." *Nutrition Reviews* 55, no. 11 (2009): 383–9.

Tritter, Jonathan, and Alison McCallum. "The Snakes and Ladders of User Involvement: Moving beyond Arnstein." *Health Policy* 76, no. 2 (2006): 156–68. https://doi.org/10.1016/j.healthpol.2005.05.008

Truth and Reconciliation Commission of Canada. *Honouring the Truth, Reconciling the Future: Summary of the Final Report of the Truth and Reconciliation Commission of Canada*. 2015. Online at http://nctr.ca/assets/reports/Final %20Reports/Executive_Summary_English_Web.pdf.

Truth and Reconciliation Commission of Canada. *Truth and Reconciliation Commission of Canada: Calls to Action*. 2015. Online at http://nctr.ca/assets /reports/Calls_to_Action_English2.pdf.

Tuck, Eve, and Wayne Wang. "Decolonization Is Not a Metaphor." *Decolonization: Indigeneity, Education & Society* 1, no. 1 (2012): 1–40.

Tullock, Gordon. "Public Decisions as Public Goods." *Journal of Political Economy* 79, no. 4 (1971): 913–19.

Tully, James. "The Crisis of Global Citizenship." *Radical Politics Today*, 2009. Online at https://core.ac.uk/download/pdf/14527443.pdf.

Tully, James. "Deparochializing Political Theory and Beyond: A Dialogue Approach to Comparative Political Thought." *Journal of World Philosophies* 1 (Winter 2016): 51–74. Online at https://www.researchgate.net/publication /312909208_Deparochializing_Political_Theory_and_Beyond_A_dialogue _approach_to_comparative_political_thought.

Tungohan, Ethel. "From Encountering Confederate Flags to Finding Refuge in Spaces of Solidarity: Filipino Temporary Foreign Workers' Experiences of the Public in Alberta." *Space & Polity* 21, no. 1 (2017): 11–26.

Tungohan, Ethel. "Intersectionality and Social Justice: Assessing Activists' Use of Intersectionality through Grassroots Migrants' Organizations in Canada." *Politics, Groups, and Identities* 4, no. 3 (2016): 347–62.

Tungohan, Ethel. "The Transformative and Radical Feminism of Grassroots Migrant Women's Movements in Canada." *Canadian Journal of Political Science* 50, no. 2 (2017): 479–94.

Turner, Dale. *This Is Not a Peace Pipe: Towards a Critical Indigenous Philosophy.* Toronto: University of Toronto Press, 2006.

Tyee, Staff. "What Is Social License"? *Tyee*, 1 March 2017. Online at https://thetyee.ca/Presents/2017/03/01/Social-Licence-Debate-Vancouver-Panel/, accessed 27 June 27 2018.

Unger, Jennifer B., Lourdes Baezconde-Garbanati, Sohaila Shakib, Paula H. Palmer, Elahe Nezami, and Juana Mora. "A Cultural Psychology Approach to 'Drug Abuse' Prevention." *Substance Use & Misuse* 39, no. 10–12 (2004): 1779–820. https://doi.org/10.1081/JA-200033224.

UNICEF (United Nations International Children's Emergency Fund). *A Manual on How to Integrate Children's Rights into Social and Economic Development Plans.* Hanoi: UNICEF Viet Nam, 2015. Online at https://www.unicef.org/vietnam/media/1386/file/A%20manual%20on%20how%20to%20integrate%20children's%20rights%20into%20socio-economic%20development%20plans.pdf.

UNICEF. *Situation Analysis of Children in Ho Chi Minh City, Viet Nam, 2017.* Hanoi: UNICEF Viet Nam, 2017. Online at https://www.unicef.org/vietnam/media/1516/file/Situation%20analysis%20of%20children:%20in%20Ho%20Chi%20Minh%20city%20-%20Viet%20Nam%202017.pdf.

United Nations. Department of Economic and Social Affairs. "Situation of Women and Girls with Disabilities and the Status of CRPD." New York, 15 September 2017, online at https://www.un.org/development/desa/disabilities/news/dspd/women-and-girls-with-disabilities-crpd.html.

United States. Environmental Protection Agency. "Environmental Justice." Washington, DC, 16 November 2017. Online at https://www.epa.gov/environmentaljustice.

Universities Canada. *Principles on Indigenous Education.* 25 June 2015. Online at https://www.univcan.ca/wp-content/uploads/2015/11/principles-on-indigenous-education-universities-canada-june-2015.pdf.

Urbinati, Nadia, and Mark Warren. "The Concept of Representation in Contemporary Democratic Theory." *Annual Review of Political Science* 11 (2008): 387–412.

Vagle, Mark. *Crafting Phenomenological Research*. Walnut Creek, CA: Left Coast Press, 2014.

Van Cuilenburg, Jan, and Denis McQuail. "Media Policy Paradigm Shifts: Towards a New Communications Policy Paradigm." *European Journal of Communication* 18, no. 2 (2003): 181–207.

Van Manen, Max. *Phenomenology of Practice: Meaning-Giving Methods in Phenomenological Research and Writing*. Walnut Creek, CA: Left Coast Press, 2014.

Van Manen, Max. *Researching Lived Experience: Human Science for an Action Sensitive Pedagogy*. London: Althouse Press, 1997.

Verba, Sidney. *Small Groups and Political Behavior: A Study of Leadership*. Princeton, NJ: Princeton University Press, 2015.

Vermette, D'Arcy. "Inclusion Is Killing Us." *Teaching Perspective* 17 (2012): 18–20.

Vertovec, Steven. "Minority Associations, Networks, and Public Policies: Re-assessing Relationships." *Journal of Ethnic and Migration Studies* 25, no. 1 (1999): 21–42.

Victoria. Department of Environment, Land, Water, and Planning. *Effective Engagement: Building Relationships with Community and Other Stakeholders*. 4th ed. Melbourne: State Government of Victoria, 2015.

Visvanathan, Nalini, Lynn Dugan, Nan Wiegersma, and Laurie Nisonof. *The Women, Gender and Development Reader*. 2nd. ed. London: Zed Books, 2011.

Waiser, Bill. *Saskatchewan: A New History*. Calgary: Fifth House, 2005.

Walia, Harsha. *Undoing Border Imperialism*. Oakland, CA: AK Press, 2013.

Walia, Harsha. "Why the B.C. Missing Women's Commission of Inquiry Fails." *Rabble.ca*. Vancouver, 11 October 2011.

Wallace, R. Jay. "Practical Reason." In *The Stanford Encyclopedia of Philosophy Archive*, 2014. Online at https://plato.stanford.edu/archives/sum2014/entries/practical-reason/.

Waller, Lori. "Union Helps Migrants Counter Worst Abuses of Temporary Foreign Worker Program." *Rabble.ca*, 20 November 2012. Online at http://rabble.ca/news/2012/11/union-helps-migrants-counter-worst-abuses-foreign-temporary-worker-program.

Walsh, Shannon. "Critiquing the Politics of Participatory Video and the Dangerous Romance of Liberalism." *Area* 48, no. 4 (2016): 405–11.

Warick, Jason. "It's not just add indigenous and stir: U of S's indigenization approach raising questions." *CBC News*, 23 September 2017. Online at http://www.cbc.ca/news/canada/saskatoon/indigenous-education-university-saskatchewan-1.4299551.

Warren, Mark E., and Hilary Pearse, eds. *Designing Deliberative Democracy: The British Columbia Citizens' Assembly*. Cambridge: Cambridge University Press, 2008.

Wehbi, Samantha. "Crossing Boundaries: Foreign Funding and Disability Rights Activism in a Context of War." *Disability & Society* 26, no. 5 (2011): 507–20.

Weinstock, Daniel, and David Kahane. "Introduction." In *Deliberative Democracy in Practice*, edited by David Kahane, 1–18. Vancouver: UBC Press, 2010.

Westley, Frances, Per Olsson, Carl Folke, Thomas Homer-Dixon, Harrie Vredenburg, Derk Loorbach, John Thompson, et al. "Tipping Toward Sustainability: Emerging Pathways of Transformation." *Ambio* 40, no. 7 (2011): 762–80. doi:10.1007/s13280-011-0186-9.

White, Erin, Valerie Bockstette, Thaddeus Ferber, Elizabeth Gaines, and Karen Pittman. *How Public Policy Can Support Collective Impact*. Boston: FSG & Collective Impact Forum, November 2014. Online at https://www.fsg.org /publications/how-public-policy-can-support-collective-impact.

Wiebe, Sarah Marie. "Decolonizing Engagement? Creating a Sense of Community through Collaborative Filmmaking." *Studies in Social Justice* 9, no. 2 (2016): 244–57.

Wiebe, Sarah Marie. *Everyday Exposure: Indigenous Mobilization and Environmental Justice in Canada's Chemical Valley*, Vancouver: UBC Press, 2016.

Williams, Stephen. "Evaluating Transition Experiments in Times of Rapid Change." Paper presented at conference, International Sustainability Transitions 2017, Gothenburg, Sweden, June 2017.

Williams, Stephen. "UN Sustainable Development Goals and Sustainability Transition: An Integrated Evaluative Framework." Paper presented at 2018 Summer Institute on Critical Studies of Environmental Governance, Toronto, June 2018.

Williams, Stephen, and Andréanne Doyon. "Just Systemic Change: Environmental Justice and System Transition." Paper presented at conference, International Sustainability Transitions 2018, Manchester, June 2018.

Wilson, Shawn. *Research Is Ceremony: Indigenous Research Methods*. Winnipeg: Fernwood, 2008.

Winseck, Dwyane. "Poster: Mapping Canada's Top Telecoms, Internet & Media Companies by Revenue and Market Share (2015)." Canadian Media Concentration Research Project, 22 November 2016. Online at http://www .cmcrp.org/poster-mapping-canadas-top-telecoms-internet-media-companies -by-revenue-and-market-share-2015/, accessed 6 January 2018.

Wise Practices. "Action Guide for Communities: Bringing Wise Practices to Life." n.d. Online at https://wisepractices.ca/wp-content/uploads/2018/10 /WisePractices_ActionGuide_v13.pdf.

Wood, Colin. "3 Forces Hindering Public-Sector Collaboration." *Government Technology*, 4 April 2013. Online at https://www.govtech.com/policy- management/3-Factors-Hindering-Public-Sector-Collaboration.html, accessed 3 November 2016.

Woodford, M.R., and S. Preston. "Strengthening Citizen Participation in Public Policy-Making: A Canadian Perspective." *Parliamentary Affairs* 66, no. 2 (2013): 345–63. doi:10.1093/pa/gsr065.

World Health Organization. "Constitution of the World Health Organization." Geneva: World Health Organization, 1946. .

World Health Organization. "Ottawa Charter for Health Promotion." Geneva: World Health Organization Europe, 1986.

Yanow, Dvora. "Interpretation in Policy Analysis: On Methods and Practice." *Critical Policy Analysis* 1, no. 1 (2007).

Yanow, Dvora, and Peregrine Schwartz-Shea, eds. *Interpretation and Method: Empirical Research Methods and the Interpretive Turn.* Armonk, NY: M.E. Sharpe, 2006.

Young, Iris Marion. "Activist Challenges to Deliberative Democracy." *Political Theory* 29, no. 5 (2001): 670–90.

Young, Iris Marion. "Communication and the Other: Beyond Deliberative Democracy." In *Democracy and Difference: Contesting the Boundaries of the Political,* edited by Seyla Benhabib, 120–35. Princeton, NJ: Princeton University Press, 1996.

Young, Iris Marion. *Inclusion and Democracy.* Oxford: Oxford University Press, 2002. doi: 10.1093/0198297556.001.0001.

Young, Iris Marion. *Justice and the Politics of Difference.* Princeton, NJ: Princeton University Press, 2001.

Young, Iris Marion. "Polity and Group Difference: A Critique of the Ideal of Universal Citizenship." *Ethics* 99, no. 2 (1989): 250–74.

Zhang, Youchun, Jane D. Brown, Kathryn E. Muessig, Feng Xianxiang, and He Wenzhen. "Sexual Health Knowledge and Health Practices of Female Sex Workers in Liuzhou, China, Differ by Size of Venue." *AIDS and Behavior* 18, no. 2 (2014): 162–70.

Index

A Luoi (Vietnam), 142, 144, 149, 150
Abelson, Julia, 256, 259, 267
able-bodied, 227
ableist, 143
Aboriginal activist, 343
Aboriginal Peoples, 271, 319, 333–4, 348, 397. *See also* Indigenous Peoples
Aboriginal Student Centre (Mount Saint Vincent University), 235, 238, 242
Aboriginal students, 332, 337–8, 341, 348, 389
Aboriginal Women's Action Network, 32
abortion, 359, 361
accessible, accessibility, 153, 173, 200, 213, 233, 242, 254, 260, 280–1, 290, 324
accountability, 79, 172, 202, 206, 244, 258, 320, 354, 360, 372, 394, 401
Ackerly, Brooke, 361
action-oriented, 289
active listening, 220, 237
activists, 3, 29, 42, 145, 149, 185, 222, 235, 242, 299, 302, 306–7, 318, 323, 343; academic, 314, 318
addiction, 190
adultism, 153
advocacy, 25, 36, 126, 150, 164, 167–8, 174, 282, 302, 307, 362, 376

aesthetics, 167, 346
affected constituency, 231
affected interests, affected parties, 5, 7, 12, 19, 20, 254, 270, 340, 382. *See also* democracy
affective communities of support, 303
affective framework for analysis, 230
affective spaces, 15, 288
agony, 340
Alberta, 3, 13, 47, 51, 52, 54, 58–64, 102, 294, 303–4, 306, 308
Alberta Climate Dialogues (ABCD), 64, 71
Alberta Energy Futures Lab (EFL), 13, 47–65
Alexander, Bruce, 190
Alexander, Chris, 299
Alianza Bolivariana para los Pueblos de Nuestra América (ALBA, Bolivarian Alliance for the Peoples of Our America), 356
alliances, 174, 297, 302, 333
allies, 26, 30, 32, 36, 38–9, 297, 303–5, 307, 308, 315, 324, 332–4, 342–4, 355, 358
alternative discourse, 367
alternative policy futures, 382
Aluminum Company of Canada, 98

Amnesty International, 32, 41, 45, 94, 388
amplify, amplifying, 49, 208
anger, 31, 121–2, 280, 342, 344
animals, 322, 323, 325
Anishnabeg, 97
anti-Black racism, 381. *See also* racism
anti-Christ, 359
anti-migrant, anti-migrant discourse, 296
anti-oppression, 6, 13, 16, 319, 376, 377
apartheid, 298
Aristotle, 192, 220
Arnstein, Sherry, 96, 112
art, arts-based engagement: drawing, 144, 146, 147, 208, 214–15, 223, 232; games, 51, 146, 209, 232; mobile art, 15, 280, 284, 286–7; mosaics, 278, 283–6, 290; music, 4, 209, 222–3, 277, 315–16; painting, 278, 283–4, 289, 316; poetry, 7, 209, 316; theatre, 209, 347
"art-ful," 14. *See also* citizen/public engagement methods
art gallery, galleries, 15, 277–91
artistic expression, 284, 378
artists, 122, 209, 214, 245, 277, 287, 288, 313, 315, 321, 330
Asian Women Coalition Ending Prostitution, 32
assemblage, 58, 283
Assembly of First Nations, 33
assimilation, 339
Association of Indigenous Women of the Atlantic, 356
atmosphere, 29, 121, 124, 132, 167, 210, 215, 262, 288, 340
Attawapiskat, 15, 312–24
attitudes, 31, 35, 100, 163, 193, 301, 340

authorities, 163, 176, 313–14, 365, 366
autonomy, 28, 164, 346
awareness of rights, 143–4, 149

Bac Tu Liem (Vietnam), 144, 147, 150, 151
Barney, Darin, 167
Barrett, Gregory, 9, 140, 143, 258
Bator, Francis, 77
Battiste, Marie, 348
BC Citizens' Assembly on Electoral Reform, 123, 132, 138. *See also* citizens' assemblies
BC Civil Liberties Association (BCCLA), 33
BC Coalition of Childcare Advocates, 33
BC Council of Women, 33
beauty, beautiful, 218, 220, 223, 290, 321
being-in-the-world, 191–2
belonging, 111, 113, 141, 149, 192, 290, 313, 320
beneficiaries, 354–5, 364–5, 369
Benhabib, Seyla, 29
Bennett, Darcie, 37
bias, 31, 39, 48, 53, 173, 240, 255, 270, 281, 335, 338–9, 410
Bickford, Susan, 219
bilingual, 256, 261
Bill C-30, Lawful Access Bill, 172
Bill C-51, 172–4
Boler, Megan, 193
Borg, Carmel, 280, 289
Botes, Annatjie, 194
Boyer, Ernest, 189
brainstorming, 34, 233, 330
bravery, 348
Brazil, 15, 277, 278–82, 291, 317
break the cycle, 322
briefing note, 299, 301

Bringing the Pieces Together (BPT), 253, 256, 267, 268
Broadcasting Act (1991), 166, 179, 185
Broadway and Commercial (Vancouver), 118, 120
Bronfenbrenner, Urie, 190
Bryce, Cheryl, 103
Buber, Martin, 192–3
Buchanan, James, 77
bureaucracy, bureaucratizing, 167, 178, 224, 229, 245, 266, 301, 354

calls for proposals, 360
campus, 14, 187–90, 192, 195–201, 235, 336–8, 341, 343, 347
Can Tho (Vietnam), 144, 147
Canada's Privacy Plan, 170, 172–4, 183
Canada Without Poverty, 257, 271, 395
Canadian Association of Sexual Assault Centres, 33
Canadian immigration policy, 297
Canadian Internet Policy and Public Interest Clinic, 173
Canadian Radio League, 169
Canadian Radio-television and Telecommunications Commission (CRTC), 166–9, 171, 172, 183. See also communication policy making
Canadian-Indigenous relations, 313
Canadians for Democratic Media (CDM), 169
CANARIE (formerly the Canadian Network for the Advancement of Research, Industry and Education), 167
capacity, capacity-building, 56–7, 61, 76, 81–2, 87, 97, 108, 117, 124, 128–32, 139–40, 144–5, 155, 167,

188, 193, 199, 220, 223, 233, 242–4, 281–4, 354, 356, 381
capitalism, 165, 280
care, caring, 106, 148, 189, 313, 320, 322, 345, 347
caregivers, 216, 297, 301
Caribbean, 297, 298, 356
Caribbean Domestics Scheme, 297
Carpentier, Nico, 178
Carrier Sekani Tribal Council, 33
Carroll, William K., 168
Casting an Open Net, 170
Cattapan, Alana, 14, 16, 17, 267, 378, 381
Caucasian, 342
Cauchi, Bernard, 289
cautionary tale, 380
celebrating culture, 321
census, 40, 256, 271
Central America Women's Network, 357
ceremony, ceremonies, 4, 7, 235, 321, 323, 325, 342, 354
Challenge for Change initiative, 229
Chaney, Nadia, 209, 212
Changing Public Engagement from the Ground Up, 226, 227, 233, 239, 244–5
Changing the Culture of Substance Use, 188, 189, 195, 196, 199, 200
Charlottetown Accord, 228
Chicago, 72, 75
Chicago Citywide Literacy Coalition, 75
Chiefs (Indigenous), 4, 33, 312, 314, 326, 330
childcare, daycare, 58, 69, 110, 242, 375–6, 383
children, 100, 106–7, 142, 150, 159, 208, 213, 218, 235, 258, 261, 307, 364, 375

Chinese railroad workers, 297, 300.
  See also racism
Chinese-language focus groups, 125
Chippewa, 97
Christian values, 359
Cincinnati, 80
citizen, citizenship, 296, 357
Citizen Power Councils, 356
citizen/public engagement methods,
  214, 230, 240, 246; citizen polls, 28,
  48, 65, 123; citizens' assembly/
  assemblies, 13, 117–18, 120–4, 129,
  131, 132–8, 253, 269 (*see also* BC
  Citizens' Assembly on Electoral
  Reform; Grandview-Woodland
  Citizens' Assembly); community
  forum, 303; consultation, public
  consultation, 4, 5, 8–10, 14, 118,
  121, 128, 136, 152, 170–3, 197, 226,
  227–9, 231–3, 238, 245, 262, 358,
  380; crowdsourcing, 164, 169–73,
  186; deliberative polling, 28, 48,
  65, 123, 175; digital storytelling,
  visual methods, 232, 313, 318,
  329–30; engagement methods and
  tools, 14, 17, 246; focus groups,
  125, 146; hashtag campaigns,
  #strongertogether, 172, 233, 324;
  mini-publics, 13, 255, 270, 344;
  mixed-media storytelling, 15,
  313, 318, 319–20, 323–6; online
  petitions, 172; participatory
  budgeting, 28, 48, 176; policy
  hacking, 14, 164, 169, 174–5;
  popular participation, 254, 380;
  public engagement experiments,
  250; public hearings, 3, 166, 172,
  211, 226; public inquiries, 28;
  questionnaires, "drag and drop"
  interactive survey, 170, 230, 246,
  259–60, 291; roundtable sessions,
  166, 257; sharing circles, 106,

378; storytelling, 15, 221, 222,
  232, 312–31, 346, 378; town halls,
  internet town halls, 170, 211, 228,
  230; web-based technologies, 230;
  workshops, 51–3, 56–9, 69, 104–5,
  134–5, 144, 151–2, 236–42, 278,
  282–6, 291, 313, 315–16, 320, 394.
  See also research methods
Citizenship and Immigration
  Canada, 301, 307–9
city hall, 277, 284, 288
civic and political knowledge, 143–4
civic engagement, civic
  participation, 27, 75, 172, 208, 209,
  214, 220, 225, 229, 278–9, 289, 291
civic imagination, 222
civic renewal, 141, 219, 257, 268, 318
civil and economic rights, 357, 366
civil society, civil society
  organizations, 15, 27, 38, 142, 143,
  147, 172–4, 228, 353, 355–9, 362–3,
  378, 380
civilizing rituals, 289, 293, 341, 401
Clark, Natalie, 243, 384–5
climate change, 8, 64, 66, 67, 71, 73,
  96, 175, 394, 411, 425
climate of distrust, 359
Clover, Darlene, 280–1
co-construction, 290, 383, 416
co-create, creation, 313, 318, 335
Coalition Ending Prostitution, 32
coalitions, 3, 32, 33, 49, 126, 169, 304,
  355, 361
Coast Salish Territory, 323
Cole, L. Arda, 280
collaboration, 8, 13, 14, 17, 47, 57, 58,
  80, 87, 91, 144, 146, 164, 209, 222–3,
  226, 245, 313, 316–19, 321, 324, 326,
  329, 363, 381
collective: action, 72–3, 76–9, 82, 88,
  89, 91, 176, 222; agenda setting,
  254; deliberation, 28, 36, 38, 39

(*see also* public deliberation); experience, 191, 367; message, 290; struggle, 237

colonial mindset, 334; neocolonial, 148, 154; as tool of oppression, 338. *See also* decolonial, anticolonial

colour, 125, 146, 210, 218, 236, 241, 312, 321

comfort zones, 286, 290, 291

common goals, 88, 334

communal judges, 366

communicative engagement, 140, 172, 219

Communist Party of Vietnam, 142, 157

community: art, art gallery, 225, 278, 287, 290; building, development, 86, 88, 278, 279, 281; creative engagement, 230; engagement, 222, 258, 313, 318, 332; expertise, 325; leaders, 279, 320; organizing, 296, 302, 305; perspectives, 313; social learning, 197

Community Inclusion Networks (CINs), 257. *See also* Economic and Social Inclusion Corporation

community-based policy research, 227, 232, 267

competitive bidding process, 360

competitive policy, 334

complementary action, 356

connections, interconnections, 10–11, 14, 17, 28, 36, 49, 58, 60, 63, 74, 75, 81, 104–5, 107, 143, 174, 191, 208–13, 218, 229, 237, 242, 255, 263, 272, 314–15, 321–4, 326, 333–4, 336, 341, 345, 347, 378

Connell, Raewyn, 149

conscientização, 278, 282, 286, 288

consciousness-raising groups, 29

consensus mobilization, 174

constellation of contextual factors, 313

constellations of concern, 4, 117, 122–3

contextual conditions/factors, 176, 256, 259, 266, 268, 358

convener, 82, 377

cooperation, 225, 254, 284, 354, 356, 369, 370, 388, 391, 393, 394, 416

cooperative spirit, 348

cooperatives, 278, 281, 282, 283, 317

Corntassel, Jeff, 103

cosmologies, 366

counterargument, 344

counternarratives, 289, 313, 316, 317, 324

countervailing power, 176, 184, 404

courage, 303, 348, 381

Cowen, Emory, 189, 192

Cowichan Valley (British Columbia), 215, 216

CRAB-Water for Life Society, 31, 33

creative arts-based methodologies, 14, 139, 152, 154, 230, 278–81, 314, 378

creative community-based policy research commitments, 232, 267

creative writing, 232

creativity, 9, 10, 11, 14, 16, 123, 135, 220, 225–33, 243, 245, 267, 280, 289, 313–18, 321, 325, 347, 378, 382, 429

Cree, 322, 326

criminal justice, 32, 33, 74, 375–6. *See also* justice

criminal justice branch, 32, 33

crises, 15, 313

critical pedagogy, 195, 280. *See also* pedagogy

critical policy studies, 18, 19, 247, 252, 383, 393, 412, 416, 419, 421

Crouch, Colin, 165

crowdsourced policy recommendations. *See* Canada's Privacy Plan; Casting an

Open Net; Our Digital Future;
Reimagine CBC; Time for an
Upgrade
Cuadra, Maria Elena, 357
cultural history, 336
Cultural Medicine Cabinet Choir,
222
cultural norms, 297
cultural politics, 280, 292, 293, 392
culturally appropriate care, 313
culturally appropriate interventions,
365
culture as being in the world, 189,
191
currents of thought, 348
curriculum, 123, 124, 204, 334, 348,
350, 402
cybersurveillance, cybersurveillance
capabilities, 172. See also Bill C-30;
Bill C-51
cynicism, 121, 166, 179, 211, 227,
265-8

dance, dancing, 232, 320-3
Datta, Kavita, 365
de Oliveira Jayme, Bruno, 15-17,
317, 378
decolonial, anticolonial: critiquing
colonialism, 321; post-colonial
politics, 141, 143, 145, 177. See also
colonial
deep listening, 194, 240
Deleuze, Gilles, 20, 288, 290, 384
deliberating reconciliation, 332-6,
341, 344, 349
deliberative oppression, 28
deliberative practices, 26, 333, 351,
379. See also public participation
democracy: counter democracy,
14, 164, 170, 175-80, 185, 425;
democratization, 142-3, 164, 179,
199-200, 266; durable democracy

of distrust, 177; knowledge
democracy, 7, 164, 368, 381;
participatory counter-democracy,
164, 177-9; participatory
democracy, 5, 6, 42, 208, 212-14,
219, 222, 356, 376-7; thin
democracy, 213
democratic participation: artistic
tools, art shows, art exhibits,
208, 233, 277-9, 283-4, 288;
collaborative decision making,
80, 87; collaborative policy
making, 381; democracy of the
arts, 288; democratic illusion,
46; participatory democratic
engagement, 357; political
listening, 14, 208, 219-23
democratic rationalization, 178
democratization, 142, 143, 164, 179,
199, 200, 266
demonstration, 4, 12, 25-30, 39, 41,
130, 288, 343
Department of Foreign Affairs,
Trade and Development (Canada),
360
Department of Social Development
(New Brunswick), 253
deputy minister, 264
designing for uptake, 264
déterritorializationés, 288
Development Assistance Committee
(OECD), 354
development cooperation,
development cooperation
landscape, 354
Dhillon, Jaskiran, 313
dialectical spaces, 278, 279, 291
dialogue: community-based,
221; culture-focused, 14, 200;
deliberative, 189, 228, 257,
317; engagement projects, 208;
generative, 211; meaningful, 211,

244, 291; multi-, 240; policy, 223, 324; public, 14, 222, 257, 259, 260, 263, 264, 268. *See also* Alberta Climate Dialogues; democratic participation; Dinner Dialogues; Imagine BC
different viewpoints, 208
difficult conversations, 145, 338
difficult-to-reach publics, 231, 244, 381. *See also* historically marginalized groups, people; marginalized
Dinner Dialogues, 198
direct participation, 270, 364, 413
disability, disabilities, 13, 139, 140, 143–9, 151–5, 159, 357
disability politics, 140, 143
Disabled Person(s) Organizations (DPOs), 139
discrimination, 34, 35, 41, 76, 146, 149, 150, 151, 227, 350, 355, 358, 368, 388, 406, 420
discursive, 42, 66, 82, 231, 316, 351, 385, 400, 403
disruption, 29, 50, 51, 56, 109, 143, 152, 211, 244, 254, 288, 303, 348, 380
dissemination, 319, 320
District of Kitimat (British Columbia), 98
diverse: communities, 16, 249; members of the public, 254; spaces, 367; stakeholders, 201, 260; voices, 111, 200, 208, 223, 262
Đổi Mới, 141, 142, 157
domestic violence, 302, 359
donors, 231, 249, 332, 354, 355, 358–61, 366, 369, 372, 396
donors club, 354
Downtown Eastside (DTES) (Vancouver), 25, 26, 28, 30–3, 35, 36–9, 222

Downtown Eastside Women's Centre (DEWC), 31, 32, 34–6, 38–9, 44, 416
dreams, 148, 151, 214, 278, 291, 311, 322, 413
drink with class, 198
drug plan, 258
drumming, 235, 321, 322
Dryzek, John, 26, 258
Duncan, Carol, 289
Durkheim, Emile, 190

early childhood education, 208, 212
earthy indicators, 192
East Vancouver, 118
Eby, David, 37, 40
Eckersley, Richard, 191
ecological restoration, 208
Economic and Social Inclusion Corporation, 257
economic development, 80–6, 91, 106, 110, 159, 166, 354, 357, 371, 392, 431
economic literacy, 357
ecosystem of relations, 322
Edmonton, 47, 56, 57, 68, 294, 304, 310
egg donors, 231
e-gov initiative, 74. *See also* governance
Elders, 100, 339, 342, 344
elected officials, 3, 19, 72, 85, 223, 262, 264, 382
electoral politics, 302
electoral reform, 123, 132, 138, 253–4, 269
elites, 29, 123, 142, 165–5, 175, 178, 193–4, 269
emancipation, 129, 130–8, 281, 282, 359
embodied practice, 147, 148, 191, 201, 237, 283, 287, 318, 345

emergency, 159, 312, 313–20
emerging directions, 121, 122
emotion, 51, 104, 113, 210, 280, 283, 322, 323, 336, 340, 347, 378
empathy, 193, 205, 214
empowerment, 8, 27–9, 82, 117, 132, 143, 144, 151, 175, 178, 194–5, 198, 213, 278, 281–2, 285–91, 367
"End the Temporary Foreign Worker Program" Coalition, 303
Ending Violence Association of BC (EVA BC), 33, 98
energy sector, 47
England and Wales, 255
English (language), 121, 125, 216, 236, 256, 260
entangled ideologies, 359
environment, 16, 48–9, 55, 59, 72, 78, 94–6, 98, 103–4, 151, 174, 179, 189, 190–1, 197–8, 266, 278–9, 280–8, 290–1, 338, 341, 359, 361
environmental agents, 279, 283, 285–8
environmental clean-up, 315
environmental education, 281–2, 285
environmental issues, 279, 281–2, 288, 291
environmental justice, 19, 25, 28, 70, 96, 103, 104, 108, 115, 269, 317, 331
epistemology, 7, 153, 245, 289, 320, 329, 343, 349, 367, 368
Epp, Jake, 189
Ermine, Willie, 348
ethics: of care, 107, 193, 194, 320, 344; ethical relations, 333; of justice, 194; research ethics, 97, 243, 244, 334. See also research ethics boards
ethnic background, 357
ethnicity, 125, 146, 149, 302
ethos of life, 335
Eurocentric, 280, 289, 290
European Union, 307, 360

evaluation, 9, 11, 13, 14, 28, 29, 48–50, 53, 56, 58, 62, 73, 80, 86, 145, 201, 228, 234, 235, 237, 253, 256–8, 262, 265–6, 268, 326, 362, 369, 377
evidence-based policies, 199
exclusion, 8, 12–15, 25–8, 32, 34, 37, 39, 95–6, 99, 100, 102–3, 107, 108–9, 139, 141–5, 148–55, 166, 230–1, 241, 266, 267–8, 291, 297, 300, 333, 355, 377–80
executive order, 223
experiential expertise, experiential knowledge, 27, 226, 230, 233, 317, 382
experiment, experimental, 49–50, 60, 133, 190, 226, 244, 265–6, 269, 290, 387
Exploited Voices now Educating, 33
external experts, 313, 320

Facebook, 324
facilitation and process methods, 51
facilitators, 145, 151, 222, 235–7, 260, 263–6, 286, 291
Falleti, Tulia, 259
Fals-Borda, Orlando, 195
family, family unit, 25, 30–2, 35–6, 39, 84, 104, 107–8, 124–5, 261, 283, 289, 321, 334–7, 357, 364
faux participation, 176
February 14th Women's Memorial March, 31
feed-forward effects, 95, 100, 110, 111
feelings, 113, 122, 128, 130, 198, 235, 306, 323, 325, 340, 343, 345, 340
Feenberg, Andrew, 178
fellowship, 55, 69, 213
Femenías, Maria Luisa, 367
feminism, feminists, 8, 14, 40, 106, 111, 116, 227–32, 237–8, 240, 244, 245, 252, 267, 302, 313, 317, 353, 356–9, 364–7, 369

feminist cinematics, 313, 317
feminist economics, 357
feminist organizations, 228, 353, 358, 359
feminist policy analysis, 227, 229
feminist political economy, 353, 357, 358
feminist research, 227, 232
femocrats, 229
fetishize the local, 368
Filipino, 15, 302, 304
film screenings, 233
filmmaker, 222, 229, 235, 242
financial crisis of 2008, 360
Findlay, Tammy, 14, 16, 17, 228, 238, 378
First Nations, 31, 33, 40, 101, 108, 114, 116, 260, 327, 328, 332, 349, 380. *See also* Aboriginal Peoples; Indigenous Peoples
First Nations Summit (FNS), 31, 33
Fischer, Frank, 345, 379
Fishkin, James, 123
forms of participation, 176, 178, 180, 208
food insecurity, 106, 375, 376, 382
food security, 104, 106, 109, 110, 119
Ford Foundation, 86
Foreign Domestics Movement, 297, 306
Forester, John, 223
forums, policy forums, 7, 13, 26–30, 35, 37, 166, 229, 233, 257, 294, 295, 303, 339, 341, 343–5, 355, 378, 381
Frank, Thomas, 165
Frank Paul Society, 33
Freire, Paulo, 195, 278, 282, 286, 288, 379
French (language), 142, 256, 260, 262
friendships, 88, 303, 347, 356, 360, 365–6
front-line interactions, 265

frustration, 3, 291, 340, 342
FSG (consulting firm), 81, 87
Fuji Johnson, Genevieve, 7, 101, 123, 175, 255, 338, 378
funding, 33, 34, 36, 37, 51, 58, 72, 73, 80–5, 90, 113, 145, 188, 243–5, 301, 315, 324, 325, 358, 359, 360–5
future generations, 4, 322

Gadamer, Hans-Georg, 193
Gauvin, François-Pierre, 256
Gaventa, John, 9
gaze, 316, 317
Geels, Frank, 49, 54, 58–9, 60
gender budgeting, 357
gender development theory, 356–7, 363–6; and development scholarship, 357
gender equality, 148, 153, 353, 355–8, 362–8
Gender Equality and Violence Against Women, 356, 358, 366
gender-sensitive indicators, 354, 358, 368
gender-sensitive policies, 230, 353, 356–7, 363
genocide, 41
geopolitical location, 230, 318
gestalt, 219
gift, 131, 320, 343, 352
Gillis, Jacqueline, 13, 16, 17, 378, 380–1
girls, 13, 33, 40–1, 94, 99, 100, 108, 139, 142, 144–56, 232, 234, 243, 377, 384
Girls Conference, 236–42
Global Affairs Canada, 360–1
global aid: architecture, 354, 357, 369, 372, 374; beneficiary countries, 354; budgets, 360; conditionality, 354, 369; effectiveness, 353–8, 362, 363,

365–9; international development
aid, 353; management, 354, 355,
360, 361; priority countries, 360;
tied aid, 354, 369
global forums, 355
global initiatives, 8
Global Partnership for Effective
Development, 355, 370
global South, 8, 148, 152–4, 297, 298,
353
Goldhammer, Arthur, 180
Goldring, Luin, 302, 305
Govender, Kasari, 37–8, 40
governance, 9, 13, 26–9, 38–40,
142, 166, 255, 273, 316, 378, 380;
hierarchies of, 9, 378. See also
e-government
governmentality, 19, 313, 384
graduate students, 209
graffiti, 277
Graham, Katherine, 230
Grandview-Woodland Citizens'
Assembly, 117, 118, 120, 121, 122,
124, 129, 131, 132, 133
Grant, John, 123
grassroots events, organizations:
community networks, 233,
315. See also CRAB-Water for
Life Society; February 14th
Women's Memorial March;
Foreign Domestics Movement;
Indigenous organizations;
International Migrants Alliance;
Men Allied with Women's
Health; Migrante Alberta; Our
Community, Our Plan (OCOP);
Still Moon Society
Gratl, Jason, 31
Guattari, Félix, 288, 290
Guildford neighbourhood (Surrey,
BC), 216
Gutmann, Amy, 254, 273

Habermas, Jurgen, 191, 193
Hacket, Robert, 168
Haisla Nation, 97–9, 101–2, 106–10
Haisla territory, 98, 99, 101, 102, 106,
107–10
Halifax, 233, 236
Hamrick, Will, 345
Hankivsky, Olena, 306
Hansen, William, 190
happiness, 151, 290
Happy Valley-Goose Bay (HV-GB)
(Newfoundland and Labrador),
97, 99, 104, 105
Haraway, Donna, 17, 365
Harding, Sandra, 368
Harper, Stephen, 171
Harvey, David, 165
Haudenosaunee, 97
head tax, 297
healing, 315, 321, 322, 323, 324
health: community health,
community health and wellness,
16, 313–15, 382; global health, 209;
health benefits, 258; mental health,
106, 110, 142, 216, 314, 315, 323.
See also Health Canada; Healthy
Minds | Healthy Campuses;
Ministry of Health (British
Columbia); Ottawa Charter on
Health Promotion
Health Canada, 231, 314, 323, 324
Healthy Minds | Healthy
Campuses, 188, 196
hearing, 17, 37, 123, 125, 126, 153,
171–3, 220, 240, 260, 262, 263, 303
heartbeat of the earth, 322. See also
Cree
hegemonic, 28, 37, 154, 174, 178,
279–81, 288, 291, 317
Heidegger, Martin, 191
Hendriks, Carolyn, 27, 29–30
Heritage Canada, 169

hesitation, 333, 341, 343
hidden politics, 232
hidden practices and structures, 333
Hintz, Arne, 174
historically marginalized groups, people, 9, 15, 39, 141, 231, 253, 258, 267
holistic, 320
home, 97, 98, 107, 122, 215 237, 256, 261, 294, 299, 300, 302, 314, 320–3, 335, 337
Honig, Bonnie, 316
Hookimaw, Tyra, 315
hope, hopelessness, 35, 72, 118, 148, 150–2, 170, 175, 196, 201, 227, 245, 259, 267, 288, 291, 299, 313–15, 322, 323, 378, 380, 382
Horizons of Friendship, 356, 360, 365, 366
horror stories, 171, 172
hospitable, hospitality, 294, 348
human dignity, 364
human rights, 33, 41, 103, 139, 143, 146, 150, 152, 173, 293, 309, 353, 358, 359, 362, 364, 366
humanity, 341
humility, 117, 137, 140, 313, 320, 322
humour, 320
hunger strike, 312, 326
Huron Wendat territory, 97

identity, identities: female, 236; pluralistic, 368; social, 104, 256, 288
ideology, 142, 153, 164, 165, 169, 298, 364
Idle No More, 312
image, 105, 151, 171, 175, 209–16, 283, 320–2
imagination, 7, 62, 222, 313, 316, 318, 382
Imagine BC, 221

immigrants, 121, 212, 214, 222, 234, 253, 295, 297, 302
immigration minister, 298, 299, 306
Impact Assessment Act (2019), 96
imperialism, 280
income generation, 279, 284, 286, 287
Indian Act, 108, 380. See also colonial
Indiana, 81, 82
indigenization, 332, 334–5, 341
Indigenous engagement, 333
Indigenous epistemology, 320
Indigenous knowledges, 338
Indigenous land rights, 177
Indigenous Peoples, 8–9, 16, 27, 42, 43, 52, 94, 102, 104, 108, 142, 312–16, 326, 348, 380, 399, 409, 415. See also Aboriginal Peoples; First Nations
Indigenous population, 256
Indigenous resurgence, 104
Indigenous rights, 94, 366
Indigenous sovereignty, 177, 245
Indigenous storytelling methodologies, 313
Indigenous ways of knowing, 334
Indigenous women, 25, 33, 36, 40–2, 94, 97, 102, 108, 111, 232–7, 240–5, 342, 356
Indigenous youth, 313, 315, 318, 323, 324, 377
Indigenous-settler engagement, 381
Industry Canada, 166, 169
inequity, inequities, 10, 376
influencing factors, 358
information and communications technology (ICT), "big five," big three, 167, 171
Information Highway Advisory Council, 167
injustice, 25, 28, 29, 34, 35, 104, 107, 280, 291, 333, 336, 361, 368, 375, 376

innovation, 6, 16, 47–58, 60–4, 76, 166, 176, 178, 208, 227, 253, 256, 259
Innu Nation, 97
Insights, 26, 27, 50, 51, 56, 58, 59, 65, 73–5, 77, 78, 139, 152, 179, 190, 193, 200, 201, 238, 241, 255, 261, 268, 319, 321, 335, 340–1, 354, 357
inspections, 300
institutional initiatives, 332
institutional policies and practices, 188, 332
institutional rifts, 333
institutionalized public engagement, 166, 272
Instituto Nicaraguense de la Mujer, 363
interaction, 51, 170, 228, 289, 346
intercultural competencies, 335
interdepartmental silos, silo effects, 187, 264
International Association for Public Participation (IAP2), 8, 96, 273
International Migrants Alliance, 306
International Monetary Fund, 358
international relations, 357
international students, 335
internationalization, 335
interpretations, 53, 77, 140, 153, 216, 227, 330, 335, 342, 366, 367, 379
interpreting, 38, 283, 346
interrogation, 229, 319
intersectionality, 6, 8, 10, 14, 16, 95, 103, 116, 144, 155, 227, 230, 237–40, 243, 253, 256, 265, 302, 306, 317, 357, 376, 378, 379
interventions, 50, 53, 56, 60, 63–4, 142, 164–5, 167, 174, 190, 200, 216, 304–5, 313, 315–18, 321, 323, 333, 345, 361–2
interweaving, 347
Inuit, 40, 97, 104, 106, 107

Inuksuk, 104, 105
investment, 167, 325
invisibility, 15, 17, 139, 146, 147, 155, 244, 319, 365, 376, 377
issue reformulation, 223
I-you word pair, 193

Jacotot, Joseph, 129
James Bay 312, 315. See also Ontario
John, Peter, 255
Jones, Melinda, 140
journalism, 170
joy, 290
jurisdiction, 5, 9, 16, 64, 134, 253, 268
Justice for Girls, 33

Kabeer, Naila, 364
Kania, John, 76, 79
Karpowitz, Christopher, 259
Kenney, Jason, 298, 304
Kentucky, 80
kindness, 333, 344–8
kinship, 347
Kitamaat Village, 98, 99, 106, 109
kitchen table discussions, 233
Knapp, Dave, 213
knowledge democracy, 7, 164, 368, 381, 382
knowledge mobilization, 280, 281, 289
knowledge systems, 6, 7, 380. See also Indigenous ways of knowing
Kovach, Margaret, 319–20
Kramer, Mark, 76, 78–80, 82
Kuokkanen, Rauna, 338, 352

labour brokerage, 301
Labour Market Impact Assessment, 294, 298
Labour Market Opinion, 298
labour unions, 303–5
Labrador, 97, 99, 105, 106, 110

land relationships, 380
land-based healing, 315
Landolt, Patricia, 302, 305
lands, 4, 97, 312, 314, 321, 325
Lang, Amy, 123
language: jargon-free, clear, accessible, 171, 173; non-agentic, 265; policy language, 171, 173; shared, 194, 209, 222; sign language, 153
Larocque, Florence, 256, 258
lasting change, 332
Latin America, 293, 302, 356; and organizing, 302
laughter, 320
lawyers, 33–7, 288
layers of myth, 4, 107, 302, 305, 338
Leach, Edmund, 191
leadership, 9, 47, 86, 154, 165, 172, 198, 216, 237, 259, 282, 293, 304, 312, 316, 320, 324, 330, 333, 335
Learmond, Meva, 238, 241, 246
learning spaces, 282
legal commitments, 380
legal framework, 9, 264
legal processes, 365
legislatures, 175, 264
legitimacy, 5, 7, 35, 55, 64, 100, 177, 178, 208, 216, 223, 229, 233, 354, 216, 291, 339, 354, 356
lenses, 10, 14, 28, 50, 51, 61, 63, 64, 76, 79, 280, 288, 307, 317, 318, 357, 382
Lerner, Josh, 211, 213
lessons learned, 87, 227, 314, 354
Levac, Leah, 13, 15, 16, 17, 231, 261, 339, 343, 380–1
Levitas, Ruth, 141
Lewin, Kurt, 195
Liberal government, 232
liberal individualism, 320
Liberman, Robert, 103, 111
Library and Archives Canada, 169

light and shadows, 321
linear, 9, 264, 290, 302, 318, 361, 362, 367
linear relationship, 302
Linklater Jr., Jack, 312, 315, 322, 326, 330, 331
listening, 4, 9, 14, 17, 88, 140, 194, 208, 219, 220–3, 237, 240, 278, 304, 313, 323, 341, 346, 347, 379
literacy, 75, 76, 81, 216, 357
lived experience, first-hand experience, 6, 33, 73, 94, 117–18, 132, 144, 148, 191, 201, 209, 216, 219, 222–4, 227–30, 245, 256, 258, 265, 268, 279–80, 291, 295, 302, 318, 333, 335, 358, 368–9, 376, 379, 382
Live-in Caregiver Program, 297
LNG Canada, 99, 101
lobbying, 303, 305
local initiatives, 86
Local Initiatives Support Corporation, 86
local municipalities, 365
local politics, 152, 302, 362
local spaces, 368
locality, 369
logics, 100, 200, 266, 301, 356, 361
Londrina (Brazil), 284, 285
longitudinal analysis, 302
Louis Bull Tribe, 58
love, 4, 223, 290, 312, 322
low income, 15, 19, 81, 103, 212, 253, 255–68, 377
Lower Churchill (Newfoundland and Labrador), 97, 98, 102
Lynch, Julia, 259

machismo, 366
Mackey, Eva, 346–7
Maclean's, 323
macro, 12, 13, 25–8, 30, 32, 36–9, 49, 192, 199, 255, 306, 338, 378

macro culture, 192, 199
macro sphere, 26, 27, 38, 378
Magnusson, Rachel, 5, 13, 16, 137, 253, 344
mainstream narratives, 302
majority group womxn, 365
male community judges, 366
malestream, 229
Malta, 289
managing for results, 354
mandate, 8, 106, 188, 190, 192, 195, 239, 257, 295, 340
Mansbridge, Jane, 26–7, 29, 35
marginalization, 9–12, 15, 26–8, 33–9, 98, 141, 153–4, 166, 196, 223, 229, 231, 234, 237, 244, 253, 254, 258, 267, 278, 279, 282, 286, 288, 289, 334, 376, 379. See also historically marginalized groups, people
market economy, 357
Martin, Carol, 34, 44
Martin, Catherine, 235, 238, 241–2
masculinity, masculinities, 6, 99, 101–2, 359, 366
Mayo, Perter, 280, 289
McBride, Stephen, 166
McCallum, John, 306
McGauley, Laurie, 281
McIlwaine, Cathy, 365
McIntyre, Maura, 280
MDG Achievement Fund, 357, 363–6
meaning-making, 280, 286
meaningful policy change, 265
media studies, 317
memorial, 26, 31–9, 235–41
Men Allied with Women's Health, 366
Mendelberg, Tali, 259
Mennonite farmers, 297
Merleau-Ponty, Maurice, 191
meso, 306
metanarratives, 320

metaphor, 52, 222, 290
Mexican and Central American farmers, 297. See also racism
micro culture, 192, 199
microsphere, 26, 27, 29, 38, 192, 255, 378
migrant activism, 302, 306–7, 393. See also activists
migrant workers, 15, 295, 297–303, 305–7, 309, 311, 381
Migrant Workers Alliance for Change (MWAC), 304–5
Migrante Alberta, 294, 303, 304, 306
Migrante International, 306
Mi'kmaq, Mi'kmaw, 235, 242, 256
military dictatorship, 282
mini-grants, 197
Ministry of Health (British Columbia), 188
Ministry of the Family, Youth and Children (Nicaragua), 364
missing and murdered women, 25, 26, 28, 30–3, 35–6, 38, 39–41, 108, 232, 235
Mississaugas of the Credit, 97
MNCR Women's Conference, 284, 285
mobilization, 31, 39, 174, 278, 280, 281, 289, 302, 306
moccasin vamps, 235
modes of communication, 141, 346
money, 122, 166, 239, 356, 360, 369
monitoring, 50, 53, 98, 361, 362, 369
Moore, Michael, 222
Moore Lappé, Frances, 213
Moose Factory, 314
more-than-human, 322
Morris J. Wosk Centre for Dialogue, 209, 212
Moscrop, David, 267, 379
Mouffe, Chantal, 176
Mount Saint Vincent University, 233, 250

mourning, 240
multiculturalism, 114, 208, 209, 222
multijurisdictional, 5, 9, 16, 64, 253, 268
multilayered analysis, 8, 230, 318–19, 343
multilayered policy problems, 8, 324, 343
multilevel actor networks, 50
multilingual, 261
multiple axes of diversity, 194
multiple perspectives, 368
multiple sites of authority, 317
Muñoz Cabrera, Patricia, 359
Museum of Modern Art, 289
Mushkegowuk territory, 312
musicians, 4, 223, 315
mutual accountability, 354
mutual respect, 262, 278
mutually reinforcing dynamics, 50, 57

Nalcor, 101
Nancy's Chair in Women's Studies (MSVU), 235, 242
nannies, 297
narratives, 12, 15, 48, 51–8, 60–4, 73, 108, 121, 152, 222, 280, 288, 290, 302, 313, 315, 316, 318, 319, 322–5
National Broadband Task Force, 167
National Congress of Black Women, 33
National Film Board of Canada, 229
National Inquiry into Missing and Murdered Indigenous Women and Girls, 41, 232, 419
National Maritime Museum, 289
National Observer, 173
National Occupation Classification, 298
National Program on Gender Equality, 364

Native American and Indigenous Studies Association, 323
Native Courtworker and Counselling Association of BC, 33
native students, 341, 350
Native Women's Association of Canada (NWAC), 33, 40
natural law, 344
Natural Step Canada, 47, 51, 65
negotiations, 124, 131, 133, 152, 176, 185, 213, 214, 221, 238, 266, 279, 280, 287, 343
neighbourhood, 28, 30–1, 37, 74, 81–2, 118–27, 133, 216–17, 220, 253, 265, 286
neoclassical economics, 12, 73
neoliberalism, 152–3, 157, 163–5, 168, 170, 176–9, 228
new aid architecture, 354, 357, 369
New Brunswick, 253, 256, 257, 260, 262, 267, 268
New York, 289
newcomers, 222, 343
Nicaragua, 15, 353, 355–9, 360–1, 363–6, 368
niche innovations, 48–50, 55–61, 64
Nicholson, Rob, 172
Nightingale, Eithne, 288
non-citizens, 15, 296
non-governmental organizations, 47, 57, 174, 260–1, 356
Non-Immigrant Employment Authorization Program, 298
non-Indigenous allies, 332
non-linear, 361–2, 367
non-profit sector, 80, 257
normalcy, 320
norms, policy norms, 30, 76, 90, 101, 154, 174, 184, 191–2, 195, 200, 204, 230, 297, 312, 333
nothing about us without us, 145
Nova Scotia, 226, 233, 236

Nunatsiavut government, 97, 105
Nunatukavut Community Council, 97
nursemaids, 297

Obar, Jonathan, 172
objectivity, 241, 368
observation, 164, 178, 234, 240–1,
    243, 256, 259, 260, 263, 295, 298
O'Keefe, Jennifer, 236, 238–9, 246
Ontario, 253, 314. *See also* James Bay
Ontario Women's Directorate, 228
open government, 9
open space, 15, 51, 57, 367
OpenMedia, 14, 121, 164, 168–80, 186
openness, 121, 142, 193, 196, 198, 211,
    214, 219, 262, 339
Oppal, Wally, 31–3, 37, 41, 44
oppression, oppressor, 6, 12, 13, 16, 24,
    25–30, 32, 34–5, 37, 39, 238, 278–83,
    287, 313, 314, 319, 338, 343–5, 376–7
oral history, 289
Ostrom, Elinor, 78
Ottawa, 166, 189, 190, 305, 315, 324,
    326, 334
Ottawa Charter on Health
    Promotion, 189
Our Community, Our Plan (OCOP),
    121, 135
Our Digital Future, 170
Overcoming Poverty Together: The
    New Brunswick Economic and
    Social Inclusion Plan, 257

PACE, 33, 76
Pacey, Katrina, 37–8, 40, 46
Pahsahwaytagwan "Sounding Echo"
    Youth Committee, 314.
    See also Indigenous youth
pain, 211, 340–1
panels, 58, 69, 96, 98, 120, 134, 215,
    217, 233, 246, 342

pan-ethnic, 302, 306
panic, 339, 341
paradigms, 179, 319, 336, 355, 366, 368
Paradis, Christian, 171
paradoxes, 6, 9, 11, 19, 109, 136, 178,
    255, 335, 353, 368, 378, 380
Paris Declaration, 354, 355, 360, 362,
    362, 365
Parkinson, John, 26, 46
Parklands shooting, 375
parliament, 3, 142, 172, 312
participant demographics, 260
participant researchers, 240–1
participation paradox, 178
participatory games, 146, 232
participatory inclusion, 7, 26, 32,
    101, 140
participatory integrated
    assessments, 48, 63
participatory politics, 164, 174–8
participatory rituals, 341
Participedia.net, 209
partner organizations, 145, 147, 149,
    152, 159, 355
partnerships, 7, 51, 80, 197, 223, 342
party culture, 198
Passamaquoddy, 256
passive empathy, 193
patchwork quilt, 290
patriarchy, 359
PaulMartin, Keisha, 316, 321, 323–4,
    330
PaulMartin, Marlen, 322–3
peace, 25, 129, 252, 290
peaceful demonstration, 25, 27, 39
pedagogy, 195, 205, 278–80, 288, 346
people-centred development, 360
people's power, 364
performance measurement, 361
permanent residency, 294, 295, 298,
    299, 306–7

permission, 3, 217, 332
Perry, Adam, 298
personal priorities, policy priorities,
    8, 16, 37, 86, 190, 213–14, 234,
    241–2, 257, 360
personal stories, life stories, 235, 260,
    265, 268, 283, 313
Pettit, Philip, 123
Philippines, 297, 301
Phillips, Susan, 230
photographs, photography, 217, 283,
    316, 321
physical disabilities, 140
Pierson, Paul, 296
pilot project, 144, 298, 382
pilot public engagement exercises,
    232–3, 237, 243–5
Pivot Legal Society, 46
place-based planning, 216
plants, 298, 325
playfulness, 146, 211–12, 291
plurality, 280, 288
Polanco, Geraldina, 299
policy areas: environmental health,
    15, 282; health, mental health,
    106, 110, 142, 216, 314, 315, 323,
    324; housing, 76, 81, 104, 106,
    109–10, 113, 118–19, 126, 185,
    203, 212, 254, 312, 336, 382, 388;
    immigration, 241, 297–9, 306–11;
    poverty reduction, 253, 256,
    264, 267–8, 362; public safety,
    73, 169, 208, 212–13, 216, 218;
    resource (extraction), 94–5, 99,
    101–2, 104, 107–11, 116, 254, 380;
    telecommunications, 14, 164, 166,
    169, 176, 178–9, 181, 185
policy design, 101, 228
policy development, 4–6, 10–12, 48,
    94, 100–1, 170, 188, 199, 227, 253–7,
    260, 268, 362, 279, 381

policy dialogue, 324
policy failures, 375
policy feedback, 380
policy history, 296, 307
policy influence, 338
policy intent, 380
policy justice, 6, 10–11, 15–17, 164,
    179, 227, 254, 317, 333–4, 375,
    376–82
policy makers, 11, 17, 28, 48, 54, 64,
    154–5, 169, 206, 219, 223–4, 239,
    283, 296–7, 303, 305–7, 314, 317–18,
    324, 326, 377
policy outcomes, 6, 8, 12–13, 48, 80,
    230, 376, 377, 380
policy participants, 380
policy process/es, policy formation:
    affected interests, 12, 254;
    agenda setting, problem finding,
    problem definition, 28, 223, 228,
    229, 231, 254, 380; bottom-up,
    ground-up, 14, 192, 226–33, 237,
    239, 244, 245, 254, 360; collective
    impact, 13, 73–4, 76–7, 79–81,
    84–5, 87–93; consensus (in policy
    making), consensus building, 7,
    26, 75, 79, 89, 101, 174, 191, 193,
    213; decision making, 5, 7, 97,
    99–101, 110, 117, 123, 166, 175–7,
    228, 230, 254, 318, 324, 377, 380;
    dialogical policy making, 6, 7,
    201, 278, 318, 341; dialogue, 223,
    324; participatory, 101, 133, 139,
    164, 174–80, 193, 201, 208, 212,
    246, 357; policy-forming activities,
    254; sensing policy, 230, 318, 329;
    social construction of policy, 12,
    13, 95, 102, 107, 110, 380; solutions
    generation, 17, 57, 75–6, 110, 140,
    196, 208–9, 213, 216, 219, 223–4,
    239, 282, 314, 323, 340; striated

spaces (of policy making), 8, 11, 20, 377–8
policy solidarities, 380–2
policy spaces, 15, 305, 339
policy windows, 174
political decisions, 318–19
political landscape, 296, 304, 358
political mobilization, 31
political participation, 100, 101, 110, 163, 166, 177–8, 228, 255, 296, 301
political quiescence, 15, 296, 300, 301
political will, 262, 265, 267, 380
positionality, 152, 319
post-modern, 290, 319, 329
post-positivist/positivism, 317
post-secondary, 14, 187–9, 192, 195–6, 332–6, 341, 348, 350, 378
poverty, poverty reduction/elimination, 31, 37, 72–4, 76, 81, 85, 149, 244, 253–72, 278–9, 283, 289, 353–5, 358, 361–2, 371–2
Poverty and Human Rights Center, 33
power dynamics, 9, 10, 11, 15, 17, 19, 101, 141, 144, 145, 154, 164, 177, 191, 201, 231, 238, 243, 244, 245, 263, 317, 368; inequalities, 37, 194; multiple power differentials, 154, 227; power-infused contexts, 8, 343, 368
Power of Women for Women, 30, 31
power structures, 357, 378
power struggles, 368
praxis, 6, 179, 232, 237, 335, 345, 376
precarity, 106, 125, 296, 300, 304, 307, 335
pre-formulation, 237
prejudice, 151, 287, 339–40
presentation, 13, 51, 53–4, 56, 60, 119, 151, 171, 289, 340
principled engagement, 332
prism, 16, 237, 316–19, 325

privilege, 8, 29, 89, 95, 145, 226–7, 237–40, 243, 297, 319, 338, 345, 381
privileged knowledge, 338
problem, 5–8, 12–13, 17, 27, 42, 49, 75–81, 87–9, 95, 99–101, 108–10, 124, 126, 128–9, 140–2, 148, 151, 161, 163, 171, 176, 182, 190, 196, 199, 208, 213, 216, 218, 220, 223, 228–38, 281, 316, 324, 334, 343, 353, 368, 377–8, 380–1
problematization, 237, 239, 281, 313, 379
procedural republic, 194
production of knowledge, 317
professional practitioners, 209
professor, 209, 337, 342
profit, 72, 80–1, 86, 164–5, 257, 356
promotoras, 365
protection, 36, 164–5, 168, 174–5, 238, 244, 313, 347
protest, protesting, 3, 5, 12, 25–9, 30, 34, 35, 39, 41–2, 109, 173, 176, 223, 255, 304, 310, 376
protest fatigue, 223
protocols, 230, 235, 320
Provincial Nominee Program, 294, 299
pseudoparticipation, 176. *See also* faux participation
psychoactive substance, 187, 199
psychological disorders, 30
public administration, 11, 268
public deliberation: macro-level, 338; multidimensional, 333. *See also* Alberta Climate Dialogues (ABCD); collective deliberation
public engagement evaluation literature, 253
public good, 5, 73–4, 77, 78, 81, 163
public official, 5, 211–13, 312, 314, 326
public pedagogy, 280

public safety, 73, 169, 208, 212–13, 216, 218
Public Safety Canada, 169
public servants, 11, 256, 259, 260, 263–6, 380, 383
public service announcement, 324
public space, 8, 132, 210, 288, 291, 335
public sphere, 29, 151, 192, 194, 213–14, 224, 255
public square, 277, 284, 288
public welfare, 12, 73, 90, 408
Puerto Cabezas (Nicaragua), 356

quality-of-life plan, 84–6
quasi-governmental context, 16, 96, 334
quasi-governmental initiatives, 16
question assumptions, 194, 200, 214, 229, 241, 341

racialization, 145, 260, 268, 297, 300, 307, 317, 381
racism, racist, race, 6, 27, 31, 35, 74, 81, 98, 116, 148, 241, 283, 297, 298, 337, 338, 340, 381. See also anti-Black racism; Chinese railroad workers; Mexican and Central American farmers
radical policy futures, 15, 244, 381, 382
radical public engagement, 379
radical representational change, 324
raise awareness, 315, 317
Raisio, Harri, 140
Rancière, Jacques, 118, 129, 130–2, 137–8
rapids, 321–2
rationality, 6, 100, 140, 164, 178, 230
Ravensbergen, Frances, 253, 265
reason, 26, 101, 110, 120, 175, 191–3, 243, 254, 280, 295, 343, 376, 378
reciprocal elucidation, 240

reciprocity, 320, 381
recognition, 32, 80, 140, 150, 177, 193, 231, 331, 335, 343, 350, 365, 366, 379
reconciliation, 15, 36, 52, 119, 332–48, 352
recycling, 277–91, 317
recycling cooperatives, 278, 281, 317
redefinition, 367
Redvers, Tunchai, 315, 323
reflection, 79, 153, 200, 214, 236, 245, 279, 290, 295, 314, 321, 322, 337, 347, 380
reflexivity, 50, 227, 232, 237, 318, 320, 325
refugee, 302, 311
refusal, 42, 343
Regan, Paulette, 338, 352
Regan Shade, Leslie, 167
regional integration, 356
Reimagine CBC, 170
Reimagining Attawapiskat, 315–24
relational engagement, 17, 38, 82, 214, 320, 325, 336, 340, 379–80
relational research, 17, 316, 319, 320, 325
relationship building, relationships of trust, 5, 6, 79, 82, 88, 102, 127, 163, 195, 211, 227, 231–2, 242, 244, 265, 267, 281, 342, 347–8, 381
religion, 357, 364
religious fundamentalism, 359
religious institutions, 359
remedies, 379
representation, 7, 11, 13, 34, 37, 58, 82, 102, 104, 108, 122–3, 125–7, 135, 137, 140, 153, 155, 167, 178, 228, 237, 261, 268, 278, 286, 289–90, 317, 324, 338, 354
repression, 168, 338
reproductive rights, 103, 359, 361, 366

research approaches:
phenomenological, 188, 192, 194,
200, 201, 333, 335; philosophical
hermeneutics, 351, 404, 405;
research as resistance, 318
research ethics boards, 97, 243–4. *See
also* educational institutions; ethics
research methods, methodology:
arts-based participatory research,
14, 139, 152, 154, 230, 278–81, 314,
378; case study, 47, 71, 85, 87, 89,
164, 179, 353, 355; community-
based participatory research
(CBPR), 195; community-centred
methods of engagement, 226;
community-engaged research,
232, 244, 325, 333, 376; discourse
analysis, 283; document reviews,
358; focus groups, 125, 146;
interpretive policy analysis, 10,
336, 376; intersectionality-based
policy analysis, 306; interviews,
36, 53, 54, 126, 127, 169, 256,
259, 260, 300, 335, 338, 343, 358,
360; iterative methodology, 318;
participatory research, 6, 139, 144,
152, 195, 291, 319; photovoice,
144, 158, 246; qualitative research,
291, 320; semi-structured
interviews, 53; sharing circles,
106, 378; storytelling, narrative
storytelling, 15, 221, 222, 232,
312–31, 346, 378
residential schools, 30, 238, 247,
352. *See also* Aboriginal Peoples;
Indigenous Peoples
resilience, 51, 61, 64, 97, 222, 322
resistance, 5, 15, 49, 85–6, 94–5, 100,
109, 147, 165, 302–4, 318, 341, 366,
368
resource extraction, 4, 90–5, 99–102,
104, 107–10, 254, 380

respect, respectful relations, 7, 26,
38, 101, 140, 145, 196, 214, 262, 278,
281, 312, 333
results, 13, 51, 56, 64, 85, 89, 96, 98–9,
137, 145, 173, 187, 219, 238, 253,
258, 262, 229, 289, 300, 319, 354,
360–2, 367
results-based management, logic
model, 360–2, 367
revelatory political protest, 39
Rheingold, Howard, 78
rhetorical, 100, 357, 367, 380
Richards, Vanessa, 222
Rideout, Vanda, 168
Rio de Janeiro, 284, 285
Rio+20 Summit, 284–5
Rittel, Horst, 74
Roach, Kent, 33
Rodriguez, Robyn, 301
Rosanvalon, Pierre, 164, 177
Rose, Jonathan, 124
Rosen, Carmen, 220
Royal Bank of Canada, 295, 303
Royal Canadian Mounted Police
(RCMP), 31, 33, 36, 41
Royal Commission on Aboriginal
People (RCAP), 319
Royal Commission on the Status of
Women, 226, 233
rupture, 367

sacred space, 240, 342
safe space, 51, 339
Samuelson, Paul, 77
Sandel, Michael, 194
Sandell, Richard, 288
Sandinista Defense Committees, 363
Sandinista Party, 363–4
São Paulo, 277, 278, 284, 287, 288
Satzewitch, Vic, 298
scale, 16, 49, 58, 61–4, 81, 98, 109, 306
scaling up, 233

scapegoat, 303
scenarios, 59, 62, 236, 245, 279, 363
Science and Economic Development
    Canada, 166
scientific paradigm, 319
Seasonal Agricultural Workers
    Program, 297, 300–1
seasons, 321
self-determination, 104, 150, 245,
    319, 339, 419
self-expression, 229
self-location, 336
self-narrative, 290
Selkirk College, 198, 200
sense of belonging, 290, 320
sense of community, 318, 319, 323
sensitivity, 230, 241, 346, 362
serial killer, 30, 32
service, 97, 106, 110, 168, 169, 171,
    228, 255, 301, 315, 319, 324, 325,
    347, 364, 366
settlement, 222, 297, 298, 300, 301,
    305–7, 334–5
settlement service organizations,
    301, 305
settler practices, 338
settler privilege, 381
settler state, 239
settler-colonial relations, 314, 321.
    See also colonial
sewage, 220
sex and gender, 256, 357, 366
sex trade, 31
sex worker organizations, 32, 39–40
sex workers, 31, 40, 196
sexism, 6, 35–6, 346
sexual health, 359, 361, 366. See also
    health
sexual orientation, 357
sexual violence, 31, 356–69, 361, 365
sexuality, 145, 239
Shaker, Lee, 259

shared identity, 209
shared intention, 341, 347
shared interests, 75, 83, 303
shared language, 194, 209, 222. See
    also dialogue
shared truths, 341
Sharma, Nandita, 298
Shisheesh, Bruce, 314
shut up, 332
silencing, 226, 338
Simon Fraser University, 209, 217,
    222
situated knowledges, 11, 17, 230,
    313, 317–19, 365–8, 382
situatedness, 227
smudging ceremony, 235
social capital, 75, 82, 222
social change, 76, 81, 89, 232, 245,
    281–2
social class, 149, 236
social determinants, 190, 195
social discrimination, 355
social disparities, 355
social ecology, 190–1
social innovation, 47–9, 58
social justice, 6, 16, 103, 154, 226, 232,
    290, 302, 304, 376
social licence, 5, 7, 8, 9, 102, 339
social location, 94, 145, 153, 240, 302,
    306, 368
social media, 169, 175, 232, 315
social movements, 7, 27, 29, 164,
    228, 281, 291, 297, 307. See also
    democracy)
social networks, 303
social norms marketing
    interventions, 200
socio-ecological health promotion,
    189–90, 197
socioeconomic status, 255
sociopolitical factors, sociopolitical
    landscape, 265

sociotechnical transitions, 5, 13, 47–50, 63
solidarity: feelings of, 306; relationships of mutual enablement, 367; solidarity-based relationships, 364
solutions, 17, 57, 75–6, 110, 140, 196, 208–9, 213, 216, 219, 223–4, 239, 282, 314, 323–4, 340
sovereignty, political sovereignty, 109–10, 177, 245, 343, 356
spaces of deliberation, 15, 275, 335, 348
spaces of inclusion, 15, 302
speaking truth to power, 279, 315
special interest groups, 26, 228
speech acts, 208
Spence, Theresa, 312, 326
Spry, Graham, 169
stakeholders, 28, 32, 51, 52, 60–4, 76–89, 147–9, 155, 179, 197–201, 232, 244–6, 295, 305
Stalker, Joyce, 281
Starr, Beatrice, 35
state of emergency, 312–16, 320
Statistics Canada, 259
status quo, 9, 35, 290, 313, 316, 317, 326, 332
sticky policy problems, 8, 343, 377. See also policy
Still Creek (Vancouver), 220
Still Moon Society, 220
Stop Online Spying, 172
Stop the Meter, 169
Stop the Squeeze, 171
strategic alliance building, 305
strategic spaces of contestation, 291
strength, 5, 30, 39, 60, 97, 143, 146, 154, 176, 201, 224, 245, 281, 302, 303, 312–15, 344
structural adjustment, 358
structural inequalities, 27–9, 39, 178

student affairs, 334–5
student housing, 336
studied ignorance, 338
subjugated discourses, 317
subjugated knowledge, 27, 38–9, 317
substance use policies, 187
subterfuge, 338
subversive, 363
suicide, suicide prevention, 190, 312–16, 321–4
surprise, 130, 219, 332
Surrey, 216–18
surrogates, 231
surveillance legislation, 173
survivor, 347
suspicion, 122, 124, 130, 338
sustainable cities, 209
Sustainable Development Goals (SDGs), 354–5. See also United Nations
sustainable energy futures, 47, 52, 316
symbolism, 100, 104–5, 191, 283, 290, 332, 336
systemic inequality, 312
systemic oppression, 314
systems change, 13, 48, 50–1, 56, 63

tact, 335, 346
talking circle, 251, 346
talking stick, 235–7
Taylor, Charles, 194
teaching, 4, 222, 285, 322, 334–7, 341–2, 347
teamwork, 222, 342, 347
technical expertise, 193, 382
technocratic and management approaches, 362, 366
Telecommunications Act (1993), 166, 179
Temporary Foreign Workers Program, 294, 299

theories: critical race theory,
317; critical theory, 144, 185,
204, 237; landscapes, 49, 64;
multilevel perspective (MLP),
13, 47–9, 53, 59, 62 (see also
multilevel actor networks);
niches, 49; political opportunity
structure, 302; regimes, 49–51,
67, 391; sociocultural theory, 291;
sociotechnical transition theory,
sociotechnical transitions, 13, 47–
50; windows of opportunity, 50, 56
theory, 5, 7, 9, 11, 12–14, 16, 17, 26,
46–9, 53–4, 56, 63, 74, 77–8, 99–100,
129, 144, 153, 175, 188–96, 216, 219,
237, 254, 267, 280, 291, 313, 316,
325, 356–7, 377
theory of change, 49, 56, 216
Thompson, Dennis, 124, 254
Thompson Rivers University, 198,
200
Three Horizons framework, 62
Tichkosky, Tanya, 141
Time for an Upgrade, 170–1, 183
tokenism, 10, 343
trade union, 304
training, 82, 85, 101–2, 109, 150, 263,
283, 286–91, 298, 339, 341, 366
transcripts, 283
transdisciplinary, 5, 7, 10–12, 141,
376–7, 379, 381
transformation, 9, 333, 344, 358,
362–3
transformative approaches, 358, 363
Transforming Disability Knowledge,
Research, and Activism (TDKRA),
139
transition dynamics, 48, 61–4
Trans-Pacific Partnership, 141
transparency, 53, 79, 121, 214, 360
trauma, 8, 240, 253
treaty people, 341

treaty relations, 312–13
Treaty Six, 335
treaty-making, 346
Tremblay, Crystal, 317
Tribe Called Red, A, 315
Trudeau, Justin, 232, 315
truth telling, 315, 316, 333, 338–41,
345, 352
Tullock, Gordon, 77
Tully, James, 240
Turner, Dale, 334

uncertainty, 7, 131–2, 211, 341, 344–5,
348
uneven relations, 317
UNICEF, 150
Unifor, 304. See also trade union
Union of BC Indian Chiefs, 33
United Nations, 41, 141, 354–5,
357, 365. See also Sustainable
Development Goals (SDGs)
United Nations Fund for Population
Activities, 363–4
United Way, 216
universalism, 367
universality, 367
Université de Montréal, 209, 224
Universities Canada, 332
unravel, 339, 341, 347
unspeakable, 340
untruths, 339–40
urban planning, 170, 175, 223
usage-based billing, 169

values, 49, 88, 99–100, 102, 119–20,
150, 176, 191–2, 195, 200–1, 213–14,
219, 221–3, 285–7, 309, 345, 356,
359, 364
van Manen, Max, 335, 346
Vancouver Island, 216
Vancouver Police Department
(VPD), 31, 35, 36

Vancouver Rape Relief and Women's
    Shelter, 33
Vancouver University Women's
    Club, 33
Vanderplaat, Madine, 253, 265
veneer, 36–7, 345
Vertovec, Steven, 301
Vezina Secondary School, 316, 320
victims, 34, 37, 40–1, 106, 139, 165,
    231, 366
video messaging, 315
Vietnam, 13, 139, 140–54, 377
vignettes, 377
violence, 25–6, 30–3, 39, 98, 106, 110,
    243, 302, 314, 356, 358, 359, 361,
    365, 366
visibility, 31, 304
visual meaning, 279
visual thought, 284–6
voluntary associations, 29
volunteers, 235, 263, 364–5
voting, 72, 83, 117, 122, 213, 227, 296,
    301
vulnerability, 14, 36–8, 40, 139, 142,
    152, 243, 313
vulnerable communities, 243. See
    also historically marginalized
    groups, people
Vygotsky, Lev, 285

Walia, Harsha, 35, 43
Walking with Our Sisters, 235, 236,
    238, 240, 241
Warren, Mark, 123, 136, 267, 379
wasteland, 321
water, 4, 31, 220, 312, 322, 325
watershed, 220
We Matter, 312, 315, 324, 326
weaving, 313, 347
web-based technologies, 230
Webber, Melvin, 75

website, 198, 231, 300, 316, 321,
    324–5, 364
well-being, wellness, 16, 94, 98–111,
    119, 165, 189, 192, 199, 291, 313–14,
    316, 321, 323–4, 357
West Coast Women's Legal
    Education and Action Fund
    (LEAF), 33
Western approaches, 337
western Canada, 297
Westley, Frances, 57
white/whiteness, 83, 87, 125, 227,
    238–41, 289, 297, 342, 375
Whiteside, Heather, 166
wicked problems, 75–8, 81, 87–9
Wiebe, Sarah Marie, 15, 89, 230, 333,
    343, 381
Wilson, Shawn, 336
wise practices, 313, 324
witness, 33, 35–7, 130, 132, 303, 325,
    330
Wolastoqiyik, 256
women/womxn: Afro-descendant,
    365; Asian, 32; as dependent,
    109, 110; as deviant, 95, 108;
    immigrant, 234; Indigenous
    and northern, 97, 100, 101, 107,
    109–11, 380; rural, 234; senior,
    103
women/womxn living in low
    income, people living in low
    income, 15, 81, 103, 212, 253, 255,
    260, 265, 267, 268, 286, 377
Women's Equality Branch (New
    Brunswick), 256
Women's Information and Safe
    House Drop-In Society (WISH), 33
women's/womxn's participation,
    253, 353, 356, 362–3, 368
women's/womxn's particular ways
    of knowing, 365

Women's Research and Action
   Forum, 233
women's/womxn's resistance,
   95
Wood, Colin, 80
Wood, Diane, 35
Woodward's Community Singers,
   222
work ethic, 84, 299
World Bank, 154, 358

World Health Organization, 189
World Trade Organization, 141, 154

xenophobia, 296

Yankelovich, Daniel, 214
Yellow-Quill, Lisa, 35
Young, Iris Marion, 27–9, 140
young women, 231, 234, 236, 239–45
youth-led solutions, 323